DEFENCES IN EQUITY

This book is the fourth in a series of essay collections on defences in private law. It addresses defences to liability arising in equity. The essays range from those adopting a mainly doctrinal perspective to others that explore the law from a more philosophical perspective. Some essays concentrate on specific defences, while others are concerned with the links between defences, or with how defences relate to the structure of the law of equity generally. One aim of the book is to shed light on equitable doctrines by analysing them through the lens of defences. The essays offer original contributions to this complex, important but neglected field of scholarly investigation. The contributors—judges and academics—are all distinguished jurists. The essays are addressed to all of the major common law jurisdictions.

Volume 4 in the series Hart Studies in Private Law: Essays on Defences

Hart Studies in Private Law: Essays on Defences

The series offers a systematic treatment of defences in private law as a connected field. It addresses tort law, unjust enrichment, contract law and equity, in that order. Its aim is to contribute to this theoretically challenging and practically important, yet understudied, area of the law. The essays that constitute each of the collections in this series are written by some of the world's leading judges and scholars. They bring together insights from several jurisdictions, including civilian jurisdictions. The series is of value to academics and practitioners alike.

Defences in Equity

Edited by
Paul S Davies
Simon Douglas
and
James Goudkamp

• HART •
OXFORD • LONDON • NEW YORK • NEW DELHI • SYDNEY

HART PUBLISHING
Bloomsbury Publishing Plc
Kemp House, Chawley Park, Cumnor Hill, Oxford, OX2 9PH, UK

HART PUBLISHING, the Hart/Stag logo, BLOOMSBURY and the Diana
logo are trademarks of Bloomsbury Publishing Plc

First published in Great Britain 2018
First published in hardback, 2018
Paperback edition, 2020

A catalogue record for this book is available from the British Library.

Library of Congress Cataloging-in-Publication data
Names: Davies, Paul S. (Law teacher), editor. | Douglas, Simon, 1983-editor. |
Goudkamp, James, 1980-editor.
Title: Defences in equity / edited by Paul S Davies, Simon Douglas and James Goudkamp.
Description: Oxford; Portland, Oregon: Hart Publishing, 2018. | Series: Hart studies in private law:
essays on defences; Volume 4 | Includes bibliographical references and index.
Identifiers: LCCN 2017053835 (print) | LCCN 2017055291 (ebook) | ISBN 9781509921027 (epub) |
ISBN 9781849467247 (hardback)
Subjects: LCSH: Equity—English-speaking countries. | Equity—England. |
Actions and defenses—English-speaking countries. | Actions and defenses—England. |
Defense (civil procedure)—English-speaking countries. | Defense (civil procedure)—England.
Classification: LCC K247 (ebook) | LCC K247.D438 2018 (print) | DDC 346/.004—dc23
LC record available at https://lccn.loc.gov/2017053835

ISBN: HB: 978-1-84946-724-7
PB: 978-1-50994-111-7
ePDF: 978-1-50992-101-0
ePub: 978-1-50992-102-7

Typeset by Compuscript Ltd, Shannon

Foreword

As this splendid collection of essays—the last in a series concerning defences in private law—makes plain, the difficulty one immediately encounters in considering defences in equity is in defining what it means to have *a defence* in equity. Most common lawyers, including me, were trained to recognise certain conventional doctrines as affording a 'defence': unclean hands, for example (*Jones v Lenthal* (1669) 1 Ch Cas 154; 22 ER 739), or laches (*Smith v Clay* (1767) Amb 645; 27 ER 419), and illegality of transaction (*Quarrier v Colston* (1842) 1 Ph 147; 41 ER 587) or of purpose (*Nelson v Nelson* (1995) 184 CLR 538). (To which list Canadians might wish to add want of causation, in reliance on Peter Turner's contribution to the collection, and on my court's decision in *Canson Enterprises Ltd v Boughton & Co* [1991] 3 SCR 534.) As I listened to the various papers being presented at Jesus College, Oxford last January, however, I was struck by how impoverished an understanding this may be of what comprises the list of equitable defences.

Just as an example, Robert Stevens's paper on equitable set-off led me to reflect on a decision of my court that I used to teach as a civil procedure instructor, *Holt v Telford* [1987] 2 SCR 193. There, A agreed to exchange land parcels, under which agreement A granted a mortgage to B of $150,000, and B granting a mortgage to A of $100,000. B assigned its rights under the mortgage to C, who sued A for payment. A pleaded legal set-off (unsuccessfully, since the assignment destroyed any mutuality of cross-obligations). Its plea of equitable set-off, however, succeeded. Citing the British Columbia Court of Appeal in *CIBC v Tuckerr Industries Inc* (1983) 149 DLR (3d) 172, the court explained that a set-off in equity can exist in the absence of mutuality of cross-obligations.

Is, then, equitable set-off a defence? The prevailing view on this side of the Atlantic (or, at least in Alberta, from which *Holt* originated) suggests that it is not, because it is asserted by counterclaim. But Stevens's arguments cast this view into some doubt, since the counterclaim is parasitic to the original claim. And so, recalling *Holt*, the only reason A could claim set-off against C was that A had been sued on a transaction which the court described as 'closely connected' to a reciprocal transfer. Since each obligation would not have existed without the other, denying set-off would in effect be tantamount to enforcing only one side of their agreement.

Similarly provocative and original insights emerge from the other papers. Each is characterised by admirable doctrinal rigour, sensitivity to taxonomy and careful examination of judgments from across the Commonwealth. Collectively, they speak to the vitality and ambition of the scholarship in the field. My thanks and congratulations to Professors Davies, Douglas and Goudkamp and all the distinguished contributors.

Russell Brown
Justice of the Supreme Court of Canada and
Honorary Professor of Law, University of Alberta

Preface

We have incurred several debts of gratitude in connection with this volume. Jesus College provided significant financial support for the project and the venue for the workshop at which most of the chapters that form this volume were presented. Support was also provided by All Souls College, Hart Publishing, the OUP John Fell Fund, the Oxford Law Faculty and the Society of Legal Scholars' Small Projects and Events Fund. We are very pleased to have welcomed as observers at the workshop Robert Chambers, David Cheifetz, Birke Häcker, Ben McFarlane and Frederick Wilmot-Smith. We are particularly grateful to the Hon Justice Russell Brown of the Supreme Court of Canada for travelling to Oxford in order to participate in the workshop and for writing the foreword. Finally, we acknowledge with thanks the support that we had from the following research assistants: Manuel González, Václav Janeček, Daniel Judd, Jia Wei Lee and Zhicheng Wu.

Paul S Davies
Simon Douglas
James Goudkamp

1 September 2017

Contents

Contributors

Michael Ashdown is a barrister at Wilberforce Chambers and Lecturer in Law at Somerville College, Oxford.

Paul S Davies is Professor of Commercial Law at University College London.

Simone Degeling is Professor of Law at UNSW Australia.

Simon Douglas is a Fellow of Jesus College, Oxford, and an Associate Professor of Law, University of Oxford.

David Fox is Professor of Common Law at the University of Edinburgh.

Joshua Getzler is a Fellow of St Hugh's College, Oxford, and Professor of Legal History, University of Oxford.

James Goudkamp is a Fellow of Keble College, Oxford, and Professor of the Law of Obligations, University of Oxford. He is also a barrister at 7 King's Bench Walk.

Christopher Hare is a Fellow of Somerville College, Oxford, and Travers Smith Associate Professor of Corporate and Commercial Law, University of Oxford.

Lusina Ho is Harold Hsiao-Wo Lee Professor in Trust and Equity, University of Hong Kong.

The Hon Justice Mark Leeming is a Judge of Appeal of the Supreme Court of New South Wales.

Ying Khai Liew is Senior Lecturer in Law at University of Melbourne.

Nicholas J McBride is a Fellow of Pembroke College, Cambridge.

Charles Mitchell FBA is a Professor of Law at University College London.

Sir Philip Sales is a Lord Justice of Appeal.

Henry E Smith is the Fessenden Professor of Law at Harvard Law School.

Robert Stevens is Herbert Smith Freehills Professor of English Private Law, University of Oxford.

PG Turner is a University Lecturer, and a Fellow of St Catharine's College, in the University of Cambridge.

Table of Cases

AUSTRALIA

CANADA

CAYMAN ISLANDS

HONG KONG

JERSEY

NEW ZEALAND

SINGAPORE

UNITED KINGDOM

UNITED STATES

Table of Statutes

Australia

Commonwealth

Australian Capital Territory

New South Wales

Northern Territory

United States

Table of Delegated Legislation

Australia

New South Wales

United Kingdom

1

Introduction

PAUL S DAVIES, SIMON DOUGLAS AND JAMES GOUDKAMP

I. DEFENCES IN EQUITY

THIS VOLUME IS the fourth in a series that addresses defences in private law. Like those that preceded it,[1] it is animated by a belief that defences comprise an important but under-theorised part of private law. The present volume's concern is with defences in equity. It is obvious that the law of equity is not usually understood through the lens of defences (by which we mean that defences are not used as a major organisational device). Indeed, defences do not usually feature prominently in tables of contents of textbooks in the field, if they feature at all.

For at least two related reasons, it is slightly puzzling that the concept of a defence has not received systematic treatment in the law of equity. The first concerns the relationship between equity and the rest of private law. A dominant theme in many recent attempts to classify private law is that there is no meaningful conceptual (as opposed to historical) distinction between equity and the common law. Peter Birks, a leading figure in articulating and promoting this viewpoint, contended, for example, that liability in equity is no different, ultimately, from liability arising in respect of common law wrongs.[2] The clear implication to be drawn from Birks's pioneering work is that liability for equitable wrongs ought to be controlled by the same rules as liability arising at common law. Andrew Burrows derives precisely this message from Birks's work. Burrows argues, writing in relation to restrictions on the award of compensatory damages and equitable compensation, 'there is no good reason for equity going its own separate way'.[3] Similarly, he contends 'that it is simply false to imagine that there are irreconcilable differences between common law and equitable defences'.[4] In another contribution, Burrows contends, 'I make no apology for reiterating that, in my opinion, there are common law counterparts to the famous

[1] The previous volumes are A Dyson, J Goudkamp and F Wilmot-Smith, *Defences in Tort* (Oxford, Hart, 2015); A Dyson, J Goudkamp and F Wilmot-Smith, *Defences in Unjust Enrichment* (Oxford, Hart, 2016); A Dyson, J Goudkamp and F Wilmot-Smith, *Defences in Contract* (Oxford, Hart, 2017).

[2] P Birks, 'The Concept of a Civil Wrong' in DG Owen (ed), *Philosophical Foundations in Tort Law* (Oxford, Clarendon, 1997).

[3] Andrew Burrows, 'We Do This at Common Law But That in Equity' (2002) 22 *OJLS* 12.

[4] ibid 14.

equitable defences'.[5] If there is no conceptual difference between common law and equitable wrongs, the strong presumption would be that just as there are many defences to liability arising in common law wrongs, the law of equity does (or should) readily recognise defences too. In these circumstances, one would expect defences to have occupied as prominent a part in the thinking of equity scholars as they have in relation to certain other major branches of private law.

The second reason why it is arguably somewhat odd that equity lawyers have tended not to organise their thinking in terms of defences is that equity recognises many rules that are widely understood as defences in other departments of the law of obligations. Illegality, limitation and consent, for instance, are regularly regarded as defences in other parts of private law. Equity also provides for a wide array of rules that are specific to the law of equity but to which the term defence could readily be (and sometimes is) applied. A good example is the rule in section 61 of the Trustee Act 1925 (UK), which provides that where a trustee has committed a breach of trust 'but has acted honestly and reasonably' the court may 'relieve him either wholly or partly from personal liability' if the court considers that he 'ought fairly to be excused for the breach of trust and for omitting to obtain the directions of the court in the matter in which he committed such breach'.[6] In his chapter in this volume, Robert Stevens singles out several rules that he considers are 'archetypal defences', including equitable set-off, laches, acquiescence and release.[7] In short, equity contains many rules that are regularly recognised as defences in other fields or which otherwise have a strong claim to having the label of defence applied to them.

If the law of equity can fairly be regarded as being populated by a wide network of defences, several important issues arise. One key question is what is meant by the term 'defence'. One message that the previous books in this series sought to communicate is that there is no uniform understanding of the concept of a defence. The term is used in a wide variety of ways. Sometimes it is used in contradistinction to the idea of a 'denial'. A denial is typically understood as an argument that attacks the existence of something that forms part of the claimant's cause of action. When contrasted with a denial, a defence is a rule that allows the defendant to escape or reduce his liability even if what the claimant alleges is true. A second way in which the notion of a defence is often understood is in terms of onuses of proof. On this view, defences are rules that the defendant must establish by proving certain facts. A third way of defining the concept of a defence is suggested by Stevens. He argues that 'Whether or not something constitutes a defence is, in private law, a purely formal question. Is it something that the defendant asserts in his pleadings,

[5] A Burrows, 'Remedial Coherence and Punitive Damages in Equity' in S Degeling and J Edelman (eds), *Equity in Commercial Law* (Sydney, Thomson Reuters, 2005) 386.

[6] See J Lowry and R Edmunds, 'Relieving the Trustee-Solicitor: A Modern Perspective on Section 61 of the Trustee Act 1925?' (2017) 133 *LQR* 223; P Davies, 'Section 61 of the Trustee Act 1925: deus ex machina?' [2015] Conv 379.

[7] ch 3 at p 50.

that is not merely a denial, in order for a claim to fail?'[8] This way of understanding is similar to but not the same as the second definition given above, since a defendant might be required to plead a certain rule but not prove the existence of facts that engage it (such as is the case in relation to limitation bars, where the claimant must show that the action was brought in time once the question of limitation has been pleaded by the defendant). All three of these ways of comprehending the concept of a defence are subtly but importantly distinct from each other. They do not exhaust the range of ways in which that notion can and has been understood.

Another important question that is of general significance concerns classification. If the concept of a defence is employed in a given field of law, one issue that arises is whether defences in the field concerned can be organised in any particular way. The classification of defences has been one of the largest research projects ever undertaken in the criminal law, for instance. It has been either the sole or main concern of several books[9] and the subject of countless articles in law reviews. It is widely thought that these endeavours have significantly advanced understanding of the criminal law. In light of this experience, it is surprising that similarly sustained efforts have not been undertaken in relation to all of the various parts of private law. It is true that efforts systematically to arrange tort defences can be traced at least as far back as Wigmore,[10] and scholars have regularly offered a variety of ways of arranging defences to liability in tort since Wigmore's time.[11] However, the situation is different in relation to private law's other departments, where scholars have not embarked on the same project. If a more complete understanding of private law is to be obtained, the question of classification also needs to be asked in relation to the law of contract, unjust enrichment and equity.

Before proceeding, we should mention one radical challenge to the entire enterprise that this book represents. We drew attention, above, to the Birksian understanding that equitable wrongs do not differ in any material way from common law wrongs and that it is thus an error to see equitable wrongs as pertaining to a separate category within private law.[12] If this view is pursued to its logical conclusion, equity is not a separate branch of private law with the result that it makes no sense to look at defences in equity as an independent category. Instead, equitable defences that affect rights to redress that would otherwise arise in contract, tort or unjust enrichment should properly be considered alongside common law defences in each of those branches of the law. Whether or not there is anything distinctive about equitable defences is considered by Henry Smith in his essay (chapter two).

[8] ibid.

[9] The leading works are GP Fletcher, *Rethinking Criminal Law* (Boston, Little, Brown & Co, 1978) chs 7, 9–10; PH Robinson, *Criminal Law Defenses* (St Paul, Minn, West Publishing Co, 1984) (two volumes).

[10] JH Wigmore, 'The Tripartite Division of Torts' (1894) 8 *Harvard Law Review* 200; JH Wigmore, 'A General Analysis of Tort-Relations' (1895) 8 *Harvard Law Review* 377.

[11] Several attempts to categorise tort defences are recounted in J Goudkamp, *Tort Law Defences* (Oxford, Hart, 2013) ch 7.

[12] See the text accompanying n 2.

II. THE NATURE OF EQUITABLE DEFENCES

Smith asks whether the jurisdictional origin of equitable defences, such as laches, equitable estoppel and unclean hands, helps us to understand these doctrines. For Smith, an important characteristic of the equitable jurisdiction is its 'second order' status. Equitable rules are 'second order' because they refer to common law rules and, hence, depend upon them for their existence.[13] In other words, they are rules about rules. Equitable rules are needed, Smith explains, to root out forms of opportunism, where individuals identify and then seek to exploit weaknesses in the apparatus of the common law. Individuals exploiting loopholes in the tax system is one example identified by Smith. Another is the case of an estoppel, where an individual acts unconscionably, but stops short of making any legally binding promise. A secondary system, Smith explains, is one that takes aim at those who opportunistically avoid the effects the general legal rules.

It is within this conception of equity as a whole that Smith attempts to place equitable defences. They are different, he argues, from defences recognised at common law because they are of a 'second order' nature. They modify the result that would otherwise obtain by the application of standard rules. This, Smith argues, explains certain features of equitable defences, particularly the fact that they tend to be discretionary. An individual who exploits a tax loophole, or encourages another to act to his detriment, might be acting in a way that is permissible pursuant to common law principles. As such, the only way to assess their behaviour is against some form of moral code. This might explain why unconscionability features so heavily in equitable defences. Given the distinct function and features of equitable defences, the project of fusion with common law defences is, Smith argues, a difficult one, and it might be preferable to recognise equitable defences as a distinct category.

Stevens is concerned in his chapter (chapter three) with the defence of equitable set-off. He begins his treatment by distinguishing equitable set-off from other species of set-off that do not have equitable underpinnings, including what he refers to as 'contractual set-off', 'insolvency set-off' and 'procedural set-off'. The defence of equitable set-off, unlike the other species of set-off, does not involve netting out claims. Rather, Stevens argues, it entails the defendant bringing a counterclaim on the basis of equitable rules, which counterclaim, if successful, would result in the failure of the claim that has been asserted against him. A defendant raises the defence of equitable set-off whenever he counterclaims, relying on equitable doctrines, on the basis that the 'claimant's conduct has caused a claim against him to arise' with the result that the claimant 'may not assert a claim which is causally related to the same conduct'.[14] *Lord Cawdor v Lewis*[15] supplies an excellent illustration of what Stevens has in mind, which case Stevens cites. The claimant landowner sued the defendant for mesne profits and the defendant successfully counterclaimed for an injunction restraining the bringing of the claimant's action on the basis that the

[13] The same proposition features prominently throughout in Stevens's chapter (ch 3).
[14] ch 3 at p 47.
[15] *Lord Cawdor v Lewis* (1835) 1 Y&C Ex 427; 160 ER 174.

claimant had stood by while the defendant had, to the claimant's knowledge, made improvements to the land.

The defence of equitable set-off, as described by Stevens, means that it has little, if anything, in common with other types of set-off, and should not, in fact, even be labelled a type of set-off in so far as the idea of set-off necessarily involves the netting out of claims. Rather, Stevens argues, the defence of equitable set-off is much more closely allied with other equitable rules generally. Equitable rules, Stevens reminds us, are rules about other rules and, as such, lack any independent vitality. They presuppose, and are only intelligible against, the backdrop of the common law's rules. The defence of equitable set-off, consistent with its equitable nature, involves the assertion of a counterclaim that the defendant would be unable to pursue absent a claim against him. It is a counterclaim that has no independent existence.

III. BONA FIDE PURCHASE FOR VALUE WITHOUT NOTICE

The bona fide purchase for value without notice plea has been described, as David Fox notes in the introduction to his chapter (chapter four), as the 'polar star' of equity. Although its origins lie in trusts (or uses) of land, it has developed into a general plea, available to any recipient of legal rights as a possible defence to pre-exiting equitable interests. The plea is available not only in the context of equitable interests arising under trusts, but to all forms of equitable interest. The features of the modern defence have been clearly articulated by the courts and are generally well understood. Where difficulty lies in the modern law is in the relationship between this defence and forms of personal liability in equity, particularly the action of knowing receipt.

Fox considers the basis and scope of the modern defence through the prism of its historical development. His approach yields surprising conclusions. In short, he argues that the modern defence has been largely uncoupled from its original purpose and scope. Fox explains that the enforceability of the early beneficial interests, or uses, depended on notions of privity and consideration. Where a trustee (the feoffor), held land for the benefit (or use) of a *cestui que use*, that use could endure against a transferee (the feoffee) of the land, in much in the same way that a modern equitable interest in land can bind a successor in title. If the feoffee had provided consideration for the transfer (ie, a sale), then one would say that the feoffee had intended to acquire the title to his own use. However, if consideration was absent, and the feoffee was aware of the *cestui que use's* interest, he was said to have acquired the title to the use of the *cestui que use*. Notions of privity and consideration, therefore, lie at the heart of the emergence of the trust, and explain how equitable interests ceased to be merely personal obligations and acquired a proprietary status.

The origin of the bona fide purchaser without notice plea, Fox explains, is closely related to the origin of uses. If land subject to a use was transferred to a feoffee, then the feoffee's notice of the use, and his failure to provide consideration, justified his being bound by the use; conversely, if a feoffee took the land without notice of the use, and he had given consideration, then there was no justification for the use persisting against the title. In its earliest form, the bona fide purchaser without notice plea was not so much a defence, but the very negation of the binding force of a use; it was the very opposite of the argument that the feoffee was privy to the use.

The way in which the bona fide purchase without notice plea developed into the modern defence, which cuts across all equitable interests (and not just equitable interests under trusts of land, where the defence has been superseded by registration principles), is the story told by Fox. Modern trusts are no longer based upon the medieval idea of privity, but more so upon the notion that third parties can be bound due to the proprietary nature of a beneficiary's interest. Yet the bona fide purchaser defence has features that can be explained only in the context of its historical origins and relation to the rules of privity of uses.

IV. CONSENT

Consent to breach of trust, as Liew and Mitchell explain (chapter five), can play a crucial role in the normal functioning of express trusts. Take the case of an overly cautious settlor who ties the hands of trustees by restricting their investment powers, by, for example, limiting them to buying government bonds. The trustees may reasonably take the view that the trust fund will fall in value unless they breach its terms and invest in other assets. One way to defend against such a breach is by invoking section 61 of the Trustee Act 1925 (UK). The other, and perhaps easier way, is to seek the consent of the beneficiary. It is this type of case that Liew and Mitchell examine. What, they ask, is the legal consequence of consent? Does it furnish the trustee with a defence against any future claim by the beneficiary, or does it alter the terms of the trust, such that there is no breach to speak of?

Liew and Mitchell examine the proposition that a beneficiary can unilaterally change the terms of the trust, and can do so merely by instructing the trustee to behave in a particular way. Support for this view can be found in the rule in *Saunders v Vautier*,[16] whereby the beneficiaries of a trust can call upon a trustee to terminate the trust and distribute the trust property. This analysis is rejected by Liew and Mitchell. Their reasoning depends upon the rules that govern the creation of trusts. A settlor might express a wish that a particular person act as trustee and take property subject to certain duties but, unless the nominated trustee accepts, those duties cannot come into existence and the court must appoint a new trustee. If a trustee's consent is necessary for the creation of trust rights, then it is equally necessary for the variation of the trust. In other words, while a beneficiary might bring the trust relationship to an end, he cannot force a different one upon the trustee without his consent. Just as the creation of a trust depends upon more than just the settlor's intention, the variation of a trust needs more than just the beneficiary's consent.

Another angle on consent is provided by Simone Degeling (chapter six). Her concern is to understand how consent functions in the context of fiduciary duties. Degeling observes that a principal and a fiduciary can contract so as to exclude fiduciary obligations and that, where a breach of fiduciary duty has occurred,

[16] *Saunders v Vautier* (1841) 4 Beav 115; 41 ER 482.

equity provides for a parallel result where the principal gave fully informed consent. The question that Degeling poses is whether the court can give the fiduciary permission to breach his fiduciary obligations. In other words, can the principal be bypassed? Degeling explores this question first by looking (primarily) at the powers that are available to the court in New South Wales to authorise trustees to exercise conflicting powers in certain circumstances. Degeling then specifically addresses whether the court can authorise a breach of a fiduciary obligation. Her ultimate conclusion is that it cannot, including where, for example, the principal is uncontactable. Degeling arrives at that conclusion based on a combination of descriptive and normative reasons. More specifically, she contends that it is 'difficult to find a general power ex ante to authorise a breach of fiduciary duty'[17] and considers that the nature of the office occupied by a fiduciary is incompatible with prior authorisation to commit a breach of duty.

V. EXEMPTION CLAUSES, PROFESSIONAL ADVICE AND EQUITABLE COMPENSATION

The next three chapters deal with situations that commonly arise where the actions of trustees cause loss to be suffered by the trust fund. Sir Philip Sales (chapter seven) focuses on exemption clauses: the trustees may be able to rely upon a clause in the trust instrument which means that they do not have to pay. Michael Ashdown (chapter eight) analyses a different contention which may made by trustees: that they were not in breach of duty because they properly took professional advice. Finally, Peter Turner (chapter nine) considers that even if there is no exemption clause or defence of having properly taken professional advice available to defaulting trustees, their liability may nonetheless be curtailed, in some circumstances, if the breach did not cause the relevant loss.

There are of course two different types of exemption clause. The most common excludes liabilities that might arise upon a breach of trust. Another category of exemption clause excludes duties that a trustee would ordinarily owe to the beneficiaries. Where a trustee relies upon the latter type of exemption clause, the trustee is in effect arguing that he has done nothing wrong. This might strictly be viewed as a denial. The former category of exemption clause is more easily characterised as a defence. Both raise similar issues as to whether the exemption clause is so extensive that what remains fails to satisfy the 'irreducible core' of a trust.[18] But it should nevertheless be borne in mind that important differences exist between the two types of clause. For example, if liability only is exempted following a breach of trust, then the trustee will still have committed a wrong, and as a result an accessory to that wrong may be liable as a dishonest assister. But where the trustee did not owe a duty in the first place as a result of the second type of exemption, then it cannot be said that

[17] ch 6 at p 112.
[18] See, notably, *Armitage v Nurse* [1998] Ch 241 (CA).

the trustee committed a wrong and therefore there is no wrong to which accessory liability might attach.

Sir Philip Sales analyses in detail a possible analogy with contract law. He highlights the importance placed upon 'freedom of contract', and considers whether 'freedom of trust' should be similarly emphasised, such that the settlor be able to agree to (almost) whatever he wishes. In some situations, the settlor and beneficiary will be the same party, and might have a contract with the trustee. In such circumstances, the contractual regimes regarding unfair terms will also be in play.[19] But in other circumstances the settlor will no longer be around, and the beneficiary will have no contract with the trustee. Sales discusses whether exemption clauses are invalid as a matter of interpretation (which issue could be overcome by clear drafting) or as a rule of law—and, if the latter, what the basis of such a rule may be.

The chapter raises fundamental questions for the law of trusts, and, indeed, more generally. For instance, the relationship between exemption clauses and the *ex post* relief from liability which may be granted under section 61 of the Trustee Act 1925 (UK) presents some interesting questions about the role of statute in the development of the common law. It is clear that exemption clauses can be valid when drafted much more broadly than the language of section 61. This perhaps shows the importance placed upon the freedom of a settlor to dispose of his property how he wishes. But some limits seem appropriate, and it is unclear whether the Court of Appeal in *Armitage v Nurse*[20] struck the right balance. Indeed, following the split decision of the Privy Council in *Spread Trustee Company Ltd v Hutcheson*,[21] it may be that the issue should be considered by the Supreme Court. Criticism of *Armitage v Nurse* has tended to contend that the decision was too generous to trustees, but, as Sales shows, it could be argued that it was too tough on settlors. This debate is clearly linked to the scope of the 'irreducible core' of a trust, without which the relationship in question is not that of beneficiary-trustee. The shift in focus (or at least litigation) from small, family trusts to larger, commercial trusts has inevitably influenced this question. If the irreducible core contains very little, then it is to be expected that very broad exemption clauses will be valid.

Michael Ashdown draws attention to a rule—acting on professional advice—which he describes as 'now one of the most important defences' in the law of equity but which is not identified as a freestanding answer to liability in the leading works in the field.[22] The rule, stated simply, involves a trustee asserting that 'I can't possibly have committed a breach of trust: I just did what my professional adviser told me to'. The rule is confined, it appears, to cases in which trustees acted within the scope of their powers. Ashdown's concern, after demonstrating how the rule obtained a foothold in English law, is to isolate its elements and

[19] Either the Unfair Contract Terms Act 1977 (UK) or the Consumer Rights Act 2015 (UK).

[20] *Armitage v Nurse* [1998] Ch 241 (CA).

[21] *Spread Trustee Company Ltd v Hutcheson* [2011] UKPC 13; [2012] 2 AC 194.

[22] See, further, M Ashdown, *Trustee Decision Making: The Rule in Re Hastings-Bass* (Oxford, OUP, 2015).

consider what each of them entails. Those elements, he says, comprise: (i) obtaining professional advice; (ii) the advice was obtained conscientiously; (iii) the advice was followed; and (iv) the advice was apparently competent.[23]

One interesting question is whether the professional advice rule is really a defence at all. There is much in Ashdown's chapter to suggest that he does not regard it as such. He refers constantly throughout his chapter to there being no breach of trust where the rule applies. That is suggestive. If the rule really were an independent doctrine and hence separate from the matters that must be shown by the claimant to establish liability, one might expect Ashdown to speak instead of the rule as precluding liability despite a breach of trust. It is strongly arguable that it is not a defence in so far as the word defence is understood in contradistinction to the idea of a denial. Except in cases in which trustees exceed their powers, where strict liability is imposed, no liability will be imposed on trustees unless they are at fault in their conduct. The professional advice rule, however, bears all of the hallmarks of a simple denial of fault on the part of the trustee. The idea is that a trustee who acts upon apparently competent advice is not at fault. But this analysis raises several puzzles. One question that arises is why, if professional advice is a mere denial of fault, does it comprise (as Ashdown argues) four elements. Why does the rule not turn, instead, on a conventional enquiry as to whether the trustee exercised reasonable care? The answer to this question may well be that the professional advice rule is merely a device that is aimed to lend greater structure to the enquiries as to whether a trustee is at fault in cases involving professional advice.

Peter Turner considers the controversial issue of monetary remedies available to beneficiaries following a misapplication of trust assets by trustees. The decisions of the House of Lords in *Target Holdings Ltd v Redferns*[24] and the Supreme Court in *AIB Group (UK) plc v Mark Redler & Co Solicitors*[25] have prompted a great deal of discussion, largely because—on at least one view—they seem to depart from long-standing equitable principles (despite the contrary protestations of Lord Toulson in the latter case). On a traditional view, trustees who misapply or misappropriate trust property immediately become liable to restore the trust property. Yet these more recent decisions perhaps suggest that rather than taking an account and falsifying improper disbursement, beneficiaries should simply sue for equitable compensation, and recover compensation for their loss (or, preferably, the loss suffered by the trust fund—at least in situations where there is not only one sole beneficiary under a bare trust).

Turner recognises that *Target* marked a shift in the law. But he explains this in a novel way. Turner argues that *Target*, and *AIB*, show that there has not been incorporated into the law a defence of 'want of causation'. As Turner puts it, 'where a trust suffers direct loss by reason of trustees' misapplication of trust moneys, the trustees' liability therefor may be reduced—even to nil—by showing that the loss

[23] There is clearly a connection of sorts between the professional advice rule and s 5 of the Trustee Act 2000 (UK), which imposes a duty on trustees who are exercising a power of investment to obtain and consider proper advice about how the power should be exercised.

[24] *Target Holdings Ltd v Redferns* [1996] AC 421 (HL).

[25] *AIB Group (UK) plc v Mark Redler & Co Solicitors* [2014] UKSC 58; [2015] AC 1503.

would have been suffered even had the moneys been properly applied'.[26] This is an unusual type of defence, and how and why the defence developed is somewhat murky, but Turner illustrates how the defence is consistent with both *Target* and *AIB*. Turner further argues that the decision of the High Court of Australia in *Youyang Pty Ltd v Minter Ellison Morris Fletcher*[27] provides support for such a defence, despite *Youyang* often being considered to show that Australian law remains grounded in traditional orthodoxy, unlike the decision of the Supreme Court in *AIB*.

Turner argues that Lord Reed's judgment should be considered to be the leading judgment in *AIB*, and this further restricts the scope and impact of *AIB* upon traditional equitable doctrine. The accounting process remains intact, but there is a defence available to trustees who manage to show that the loss would have been suffered regardless of the breach of duty. It will be interesting to see whether such a defence comes to be explicitly recognised by the courts. If it is, the outlines of the defence as sketched by Turner will no doubt prove to be helpful. In any event, recent judgments appear to show some inclination to restrict the scope of *AIB*,[28] and the pressures to fit *Target* and *AIB* within traditional equitable learning are considerable. It may be that a clear break has been made with the law prior to 1995, and it may also be that this has really been through adopting a 'want of causation' defence as Turner suggests.

VI. CO-TRUSTEES AND CREDITORS

Co-trustee liability is the focus of Joshua Getzler's contribution (chapter ten). Co-trustees are not agents the one for the other, and neither is one trustee vicariously liable for the acts of another. The liability of trustees is said to be 'joint and several', and Getzler carefully analyses what this means, and its implications. Getzler considers instances where an 'innocent' co-trustee seeks to escape liability because he simply followed an 'active' co-trustee, and whether this can be characterised as a defence. As Getzler suggests, the claim of the 'innocent' co-trustee might also be considered to be a denial, or amount to a dilution of liability, and classification of this issue is not entirely straightforward.

However, the issue remains important. In *Central Bank of Nigeria v Williams*[29] the Supreme Court had to decide upon the limitation regime applicable to dishonest assisters and knowing recipients. But in the course of his judgment, Lord Sumption made his view clear that an innocent co-trustee's joint liability for a co-trustee's fraudulent breach could still be shielded by limitation. Getzler questions why this should be so, and whether a co-trustee who tolerates or ignores the breaches of another should really be treated so generously.

Getzler combs through the origins of co-trustee liability, and highlights that a proper understanding of the modern law should rest upon its historical roots.

[26] ch 9 at p 155.
[27] *Youyang Pty Ltd v Minter Ellison Morris Fletcher* [2003] HCA 15; (2003) 212 CLR 484.
[28] See, eg, *Various Claimants v Giambrone and Law (A Firm)* [2017] EWCA Civ 1193.
[29] *Central Bank of Nigeria v Williams* [2014] UKSC 10; [2014] AC 1189.

Indeed, one reason why there are not very many modern cases discussing the issue of co-trustee liability appears to be that the law has already been well settled. That in turn has perhaps been one prompt for the rise of indemnity clauses, the broad nature of which causes Getzler some concern.[30] In any event, Getzler's exposition of the leading cases emphasises the importance of each trustee not hiding behind the decision of another trustee, and that each trustee should ensure personal knowledge of the state of the trust assets. As Getzler puts it, '[t]he duty of the co-trustee was apparently to mistrust the other co-trustees'. A trustee who fails to meet this duty should in general be equally liable with the other co-trustees, and only rarely should the principle of equal liability be departed from in contribution proceedings.

Christopher Hare (chapter 11) tackles the difficult doctrine of marshalling. Marshalling has long defied juridical classification and it is perhaps for this reason that it has not received the attention that it deserves. Hare analyses the problems inherent in treating marshalling as a 'right' or a 'remedy', and suggests that greater clarity can be achieved by considering at least some instances of marshalling to be an example of an equitable defence. Hare argues that no matter which explanation of marshalling is favoured, the doctrine operates as an essentially defensive tool in the hands of the junior secured creditor.

The recent decision of the Supreme Court in *National Crime Agency (formerly Serious Organised Crime Agency) v Szepietowski*[31] perhaps highlights that a reconsideration of marshalling comes at an opportune moment. Although the Supreme Court's decision was unanimous in result, the reasoning of the Justices diverged and the lack of agreement about the basis of marshalling leads to problems in its application.[32] Hare examines the roots of marshalling to illustrate that Equity has traditionally taken a broad view of 'unconscionability', and that, in its origins, marshalling could operate against both the senior secured creditor and the debtor. It might therefore be viewed as an equitable defence that a junior secured creditor could raise directly against the senior secured creditor, in order to restrict the latter's enforcement options against assets that the former viewed as collateral, but also as a defence raised against the debtor—or more likely the debtor's representatives, especially where the liquidator or administrator seeks directions from the court as to how to distribute the surplus from the sale of an asset by the senior security-holder.[33] It would seem that both possibilities can exist in tandem, and that adopting a 'hybrid' approach helps to maintain the doctrine's traditional flexibility. Greater appreciation of the historical origins of marshalling may well help to elucidate the modern law.

However, it is to be hoped that the flexibility sought does not lead marshalling to merge with subrogation. Functionally, the two doctrines appear similar: the junior creditor may effectively end up standing *pro tanto* in the shoes of the senior creditor

[30] *cf* Sales's chapter (ch 7).

[31] *National Crime Agency (formerly Serious Organised Crime Agency) v Szepietowski* [2013] UKSC 35; [2014] AC 338.

[32] There are other difficulties raised by the decision of the Supreme Court: for discussion of the relationship between a debt and a charge see, eg, N Hopkins, 'Marshalling Arguments: The Relationship Between a Debt and a Charge' [2014] Conv 344.

[33] See, eg, *McLean v Berry* [2016] EWHC 2650 (Ch); [2017] Ch 422.

in relation to an asset in which the junior creditor did not originally have a security interest. But such apparent equivalence should not obscure the different origins and purposes of the two doctrines. This seems particularly important given the complications that have recently surrounded subrogation following the decision of the Supreme Court in *Menelaou v Bank of Cyprus UK Ltd.*[34]

VII. ILLEGALITY AND UNCLEAN HANDS

The volume contains chapters that address the illegality and unclean hands doctrines respectively. These rules, in our view, are animated, at least superficially, by similar concerns,[35] and it is thus somewhat curious that the connection between them is not something that has been subjected to sustained critical examination to date. They are often treated in separate silos and we hope that presenting the chapters side by side in this volume will facilitate understanding regarding the nature of their relationship.

The illegality doctrine is addressed by Paul Davies (chapter 12). The law of illegality has been the subject of intensive investigation recently[36] and has been considered repeatedly over the course of the last few years at the ultimate appellate level. Matters came to a head when the Supreme Court handed down judgment in *Patel v Mirza*.[37] In that landmark decision, the Supreme Court opted for a 'range of factors' approach to the illegality doctrine in preference of the reliance test, which test was embraced by the House of Lords in *Tinsley v Milligan*.[38] Although *Patel* is a case in the law of unjust enrichment, the explicit rejection by the majority of the reasoning in *Tinsley*, a case in the law of trusts, leaves little room for any suggestion that the 'range of factors' analysis does not now govern the illegality doctrine as it applies in equity.[39]

Davies's primary concern in his chapter is to consider the impact of *Patel* in the bribery context in light of Lord Toulson's remark that the 'range of factors' approach to the law of illegality will rarely result in the denial of a claim in

[34] *Menelaou v Bank of Cyprus plc* [2015] UKSC 66; [2016] AC 176.

[35] According to *Snell's Equity*, the unclean hands 'maxim is closely related to the common law maxim ex turpi causa non oritur actio ("no action can arise from a bad cause")': J McGhee (ed), *Snell's Equity* 33rd edn (London, Sweet & Maxwell, 2016) para 5-010.

[36] Recent contributions include G Virgo, 'Illegality's Role in the Law of Torts' in M Dyson (ed), *Unravelling Tort and Crime* (Cambridge, CUP, 2014); B McLachlin, 'Weaving the Law's Seamless Web: Reflections on the Illegality Defence in Tort Law' in Dyson, Goudkamp and Wilmot-Smith (2015) (n 1); RA Buckley, 'Illegality in the Supreme Court' (2015) 131 *LQR* 341; J Fisher, 'The Ex Turpi Causa Principle in Hounga and Servier' (2015) 78 *MLR* 854; J Goudkamp, 'The Doctrine of Illegality: A Private Law Hydra' (2015) 6 *United Kingdom Supreme Court Yearbook* 254; N Strauss, 'Ex Turpi Causa Oritur Actio?' (2016) 132 *LQR* 236; S Erbacher, *Negligence and Illegality* (Oxford, Hart, 2017); A Grabiner, 'Illegality and Restitution Explained by the Supreme Court' (2017) 76 *CLJ* 18.

[37] *Patel v Mirza* [2016] UKSC 42; [2017] AC 467.

[38] *Tinsley v Milligan* [1994] 1 AC 340 (HL).

[39] Davies opines that the 'range of factors' approach applies to private law generally: ch 12 at p 250.

unjust enrichment.[40] Davies's thesis is that bribers should generally be unable to recover the payments that they made and he casts doubt on the merits of *Patel* to the extent that it suggests that the bribes might be more readily recoverable by the payor than was previously the case. Davies also contends that *Patel* should neither be construed as obstructing a claim by a beneficiary to recover a bribe under a constructive trust nor as standing in the way of any personal claims that the beneficiary may have against bribers and bribees.

One important issue is what (if anything) justifies the illegality doctrine. *Patel* does not endeavour to answer to that question.[41] The Supreme Court's concern was not with the justifiability of the illegality doctrine—it was essentially assumed that the doctrine was justified—but with the test that should be applied to determine when illegality on the part of the claimant is sufficiently associated with the claimant's cause of action that the claim should fail. The question of what justifies the doctrine is separate from that of pursuant to which test the doctrine (if it is justified) falls to be governed. Davies is more concerned in his chapter with the former issue. He sees rather more promise than do many other writers in the concept of deterrence as one potential rationale (among several), although his remarks are intended to be suggestive rather than a fully-developed argument on this score.

Nicholas McBride (chapter 13) asks whether the unclean hands doctrine should remain part of the law or whether it should be swallowed up by the defence of illegality. McBride thus engages with a familiar but important debate, namely, whether it is desirable that an equitable counterpart to a common law defence should continue to be recognised. McBride proceeds by organising remedies into three groups: (1) remedies to which a claimant is 'entitled', (2) remedies that are 'necessary' to grant in order to preserve the legitimacy of the legal system, and (3) 'supererogatory' remedies that are neither remedies to which the claimant is entitled nor remedies that it is necessary to award and which are awarded on the basis that granting them does more good than harm. McBride places within category (3) specific performance, most injunctions and aggravated damages. He seems to suggest that it is unclear whether rescission and remedies for unjust enrichment fall within category (2) or category (3). Having put this taxonomy in place, McBride argues that it is proper for the law to take into account the uncleanliness of the claimant's hands where the claimant seeks a category (3) remedy. He writes: 'in determining whether awarding a [supererogatory remedy] would do more harm than good, it would seem irrational not to have regard to the question of whether awarding [the claimant] a [supererogatory remedy] would encourage people to engage in undesirable forms of behaviour'.[42] Once this is appreciated,

[40] *Patel* (n 37) [116].

[41] Although note Lord Toulson's brief remark at, ibid, [99] that 'there are two broad discernible policy reasons for the common law doctrine of illegality as a defence to a civil claim. One is that a person should not be allowed to profit from his own wrongdoing. The other, linked, consideration is that the law should be coherent and not self-defeating, condoning illegality by giving with the left hand what it takes with the right hand.'

[42] ch 13 at p 287.

McBride says, it becomes clear that room must be preserved for the unclean hands doctrine. As he puts it:[43]

> The law on illegality should be seen as being concerned with whether awarding a remedy would normally be awarded in order to preserve the legitimacy of the law will in fact do more harm than good *to the law's legitimacy*. By contrast, the law on clean hands should be seen as being concerned with whether awarding a supererogatory remedy will do more harm than good *in general*, given the way that the person seeking that remedy has behaved in the past.

It would appear to be necessary to make various changes to both the illegality and unclean hands doctrines in order for McBride's analysis to fit the positive law regarding these rules. It is tolerably clear that the law of illegality, as recast by the Supreme Court in *Patel*, is sensitive to matters that do not immediately relate to the preservation of the law's legitimacy. Similarly, it is fairly obvious that the application of the unclean hands does not turn on an enquiry as to whether utility would be maximised by denying the remedy sought. None of this necessarily impugns McBride's treatment. The point is merely that his argument appears to require that certain changes be made to the law.

VIII. STATUTE, LIMITATION AND LACHES

The burden of Mark Leeming's chapter (chapter 14), is to examine the relationship between equity and statutes of limitation. The analysis is motivated mainly by the fact that equity sometimes 'follows' limitation statutes even where those statutes do not apply in terms. Leeming's concerns are several but a key issue for him is the circumstances in which equity should deny its assistance in view of a relevant statute of limitation even though the statute does not, properly construed, apply directly. It may well be that Leeming's analysis will assist in understanding the intersection between equity and statutory law more generally, even though limitation statutes are his focus.

It is important to appreciate that Leeming's chapter is concerned with just one facet of what is a much wider problem, namely, the circumstances in which judge-made law can and should be developed by analogy with statutory law.[44] That problem is magnified in Australia (as Leeming's chapter amply demonstrates) on account of Australia's unique federal arrangements and the major differences in the statutory law that prevail in different states and territories. It is on account of these and certain other considerations that Australian courts, perhaps more so than the courts in any other common law country, are required to dedicate significant resources to statutory construction and grappling with the interplay between statutory and judge-made law.

[43] ibid at p 288.

[44] Classic treatments of this subject include R Pound, 'Common Law and Legislation' (1908) 21 *Harvard Law Review* 383; PS Atiyah, 'Common Law and Statute Law' (1985) 48 *MLR* 1.

Leeming's overarching thesis is, ultimately, fairly modest; namely, that everything depends upon the precise parameters and objectives of the legislation in issue and the particular equitable doctrine that is under consideration. In his words, the matter in the end entails 'a contestable question of judgment, based upon the nature and purpose of the statue in question, as well as the similarity or otherwise of the equitable claim to the legal claim which engages the statute'.[45] The modesty of this thesis does not, of course, diminish the complexity or importance of the tasks that Leeming isolates.

Complexity in this area of defences is not merely a product of the interaction between case law and statute but also a consequence of the multiplicity of defences that are closely related to limitation bars. The effluxion of time seems to form the basis of, in addition to limitation bars, several other defences, including laches, estoppel, acquiescence and release. These defences, as Lusina Ho demonstrates in her chapter (chapter 15), overlap to a considerable extent. For instance, a promise not to sue on a past breach might in one particular case be pleaded as a release, acquiescence and even laches. This can be a source of confusion. One possible way of reducing the complexity of the law in this regard that is alluded to in some cases[46] but rejected by Ho is to roll the various defences into a single principle of estoppel. By delaying bringing a claim, the argument goes, the claimant represents to the defendant that he will not stand upon his rights, and the defendant might then rely upon this representation to his detriment. This overarching principle of estoppel, based upon a broad notion of unconscionability, is dismissed by Ho as being overly simplistic. In her chapter, she pulls apart the separate threads underpinning these defences, and shows that they each recognise various moral duties. These moral duties, Ho contends, are distinct and ought not to be subsumed by a generic principle of unconscionability.

Delay in bringing a claim is not normally a reason, in and of itself, to deny that claim. Rather, it is the further facts that tend to follow from delay that do the normative work in this field. Ho distinguishes between three types of case. First, where there has been undue delay it might be the case that the claimant has, expressly or impliedly, promised not to sue the defendant for a past breach. The claimant's moral duty to do as he promised, and not sue, bars the claim. Second, a delay might be evidence that a claimant has represented to the defendant that he does not have a cause of action against the defendant. The defendant's detrimental reliance upon this representation might furnish him with a good reason to bar the claim. Third, delay might, independently of what the claimant has promised or represented, encourage the defendant to believe that he is free from liability. Any subsequent claim might cause irreversible prejudice to the defendant. These are the normative reasons identified by Ho for denying a claim.

Ho's approach avoids the arguably unsatisfactory overlap between the actions by linking them to the three principles identified in the chapter. This requires a fair amount of re-arranging. Laches, for instance, can be disaggregated into cases where

[45] ch 14 at p 309.
[46] Eg, *Orr v Ford* (1989) 167 CLR 316, 339 (Deane J).

delay amounts to a representation that the claimant holds no rights, and cases where there is no representation, but the defendant will suffer irreversible prejudice. Acquiescence can similarly be split up between cases where the silence amounts to a promise not to sue and a representation that the claimant holds no cause of action against the defendant. Under Ho's analysis these cases ought to be treated separately. This is an ambitious project but Ho makes a compelling case for a more coherent taxonomy of defences arising in cases of undue delay.

2

Equitable Defences as Meta-Law

HENRY E SMITH*

I. INTRODUCTION

IS THERE ANYTHING special about equitable defences? Historically, equity courts developed defences that displayed certain characteristics. Equitable defences tended to be more discretionary, to sound in morality and to defeat remedies—themselves denominated equitable—rather than cutting off liability altogether. Nevertheless, treating these defences as more than an historical happenstance or institutional artifact is difficult, because common law defences sometimes involve discretion and reflect moral considerations. And saying that an equitable defence is paired with an equitable remedy leaves us with the question of what is uniquely equitable about remedies like an injunction, reformation or accounting. Conversely, many equitable defences do not look all that discretionary or uniquely infused with morality. And after the fusion of law and equity, the pairing of equitable defences with 'equitable' remedies has partially broken down, and looks ripe for further assimilation.[1] So it would appear that treating equitable defences as an interesting or justifiably separate category would be a tall order.

In this chapter, I argue that there is an interesting and functionally justified notion of 'equitable defence'. It is not coextensive with what went under that heading when there were separate equity courts. And yet I will argue that the law-equity divide is not irrelevant to a functional theory of equitable defences. Because equity drew on a tradition in which equity corrects law where law fails owing to its generality and because equity intervened literally from outside the law, functional equity and functionally equitable defences in particular tended (but only tended) to originate in equity jurisdiction.

What is an equitable defence, functionally speaking? In related work I develop a theory of the equitable function, in which equity serves as a second-order safety

* Fessenden Professor of Law and Director of the Project on the Foundations of Private Law, Harvard Law School. For helpful questions and comments, I would like to thank participants at the Workshop on Defences in Equity, Jesus College, Oxford, and a faculty workshop at the Harvard Law School. Thanks to Molly Brown for excellent research assistance. All errors require a defence on my part.

[1] See, eg, A Burrows, 'We Do This at Common Law But That in Equity' (2002) 22 *OJLS* 1; D Laycock, 'The Triumph of Equity' (Summer 1993) 56 *Law and Contemporary Problems* 53; A Mason, 'Fusion' in S Degeling and J Edelman (eds), *Equity in Commercial Law* (Sydney, Lawbook Co, 2005). See also A Schwartz, 'The Case for Specific Performance' (1979) 89 *Yale Law Journal* 271, 298–303.

valve on the regular law.[2] The 'regular' part of the law, precisely because it aspires to be general, faces difficulties with hard-to-foresee problems that disturb the stable relationships between activities. Equity on this account is a function that consists of second-order intervention into the rest of the law. That is, equity is law about law; equity refers to law but not vice versa. Some defences serve this equitable function, and for that reason deserve the name 'equitable'.

This chapter will begin in section II by setting out how some law can function as meta-law and why historically equity courts focused on serving this function. Section III turns to special considerations that arise when defences, many of them historically equitable, serve a second-order function in solving problems of uncertainty and variability, especially party opportunism. Section IV explores the dynamic dimension of equity and shows how the equitable function leads to new law. The chapter ends with some thoughts on the implications of equitable defences as meta-law for the debates over the fusion of law and equity.

II. EQUITY FUNCTIONING AS META-LAW

Many aspects of law are second or higher order—they operate at a meta level. For example, a power is second order in the sense that one who has a power can change legal relations: the power refers to (and potentially changes) these legal relations. But not vice versa: those lower-order legal relations do not make reference to the power that might change them.[3] Thus, a power to transfer is the power to change who holds a right (and who bears the corresponding duties). A power to legislate is the power to create law. Even courts in the common law when adjusting legal rules to fit new conditions, in a sort of quasi-legislation, are exercising a power—a power to change the law.[4] They are engaged in a 'meta' enterprise: the judicial law-creating process makes reference to the law, which by its terms need not make reference to this (higher-order) process. Thus, there are many aspects of law and the legal system that could be termed 'meta'.[5]

[2] HE Smith, 'Why Fiduciary Law Is Equitable' in AS Gold and PB Miller (eds), *Philosophical Foundations of Fiduciary Law* (Oxford, Oxford University Press, 2014) 261–84; HE Smith, 'Fusing the Equitable Function in Private Law' in K Barker, K Fairweather, and R Grantham (eds), Private Law in the 21st Century (Oxford, Hart Publishing, 2017); HE Smith, 'Equity as Second-Order Law: The Problem of Opportunism' (unpublished manuscript, 15 January 2015) <http://ssrn.com/abstract=2617413>.

[3] See WN Hohfeld, 'Fundamental Legal Conceptions as Applied in Judicial Reasoning' (1913) 23 *Yale Law Journal* 16, 44–58; U Pagano, 'Public Markets, Private Orderings and Public Governance' (2000) 20 *International Review of Law and Economics* 453, 459–65; TM Sichelman, 'Quantifying Legal Entropy' (2013) San Diego Legal Studies Paper No 13-128, available at http://ssrn.com/abstract=2293015. Although I do not rule out that there may be higher orders than second, for present purposes I will deal with questions of meta-law as involving a second order.

[4] It is interesting that the traditional aversion to admitting this casts this function as sounding as if it were not second order at all.

[5] The 'rules about rules' in Robert Stevens' chapter in this volume (ch 3) are meta, and it worth pointing out that equitable set-off involves adjustment to primary claims in the light of relationships between claims that are variable, complex and hard to foresee. Also 'meta', in a sense, are equitable rights if one views them as rights against rights. See B McFarlane and R Stevens, 'The Nature of Equitable Property' (2010) 4 *Journal of Equity* 1.

I argue that there is a special kind of meta-law that deals with problems that become too complex and unforeseeable to be easily handled at the primary level on which they arise. The most compelling and immediate problem faced by a system of 'general' law is efforts by actors within the system of finding its weak points and exploiting them. This is a familiar problem in tax law but is true across law.[6] For example, what happens when someone uses the possibility of an injunction solely to extract payment from a rights violator out of all proportion to the actual injury suffered? What if someone invokes the letter of a contract in order to evade payment for the full value received, as where a builder inadvertently uses a pipe that is the wrong brand but that is of equal quality?[7] One could always imagine the law being better spelled out, contracts covering more contingencies, or some source supplying better and more complete information to primary actors, but none of this is costless. The fear is that as soon as these holes are plugged, opportunists will find yet others to exploit.[8] One option is to do the best one can at the primary level and then tolerate whatever bad behaviour falls through the cracks.

There is yet another solution: equity. By 'equity' I mean a part of the law serving a particular function.[9] For historical and institutional reasons this function was a theme—but only one theme and not the exclusive preserve of equity courts.

What is the equitable function and how is it served? In systems theory, problems of high variance and uncertainty sometimes call for a solution at a higher level.[10] In hierarchy, the higher-order component makes reference to the primary component but not vice versa.[11] Think of part of a computer program that keeps values at a primary level within a certain range. Or a safety valve that kicks in when a threshold is reached. I argue that equity serves a function much like this in law.

Equity is a second-order safety valve on the law, which responds to problems of special complexity and unforeseeability. These include not only opportunism,

[6] DA Weisbach, 'Formalism in the Tax Law' (1999) 66 *University of Chicago Law Review* 860. See also SB Lawsky, 'Probably? Understanding Tax Law's Uncertainty' (2009) 157 *University of Pennsylvania Law Review* 1017, 1032, arguing that tax law uses probabilistic doctrines because 'the essence of a tax shelter is that it technically complies with the law while nonetheless violating the substance or intent of the law, which is no easy thing to determine'; SS Surrey, 'Complexity and the Internal Revenue Code: The Problem of the Management of Tax Detail' (1969) 34 *Law and Contemporary Problems* 673, 707, fn 31.

[7] *Jacob & Youngs v Kent* 129 NE 889 (NY 1921); VP Goldberg, 'Rethinking *Jacob & Youngs v. Kent*' (2015) 66 *Case Western Reserve Law Review* 111; HE Smith, 'Is Equitable Contract Law a Pipe Dream?' (*New Private Law*, 9 June 2016) <http://blogs.harvard.edu/nplblog/2016/06/09/is-equitable-contract-law-a-pipe-dream-henry-smith/>.

[8] This is one reason why parties may contract in anticipation of some opportunism, but the law will not allow parties to bargain out of the duty of good faith. Opportunism may also arise in the context of litigation over remedies. See *Ruxley Electronics and Construction Ltd v Forsyth* [1996] AC 344 (HL), in which the judge took the plaintiff's offer to use the damages to rebuild a swimming pool, which did not conform to the contract but was equivalent in market price, as vindictive and extortionate. See also Smith (n 7).

[9] See the sources cited above at n 2.

[10] See, eg, AY Aulin-Ahmavaara, 'The Law of Requisite Hierarchy' (1979) 8 *Kybernetes* 259; F Heylighen and C Joslyn, 'Cybernetics and Second-Order Cybernetics' in RA Meyers (ed), *Encyclopedia of Physical Science and Technology* 3rd edn (San Diego, Academic Press, 2002).

[11] See, eg, KL von Bertalanffy, *General System Theory* (New York, Braziller, 1968). See also JH Holland, *Hidden Order* (Reading MA, Addison-Wesley, 1995) 11–12, discussing second-order agents and properties.

but also conflicting rights and multipolar interactions.[12] For example, certain problems in nuisance require an equitable style of analysis in which the interaction between two potential uses is analysed in terms of what maximises mutual freedom or utility, in a symmetric fashion.[13] Multipolar problems, which Lon Fuller, borrowing from Michael Polanyi, called 'polycentric', involve multiple parties and many interdependencies. Fuller gave as an example the problem of dividing up a collection of paintings left under a will to two museums without instructions as to which paintings would go to which museum.[14] The problem is complex because the value to a museum of each painting depends on the other paintings it gets. The interdependencies here make this a problem like those familiar from complexity theory, in which the time required to solve the problem sometimes increases exponentially in the size of the problem.[15] In complexity theory, such problems tend to call for approximate solutions.

They also often call for solutions at a higher level. Consider opportunism. Anticipating opportunism is inherently difficult. By evaluating it ex post, the court or other decision-maker has the advantage of moving second. The opportunist in some sense operates at a higher level than other parties: such actors have the entire system in view and exploit it accordingly. By moving to the same higher level, courts and other decision-makers can occupy the same ground. Ex post and somewhat context-dependent decision-making also can be tailored to the problem presented by a specific instance of opportunism.

Unconstrained, such a second-order intervention is a powerful tool, and it is correspondingly destabilising. If it could in principle have any effect based on any combination of circumstances at the primary level, it would create a great deal of uncertainty in its results and would undermine the guidance function of the law. Opponents of equity were quick to point out this tendency, and accused equity courts of going too far down this road. Hence the gibe about the 'Chancellor's Foot'.[16]

[12] Smith, 'Fusing the Equitable Function in Private Law' (n 2); Smith, 'Equity as Second-Order Law' (n 2).

[13] JCP Goldberg and HE Smith, 'Wrongful Fusion: Equity and Tort' in JCP Goldberg, HE Smith and PG Turner (eds), *Equity and Law: Fusion and Fission* (Cambridge, Cambridge University Press, forthcoming). A limited equitable function within and around the law of tort does not amount to general equitable jurisdiction over torts, much less crimes.

[14] LL Fuller, 'The Forms and Limits of Adjudication' in KI Winston (ed), *The Principles of Social Order: Selected Essays of Lon L. Fuller* (Oxford, Hart Publishing, 2001) 126–36, introducing the concept of polycentric tasks. See also M Polanyi, *The Logic of Liberty; Reflections and Rejoinders* (Chicago, University of Chicago Press, 1965) 171.

[15] A famous similar problem is the so-called 'knapsack problem', in which one is required to choose the combination out of a given set of n items that will maximise value under a given weight limit. This problem requires exponential time (as n increases) and is in the class of probably intractable problems known as 'NP-complete'. See R Greenlaw and HJ Hoover, *Fundamentals of the Theory of Computation: Principles and Practice* (San Francisco, Morgan Kaufmann, 1998) 287–313; K Devlin, *The Millennium Problems: The Seven Greatest Unsolved Mathematical Puzzles of Our Time* (New York, Basic Books, 2002) 105–30.

[16] The most famous critique of equity is that of John Selden, 'Equity' in R Milward (ed), *Table-Talk: Being the Discourses of John Selden, Esq* (London, JM Dent & Co, 1898) 43, 43–44: 'Equity is a Roguish thing: for law we have a measure, know what to trust to; Equity is according to the Conscience of him that is Chancellor, and as that is larger or narrower, so is Equity. 'Tis all one as if they should make the Standard for the measure we call a Foot, a Chancellor's Foot; what an uncertain Measure would be this. One Chancellor has a long Foot, another a short Foot, a Third an indifferent Foot: 'Tis the same thing in the Chancellor's Conscience'. See generally JH Baker, *An Introduction to English Legal History* 4th edn (London, Butterworths LexisNexis, 2002) 96–115.

As with second-order interventions generally, the conditions for going to the second level can prevent this unravelling. In a safety valve, there are conditions that delimit when it becomes relevant. So too in equity, the basic presumption is for law, and it can only be overcome when some triggering conditions are met. Some of these triggers are proxies for opportunism, which in turn operate in a domain of potential application.

In traditional equity, then, the domain of potential applicability of equity was the familiar trio of 'fraud, accident, and mistake'.[17] Crucially, equity has no roving commission to root out opportunism wherever it can be found. On the contrary, equity only kicks in when it is triggered. The triggers for equity as an anti-opportunism device sound in bad faith and disproportionate hardship. The exact triggers differ somewhat depending on the class of problems involved. Thus in building encroachments, a continuing trespass gives rise to a presumption for an injunction. But if the injunction would visit much greater hardship on the defendant than on the plaintiff, a court may withhold the injunction, leaving the plaintiff to a damages remedy.[18] Nevertheless if the encroachment was in bad faith, which in the context of building means knowledge of the boundary, the defence of disproportionate (or undue) hardship would be unavailable and the injunction would issue. In contracts, the unconscionability defence works similarly, the trigger being a combination of a startlingly one-sided result and a vulnerable party. Once this trigger has been satisfied, the contract is subjected to some version of a closer scrutiny on fairness grounds, an analysis in which conscious exploitation plays an important role.

Much of the danger in fraud, accident, and mistake comes from the opening they afford for advantage-taking. In traditional parlance, the problem was 'constructive fraud', which not atypically takes up the bulk of Justice Story's treatise. He describes constructive fraud:[19]

> There is always fraud presumed or inferred from the circumstances or conditions of the parties contracting, weakness on one side, usury on the other, or extortion or advantage

[17] *American Jurisprudence* 2nd edn (2016) vol 47, 'Judgments' § 718, Westlaw (database updated November 2015): 'Generally, claimants seeking equitable relief from judgments through independent actions must meet three requirements [the third of which is that] they must establish a recognized ground, such as fraud, accident, or mistake, for the equitable relief' (footnotes omitted, citing cases). See also WF Walsh, *A Treatise on Mortgages* (Chicago, Callaghan and Co, 1934) 6, 11, regarding relief from mortgages in equity on grounds of fraud, accident or mistake; VD Ricks, 'American Mutual Mistake: Half-Civilian Mongrel, Consideration Reincarnate' (1998) 58 *Louisiana Law Review* 663, 717, and see also at fn 277, speculating that Chief Justice Allen in *Swift v Hawkins* 1 Dall 17 (Pa 1768) 'considered "mistake" to be representative of all categories of equity'. A poetic version is attributed to Thomas More, the first lawyer to serve as Chancellor: 'Three things are to be helpt in Conscience; Fraud, Accident and things of Confidence', 1 Rolle's Abridgement 374. See also *Coco v AN Clark (Engineers) Ltd* [1969] RPC 41, 46 (Ch) (Megarry J), quoting More's couplet; A Laussat Jr, *An Essay on Equity in Pennsylvania* (Philadelphia, Robert Desilver, 1826) 67, stating that 'Sir Thomas More used to say that the following doggerel contained all the heads of chancery jurisdiction'.

[18] *American Jurisprudence* 2nd edn (2005) vol 42, 'Injunctions' § 35: 'Even if the wrongful acts are indisputable, an injunction may be denied if the payment of money would afford substantial redress and if the injunction would subject the defendant to grossly disproportionate hardship'; D Laycock, 'The Neglected Defense of Undue Hardship (and the Doctrinal Train Wreck in Boomer v. Atlantic Cement)' (2011) 4 *Journal of Tort Law*, Issue 3, Article 3.

[19] J Story, *Commentaries on Equity Jurisprudence, As Administered in England and America* (Boston MA, Hilliard, Gray & Co, 1836) § 334. See also *Nocton v Ashburton* [1914] AC 932, 954 (Viscount

taken of that weakness. There has always been an appearance of fraud from the nature of the bargain, even if there be no proof of any circumvention, but merely from the intrinsic unconscionableness of the bargain.

The notion of constructive fraud is how the law captures opportunism. Whether opportunism is a useful category at all has been controversial in economics for reasons analogous to the debate about equity. Elsewhere I have defined opportunism as 'behavior that is undesirable but that cannot be cost-effectively captured—defined, detected, and deterred—by explicit ex ante rulemaking … It often consists of behavior that is technically legal but is done with a view to securing unintended benefits from the system, and these benefits are usually smaller than the costs they impose on others'.[20] The nature of opportunism often calls for second-order treatment, which will inevitably be somewhat ex post and open-ended.[21] As Story put it his treatise, equity had to be open-ended and flexible because '[f]raud is infinite' given the 'fertility of man's invention'.[22]

The debate among economists about opportunism offers instructive parallels. The most famous invocation of opportunism can be found in the work of Nobel laureate Oliver Williamson, who defines opportunism as 'self-interest seeking with guile'.[23] Apparently Williamson sees any rule-breaking as opportunism. And yet because not all rule-breaking causes the kind of complexity and uncertainty at issue here, not all rule-breaking calls for extraordinary intervention, much less at a meta level. It is Williamson's 'guile' that seems special. Likewise in other definitions of opportunism based on defeating legitimate expectations and the like, we see undistilled hints of what calls for meta level treatment.[24]

Haldane LC): 'What it really means in this connection ["constructive fraud"] is, not moral fraud in the ordinary sense, but breach of the sort of obligation which is enforced by a Court which from the beginning regarded itself as a Court of conscience'; JN Pomeroy, *A Treatise on Equity Jurisprudence* (San Francisco, Bancroft-Whitney Co, 1907) §§ 922–23. One modern approach is to sever the connection with fraud by replacing the notion of 'constructive fraud' with undue influence and unconscionable transactions. See John McGhee (ed), *Snell's Equity* 33rd edn (London, Sweet and Maxwell, 2015) ch 8.

[20] Smith, 'Equity as Second-Order Law' (n 2) 14–15.

[21] Smith, 'Fusing the Equitable Function in Private Law' (n 2); Smith, 'Equity as Second-Order Law' (n 2).

[22] Story (n 19) § 186 (at 196) fn 4, quoting a letter from Lord Hardwicke to Lord Kames (June 30 1759). Chancellor Ellesmere made a similar point in *The Earl of Oxford's Case* (1615) 1 Ch Rep 1, 6; 21 ER 485, 486: 'The Cause why there is a Chancery is, for that Mens Actions are so divers and infinite, That it is impossible to make any general Law which may aptly meet with every particular Act, and not fail in some Circumstances'.

[23] OE Williamson, *The Economic Institutions of Capitalism* (New York, Free Press, 1985) 47.

[24] See, eg, GM Cohen, 'The Negligence-Opportunism Tradeoff in Contract Law' (1992) 20 *Hofstra Law Review* 941, 957, defining 'opportunism' as 'any contractual conduct by one party contrary to the other party's reasonable expectations based on the parties' agreement, contractual norms, or conventional morality' (footnotes omitted); TJ Muris, 'Opportunistic Behavior and the Law of Contracts' (1981) 65 *Minnesota Law Review* 521, 521, defining 'opportunism' as conduct that is 'contrary to the other party's understanding of their contract, but not necessarily contrary to the agreement's explicit terms'. See also, eg, SW Buell, 'Good Faith and Law Evasion' (2011) 58 *UCLA Law Review* 611, 623: 'In common parlance, the evasive actor is one whose project is to get around the law. She seeks to avoid sanction while engaging, in substance, in the very sort of behavior that the law means to price or punish'. For a wider definition, see, eg, RA Posner, *Economic Analysis of Law* 5th edn (New York, Aspen Law & Business, 1998) § 4.1 (at 103), defining 'opportunism' in the contracting context as 'trying to take advantage of the vulnerabilities created by the sequential character of contractual performance'.

On the other side are economists who think that opportunism is uninteresting and unimportant. All behaviour is self-interested and any such behaviour within the constraints offered by institutions is legitimate; if not, then the rules of the game need to be changed.[25] In a sense, these economists are arguing that behaviour and institutions should be evaluated on one level. Behaviour is behaviour and sets of rules either constrain it cost-effectively or they do not. This view also resonates with a view about rights: that a right is not a right if one cannot exercise it without being second-guessed as to motive.[26] For some, abuse of a right is not a legitimate doctrine; if there is a problem with certain exercises of the right, then the only choices are to redefine rights or to tolerate the behaviour in question.

In the present account of equity, the ambition is not to capture it perfectly. Instead, the presumptions and the triggers that overcome them aim to sweep in a mix of behaviour that contains enough opportunism that closer and more open-ended scrutiny will do more good than harm. If this is how the equitable function works it is understandable that it is often mistaken for something else. A determinate approach at the primary rather than a meta level would require something very different. Modern commentators such as Douglas Laycock tend to dismiss notions like the irreparable injury 'rule' as not constraining because one can point to a wide variety of situations in which it does not prevent a court from ordering specific performance or issuing an injunction.[27] These critiques are well-taken if equity were first order, and yet invocations of irreparable injury may make sense as a signal that a court is overcoming the presumption against equity. Indeed, if as Laycock argues, it would be better to replace notions like irreparable injury and equity with functionally justified substitutes, we should consider whether something like the irreparable injury requirement—and equity—can be justified as a method of implementing the two-tier architecture.

Interestingly, the architecture of presumptions and meta levels surfaces occasionally in moral philosophy as well. In threshold deontology a moral principle holds until one crosses some threshold: in an extreme enough situation, other (for example, consequentialist) considerations can come into play. Quite parallel to the idea of an equitable safety valve in law is Philip Pettit's idea that we should be guided by general dispositions until certain 'contextual cues', 'red lights' or 'alarm bells' go off and then we should be guided by the 'stand-by guide' of general principles of right.[28]

[25] Y Barzel, 'Transaction Costs: Are They Just Costs?' (1985) 141 *Journal of Institutional and Theoretical Economics* 4, 10–11, arguing that because it is costly to tell whether someone is acting in a self-seeking manner and not 'as he should', the concept of opportunism does not help in understanding behaviour and only confuses; P Klein, 'Does Transaction Cost Economics Need Opportunism?' (*Organizations and Markets*, 6 October 2006) <http://organizationsandmarkets.com/2006/10/06/does-transaction-cost-economics-need-opportunism/>. See also OE Williamson, 'Opportunism and Its Critics' (1993) 14 *Managerial and Decision Economics* 97, defending the usefulness of the notion of opportunism against social science critics.

[26] See, eg, L Smith, 'The Motive, Not the Deed' in J Getzler (ed), *Rationalizing Property, Equity and Trusts: Essays in Honour of Edward Burn* (London, LexisNexis UK, 2003) 66; N Shoked, 'Two Hundred Years of Spite' (2016) 110 *Northwestern University Law Review* 357, 371.

[27] D Laycock, *The Death of the Irreparable Injury Rule* (Oxford, Oxford University Press, 1991); D Laycock, 'The Death of the Irreparable Injury Rule' (1990) 103 *Harvard Law Review* 687, 688–701.

[28] P Pettit, *The Robust Demands of the Good: Ethics with Attachment, Virtue, and Respect* (Oxford, Oxford University Press, 2015) 221.

Pettit offers as an example the old joke that a good friend will help you move an apartment but only a very good friend will help you move a body.[29] One should be guided by an automatic loyalty to friends until a red light goes off—as when a murder might be involved. Pettit develops a model of moral psychology in which the sensitivity to cues for switching to the stand-by strategy is a skill, which he likens to Aristotle's 'phronesis' and Aquinas' 'prudentia'.[30] To this we can add that the skill also requires knowing how not to switch to the stand-by strategy too quickly. This kind of wisdom helps connect the general and particular.

Equity works similarly. A certain prudence or practical wisdom is necessary for the implementation of equity. Only when certain contextual cues—I have been calling them proxies or triggers—are invoked does one switch from relatively general and simple rules to a more open-ended and direct employment of principles.

Note that the stand-by—or safety-valve—role for equity implements a kind of modularisation and specialisation. The two-tier structure can help to overcome complexity. The second-order safety valve is a specialised module connected by an interface of the proxies and presumptions, the triggers for going from 'law' to 'equity'. Modularity in general helps manage complexity by breaking a complex system into parts and allowing them to interact only in certain ways.[31] A complex system is one in which it is hard to predict the properties of the whole from the properties of its parts, and the effect of modularity is to contain such ripple effects. A two-tiered or hierarchical structure of modules is a familiar one that is suited for certain kinds of problems involving uncertainty and variability. In functional equity, it is the reservation of some problems, such as opportunism or multipolar problems, to be solved at the second, equitable level that allows first-order rules to be more formal—less contextual and less complex—than they would otherwise be. In other words, functional equity is a module with a largely one-way connection (interface) to the rest of the law. It is triggered by proxies (the stand-by system is conditioned on an alarm) and once triggered it makes use of a wide range of information at the primary level. That primary level does not make reference to the second level. The primary level can be simpler, more general and hence easier to use, if it is backstopped with a resort to general considerations. The triggers (alarm bells) are a simple method for cabining the powerful and complex tool of applying general considerations—freer use of context. Because the freer use of context is confined in this manner, it can be more thoroughgoing and effective than if it were used more generally.

[29] ibid.

[30] ibid 222. RC Bartlett and SD Collins (trs), *Aristotle's Nicomachean Ethics* 3rd edn (Chicago, University of Chicago Press, 2011) 120–21 [Book 6 ch 5, 1140a24ff]; St T Aquinas, *Summa Theologiae*, (Fathers of the English Dominican Province trs, Westminster, Christian Classics, 1981) IIaIIae 47.2 ad 1, IIaIIae 47.4.

[31] See, eg, CY Baldwin and KB Clark, *Design Rules: The Power of Modularity*, vol 1 (Cambridge MA, MIT Press, 2000); R Garud, A Kumaraswamy and RN Langlois (eds), *Managing in the Modular Age: Architectures, Networks and Organizations* (Malden MA, Blackwell, 2002); HA Simon, *The Sciences of the Artificial* 2nd edn (Cambridge MA, MIT Press, 1981) 195–200; RN Langlois, 'Modularity in Technology and Organization' (2002) 49 *Journal of Economic Behavior & Organization* 19; R Sanchez and JT Mahoney, 'Modularity, Flexibility, and Knowledge Management in Product and Organization Design' (1996, Winter Special Issue) 17 *Strategic Management Journal* 63.

It is probably no accident that equity and moral psychology would share such a structure. A possible reason for their similarity is that they both respond to the same considerations of system organisation. The demands of managing complexity and achieving the goals of 'correct' decision-making lead to hierarchy and specialisation through modularity. Using the stand-by system only—all equity all the time—would be complicated and prone to error. And using the general rules would fail spectacularly in extreme circumstances.

Indeed, the idea that equity saves law from bad results in extreme situations resonates with aspects of the equitable tradition. Much of that tradition, including cases and commentary, invokes the Aristotelian idea that equity is 'a correction of law in the respect in which it is deficient because of its being general'.[32] What sets theories of equity apart is what counts as a failure of law owing to its generality. The broadest version of equity would aspire to capture every occurence of unfairness or every ex post instance of lack of fit between rules and their purposes. On the safety-valve account offered here, equity is not primary. Instead, primary law is meant to guide conduct and to apply generally, not on a case-by-case basis. But the attempt to be general runs up against limits from complexity and lack of foreseeability.

Modularity allows equity to specialise as well in its degree of formalism relative to law. Within the domain of equity, decision-makers are able to make freer use of context than they usually can. It is a truism that equity is less formal than law, but it is true in a deep sense. Formalism can be defined as relative invariance to context.[33] Thus English is less formal than computer languages, and the notation of everyday mathematics is less formal than that of published proofs. In everyday speech, pragmatic meanings like 'Please close the window' when actually uttering 'It's cold in here', make colloquial speech very context-dependent. Law strips a lot of context out in order to apply across situations and in order to achieve uniformity, in accordance with the rule of law. Litigants' hair colour is almost never a relevant consideration, and often motive or even ethical behaviour is not factored in either. Equity by contrast unabashedly employs context. Aristotle captured this aspect of equity when he likened equity to the leaden ruler used by the builders on the island of Lesbos; being soft, a leaden rule would mould around a stone and allow an exactly fitting stone to be chosen to fit next to it.[34] This process requires a kind of fine judgment.[35]

Because it is a stand-by system, equity allows the law to be more formal. Instead of necessarily undermining the guidance function of the law, equity can allow the law to be simpler, more general and easier to follow—most of the time. The functional separation into law and equity also allows equity to target certain problems such as opportunism, without needless destabilisation. By using triggers based on proxies for problems like opportunism—fire alarms, if you will—equity is not hanging over every actor and every transaction all the time. While it is true that equity tends to

[32] Bartlett and Collins (n 30) 112 [Aristotle, *Nicomachean Ethics* 1137b, lines 26–28].

[33] F Heylighen, 'Advantages and Limitations of Formal Expression' (1999) 4 *Foundations of Science* 25, 25, 37; HE Smith, 'The Language of Property: Form, Context, and Audience' (2003) 55 *Stanford Law Review* 1105, 1112–13, 1135–39, 1181–90.

[34] Bartlett and Collins (n 30) 112 [Aristotle, *Nicomachean Ethics* 1137b, lines 29–31].

[35] ibid 129–30 [1143a, lines 19–35].

look to custom and very basic consensus morality to keep its analysis within bounds, the use of triggers based on proxies means that we need not define opportunism with exactitude or build the limits of equity into the notion of morality or conscience.[36] Indeed, because it sounds in basic consensus morality, equity performs a kind of 'acoustic separation': with the same message, equity threatens the potential opportunist and reassures the garden-variety rule follower.[37] Again, by preventing evasion of the law, equity prevents it from unravelling: either by becoming too complex or falling into disrepute.[38]

Finally, the idea that this stand-by system is second order also has points of contact with the historical tradition of equity. Aristotle's equitable function can be interpreted this way: the law need not make reference to equity, but equity does involve evaluation and intervention into the law. The early seventeeth-century conflict between law and equity pitting Coke against Ellesmere, solidified equity courts' ability to intervene from outside and to have the last word.[39] This jurisdictional structure dovetailed with a more substantive point: equity presupposed law and not vice versa. As Maitland pointed out, without equity 'in some respects our law would have been barbarous, unjust, absurd', but still 'the great elementary rights, the right to immunity from violence … the rights of ownership [and so on] would have been enforced', but abolishing common law would have meant 'anarchy', because '[a]t every point equity presupposed the existence of common law'.[40] Maitland formulated this relationship in the famous aphorism that 'Equity without common law would have been a castle in the air, an impossibility'.[41]

The second-order aspect of equity is also reflected in how fusion happened. Generally speaking in both general legislation and more piecemeal forms of fusion the equitable element 'wins' whenever the two conflict.[42] This is true both substantively

[36] For examples of more direct definitions of equity, see D Klimchuk, 'Equity and the Rule of Law' in LM Austin and D Klimchuk (eds), *Private Law and the Rule of Law* (Oxford, Oxford University Press, 2014) 247–68; I Samet, 'What Conscience Can Do for Equity' (2012) 3 *Jurisprudence* 13.

[37] Y Feldman and HE Smith, 'Behavioral Equity' (2014) 170 *Journal of Institutional and Theoretical Economics* 137. *cf* M Dan-Cohen, 'Decision Rules and Conduct Rules: On Acoustic Separation in Criminal Law' (1984) 97 *Harvard Law Review* 625. Emily Sherwin argues that equity may achieve acoustic separation in the sense of deceptively telling actors the law is rule-like and then actually applying fairness review: EL Sherwin, 'Law and Equity in Contract Enforcement' (1991) 50 *Maryland Law Review* 253, 300–14. See also EL Sherwin, 'Equity and the Modern Mind' in Goldberg, Smith and Turner (n 13). The acoustic separation I am arguing for does not involve two messages or any deception.

[38] HE Smith, 'Property, Equity, and the Rule of Law' in Austin and Klimchuk (n 36) 224–46; M Harding, 'Equity and the Rule of Law' (2016) 132 *LQR* 278.

[39] See Baker (n 16) 125–26.

[40] FW Maitland, *Equity: A Course of Lectures* (AH Chaytor and WJ Whittaker eds, Cambridge, Cambridge University Press, 1936) 19. This view stands in contradiction to the views of those like Hohfeld who see equity as a complete and parallel system of law. See WN Hohfeld, 'The Relations Between Equity and Law' (1913) 11 *Michigan Law Review* 537, 557: 'Since, in every sovereign state, there must, in the last analysis, be but a single system of *genuine law*, since the various rules and principles of that system must be consistent with one another, and since, accordingly, all *genuine* jural relations must be consistent with one another, two conflicting rules, the one "legal" and the other "equitable", cannot be valid at the same moment of time: one must be valid and determinative to the exclusion of the other.'

[41] ibid.

[42] For the United States, see Federal Rules of Civil Procedure (1938); New York Code of Procedure of 1848, NY Laws c 379 (Field Code); RE Kharas, 'A Century of Law-Equity Merger in New York' (1949) 1 *Syracuse Law Review* 186. For England, see Supreme Court of Judicature Act 1873; Supreme Court

and procedurally, with the rise of notice pleading and free discovery, among many generalised equitable devices. Fusionists tend to see this as a one-time affair, but there should be a question of whether the 'conflicting' law is simply eliminated. If instead equity is a distinct function, one may be able to formulate the law as general enough to cover a large range of cases and then let equity override or suspend the law in some of them. If so, to the extent equity is dialled back the law automatically springs back to cover the situation in question. I will argue that sometimes this is exactly the right way to think about some equitable defences.

III. FIRST ORDER VERSUS SECOND ORDER DEFENCES

Defences have always constituted an important part of equity historically, and a functional account dovetails partially with the familiar picture and helps make partial sense of it. Equity both restrained litigants from enforcing their rights in an inequitable manner and imposed equitable limits on the special remedies that equity offered. Both can be thought of as defences, and in a fused system that is their natural place. Like the rest of equity, equitable defences often, but not always and not exclusively, served a safety-valve function as meta-law.

Regular parts of the law are first order, such as the operation of causes of action and defences like consent to battery or necessity to trespass. Defences like consent and necessity are rules or standards that operate as part of the 'regular' or first-order law: the defence requires no special comprehensive view of the law and relatively little discretion. The triggers for the defence are expressed in the same terms as the claims they defeat. Emily Sherwin notes that in contract, legal defences—'includ[ing] fraud, variations on fraud, certain types of mistake, incapacity, duress, impossibility, and undue influence'—tend to be 'standardized' and, compared to the 'equitable fairness' defence, 'relatively narrow and concrete'.[43]

A. General Considerations

In considering how equitable defences function as meta-law, we need first to show how conventional views of equity and equitable defences tend to reduce them to something first-order and thereby miss the equitable function that is our concern here.

In much of the law and economics literature, a great deal of what went under the heading of law versus equity is captured by rules versus standards. In Louis Kaplow's model of the distinction, the difference is in the timing of decision-making.[44]

of Judicature Act 1875; Baker (n 16) 108–09; S Waddams, 'Equity in English Contract Law: The Impact of the Judicature Acts (1873–75)' (2012) 33 *Journal of Legal History* 185; PI McMahon, 'The Fusion Fallacy Revisited: A Purposive Approach to the Fusion of Law and Equity Under the Judicature Acts, 1873–1875' (unpublished manuscript, 30 Sept 2015).

[43] Sherwin, 'Law and Equity in Contract Enforcement' (n 37) 266–67 (footnotes omitted).

[44] L Kaplow, 'Rules Versus Standards: An Economic Analysis' (1992) 42 *Duke Law Journal* 557.

Rules involve more ex ante specification than standards, and the latter leave more content to be filled in at the application stage. Thus, in the classic example, a flat speed limit is a rule, whereas a directive to drive reasonably under the conditions is a standard. (Actual laws tend to be a hybrid of the two.) The kinds of problems that call for special treatment by equity—opportunism, conflicting rights and multipolar problems—tend to require at least some use of standards. In Kaplow's model, rules are more expensive to set up but cheaper to apply, whereas standards are the reverse: they leave most of the cost for the ex post time of application. The 'equitable' problems are ones in which it is difficult to come up with tailored ex ante rules, which pushes decision making towards standards. But both rules and standards can be either first or second order, and the two distinctions sometimes come apart in the face of the equitable problems. Thus, extreme opportunism, as in misfeasance by a fiduciary, calls for broad and simple ex ante rules and no filling in later through standards.[45] More usually, opportunism tends to defeat efforts to combat it on the same level. Ex ante rules are manipulable, and broad first-order standards are potentially very destabilising.

To see how going to a second level is different from replacing a rule by a standard, let's return to the speed limit example. Software for adaptive traffic control and autonomous vehicles that can build more fine-grained traffic rules into the system is being developed.[46] One potential problem is that human agents or software can anticipate the system and evade it, by performing dangerous self-serving manoeuvers that satisfy the constraints imposed by the system.[47] One response can be to plug the loopholes. Another would be to make the rules more standard-like but at the cost of greater uncertainty and slack in the system (more margin for error must be built in). Another alternative is to go one level up. This can be done by redesigning the system or building an extra layer of adaptation into it, by enabling the system to evolve in response to driver behaviour: the goal is for the system to make reference to primary rules and behaviour and change the primary rules in response to bad results stemming from opportunistic behaviour. This allows the system to make use of tightly interconnected rules and aim for closely meshing behaviour while at the same time addressing misuse of the system in a targeted fashion. It is the equitable function on wheels.

Going to a second-order level presents advantages but at the cost of significant disadvantages. Both the advantages and disadvantages form an answer to those who might argue that there is no difference between first-order and second-order law. It is a set of entwined advantages and disadvantages that is at stake. From a higher level, the higher-order components can control the variability at the primary level in a fashion that is comprehensive—it takes into account a wide range of information at the primary level—without thereby making that information available to all

[45] Smith, 'Why Fiduciary Law is Equitable' (n 2).

[46] Thanks to Ted Sichelman for suggesting this example. See, eg, P Gora and P Wasilewski, 'Adaptive System for Intelligent Traffic Management in Smart Cities' in D Ślęzak, G Schaefer, ST Vuong and YS Kim (eds), *Lecture Notes in Computer Science, Book 8610—Active Media Technology: 10th International Conference, AMT 2014, Proceedings* (Springer, 2014).

[47] For a humorous take on this problem, see 'Engineers Unveil New Driverless Car Capable of Committing Hit-And-Run' (*The Onion*, 2 April 2015) available at http://www.theonion.com/article/engineers-unveil-new-driverless-car-capable-of-com-38358, describing an 'advanced Culpability-Evasion-System'.

the first-order processes. By definition, first-order processes make use of whatever information they are formulated to take into account. They need not—but can be—formal, in terms of relative invariance to context.

In terms of equitable defences, such defences only operate when triggered, they make relatively free use of contextual information, and they (and that wide context) are not part of or referred to by the primary part of the law. Whether to formulate a defence as first order or second order involves a trade off familiar from systems theory. Setting up a second level gives rise to start-up costs and causes uncertainty relative to a system that does not make use of the contextual information it uses. There will also be uncertainty around the edges in whether the triggering condition for equity's second level has been met. And yet, the second level allows better tailoring—for example better containment of opportunism—than either a system that does make the attempt (no context, lots of opportunism) or a system that tries to accomplish everything on the same level. The latter can under some circumstances involve a greater degree of uncertainty than the uncertainty created by a second level of equity. If in principle it is all context all the time at the primary level, that can be more destabilising than triggered use of free context at an equitable meta level. There are all sorts of systems that combine different formulations of the two levels and their interface: how much context at level one, how much at level two, and what are the triggers. Which combination is best is an empirical question. For example, if opportunism is a very small problem, tolerating it would be less costly than using a lot of context at level one or level two. If the opportunism problem comes up rarely and can be dealt with by moderate amounts of context, formulating a standard at level one is a viable option. And so on. This is a problem quite familiar from systems theory, where all sorts of combinations of levels are employed in practice.

Returning to defences, we can now see how different first- and second-order defences are. First-order defences are conditioned on the same kinds of information and use the same kind of reasoning in their application as other parts of the law. Consider contributory and comparative negligence: each is conditioned on the same kinds of information as is the tort of negligence itself. Like the regular law, legal defences purport to offer guidance to actors' future behaviour. Thus, it makes sense to ask what the general effect on incentives of a given defence is, and the defence is no different in its terms than the claim it qualifies.

Consider first non-equitable, regular or, to use the historic (but not entirely accurate) term, 'legal' defences. Because they operate on the same level in this way, first-order defences are more likely to lead to controversy over whether they are defences at all: is the doctrine in question a defence or part of the main case? Is permission a defence to the tort of trespass to land or is lack of permission part of the main case? In the United States, this is a surprisingly unclear proposition.[48]

[48] See, eg, *Environmental Processing Systems LC v FPL Farming Ltd*, 457 SW 3d 414, 425 (Tex 2015), holding that a plaintiff must plead and prove lack of authorisation; *Perkins v Blauth*, 127 P 50 (Cal 1912): '[W]e are not advised of any rule of pleading which requires a declaration from plaintiff that an unlawful trespass was committed without his acquiescence. There is no presumption that a plaintiff consents to an unwarranted invasion of his personal rights or rights of property'; *Moore v Walter Coke Inc*, No 2:11-cv-1391-SLB, US Dist ND (Ala 2012) 34, holding that a trespass plaintiff's burden regarding lack of authorisation was met by lack of facts pleaded suggesting consent.

The defences that are functionally equitable are different. They are second order in the sense that they are in principle conditioned on the whole of the regular law and modify the result that would otherwise obtain. They are more discretionary and more context-dependent, and they make more reference to moral considerations. It is thus harder to confuse them with the main case. And, as we will see, this corresponds to one barrier to their fusion with the regular law: equitable defences differ in terms of how easily they can be recast at the primary ('legal') level. The easier that is, the easier it is both to fuse them with the law and to entertain the possibility that they are really not defences at all but part of the main case.

B. Functionally Equitable Defences

Some defences are second order, and reflect an equitable function. This is loosely, and only loosely, associated with historic equity jurisdiction. The separate courts did promote second-order defences, but second-order defences do not require separate courts. The traditionally equitable defences served a variety of second-order roles, which makes them differ in their degree of fusability with regular law.

i. Unconscionability

Illustrative of equitable defences that serve an equitable function is unconscionability. Unconscionability comes in many varieties, some of which are very narrow and others of which verge on a completely unconstrained fairness review. Equity courts treated unconscionability as a prototypical instance of constructive fraud, involving advantage-taking,[49] especially of the vulnerable, and, among modern accounts, those offered by Arthur Leff and Richard Epstein come closest to capturing the traditional approach, including (unconsciously) its second-order aspect.[50] The trigger for unconscionability is a combination of disproportionate hardship and a vulnerable party, with overtones of conscious behaviour or bad faith lowering the threshold. In terms of the specific proxies used under the heading of vulnerability, certain classes of people, such as the very young and very old, sailors on leave, and so on, triggered a presumption of opportunism.[51] Once this threshold has been met, a more freewheeling fairness analysis with the presumption against the potential advantage-taker would ensue; if the transaction flunks, the contract is not enforceable, originally by specific performance and latterly also by damages. Epstein points to a similarity to the Statute of Frauds: some transactions contain a high enough degree of danger of being fraudulent that it makes sense not to enforce that class of

[49] Story (n 19) § 221.

[50] AA Leff, 'Unconscionability and the Code—The Emperor's New Clause' (1967) 115 *University of Pennsylvania Law Review* 485, 539; RA Epstein, 'Unconscionability: A Critical Reappraisal' (1975) 18 *Journal of Law and Economics* 293, 293–301. See also HE Smith, 'The Equitable Dimension of Contract' (2012) 45 *Suffolk University Law Review* 897, 902–07.

[51] Leff (n 50) 532.

transactions—even if some legitimate deals will be swept in the dragnet.[52] The point is that banning a class of transactions can be better than doing nothing or further tailoring of the law itself. The difference with the Statute of Frauds is that equity is typically second order and, once triggered, it involves (even on Epstein's somewhat narrow version) a more holistic and context-dependent analysis than is required under the rule-like Statute of Frauds.[53]

One might think—and many do think—that unconscionability is irrelevant for sophisticated parties.[54] One can grant that it is less needed in the case of sophisticated parties, but it is an open question whether it can ever be eliminated altogether. In such contexts, the possibility that a party will come up with an as yet unheard of method of committing near-fraud is not implausible. Perhaps the courts' unwillingness to allow any parties to bargain away the duty of good faith is a recognition that courts need this ultimate trump card for such rare occasions—and that the benefits of legitimate instances of bargaining away do not outweigh the danger of opportunism that it presents elsewhere. Again, this is an empirical question, and invocation of parties' sophistication will not resolve it. Nor does this represent a commitment of courts to root out opportunism wherever it might lurk.[55] As always, the question is whether the presence of the stand-by system is cost-effective or not, considering the possibility of error in both directions.

Consonant with its being a prototypical instance of constructive fraud, unconscionability should not be tied to equitable remedies. As we will see, there may be more need of second-order adjustment in the case of remedies like specific performance that lead to cliffs: beyond a certain point of primary activity the liability takes a sudden jump. And yet if one can commit constructive fraud—can engage in opportunism—through insistence on a damages remedy, the defence of unconscionability should be available there too. This is a case where a functional account of equity points to the desirability of fusion.

ii. Estoppel

Estoppel is a prototypical equitable defence, in which a court will refuse to allow someone to create an expectation and then defeat it to the prejudice of the other party. Unlike unclean hands, estoppel can be used affirmatively to enjoin someone from enforcing a legal right:[56]

> Equitable estoppel is the effect of the voluntary conduct of a party whereby he is absolutely precluded both at law and in equity, from asserting rights which might perhaps

[52] Epstein (n 50) 302.

[53] That is, the Statute of Frauds was rule-like until equity encrusted it with exceptions and modifications.

[54] See, eg, JS Kraus and RE Scott, 'Contract Design and the Structure of Contractual Intent' (2009) 84 *New York University Law Review* 1023; A Schwartz and RE Scott, 'Contract Theory and the Limits of Contract Law' (2003) 113 *Yale Law Journal* 541, 609–10.

[55] But see RE Scott, 'Contract Design and the Shading Problem' (2015) 99 *Marquette Law Review* 1.

[56] *Cunninghame v Cunninghame*, 772 A 2d 1188, 1201 (Md 2001), citing 3 J Pomeroy, *Equity Jurisprudence* 5th edn (Spencer Symonds, 1941) § 804. See also TL Anenson, 'The Triumph of Equity: Equitable Estoppel in Modern Litigation' (2008) 27 *Review of Litigation* 377.

> have otherwise existed, either of property, of contract, or of remedy, as against another person, who has in good faith relied upon such conduct, and has been led thereby to change his position for the worse and who on his part acquires some corresponding right, either of property, of contract, or of remedy.

The situation of someone trying to benefit from this kind of inconsistent representation or behaviour is rife with the danger of opportunism. The triggers for estoppel are like those for unconscionability: a combination of extreme result, bad intent and vulnerability, the mixture of which varies by context (leading to an open question whether various forms of estoppel can be treated as one category).[57] It often requires a second-order approach: the net effect of the opportunism is hard to evaluate except in light of a wide range of interacting circumstances.

Like many equitable defences, estoppel allows for compromise between all or nothing in remedies. This is especially important for equitable remedies.[58] The injunction leads to large cliffs in liability: the difference between being ordered to do something under threat of contempt and not being ordered is not a matter of degree, despite the ability of courts to tailor or delay injunctions. Injunctions can lead to very lopsided results, leading to the defence of undue hardship.[59] The on/off jump in liability and the potential lopsided results of equitable remedies like injunctions themselves carry a danger of opportunism. This is why the traditional rules of thumb for injunctions are sensitive to the potential for opportunism on both sides: the defendant may be in bad faith and the plaintiff may be an extortionist.[60]

Estoppel is not limited to being a defence to equitable relief. It also relates to the use of equity to enjoin the enforcement of legal rights. As such, it is still second order, but this does not require it to be paired with an equitable remedy. Someone can opportunistically create reliance and disappoint it in such a way that the put-upon party would owe damages. For example, someone might lead another to believe that he will not enforce a right and then sue in damages for its violation.[61]

Much of what is special about estoppel is captured by regarding it as second order. Mark Gergen argues that mysterious statements that estoppel is a shield and not a sword may not have much content but they do reflect something: estoppel can be deep because it is narrow remedially.[62] Within its narrow remedial ambit, estoppel involves broad evaluation, for example asking which party did more to create a risk.[63] These features of estoppel are consistent with estoppel being triggered as

[57] See E Cooke, *The Modern Law of Estoppel* (Oxford, Oxford University Press, 2000); MP Gergen, 'Towards Understanding Equitable Estoppel' in C Rickett and R Grantham (eds), *Structure and Justification in Private Law: Essays for Peter Birks* (Oxford, Hart Publishing, 2008) 319–37. See also B McFarlane and P Sales, 'Promises, Detriment and Liability: Lessons from Proprietary Estoppel' (2015) 1341 *LQR* 610.

[58] This is one of the main arguments Edward Yorio made for keeping equitable defences separate: see E Yorio, 'A Defense of Equitable Defenses' (1990) 51 *Ohio State Law Journal* 1201. See also HL McClintock, *Handbook of the Principles of Equity* 2nd edn (St Paul MN, West Publishing Co, 1948) § 23 (at 51); SL Bray, 'The System of Equitable Remedies' (2016) 63 *UCLA Law Review* 530.

[59] See sources cited at n 18.

[60] MP Gergen, JM Golden and HE Smith, 'The Supreme Court's Accidental Revolution? The Test for Permanent Injunctions' (2012) 112 *Columbia Law Review* 203.

[61] *American Jurisprudence* 2nd edn (2016) vol 28, 'Estoppel and Waiver' § 27.

[62] Gergen (n 57) 330–37.

[63] ibid 328–30.

a second-order intervention and, once triggered, ranging broadly over the primary situation.

Although it is true that equitable remedies will often call for second-order defences, it is not the case that second-order defences are only of relevance to traditionally equitable remedies. When it comes to both traditionally equitable and traditionally legal remedies, we need to ask whether we can formulate triggers and engage in a worthwhile evaluation of the whole situation in order to solve problems like opportunism. Otherwise defences need not be functionally equitable. When it comes to estoppel, defeating expectations to the detriment of another is a good proxy for the danger of opportunism, whether that trigger comes from the historic equity or law side of the old jurisdictional divide.

iii. Unclean Hands

Unclean hands is a defence related to a famous maxim of equity: 'One who comes into equity must come with clean hands' means that one cannot get an equitable remedy if one has acted immorally in the transaction in question. General bad behaviour or ill repute is not enough.[64] The unclean hands defence is of relatively recent vintage,[65] but like estoppel it allows a flexible and comprehensive view of the transaction in question. A useful counterpoint is the common law doctrine of *in pari delicto*, which operated more mechanically: it looked for equal guilt and invalidated the entire cause of action.[66]

The hallmark of the unclean hands defence is flexibility. Unclean hands, like estoppel, can blunt the on/off quality in response to the overall situation. Unclean hands is neither a rule nor an all-things-considered first-order standard. It is triggered by bad behaviour in the transaction in question and freely makes use of context within that transaction. It is narrow and intense, like equity generally.

Perhaps the best argument for keeping unclean hands cabined in various ways is the difficulty of getting it right. Although there are not a great many cases in which someone manages to get a legal remedy after being denied an equitable remedy for unclean hands,[67] one of the most famous equity cases involved just such a situation. In *Carmen v Fox Film Corp*,[68] actress Jewel Carmen repudiated a contract she had entered into just before the age of majority (invoking the legal defence of minority), and sought to sue the disappointed party for an injunction against interference with her new more lucrative contract. The court found the behaviour

[64] *Scattaretico v Puglisi*, 799 NE 2d 1258, 1261–62 (Mass App Ct 2003): 'A person is not to be deprived of civil justice merely because he has sinned in the past; his wrongdoing must have been related directly to the present situation to justify his being barred'. See also at 1262, fn 16: 'Chief Baron Eyre who, according to Chafee ... first uttered the maxim, "A man must come into a Court of Equity with clean hands," was well aware of the point: "it does not mean a general depravity; it must have an immediate and necessary relation to the equity sued for"', citing *Dering v Earl of Winchelsea* (1787) 1 Cox Eq 318, 319; 29 ER 1184, 1185.

[65] Z Chafee Jr, 'Coming into Equity with Clean Hands' (1949) 47 *Michigan Law Review* 877, 880–84.

[66] TL Anenson, 'Treating Equity Like Law: A Post-Merger Justification of Unclean Hands' (2008) 45 *American Business Law Journal* 455, 489.

[67] Sherwin, 'Law and Equity in Contract Enforcement' (n 37) 259, fn 26 (citing cases).

[68] *Carmen v Fox Film Corp* 269 F 928 (2d Cir 1920).

in question to be unethical even if legal, and denied the injunction. Carmen later sued and obtained substantial damages. The case is set against the backdrop of the collusion among movie companies in the studio system of early and mid-twentieth-century Hollywood. Perhaps, courts are not well equipped to deal with a problem on that scale, and so contract enforcement should not be conditioned on it. It is even possible that preventing Carmen from getting an injunction but allowing damages is the least bad response to an opportunist acting in a sea of opportunism. The right question to ask is what the best rules of thumb are and at what level of generality. The current state of the rules of thumb is to allow unethical behaviour more easily to block access to the most troubling remedies, and to allow for a more continuous type of modulation for damages.

iv. Laches

In laches, a defendant can get a claim dismissed because of the plaintiff's unreasonable and prejudicial delay in filing suit, even if the statute of limitations has not yet run. Traditionally, the defence of laches only precluded equitable relief—such as injunctions, specific performance and accounting—but would not affect legal remedies like damages.[69] Recently, a few courts have extended laches to legal claims.[70] From a doctrinal point of view, there is good reason to apply laches to equitable remedies, even under recent federal legislation containing statutes of limitation. The extension to legal claims is more difficult, and I will consider it from a purely normative point of view. (This is the point of view that is available to English courts and most American state courts under state law, and would be available under US federal law but for a narrow view of the nature of equity at that level.[71])

Laches clearly takes more context into account than does a statute of limitations: it is a standard and not a rule. Like estoppel, it can also be used to police for opportunism, and some of its applications can involve hard-to-foresee and unfair advantage-taking. The latter make laches look more second order.

Should laches apply to legal remedies? Laches originally was equity's response to a lack of statutes of limitations.[72] Modern statutes of limitations are often argued to reflect a legislature's considered judgment of a reasonable time for bringing suit—full stop. And yet, it is not impossible for someone to engage in opportunism in lulling another into reliance on the prospect of not being sued in damages.

[69] *Landreth v First National Bank of Cleburne County*, 45 F 3d 267, 271 (8th Cir 1995); *Erwin v City of Palmyra*, 119 SW 3d 582, 586–87 (Mo App ED 2003).

[70] *Harris v Beynon*, 570 F Supp 690, 692, fn 3 (ND Ill 1983); *Sutton v Davis*, 916 SW 2d 937, 940–41 (Tenn Ct App 1995). See also E Fetter, 'Laches at Law in Tennessee' (1997) 28 *University of Memphis Law Review* 211.

[71] The US Supreme Court looks to what courts of equity did in 1789: *Grupo Mexicano de Desarrollo SA v Alliance Bond Fund Inc*, 527 US 308 (1999), and see SL Bray, 'The Supreme Court and the New Equity' (2015) 68 *Vanderbilt Law Review* 997.

[72] *Petrella v Metro-Goldwyn-Mayer Inc*, 134 S Ct 1962, 1973 (2014), citing 1 D Dobbs, *Law of Remedies* 2nd edn (St Paul MN, West Publishing Co, 1993) § 2.4(4) (at 104): 'laches ... may have originated in equity because no statute of limitations applied ... suggest[ing] that laches should be limited to cases in which no statute of limitations applies'.

As with other equitable defences, it is not hard to see why they not only arose in equity but are most compelling when it comes to equitable remedies. As Sam Bray points out, the equitable remedies are often burdensome on the enjoined party, require management of the parties and are particularly costly, whereas damages often (but not always) involve a sliding scale.[73] Again, the on/off quality and large cliffs argue for stepping back in a second-order way. Indeed, the whole theme of 'management' of the parties and of the litigation that Bray identifies in equity is naturally performed at a meta level. Bray argues further that the equitable defences like laches are costly in terms of uncertainty and especially compelling for equitable remedies such that drawing the line at the law-equity divide makes sense. In the recent case of *Petrella v Metro-Goldwyn-Mayer Inc*,[74] the US Supreme Court took this middle route—reserving laches for equitable remedies—and not extending the defence to legal remedies as urged by leading pro-fusion scholars.[75]

Moreover, as many have noted, for the more extreme cases of opportunistic delay of suit within the statute of limitations, the defence of estoppel is uncontroversially available.[76] Because estoppel directs the court to a more explicitly second-order and constrained equitable analysis and a generalised laches defence would invite a great deal of uncertainty, it is reasonable to cabin laches to equitable remedies and rely on estoppel for the worst abuses. This is not because damages and other legal remedies never present problems that could benefit from 'meta' treatment or that some applications of laches could not be performed at the primary level. Rather, it would seem that the current system gets much of the envisioned benefit without courting the all-too-familiar danger of equity filling the entire space. Given that second-order power is not easy to cabin, we should ask for more than the tidiness of complete fusion or a 'why not' style presumption before extending laches further. Unlike in the pro-fusion commentary, the burden at this point should be on those advocating extension.

v. Fraud and Constructive Fraud

Many defences appear to be a little ambiguous as to whether they are functionally legal or equitable, and this is especially true after the fusion of law and equity. A microcosm of this picture comes from fraud in contract.[77]

[73] SL Bray, 'A Little Bit of Laches Goes a Long Way: Notes on *Petrella v. Metro-Goldwyn-Mayer Inc.*' (2014) 67 *Vanderbilt Law Review En Banc* 1.

[74] *Petrella* (n 72). *Petrella* involved a copyright claim. The Court has recently decided that laches does not apply to claims for damages from patent infringement during the statutory period under 35 USC § 286: *SCA Hygiene Products Aktiebolag v First Quality Baby Products*, 137 S Ct 954 (2017).

[75] See 'Brief of D Laycock, MP Gergen, and D Rendleman as Amici Curiae in Support of Neither Side' (2013) WL 6213269 (US, Appellate Brief) and 'Brief of TL Anenson as Amicus Curiae in Support of Respondents: *Petrella v Metro-Goldwyn-Mayer*' No 12-1315.

[76] Bray (n 73) 8.

[77] Contractual mistake presents a similar picture, with a broader and more complex approach to mistake in equity than at law: McClintock (n 58) § 88 (at 238). This has given way to an extension of mistake to claims for legal remedies: *Restatement (Second) of Contracts* (1981) ch 6, Introductory Note, 152–55. In English law, mistake may in cases of great hardship lead to a refusal of an injunction but allowance of damages. There are, however, no special equitable grounds to rescind contracts on grounds of mistake, a contract being either valid or invalid. See McGhee (n 19) para 15-002.

Although the relation between legal and equitable fraud is a large subject—too large a subject for thorough treatment here—aspects of this relationship are very telling from the point of view of the equitable function. As already discussed, equity's notion of constructive fraud was not just wider but more open-ended and the devices for dealing with it are structured as a second-order safety valve.

From the point of view of fusion, the types of fraud present a complex picture. At first blush, it looks as if law and equity are concerned with the same thing and that this area is ripe for reconciliation and consolidation. And yet fraud is not all of one piece. Some of it is easy to specify—lying to get someone to give you their property and the like—but some of it is highly uncertain. The main idea of constructive fraud is the difficulty of proving and especially anticipating new ways of abusing and evading the law.[78] This suggests that some residuum of second-order intervention will be needed. And yet relying only and always on second-order intervention would be needlessly uncertain. Again, a division of labour even within the domain of fraud carries its advantages.

Definitions of fraud have shifted over time as well. This too is no argument against an equitable function. Quite the contrary. As the equitable function is applied to categories of fraud, they become known and amenable to first order ('legal') treatment. Thus, yesterday's purely equitable fraud sometimes becomes today's legal fraud, notably in the law's late recognition of fraud in the inducement, first dealt with in equity.[79] This pipeline of fraud from equity to law is an instance of the temporal dimension of the equitable function. It is to this dynamic aspect that we now must turn.

C. Patterns of Equitable Defences

Looking at the defences through the lens of an equitable function allows us to discern a number of patterns in defences.

First, we should expect that equitable defences will tend to respond to opportunism, polycentric problems and other complex and hard-to-foresee situations. From a functional point of view, this means that we should see a tendency for these problems to be solved with second-order interventions set off by triggers, especially those relating to disproportionate hardship and bad faith. There is nothing historical or jurisdictional about this, nor is it peculiar to the 'common law' world. And indeed civilian doctrines like abuse of right, abuse of law and good faith bear some resemblance to the equitable interventions and defences, from a functional point of view.[80]

[78] See above n 22 and accompanying text.

[79] DJ Ibbetson, *A Historical Introduction to the Law of Obligations* (Oxford, Oxford University Press, 199) 208–09.

[80] See, eg, A di Robilant, 'Abuse of Rights: The Continental Drug and the Common Law' (2010) 61 *Hastings Law Journal* 687; LM Katz, 'Spite and Extortion: A Jurisdictional Principle of Abuse of Property Right' (2013) 122 *Yale Law Journal* 1444; JM Perillo, 'Abuse of Rights: A Pervasive Legal Concept' (1995) 27 *Pacific Law Journal* 37.

A correlation of such defences with historic and jurisdictional equity is not unexpected though. Because equity courts did intervene from outside and won the battle with the law, and because they focused on problems that such a tool was suited for, it is no accident that second-order safety-valve-style intervention was the order of the day for equity courts.

More specifically, where a defence is both legal and equitable, the equitable version can be expected to be more second order and to respond to those kinds of problem. This is simply a corollary of the general distinction between defences. This apparent duplication need not be duplication at all. Instead, the legal and equitable versions of the defences may be serving different functions in different ways. Fraud and constructive fraud cannot be collapsed into each other.

We also should expect some—but only some—correlation of traditional equitable defences and equitable remedies. As many have noticed, equitable remedies can lead to extreme results and equitable defences allow for compromise.[81] To this we can add that the method for doing so is targeted, in a second-order fashion.

When it comes to fusion, equitable defences are special. The ones that do indeed serve a second-order role should be hardest to fuse completely, and this does seem to be the case. Alternatively, when they are fused they will lead to the most complication or uncertainty. The reluctance of courts to fuse unclean hands and laches may receive some explanation here. The attempt to capture estoppel with proliferations of multifactor tests is a possible example of the latter.[82] In other common law countries, fusion has led to a combination of standards and complex rules—what we would expect from an attempt to replace equity with something more first order.[83]

IV. THE DYNAMICS OF EQUITABLE DEFENCES

Legal and equitable defences do not stay that way. Equitable defences, like other aspects of equity, have often been adopted by the common law courts and have become regular law.[84] Fusionists sometimes take this as further evidence of the arbitrariness of the law-equity distinction: any such distinction in the area of defences must be a happenstance, path dependence or the like.

It is actually this fusionist conclusion that is too static. This development of equitable into legal defences reflects the operation of the equitable function over time. First note that the traffic was one way: equitable defences and other equitable

[81] See above n 58.

[82] Smith, 'Fusing the Equitable Function' (n 2). On multifactor tests for estoppel, see Gergen (n 57) 325.

[83] The multifactor test seems to be particularly prevalent in the United States. In jurisdictions without a tradition of Realism, there is a tendency to combine standards with finely tuned complex doctrine. See J Getzler, 'Patterns of Fusion' in P Birks (ed), *The Classification of Obligations* (Oxford, Clarendon Press, 1997) 192–93. This too can be seen as an attempt to do on one level that which, prior to fusion, was done on two.

[84] See, eg, *Spect v Spect*, 26 P 203, 205 (Cal 1891) (Harrison J), quoting Lord Redesdale; Anenson (n 66) 463–64; RS Stevens, 'A Plea for the Extension of Equitable Principles and Remedies' (1956) 41 *Cornell Law Quarterly* 351, 352, 354.

interventions became law but not vice versa. This was widely recognised by courts, especially as equitable treatment of mortgages became a matter of law:[85]

> The distinction between strict law and equity is never in any country a permanent distinction. Law and equity are in continual progression, and the former is constantly gaining ground upon the latter. A great part of what is now strict law was formerly considered as equity, and the equitable decisions of this age will unavoidably be ranked under the strict law of the next.

The statutes effecting fusion also gave primacy to equity whenever there was a conflict.[86] Commentators too have noticed this progression, especially in the area of defences.[87]

Looking at these developments through the lens of equity as a second-order function helps explain and justify some of these dynamic patterns. First of all, the one-way traffic is what we would expect: equity is a power ranging over the law so that its output can be formulated in a first-order fashion. If, for example, interventions to prevent murders by heirs—using the principle that one will not be allowed to profit from his own wrong—are recognised as a class of problems, a rule (the slayer rule) can replace the equitable intervention.[88] Likewise, when varieties of fraud (notably fraud in the inducement) were recognised as being amenable to first-order treatment they could become 'legal'. It is hard to see how or why on the two-tier model that legal defences would become equitable in the same fashion. Further, Rose's model of oscillation of 'crystals' and 'mud' is not universal; sometimes the mix of law and equity (in a functional sense) can be stable, where aspects of equity become regularised and a local equilibrium is reached, in a process I call 'sedimentation'.[89] Arguably this has happened with the role of notice in real property recording acts and more generally with good faith purchaser rules.

To the extent it reflects an equitable function, equity is thus a moving frontier. The function is needed for problems of great uncertainty and variability. The same 'problem' need not be static in terms of its uncertainty and variability: especially if it becomes more certain, the equitable function need not be used on an ongoing basis, or it can be reserved for the residuum of the problem that retains its uncertain and variable character.

Far from providing an argument for the arbitrariness and hence undesirability of distinct equity, this dynamic picture provides powerful evidence for recognising

[85] *Spect* (n 84) 205 (Harrison J), quoting Lord Redesdale.

[86] See the sources cited above at n 42.

[87] JB Ames, 'Specialty Contracts and Equitable Defenses' (1896) 9 *Harvard Law Review* 49; Anenson (n 66) at 463–66. Even in Carol Rose's model of oscillation between 'crystals' and 'mud', bright-line law ('crystal') becomes less determinate and more standards-based ('mud') through judicial interpretation and modification; courts' mud is replaced with crystal by legislatures and parties, not by courts. CM Rose, 'Crystals and Mud in Property Law' (1988) 40 *Stanford Law Review* 577, 588.

[88] The chestnut in the United States is *Riggs v Palmer*, 22 NE 188 (NY 1889), which I have argued is an example of hyperfusion. See Smith, 'Fusing the Equitable Function in Private Law' (n 2). The Wills Act was probably passed against a background of equity and earlier English ecclesiastical law which would have reached the same result.

[89] HE Smith, 'Rose's Human Nature of Property' (2011) 19 *William & Mary Bill of Rights Journal* 1047, 1047–55.

an equitable function, both descriptively and normatively. The patterns themselves are what one would expect from the use of the equitable function over time and the building up of experience with applications. From a normative point of view, it makes sense to treat categories of problems in a less complicated way at the primary level if they are amenable to primary-level treatment. This is what we mean by the presumption for the first level (roughly, law) and the exceptional character of the equitable second level.

V. CONCLUSION

Fusionism often calls for refashioning defences according to their function. In this chapter I have suggested that recognising a second-order safety-valve function makes some sense of the traditional category of equitable defences. Because the equity courts were structured as separate and they wound up in a position to override the law, it was natural for them to focus on this equitable function. This is not all they did, however, and the law itself contains within it instances of second-order functions as well. It would be a mistake to draw the conclusion that freezing the jurisdictional line is any way justified. And yet, the rough allocation of defences to one side or the other, as with lack of capacity and statutes of limitation on one side and unconscionability and laches on the other, serves some purpose and should not be lightly tossed aside. Further, the idea that some defences straddle the line or are in the process of being adapted in a more formal way—as with fraud over a long period of time—should be welcomed and accepted. A second-order function can in principle be kept separate enough without separate courts. And yet, in a legal culture where the only boundaries to the judicial function are the brightest of bright lines with everything else up for grabs is not one that is very hospitable to equity. And in the United States, the process of replacing equity, including the equitable defences, with first-order standards, including multifactor tests, is well under way. The functional account of equity offered in this chapter implies that we should call these developments into question rather than celebrating them unthinkingly as the pure dawn of enlightenment. The lessons of systems theory suggest that we will never get away from some version of equity, and certainly not the problems it is suited to address.

3

Set-Off and the Nature of Equity

ROBERT STEVENS

I. EQUITY

LAW IS NOT a science, thankfully. Scientists are solely concerned with facts. Physicists are unconcerned with what gravity ought to be, but want to know what it is. Zoologists do not condemn wolves for their lupine behaviour.[1] Scientists classify animals and plants according to facts in the world that have no moral significance. Some animals are carnivores, and there is no blame attached to that.

It might be thought that lawyers classify law in much the same way, by grouping cases together that have the same facts in common. In his work Peter Birks implied at certain points that this is so when he sought to classify duties in private law according to certain kinds of events (manifestations of consent, wrongs, unjust enrichment and other events). But if we really thought that was all there was to it then there would seem to be nothing better or worse about selecting another kind of fact that claims have in common (days of the week, height of litigant, etc).

Many legal categories take their unity from the moral or normative reason why particular rights of that kind exist. That moral or normative reason cannot be found just by looking at the positive law itself (although judges in deciding cases often articulate those reasons). Obligations to pay damages following a wrong take their unity from the persistence of the reason underlying the initial primary duty that has been breached. This now takes the form of a duty of next-best compliance: pay damages to ensure the claimant is placed in the position, as near as money can do it, to the wrong not having been committed. Contracts takes its unity from the moral force of the idea that rights created by agreements ought to be respected. If unjust enrichment were a single subject, there would be a reason of this kind unifying it. In classifying the legal obligations in this way, which is essential to ensuring that (morally) like cases are treated alike, lawyers are inevitably engaged in a quite different endeavour from the scientist.

Equity as found within our law in common does not seem to fit within this kind of approach. It is the body of law developed in the English Court of Chancery before 1875, and that has since developed from it since that time. It seems to have no more

[1] *cf* T Macklem and J Gardner, 'Human Disability' (2014) 25 *King's Law Journal* 60, 69: 'we should take a dim view of life as a hyena'.

unity than that. Nowadays when we administer law and Equity together, should not we instead group all cases according to the (normative) reason why a claim exists? Just as large amounts of 'Equity' now appear in books on contract (undue influence, injunctions, specific performance etc), should we not re-allocate the other rules of Equity to other areas given unity in ways that are not specific to the peculiar history of one particular kind of legal system? Although it may be true that the rules as they exist can only be understood in the light of their historical origin, should these differences not yield to the higher force of whatever moral reasons underlie the various rules that there are? Equitable set-off is now dealt with within general works of set-off. Is there any longer any justification for treating the equitable species separately?

If the *only* unity that the rules of Equity had were their historical origin, we should perhaps agree that there should be 'No More Snells'. It is not the case, however, that lawyers are *always* engaged in a different endeavour from scientists. Often the classifications we adopt are useful, and not driven by the moral distinctiveness of any particular kind of claim. So, in dividing rights into those that are *in rem* and those that are *in personam*, nothing at all is said about *why* such kinds of rights exist, or indeed whether any should exist at all. We are (or at least were) merely observing that some duties are owed to other individuals, whilst others relate to physical things and give rise to duties owed to the rest of the world. Hohfeld in dividing rights into claim-rights, privileges, powers and immunities was drawing conceptual distinctions that are useful for lawyers (and others) but which are not related to the reasons why such different species of 'rights' should exist. Similarly, in arguing alongside my co-author Ben McFarlane that equitable property has a particular kind of formal structure[2] it was not part of our endeavour to articulate the normative reasons why rights of that kind arise. Such rights are not given their unity from the multiplicity of reasons underlying their existence.

Most of Equity has a conceptual unity and it is useful for lawyers to grasp that this is independent of, although caused by, its historical development. It concerns rules about rules. It is a form of meta-law. Equitable set-off can only be understood as being of this form. This formal difference from other kinds of set-off has the result that the substantive kinds of reason that justify it are also quite different.

II. META-LAW

One view of Equity is that it takes the form of a kind of discretionary power in the judges to do justice in particular cases where the application of the strict rules of law would be harsh in an individual case. On this view, Equity fulfils the kind of function that 'good faith' seems to an outsider to perform in some civilian jurisdictions. A kind of *deus ex machina*. Put rudely, it allows the judges to cheat.

There are several reasons why this model of Equity still has a hold upon us.

First, it gives Equity a kind of conceptual distinctiveness. It is not just a historical curio.

[2] B McFarlane and R Stevens, 'The Nature of Equitable Property' (2010) 4 *Journal of Equity* 1.

Second, it has analogues within other legal systems outside of the common law tradition. Since at least Aristotle's *Nicomachean Ethics* the problem of making general definite rules cover the whole range of unforeseen possible factual scenarios has been recognised, creating the need for exceptions.

Third, it was, at one time, partially true. The body of judge-created law that we call Equity arose later in time. Inevitably, therefore, it initially involved judges having more freedom of choice than they then possessed at common law in setting down rules.

Fourth, it is still the case that judges often speak of equitable rules involving a discretion: one common example is the decision whether to award or refuse an injunction or specific performance. However, it may be queried in what sense this is meant. If a decision is truly within the ambit of discretion of a decision maker, it cannot be wrong. The decision to award an injunction would be just as correct as the decision to refuse it. If this were so, the decision of a trial judge whether to award or refuse an injunction would be amenable to being successfully challenged on appeal, just so long as it was within the range of available options. This is not, however, how appellate courts have treated the question of the availability of these remedies. They have not shown deference to the decisions of trial judges in this way.

Anyone who picks up a textbook on the law of trusts will see that it is a body of law that is suffused with detailed rules. It is not the abandonment of rule by law but its embodiment. This process of crystallisation was and is inevitable. In any legal system where the doctrine of *stare decisis* applies, over time rules must form. As the courts of Equity accepted the binding nature of past precedents, judges created law. This was especially so in the absence of juries, as all questions were for the judges and every decision had the force of precedent. If it really were the case that Equity was distinguished by the absence of rules but rather with the vesting of discretionary power in the individual judge it would seem to offend the rule of law. Fortunately, that is a gross mischaracterisation.

The entire point of Equity is to be different from the Common Law. If it were the same, it would not exist. Some of the justifications for difference, such as the different rules of evidence and procedure, do not survive today.[3] But in order to justify its continuing treatment as a separate body of rules that difference alone cannot be enough.

Equity primarily concerns rules about other rules. The easiest example is the trust. As I and several others have argued, the subject matter of a beneficiary's rights under a trust is never a thing, such as an area of land, items of furniture or pieces of paper labelled 'share certificates'. Rather the beneficiary's rights relate to other rights. We do not hold land on trust, but the right to land. Without the prior recognition of such rights, trusts could not exist. The trust is entirely dependent upon the common law's prior recognition of rights to land, furniture, share certificates and so on. Equity does not, and never has, contradicted the common law as to who owns what. Equity does not determine who is the owner of land, furniture, share certificates and so on.

[3] M Macnair, 'Equity and Conscience' (2007) 27 *OJLS* 659.

Other forms of equitable property are similarly dependent upon there being rights recognised at common law upon which they are ultimately dependent. So, when a charge is granted, the debtor comes under a duty (is charged) to hold property by way of security for another. This entails that he is not free to use it for his own benefit until the secured obligation is discharged. If I charge my house to the bank, what is charged is not the bricks and mortar, but the right to the bricks and mortar. If I mortgage the property, I transfer the right to it but have a power to compel re-transfer back to me of that right upon discharge of the obligation secured (the '*equity* of redemption').

The picture is slightly complicated because Equity also allows the rights that it recognises to be held on trust (or charged). This enables sub-trusts, and sub-sub-trusts and so on. Ultimately, however, there must be a right at common law at the end of the chain to which these equitable rights relate. Another useful metaphor is the ivy on the wall. Equity (the ivy) is entirely dependent upon the rights at common law (the wall) for its support. The common law, by contrast, would function in the same way without the equitable overlay.

Other examples of Equity's parasitic nature are those cases where it has restrained the enforcement of legal rights. The classic example of this is estoppel. It is possible to be estopped from asserting two kinds of things: facts and rights. Where a party is estopped from asserting a fact, estoppel is operating as a rule of evidence. This rule is common to the courts of Equity and the common law. Equitable estoppel, by contrast, is an extension of the common law doctrine of waiver, and bars the assertion of rights. In the modern era (ie, from the late 1960s onwards) 'equitable estoppel' has taken on a quite different usage, particularly in the context of 'proprietary estoppel'. At one time, the latter merely referred to being estopped from asserting a proprietary right (as opposed to say a contractual or statutory right). Today, it has become freestanding source of proprietary claims where the normal rules for the acquisition of proprietary rights can be dispensed with. What the normative justification for this might be is, to me, obscure. At a minimum, we should discard the label 'estoppel' where nobody is being estopped from asserting anything.

More problematic, because creating a sharper inconsistency between the common law and Equity, are those cases where Equity has recognised defeating reasons for what would otherwise be valid legal rights. So, despite all the necessary conditions for the recognition of enforceable contractual rights being fulfilled (offer/acceptance, consideration, certainty, intention to create legal relations) Equity allows the setting aside of the transaction for other defeating reasons that are not recognised at common law (undue influence, innocent misrepresentation, relief against forfeiture etc). Again, Equity is still not operating as a freestanding body of rules, but the conflict with the common law's decision that such transactions are valid is stark. Indeed, in some cases Equity has gone too far, as it did in enabling a transaction to be rescinded for a wholly innocent misrepresentation that merely influenced the misrepresentee's decision-making process, and this required correction by legislation.[4]

Not all of the rules that were applied in the Court of Chancery in 1875 that have been developed by the modern court system since that time fall into this pattern of

[4] Albeit incompetently, by the Misrepresentation Act 1967 (UK), s 2(2).

being rules about rules. The modern law of breach of privacy, which originated in the old action for breach of confidence, cannot be seen in this way, and has become a new freestanding tort. In England at least, there no longer seems to be anything specifically equitable about it.

Equitable set-off does however follow the pattern of concerning rules about other rules. This enables us to see how it is different from the other rules travelling under the label of set-off.

III. OTHER KINDS OF SET-OFF

In order to clear the ground, it is necessary to set out the other kinds of set-off that are not equitable and their distinct rationales. Once this has been done, the distinctive role and need for equitable estoppel will become clearer.

A. Contractual Set-Off

The easiest category of set-off to justify is contractual set-off. The justification for recognising such rights of set-off is the same as for the recognition of any other kind of rights created by agreement. The set-off may be automatic upon the happening of an event (eg, a day in the month) or triggered by the giving of notice by one or both parties. All depends upon the terms of the agreement. The banker's right to combine current accounts operated for the same customer is a species of this form, based upon an implied agreement. Contractual set-off is substantive: the parties' rights as they otherwise would be are changed (netted off) by the operation of their agreement.

B. Insolvency Set-Off

If one of the parties to a cross-demand is a person who is bankrupt, or a company in liquidation or administration, insolvency set-off applies and the two claims are netted off.[5] Insolvency set-off is automatic, self-executing, retrospective[6] and mandatory. It applies to liquidated and unliquidated claims alike. These rules originated in statutes going back to the time of Queen Anne.

Insolvency set-off is somewhat difficult to justify. Its substantive effect is to ensure that one creditor is paid, whilst others are left to prove for a dividend. It is usually said that it would be unfair if a creditor of an insolvent party were forced to pay all that he owes, whilst being left merely to prove for a dividend on what is owed to him by the insolvent. But the unfairness here is not in the creditor paying what

[5] For individuals, Insolvency Act 1986 (UK), s 323. For corporations, Insolvency Rules 1986 (UK), rr 2.85, 4.90.

[6] The netting takes place at the date of the commencement of the insolvency proceeding, but subsequent events relevant to the valuation of the claims are taken into account.

he owes, but in only receiving a dividend, something that does not distinguish him from the other creditors of the company. Set-off here operates as a form of hidden unbargained-for security. Other jurisdictions (eg, France) not only have no equivalent expansive provisions but *exclude* the operation of set-offs that would operate outside of the insolvency proceeding.

An alternative justification is that it makes the carrying out of the realisation and distribution of assets to creditors more efficient. If a trustee in bankruptcy or liquidator had to pay out dividends to a creditor, whilst pursuing counterclaims against them potentially in other jurisdictions and possibly fruitlessly, this would prejudice other creditors. However, there is no need for insolvency set-off specifically to meet this problem. Under the rule in *Cherry v Boultbee*[7] a person is not entitled to participate in a fund until he has fulfilled his duty to contribute. This adequately meets the efficiency concerns of other creditors without requiring a separate insolvency set-off rule.

Regardless of its justification, insolvency set-off is the most significant form of set-off as it is upon one party's insolvency that set-off has its largest commercial significance.

C. Procedural Set-Off

Outside of insolvency, set-off between solvent parties also originated in statutes of Queen Anne.[8] This form of set-off does not affect the substantive rights of the parties until both causes of action have been merged in a judgment of a court. Its purpose was and is to allow a defendant to require his cross claim to be tried together with the claimant's claim. This entails that judgment will be given simultaneously, so that one party is not required to satisfy the claim against him first. Unfortunately, this rule is confined to liquidated claims, and this has led to pressure to expand the equitable form of set-off.

IV. EQUITABLE SET-OFF

A. Misnomer

The classic examples[9] of equitable set-off reveal its normative basis. In *Beasley v Darcy*[10] a tenant had an unliquidated claim for damages against his landlord for cutting timber on his land. The landlord sued for rent and sought the ejectment of

[7] *Cherry v Boultbee* (1838) 2 Keen 319; 48 ER 651 (Court of Chancery); (1839) 4 My & Cr 442; 41 ER 171 (Chancery Division).

[8] Set-off of Debts Act 1728 (2 Geo 2 c 22); Set-off of Debts Act 1734 (8 Geo 2 c 24).

[9] Given by Lord Cottenham in *Rawson v Samuel* (1841) Cr & Ph 161; 41 ER 451 (High Court of Chancery).

[10] *Beasley v Darcy* (1800) 2 Sch & Lef 403 (Ireland).

the tenant. The tenant was granted relief from forfeiture. This is a strong and easy case because the trespass of the landlord had rendered the land less valuable, thereby inhibiting the tenant's ability to extract rent from it. The cross claim that was set up as a defence was *causally* related to the claim the claimant wished to assert.[11]

Similar is *Piggott v Williams*.[12] The defendant was sued by his solicitor for the recovery of his costs, foreclosure being sought of an estate pledged as security for costs. The defendant set up a counterclaim for negligence asserting that the fees would never have been incurred but for the solicitor's negligence. Foreclosure was denied. Again, the wrongful action of the claimant was causally related to the claim he wished to assert.

Finally, in *Lord Cawdor v Lewis*[13] an owner of land who had stood by while another person made improvements to it, brought a claim for mesne profits for its use. The defendant brought a cross claim for the money expended upon the land, and an injunction was granted restraining the bringing of the action for mesne profits at common law. Again, the claimant's conduct which formed the basis of the counterclaim was causally related to the claim that the claimant sought to assert.

In none of these classic examples do the words 'set-off' appear in the judgments. The reason why not should be apparent. In each case the causal relation between the counterclaim and the claim sought rendered it unfair that the claimant should obtain judgment in his favour before the counterclaim against him was resolved. As the counterclaim was for an unliquidated sum, without a mechanism for determining its value before a court judgment (as exists today where a debtor is bankrupt) there was and is no way of netting out the claims. If by 'set-off' we mean some kind of netting out of mutual claims so that only the balance remains payable (as is true of all other forms of set-off) 'equitable set-off' is a misnomer for this rule.[14] Where the claimant's conduct has caused a claim against him to arise he may not assert a claim which is causally related to the same conduct.

Further it may be that the counterclaim that is asserted ultimately fails, so long as it is asserted reasonably and in good faith.[15] Where a claim is ultimately valueless, no reduction will be made. Equitable set-off may result in a netting out at the end of the story, but there is no necessary reason why it should.

It also follows that equitable set-off shares none of the core features of insolvency set-off. It is not automatic or self-executing: it must be asserted. It is not retrospective. It is not mandatory: the parties may contract out of it in advance. Its basis is not agreement, and its operation is substantive not procedural.

[11] See *Stimson v Hall* (1857) 1 H & N 831; 156 ER 1436 1438 (Bramwell B).

[12] *Piggott v Williams* (1821) 6 Madd 95; 56 ER 1027 (High Court of Chancery).

[13] *Lord Cawdor v Lewis* (1835) 1 Y & C Ex 427; 160 ER 174 (Exchequer).

[14] See also *Aries Tanker Corporation v Total Transport Ltd* [1977] 1 WLR 185 (HL) 192 (Lord Salmon); *Fearns v Anglo-Dutch Paint & Chemical Co Ltd* [2010] EWHC 2366 (Ch); [2011] 1 WLR 366, [11] (George Leggatt QC).

[15] *Santiren Shipping Ltd v Unimarine SA* [1981] 1 All ER 340 (QBD) 346 (Mocatta J); *SL Sethia Liner Ltd v Naviagro Maritime Corpn* [1981] 1 Lloyd's Rep 18 (QBD) 26 (Robert Goff J); *Fearns v Anglo-Dutch Paint & Chemical Co Ltd* [2010] EWHC 2366 (Ch); [2011] 1 WLR 366 [30] (George Leggatt QC).

An illustration of the situation where no equitable set-off should be or is allowed is the decision of the House of Lords in *Aries Tanker Corporation v Total Transport Ltd*.[16] The voyage charterers of a vessel sought to set up an equitable set-off of their claim for short delivery of oil, against the carrier's claim for freight. This was refused. Despite the fact that the two claims arose from the same transaction, there was no causal relation between the claim for freight and the short delivery. A charterer who thereby paid less than the freight on the due date was not thereby in breach of contract.

This may be contrasted with the subsequent decision of the Court of Appeal in *Federal Commerce Navigation Ltd v Molena Alpha Inc ('The Nanfri')*.[17] Under a time charter contract where the carriers deprived the charterers of the use of the vessel or prejudiced their use of the vessel through, for example, breaching a speed warranty, a right to an equitable set-off, entitling them to make a deduction from the hire payable, arose. Here the claimant's conduct which formed the basis of the counterclaim (taking the vessel off hire) is causally related to the claim that he wishes to assert (the claim for hire).

B. A Causal Not a Transactional Link

In the light of the above cases and justification, it should be plain that what is required is a causal relationship between the two claims. That they arise from the same transaction should be neither necessary nor sufficient. If a purely transactional relation sufficed, then *Aries Tanker*, where the claims arose under the same contract, is wrongly decided. If a transaction is required, those cases of equitable set-off where there has been no transaction at all between the parties would be wrongly decided. What we are searching for is a reason why it is unfair to allow an otherwise valid claim to be asserted. The mere existence of a counterclaim, even one arising out of the same contract, is not such a reason.

The modern law in England has not, however, conformed to this traditional approach, and is now both difficult to state and to justify. For present purposes, it suffices to fast-forward[18] to the two most recent English Court of Appeal decisions: *Geldof Metaalconstructie NV v Simon Carves Ltd*[19] and *Bibby Factors Northwest Ltd v HFD Ltd*.[20]

In *Geldof*, the defendants were the main contractors for the construction of a bioethanol plant in Teesside. They entered into two separate contracts with the claimants. Under one contract they agreed to *supply* pressure vessels, under another they agreed to *install* storage tanks. There was no connection between these items save that they were necessary for the completion of the plant. The claimants

[16] *Aries Tanker* (n 14).

[17] *Federal Commerce Navigation Ltd v Molena Alpha Inc ('The Nanfri')* [1978] QB 927 (CA).

[18] For earlier departures, see *Dole Dried Fruit and Nut Co v Trustin Kerwood Ltd* [1990] 2 Lloyd's Rep 309 (CA).

[19] *Geldof Metaalconstructie NV v Simon Carves Ltd* [2010] EWCA Civ 667; [2010] 1 CLC 895.

[20] *Bibby Factors Northwest Ltd v HFD Ltd* [2015] EWCA Civ 1908; [2016] 1 Lloyd's Rep 517.

supplied the vessels, and sought payment. The defendants sought to set off a claim for damages for wrongful repudiation of the contract to *install*.

The modern language of the courts has required that there be a 'close connection' between claim and counterclaim and that it be 'manifestly unjust' not to allow a set-off. The older language that one claim must 'impeach' the other has upon occasion been deprecated. But these opaque tests tell us nothing at all. What is a close connection, if not some kind of causal relationship? What is the 'manifest injustice' which is not simply that there are cross claims? Who knows without more.

The Court of Appeal concluded that the suppliers, by insisting upon payment under the supply contract before continuing to perform the instalment contract, created the necessary connection.[21] However, this conduct was irrelevant to their entitlement to payment under the supply contract. It is obscure what the injustice was in allowing the supplier to claim the sum it was owed. If the defendant had wrongfully not paid what he owed, and this had caused the claimant to refuse to continue to perform, this may have been a good reason for refusing to allow a claim for damages for non-performance to proceed. The converse does not follow.

The result in *Geldof* can be justified on the basis that there was a separate express contractual right of set-off under the terms of the supply contract. No such express entitlement existed in *Bibby Factors*.

Here, the defendants bought goods from a supplier, who subsequently assigned all claims to the claimant factors (for our purposes the assignment can be ignored). Under the terms of the overarching agreement between buyer and supplier, the supplier was entitled to a 10 per cent rebate at the end of each calendar year for every supply made, payable in January. If, however, there was no *contractual* entitlement to set off the sums owing under the supply contracts, and the sum owing by way of rebate, it is unclear how equitable set-off could assist. The entitlement to be paid for supplies was causally independent of any counterclaim to a rebate. The better view is that there was such an implied contractual right of set-off. It was indeed 'manifest'[22] that the supplier could not demand payment without giving credit for the rebate it had promised once accrued, but this was because this was what the parties had through their arrangement implicitly agreed.

In Australia and Canada, the old-learning that one claim must 'impeach' the other still lives on, but it may be that in England it has been lost. Perhaps the law now is that the decision of the House of Lords in *Aries Tanker Corporation v Total Transport Ltd*[23] is an anomalous one confined to cases of voyage charters. The change between the old language of 'impeachment' to the new of 'close connection' was not merely semantic. The courts in England seem to have lost sight of the justification for equitable set-off, as an entitlement to restrain the assertion of another right. If, in *Geldof*, we concluded that there were no contractual right of set-off, why should it suffice that the two claims arose from the same transaction?

[21] *Geldof* (n 19) [46].
[22] *Bibby Factors* (n 20) [39].
[23] *Aries Tanker* (n 14).

C. Mutuality

A divergence among textbook accounts of equitable set-off concerns the requirement of mutuality. Professor Goode[24] insists that it is required, as it no doubt is for all other forms of set-off, whilst Professor Derham[25] and the authors of *Meagher, Gummow and Lehane*[26] deny it. The former view has also been expressed in *obiter dicta* by the English Court of Appeal.[27]

If equitable set-off involved the netting out of claims, as do all other forms of set-off, then it would follow as a matter of course that mutuality should be required. But it does not. Ordinarily it will be the case that it will only be unfair to enforce a claim where the very party that the claimant seeks to enforce against has a right by way of counterclaim rendering this unfair, but this will not always be so.

One illustration is that of *Hamp v Jones*.[28] A landlord acting through a bailiff levied distress for unpaid rent upon the tenant's goods. The tenant then obtained judgment against the landlord and bailiff for irregularities in the distress and sale. The bailiff had no counterclaim, but the landlord had a claim for the rent arrears. At law, the fact that one claim was against the landlord and bailiff jointly, whilst the other was not, destroyed the mutuality between them.[29] As the landlord had agreed to indemnify the bailiff, so that he would bear the cost of any judgment made, the Vice Chancellor regarded this as sufficient to raise an Equity to restrain the proceedings against them both.

D. Is It Always a Defence?

Whether or not something constitutes a defence is, in private law, a purely formal question. Is it something that the defendant asserts in his pleadings, that is not merely a denial, in order for a claim to fail? Ordinarily, 'equitable set-off' is, alongside laches, acquiescence and release, an archetypal defence. However, it may be that in some situations it does not operate as such. Derham gives the example of a time charter under which the carrier is entitled to withdraw the vessel for non-payment of hire, but where the charterer has a valid equitable set-off against the claim to hire. Here, the charterer ought to be able to obtain an injunction restraining the use of the vessel in a manner inconsistent with the time charter. The set-off allows a claim that would otherwise fail to succeed. It is operating as part of a reply. The pleadings proceed in three stages.

[24] See L Gullifer (ed), *Goode on Legal Problems of Credit and Security* 5th edn (London, Sweet & Maxwell, 2013) [7–53].

[25] R Derham, *The Law of Set-Off* 4th edn (Oxford, Oxford University Press, 2010) [4.67].

[26] JD Heydon, M Leeming, PG Turner, *Meagher, Gummow and Lehane's Equity: Doctrines and Remedies* 5th edn (NSW, LexisNexis Butterworths, 2015) [39-060].

[27] *R (on the application of Burkett) v Hammersmith and Fulham LBC* [2004] EWCA Civ 1342; [2005] CP Rep 11 [57]–[58].

[28] *Hamp v Jones* (1840) 9 LJ Ch 258.

[29] The meaning of mutuality for purposes of insolvency set-off is not the same, adding to the difficulty.

(1) Charterer's Claim: I have a right to restrain the use of the vessel in a way inconsistent with the charter.
(2) Carrier's Defence: I have a right to withdraw the vessel for non-payment of hire.
(3) Charterer's Reply: I have a right to resist the claim for hire because of a counterclaim that operates as an equitable set-off.

The set-off is never, however, an independent claim in its own right. In this it resembles an equitable estoppel, properly understood. It is a shield not a sword, but one that may enable a claim that would otherwise fail to succeed.

V. CONCLUSION

Confusion in the law has three sources. First, the label 'equitable set-off' is misleading as it implies it involves some kind of netting out as do other forms of set-off. In fact, it involves a right in the defendant to restrain the claimant from enforcing his claims against him. It is a traditional equitable rule about another rule. Second, the procedural form of set-off is unduly restricted to liquidated claims, creating an incentive to expand 'equitable' set-off to cover the gap, a role for which it is ill-suited. This may be the reason for the change in the law we have seen in England. Third, and most seriously, the normative basis for the equitable rule has been lost sight of and the courts are now using hopelessly opaque formulas about 'close connections' and 'manifest injustice' that shed no light on what the right result ought to be.

Properly understood, equitable set-off has more in common with other rules of Equity than it does with other rules of set-off. The formal structure of both enables us to understand this.

4

Purchase for Value Without Notice

DAVID FOX

I. INTRODUCTION

PURCHASE FOR VALUABLE consideration without notice is the paradigmatic equitable defence. In *Stanhope v Earl Verney* (1761) Lord Henley LC described it as the 'polar star of equity'.[1] As his metaphor suggested, the purchase of a legal estate for value and without notice was the central point around which the jurisdiction of the Court of Chancery revolved. It defined the jurisdictional divide between the Chancery and the common law courts, which litigants had to navigate as they proceeded in each system. Even today, after the abolition of the separate equity and common law jurisdictions, it remains central to our understanding of trusts, equitable property and the conditions for the grant of equitable relief.

This chapter takes a long view of the development of the defence, from its origins in the early modern law of uses down to its current place in the law of property. Although we now call purchase for value without notice an equitable 'defence', with the burden of raising and proving it on the defendant, it was known for most of its life to Chancery practitioners as a 'plea'.[2] It served as a single answer sufficient to bar the claimant's suit for equitable relief.[3] In the field where it operates today that is still the result.

Its status as a plea was clearly articulated in the seventeenth century, through the systematising work of Lord Nottingham LC. Before then it had a narrower scope. It was confined to, and took shape within, the early law of uses. The purchase of a freehold estate for good consideration and the lack of notice combined as reasons why the purchaser was not privy to any use assumed by an earlier proprietor of the estate. The elements of the plea had more to do with formalised inferences about the parties' intentions than default rules of general property law. The place of the defence in the current law of property is now entirely different from its origins. Not only is it a bar to the enforcement of trusts, but also to the many other kinds of equitable interest that have proliferated since the early modern period. The limitation of the defence to purchasers of a legal estate was rooted in the old theories of land tenure

[1] *Stanhope v Earl Verney* (1761) 2 Eden 81, 85; 28 ER 826, 828.

[2] *Re Nisbet and Potts' Contract* [1906] 1 Ch 386, 404 (Collins MR); *Barclays Bank plc v Boulter* [1999] 1 WLR 1919, 1925 (Lord Hoffmann).

[3] See further section III.A below.

distinctive to real property. Statutory reforms throughout the twentieth century have made the defence almost irrelevant to real property. A few rare exceptions aside, it now operates to resolve competing claims to personal property, such as money or securities. Although the defence now operates far from its origins, traces of the old law of uses still leave wrinkles in the modern law. These can only be smoothed, or at least seen for what they are, by understanding the origins of the defence.

II. USES AND PRIVITY

The classical eighteenth-century form of the defence described by Lord Henley LC was nearly three centuries in the making. Its origins are traceable to the late fifteenth and early sixteenth-century rules on the raising of uses on the feoffment of a legal estate.[4] It was not obviously a plea in defence to the enforcement of a right that might now be analysed as an equitable interest in land. The existence of consideration and the feoffee's notice of any prior use affecting the estate determined when the personal confidence first undertaken by the original feoffee to use might bind a stranger who had not given the same undertaking. They explain how the use or the trust of land later evolved as an arrangement where the beneficiary took an equitable right *in rem* in the legal estate. The broad outlines of this story have been told most famously by FW Maitland in his lectures on *Equity* (1909).[5] This section fills in the detail of Maitland's outline.

A. Uses in the Early Modern Common Law of Property

It is convenient to begin at the mid-point of the development of the plea in the late sixteenth and early seventeenth centuries. The printed sources and the case reports of this period give a reasoned analysis about the nature of the use that is largely absent from—or undiscoverable in—the Year Book or manuscript reports of the earlier sixteenth century. Foremost among these are Francis Bacon's *Readings on the Statutes of Uses* delivered early in the seventeenth century and published in 1642,[6] and *Coke's First Institutes of the Laws of England or Commentary upon Littleton* (c1628).[7] Both draw heavily on the argument and reasons reported by Sir Edward Coke

[4] See generally SFC Milsom, *Historical Foundations of the Common Law* 2nd edn (Oxford, Oxford University Press, 1981) ch 9; JH Baker, *The Oxford History of the Laws of England* vol VI (Oxford, Oxford University Press, 2003) ch 35; and for the medieval and Tudor periods, J Biancalana, 'Medieval Uses' and N Jones, 'Trusts in England after the Statute of Uses: A View from the 16th Century' in R Helmholz and R Zimmermann (eds), *Itinera Fiduciae* (Berlin, Duncker & Humblot, 1998).

[5] FW Maitland, *Equity: A Course of Lectures* 2nd edn revised by J Brunyate (Cambridge, Cambridge University Press, 1936), Lectures III, IX.

[6] References are given to F Bacon, *The Learned Reading of Sir Francis Bacon upon the Statute of Uses* (London, Walbancke & Chapman, 1642).

[7] References are given to F Hargrave and C Butler (eds), *Coke's First Institutes of the Laws of England or Commentary upon Littleton* 17th edn (London, W Clarke & Sons, 1817).

in *Chudleigh's Case* (*Dillon v Freine*) (1589–95),[8] although the threads extend at least 60 years earlier. Coke described a use as follows:

> [A] trust or confidence reposed in some other, which is not issuing out of the land, but as a thing collaterall, annexed in privitie to the estate of the land and to the person touching the land, *scilicet*, that *cesty que use* shall take the profit, and that the terre-tenant shall make an estate according to his direction. So as *cesty que use* had neither *ius in re*, nor *ius ad rem*, but only a confidence or trust, for which he had no remedie by the common law, but for breach of trust his remedie was only by *subpoena* in chancerie.[9]

Coke's point was not so much to demonstrate that the use defied straightforward labelling under the civil law categories of *ius* but to demonstrate its tenuous status outside the common law theory of estates or interests in land.[10] The point was developed by Bacon, who identified *ius in re* with a common law estate and *ius ad rem* as 'a demand' enforceable against land such as a pernancy of profits. The use was neither.[11] The Tudor case law from which Coke and Bacon drew their explanations emphasised that the use was almost a non-legal arrangement. The enforcement of uses by subpoena in Chancery, where jurisdiction was exercised according to an extra-legal rationale of conscience, confirmed this understanding. The description of uses in common law cases was often negative, almost dismissive, of their substance. Uses could thus be described as 'but imaginations';[12] 'not a thing issuing out of land but only a trust or confidence collateral';[13] or 'nothing in law but a confidence'.[14] The recognition of the use at common law did not derive from any consistent theory about its substantive status. The incidents of the use had to be gathered incrementally from the statutes or judicial decisions which resolved, from case to case, that some aspect of the beneficiary's status warranted legal recognition.[15]

The use was a personal confidence reposed by a feoffor when he made a feoffment of an estate. It bound the feoffee to hold the land for the *cestui que use*. Its main incidents were two-fold: that, although the estate and possession had passed to the feoffee to use, the feoffee would yield up the profits of the land to the *cestui que use*;[16] and that in accordance with a statute of 1484 the feoffee would convey the legal estate at the *cestui que use*'s direction. The *cestui que use* thus had a statutory power of disposition over an estate vested in another.[17] After 1536 this second incident was qualified by the Statute of Uses.[18] It 'executed' the use of freeholds by

[8] *Chudleigh's Case* (*Dillon v Freine*) (1589–95) 1 Co Rep 120a; 76 ER 261.

[9] Hargrave and Butler (eds), *Coke's First Institutes of the Laws of England* (n 7) [272b].

[10] On the personal character of the early use, see Jones, 'Trusts in England after the Statute of Uses' (n 4).

[11] Bacon, *Statute of Uses* (n 6) 4–5.

[12] *Chudleigh's Case* (*Dillon v Freine*) (1589–95) 1 Co Rep 120a, 140a; 76 ER 261 (Periam CB).

[13] ibid 121b (in argument).

[14] *Bury (Abbot of) v Bokenham* (1536) 1 Dyer 7b, 12a; 73 ER 19, 26 (in argument). See also *Gervys v Cooke* (1522) YB Mich 14 Henry VIII, fol 4b, pl 5; (2002) 119 *Selden Society* 108, 114 (Fitzherbert J) ('nothing other than a trust and confidence'); *Anon* (1549) *William Yelverton's Notebook* (2004) 121 *Selden Society* 347-[73] (CP).

[15] See generally the instances gathered in Bacon, *Statute of Uses* (n 6) 5–6.

[16] See generally St German, *Doctor and Student* cap 23, [54b]–[55a].

[17] Statute 1 Richard III, c 1 (1484).

[18] Statute 27 Henry VIII, c 10 (1536).

vesting the legal estate in the *cestui que use*. The effect was to reunite the legal estate and the power of disposition over it in the same person.

The personal nature of the confidence explained the range of its enforcement. To repeat Coke's explanation, it was 'annexed in privitie to the estate of the land and to the person touching the land', as 'a thing collateral' to it but 'not issuing out of the land' itself.[19] The use was only enforceable against the original feoffee to use or against one who was in privity of estate with him. It did not directly bind on the land itself. So although its main practical incident was to give the *cestui que use* the profits of the land, it differed fundamentally from a pernacy of profits or a rent charge. The pernor or grantee of a charge had a legal right against the land to take the fruits or money rents generated from the land.[20]

The extension of the use to those in privity with the original feoffee is the same process that Maitland later explained as the incremental evolution of a trust beneficiary's equitable right of property.[21] From about the 1460s the Chancellor would issue a writ of subpoena against the heir of the original feoffee and enforce the use against him as he had against the ancestor. Likewise, those taking an interest by grant or an estate by feoffment from the original feoffee might also be bound by the use, provided, as we shall see, that there was no good reason to bar the continuing enforcement of the use against them.[22] The justification for this extension might first have been found in the terms of the original feoffment creating the use. As Fitzherbert J said in *Gervys v Cooke* (1522):

> For, if I enfeoff B to have unto him and his heirs and assigns, my trust and confidence is in him and in his heirs and assigns; and that is easily proved, because the heirs shall be as bound to perform the feoffor's will as [their] father was; and likewise the second feoffee is just as bound as the first (unless there is consideration).[23]

The use was unenforceable against those holding an estate or interest that did not depend on privity with the original feoffee to use. One who took the land by disseisin or on an escheat of the feoffee's estate held it free of any confidence to observe the use.[24] The disseisor or the superior lord had not undertaken the confidence for themselves nor did they derive title through one who had. This privity limitation was eventually summed up in the maxim that the use bound those who took title in the *per* from the original feoffee but not those taking in the *post*.[25] It also explains why the plea applied specifically to a purchaser of an estate or interest in the land. A 'purchaser' is one who takes an estate or interest by an act of the parties rather

[19] Hargrave and Butler (eds), *Coke's First Institutes of the Laws of England* (n 7) [272b].

[20] Bacon, *Statute of Uses* (n 6) 5.

[21] Maitland, *Equity: A Course of Lectures* (n 5) Lectures IX.

[22] The case law is summarised in AWB Simpson, *A History of the Common Law of Contract* 2nd edn (Oxford University Press, Oxford, 1987) 357–61.

[23] *Gervys v Cooke* (1522) YB 14 Henry VIII fol 4, pl 5, as reported in (2002) 119 *Selden Society* 108, 115 (Fitzherbert J).

[24] *Chudleigh's Case* (*Dillon v Freine*) (1589–95) 1 Co Rep 120a, 121a–121b, 139b; 76 ER 261.

[25] DEC Yale (ed), *Lord Nottingham's 'Manual of Chancery Practice' and 'Prolegomena of Chancery and Equity'* (Cambridge, Cambridge University Press, 1965) Ch XII, para 12, Ch XIV, para 3 ('Yale, *Manual and Prolegomena*').

than by operation of law.[26] The protection afforded by the plea was unnecessary for one taking by operation of law. He would not have been in privity with the original feoffee to use so the use would not have bound him at any rate.

It is easy to read the old cases with the distorting perspective of hindsight and find in them a default rule of property law that the use ran with the estate. But that conclusion would be mistaken because its premises are wrong. The use lay outside any formal conception of property recognised at common law. The explanation for the 'running' of the use lay partly in the intention of the original feoffor to use to bind his heirs and assigns, and partly in the intention of each subsequent feoffee or grantee. The personal confidence was re-imposed with each new transaction. So far as default rules figured at all, they were only standard presumptions about the party's intentions as to the running of the confidence, which necessarily confined them to transactions linked by privity. The corollary was that each subsequent feoffee could evince a transactional intention that was inconsistent with the terms of the original use. This explains Fitzherbert J's parenthetic qualification in *Gervys v Cooke* (1522) about consideration.[27] As the next section shows, the consideration for a transaction evolved as a key reason determining whether the use still bound the estate after the original feoffee had conveyed it to a stranger.

B. Uses and Consideration

The formation of the plea of purchase for value without notice was linked to, and found its rationale in, the early sixteenth-century rules on consideration. Vestiges of those rules survive in the modern presumptions of advancement and resulting trust, and hint at the original relevance of consideration to the plea. The presumptions of advancement and resulting trust now serve as default equitable rules for ascertaining an owner's intention about the beneficial interest in property on a transfer of the legal title.[28] The sixteenth-century rules of consideration determined whether the use of property passed to a feoffee when the land was conveyed, or whether it remained instead in the person who previously had the use of the property.

The late medieval understanding of consideration was grounded in the reasons motivating a person to perform a legal act.[29] The word 'consideration' is best taken literally: the consideration for a transaction was the reason or the circumstance that a person held in his mind and which prompted him to enter into the transaction. The consideration was evidence of the person's intentions about the true effect of an equivocal transaction or where those intentions might not have warranted protection in law. Consideration was directly relevant to the rules governing the raising

[26] RE Megarry and HWR Wade, *Law of Real Property* 1st edn (London, Stevens & Sons Ltd, 1957) lxxxii; Hargrave and Butler (eds), *Coke's First Institutes of the Laws of England* (n 7) 18b.

[27] *Gervys v Cooke* (2002) 119 *Selden Society* 108, 115 (Fitzherbert J). See text at n 23.

[28] See generally J McGhee (ed), *Snell's Equity* 33rd edn (London, Sweet & Maxell, 2015) ch 25.

[29] The best account of consideration in the early law of uses remains Simpson, *A History of the Common Law of Contract* (n 22) 327–74.

and extinction of uses. It determined which party had the use of land where the conveyancing documents were silent or where the court had to decide if the party's expressed intentions were legally enforceable. Some considerations were good. The law would regard them as valid reasons for recognising that the feoffee or some third party had the use of the property, as the feoffor intended. The most obvious were conveyances made in consideration of marriage, close family ties or the payment of money. Other considerations were not good reasons for enforcing the party's intentions and so did not pass the use as the feoffor might have wished.[30] Illegal uses were the extreme example. A use made to defraud the feoffor's creditors was unlawful and outside any enforcement by the law.[31]

The ascertainment of the feoffor's intention depended on formalised rules. Most relevant here, and on one side of a line, were the rules about which kinds of consideration would pass the use of the land to the feoffee or some third party for whom the feoffor instructed the feoffee to hold.[32] On the other side were the rules where the use of the land was unchanged despite the feoffment. The use remained in the feoffor or in a *cestui que use* in whom it was already vested by some prior transaction.

The usual kinds of consideration that passed the use to the feoffee were those which provided some *quid pro quo* for the feoffment.[33] This might consist in a bargain and sale between the feoffor and feoffee, or more generally in some 'recompense' paid to the feoffor in return for the feoffment.[34] It was in the very nature of a bargain and sale that the bargainor had to pass the entire use of the land to the bargainee. He could not with one hand bargain the land away and with the other reserve the use of the land for himself.[35] The Year Books and nominate reports of the early Tudor period are replete with examples,[36] some dealing with the details of the rule. A bargain and sale of land for payment of certain money was good to pass the use immediately to the buyer even though the buyer paid only part of the price, or postponed payment until a fixed future day.[37] The rule applied where the *cestui que use* sold his interest under the use. If the *cestui que use* bargained all his interest to a third party, the feoffees were immediately seised to the use of the buyer. If the original *cestui que use* then attempted to enter and make a feoffment of the land,

[30] eg, *Masterson v Brokesby* (1599) reproduced in 'Richard Powle's Reports' (2000) 117 *Selden Society* 117-[362] (where a covenant to stand seised to the use of a grandfather and grandfather in law was not a good consideration to raise a present use in them. They fell outside the blood descendants of the covenantor for whom he had an interest in providing).

[31] Bacon, *Statute of Uses* (n 6) 7.

[32] The cardinal importance of intention and the relevance of consideration to the raising or passing of a use on a feoffment were extensively considered in the second dialogue of Christopher St German's *Doctor and Student* (1530) chs xxi–xxiii. See (1974) 91 *Selden Society* 219–28.

[33] *Lord Audley's Case* (1572) 3 Dyer 324b, 325a; 73 ER 734.

[34] R Brooke, *La Graunde Abridgement* (R Tottel, London, 1573), 'Feffements al uses' pl 54 (1544–45).

[35] Similarly, a conveyance creating an entail was presumed to pass the use to the heirs (*Anon* (1573) Dalison 88, pl 3; 123 ER 297), and the creation of a lease passed the use to the lessee (*Bury (Abbot of) v Bokenham* (1536) 1 Dyer 7b, 10a; 73 ER 23 (in arg)).

[36] See, eg, the cases noted in Brooke, *La Graunde Abridgement* (n 34), 'Feffements al uses' pl 7 (1535–36), pl 15 (1505–06). *Re Nisbet and Potts' Contract* [1906] 1 Ch 386.

[37] *Anon* (c 1520) *Richard Pollard's Notebook* (2003) 120 *Selden Society* 135-[125] (CP); *Southwall v Huddleston* (1522) *Richard Pollard's Notebook* (2004) 121 *Selden Society* 253-[16] (CP); eg, *Anon* (1557) Benloe 61; 123 ER 48.

the prior bargain made him a disseisor.[38] The rule even applied in the face of an expressed intention to the contrary. The bargainor could not hold mutually repugnant intentions. A bargainor could not sell land to his own use,[39] or sell it to the buyer on the understanding that buyer would hold to the bargainor's use for life.[40] A use of property intentionally yielded up by sale could not be intentionally reserved in the same transaction.

On the other side were the transactions where there was no consideration to pass the use to the feoffee. If the feoffor provided that the feoffee took the estate on an expressed use, then his intention was respected. The feoffee held the estate according to the expressed use. But where the feoffment was silent about the use, and there was no good reason in the transaction to take it forward to the feoffee, then the use simply stayed where it was.[41] The feoffee held the land to the use of the feoffor if he had already had the use in the land before the feoffment. So strong was the pull of consideration in changing the use, that the lack of any consideration for a transaction suggested that the feoffor intended to maintain the status quo. Again the reports are replete with statements of the rule:

> But the law is otherwise of a feoffment, for if no use is expressed in the deed of feoffment the feoffee shall be seised to the use of the feoffor and not to his own use. However, if any use is expressed in the deed, the use shall always be as it is expressed in the deed.[42]

These standardised rules about consideration in the raising or passing of the use on a feoffment became the foundation for the plea of purchase for value without notice. If a feoffee holding a freehold on an existing use enfeoffed it for a good consideration to a stranger then that implied—or at least gave grounds for arguing—that the feoffee and the stranger intended the stranger to hold to his own use rather than for the original *cestui que use*. The consideration for the feoffment tested the limits of the personal confidence that the original feoffor had imposed on the feoffee to use and on those who were in privity of estate with him. This leads to a detailed study of *Gervys v Cooke* (1522) and the early cases on conveyances to a stranger.[43]

C. *Gervys v Cooke* (1522)

Gervys v Cooke (1522) was not the earliest case to discuss consideration and notice after a feoffee to use conveyed the land to a stranger. Maitland has traced the first reference to 1471: '[I]f my feoffee on trust etc enfeoffed another who knew well that

[38] *Anon* (1524) *Roger Yorke's Notebook* (2003) 120 *Selden Society* 138-[132].

[39] Brooke, *La Graunde Abridgement* (n 34), 'Feffements al uses' pl 54 (1544–45).

[40] *Anon* (1557) Benloe 61; 73 ER 48.

[41] eg, *Anon* 1 Anderson 37; 123 ER 340.

[42] *Anon* (1549) *William Yelverton's Notebook* (2004) 121 *Selden Society* 347-[73] (CP). Traces of the rule date as early as the 1460s: see R Brooke, *La Graunde Abridgement* (n 34), 'Feffements al uses' pl 36 (1465–66); and pl 37 (1467–68). See also (c 1530) Note, *Reports of John Caryll Jnr* (2004) 121 *Selden Society* 392-[54]; *Villers v Beamont* (1556–37) 2 Dyer 146b; 73 ER 319; *Audley's Case* (1579) 2 Leonard 160; 74 ER 442; (1558) 2 Dyer 166a; 73 ER 363.

[43] *Gervys v Cooke* YB 14 Henry VIII fol 4, pl 5, as reported in (1522) (2002) 119 *Selden Society* 108.

[the first feoffee] had nothing except to my use, then a subpoena would lie against the [second] feoffee as well as against the [first feoffee] ... because in conscience it is my land that he purchases.'[44] The relevance of consideration and notice was worked out separately, a development which still puts wrinkles in modern attempts to find a consistent explanation for the enforcement of equitable entitlements against innocent transferees of trust property.[45] By the second decade of the sixteenth century the courts were considering the connection between the two elements. The notebook of Roger Yorke, Serjeant at Law (c1513–35) records two cases on the issue from before 1520. In one, Yorke's note reads:

> Note that if someone has feoffees to his use, and the feoffees made a feoffment over to strangers without any consideration, they are now seised as their feoffees were previously, in accordance with the first use. But if the second feoffment was made upon certain considerations, then if the last feoffees have no knowledge of the first use, so that the cestuy que use would suffer wrong and lose his use, then they shall be seised to their own uses and not in accordance with the first use.[46]

The second note from about the same time records a general discussion about the enforcement of uses against strangers, including the effect of granting a rent charge out of the land: 'if I make a feoffment to someone to my use, and the feoffee grants a rent charge to a stranger, or marries a wife and dies, she shall be endowed and also the grantee of the rent shall be deemed to be seised to the first use and shall hold charged'.[47] The note does not refer to the chargee's state of mind or to any consideration for the grant of the rent charge.

These very points did, however, figure on similar facts in *Gervys v Cooke* (1522), a decision of the Court of Common Pleas. Their connected relevance was considered fully by counsel and the court. Gervys' action was a replevin for cattle taken in exercise of a right of distress under a rent charge of land. The land originally belonged to one William Stoneacre. He made a gift and feoffment of this land to four feoffees to the use of himself, William. The feoffees then granted an annual rent charge of £4 to William's wife, Alice, for her life. She had notice of the prior use of the land for William. There was no consideration for the grant: she paid the feoffees no money for the rent; it was not sold to her by bargain; and she was not then in any family relationship with the feoffees that would have raised a presumption that the use passed to her. William died and Alice then married the defendant, Robert Cooke. He distrained the cattle on the land for unpaid rent due under the charge to Alice.

[44] YB (1471) 11 Edward IV, pl 14, f 8a, discussed in 'Trust and Corporation' in HD Hazeltine et al (eds), *Maitland: Selected Essays* (Cambridge, Cambridge University Press, 1936) 166. See also *Marshall's Case* (1506) Keilway 84; 72 ER 247.

[45] See *Westdeutsche Landesbank Girozentrale v Islington LBC* [1996] AC 669, 705 (Lord Goff). An innocent transferee of trust property holds it subject to the beneficiary's interest even though he has no notice of the trust. A voluntary transfer of property creates a resulting trust for the transferor even if he is unaware that he takes it for no consideration. The mistake is to reduce the explanation for enforcing the equitable claimant's interest against a transferee to a single test of unconscionability. Pre-modern lawyers would have found as much relevance in the consideration for the transfer as the transferee's state of mind. See further section V below.

[46] *Anon* (c 1520) *Roger Yorke's Notebook* (2003) 120 *Selden Society* 141-[142].

[47] ibid 142-[143].

The outcome turned on whether the feoffees had granted the rent to Alice subject to the prior use for William or for Alice's own use, in which case she and Robert would have been justified in seizing the cattle. The majority view was against the distress. Alice held her rent subject to the prior use. The reported arguments centred on whether Alice was linked by privity to the original use of the land and the degree to which the rent should 'follow the nature of the land' in being subject to it.[48]

As reported the second argument fell away in the judges' reasoning. They were mainly concerned with the relevance of consideration and notice to the relation of privity between the original feoffor who created the use and the grantee of the rent. Fitzherbert J said that privity raised a presumption that the feoffees for use intended to preserve the trust and confidence imposed on them. He worked through the usual relationships of privity. An original use would bind an heir. An heir was bound to perform the father's will, including his promise to observe the use. All other things being equal, it would also bind a stranger to whom he enfeoffed the land, unless there was consideration for the feoffment:

> For the law will presume that, since he parted with the land of which he was seised to the use, without consideration, he parted with it in the most due form he could, namely just as he had it before. Whenever an act rests upon presumption, and is equivocal, the law will judge it the best way ... So here, when he makes a feoffment or grant without any consideration, the law will presume the best: namely that he did it lawfully.[49]

The feoffees' grant to Alice was equivocal about their intention as to who had the use of the rent. In the absence of any consideration to resolve that evidential uncertainty, the court presumed an honest intention to preserve the confidence. But it would have lain in the feoffees' power to destroy the use by evincing a contrary intention. If the incidents of the grantee's right were incompatible with the use, it could not have been their intention to bind the grantee to observe the use. Fitzherbert J added: 'If, however, the feoffee grants a way across my land, or a right of common, or a stewardship, this is not to the first use, for in this case the grant (and his act) is expressly to the contrary.'[50] It seems he would have taken the same view if the grant of the rent was expressed for the use of the grantee.

The presence or absence of consideration for the transaction with the stranger must also have related to proving the feoffees' intention to bind the stranger with the use. Since the grant of the rent was for no consideration, the law presumed the parties' intention to leave the existing use unchanged, as it would with any other feoffment of land for no consideration. Broke J was explicit in making this connection: 'because these grants are without consideration the law presumes them to be made to the first use'.[51] If the grant had been supported by consideration, the presumption would have gone the other way. The parties could not have meant the grantees to

[48] *Gervys v Cooke* (2002) 119 *Selden Society* 108, 110–11 (Brown and Spelman JJ) (in argument).

[49] ibid 115 (Fitzherbert J).

[50] ibid.

[51] ibid 116 (Broke J). See also ibid 119 (Pollard J): 'And if the feoffees enfeoff someone without consideration, this is to the first use, even though there is no notice.'

assume the confidence. All other things being equal, Alice would have held the rent for her own use.

But all things were not equal: Alice had notice of the prior use, which tipped the balance back in favour of the *cestui que use*. Even if there had been a good consideration for the grant to her, she would have held the rent subject to the prior use. The point is developed most fully in Broke J's judgment. A person who was in privity of estate with the original feoffee to use and who took with notice was *particeps criminis* in the feoffee's intention to defeat the use. 'Those who consent to an act shall have equal punishment with those who perform it.'[52] 'In this case the notice makes the use, and otherwise not. For without notice the feoffee was innocent in not knowing other than that the land belonged to the feoffee himself, and innocent persons shall not be hurt or prejudiced.'[53] It was not enough that he might benefit from the operation of a legal rule that destroyed the prior use and allowed him to enjoy the legal estate for himself. A lord taking by escheat or a widow taking by dower from the original feoffee to use enjoyed the land for their own use.[54] Notice was irrelevant to them since their title did not derive through privity of estate with the feoffor who created the use.

The reason for binding a grantee with notice was not necessarily any distinctive theory of conscience enforced by the Chancellor. This may be how the rule was eventually rationalised as it developed in Chancery jurisprudence. So Francis Bacon said that privity was 'nothing else but a continuance/Of the Confidence without interruption and ordered and guided by Conscience: either by the private Conscience of the Feoffee; Or the general Conscience of the Estate which is *Chancery*'.[55] But the understanding of the use articulated by the judges in *Gervys v Cooke* (1522) belonged as much to the common law as to anything in the Chancellor's own jurisdiction. To be sure, Broke J understood that uses should bind proprietors who were 'chargeable in conscience'. But he also gave other examples from the common law where a proprietor was barred from enjoying the benefits of a fraudulent conspiracy to destroy another's legal rights.[56]

D. The Formation and Rationale of the Plea

The coalescence of consideration and absence of notice happened rapidly. Dyer's report of *Abbot of Bury v Bokenham* (1536) reports a submission about the kinds

[52] ibid 117 (Broke J).

[53] ibid.

[54] ibid (Broke J), translating the maxim *Consentientes et agentes pari poena plecentur* which the editor of the translation, Professor JH Baker, attributes to a collection of maxims by the thirteenth-century canonist Damascus: ibid n 1.

[55] Bacon, *Statute of Uses* (n 6) 8–9, citing Walmesley J, possibly in *Chudleigh's Case* (*Dillon v Freine*) (1589–95) 1 Co Rep 120a; 76 ER 261. *Westdeutsche Landesbank Girozentrale v Islington LBC* [1996] AC 669, 705 (Lord Goff). Maitland was sensitive to the generality of the rationale: Maitland, *Equity: A Course of Lectures* (n 5) 113; Hazeltine et al (eds), *Maitland: Selected Essays* (n 44) 166.

[56] *Gervys v Cooke* (2002) 119 *Selden Society* 108, 116–17 (Broke J) (eg, a collusive theft and purchase of stolen good in market overt).

of transaction where a feoffee to use might divest and alter the use of their feoffor. One was where 'by reason of feoffment made for money bona fide to one who hath not notice of the use; but if he hath notice of the use, although he hath given money, that shall not change the use'.[57] Coke's report of the argument in *Chudleigh's Case* (*Dillon v Freine*) (1589–95) refers to instances where a feoffee to use 'made a feoffment, upon good consideration to him who had no notice of the use' or where 'the land be aliened bona fide, upon consideration to one who hath no notice'.[58] These formulations were ambiguous about the relevance of bona fides to the plea. A finding of bad faith in the purchaser meant he had notice of the use and was bound by it.[59] But the second of these formulations implies the bad faith of the feoffee to use was also relevant as indicating an illegal consideration for the transaction.[60] The point was resolved only later in the eighteenth century when the treatise writers refined the precise details of the combined plea.[61]

Bacon rationalised the plea. The reason why a stranger who took with notice stood seised to the original use was that Chancery looked

> further than the Common Law, to the corrupt Conscience of him that will deale in the Land, knowing it in equity to bee anothers, and therefore if there were *Radix Amaritudinis* ["a root of bitterness"],[62] the consideration purgeth it not, but it is the peril of him that giveth it, so that consideration, or no consideration is the issue at the Common Law, but notice or no notice is an issue in the *Chancery*, and so much so for the preserving of uses.[63]

His Biblical allusion to 'a root of bitterness' emphasised the taint on the stranger's conscience and the possibility that it might spread like a contagion. The use would bind the stranger and any other to whom he then conveyed the land.

Bacon's comparison with the common law emphasised the similarities and differences between the common law and equity to the liability of a stranger who became implicated in the primary wrong of another. The use bound a stranger with notice because, as Broke J had said in *Gervys v Cooke* (1522), the stranger was *particeps criminis* in the wrong of the feoffee in conveying the land to him. He was party to a fraudulent covin designed to defeat the *cestui que use*'s claim. But the courts adopted different standards of complicity. 'There is no Case in the Common Law, wherein notice simply and nakedly is materiall to make a Covin.'[64] The common law set a

[57] *Bury (Abbot of) v Bokenham* (1536) 1 Dyer 7b, 8b (in argument). See also *Dalamere v Barnard* (1557) 1 Plowden 346, 351; 75 ER 525.

[58] *Chudleigh's Case* (*Dillon v Freine*) (1589–95) 1 Co Rep 120a, 121b, 126b; 76 ER 261. By the early seventeenth century, the rule was expressed as a standard formula: eg, *Foliambe v Rokeby* (c 1608–c 1620) 117 *Selden Society* 382-[167.742]; *Peacock v Reynellote* (1612) 117 *Selden Society* 400-[196].

[59] *cf Chudleigh's Case* (*Dillon v Freine*) (1589–95) 1 Co Rep 120a, 124b(5); 76 ER 261 which refers to the bona fides of the purchaser.

[60] The formulation might have been influenced by the terms of the Statute (1585) 27 Elizabeth I, c 4 which rendered void a fraudulent conveyance made to deceive subsequent purchasers. The Act did not touch a conveyance made 'upon or for good consideration and *bona fide*'.

[61] See section III.B below.

[62] An allusion to St Paul's Epistle to the Hebrews, 12, 15: 'Looking diligently lest any man fail of the grace of God; lest any root of bitterness springing up trouble you, and thereby many be defiled.'

[63] Bacon, *Statute of Uses* (n 6) 13.

[64] ibid 12.

high standard of fault before the stranger did enough to implicate himself in the wrong: '[T]he Common Law looketh no further then to see whether the Act were meerely *Actus fictus in fraudem legis*, and wheresoever it findeth consideration given it dischargeth the covin.'[65] Unless the stranger colluded in fraudulent covin to defeat the rights of the person truly entitled, then he might escape liability. This standard at least required the stranger to have actual knowledge.[66] A buyer of stolen goods in market overt would defeat the original owner's title so long as he bought in good faith and the purchase would not be tainted merely because he had the means of discovering the seller's wrongdoing.[67]

The outlines of distinctive Chancery doctrine of notice were beginning to form by the time Bacon delivered his lectures near the turn of the seventeenth century. Dr Jones has shown how earlier cases seemed to use the terms 'notice', 'knowledge' or 'privity' interchangeably.[68] By the 1590s, however, some credible and substantial ground was necessary to fix the stranger with notice. Rumours or a simple allegation of a trust would not do.[69] Traces of a formalised understanding of constructive notice can also be found: a purchaser might be fixed with notice of a pending suit concerning a trust.[70] All these points were to be refined during the next century as Lord Nottingham systematised the plea, giving it its classical form.

III. LORD NOTTINGHAM AND SYSTEMISATION

Heneage Finch, first earl of Nottingham, was Lord Keeper 1673–75 and Lord Chancellor 1675–82.[71] His decisions and extra-curial writings were the foundation of the courts' and treatise writers' understanding of purchase for value without notice down to the Chancery reforms of the nineteenth century. Their significance goes beyond his neat restatements of the rule as a single verbal formula distilled from the old sixteenth-century authorities on uses. Lord Nottingham wrote for example in his *Prolegomena* (1674) that 'in conveyance for valuable consideration, there the purchaser is not charged with any former trust without notice'.[72] Under Lord

[65] ibid.

[66] ibid.

[67] *Wikes v Morefoots* (1587) Cro Eliz 86; 78 ER 344. See also *Anon* YB (1455) Hil 33 Henry VI, pl 15, fol 5 (requiring a covin between the buyer and the seller to defeat the true owner's title); *cf* also Statute (1589) 31 Elizabeth, c 12, enacting an exception for the buyer of a stolen horse at market who 'paid for the same bona fide, without Fraud or Collusion'.

[68] For a reference to a purchase without 'notice' although not clearly analysing its meaning, see *Rooke v Staples* (1579) Cary 76; 21 ER 40.

[69] For a twentieth-century application of the same principle, see *Carl Zeiss Stiftung v Herbert Smith & Co (No 2)* [1969] 2 Ch 276.

[70] See Jones, 'Trusts in England after the Statute of Uses' (n 4) 196–99, discussing particularly *Cornwallis's Case* (1595) Tothill 186; 21 ER 163; *Wildgoose v Wayland* (1601) Gouldsborough 147; 75 ER 1056; *Diggs v Boys* (1598) Tothill 186; 21 ER 163.

[71] See DEC Yale, *Lord Nottingham's Chancery Cases*, vol I (1954) 73 *Selden Society*; vol II (1961) 79 *Selden Society*. For Lord Nottingham's contribution to developing the law of trusts, see M Macnair, 'The Conceptual Basis of Trusts in the Later 17th and 18th Centuries' in Helmholz and Zimmermann (n 4) 203–36.

[72] See Yale, *Manual and Prolegomena* (n 25) Ch XIV, paras 1, 2, Ch XV, para 1.

Nottingham purchase for value without notice ceased to be an outworking of the old privity rules governing the law of uses and trusts. It developed a recognisable procedural shape as an equitable defence. It became a plea in bar to proceedings initiated by a Chancery bill. It was established as a central doctrine in real property conveyancing, applying not just to trusts but to the great variety of equitable interests that had come to be recognised as binding on real property. The plea also had a special jurisdictional relevance. It marked the boundary between the Court of Chancery and the common law courts. It determined the limits of the Chancellor's jurisdiction to grant relief, whether the plaintiff was suing on a legal or an equitable title. Surprising as it may now seem, many of the leading seventeenth and eighteenth-century cases on purchase for value without notice have nothing to do with trusts or, indeed, with equitable property at all. They are cases in what later lawyers dubbed the 'auxiliary' jurisdiction of Chancery.

A. Purchase for Value Without Notice as a Plea

Chancery litigants raised purchase for value without notice as a plea to a plaintiff's bill for relief. A plea was a specialised kind of defence. The treatise writers have explained its procedural significance, refining the more obliquely expressed understanding of the contemporary Chancery judges. John Mitford's *Treatise on the Pleadings in the Suits in the Court of Chancery* (1780) defined a plea as

> a special answer showing or relying upon one or more things why the cause should be either dismissed, delayed or barred. The defence proper for a plea is such as reduces the cause, or some part of it, to a single point, and from thence creates a bar to the suit, or to the part to which the plea applies.[73]

Mitford enumerated a list of categories of plea. The ground of the plea of purchase for value without notice was that the defendant had 'an equal claim to the protection of a court of equity to defend his possession, as the plaintiff has to the assistance of the court to assert his right'.[74] John Beames' work on Chancery pleading (1818) explained that a plea differed 'from a demurrer in being a mode of defence founded on an objection to a suit not apparent on the face of the bill itself, but arising … "*dehors* the bill"'.[75]

Mitford's explanation of the plea is traceable to Finch LK's decision in *Bassett v Nosworthy* (1673).[76] The plaintiff, Bassett, was the heir by descent from the owner of an estate in Cornwall originally belonging to Henry Killigrew. The defendant, Nosworthy, purchased the estate through the beneficiary of Killigrew's will. Bassett alleged that Killigrew had previously revoked the will so that the estate rightfully

[73] Citing from J Mitford, *Treatise on the Pleadings in the Suits in the Court of Chancery* 5th edn by JW Smith (London, Stevens and Norton, 1847) 258.

[74] ibid 259, 319–25.

[75] Citing from J Beames, *The Elements of Pleas in Equity* 1st American edition by W Halstead (New York, O Halsted, 1824) 2.

[76] *Bassett v Nosworthy* (1673) Rep temp Finch 102; 23 ER 55.

passed to him by descent. He brought a bill for discovery of the revocation so that he might bring proceedings at law to try his title to the estate against the title of the defendant, Nosworthy. He accepted that Nosworthy was 'a Purchaser, *bona fide*, without Notice of any Defect in his Title at the Time of the Purchase'. He had therefore brought himself within the protection of the Court of Chancery. Equity would not

> disarm a *Purchaser*, but assist him … And this Rule, in a Court of Equity, is agreeable to the Wisdom of the common Law, where the Maxims that refer to *Descents*, *Discontinuances*, *Nonclaims*, and to *collateral Warranties*, are only to the wise Arts and Intentions of the Law to protect the Possession, and to strengthen the rights of *Purchasers*.[77]

Like the common law, equity's default policy was to protect a party's settled possession of property, laying the burden of disturbing it on to the other party who was out of possession. A mid-eighteenth-century maxim summarised the long-standing practice: *In aequali jure melior est conditio possidentis*.[78] If, indeed, the plaintiff had a superior legal title to the estate then he was still free to establish it by separate proceedings in the common law courts. Against a purchaser for value without notice, however, he could not rely on the assistance of Chancery to discover additional evidence that might support that action. In equity, possession might not have been a root of title as it was later said to be at law.[79] But the acquisition of possession by purchase for value without notice was at least a reason for letting that possession stay where it lay.

Finch LK's explanation was recast a century later in the familiar Chancery rationale of conscience. A purchaser for value without notice 'was not bound, in conscience, to assist the rightful owner in the legal recovery of the subject purchased under such circumstances'.[80] 'The doctrine of the jurisdiction of this Court is this: you cannot attach upon the conscience of the party any demand whatever, where he stands as a purchaser having paid his money, and denies all notice of the circumstances set up in the bill.'[81] The jurisdictional explanation tilted the emphasis to the justification for intervention against the person of the defendant and away from a default rule of protecting settled possession of property, as Finch LK had first explained it in *Bassett v Nosworthy* (1673). The question became why a defendant had to be exposed to a greater degree of curial intervention in the Court of Chancery than he would have encountered at common law: '[A] man, who has honestly dealt for valuable consideration, without notice, shall not be called upon by confessions wrung from his conscience to say, he has missed his object in the extent, in which he meant to acquire it', said Lord Eldon LC.[82] The plea justified refusing a bill for

[77] ibid 103–04.

[78] Anon, *Grounds and Rudiments of Law of Equity, Alphabetically Digested* (London, H Lintot, 1749) maxim 190.

[79] F Pollock and RS Wright, *Essay on Possession in the Common Law* (Oxford, Clarendon Press, 1888) 20–25.

[80] *Hoare v Parker* (1785) 1 Bro CC 578, 581; 28 ER 1308, 1310. The plea seems to have failed on the facts since the defendant, a pawnee of jewels, might have had notice: (1785–86) 1 Cox 224; 29 ER 1139.

[81] *Jerrard v Saunders* (1794) 2 Ves Jun 454, 458; 30 ER 721, 723 (Lord Loughborough).

[82] *Wallwyn v Lee* (1803) 9 Ves Jun 25, 34; 32 ER 509, 512 (Lord Eldon).

discovery of title deeds or to perpetuate testimony against him, even when he was a mortgagee in possession of the title deeds but was not in fact in possession of the land actually in dispute.[83]

Talk of 'jurisdiction' gave the explanation its strongest rhetorical force. This was not to say that the plaintiff's filing of the bill in Chancery was a procedural error. Mitford had reserved his category of 'plea to jurisdiction' for cases where the plaintiff's suit belonged in an entirely different court. Instead, he treated purchase for value without notice as belonging to the more general category of a 'plea in bar to relief'.[84] But the bar against the purchaser for value without notice was absolute. It cut across what Joseph Story later called the 'auxiliary jurisdiction' (where the plaintiff sued in Chancery for procedural relief supplementary to a claim at law) and 'the exclusive jurisdiction' (where he sued on an equitable title where only the Chancery had jurisdiction to grant relief).[85] The classical statements of the rule quoted above were all cases in the auxiliary jurisdiction where a plaintiff brought a bill for discovery of title deeds. They might assist the plaintiff's prior action at law by disclosing some weakness in the defendant's legal title to the property.[86]

Either way, the plea went to the rationale of the Court of Chancery's existence. As a court, its jurisdiction was parallel with, but secondary to, the primary jurisdiction of the common law courts. Chancery could not justify intervention against a defendant whose conscience was not affected in a formal sense. The plaintiff therefore had to pursue whatever remedies might be available to him in the common law courts (if indeed he had any remedies there at all). A plaintiff suing on a legal title, who was merely seeking auxiliary relief in Chancery, was left to his remedy at law and had to make do, despite any procedural limitations that the common law process might throw in his way. Those limitations might prevent his claim from succeeding. The outcome was simpler for a plaintiff suing on an equitable title, such as the beneficiary of a trust. He would generally have no standing to sue at law.[87] In a system where the existence of rights still depended on the availability of remedies, his equitable title was extinguished against a purchaser for value without notice. The extinction was permanent: his interest would not revive if the property next passed to a second purchaser with notice.[88]

[83] ibid.

[84] Mitford, *Treatise on the Pleadings in the Suits in the Court of Chancery* (n 73) 259–60.

[85] J Story, *Commentaries on Equity Jurisprudence as Administered in England and America* 1st edn (Boston, Hilliard, Gray & Co, 1836) vi, 92. As to the origins and reality of the distinction, see D Yale, 'A Trichotomy of Equity' (1985) 6 *Journal of Legal History* 194.

[86] See also *Churchill v Grover* (1663–64) Nelson 89; 21 ER 797; *Sherly v Fagg* (1665) 1 Chan Cas 68; 22 ER 669; *Brereton v Gamul* (1741) 2 Atk 240; 26 ER 548; *Glegg v Legh* (1819) 4 Madd 193; 56 ER 678; *Gait v Osbaldeston* (1826) 1 Russ 158; 38 ER 62; (1820) 5 Madd 428; 56 ER 959. This auxiliary aspect of Chancery jurisdiction was abolished in the Judicature reforms of 1873–75: Supreme Court of Judicature Act 1873, s 24(7).

[87] But note the exceptional instances where common law courts applied equitable titles: JD Heydon et al, *Meagher Gummow and Lehane's Equity Doctrines and Remedies* 5th edn (Chatswood, NSW, Butterworths, 2015).

[88] *Harrison v Forth* (1695) Prec Ch 51; 24 ER 26; *Brandlyn v Ord* (1738) 1 Atk 571; 26 ER 539. Exceptionally, however, the trust would revive if the land was reconveyed to the original trustee: *Bovey v Smith* (1682) 1 Vern 60; 23 ER 310.

B. Refining and Extending the Plea

The same period saw the refinement of the elements of the plea and its extension beyond the rules of priority in real property conveyancing until the property reforms of 1925. First was the refinement in the definition of consideration. By the Chancellorship of Lord Nottingham, consideration had long shaken off the generality of its late medieval meaning as the formal motivation for a transaction. The references to categories of consideration—marriage or bargain and sale—in the later Tudor cases show that the reservation or passing of the use in property had come to depend on settled rules. The consideration ceased to be a circumstantial ground from which the court might infer the feoffor's intention about the location of the beneficial rights in the feoffment. In *Bassett v Nosworthy* (1673) Finch LK confirmed that the primary consideration to found the plea was 'valuable' consideration.[89]

Statute became the analogy for fixing the limit of the equitable plea and showed something of its rationale: 'for if it be such a Consideration as will make the Defendant a Purchaser within the Statute [(1585) 27 Elizabeth, c 4] and bring him within the protection of that Law, he ought not to be impeached in Equity'.[90] The Statute of Elizabeth struck down conveyances, grants or limitations of use made with the intent of deceiving subsequent purchasers of the land even where the parties expressly declared the uses under which the property was to be held. It also targeted collusive transactions where the vendor of land retained the use and free disposition over his lands despite a feigned 'Countenance and Shew of Words and Sentences, as though the same were made bona fide, for good Causes, and upon just and lawful Considerations'. Such transactions were made void against any person who purchased 'for Money or other good Consideration'. The immediate point of Finch LK's analogy was that the consideration need be no more adequate for the plea to succeed in equity than it did to secure it against objections under the Statute of Elizabeth.[91] The analogy with the statute also indicated a subtle shift in the rationale of the plea. The requirement of valuable or other recognised consideration favoured the security of purchasers who had irrevocably altered their circumstances by entering into the transaction. It favoured what would later be thought of as security of transaction over security of interest. But the benefit of the plea was not confined to transactions that we might now crudely characterise as commercial in character.[92] Marriage consideration also supported the plea, as it probably always had.[93]

[89] *Bassett v Nosworthy* (1673) Rep Temp Finch 102, 104; 23 ER 55, 56.

[90] ibid, Rep Temp Finch 102, 104; 23 ER 55, 56.

[91] See *Mildmay v Mildmay* noted in DEC Yale, *Lord Nottingham's Chancery Cases*, vol I (1954) 73 *Selden Society* [474]. But the consideration might be so small that the plaintiff's bill nonetheless needed an answer because it put in doubt his lack of notice: *Solly v Whitfield* (1674) *Lord Nottingham's Chancery Cases*, vol I (1954) 73 *Selden Society* [169].

[92] Besides, a clear distinction between commercial transactions based on the exchange of monetary value and marriage transactions based on sentiment would be an anachronism for any period except perhaps our own.

[93] *Reynell v Peacock* (1619) 2 Rolle 105; 81 ER 688, noted sub nom *Reynolds v Peacock* in Yale, *Manual and Prolegomena* (1965), Ch XIV, para 2. For later confirmation, see *Jackson v Rowe* (1826) 2 Sim & St 472; 57 ER 427.

The transformation of the plea from an aspect of privity in the law of uses to a rule limiting the jurisdiction of the Chancery to grant relief meant also that it was no longer confined to interests arising under uses or trusts. By early in the eighteenth century the plea would bar, for example, the enforcement of an equity of redemption,[94] an equitable lien,[95] an annuity[96] or the right to impugn an outright conveyance for fraud and imposition.[97] The extension of the plea's range of application mapped the gradual recognition in Chancery of various pleas for relief in respect of property transactions as equitable interests in the property itself. From the Chancellorship of Lord Nottingham onwards, interests under trusts were modelled by analogy with common law estates. The equity of redemption took on features that would eventually allow it to be characterised as an equitable interest in the mortgaged estate.[98] By the nineteenth century, even the trust had shaken off the last limitations of privity which characterised the use. A superior lord who took the land on the escheat[99] or a squatter who dispossessed the lawful proprietor were bound by a prior trust interest affecting it.[100] Neither could claim the benefit of the plea since they did not derive their legal title by purchase from the original trustee of the land. The plea was no longer the inverse opposite of the privity rule that had once determined the binding force of the use. It became tenable to treat purchase for value without notice as a rule determining the priority between legal interests and equitable interests in property.

C. Notice Systematised as a Conveyancing Norm

The most enduring refinement of the plea made by Lord Nottingham was his development of the doctrine of notice. He began a process that transformed the plea from a general principle of conscience, loosely identified with a collusive intent to defraud, into a body of technical rules controlling the norms of real property conveyancing. Two hundred years later, the original ethical character of the rule was largely lost, as was its distinctive character as a defence according to the procedural practices of Chancery. True, it still lay with the defendant to raise the plea.[101] But the conveyancing setting where it was pleaded gave it a different character. It became more relevant as a rule for resolving priority conflicts between competing interests affecting the legal fee. By the nineteenth century the most elaborate descriptions of notice appeared in the textbooks on real property conveyancing. These had their own

[94] *Cottingham v Lord Cornbury* (1673) in Yale, *Manual and Prolegomena* (n 25) Ch XV, para 11.

[95] *Tourville v Naish* (1734) 3 P Wms 307; 24 ER 1077.

[96] *Holms v Atkins* (1673) in Yale, *Manual and Prolegomena* (n 25) Ch XV, para 13; *Mildmay v Mildmay* (1676) noted in DEC Yale, *Lord Nottingham's Chancery Cases*, vol I (1954) 73 *Selden Society* [474].

[97] *Maitland v Wilson* (1754) 3 Atk 814; 26 ER 1265.

[98] See generally Macnair, 'The Conceptual Basis of Trusts in the Later 17th and 18th Centuries' (n 71) 221–24.

[99] (1800) 39 & 40 Geo III c 88, s 12 as amended by (1807) 47 Geo III Session 2 c 29, (1819) 59 Geo III, c 92, s 1.

[100] *Scott v Scott* (1854) 4 HLC 1065; 10 ER 779; *Re Nisbet and Potts' Contract* [1906] 1 Ch 386.

[101] *Re Nisbet and Potts' Contract* [1906] 1 Ch 386.

systematising influence on the case law.[102] The relevance of purchase for value without notice in justifying the distinctive relief available through the Court of Chancery's auxiliary jurisdiction ceased to matter after the Chancery and common law jurisdictions were 'fused' by the Judicature Acts 1873–75.

The early eighteenth-century rationalisation of the plea in terms of fraudulent collusion would still have been recognisable to the judges in *Gervys v Cooke* (1522) and to Francis Bacon in his *Reading on the Statute of Uses* (c1600, 1642).[103] Henry Ballow's *Treatise of Equity* (c 1737) restated the idea that one who took with notice of the *cestui que use*'s right was implicated in the feoffee's fraudulent disposal of the land: 'for then he is *particeps criminis, et dolus et fraus nemini patrocinantur*, since in conscience he purchased my land or my goods'.[104] Notice was part of a larger principle that a party must be denied the benefit of any property or judgment obtained by fraudulent collusion to defeat another's legitimate title or to subvert a relationship of confidence.[105] At about the same time as Ballow wrote, Lord Hardwicke LC was explicit at identifying notice as a 'species of fraud, and Dolus Malus itself'. He cited the definition of the Roman jurist Ulpian, commenting on the classical Roman *actio doli*.[106]

But attempts at general rationalisation may lag behind the incremental processes that eventually overturn them. Lord Nottingham's 'Prolegomena' (1674) had already begun to systematise notice into a formal doctrine, operating independently of any generic or moral rationale. He distinguished what he called 'actual' from 'legal' notice. He must have thought that the meaning of actual notice was so obvious that it needed no definition. He did, however, seek to distinguish the circumstances that would be too unspecific to require the purchaser to inquire into a possible encumbrance or claim.[107] Lord Nottingham accepted that actual notice of a prior claim or encumbrance could not be based on unsubstantiated rumours: 'notice ought not to be defective'.[108] The doctrine of notice by *lis pendens* developed to prevent the

[102] Most comprehensively in the many editions of EB Sugden, *Practical Treatise on the Law of Vendors and Purchasers of Estates* 1st edn (London, Brooke & Clarke, 1805) ch 16 (cited in *Jones v Smith* (1841) 1 Hare 43, 56; 66 ER 943), the outlines of which were followed in JH Howard, *The Duties of Solicitors in Sales by Auction or Private Contract* (London, Butterworth & Son, 1827) ch 6; S Atkinson, *A Practical Treatise on Conveyancing* (London, S Sweet, Stevens & Sons, 1829) ch 34; and in the many editions of the standard textbooks, eg, JH Dart, *Compendium of the Law and Practice of Vendors and Purchasers of Real Estate* (London, Stevens & Norton, 1851) ch 15; EHT Snell, *Principles of Equity* 1st edn (London, Stevens & Haynes, 1868) 28–33. Still later, instances of notice were stated as general rules in the many editions of LE Emmet, *Notes on Perusing Titles* (London, Jordan & Sons, 1895) ch 5.

[103] See text at n 52 above.

[104] *A Treatise of Equity* 4th edn by J Fonblanque, (London, W Clarke & Sons, 1812) vol 2, ch VI, § 3. The book was originally published anonymously and attributed to Ballow by its later editor Fonblanque. See Macnair, 'The Conceptual Basis of Trusts in the Later 17th and 18th Centuries' (n 71) 210–11.

[105] The two cases cited by Ballow for the principle were unrelated to notice of uses: *Fermor's Case* (1602) 3 Co Rep 77a, 79b; 76 ER 800 (a lessee who secretly obtained a fine in fraud of the lessee could not defeat the reversion and obtain the fee); *Sir John Webb's Case* (1620) Palmer 157; 81 ER 1025 (judgment obtained by fraudulent collusion between attorneys made be set aside even after entry on the record).

[106] *Le Neve v Le Neve* (1748) 3 Atk 647, 654–55; 26 ER 1172, citing D.4.3.1.2.

[107] See the cases cited at n 70 above.

[108] '*[N]otitia non debet claudicare*' citing *Green's Case* (1601) 6 Co Rep 29a, 29b; 77 ER 295 (concerning lack of particularity in a written notice given to the patron of a living); and citing the cases discussed at n 70 above.

proprietor of lands subject to Chancery proceedings from defeating a decree that the court might subsequently make affecting the lands. The plaintiff's filing of the subpoena and bill was said to fix the world with notice of his claim for relief.[109] This was acknowledged to be a 'hard fiction' on a purchaser who might have taken the lands in good faith and with no easy means of discovering the plaintiff's claim by searching a public register.[110] Some decades later, the anonymous *Abridgment of Cases in Equity* (1732) grouped other cases under the category of 'presumptive notice'.[111] Within these were cases that would eventually be categorised separately as instances of imputed notice and constructive notice. Thus it was accepted that one for whom land was purchased through an intermediary was fixed with the same notice as the intermediary might have had.[112] He could not rely on his own personal lack of notice to take the land free of the plaintiff's claim. By 1706 Lord Cowper LK could state as a rule that 'notice to the agent is good notice to the party'.[113]

The seeds of the mature nineteenth-century doctrine of constructive notice were also set in Lord Nottingham's time. A purchaser was taken to know the legal effect of a document under which he claimed title (even if the notice was in a sense 'notional'), and was also bound by a trust referred to in a document through which he derived his title.[114] He was said to be guilty of *crassa negligentia* in failing to seek after a fact mentioned in a document in his possession.[115] The association of notice with *crassa negligentia* shows how the Chancery's understanding of constructive notice still kept something of its original ethical character, where the purchaser's conduct was tainted by fraud. *Crassa negligentia* was a standard of actionable fault commonly identified at common law and in equity with agents or delegates undertaking tasks on behalf of others.[116] In its civil law guise, *culpa lata*, it was treated as equivalent

[109] eg, *Culpepper v Aston* (1682) 2 Chan Cas 116. It was eventually settled that the rationale of *lis pendens* lay outside the equitable doctrine of implied or constructive notice. In the interests of finality of litigation a purchaser must take subject to pending actions and claims, regardless of his awareness of them: see *Sorrell v Carpenter* (1728) 2 P Wms 482; 24 ER 825; *Bellamy v Sabine* (1857) 1 De G & J 566; 44 ER 842.

[110] *Anon* (1685) 1 Vern 318; 23 ER 494. The hardship to purchasers was eventually mitigated by a statutory system of registration. Thenceforward *lis pendens* would only bind a purchaser by express notice or entry in the records of the Court of Common Pleas: Judgments Act 1837, s 7. It had long been settled that actual notice of a registrable but unregistered instrument would bind a purchaser: *Le Neve v Le Neve* (1748) 3 Atk 647; 26 ER 1172. The Land Charges Act 1925, Part I rendered notice by means other than registration irrelevant to the purchaser for valuable consideration. See *Midland Bank Trust Co Ltd v Green* [1981] AC 513 and section IV below.

[111] See the version published in 21 ER 828 as *Equity Cases Abridged*, vol 1 (1667–1744) ch 42(A).

[112] *Merry v Abney* (1663)1 Chan Cas 38; 22 ER 682.

[113] *Brotherton v Hatt* (1706) 2 Vern 574, 574–75; 23 ER 973, 973–74; similarly *Jennings v Moore* (1708) 2 Vern 609; 23 ER 998.

[114] *Bovey v Smith* (1682) 1 Vern 149, 150; 23 ER 377, 379 (North LK); *Dunch v Kent* (1685) 1 Vern 385; 23 ER 494; and later *Drapers v Yardley* (1710) 2 Vern 662; 23 ER 1031.

[115] *Moore v Bennett* (1678) 2 Chan Cas 246; 22 ER 929.

[116] eg, *Masters of Trinity House in Deptford Strond v Crispin* (1680) Jones, T 144; 84 ER 1188 (notice of a published bye-law is equivalent to *crassa negligentia* in failing to observe it); *Charitable Corporation v Sutton* (1742) Atk 400; 26 ER 642 (active and passive breaches by the trustees of a charitable corporation); *Belchier v Parson* (1754) Kenyon 38; 96 ER 908 (neglect by an assignee in bankruptcy to make her chargeable for moneys not received); *Pitt v Yalden* (1767) 4 Burr 2060; 98 ER 74 (standard of care of a country attorney in failing to pursue payment of a debt due to his client); *Ballejo v Wheeler* (1774) 1 Cowp 143; 98 ER 1012 (*crassa negligentia* equated to fraud and knavery in action against the master of ship for barratry).

to *dolus*: a grossly careless failure to act was treated as equivalent to a fraudulent intent to do a positive act.[117] It figured in the classical and Justiniac Roman law to define the standard of care of a depositary or mandatary gratuitously undertaking a task for another.[118] It lent itself naturally, with some modification, to a standard of fault in land transactions, which were usually undertaken by attorneys acting for purchasers. The stock example of *crassa negligentia* from the English cases was of the gaoler who carelessly left the prison doors unlocked so that the prisoners escaped. The gaoler's neglect was equivalent to voluntarily permitting the prisoners to escape.[119]

The authoritative systemisation of constructive notice eventually made by Sir James Wigram V-C in *Jones v Smith* (1841) kept something of the old taint of fraudulent collusion in a transaction to defeat the prior equitable interest.[120] He ordered the earlier cases into two categories which are still observed.[121] First was the notice imputed to a purchaser who had actual notice that the property in question was in fact charged or encumbered. The purchaser would be fixed with constructive notice of other facts or interests which he would have discovered had he made inquiries following on from those charges or encumbrances. The definition was grounded in the practices of real property conveyancing. It supposed that the vendor's title depended on a chain of documentary evidence. The purchaser was fixed with notice of that which he would have been led to discover 'deed by deed'.[122] Secondly, constructive notice was imputed to a purchaser who designedly abstained from inquiry for the very purpose of avoiding notice.[123] It suggested that the purchaser committed a fraud by turning away from the knowledge of facts that the circumstances would have suggested to a prudent purchaser. A mere want of caution was not the same as constructive notice.[124] Lord Nottingham's old test was preserved, at least in name: the purchaser was only fixed with notice of facts that he would have acquired but for his gross negligence, equivalent to *culpa lata*.[125] But the lines between carelessness, gross negligence and fraud were not easily drawn. Their usage in cases of notice was as uncertain as in the many other cases of medical, professional or trustee liability where the courts of common law and equity applied them as standards of fault in

[117] *cf* the Classical Roman definition: D.50.16.223.pr.

[118] *J Inst* III.14.3; D.50.17.23. See generally R Zimmermann, *Law of Obligations: Roman Foundations of the Civilian Tradition* (Oxford, Oxford University Press, 1996) 208–12, 426–30. Similarly in the Scots law of the same period, the standard of 'supine neglect' was applied to the liability of executors: see J Erskine, *An Institute of the Law of Scotland* (1773), III.2.21. For the equation of 'supine' with 'gross' neglect in English law, see *Charitable Corporation v Sutton* (1742) Atk 400; 26 ER 642.

[119] *R v Rooks* (1637) Cro Car 491, 492; 79 ER 1024, 1025 followed in Scotland in *Cuming v Kennedy* (1707) Mor 4433, 4438.

[120] *Jones v Smith* (1841) 1 Hare 43; 66 ER 943. See C Harpum, 'The Stranger as Constructive Trustee' (1986) 102 *LQR* 114, 123–24.

[121] See generally *Re Montagu's Settlement Trusts* [1987] Ch 264, 277 (Megarry V-C); *Eagle Trust plc v SBC Securities plc* [1993] 1 WLR 484, 493–95; and McGhee (ed), *Snell's Equity* (n 28) paras 4-027–4-039.

[122] *Jones v Smith* (1841) 1 Hare 43, 55, 66–67; 66 ER 943, 952.

[123] ibid, Hare 55; ER 948.

[124] ibid, Hare 56; ER 949.

[125] *Ware v Lord Egremont* (1854) 4 De G M & G 460, 467; 43 ER 546, 589 (in argument); (1854) 4 De G M & G 473; 43 ER 592 (Lord Carnworth LC).

the early decades of the nineteenth century.[126] Two years later in *West v Reid* (1843) Wigram V-C had to clarify his remarks. A finding of constructive notice did not require the purchaser to have had any fraudulent motive for his failure to inquire. But gross negligence might be visited with the 'same consequences as fraud, although (morally speaking) the party charged may be perfectly innocent'.[127]

Throughout the middle decades of the nineteenth century, notice developed into a formal doctrine. Adherence to ordinary standards of commercial conduct became the end in itself rather than a proxy for some substantive taint on purchaser's conscience. Throughout this period the epithet 'gross' came to be associated with the failure to observe the special standard of care undertaken by a professional person or one who fell below the habitual standard of his calling.[128] The 'turning away' from discoverable knowledge might have consisted in no more than a wrongly exercised judgment about an identified conveyancing risk. The courts were sensitive to the efficiency of transacting. The elaboration of standards of notice was as much concerned with defining when a purchaser would not be bound by an encumbrance as when he would be. So the purchaser was not fixed with notice of the contents of instruments not connected to his title, and he was not expected to act with extreme caution.[129]

It was an easy next step for notice to be recast as a morally neutral standard identifying it with the ordinary procedures observed by conveyancing practitioners. The definitive recognition of this transition was s 3(1) of the Conveyancing Act 1882 which fixed the standard of inquiry expected of the purchaser in terms of the inquiries 'as ought reasonably to have been made by him'. The subsection was framed negatively to emphasise that there were no other criteria for fixing the purchaser with constructive notice. The Court of Appeal in *Bailey v Barnes* (1893) read the provision as restating the existing law.[130] But even at this stage, traces of the old fraud rationale clung on, and required some inquiry into the knowledge and disposition of the individual purchaser. Lindley LJ said that the purchaser was still held to a standard of gross or culpable negligence before notice was attributed to him:

> in dealing with real property, as in other matters of business, regard is had to the usual course of business; and a purchaser who wilfully departs from it in order to avoid acquiring a knowledge of his vendor's title is not allowed to derive any advantage from his wilful ignorance in the defects which would have come to his knowledge if he had transacted his business in the ordinary way.[131]

The identification of notice with ordinary conveyancing norms was continued in the property reforms of 1925. The Law of Property Act 1925 continued the effect of s 3 of the Conveyancing Act 1882. A purchaser was not to be prejudicially affected

[126] See D Ibbetson, '"The Law of Business Rome": Foundations of the Anglo-American Tort of Negligence' (1999) 52 *CLP* 74, 92–104.

[127] *West v Reid* (1843) 2 Hare 249, 257; 67 ER 104, 107.

[128] J Getzler, 'Duty of Care' in P Birks and A Pretto (eds), *Breach of Trust* (Oxford and Portland, OR, Hart Publishing, 2002) 53–59.

[129] *West v Reid* (1843) 2 Hare 249, 259; 67 ER 104, 108.

[130] *Bailey v Barnes* [1894] 1 Ch 25.

[131] ibid 35.

by notice of any instrument, matter or fact unless it was within his own knowledge or would have come within his knowledge if he had made reasonable inquiries and inspections.[132] Beyond that, however, the property reforms of 1925 entirely recast the relevance of the plea. They were instrumental in defining its place in current law.

IV. AFTER 1925

The presence of consideration and the absence of notice began, as we saw, as inverse opposites of the old privity rules determining the binding force of a use on a conveyance of real property.[133] They implemented presumptions about the parties' intentions as to the effect of the conveyance and were hedged about by rules of privity of estate associated with the common law theory of land tenure. By the nineteenth century, the combined elements of the plea had evolved into a general rule of property law, operating in default of any expressed stipulation to the contrary in a trust instrument, and determining the priority of competing interests in property. All trace of privity as a doctrine to determine the running of uses and trusts was lost.

The 1925 property legislation caused another great shift in purchase for value without notice, separating it from its late medieval rationale and changing its area of operation. Apart from rare residual cases, the plea now only has a practical relevance to the determination of priority disputes in personal property and, unlike land, a proprietor can have a direct ownership interest in personal property. In a strange inversion of history, the theories of estate tenure, which were so influential in shaping the early form of the plea, have never applied to personal property.[134] Systems of title and deeds registration have almost entirely superseded purchase for value without notice in relation to real property. The defence now has more to do with cases of asset recovery by following and tracing than the determination of priorities in conveyancing transactions.

The property reforms of 1925 were the turning point in the gradual extinction of purchase for value without notice as far as land is concerned. At one level, they caused a potential proliferation of equitable interests affecting real property. The Law of Property Act 1925 converted some former kinds of legal estate and interest to equitable interests. The variety of estates and interests capable of subsisting or being conveyed in real property was reduced to a closed list and '[a]ll other estates, interests, and charges in or over land take effect as equitable interests'.[135] But the classical doctrine of notice was left with an attenuated place in determining the priority of those interests against both registered and unregistered legal estates.[136] Against disponees of a registered legal estate for value, the priority of any subsisting equity is determined by statutory rules for the registration of interests or by

[132] Law of Property Act 1925, s 199(1), (3).
[133] See section II above.
[134] J Crossley Vaines, *Personal Property* 5th edn (London, Butterworths, 1973) 6.
[135] Law of Property Act 1925, s 1(1)–(3).
[136] See the summary in RE Megarry and HWR Wade, *Law of Real Property* 8th edn by C Harpum, S Bridge and M Dixon (London, Sweet & Maxwell, 2012), paras 6-057–6-063.

the residual category of overriding interests.[137] Notice has no place in determining priorities in registered land.[138] Even in relation to unregistered land, the 1925 land charges registration system, which drew together the piecemeal registration regimes of the nineteenth century, has superseded the classical doctrine of notice as it once applied to most kinds of equitable interest.[139] The Land Charges Acts of 1925 and 1972 defined a fixed list of instruments or interests capable of registration. The fact of registration against the name of the estate owner constitutes actual notice to all persons of the interest or instrument.[140] Unless registered, the interest or instrument is void against him. It is irrelevant that a purchaser might have acquired notice of it in the classical sense.[141] The classical doctrine of notice was left to determine the priority of trust interests affecting an unregistered legal estate,[142] and a small residue of interests, such as restrictive covenants made before 1926. Its useful role in protecting such interests wanes as dealings with unregistered titles in land become ever fewer.[143]

As its relevance to real property conveyancing wanes, purchase for value without notice has found new prominence in the rules on the recovery of misapplied trust assets. These are usually money or transferable securities.[144] A twenty-first century reader who wants to learn about the plea now consults the books on trusts, and finds it described in the chapters on proprietary remedies against the transferees of misapplied trust assets.[145] This, for example, is where it belongs in the current, 33rd edition, of *Snell's Equity* (2015).[146] The first edition of *Snell* (1868) did not even include a chapter on breach of trust, and it discussed the plea as an aspect of the maxim 'where the equities are equal, the law prevails'.[147] That account drew mainly

[137] Land Registration Act 2002, s 29(1)–(2), Part 4, Sched 3, superseding Land Registration Act 1925, ss 20, 23, Part IV, s 70.

[138] eg, *Barclays Bank plc v Boulter* [1998] 1 WLR 1, 11 (Mummery LJ); *Williams & Glyn's Bank v Boland* [1981] AC 487, 504 (Lord Wilberforce) (commenting on the Land Registration Act 1925). Exceptionally, it remains relevant to dispositions of registered land by a bankrupt: Land Registration Act 2002, s 86(1), (5).

[139] For its operation and nineteenth-century antecedents, see Megarry and Wade, *Law of Real Property* 1st edn (n 26) 916–30.

[140] Law of Property Act 1925, s 198(1); Land Charges Act 1972, ss 1–7, superseding Land Charges Act 1925, ss 2–14.

[141] *Midland Bank v Green* [1981] AC 513.

[142] eg, *Kingsnorth Finance Co Ltd v Tizard* [1986] 1 WLR 783.

[143] Law Commission for England and Wales, *Land Registration for the Twenty-First Century* (LawCom 254) paras 1.5–1.6, 2.8–2.9.

[144] To name just a few of many possible examples: *Barclays Bank Ltd v Quistclose Investments Ltd* [1970] AC 567; *Macmillan Inc v Bishopsgate Investment Trust plc (No 3)* [1995] 1 WLR 978; *Sinclair Investments (UK) Ltd v Versailles Trade Finance Ltd (In Administration)* [2011] EWCA Civ 347; [2012] Ch 453. The defence is relevant, by its absence, whenever the claimant traces against a transferee who gives no value: eg, *Re Diplock* [1948] Ch 465; *Foskett v McKeown* [2001] AC 102.

[145] See G Thomas and A Hudson, *The Law of Trusts* 2nd edn (Oxford, Oxford University Press, 2010) paras 33.92–33.112; *Lewin on Trusts* 19th edn by L Tucker, N Le Poidevin and J Brightwell (London, Sweet & Maxwell, 2016) paras 41.117–41.142; *Underhill and Hayton, Law Relating to Trusts and Trustees* 19th edn (London, Lexis Nexis, 2016) paras 99.13–99.59.

[146] McGhee (ed), *Snell's Equity* (n 28) ch 30.

[147] See EHT Snell, *Principles of Equity* 1st edn (London, Stevens & Haynes, 1868) 18–33.

on issues in real property conveyancing and took its shape from Sugden's *Law of Vendors and Purchasers of Estates*.[148]

The new place of the defence in the law of personal property has presented difficulties of its own. A defence developed to its most refined form in real property transactions would make a bad fit if it were applied unmodified to the wrongful disposal of trust assets consisting in money or securities. The gist of the problem is expressed in Lindley LJ's observation that 'if we were to extend the doctrine of constructive notice to commercial transactions we should be doing infinite mischief and paralyzing the trade of the country'.[149] The observation is unhelpful in its obliqueness. It fails to define the difference between commercial and non-commercial transactions, and overlooks that many land transactions are made between parties who could be labelled as 'commercial' on any ordinary understanding of the word.[150] It belongs to that traditional current of thought, now long past, that treated mercantile dealings as the sole province of the common law and customary mercantile practices.[151] Lindley LJ's observation is most sensibly taken as a warning against imposing the same onerous inquiries of title on the recipients of money, goods and securities in equity as were accepted as the norm in real property transactions.[152] In generic transactions with a high turnover, the risks of dealing with property subject to a defective title may be better weighted in favour of the recipient and against some unknown claimant to the property. The conclusion commonly reached is that the standard of diligence needed to trigger a finding of notice should be defined more narrowly than it would be in a land transaction. What is required of a purchaser in buying land is not the same as a banker opening a new customer account or combining the accounts of an existing customer.[153]

Allowing for this difference in the kinds of inquiries made, the courts' approach has been fundamentally similar to that of the nineteenth-century judges in the conveyancing cases. The recipient owes no duty of inquiry as such (other than those separately imposed by any relevant money-laundering regulations). Like a purchaser of land, a recipient of money acts from a self-interested concern to avoid the risk of being bound by the adverse claim or interest of another.[154] The due level of inquiry is defined by the norms commonly accepted as usual and proper in the kind of transaction in question. This is not so different from the old Conveyancing Act 1888 standard of the inquiries 'as ought reasonably to have been made'. Notice resolves itself

[148] Sugden, *Practical Treatise* (n 102) and subsequent editions.

[149] *Manchester Trust v Furness* [1895] 2 QB 539, 545 (Lindley LJ).

[150] *Macmillan Inc v Bishopsgate Investment Trust plc (No 3)* [1995] 1 WLR 978, 1000 (Millett J). An example of a mixed commercial and private transaction would be a mortgage security taken over a family home to secure a business loan: *Barclays Bank v O'Brien* [1994] 1 AC 180.

[151] *cf* PJ Millett, 'Equity's Place in the Law of Commerce' (1998) 114 *LQR* 214.

[152] Read in context, this was the very point of Lindley LJ's remark. He was arguing against the conclusion that a party who saw a reference to a charterparty in a bill of lading was fixed with notice of its terms. The analogy in real property conveyancing is *Jones v Smith* (1841) 1 Hare 43, 66 ER 943 discussed in section III.C above.

[153] eg, *Sinclair Investments (UK) Ltd v Versailles Trade Finance Ltd (In Administration)* [2011] EWCA Civ 347; [2012] Ch 453; *Papadimitriou v Crédit Agricole Corpn and Investment Bank* [2015] UKPC 13; [2015] 1 WLR 4265.

[154] *Bailey v Barnes* [1894] 1 Ch 25, 35 (Lindley LJ); *Papadimitriou v Crédit Agricole Corpn and Investment Bank* [2015] UKPC 13; [2015] 1 WLR 4265, [33] (Lord Sumption JSC).

into a mixed question of industry practice and the commercial propriety of taking risks in relation to unknown third-party interests which may well be affected by a bilateral payment transaction.[155] The recipient can start with the assumption that it is dealing with honest people.[156] It must make inquiries if there is a serious possibility of a third party having a proprietary right to the money received or if the facts known to it would give a reasonable banker in its position serious cause to question the propriety of the transaction. It may be expected to question the purpose of a transaction that is carried out in an unusual or unnecessary form.[157] None of this requires the recipient to know of the claimant's proprietary interest. But it supposes that the recipient has made a considered choice to look no further, which resonates with the nineteenth-century understanding that constructive notice involved gross negligence in failing to inquire into a fact.

V. DONEES AND PERSONAL LIABILITY

The current equitable rules on recovery of assets still show some odd doctrinal wrinkles. These only makes sense when compared with the early modern formulations of the plea, and the theory of the use where it evolved. They bring the history of the plea full circle from its origins.

One such problem is to explain the status of an innocent volunteer who has received misapplied trust assets. The most prominent example is the charities which received the testamentary gifts under the invalid will in *Re Diplock*, but the problem would apply whenever a person receives and then disposes of trust assets before he has been made aware that they were the proceeds of a breach of trust.[158] Obviously, the charities in *Re Diplock* could not rely on the defence since they gave no consideration for the gifts. But explaining the ground of their equitable liability to restore the traceable residue of the void gifts was difficult according to any general theory of conscience. The charities were innocent of any knowledge that the gifts made to them were invalid so, in a substantive sense, their consciences were unaffected. The point was made by counsel for the charities when he argued that they took free of any claim by the estate.[159] Lord Greene MR disagreed. The charities' failure to give consideration was enough to bind their conscience. Between them and the estate the equities were weighted in the estate's favour. The estate's claim against them had evolved into an equitable right of property. Absent some reason to extinguish it, it persisted against the charities.[160]

[155] Compare the approach to dishonest risk-taking in claims for dishonest assistance in breach of trust: *Royal Brunei Airlines Sdn Bhd v Tan* [1995] AC 378, 389–90 (Lord Nicholls); and *Cowan de Groot Properties v Eagle Trust* [1992] 4 All ER 700, 707 (Knox J).

[156] *Macmillan Inc v Bishopsgate Investment Trust plc (No 3)* [1995] 1 WLR 978, 1014 (Millett J).

[157] *Papadimitriou v Crédit Agricole Corpn and Investment Bank* [2015] UKPC 13; [2015] 1 WLR 4265 [20] (Lord Clark JSC).

[158] *Re Diplock* [1948] Ch 465, 476 (Gray KC).

[159] ibid 488, 524 (Greene MR).

[160] ibid 539. See also the recent explanations of equitable property rights in *Independent Trustee Services Ltd v GP Noble Trustees Ltd* [2012] EWCA Civ 195; [2013] Ch 91; and *Akers and others v Samba Financial Group* [2017] UKSC 6; [2017] 2 WLR 713, [16] (Lord Mance JSC), [82]–[83] (Lord Sumption JSC) (noted RC Nolan (2017) 133 *LQR* 353).

The judges of the early modern period must have sensed the same explanatory problem. Innocent feoffees of land subject to a prior use were not natural candidates for a jurisdiction founded on unconscionable conduct. But at a technical level, such recipients were presumed to hold subject to the use because they had not given any consideration to pass the use to themselves.[161] By late in the sixteenth century a fiction gained general acceptance that the law implied notice into a feoffment made for no consideration.[162] The conscience of any donee was presumptively bound by the prior use even, it seems, if he was actually innocent of any notice that he was implicated in the feoffor's breach. The substantial effect of the presumption was to place the burden of proving the purchase for value without notice on the defendant. A donee of land subject to a prior use was bound in conscience to answer to the jurisdiction of Chancery unless he succeeded on the distinctive plea that would put him outside its reach.

For want of any better name, the current consensus is that innocent donees of misapplied trust property can be called 'constructive trustees'.[163] It is understood, however, that this term only describes their liability to an equitable proprietary claim to yield up the legal ownership of the property. They do not owe any additional personal duties to account for the proceeds they received unless and until they have notice that these derived from a breach of trust. The early modern lawyers would have reached a like result: a donee from a feoffee to use would also have held the land as a feoffee to use for the original beneficiary. The donee gave no consideration so the first feoffee cannot have meant to pass the use to him.[164] But they would not have had the same analytical problems of separating the beneficiaries' personal and proprietary claims against the transferee that characterise the modern misgivings about calling an innocent donee of property a 'trustee' to the claimant.[165] As we saw, the sole duties of a feoffee to use were to yield up the profits of the land to the beneficiary and to deal with the legal estate as he directed.[166] As such, he had to do no more than yield up the property or convey it away at the beneficiary's direction. His duties were hardly different from those of an innocent donee on the modern analysis. The trustee in the full modern sense—one who undertakes asset management duties for beneficiaries with various entitlements against him—was a later development.

The modern law of trusts is still shackled by forms of analysis bound to the old law of uses even though uses and trusts are substantively different in their incidents. If we allowed ourselves the anachronism of calling an innocent donee a 'transferee to the use of the equitable claimant' then we might capture the gist of donee's liability

[161] See section III.B above.

[162] *Chudleigh's Case* (1589–95) 1 Co Rep 120a, 122b; 76 ER 261 (in argument); Yale, *Manual and Prolegomena* (n 25) Ch XIV, para 1.

[163] *Independent Trustee Services Ltd v GP Noble Trustees Ltd* [2012] EWCA Civ 195; [2013] Ch 91 [77]–[81] (Lloyd LJ), (querying the dicta of Lord Goff in *Westdeutsche Landesbank Girozentrale v Islington LBC* [1996] AC 669, 705); C Mitchell and S Watterson, 'Remedies for Knowing Receipt' in C Mitchell (ed), *Constructive and Resulting Trusts* (Oxford and Portland, OR, Hart, 2010) 116–120; *Underhill and Hayton* (n 145) paras 28.1–28.11; 99.13–99.14.

[164] See section II.B above and *Gervys v Cooke* (1522) (2002) 119 *Selden Society* 108, 119 (Pollard J).

[165] *Independent Trustee Services Ltd v GP Noble Trustees Ltd* [2012] EWCA Civ 195; [2013] Ch 91 [80] (Lloyd LJ).

[166] See section II.A above.

in a way that calling him a 'trustee' no longer can. That word has moved on to a different sense. As Lord Browne Wilkinson said, whether we call the innocent donee of a misapplied trust asset a 'trustee' may be just a 'question of semantics'.[167] The point is that the word 'trustee' causes confusion precisely because the modern institution it relates to is substantively different from the use, which is the institution from which it traces its lineage.

A second question relates to the place of wrongful complicity in a breach of trust. As we saw, the early modern explanation of why a third-party feoffee from the original feoffee to use held subject to a beneficiary's claim was that he was *particeps criminis* in the original feoffee's fraudulent breach of undertaking.[168] By the nineteenth century that requirement of fraud lost its direct substantive content, surviving only in the rule that the third party was fixed with constructive notice of the breach of trust if he was guilty of gross negligence. The binding force of the trust beneficiary's claim depended on tests of priority between competing proprietary claims to the same legal estate.[169]

Since the nineteenth century wrongful complicity in the original trustee's breach has taken a new turn. It now serves as the rationale for imposing personal duties to account on a third party who implicates himself in the trustees' breach by assisting the trustee to commit it or by receiving its traceable proceeds.[170] An early recognition of this explanation was *Re Blundell* (1889), where a claim was brought against a solicitor as a constructive trustee for receiving money paid in breach of trust.[171] In England at least, a third party must now account as a constructive trustee for gains or losses accruing from or caused by his dishonest assistance in the breach.[172] He is also liable to account as a constructive trustee for any money he received when his knowledge was such that it would be unconscionable for him to retain the benefit of the receipt.[173] The claim for knowing receipt requires that the third party received money in which the trust claimant had an interest. Unlike a pure proprietary claim, it survives against the recipient even if he dissipates or transfers away the proceeds of the claimant's property.[174]

All this is well known. But the difference between enforcing the trust claimant's primary proprietary right against the recipient and his secondary right to make the recipient personally accountable to him explains—and justifies—the difference in fault necessary to enforce the two kinds of right.[175] Unless the recipient is a purchaser

[167] *Westdeutsche Landesbank Girozentrale v Islington LBC* [1996] AC 669, 705.

[168] See section II.C above.

[169] See section III.C above.

[170] *Westdeutsche Landesbank Girozentrale v Islington LBC* [1996] AC 669, 705, 707.

[171] *Re Blundell* (1889) LR 40 Ch D 370, 381 (Stirling J).

[172] *Royal Brunei Airlines Sdn Bhd v Tan* [1995] AC 378; *Novoship (UK) Ltd v Mikhaylyuk* [2014] EWCA Civ 908; [2015] QB 499.

[173] See section IV above.

[174] *Bank of Credit and Commerce International (Overseas) Ltd v Akindele* [2001] Ch 437.

[175] But compare the recent suggestion that the approach to constructive notice in proprietary claims and unconscionability in knowing receipt claims should be the same: *Papadimitriou v Crédit Agricole Corpn and Investment Bank* [2015] UKPC 13; [2015] 1 WLR 4265, [33] (Lord Sumption JSC). This is correct as long as it means that the standard of inquiry expected should depend on the context. It is best not read to mean that all aspects of the technical doctrine of notice should be applied to knowing receipt cases.

for value without notice, he is bound by the claimant's proprietary claim while the asset or its traceable proceeds remain in his hands. The technical doctrine of notice, as developed from Lord Nottingham's time down to the late nineteenth century, would apply (although with some adjustment to the expected standards of inquiry if the property was money or securities rather than land).[176] The question is purely one of priority of interests. But the 'cold calculus of constructive notice' should not be enough to fix the recipient with a personal claim in knowing receipt.[177] Personal liability should depend on a more serious degree of fault, sufficient to implicate the recipient as a party to the trustee's breach. Broke J in *Gervys v Cooke* (1522) and Sir Francis Bacon in his *Readings on the Statute of Uses* (c1600, 1642) captured the gist of the idea when they spoke of the transferee from the original feoffee to use being *particeps criminis* or party to a fraudulent 'covin' with the feoffee.[178] Granted, Broke J and Sir Francis Bacon were describing the conditions where a use might bind a third-party feoffee. But the parallel between the early modern explanation for the running of a use and the post-nineteenth-century explanation for personal liability in equity holds good. The use of the early modern period was a personal undertaking given by a feoffee—actually or presumptively—to hold the legal estate for the beneficiary rather than a proprietary interest binding the estate *in rem*.[179] Since then the proprietary and personal claims against trustees have separated and hardened into distinct elements. The early modern intuition about complicity still applies to explain the personal liability of the third-party recipient from the original trustee. A degree of fault graver than technical constructive notice should be necessary to make the recipient fraudulent for this purpose. One who receives property subject to the beneficiary's equitable proprietary right is not necessarily *particeps criminis* in the original trustee's breach. He may be just an innocent recipient of an asset that still belongs in equity to another.

[176] See section IV above, discussing *Papadimitriou v Crédit Agricole Corpn and Investment Bank* [2015] UKPC 13, [2015] 1 WLR 4265.

[177] *Re Montagu's Settlement Trusts* [1987] 2 Ch 264, 272–73 (Megarry V-C).

[178] Bacon, *Statute of Uses* (n 6) 12 and *Gervys v Cooke* (1522) (2002) 119 *Selden Society* 108, 117 (Broke J), discussed in section II.D above.

[179] See section II.A above.

5

Beneficiaries' Consent to Trustees' Unauthorised Acts

YING KHAI LIEW AND CHARLES MITCHELL

I. INTRODUCTION

TRUSTEES ARE NOT liable for breach of trust to a sui juris and fully informed beneficiary who has consented to the breach.[1] Moreover, such a beneficiary may have his interest impounded to indemnify the trustees against any liability which they incur to other beneficiaries who have not consented to the breach.[2] For the purposes of these rules, the beneficiary's 'consent' can take various forms, including instigation, concurrence, acquiescence, adoption, confirmation and release, and the rules shielding trustees from liability may work differently according to the type of 'consent' which the beneficiary has given.[3] Many cases, such as the instigation and concurrence cases, can be explained as an application of estoppel doctrine, but some, such as the acquiescence cases, do not lend themselves so readily to this analysis.[4]

This chapter concerns one group of cases which are governed by these rules, namely cases where the trustees perform acts which are unauthorised by the trust deed with the unanimous consent of the beneficiaries who are all sui juris and fully informed and collectively the owners of the entire beneficial interest.[5]

[1] *Walker v Symonds* (1818) 3 Swan 1; 36 ER 751; *Stafford v Stafford* (1857) 1 De G&J 193; 44 ER 697; *Evans v Benyon* (1887) 37 Ch D 329; *Re Jarvis* [1958] 1 WLR 815; *Re Pauling's ST (No 1)* [1964] Ch 303; *Pullan v Wilson* [2014] EWHC 126 (Ch); [2014] WTLR 669.

[2] Trustee Act 1925, s 62; *Re Pauling's ST (No 2)* [1963] Ch 576; *Brudenell-Bruce v Moore* [2014] EWHC 3679 (Ch); [2015] WTLR 373 [250]. Relief under s 62 can only be granted after a finding that a breach of trust has been committed, and so relief cannot be granted for contemplated future acts: *Mitchell v Halliwell* [2005] EWHC 937 (Ch) [64].

[3] J Payne, 'Consent' in P Birks and A Pretto (eds), *Breach of Trust* (Oxford, Hart Publishing, 2002) 301: '"consent" to breach of trust is not a single, simple concept to which a single, simple set of rules can necessarily be applied in order to determine whether the beneficiary should be allowed to sue the trustee'.

[4] For further discussion, see *Spellson v George* (1992) 26 NSWLR 666 and *Byrnes v Kendle* [2011] HCA 26, (2011) 243 CLR 253, critiqued in T Economou, 'The Defence of Acquiescence to a Breach of Trust' (2013) 15 *Flinders Law Journal* 115. See also Lusina Ho, ch 15 in the present volume.

[5] In other words, we do not discuss cases where trustees commit a breach of duty other than a duty to comply with the terms of the trust instrument, nor do we discuss cases where not all of the beneficiaries are sui juris and fully informed and in agreement.

Nowadays these conditions are not often satisfied because many trusts are drafted as discretionary settlements with wide classes of beneficiaries, including contingent beneficiaries such as future children in the case of family trusts and future spouses and dependents in the case of pension trusts.[6] However, trusts with fewer beneficiaries, all of whom had vested interests, were once much more common. Furthermore, trustees' investment powers and powers of delegation were once much more limited than they are today. Hence it often happened in the nineteenth century that trustees deliberately acted beyond the scope of their authority 'at the instigation of the beneficiaries' and that such breaches were 'the result of considered agreement' between trustees and beneficiaries who were sui juris and the owners of the whole beneficial interest.[7]

In cases of this kind, as in the more general run of cases, the trustees are not liable for their breaches of trust to the consenting beneficiaries. Unlike the more general run of cases, however, our cases also possess the unusual feature that the trustees' unauthorised actions, when performed with the beneficiaries' consent, take effect as though they were authorised. This is noticed in the main practitioner works on trusts law. *Lewin on Trusts*, for example, contains a discussion of the rules shielding trustees from liability to consenting beneficiaries in Chapter 39, under the heading 'Defence of Concurrence, Acquiescence or Release and Confirmation by a Beneficiary'; but the cases with which we are concerned then reappear in Chapter 45, on 'Lawful Departure from the Trusts', under the heading 'By Agreement'.[8]

This suggests that while estoppel reasoning (or some close variant of it) can be used to explain the trustees' escape from liability in all the 'consent' cases, a different explanation can also be given for our cases that does not work for the others. This is that the trustees' duties are changed as a result of the beneficiaries' consenting to their unauthorised actions, with the result that the trustees commit no breach of duty although they act in a way that is not permitted by the trust deed. This point was made by Master Matthews in *Pettigrew v Edwards*, where he said that in cases where beneficiaries all give their informed consent to a course of action taken by the trustees:[9]

> I do not think it is necessary to resort to any kind of estoppel. The beneficiaries have given their (fully informed) consent to the action. They have licensed the trustees to do what might otherwise be a wrong. So it is not a breach of trust and they cannot complain of it as such thereafter.

This is interesting from a theoretical point of view because it tells us something about the ways in which new rights and duties can be created under existing trusts.

[6] But see *Re Barton (Deceased)* [2002] EWHC 264 (Ch); [2002] WTLR 469; *Hughes v Bourne* [2012] EWHC 2232 (Ch); [2012] WTLR 1333.

[7] C Stebbings, *The Private Trustee in Victorian England* (Cambridge, Cambridge University Press, 2002) 96.

[8] L Tucker, N Le Poidevin and J Brightwell, *Lewin on Trusts* 19th edn (London, Sweet and Maxwell, 2015) [39.106]–[39.126], [45.03]–[45.04]. See too D Hayton, P Matthews and C Mitchell, *Underhill & Hayton: Law Relating to Trusts and Trustees* 19th edn (London, LexisNexis, 2016) [43.12], [95.1]–[95.24].

[9] *Pettigrew v Edwards* [2017] EWHC 8 (Ch); [2017] WTLR 675 [46].

It also has practical consequences, not because it affects the outcome of claims by the beneficiaries against the trustees (since the beneficiaries will lose either way), but because it affects the position of third parties with whom the trustees have dealt and the content of the beneficiaries' rights and the trustees' duties going forward. As James Penner has written, the 'substance' of a trust subsists for as long as there are trustee duties, and their character determines the nature of the trust whether or not the trustee incurs any liability for breaching them; furthermore, 'dealings with trust property in compliance with the terms of the trust are the justification in law for those transactions being valid for the parties involved'.[10]

It follows that the rules laid down in our cases merit consideration for two different reasons: first, because they can be understood to shield the trustees from liability for breach of trust in an unusual way, and, second, because they enable the trustees and beneficiaries to create new rights and duties under the trust. To analyse the first of these effects, one could adopt the method used by James Goudkamp in his study of tort defences, and ask whether the rule shielding the trustees from liability is a 'denial' that all the elements of a claim are present or a 'defence' which concedes that these elements are present but identifies another reason why there is no liability.[11] One would then have to identify the elements of the beneficiaries' claim where the trustees have done an unauthorised act, and discuss what difference it makes whether trustees owe a duty to hold and produce the trust property in an authorised form when called on to do so, exigible through an order for specific performance or an order for substitutive performance by money payment, or owe a duty not to dispose of the property in an unauthorised way, breach of which triggers a secondary duty to pay compensation.[12]

Whichever of these explanations of the trustees' liability is correct, it seems most likely that in our cases (but not in the more general run of cases) the beneficiaries' consent would enable the trustees not to invoke a 'defence' but rather to deny that they owed the relevant duty in the first place. Interesting as it would be to work through the details of this argument, however, our purpose in this chapter is to discuss the second effect, and to consider the rules which produce it alongside other rules which determine when settlors, trustees, beneficiaries and other parties can validly create new rights and duties under existing trusts. We examine these other rules in sections II to IV, before returning to our rules in sections V and VI.

[10] J Penner, 'Exemptions' in Birks and Pretto (n 3) 252.

[11] J Goudkamp, *Tort Law Defences* (Oxford, Hart Publishing, 2013). See too J Goudkamp and C Mitchell, 'Denials and Defences in the Law of Unjust Enrichment' in C Mitchell and W Swadling (eds), *The Restatement Third, Restitution and Unjust Enrichment: Critical and Comparative Essays* (Oxford, Hart Publishing, 2013).

[12] Following *Target Holdings Ltd v Redferns (a firm)* [1996] AC 421 and *AIB Group (UK) plc v Mark Redler & Co (a firm)* [2014] UKSC 58; [2015] AC 1503, most cases on trustee liability to reconstitute improperly depleted trust funds must still be analysed as though the first formulation were correct, but some cases must now be analysed as though the second formulation were correct, namely cases where the trust has been exhausted and the trust fund has become absolutely vested in possession and/or where money has been paid out of a bare trust arising as an incident of a wider commercial transaction: *Underhill* (n 8) [87.31]–[87.42].

II. EXERCISE OF POWERS CONFERRED BY THE SETTLOR

We start by observing that when an express trust is first created, the settlor may reserve powers to himself, or grant powers to others, the exercise of which at some later date will create new rights and duties under the trust. Modern settlors often seek to achieve flexibility accompanied by ongoing control over the exercise of dispositive and administrative discretions by the trustees. The devices used by trust drafters to achieve these objectives include vesting wide powers in the settlor, trustees, beneficiaries and/or other parties such as protectors. Examples are powers to revoke the trust, amend the trust instrument,[13] change the governing law of the trust, appoint or resettle trust property, buy or sell trust property, add or remove beneficiaries, appoint or remove trustees, and so on.[14] One can also have a power of veto over the exercise of a power by another power-holder, so that, for example, the trustees can only exercise powers of sale and investment or a power of appointment with the consent of the settlor or beneficiaries.[15]

Where the valid exercise of a power depends on another person's consent, a purported exercise of the power is void if the consent is not given. If the trust deed permits consent to be given retrospectively this problem may be cured by subsequent ratification.[16] Otherwise it cannot be,[17] and if trustees bring transactions into the trust account which are unauthorised for this reason, the account can be falsified and the trustees can be subjected to a personal liability to make up the shortfall.[18] Where the person upon whose consent the valid exercise of a power is predicated cannot give his consent it may be that the power can never be exercised; but although the court has no general power to dispense with consents required by a trust deed or statute,[19] it may do so where this is permitted by statute,[20] or even in exceptional cases when acting under its inherent jurisdiction—as it might do, for example, where the person whose consent is required cannot give it owing to a disability.[21]

[13] Much litigated in the pensions context: D Pollard, *The Law of Pensions Trusts* (Oxford, Oxford University Press, 2013) ch 17.

[14] M Hubbard, *Protectors of Trusts* (Oxford, Oxford University Press, 2013) ch 6; J Kessler, *Drafting Trusts and Will Trusts: A Modern Approach* 12th edn (London, Sweet and Maxwell, 2015) ch 12; *Underhill* (n 8) ch 14.

[15] G Thomas, *Thomas on Powers* 2nd edn (Oxford, Oxford University Press, 2012) paras 7.107–7.128; Hubbard (n 14) paras 6.126–6.146; Kessler (n 14) paras 7.21, 7.23–7.24. Legislation also provides in some cases that the consent of beneficiaries is needed before trustees can exercise a statutory power: eg the Trustee Act 1925, s 32(1)(c) requires the trustees to obtain the life tenant's consent to the exercise of their statutory power of advancement.

[16] *Offen v Harman* (1859) 29 LJ Ch 307.

[17] *Bateman v Davis* (1818) 3 Madd 98; 56 ER 446; *Greenham v Gibbeson* (1834) 10 Bing 363, 374–75; 131 ER 944, 949; *Gilbey v Rush* [1906] 1 Ch 11, 22–23; *Whitmore-Searle v Whitmore-Searle* [1907] 2 Ch 332; *Re Courage Group's Pension Schemes* [1987] 1 WLR 495, 504–07.

[18] *Cocker v Quayle* (1830) 1 Russ & M 535, 538; 39 ER 206, 207; *Re Massingberd's Settlement* (1890) 63 LT 296. However, a beneficiary cannot ask for the accounts to be falsified if he knowingly acquiesced in the trustee's unauthorised act: *Stevenson v Robinson* (1868) 37 LJ Ch 499.

[19] *Re Forster's Settlement* [1942] Ch 199.

[20] eg, Trusts of Land and Appointment of Trustees Act 1996, s 14, considered in *Bagum v Hafiz* [2015] EWCA Civ 801; [2016] Ch 241.

[21] *Re Cardross's Settlement* (1878) 7 Ch D 728; *Re Cooper* (1884) 27 Ch D 565; *Saipem SpA v Rafidain Bank* [1994] CLC 253, further proceedings [2007] EWHC 3119 (Ch).

The decision whether to exercise a power of veto may also be taken by the court in the place of a fiduciary power-holder who is prevented from exercising the power by an inescapable conflict of interest.[22]

The creation of new rights and duties under a trust by the exercise of a power is not only sourced in the power-holder's intention to produce this effect: it is also sourced in the settlor's intention that the power-holder should be able to do this. Like the rules which determine whether a settlor has intended to create rights and duties under an express trust,[23] the rules which determine whether a settlor has intended to create powers require this question to be tested objectively: the question is whether a reasonable person would consider this to be the meaning of the settlor's words, or to follow from the settlor's words by necessary inference.[24] To decide whether a power has been created by a trust deed, and if so, what are the conditions for its exercise, its content and duration, etc, the court is therefore thrown upon 'the ordinary canons of construction; the instrument will need to be construed as a whole against the factual matrix from which it emerged'.[25]

Powers may not be forced onto the intended donees of powers who do not want them. Thus, the Law of Property Act 1925, s 156(1) provides that:

> A person to whom any power, whether coupled with an interest or not, is given may by deed disclaim the power, and, after disclaimer, shall not be capable of exercising or joining in the exercise of the power.

If a settlor purports to confer a power on several people whom he intends to be the trustees of a settlement, and one disclaims the office while the others accept it, the power never vests in the 'disclaiming trustee', but as a general rule the power vests in the others who may then exercise it.[26] However, if a settlor intends that rights and duties under an express trust should arise only if a power is exercised by a particular person, then these rights and duties may never come into existence if that person is unable to act or declines to do so.

The question whether a power-holder may exercise the power in a self-interested way depends on whether it is held in a personal or fiduciary capacity. This in turn depends on the settlor's intention, discoverable by examination of his words and the

[22] *Scully v Coley* [2009] UKPC 29, [2009] All ER (D) 10 (Nov) [47]–[49], noting *Mettoy Pension Trustees Ltd v Evans* [1990] 1 WLR 1587.

[23] *Byrnes v Kendle* [2011] HCA 26; (2011) 243 CLR 253.

[24] *Re Pope's Contract* [1911] 2 Ch 442: a power to vary trust investments and so a power to sell these can be implied from a power to invest. *cf Re Evans's Settlement* [1967] 1 WLR 1294: a power vested in trustees to advance out of the trust fund a sum 'not exceeding £5,000' necessarily excluded a simultaneous exercise of the trustees' power of advancement under the Trustee Act 1925, s 32.

[25] *Howell v Lees-Millais* [2009] EWHC 1754 (Ch); [2009] WTLR 1163 [8]. See also *National Grid Co plc Mayes* [2001] UKHL 20, [2001] 1 WLR 864 [16]–[63]. Earlier times: *Bishop of Oxford v Leighton* (1700) 2 Vern 376, 377; 23 ER 837, 838: 'although the proviso be unskilfully penned, it amounts unto a power of revoking, and limiting new uses'; *Thornton v Hawley* (1804) 10 Ves Jun 129, 137; 32 ER 793, 796: words annexed to a clause empowering trustees of marriage settlement to purchase land 'after request' from a married couple 'tend strongly to shew, the meaning could not be, that request should be a condition precedent'.

[26] *Adams v Taunton* (1820) 5 Madd 435; 56 ER 961; *Sands v Nugee* (1836) 8 Sim 130; 59 ER 52; *Earl Granville v M'Neile* (1849) 7 Hare 156; 68 ER 64; *Crawford v Forshaw* [1891] 2 Ch 261.

context in which they were expressed. If the settlor intended that the power-holder should be able to exercise the power to benefit himself then he can do that;[27] if the settlor intended that the power-holder should exercise the power exclusively in the interests of the beneficiaries then he cannot validly exercise it in his own interest where this differs from the beneficiaries' interest.[28]

The rules governing the question whether a power may be released also turn on the question whether the power is held in a fiduciary capacity. This is so despite the wide wording of the Law of Property Act 1925, s 155, which states: 'A person to whom any power, whether coupled with an interest or not, is given may by deed release, or contract not to exercise, the power.'

This rule holds good where the power has been given to a power-holder in a personal capacity: consistently with the rule which says that such a power-holder need not even consider whether to exercise the power,[29] he is free to release the power if he wishes and the effect of doing so is to destroy the power.[30] However, where the power has been given to him in a fiduciary capacity, the power-holder must consider whether to exercise it from time to time,[31] and so he cannot release it unless release is authorised by the terms of the trust.[32]

In *Re Wills' Trust Deeds* Buckley J distinguished cases where the settlor confers a power to benefit the power-holder, who can therefore exercise it as he chooses, or not at all, from cases where the settlor means to constitute the power-holder as his 'mandatory' (meaning his agent), where the power-holder is subject to constraints. In the latter case, if:[33]

> the power is granted as a means of achieving an end which the settlor desires but which involves making a selection or decision which at the time of the creation of the trust the settlor feels unable to make, or of a kind which the settlor considers the donee to be better qualified to make than he himself is, then the proper inference may be that the settlor confers the power on the donee because he reposes a confidence in him to perform vicariously on his, the settlor's, behalf a function which the settlor would himself perform were it not that the circumstances are, or may turn out to be, such that he is bound to entrust its performance to someone else, or that they are such that he chooses to entrust it to the donee because of his peculiar qualifications to perform it. … [Whereas] in respect of what I have called beneficial powers the donee is unlikely to be under any obligation to the settlor, either legal or moral, to exercise such a power, and so could not be regarded as acting

[27] *Re Ryder* [1914] 1 Ch 865; *C v C (Ancillary Relief: Trust Fund)* [2009] EWHC 1491 (Fam); [2010] 1 FLR 337 [15], [19].

[28] *Re Skeats' Settlement* (1889) 42 Ch D 522; *Eclairs Group Ltd v JKX Oil & Gas plc* [2014] EWCA Civ 640; [2014] Bus LR 835 [119]: 'the exercise of a fiduciary power for reasons which are even in part based on the trustee's self-interest will be voidable, even if the trustee was actuated by other legitimate considerations'.

[29] *Re Park* [1932] 1 Ch 580, 582.

[30] *Smith v Houblon* (1859) 26 Beav 482; 53 ER 984; *Re Hancock* [1896] 2 Ch 173, 183, approving Sir G Farwell, *A Concise Treatise on Powers* 2nd edn (London, Stevens & Sons, 1893) 15; *Re Gestetner Settlement* [1953] Ch 672, 687.

[31] *Re Gulbenkian* [1970] AC 508, 518; *Re Baden's Deed Trusts* [1971] AC 424, 456.

[32] *Re Mills* [1930] 1 Ch 654, 661; *Muir v IRC* [1966] 1 WLR 1269, 1283.

[33] *Re Wills' Trust Deeds* [1964] Ch 219, 228–29.

> unconscientiously in debarring himself from its use, in the case of what I have called a vicarious power the donee, even if under no legal or moral obligation to exercise the power, ought not in good conscience to deprive himself of the capacity to exercise it until the period within which it must be exercised, if at all, has run out ...

When the donee of a power exercises it to create new rights and duties under a trust, and the trustees act in accordance with these new rights and duties, no question arises of the trustees committing a breach of the duties which they previously owed but no longer owe following the donee's exercise of the power. This is consistent with the settlor's and trustees' intentions when the trust was created, on terms which authorised future variations; nor can the beneficiaries complain if their rights are altered or destroyed in this way since these rights were always inherently amenable to authorised alteration or destruction. As Barrett JA said in the New South Wales Court of Appeal, in *Re Dion Investments Pty Ltd*:[34]

> Where the trust instrument contains a provision allowing variation by a particular process, the situation is one in which the settlor, in declaring the trust and defining its terms, has specified that those terms are not immutable and that the original terms will be superseded by varied terms if the specified process of variation (entailing, in concept, a power of appointment or a power of revocation or both) is undertaken. The varied terms are in that way traceable to the settlor's intention as communicated to the original trustee.

III. ACTIONS BY THE SETTLOR

Once a trust is up and running the settlor has no power to create new rights and duties under it unless he expressly reserved such a power to himself at the time when the trust was created. As Cory J held in the Supreme Court of Canada, in *Air Products Canada Ltd v Schmidt*:[35]

> The settlor of a trust can reserve any power to itself that it wishes provided the reservation is made at the time the trust is created. A settlor may choose to maintain the right to appoint trustees, to change the beneficiaries of the trust, or to withdraw the trust property. Generally, however, the transfer of the trust property to the trustee is absolute. Any power of control of that property will be lost unless the transfer is expressly made subject to it.

If a settlor has no reserved powers and he directs trustees to exercise a discretionary power in a certain way and they act in accordance with his instructions without using their own independent judgment, their acts can be set aside.[36] If a settlor has no reserved powers and he directs trustees to apply the trust property in a manner that is not authorised by the trust deed, and they obey his instructions, one of two possible conclusions may be drawn. Either the trustees commit a breach of trust or the trust deed is a sham, and does not accurately record the arrangement which the settlor and trustee made at the outset regarding the property.

[34] *Re Dion Investments Pty Ltd* [2014] NSWCA 367; (2014) 87 NSWLR 753 [45].
[35] *Air Products Canada Ltd v Schmidt* [1994] 2 SCR 611, 643.
[36] *Turner v Turner* [1984] Ch 100.

The settlor and the trustee must have had a common intention to deceive before the sham doctrine will apply. As Rimer J held in in *Shalson v Russo*:[37]

> When a settlor creates a settlement he purports to divest himself of assets in favour of the trustee, and the trustee accepts them on the basis of the trusts of the settlement. The settlor may have an unspoken intention that the assets are in fact to be treated as his own and that the trustee will accede to his every request on demand. But unless that intention is from the outset shared by the trustee (or later becomes so shared), I fail to see how the settlement can be regarded as a sham.

Where the settlor and trustee share a common intention to deceive, the rights and duties specified in the trust deed never come into existence and instead the property is held from the outset in accordance with some other arrangement agreed by the settlor and trustee. The parenthesised words in the foregoing passage of Rimer J's judgment suggest that rights and duties recorded in a trust deed can come into existence, but can be altered or extinguished if the settlor and trustee later form a different common intention respecting what should happen to the trust property. As Justice David Hayton has observed, however, in extra-judicial writing endorsed by His Honour Judge Weeks QC in *Hill v Spread Trustee Co Ltd*,[38] there can be no 'halfway house': a trust deed cannot accurately record the settlor's initial intention to create a trust, but afterwards become a sham document if the settlor changes his mind and agrees with the trustee that the trustee will do something else with the property.[39] Once a trust has been created it cannot be revoked by the settlor, even with the trustee's agreement, unless the settlor has a reserved power of revocation.[40] Unless the settlor is a beneficiary of the trust he has no standing to enforce its terms against the trustee,[41] and a fortiori he cannot validly direct the trustee to commit an act that is unauthorised by the terms of the trust deed.

It follows that the true position in relation to shams is as Munby J stated in *A v A*:[42]

> [As] a matter of principle a trust which is not initially a sham cannot subsequently become a sham. ... Once a trust has been properly constituted, typically by the vesting of the trust property in the trustee(s) and by the execution of the deed setting out the trusts upon which the trust property is to be held by the trustee(s), the property cannot lose its character as

[37] *Shalson v Russo* [2003] EWHC 1637 (Ch); [2005] Ch 281, 342. See too *Hitch v Stone* [2001] EWCA Civ 63; [2001] STC 214 [69]; *Re Esteem Settlement* [2003] JRC 092; 2003 JLR 188 [53]; *A v A* [2007] EWHC 99 (Fam); [2007] 2 FLR 467 [34].

[38] *Hill v Spread Trustee Co Ltd* [2005] EWHC 336 (Ch); [2005] BPIR 842.

[39] D Hayton, 'Shams, Piercing Veils, Remedial Constructive Trusts and Tracing' (2004) 8 *Jersey LR* 1, 8.

[40] Lindsay J described this as an 'elementary proposition' in *Dhingra v Dhingra* (1999) 2 ITELR 262, 265. See also *Naas v Westminster Bank Ltd* [1940] AC 366, 389.

[41] *Barclays Bank Ltd v Attorney General* [1944] AC 372, 380.

[42] *A v A* (n 37) [42]–[43]. See too *Re Reynolds* [2008] NZCA 122; [2008] 3 NZLR 45 [57]; *Lewis v Condon* [2013] NSWCA 204; (2013) 85 NSWLR 99 [80]–[82]. In *A v A* Munby J added at [44] that '[t]he only way ... in which a properly constituted trust which is not, ab initio, a sham could conceivably become a sham subsequently would be if all the beneficiaries were, with the requisite intention, to join together for that purpose with the trustees'. However, this would not only require that the trustees and beneficiaries must have agreed that the terms of the trust should be changed (as discussed in section VI), but also that they must have agreed to conceal this change from others.

trust property save in accordance with the terms of the trust itself, for example, by being paid to or applied for the benefit of a beneficiary in accordance with the terms of the trust deed. Any other application of the trust property is simply and necessarily a breach of trust; nothing less and nothing more.

> A trustee who has bona fide accepted office as such cannot divest himself of his fiduciary obligations by his own improper acts. If therefore, a trustee who has entered into his responsibilities, and without having any intention of being party to a sham, subsequently purports, perhaps in agreement with the settlor, to treat the trust as a sham, the effect is not to create a sham where previously there was a valid trust. The only effect, even if the agreement is actually carried into execution, is to expose the trustee to a claim for breach of trust and, it may well be, to expose the settlor to a claim for knowing assistance in that breach of trust.

The same points were also made by Barrett JA in *Re Dion Investments Pty Ltd*:[43]

> Where an express trust is established ... by a deed made between a settlor and the initial trustee to which the settled property is transferred, rights of the beneficiaries arise immediately the deed takes effect. The beneficiaries are not parties to the deed and, to the extent that it embodies covenants given by its parties to one another, the beneficiaries are strangers to those covenants and cannot sue at law for breach of them. The beneficiaries' rights are equitable rights arising from the circumstance that the trustee has accepted the office of trustee and, therefore, the duties and obligations with respect to the trust property (and otherwise) that that office carries with it.

> Any subsequent action of the settlor and the original trustee to vary the provisions of the deed made by them will not be effective to affect either the rights and interests of the beneficiaries or the duties, obligations and powers of the trustee. Those two parties have no ability to deprive the beneficiaries of those rights and interests or to vary either the terms of the trust that the trustee is bound to execute and uphold or the powers that are available to the trustee in order to do so. The terms of the trust have, in the eyes of equity, an existence that is independent of the provisions of the deed that define them.

> Let it be assumed that on Monday the settlor and the trustee execute and deliver the trust deed (at which point the settled sum changes hands) and that on Tuesday they execute a deed revoking the original deed and stating that their rights and obligations are as if it had never existed. Unless some power of revocation of the trusts has been reserved, the subsequent action does not change the fact that the trustee holds the settled sum for the benefit of beneficiaries named in the original deed and upon the trusts stated in that deed. The ... equitable rights and interests of a beneficiary cannot be taken away or varied by anyone unless the terms of the trust itself (or statute) so allow.

IV. ACTIONS BY THE TRUSTEES

As the foregoing passages of Munby J's and Barrett JA's judgments indicate, trustees are prima facie in the same position as the settlor once the trust is up and running: they cannot unilaterally create new rights and duties under the trust unless

[43] *Dion* (n 34) [41]–[43].

the settlor gave them a power to do this at the time when the trust was created. They are bound to observe the limits on their authority,[44] and in particular they may not enter unauthorised transactions affecting the trust property or make unauthorised appointments of the trust property.[45]

Situations may arise, however, where trustees believe that it would be in the beneficiaries' best interests to enter an unauthorised transaction—in Lord Lindley's phrase, where trustees wish to commit what they believe to be a 'judicious breach of trust'.[46] It may be, for example, that a limit on their investment powers prevents the trustees from managing the trust fund in the way that they believe would produce the best financial return for the beneficiaries.[47] Where they cannot obtain the beneficiaries' consent, the question arises whether there is anything else that they can do?

Three possibilities are worth mentioning. First, the trustees might be protected by an exemption clause if the clause covers deliberate breaches of duty done in good faith and the reasonable belief that the beneficiaries will benefit from them.[48] Whether a court would find that the trustees were protected in such a case might be an uncertain matter, however. Second, the court might relieve the trustees from liability after (but not before[49]) they have performed their unauthorised action under the Trustee Act 1925, s 61. Again, though, the exercise of the court's power to relieve the trustees under the section is unpredictable because everything turns on the facts.[50] The third and safest course for the trustees would therefore be to make an application for prior approval from the court under the Trustee Act 1925, s 57.[51] This section applies where trustees lack the power under the trust deed and the general law to enter transactions in the course of managing and administering the trust property which the court accepts to be expedient, and it authorises the court to make an order conferring the necessary power on the trustees, either generally or in a particular instance.[52]

[44] *Youyang Pty Ltd v Minter Ellison Morris Fletcher* [2003] HCA 15; (2003) 212 CLR 484 [32]: 'Perhaps the most important duty of a trustee is to obey the terms of the trust.'

[45] *Re Hay's Settlement Trusts* [1982] 1 WLR 202, 210; *AIB* (n 12) [51].

[46] *Perrins v Bellamy* [1899] 1 Ch 797, 798 (Lindley MR): 'My old master, the late Lord Justice Selwyn, used to say, "The main duty of a trustee is to commit judicious breaches of trust"'; amended in *National Trustees Co of Australasia Ltd v General Finance Co of Australasia Ltd* [1905] AC 373, 375–76 (Lord Lindley): 'The words "main duty" are a mistake. They ought to be "great use".' See also *Lewis v Lynch* (CA, 13 March 1980).

[47] A common event prior to the Trustee Act 2000 reforms of trustee investment powers: J Holmes and P Milner, 'Trust Law Reforms: Are We Nearly There Yet?' [2000] *Private Client Business* 114, 119. See also *Target* (n 12) 433 (Lord Browne-Wilkinson): it 'often occurs' that 'a trustee commits a judicious breach of trust by investing in an unauthorised investment'.

[48] *Armitage v Nurse* [1998] Ch 241, 250–51; *Walker v Stones* [2001] QB 902, 935, 939–41.

[49] *Perrins v Bellamy* [1898] 2 Ch 521, 527; *Re Rosenthal* [1972] 1 WLR 1273, 1277–78.

[50] For cases where trustees have been relieved of liability for unauthorised acts, see *Perrins v Bellamy* [1898] 2 Ch 521, affirmed [1899] 1 Ch 797; *Re Allsop* [1914] 1 Ch 1. For cases where they have not, see *Santander UK v RA Legal Solicitors* [2014] EWCA Civ 183; [2014] PNLR 420; *AIB* (n 12).

[51] Recommended in eg S Laing, 'To Whom Do the Accumulations Under an A & M Trust Belong? The Impact of Section 31 of the Trustee Act 1925' [1998] *Private Client Business* 323, 330; R Williams and I Lambert, 'Exemption Clauses Under Scrutiny' [1999] *Private Client Business* 87, 93; R Wilson, 'How Safe Is a "Judicious Breach of Trust"?' (2010) 121 *Trusts and Estates Law & Tax Journal* 9.

[52] Section 57 puts into statutory form a power which formerly devolved on the courts as part of their inherent jurisdiction: the leading case before 1925 was *Re New* [1901] 2 Ch 534, approved in *Chapman v Chapman* [1954] AC 429. The courts continue to exercise their non-statutory inherent jurisdiction to

Where trustees successfully take one of these three routes to perform unauthorised acts without incurring liability, the question arises whether the exemption clause or the court order changes the duties that the trustees would otherwise owe, or merely exempts them from liability for breach of their duties? So far as exemption clauses are concerned, the answer depends on their wording. Many clauses exclude liability for breach of trustee duties without changing the content of the duties, but clauses can also be drafted to achieve the latter effect. An example is provided by *Hayim v Citibank NA*,[53] where Citibank was appointed executor of a testator's American will on terms that it 'shall have no responsibility or duty with respect to' a Hong Kong house until the deaths of the testator's elderly brother and sister who resided in the house. This house was given by a Hong Kong will to another executor on trust for Citibank as executor of the American will. Citibank declined to take steps to have the house sold for the benefit of the beneficiaries under the American will who wanted the house to be sold and the siblings to be evicted from it. Substantial losses flowed from the delayed sale of the house, but the Privy Council held that the clause enabled Citibank to permit the siblings to remain living in the house without incurring any liability for losses because it owed no duties regarding the house (other than a duty not to use it for Citibank's own purposes).

The wording of the Trustee Act 1925, s 61 makes it clear that the section authorises the court to excuse a trustee from liability for breach of trust but does not negate the trustee's duty.[54] It follows that court orders relieving trustees from liability under the section do not change the content of the trustees' duties and the beneficiaries' corresponding rights against them. In contrast, the Trustee Act 1925, s 57 authorises the court to change the scope and content of the trustees' powers and hence of the trustees' duties and the beneficiaries' rights. In *Chapman v Chapman*,[55] the House of Lords held that the object of the section is to make it possible for trust property to be managed as advantageously as possible for the beneficiaries, but that it does not empower the court to alter the beneficial interests under trusts—a finding which led to the enactment of the Variation of Trusts Act 1958 because Parliament considered that the courts should be able to sanction such alterations in cases where the beneficiaries could not do it for themselves because they were not all sui juris and owners of the entire beneficial interest.[56] However the courts have also held that the partitioning and sale of trust property in the interest of good administration and management may be sanctioned under s 57 even though the result of this is to vary the beneficiaries' interests, provided that this is only an 'incidental' effect of the court's order.[57] This rule leaves them with the difficult task of deciding when a

sanction transactions which are authorised by the trust deed but objected to by the beneficiaries, as in eg *Cotton v Earl of Cardigan* [2014] EWCA Civ 1312; [2015] WTLR 39.

[53] [1987] AC 730. See also *Citibank NA v MBIA Assurance SA* [2007] EWCA Civ 11; [2007] 1 All ER (Comm) 475, discussed by Philip Sales in ch 7 in the present volume.

[54] *MCP Pension Trustees Ltd v AON Pension Trustees Ltd* [2010] EWCA Civ 377; [2012] Ch 1 [18].

[55] *Chapman v Chapman* [1954] AC 429, affirming [1953] Ch 218, 248.

[56] Discussed in section V below.

[57] *Re Z Trust* [2011] WTLR 735; *Sutton v England* [2011] EWCA Civ 637; [2012] 1 WLR 326; *Dion* (n 34).

variation of the beneficial interests is merely 'incidental'. For present purposes the significance of this rule is that trustees can sometimes win orders whose effect is to alter the beneficiaries' rights in the trust property even if the beneficiaries themselves have not all consented to this.

V. ACTIONS BY THE BENEFICIARIES

The rule in *Saunders v Vautier* permits beneficiaries to terminate trusts and call for the transfer of legal title to the trust property if they are all sui juris and in agreement and owners of the entire beneficial interest.[58] Whether the rule also permits such beneficiaries to create new rights and duties under existing trusts is another matter.

Joel Nitikman has argued that it does.[59] He contends that if one ignores the tax consequences as irrelevant to the trust analysis, there is no difference in principle between a case where the beneficiaries wish to end the trust, take the property and create a new trust (something which they are clearly able to do) and a case where the beneficiaries wish to keep the trust on foot and create new rights and duties under it. He derives support for this proposition from the many cases which hold that the Variation of Trusts Act 1958 and equivalent Commonwealth legislation are underpinned by the rule in *Saunders v Vautier*, insofar as they empower the court to supply the consent of beneficiaries who cannot consent for themselves (for example, because they are not yet born), and which hold that this is the only thing needed for the variation to take effect when taken in combination with the consent of all the sui juris beneficiaries who can (and must[60]) speak for themselves.

Thus, for example, Nitikman instances *Goulding v James*, where Mummery LJ extracted the following propositions from the authorities:[61]

> First, what varies the trust is not the court, but the agreement or consensus of the beneficiaries. Secondly, there is no real difference in principle in the rearrangement of the trusts between the case where the court is exercising its jurisdiction on behalf of the specified class under the 1958 Act and the case where the resettlement is made by virtue of the doctrine in *Saunders v Vautier* ... and by all the adult beneficiaries joining together. Thirdly, the court is merely contributing on behalf of infants and unborn and unascertained persons the binding assents to the arrangement which they, unlike an adult beneficiary, cannot give. The 1958 Act has thus been viewed by the courts as a statutory extension of the consent principle

[58] The rule is named for *Saunders v Vautier* (1841) 4 Beav 115; 49 ER 282, although the principle is older. The definitive account is P Matthews, 'The Comparative Importance of the Rule in *Saunders v Vautier*' (2006) 112 *LQR* 266.

[59] J Nitikman, 'Variation Under the Rule in *Saunders v Vautier*: Yes or No?' (2015) 21 *Trusts & Trustees* 923.

[60] The court cannot supply the missing consent of sui juris beneficiaries: *Knocker v Youle* [1986] 1 WLR 934. But note the mechanism devised to circumvent this problem in *A v B* [2016] EWHC 340 (Ch); [2016] WTLR 745.

[61] *Goulding v James* [1997] 2 All ER 239, 247. See too *IRC v Holmden* [1968] AC 685, 701, 710–11, 713; *Re Holt's Settlement* [1969] 1 Ch 100, 120; *Muhling v Perpetual Trustees WA Ltd* [2001] WASC 225 [25]–[26]; *Sutherland v Hudson's Bay Co* (2005) 74 OR (3d) 608; *Re IMK Family Trust* [2008] JRC 136; [2009] 1 FLR 664; *Wright v Gater* [2011] EWHC 2881 (Ch) [11]; *Perpetual Trustees Victoria Ltd v Barns* [2012] VSCA 77 [27].

embodied in the rule in *Saunders v Vautier*. The principle recognises the rights of beneficiaries, who are sui juris and together absolutely entitled to the trust property, to exercise their proprietary rights to overbear and defeat the intention of a testator or settlor to subject property to the continuing trusts, powers and limitations of a will or trust instrument.

The role of the court is not to stand in as, or for, a settlor in varying the trusts. [Rather] ... the court acts 'on behalf of' the specified class and, in appropriate cases, supplies consent for persons incapable of consenting.

The opposing view, that the rule in *Saunders v Vautier* does not empower beneficiaries to create new rights and duties under existing trusts, has been taken by Donovan Waters,[62] whose reasons centre on the principle established by *Re Brockbank*.[63] It was held there that beneficiaries could not force one of two trustees, in whom a power to appoint new trustees was vested, to concur in the appointment of a new trustee which was demanded by the other trustee and all the beneficiaries, although these beneficiaries were sui juris and together entitled to the whole beneficial interest. This finding was later endorsed by Walton J in *Stephenson v Barclays Bank Trust Co Ltd*, who said that beneficiaries cannot 'at one and the same time override the pre-existing trusts and keep them in existence', and who thought that it also followed that 'the beneficial interest holders [are not] entitled to direct the trustees as to the particular investment they should make of the trust fund'.[64]

VI. BENEFICIARIES AND TRUSTEES ACTING TOGETHER

The fact that creating new rights and duties under an existing trust would be contrary to the settlor's wishes does not suffice to justify a rule forbidding beneficiaries to do this, given that termination of the trust is permitted even though this would run counter to the settlor's wishes. However, the courts have held that the wishes of the trustees must also be taken into account: the trustees only agree to take office on the basis that they will have a particular set of discretionary powers and duties owed to a particular set of beneficiaries, and so it would be unfair to them if the beneficiaries could rewrite the terms of the 'deal' which the trustees made with the settlor, regardless of whether the trustees themselves agreed to this. This was also brought out by Walton J in *Stephenson*, where he said that:[65]

[O]nce the beneficial interest holders have determined to end the trust they are not entitled, unless by agreement, to the further services of the trustees. Those trustees can of course be

[62] D Waters, 'Does the Rule in *Saunders v Vautier* Include the Power of Beneficiaries to Vary the Terms of the Trust?' (2014) 33 *Estates, Trusts & Pensions Journal* 78. See also *Lewin* (n 8) [24.024]–[24.026]; *Underhill* (n 8) [66.27]–[66.30].

[63] *Re Brockbank* [1948] Ch 206.

[64] *Stephenson v Barclays Bank Trust Co Ltd* [1975] 1 All ER 625, 637. See too *Napier v Light* (1974) 236 EG 273, 278; *Holding & Management Ltd v Property Holding and Investment Trust plc* [1989] 1 WLR 1313, 1324; *Ingram v IRC* [1997] 4 All ER 395, 424; *Hotung v Ho Yuen Ki* [2002] 3 HKLRD 641; *Harb v Harb* [2010] NSWSC 1251; 17 BPR 33295 [13]; *Hancock v Rinehart* [2015] NSWSC 646; 106 ACSR 207 [161]–[162]; *Pettigrew v Edwards* [2017] EWHC 8 (Ch); [2017] WTLR 675 [45].

[65] *Stephenson* (n 64) 637. See too *Tempest v Lord Camoys* (1882) 21 Ch D 571, 578 (Jessel MR): 'It is settled law that when a testator has given a pure discretion to trustees as to the exercise of a power, the court does not enforce the exercise of the power against the wish of the trustees'.

> compelled to hand over the entire trust assets to any person or persons selected by the beneficiaries against a proper discharge, but they cannot be compelled, unless they are in fact willing to comply with the directions, to do anything else with the trust fund which they are not in fact willing to do.

This suggests that the difference of opinion described in the previous section can be resolved if we distinguish between acts done by beneficiaries acting unilaterally without the trustees' agreement and acts done by beneficiaries with the trustees' agreement. The rule in *Saunders v Vautier* permits beneficiaries to override the wishes of the settlor and terminate the trusts and they do not need the trustees to agree to this because the trustees will have no further duties to perform once the trust has been ended.[66] However, the rule does not entitle the beneficiaries to require the trustees to keep the trust going on different terms, or to serve as the trustees of a new trust declared by the beneficiaries,[67] because although it empowers the beneficiaries to override the wishes of the settlor it does not empower them to force new duties onto the trustees which the trustees do not wish to perform and did not agree to perform when they took office.

This understanding of the law is supported by judicial statements which envisage that the beneficiaries can change the terms of existing trusts, or declare new trusts which will be operated by their existing trustees, provided that the trustees consent to this arrangement. This principle is sometimes said to be grounded in the rule in *Saunders v Vautier*, but it would be more accurate to say that it is an extension of the rule, which depends on the trustees' consent as well as the beneficiaries' consent to the new arrangement.

For example, Lord Wilberforce said in *IRC v Holmden* that:[68]

> If all the beneficiaries under [a] settlement [are] sui juris, *they [can join] together with the trustees* and [declare] different trusts which would supersede those originally contained in the settlement.

Likewise, in *Re Dion Investments Pty Ltd*, Barrett JA said that:[69]

> Under the principle in *Saunders v Vautier* ... beneficiaries ... are entitled to put an end to the trust and to require that the trust property be transferred to them. Their capacity to produce that result also enables them to require, as an alternative, that the property be held by the trustee upon varied trusts; but, if they do so require, the situation may in truth be

[66] *cf* JW Harris, 'Trust, Power and Duty' (1971) 87 *LQR* 31, 63: '[b]y breaking up the trust, the beneficiaries do not compel the trustees to carry out any part of their office as active trustees; on the contrary, they bring that office to an end'.

[67] If these are different, as to which note Lord Wilberforce's comments in *Holmden* (n 61) 713, and Megarry J's findings in *Holt* (n 61) both discussed in P Luxton, 'Variation of Trusts: Settlors' Intentions and the Consent Principle in *Saunders v Vautier*' (1997) 60 *MLR* 719, 721–22, concluding that 'an arrangement approved under the [1958] Act has the same effect as a variation by sui juris beneficiaries under *Saunders v Vautier*' and that 'a variation under the Act ... gives rise to new trusts replacing the old'.

[68] *Holmden* (n 61) 713 (emphasis added). See also *Re Chrimes* [1917] 1 Ch 30; *Timpson's Executors v Yerbury* [1936] 1 KB 645, 664; *Grey v IRC* [1960] AC 1; *Westpac Banking Corp v Bell Group Ltd (No 3)* [2012] WASCA 157; 44 WAR 1 [2495]: beneficiaries can declare new trusts of the trust property 'with the consent of the trustee'.

[69] *Dion* (n 34) [46] (emphasis added).

one of resettlement upon new trusts rather than variation of the pre-existing trusts *(and the trustee may not be compellable to accept and perform those new trusts)*.

Law reform bodies around the Commonwealth have made the same point. Thus, the Scottish Law Commission has argued that:[70]

> [I]f a beneficiary has a right to direct that trust assets be made over to him absolutely, it must follow that this right extends to directing that these assets be made over to a third party (such as new trustees) or, *provided that the trustees are willing to continue to act as such*, that the assets be held by them for new or amended purposes.

Similarly, the New Zealand Law Commission has recommended codifying legislation to make it clear that in their jurisdiction the rule in *Saunders v Vautier* empowers legally capable adult beneficiaries to effect a resettlement of a trust, as well as a variation or revocation, and that:[71]

> The agreement of the trustee will always be required in cases where the original trusts continue, to avoid the trustees being burdened by obligations to which they may not have agreed.

In this respect the position of the beneficiaries is analogous to the position of a settlor who wishes to create an express trust for the first time. A settlor can express the wish that certain parties should act as the trustees and hold the trust property subject to certain duties, and if the nominated parties agree these duties will become enforceable and the beneficiaries will have corresponding rights against them in their capacity as trustees of the settlement. However, the nominated parties can refuse to accept these duties: they can disclaim and the settlor or court must then find other people who are willing to accept the trusteeship.[72] In just the same way, the beneficiaries of an existing trust can express the wish that the trustees should become subject to new duties, either under a varied trust or under a new settlement, and if the trustees agree then new rights and duties will be created.[73] But the trustees can

[70] Scottish Law Commission, *Report on Variation and Termination of Trusts* (Scot Law Com No 206, 2007) para 2.6 (emphasis added).

[71] New Zealand Law Commission, *Review of the Law of Trusts: A Trusts Act for New Zealand* (NZLC R130, 2013) para 10.6. See also para 10.3, where they cite *Re Philips New Zealand Ltd* [1997] 1 NZLR 93, 101 for the proposition that the law of New Zealand already permits beneficiaries 'to use the rule to confer new powers upon trustees or deviate from, or vary, the terms of the trust where the trustees are in agreement with the change'. See now New Zealand Ministry of Justice, *Draft Trusts Bill* (2016), s 109, especially s 109(2)(d).

[72] Discussion in YK Liew and C Mitchell, 'The Creation of Express Trusts' (2017) 11 *Journal of Equity* 133.

[73] As stated in n 67, a 'varied trust' may be functionally identical with a 'new settlement'. However, different formality rules may apply, depending on the mechanism by means of which the beneficiaries and trustees agree to effect the new arrangement. A variation authorised under the 1958 Act is not caught by the Law of Property Act 1925, s 53(1)(c) (which requires signed writing for 'dispositions' of equitable interests): *Holt* (n 61) 115. Nor can the sub-section be engaged if the beneficiaries take a conveyance of legal title to themselves (since it concerns dispositions of 'equitable' and not 'legal' interests) and then transfer this legal title to the trustees of a new settlement. This consideration seems to have led the judges in *Vandervell v IRC* [1967] 2 AC 291 to hold that s 53(1)(c) is not engaged where an absolute beneficial owner directs his trustee to transfer legal title to another person with the intention that his equitable interest shall thereby be extinguished. This finding should also logically extend to a case where the recipient of the legal title has previously agreed to hold it on a new trust. However, these were effectively the facts of *Grey* (n 68), which held that such an arrangement is caught by s 53(1)(c), although it is hard to see this

decline to act on these new terms, and if the beneficiaries insist on the new or varied terms then either the trustees may choose to retire or the beneficiaries can force them to retire and appoint more compliant trustees under the Trusts of Land and Appointment of Trustees Act 1996, s 19.

Further support for the view that new rights and duties under existing trusts can be created by trustees and beneficiaries acting together can be drawn from a long line of cases which hold that where trustees wrongfully sell trust property or buy new property with trust money, the beneficiaries can adopt the sale or purchase. The sale proceeds or the new asset are then treated as having been acquired by the trustees in an authorised transaction and form part of the trust fund thereafter, to be held by the trustees in accordance with the trust terms. Cases to this effect include *Wright v Morgan*, where Viscount Dunedin held that 'if a trustee has made an improper investment, the law is well settled. The cestuis que trustent as a whole have a right, if they chose, to adopt the investment and to hold it as trust property'.[74]

Likewise, in *Libertarian Investments Ltd v Hall*, Lord Millett NPJ said that if an account of a trustee's dealings with trust property discloses an unauthorised disbursement:[75]

> the [beneficiary] may falsify it, that is to say ask for the disbursement to be disallowed. ... But [he] is not bound to ask for the disbursement to be disallowed. He is entitled to ask for an inquiry to discover what the [trustee] did with the trust money ... [and if he] invested the money at a profit, the [beneficiary] ... can treat it as an authorised disbursement, treat the property in which it has been invested as acquired with trust money, and follow or trace the property and demand that it or its traceable proceeds be restored to the trust in specie.

The trustees' unauthorised dealings with the trust property may precede the giving of the beneficiaries' consent, or they may not, since the trustees and beneficiaries may all agree in advance that the trustees will make the relevant sales and investments. Cases of the latter sort more obviously resemble cases where the trustees agree to take on new duties at the beneficiaries' request, but cases where the beneficiaries give their consent after the trustees' dealings are essentially no different from cases where they consent to these dealings beforehand. In either case, the trustees'

because in *Grey* the trustees effectively 'conveyed' legal title from themselves in their capacity as trustees for the settlor to themselves in their different capacity as trustees of other pre-existing settlements for the settlor's grandchildren. This is well explained in B Green, '*Grey*, *Oughtred* and *Vandervell*—A Contextual Reappraisal' (1984) 47 *MLR* 385, especially at 389–90, 408–11.

[74] *Wright v Morgan* [1926] AC 788, 799, adding that 'if there is not unanimity then it is not trust property, but the trustee who has made it must keep the investment himself. He is debtor to the trust for the money which has been applied in its purchase'. See also *Harrison v Harrison* (1740) 2 Atk 121; 26 ER 476; *Bostock v Blakeney* (1794) 2 Bro CC 653, 656; 29 ER 362, 364; *Pocock v Reddington* (1801) 5 Ves Jun 794, 800; 31 ER 862, 865; *Scott v Scott* (1963) 109 CLR 649, 660.

[75] *Libertarian Investments Ltd v Hall* [2013] HKCFA 93; (2013) 16 HKCFAR 681 [168]–[169]. Other recent statements of the principle can be found in *Ultraframe (UK) Ltd v Fielding* [2005] EWHC 1638 (Ch); [2006] FSR 17 [1513]; *Sinclair Investment Holdings SA v Versailles Trade Finance Ltd (in Administrative Receivership)* [2007] EWHC 915 (Ch); [2–7] 2 All ER (Comm) 993 [113]; *Independent Trustee Services Ltd v GP Noble Trustees Ltd* [2012] EWCA Civ 195; [2013] Ch 91 [102]; *Tang v Tang* [2017] HKCFA 3; [2017] 2 HKC 502 [23]–[25].

motives for entering the relevant transaction do not matter, in the sense that it makes no difference whether they deal with the trust property with the subjective intention of acting for the beneficiaries, for themselves, or for someone else. All that matters is that the trustees have in fact sold the trust property or invested trust money in a transaction which is unauthorised by the trust deed but which the beneficiaries choose to adopt. This suggests that it may not be quite right to say that the sale proceeds or newly acquired investment become part of the trust fund because the beneficiaries and trustees have agreed that this should happen. In some cases there is no real agreement, and although the courts could deem an agreement to have taken place (for example, by refusing to let the trustees say that they acted with a contrary motive), there is no need for the courts to explain the cases in this way, since there is no need for an agreement at all: the beneficiaries and trustees need only to have 'acted together' in the sense that the trustees have in fact done something and the beneficiaries have consented to it.

In cases where beneficiaries adopt unauthorised sales or investments by trustees, some thought must also be given to the position of the third parties with whom the trustees have dealt. Unauthorised sales of trust property are not generally capable of overreaching the beneficiaries' equitable interests in the property because overreaching only occurs as a result of the trustees' exercise of their powers under the trust deed to subordinate the beneficiaries' interests to those of a purchaser.[76] Suppose, however, that a trustee sells trust property to a third party purchaser in an unauthorised transaction which the beneficiaries subsequently adopt. In such a case overreaching comes into play again because the beneficiaries' adoption of the sale retroactively confers the necessary authority on the trustees to overreach their beneficial interest.[77] Support for this can be drawn from Jessel MR's statement in *Re Hallett's Estate* that the beneficiaries' ability to treat the proceeds of an unauthorised sale as trust property is the same as for an authorised sale.[78] Since the beneficiaries' ability to do this is the corollary of the overreaching doctrine, it follows that the purchaser's position is also the same in both cases. Jessel MR's words were as follows:

> The modern doctrine of Equity as regards property disposed of by persons in a fiduciary position is a very clear and well-established doctrine. You can, if the sale was rightful, take the proceeds of the sale, if you can identify them. If the sale was wrongful, you can still take the proceeds of the sale, in a sense adopting the sale for the purpose of taking the proceeds, if you can identify them. There is no distinction, therefore, between a rightful and a wrongful disposition of the property, so far as regards the right of the beneficial owner to follow the proceeds.

[76] *State Bank of India v Sood* [1997] Ch 276, 281 (Peter Gibson LJ), endorsing C Harpum, 'Overreaching, Trustees' Powers and the Reform of the 1925 Legislation' [1990] *CLJ* 277, especially at 294–95. Note that the Trusts of Land and Appointment of Trustees Act 1996, s 6 gives trustees of land 'all the powers of an absolute owner' in relation to the land when exercising their functions as trustees.

[77] D Fox, 'Overreaching' in Birks and Pretto (n 3) 106–07. See also RC Nolan, 'Property in a Fund' (2004) 120 *LQR* 108, 111–16.

[78] *Re Hallett's Estate* (1880) 13 Ch D 696, 708–09.

VII. CONCLUSION

It may seem perverse to have written an account of the circumstances in which new rights and duties can be created under existing trusts for a collection of essays concerned with 'Defences in Equity'. One point of our study, however, has been to show that legal rules can produce more than one effect, and that their significance for litigants may depend on the context in which they are invoked. It may suit trustees to defend a claim for breach of trust by arguing that they never committed a breach of duty because the effect of the beneficiaries' unanimous consent to their actions was to change the content of the duties which the trustees owed. Or it may suit beneficiaries to say that they acquired new rights against trustees when they agreed with the trustees that the trust property should be held on different terms, or when they adopted the trustees' unauthorised dealings with the trust property.

A wider point which emerges from this chapter is that rights and duties under express trusts are not only sourced in the intentions of settlors that they should come into existence. Settlors can only realise their intentions with the cooperation of other parties, such as their intended trustees and beneficiaries who must choose to accept (and not to disclaim) their duties and rights, and such as the intended donees of powers who must choose to exercise their powers, as discussed in this chapter in section II. The intentions of settlors can also be overridden, and new rights and duties can be created which the settlor may not have contemplated and may not have wished to be brought into existence. As discussed in sections IV and V, trustees and beneficiaries have limited ability to achieve such effects if they act unilaterally, but as discussed in section VI, they have more power if they act together.

6

Breach of Fiduciary Duty: Consent and Prior Court Authorisation

SIMONE DEGELING*

I. INTRODUCTION

EQUITY'S PROSCRIPTIVE FIDUCIARY duties against unauthorised profit and conflict operate to impose a duty of loyalty on the principal.[1] As is well known, the fiduciary may not put herself in a position of conflicting duties where there is a conflict or serious possibility of conflict between duty and self-interest or duties to multiple principals.[2] There is likewise a prohibition against

* I am indebted to the organisers and other participants of the Defences in Equity Workshop held at Jesus College Oxford in January 2017, as well as to Jessica Hudson and Matthew Harding, for their helpful comments on an earlier draft of this chapter. I am also grateful for the generous support of private law research at UNSW Law by Whittens & McKeough which made this chapter and my attendance at the workshop possible. Maximus Jones provided excellent research assistance and Nuncio D'Angelo discussed some of the ideas in this chapter with me. All remaining errors are mine.

1 There is a debate as to the true nature of the fiduciary's obligation(s) of loyalty which lies outside this discussion. For present purposes, all that must be noticed is that the fiduciary owes an obligation of loyalty which carries with it the no profit and no conflict rule. For example, Lionel Smith in 'Fiduciary Relationships: Ensuring the Loyal Exercise of Judgment on Behalf of Another' (2014) 130 *LQR* 608 argues that the no conflict rules 'tell a fiduciary when judgment cannot be safely exercised in relation to a fiduciary power' (ibid 625) and breach renders transaction, inter alia, voidable by the principal. The no-conflict rule is thus about the vitiation of the principal's consent. Smith views the no-profit rule as a rule of primary attribution pursuant to which profit obtained in breach of duty is attributed to the principal from the moment of acquisition. It is a rule about the principal's primary entitlement to the profit (ibid 628). See also J Penner, 'Is Loyalty a Virtue, and Even if It Is, Does It Really Help Explain Fiduciary Liability?' in AS Gold and PB Miller (eds), *Philosophical Foundations of Fiduciary Law* (Oxford, Oxford University Press, 2014) 171: '[T]he law of fiduciary accountability is akin to the law of unjust enrichment. Both are cases of *primary, remedial* duties. … [A] fiduciary has no duty not to act in conflict of interest, but when they do and acquire a gain thereby, they fall under a duty to account for the gain to their principal' (emphasis in original, footnote omitted).

2 *Birtchnell v Equity Trustees and Agency Co Ltd* (1929) 42 CLR 384 (HCA) 408 (Dixon J); *Boardman v Phipps* [1967] 2 AC 46 (HL) 67 (Lord Upjohn); *Breen v Williams* (1996) 186 CLR 71 (HCA) 135–36 (Gummow J); *Bristol and West Building Society v Mothew* [1998] Ch 1 (CA) 18 (Millett LJ; *Commonwealth Bank of Australia v Smith* (1991) 42 FCR 390 (FCA) 392 (the Court); *Hospital Products Ltd v United States Surgical Corp* (1984) 156 CLR 41 (HCA) 103 (Mason J); *Pilmer v Duke Group Ltd (in liq)* [2001] HCA 31; (2001) 207 CLR 165 [79] (McHugh, Gummow, Hayne and Callinan JJ).

profit. However, equity mediates the strictness of these obligations. As stated by Gummow J in *Breen v Williams*:[3]

> [O]ne answer to what otherwise would be breach of [fiduciary] duty is the presence of informed consent. Further, a court of equity has inherent jurisdiction or power to authorise, at least in some cases, entry into transactions which otherwise would be in breach of duty.

The modern *zeitgeist* may command that it is 'easier to ask forgiveness than get permission'[4] but in equity both paths are mandated. In relation to action by the principal, we know that by contract the parties may agree that fiduciary obligations are excluded, 'particularly where no prior fiduciary relationship existed and the contract defines the rights and duties of the parties'.[5] Once a breach of fiduciary duty has occurred, equity similarly provides for exculpation from the principal via the giving of fully informed consent.[6] But may a court give the fiduciary the necessary permission in advance?

In *Regal (Hastings) Ltd v Gulliver*[7] the House of Lords unanimously held the directors of Regal accountable for their personal profit in selling their shares in Regal's subsidiary Hastings Amalgamated Cinemas Ltd (Amalgamated). The directors used their position to acquire the Amalgamated shares which 'were acquired at par and were sold three weeks later at a profit of £2 16s. 1d. per share'.[8] Unlike Regal's solicitor Garton, who acquired the shares with the consent and at the request of Regal,[9] the directors did not have the consent of the Regal shareholders to the conflicted transaction. As Lord Russell stated:[10]

> They could, had they wished, have protected themselves by a resolution (either antecedent or subsequent) of the Regal shareholders in general meeting. In default of such approval, the liability to account must remain.

[3] *Breen* (n 2) 135 (Gummow J) (footnotes omitted), referring in fn 243 to *Re Drexel Burnham Lambert UK Pension Plan* [1995] 1 WLR 32 (Ch).

[4] Attributed to Rear Admiral Grace Hopper, United States Navy.

[5] *ASIC v Citigroup Global Markets Australia Pty Ltd (No 4)* [2007] FCA 963; (2007) 160 FCR 35 [280] (Jacobson J). If a prior fiduciary relationship exists, such as a status based relationship, any attempt to contract out, if within the scope of that relationship, would be a conflicted exercise of fiduciary power and thus a breach of the prior fiduciary relationship. Refer to *United Dominions Corp v Brian Pty Ltd* (1985) 157 CLR 1, 12 (Mason, Brennan and Deane JJ) confirming that '[a] fiduciary relationship can arise and fiduciary duties can exist between parties who have not reached, and who may never reach, agreement upon the consensual terms which are to govern the arrangement between them'. See also 7–8 (Gibbs CJ) and 16 (Dawson J). *United Dominions Corp v Brian Pty Ltd* was not relied on by ASIC in *ASIC v Citigroup Global Markets Australia Pty Ltd (No 4)*.

[6] *Maguire v Makaronis* (1997) 188 CLR 449, 466 (Brennan CJ, Gaudron, McHugh and Gummow JJ); *Farah Constructions Pty Ltd v Say-Dee Pty Ltd* [2007] HCA 22; (2007) 230 CLR 89 [107] (Gleeson CJ, Gummow, Callinan, Heydon and Crennan JJ). See also *CBA* (n 2) 393 (Gummow J); *Blackmagic Design Pty Ltd v Overliese* [2011] FCAFC 24; (2011) 191 FCR 1 [110] (Besanko J, with whom Finkelsten and Jacobson JJ agreed); *Hasler v Singtel Optus Pty Ltd* [2014] NSWCA 266; (2014) 87 NSWLR 609 [135] (Leeming JA); *Barescape Pty Ltd v Bacchus Holdings Pty Ltd (No 9)* [2012] NSWSC 984 [152]–[154] (Black J).

[7] *Regal (Hastings) Ltd v Gulliver* [1967] 2 AC 134 (HL).

[8] ibid 145 (Lord Russell).

[9] ibid 152 (Lord Russell), 153 (Lord Macmillan) and 157 (Lord Wright).

[10] ibid 150 (Lord Russell).

Could the directors instead have approached a court exercising equitable jurisdiction to seek prior authority for the transaction? This chapter asks to what extent is a fiduciary *generally* able to ask a court to authorise a breach of fiduciary obligation where that authority is sought by the fiduciary *prior* to the breach. May the fiduciary sidestep the need for the principal's consent by approaching the court?

II. AUTHORISATION BY A COURT

In interrogating authorisation of fiduciary conflict by a court, two difficulties fall immediately into view. The first is one of overlapping categories. As is discussed below, equity has in its exclusive jurisdiction, and by statute, the power to provide for the proper administration of trusts, including the power to secure the competent administration of trust property, and the limited power to authorise entry into transactions which would otherwise be in breach of duty.[11] Such power regulates the conduct of trustees[12] and in some instances receivers, for example in permitting a 'salary ... or some other allowance made ... for ... care and pains in the execution of ... duties'.[13] Notwithstanding arguments that some trustees are not fiduciaries,[14] it is generally accepted that express trustees, who are the subject of equity's jurisdiction to administer and advise, are also fiduciaries. As stated by Mason J in *Hospital Products*:[15] '[t]he accepted fiduciary relationships ... [include] trustee and beneficiary'. Gibbs CJ stated the position more strongly, opining that '[t]he archetype of a fiduciary is of course the trustee'.[16]

Of interest to this discussion, however, is equity's regulation of the conduct of fiduciaries, not trustees. It is therefore important to notice at the outset that the evidence being presented in some instances comes from equity's parallel categories of trustee and other officers of the court including solicitor and receiver.

[11] *Chapman v Chapman* [1954] AC 429 (HL) (not explicitly overturned by statute in NSW); *Re New* [1901] 2 Ch 534 (CA); *Tickle v Tickle* (1987) 10 NSWLR 581 (SC) 586 (Young J) (inherent jurisdiction of court to confer power on trustees); Trustee Act 1925 (NSW), s 81 (statutory power in the court to confer power on trustees). See also the court's general inherent power to administer the trust: *McLean v Burns Philp Trustee Co Pty Ltd* (1985) 2 NSWLR 623 (SC) 636 (Young J); Uniform Civil Procedure Rules 2005 (NSW), r 54.3 (originating summons to construe trust instrument without general order of administration). Trustees may in limited circumstances approach the court for judicial advice. See, eg, *Macedonian Orthodox Community Church St Perka Inc v His Eminence Petar The Diocesan Bishop of the Macedonian Orthodox Diocese of Australia and New Zealand* [2008] HCA 42; (2008) 237 CLR 66, 89–93 (Gummow A-CJ, Kirby, Hayne and Heydon JJ); *Re Estate Late Chow Cho-Poon* [2013] NSWSC 844 [198]–[200] (Lindsay J); *In the application of the NSW Trustee & Guardian* [2014] NSWSC 423 [25]–[26] (Kunc J); Trustee Act 1925 (NSW), s 63 (right of trustee to get directions from the court).

[12] An overview of these heads of power is outlined above (n 11).

[13] SE Williams and F Guthrie-Smith (eds), *Daniell's Chancery Practice* vol 2 8th edn (London, Stevens and Sons, 1914) 1485. See also JD Heydon and MJ Leeming, *Jacobs' Law of Trusts in Australia* 8th edn (Chatswood, LexisNexis Butterworths, 2016) para 23–05; *Harris v Sleep* [1897] 2 Ch 80 (CA) 84–85 (Lindley LJ) and 85–86 (Rigby LJ).

[14] JE Penner, 'Distinguishing Fiduciary, Trust and Accounting Relationships' (2014) 8 *Journal of Equity* 202.

[15] *Hospital Products* (n 2) 68 (Mason J).

[16] ibid 28 (Gibbs CJ). See also *Breen* (n 2) 92 (Dawson and Toohey JJ), 107 (Gaudron and McHugh JJ), 137 (Gumow J); *Maguire* (n 6) 463 (Brennan CJ, Gaudron, McHugh and Gummow JJ).

This observation is important because, as is explored below, not only are the doctrinal foundations of equity's jurisdiction(s) distinct, but arguably so are the normative justifications which may underpin any ability to sanction a breach of fiduciary duty.

The second issue is temporal. As is discussed below, judicial authorisation mechanisms potentially operate both before and after breach of fiduciary duty. For example, at least in relation to a trustee, a court may, following a trustee's request for judicial advice, provide counsel prior to trustee action. Similarly, as pointed out by Professor Conaglen, implicit in the calculation of equitable money remedies following breach of fiduciary duty may be a sanctioning of that conduct.[17] This might be visible, for example, to the extent that the *whole* of a profit is not required to be given up by the fiduciary in breach.[18] Therefore, leaving to one side an allowance for the fiduciary's 'skill, expertise and effort',[19] such adjustments, were they to be ordered, may also constitute a form of judicial authorisation of fiduciary breach. However, the primary focus of the discussion in this chapter is the possibility of judicial authorisation of the fiduciary *prior* to breach.

The court has both inherent and statutory jurisdiction to authorise conflicted exercises of power by trustees. Such controls are both direct and indirect. These controls thus provide a route of protection for the trustee. The discussion below outlines these various mechanisms by reference to the law in New South Wales. The material is presented by reference to: (1) judicial advice (section II.A); (2) administration of estates (section II.B); and (3) variation of trusts (section II.C), in recognition of the fact that specific bodies of case law and rules of practice and procedure have developed around each of these silos. However, it should not be overlooked that the wellspring of principle in each is equity's overarching warrant to secure the administration of trusts and estates.[20] Section II.D deals with examples outside trusteeship.

A. Judicial Advice

A trustee may seek judicial advice and direction. This procedure has the advantage that it is a direct means of the trustee obtaining counsel about a proposed course of action. As is discussed below, section 63 of the Trustee Act 1925 (NSW) confers

[17] M Conaglen, 'The Extent of Fiduciary Accounting and the Importance of Authorisation Mechanisms' (2011) 70 *CLJ* 548.

[18] ibid 553–54 (pointing to the unsuccessful arguments of counsel for the breaching fiduciary in *Murad v Al Saraj* [2005] EWCA Civ 959, [24], [55] (Arden LJ) who suggested that the account should only capture profit to which the principals would *not* have given informed consent if afforded the opportunity) and 565–73. There are, of course, limits to this argument. It does not take cognisance of other explanations for the court's award, relevantly, that the profit may not be causally linked to the breach, may be too remote etc.

[19] *Warman International Ltd v Dwyer* [1995] HCA 18; (1995) 182 CLR 544 (HCA), 568 (Mason CJ, Brennan, Deane, Dawson and Gaudron JJ). Note that the normative basis of equitable allowances is contested. See, generally, M Harding, 'Justifying Fiduciary Allowances' in A Robertson and HW Tang (eds), *The Goals of Private Law* (Oxford, Hart Publishing, 2009).

[20] See, eg, *Re New* (n 11) 545 (Romer LJ) (variation of trusts).

a broad statutory jurisdiction to obtain advice which protects the trustee from any subsequent claims by the beneficiary arising from that conduct. The procedure contemplates judicial advice, and thus authorisation, prior to action by the trustee in the matter the subject of advice.

The judicial power to give advice is enlivened if there is a question concerning the management or administration of trust property, or one concerning the interpretation of the trust instrument. Thus, for example, whether or not a conflicted exercise of trustee power is authorised or would otherwise be in breach of fiduciary duty may fall within this remit.[21] Independently of the jurisdictional hurdles identified above, the court is not bound to give advice, but rather retains an independent discretion in the matter.[22] As a majority of the High Court emphasised in *Macedonian Church* (where the subject of advice was whether the trustee of a charitable trust would be justified in defending proceedings for breach of trust made against it):[23]

> [T]he application of s 63 will tend to vary with the type of trust involved. Where there is a non-charitable private trust involving a conflict between beneficiaries, or between beneficiaries alleging a breach of trust out of which a trustee has profited and that trustee, and where the defendants in those proceedings have a personal capacity to fund the defence, *it might not be correct to give the trustee an opinion, advice or direction.*

The judicial advice procedure thus has two purposes. First, the role of the court is to protect the interests of the trust[24] or to order what it perceives to be in the best interests of the trust estate.[25] Second, the procedure is 'beneficial … for the protection of trustees'.[26] It provides a means for trustees obtaining private advice, the effect of which is to relieve them from later allegations of impropriety.[27] As explained by Kunc J in *In the application of the NSW Trustee & Guardian*,

[21] See, eg, *Marley v Mutual Security Merchant Bank & Trust Co Ltd* [1991] 3 All ER 198 (PC (Jam)) 201 (Lord Oliver): 'A trustee who is in genuine doubt about the propriety of any contemplated course of action in the exercise of his fiduciary duties and discretions is always entitled to seek proper professional advice and, if so advised, to protect his position by seeking the guidance of the court.' In any case, as pointed out in *Re Perpetual Investment Management Ltd* [2011] NSWSC 133 [46]–[51] (White J), the statutory jurisdiction 'in respect of the administration of trust property' is very wide.

[22] *Re Application of Perpetual Trustee Company* [2003] NSWSC 1185. Thus, there is no right in the trustee to advice nor no duty on the court to give it. The court, if it considers 'that it is an inappropriate case to give advice, is at liberty to give no advice and to dismiss the summons' (ibid [8] (Young CJ in Eq)).

[23] *Macedonian Church* (n 11) [67] (Gummow A-CJ, Kirby, Hayne and Heydon JJ) (emphasis added).

[24] *Application of Gnitekram Marketing Pty Ltd* [2010] NSWSC 1328 [10] (Hallen, AsJ).

[25] *Macedonian Church* (n 11) [60] (Gummow A-CJ, Kirby, Hayne and Heydon JJ); *Application by Marilyn Joy Cottee re Estate of Gwyneth Shirley Smith* [2013] NSWSC 47 [35] (Hallen J) (*Joy Cottee* case); *Application by Karellas Investments Pty Ltd* [2016] NSWSC 1578 [23] and [38] (Hallen J). This reflects the ultimate conceptual source of the jurisdiction, which is equity's jurisdiction to administer trusts. See also the application by trustees for directions in *Drexel* (n 3) 41 (Lindsay J).

[26] *Re Perpetual Investment Management Ltd* (n 21) [46] (White J); *Application by Karellas Investments Pty Ltd* (n 25) [23] (Hallen J).

[27] See s 63(2) of the Trustee Act 1925 (NSW) which precludes any trustee, who acts in accordance with the judicial opinion, advice or direction, from 'being held liable for breach of trust in the event that in conventional proceedings it is later held that the legal position does not correspond with the advice given, so long as the proviso to s 63(2) [trustee guilty of fraud, wilful concealment or misrepresentation in obtaining advice] is satisfied'. *Joy Cottee* (n 25) [37] (Hallen J).

'[t]he order is permissive and not mandatory … it is usually in the form that the trustee "is justified" in acting in a particular way'.[28]

Section 63 is interpreted broadly and is *not* limited to '"non-adversarial" proceedings, or proceedings other than those in which the trustee is being sued for breach of trust, or proceedings other than those in which one remedy sought is the removal of a trustee from office'.[29] In the exercise of the court's discretion whether or not to give advice,

> the discretion of the court to consider applications … "should not be yoked to a general first principle that, where there is a contest or where there are adversaries, it is not appropriate to give advice." … The question is whether it is in the interests of the trust estate that advice be given.[30]

The procedure is available both in NSW and also in courts of federal jurisdiction where the same substratum of facts supporting a claim in the federal jurisdiction also gives rise to the judicial advice application in the accrued federal jurisdiction.[31]

The only necessary party to the initial proceedings is the trustee, although a beneficiary may subsequently apply to the court, under section 63(10), for orders or directions as the circumstances require.[32] Section 63(8) sets out the circumstances pursuant to which notice of the proceedings must be given to others, which thus relevantly include 'any person whose rights as beneficiary may be prejudiced' by a conveyance or distribution in accordance with the judicial advice. Similarly, section 63(4) contemplates that the rules of court or a further court direction may require notice of the application for judicial advice to be served on another person. However, such a person is not, by the mere giving of notice, a party to the proceedings.[33] Nonetheless, if a beneficiary or other party has an opposing or competing interest, the court may well require that party to be joined to the proceedings in order that the court may give 'well measured advice' to the trustee,[34] particularly since by doing so such parties might 'inform the Court of a perspective different from

[28] In *In the application of the NSW Trustee & Guardian* (n 11) [24]. See, eg, the order made by Hallen J in *Joy Cottee* (n 25) [58]: 'The plaintiffs, as trustees, would be justified: 1. In making an advance of maintenance …'.

[29] *Macedonian Church* (n 11) [56] (Gummow A-CJ, Kirby, Hayne and Heydon JJ).

[30] *Re Perpetual Investment Management Ltd* (n 21) [55] (White J) quoting from *Macedonian Church* (n 11) [60] (Gummow A-CJ, Kirby, Hayne and Heydon JJ).

[31] *Hodges v Waters (No 7)* [2015] FCA 264; (2015) 232 FCR 97 [48] (Perram J). The court also held that a claim for advice under Trustee Act 1925 (NSW), s 63 would in any case be within federal jurisdiction, even if not within the court's accrued jurisdiction, since the advice involved the trustee (Wellington Capital) deciding whether or not to compromise for the purposes of a class action settlement federal causes of action under the Corporations Act 2001 (Cth) and the Australian Securities and Investments Commission Act 2001 (Cth). Therefore, the advice under s 63 was also within federal jurisdiction. See ibid [47] (Perram J).

[32] See also the Uniform Civil Procedure Rules 2005 (NSW), rr 7.11 and 7.12.

[33] *Application of Gnitekram Marketing Pty Ltd* (n 24) [17] (Hallen, AsJ). However, see the Trustee Act 1925 (NSW), s 63(10) and the Uniform Civil Procedure Rules 2005 (NSW), r 55.3 (Application by a beneficiary).

[34] *Chow* (n 11) [199] (Lindsay J). See also the Uniform Civil Procedure Rules 2005 (NSW), r 6.24 (Court may join party if proper or necessary).

that presented by a trustee appearing *ex parte*'.[35] Judicial advice does not create res judicata; it does not finally determine the rights of the parties.[36] Judicial statements to this effect must be construed carefully. As emphasised in the *Macedonian Church* case, advice pursuant to section 63 of the Trustee Act 1925 (NSW) is concerned with 'what ought to be done in the best interests of the trust estate, and that while it … [is] not the court's purpose to determine the rights of adversaries, that could be done as a necessary incident of determining what course ought to be followed in the best interests of the trust estate'.[37]

B. Proceedings for Administration of Estates

Equity supervises the administration of trusts. As described by Young J in *McLean v Burns Philp Trustee Co Pty Ltd*:[38] 'it is always open for a beneficiary to … [approach the court] and say: "This trust has not been properly administered. Please make sure that the … [trustee] who has assumed these obligations carries them out."' Orders for general administration are also available to trustees, and, in the case of testamentary trusts, personal representatives and creditors.[39] Young J in *McLean* extends those with standing and suggests that modern equity 'would listen to a creditor's application in a case involving an inter vivos trust'.[40] The effect of an order for general administration is to suspend the administration of the trust placing the matter in the hands of the court which is then required to sanction all dealings with trust property.

Even if an order for general administration is not sought, other evidence suggests equity's ability to authorise a conflicted exercise of trustee power. Specifically, the court's 'ancient jurisdiction to secure the competent administration of the trust property'[41] supports the court's power to authorise or vary the payment of remuneration to a trustee even though no such power exists in the trust instrument.[42] Starting from the position that the office of trustee is gratuitous, trustee remuneration must as a general matter be authorised in the trust deed. Absent such authority,

[35] *Chow* (n 11) [199] (Lindsay J). In addition, 'in almost all cases an application for judicial advice should be accompanied by counsel's opinion. The content of that opinion will be a significant matter which the Court will take into account in determining whether or not to give the advice sought'. *In the application of NSW Trustee & Guardian* (n 11) [27] (Kunc J). The practice of providing counsel's opinion is not referred to in either the Trustee Act 1925 (NSW) or the Uniform Civil Procedure Rules 2005 (NSW). See also *Chow* (n 11) [110]–[120] (Lindsay J).

[36] *Joy Cottee* (n 25) [40] (Hallen J).

[37] *Macedonian Church* (n 11) [105] ((Gummow A-CJ, Kirby, Hayne and Heydon JJ) referring to the advice of the Privy Council in *Marley v Mutual Security Merchant Bank* (n 21) the same conclusion being in High Court's opinion supported by s 63(3)–(4) of the Trustee Act 1925 (NSW).

[38] *McLean* (n 11) 633 (Young J).

[39] Heydon and Leeming (n 13) para 23–06; the Uniform Civil Procedure Rules 2005 (NSW), r 54.6 (Supreme Court not required to order general administration unless order is necessary for the determination of questions arising between the parties) and the Uniform Civil Procedure Rules 2005 (NSW), r 54.7 (Supreme Court may order general administration if it is necessary).

[40] *McLean* (n 11) 637 (Young J).

[41] *Re Duke of Norfolk's Settlement Trusts* [1982] 1 Ch 61 (CA) 78 (Fox LJ).

[42] ibid 79 (Fox LJ).

trustee remuneration is thus an example of conflict between duty and self-interest. Equity's 'ancient jurisdiction' was invoked in *Drexel*,[43] a case cited by Gummow J in the extract from *Breen v Williams* referred to at the start of this chapter.[44] In *Drexel*, pension fund trustees were all also beneficiaries under the trust scheme which was in actuarial surplus and being wound up. The rules being applied in the winding up provided for augmentation of the benefits of scheme members, including the trustees. This placed the trustees in a position of possible, if not actual, conflict between duty and self-interest. Lindsay J pointed to equity's jurisdiction to secure the competent administration of trust property and the 'adaptability of the rules of equity'[45] in confirming the court's jurisdiction to give directions to implement the proposed winding up scheme.[46]

Without requiring a claim for the administration of the estate,[47] the Uniform Civil Procedure Rules 2005 (NSW) Part 54 (Relief without general administration) provides an independent procedure by which the court may on an originating summons grant any relief which could be granted in administration proceedings,[48] or the determination of any question which could be determined in administration proceedings,[49] including any question arising in the administration of an estate or exaction of a trust,[50] and for an order directing any trustee to do or abstain from doing any act.[51] Rule 54.3(4) separately provides that proceedings may be brought, inter alia, for an order approving any sale by a trustee and directing any act to be done in the administration of the estate or execution of a trust that could be done if the same were being carried out under the direction of the court. These rules similarly appear to confer jurisdiction on the court to authorise what would otherwise be conflicted acts by the trustee. The claimant in the proceedings may be a beneficiary or trustee.[52] All trustees must in any case be parties.[53]

C. Variation of Trust Powers

Finally, there is limited evidence in those cases which recognise the power of a court to vary trust powers, including conferring power on the trustee where there is none provided for in the trust instrument. The possibility thus arises that such power may include the power to do acts which place the trustee's duty to avoid conflict under pressure. There are two routes for relief: the court's inherent power and that provided under statute.

[43] *Drexel* (n 3) 41 (Lindsay J).
[44] *Breen* (n 2) 135 (fn 243) (Gummow J).
[45] *Drexel* (n 3) 41 (Lindsay J).
[46] RSC Ord 85, r 2(3)(d) and (e).
[47] Uniform Civil Procedure Rules 2005 (NSW), r 54.3(6).
[48] ibid r 54.3(1).
[49] ibid r 54.3(2).
[50] ibid r 54.3(3)(a).
[51] ibid r 54.3(3)(d).
[52] ibid r 7.12 and a beneficiary may represent all (ibid r 7.6) and any judgment or order binds beneficiaries (ibid r 7.9).
[53] ibid r 7.11(2).

Re New[54] confirms that there is no general jurisdiction to vary the trust merely because to do so would be for the benefit of the beneficiaries. However, the case asserts an exceptional power in the court to sanction certain types of conduct not authorised by the trust instrument, Romer LJ stating '[i]t is impossible to ... state or define the circumstances under which, or the extent to which, the Court will exercise the jurisdiction'.[55] Nonetheless, it is clear that the court's discretion may be exercised where there is an emergency not foreseen by the settlor and it is 'in the interests of all the cestuis que trust, that certain acts should be done by the trustees which in ordinary circumstances they would have no power to do'.[56] The House of Lords in *Chapman v Chapman*[57] articulated the four situations which satisfy this requirement of 'emergency': changes in minor's property, salvage cases, cases where minors are allowed maintenance out of cumulated income, and approvals of compromises.[58]

Appellate authority in Australia confirms the existence of the inherent jurisdiction in *Re New*, albeit describing it of 'uncertain provenance'[59] and Mason P in *Gonzales v Claridades* noting that '[t]he line is shaky, but it stands'.[60] The High Court of Australia has applied the inherent jurisdiction identified in *Re New*,[61] although there has been no considered appellate discussion of whether *Chapman v Chapman* should be applied in Australia and judicial practice has been to respect its relatively narrow confines.[62] In *Tickle v Tickle*,[63] however, Young J suggested that the examples of emergency in *Chapman v Chapman* were too restrictive and that the inherent jurisdiction to vary the trustee's powers may exist in *any* case 'where there is an element of salvage and a flavour of compromise and the combination of these factors may make it a proper case'[64] for the court to intervene, thus allowing in his judgment 'at least a fifth exception to the general rule that a court has no power to vary a trust'.[65] Therefore, variation was also permitted where circumstances have occurred that would otherwise tend to thwart the intentions of the settlor or testator and the parties or guardians consent to the giving effect such intentions cy-pres.[66]

[54] *Re New* (n 11) 545 (Romer LJ) who delivered the judgment of the Court.
[55] ibid.
[56] ibid. Note Romer LJ also specifies a further condition which is that 'the consent of the beneficiaries cannot be obtained'.
[57] *Chapman v Chapman* (n 11).
[58] As enumerated in *Tickle v Tickle* (n 11) 583 (Young J).
[59] *Re Dion Investments Pty Ltd* [2014] NSWCA 367; (2014) 87 NSWLR 753 [47] (Barrett JA).
[60] *Gonzales v Claridades* [2003] NSWCA 227, (2003) 58 NSWLR 211 [35] (Mason P) with whom Beazley JA and Foster AJA agreed.
[61] *Templeton v Leviathan Pty Ltd* (1921) 30 CLR 34 (HCA) 68 (Higgins J) and 74–76 (Starke J). Knox CJ contra at 56. *Riddle v Riddle* (1952) 85 CLR 202 (HCA) 228 (Fullager J) and 235 (Kitto J) also considers the principle in *Re New*, but was itself about the statutory power of the court.
[62] See, generally, *Gonzales v Claridades* (n 60) [37] (Mason P).
[63] *Tickle v Tickle* (n 11).
[64] ibid 586.
[65] ibid. Subsequent cases have read down Young J's dictum, apparently limiting it to the exact fifth exception. See, eg, *James N Kirby Foundation v Attorney General NSW* [2004] NSWSC 1153, (2004) 62 NSWLR 276 [9] (White J) pointing out that the case involved infants, where circumstances had thwarted the settlor's intentions and guardians had consented to alterations to the trust instrument as would give effect to these intentions, and *Paloto Pty Ltd v Herro* [2015] NSWSC 445 [26] (Darke J).
[66] *Tickle v Tickle* (n 11) 586 (Young J).

Re New was applied in *Fomsgard v Fomsgard*.[67] The will of Frederich Fomsgard created a testamentary trust which appointed as trustee his wife and two others who were also managers of his business. Frederich's will directed that the business should be carried on for ten years, and authorised payment to his trustees/managers a salary for their work as managers together with one-twentieth of the profits of the business. The business was successful and the managers came before the court seeking an increase in salary. Two out of the three trustees were also managers, so the issue was whether these trustees, with the consent of the other trustee '[could] pay themselves what they please'.[68] Reasoning that the circumstances were not something the testator could have foreseen, and pointing to an emergency on the facts, particularly that which would arise if the managers resigned from their post(s) and the business was sold or 'coming to ruin',[69] with the consequent adverse impact on the interests of beneficiaries, Hodges J sanctioned an additional 15 per cent of net profits for the managers.[70] The beneficiaries also consented to this course of action.[71]

Section 81 of the Trustee Act 1925 (NSW) empowers the court to depart from the terms of the trust in authorising various dealings including 'transactions'[72] 'in the management or administration of trust property' where the act is 'in the opinion of the Court expedient',[73] including by reason of an absence of trustee power to act.[74] The statute expressly permits the doing of an act which would otherwise be a breach of trust.[75] *Re Ebbett*[76] is an example where a similar provision[77] was invoked to order rearrangement of trust funds under a testamentary trust, in which the trustee under the will had power to act, but from which the trustee might or would profit if carried out. Apart from the usual requirement that the proposed action be 'expedient', the section focused on action which was 'impracticable' without the assistance of the court. Perry J held that the risk that the trustee might have to account for his profits satisfied the requirement of 'impracticability'.[78] Notably in *Re Ebbett* the beneficiaries ultimately consented to the proposed orders.[79] Section 81 of the Trustee Act 1925 (NSW) has been the subject of judicial consideration as to the extent that the proposed transaction be beneficial to the trust as a whole.[80]

[67] *Fomsgard v Fomsgard* [1912] VLR 209 (SC).
[68] ibid 211 (Hodges J).
[69] ibid 213 (Hodges J).
[70] ibid.
[71] ibid.
[72] *Re Dion Investments Pty Ltd* (n 59).
[73] See, generally, *Riddle v Riddle* (n 61) 224 (Williams J); *Arakella Pty Ltd v Paton* [2004] NSWSC 13; (2004) 60 NSWLR 334, 360–61 (Austin J); *Stein v Sybmore Holdings Pty Ltd* [2006] NSWSC 1004, [53] (Campbell J).
[74] Trustee Act 1925 (NSW), s 81(1).
[75] ibid s 81(2).
[76] *Re Ebbett* [1974] 1 NZLR 392 (SC).
[77] Trustee Act 1956 (NZ), s 64 which appears in *Re Ebbett* (n 76) 397.
[78] ibid 398.
[79] ibid, although infants born and unborn were apparently entitled to a portion of the residuary estate.
[80] *Stein v Sybmore Holdings Pty Ltd* (n 73) [48]–[50] (Campbell J) taking the view that '[t]he wording of section 81 does not actually say that an exercise of power is expedient only if it is expedient for the trust as a whole. Williams J was the only judge in the majority in *Riddle* who adopted such a test.

D. Examples Outside Trusteeship

There are examples of court sanctioned breaches of fiduciary duty, outside the trustee beneficiary relationship, where that permission is obtained in advance. However, such evidence appears to fall into particular pockets of cases. Research has revealed examples from solicitors and receivers, significant perhaps since both are officers of the court[81] and independently subject to equity's jurisdiction. The Court of Chancery had an inherent power to appoint receivers and to receive and preserve assets.[82] Similarly solicitors are officers of the court. The other area of activity is in the protective jurisdiction of the court.

Solicitor cases cut both ways on the question. Lord Eldon in *Ex Parte James*[83] considered whether a court would permit the solicitor under the Commission to bid at an auction of the property of the estate of the bankrupt. The permission was denied:[84]

> With respect to the question, now put, whether I will permit Jones to give up the office of solicitor, and to bid, I cannot give that permission. If the principle is right, that the solicitor cannot buy, it would lead to all the mischief of acting up to the point of the sale, getting all the information, that may be useful to him, then discharging himself from the character of solicitor, and buying the property. Infinite mischief would be the consequence in a number of cases. On the other hand I do not deny, that those interested in the question may give the permission.

Later Lord Eldon stated that 'no Court can say *ab ante*, they will permit this: for circumstances, may exist at the time of the second sale, that the Court cannot know'.[85]

However, *Sidny v Ranger*[86] contemplates that a court might give advance approval for a solicitor to bid. Similarly, *Popham v Exham*[87] concerned the claimant enforcing a charge and who had carriage of a subsequent court-ordered sale of real estate. Exham 'was in effect the solicitor as well as the plaintiff in the suit … [and] did not obtain any order giving him liberty to bid, and the fact that he was the real purchaser was unknown to the Court … or the parties in the cause'.[88] However, in recognition of the direct conflict between interest and duty, and the risk that this may product

I would prefer to leave out any such gloss on the statute' (ibid [50]). *cf Riddle v Riddle* (n 61) 222 and 224 (Williams J). See now *Re Dion Investments Pty Ltd* (n 59) [92]–[100] (Barrett JA) with whom Beazley P and Gleeson JA agreed.

81 On receiver, see *Angel v Smith* (1804) 9 Ves Jr 335; 32 ER 632; *Re Maidstone Palace of Varieties Ltd* [1909] 2 Ch 283 (Ch D).

82 See, generally, Williams and Guthrie-Smith (n 13) ch XXVII. See now Supreme Court Act 1970 (NSW), s 67 in addition to the court's inherent jurisdiction.

83 *Ex Parte James* (1803) 8 Ves Jr 338; 32 ER 385. See also *Guest v Smythe* (1870) LR 5 Ch App 551 (CA) 556 (Giffard LJ).

84 *Ex Parte James* (n 83) 352.

85 ibid 353.

86 *Sidny v Ranger* (1841) 12 Sim 118 (Ch) 120; 59 ER 1076, 1077.

87 *Popham v Exham* (1860) 10 Ir Ch Rep 440.

88 ibid 446 (Smith MR). See also *Coaks v Boswell (No 1)* (1886) 11 App Cas 232 (HL) 245 (Lord FitzGerald): '[I]f the result of such an order is to place the trustee, solicitor, or other fiduciary party in the same position as an ordinary purchaser, and subject only to the same obligations and duties to the Court or vendor as if he had been but an ordinary purchaser, then I should say that the making of such an order ought to be rare and exceptional.'

a sale at an undervalue,[89] the court contemplates an order may be made giving the solicitor liberty to bid subject to the order 'that the carriage of the proceedings should be given to some other party or incumbrancer'.[90]

Equity has an inherent[91] protective jurisdiction which, inter alia, supervises the administration of estates of incapable persons. It is in the nature of this jurisdiction that the wishes of those it protects, as well as other family members, may be overridden. The focus is, rather, to determine the best interests of the protected person.[92] In exercising this jurisdiction, a court may give the manager of a person's estate authority to receive remuneration from the fund. In *Ability One Financial Management Pty Limited v JB by his Tutor AB*[93] Lindsay J confirmed that the manager is a fiduciary, and also that the authority to obtain remuneration may be sought at the commencement of the office. This category of case therefore provides an example in which, exceptionally, a court is empowered to authorise a breach of fiduciary duty in advance.

Ability One concerned the defendant who had previously obtained damages in negligence against a hospital for his injuries incurred when he had been treated for a cardiac arrest thereby suffering brain damage. The defendant was subsequently, on the application of a member of his family, declared by the court to be incapable of managing his own affairs. Ability One Financial Management ('Financial Management') was appointed as manager of the defendant's estate, including the damages obtained in the negligence action. It emerged that Financial Management proposed to charge an 'establishment fee' and a 'management fee' if appointed to management of the defendant's estate. The total combined fees in the first year of management would be $73,700[94] with every subsequent year capped at $41,800.[95] Financial Management was not a licenced trustee company and had not at the time of appointment as manager applied for remuneration.

In permitting Financial Management's application for remuneration out of the defendant's estate as was 'just and reasonable'[96] Lindsay J noted:[97]

> It may be best to regard the office of a manager of the estate of a protected person as unique, but taking colour from the terms of his or her appointment, governed by the

[89] *Popham v Exham* (n 87) 451 (Smith MR).

[90] ibid 451 (Smith MR).

[91] There is a debate about the origins of the jurisdiction and its connection to the *parens patriae* jurisdiction exercised by courts of equity. See, generally, PW Young, CE Croft and ML Smith, *On Equity* (Sydney, LawBook Co, 2009) 216–20. Modern case law is generally content to refer to it as the 'inherent' jurisdiction: *Ability One Financial Management Pty Ltd v JB by his Tutor AB* [2014] NSWSC 245 [11] (*Ability One* case).

[92] *Secretary, Department of Health and Community Services v JWB and SMB (Marion's Case)* (1992) 175 CLR 218 (HCA) 258–59 (Mason CJ, Dawson, Toohey and Gaudron JJ) and 270–73 (Brennan J). The case was brought to consider the decision to sterilise an intellectually disabled minor. It was necessary to determine whether the Family Law Act 1975 (Cth) conferred jurisdiction similar to *parens patriae*. In the course of judgment, the court gave an extensive exegesis on the protective jurisdiction and the boundaries of the 'best interests' of the protected person.

[93] *Ability One* (n 91).

[94] ibid [307] (Lindsay J).

[95] ibid [308] (Lindsay J).

[96] ibid [333] (Lindsay J).

[97] ibid [174].

> Court's protective jurisdiction and informed by the nature, purpose and historical origins of that jurisdiction. This is consistent with the decision of Hodgson CJ in *Equity in MB v Protective Commissioner* (2000) 50 NSWLR 24 at 32 [34] and 33 [38]. It is also consistent with the High Court's analysis in *Clay v Clay* (2001) 202 CLR 410 at 428 [37]–429 [38] and 430 [40]. The relationship between a manager of a protected estate and the protected person is 'a fiduciary relationship with particular characteristics'.

The manager of the protected estate, 'absent a legislative warrant'[98] has 'no entitlement to remuneration out of the estate of the protected person unless a determination is made by the Court'[99] that such remuneration be permitted. Leaving to one side the true juridical basis of any right to remuneration,[100] the point to notice is that the manager's conflicted remuneration is authorised by the court, not the principal. Equity does not ask the principal to do so since 'by reason of ... incapacity [he or she] is unable to protect his or her interests'.[101]

In determining whether to permit conflicted remuneration, the court will consider the following factors:[102] whether the allowance is just and reasonable; whether the manager remains liable to account for estate property; and whether there has been due performance by the manager of their obligations. The paramount consideration, both for the court and for the manager in the discharge of its obligations, is the welfare and interests of the protected person. The court is enjoined to take a 'large and liberal view of what that benefit is, doing on behalf of the ... [protected person] ... not only what may directly benefit him or her but what, if he or she were capable of self-management, he or she would, as a right minded and honourable person, desire to do'.[103]

III. AUTHORISATION BY PRINCIPAL

In relation to a breach of fiduciary duty, the fiduciary may seek exculpation via the fully informed consent of the principal. The position is stated in *Maguire v Makaronis*:[104]

> [w]hat is required for a fully informed consent is a question of fact in all the circumstances of each case and there is no precise formula which will determine in all cases if fully

[98] ibid [265].

[99] ibid [266].

[100] It might be argued that the remuneration of the manager is to reverse the unjust enrichment which would otherwise remain, having provided necessary services to the incapacitated person. This possibility is acknowledged by Lindsay J at [70]: 'Any such entitlement is probably grounded in the law of restitution rather than contract.'

[101] ibid [80]. Note also the point made at [175] which is that pursuant to the statutory scheme of the NSW Trustee and Guardian Act 2009 (NSW) 'a protected person ordinarily retains title to property managed on his or her behalf by the person appointed as manager or his or her estate'.

[102] ibid [11], [268]. See also *C v W (No 2)* [2016] NSWSC 945 [45]–[47] (Lindsay J).

[103] *C v W (No 2)* (n 102) [45] (Lindsay J).

[104] *Maguire* (n 6) 466 (Brennan CJ, Gaudron, McHugh and Gummow JJ) (footnotes omitted). See also *CBA* (n2) 393 (Gummow J); *Blackmagic* (n 6) [110] (Besanko J, with whom Finkelsten and Jacobson JJ agreed); *Hasler* (n 6) [135] (Leeming JA); *Barescape* (n 6) [152]–[154] (Black J); *Crossman v Sheahan* [2016] NSWCA 200 [366] (Ward JA).

informed consent has been given. The circumstances of the case may include ... obtaining independent and skilled advice from a third party.

Further, 'the sufficiency of disclosure can depend on the sophistication and intelligence of the persons to whom disclosure must be made'[105] as some principals may be 'shrewd and astute'[106] and others 'babes in the woods'.[107] The effect of informed consent is to 'negate what would otherwise be a breach of duty'.[108] In this sense, consent might be understood as a form of ratification or excuse of breach.[109] However, informed consent may be made at 'different times',[110] and may therefore include disclosure and consent *prior* to fiduciary action. In this latter instance, assuming the parties already stand in a fiduciary relationship, the principal's permission may therefore operate to redraw the scope of the existing fiduciary duty 'to avoid conduct amounting to breach of duty'.[111]

IV. PRIOR COURT AUTHORITY TO ENTER TRANSACTION?

The focus of this chapter is to determine the extent to which a fiduciary ought to be able to ask a court to authorise a breach of fiduciary obligation where that authority is sought by the fiduciary *prior* to the breach. The tentative general answer is: no. The reasons for this position are both doctrinal and normative.

The strongest evidence in favour of jurisdiction comes from trustee cases, which have at their root the general jurisdiction of equity to secure the administration of estates and the examples drawn from the protective jurisdiction. Similarly, it is perhaps significant that other cases—solicitors and receivers—appear to be drawn from categories in which the court would otherwise have an inherent power. Absent this mandate, it is difficult to find a general power ex ante to authorise a breach of fiduciary duty. Unless all necessary parties are before the court in some type of adversarial proceeding, which would include the principal, there is little support for a general jurisdiction beyond a trustee fiduciary. However, even were a determined court to find the existence of jurisdiction, deeper structural difficulties remain. These are principally a function of the fact that fiduciary obligations do not exist in a vacuum. They have scope and an object: the principal. Additionally, there are differences which arise in virtue of trusteeship being an office and of the nature of the obligations of trustee.

105 *Farah* (n 6) [107] (Gleeson CJ, Gummow, Callinan, Heydon and Crennan JJ).

106 ibid [108].

107 ibid.

108 *Maguire* (n 6) 453 (Brennan CJ, Gaudron, McHugh and Gummow JJ). See also *Hasler* (n 6) [135] (Leeming JA).

109 *Barescape* (n 6) [153] (Black J).

110 *Farah* (n 6) [107] (Gleeson CJ, Gummow, Callinan, Heydon and Crennan JJ). See also *Blackmagic* (n 6) [110] (Besanko J, with whom Finkelsten and Jacobson JJ agreed) referring to the need to keep the principal 'fully informed of the real state of things' (citing *Gray v New Augarita Porcupine Mines Ltd* [1952] 3 DLR (2d) 1 (PC (Can)) 14 (Lord Radcliffe), which suggests a timeliness to the need to disclose.

111 *Barescape* (n 6) [153] (Black J). This will depend on the circumstances of the case and the context of any fiduciary disclosure and consent by the principal.

The obligations of the fiduciary are to avoid placing themselves in a position where their personal interest conflicts with their duty in that capacity, or 'there is a real risk of that being so'.[112] Similarly, a fiduciary must not place herself in a position of conflict between duties to multiple principals. Careful construction of the scope of the relevant duty in each case is vital.[113] In the case of a duty-interest conflict configuration, '[t]here is no such conflict where the personal interest is sufficiently remote from the subject matter of the duty, or insubstantial in the sense that it is "too feeble an inducement to be determining motive": per Mason J in *Hospital Products*'.[114] Similarly, in a duty-duty conflict, the risk of breach arises where the interests of multiple principals are insufficiently aligned or insufficiently differentiated.[115] The fiduciary prohibitions catch not only actual conflicts but potential conflicts,[116] such conflict to be 'determined from the standpoint of an objective observer, with knowledge of all the material facts and circumstances'.[117] The fiduciary must also avoid making any unauthorised profit from the relationship.[118] Fiduciary disclosure and the consent of the principal is the fiduciary's defence to a breach of fiduciary duty. This discussion further takes the position that such fiduciary disclosure is the necessary background to any court sanction of a breach of fiduciary duty. Therefore, the outer limits of this argument may mean that a court which is unable to determine the nature and extent of the conflict between duty and interest, or duty and duty, will not be amenable to making the orders sought.

Even if we take a minimalist position and rely only on the footholds in the edifice presented by the capacity of equity to vary trustee's powers in cases such as *Re Ebbett*,[119] and *Fomsgard v Fomsgard*[120] and to authorise trustee remuneration in the administration of estates shown by *Drexel*, in all of these cases, the object of

[112] *Hart Security Australia v Boucousis* [2016] NSWCA 307 [94] (Meagher JA, with whom Spigelman CJ and Beazley P agreed).

[113] *Howard v Federal Commissioner of Taxation* [2014] HCA 21, (2014) 253 CLR 83 [34] (French CJ and Keane J).

[114] *Hart Security Australia v Boucousis* (n 112) [94] (Meagher JA, with whom Spigelman CJ and Beazley P agreed), referring to *Hospital Products* (n 2) 104.

[115] *Farrington v Rowe McBride & Partners* (1985) 1 NZLR 83 (CA) 90 (Richardson J) referred to with approval in *Maguire* (n 6) 465 (Brennan CJ, Gaudron, McHugh and Gummow JJ); *CBA* (n 2) 393 (the Court).

[116] *CBA* (n 2) 392 (the Court); *Breen* (n 2) 135 (Gummow J); *Birtchnell* (n 2) 408 (Dixon J); *Boardman v Phipps* [1967] 2 AC 46 (HL) 124 (Lord Upjohn); *Hospital Products* (n 2) 103 (Mason J); *Pilmer* (n 2) [79] (McHugh, Gummow, Hayne and Callinan JJ).

[117] *Australian Careers Institute Pty Ltd v Australian Institute of Fitness Pty Ltd* [2016] NSWCA 347 [132] (Sackville JA with whom Meagher JA agreed).

[118] *Breen* (n 2) 113 (Gaudron and McHugh JJ), approved in *Pilmer* (n 2) [74] (McHugh, Gummow, Hayne and Callinan JJ) and *Youyang Pty Ltd v Minter Ellison Morris Fletcher* [2003] HCA 15, (2003) 212 CLR 484 [41] (Gleeson CJ, McHugh, Gummow, Kirby and Hayne JJ). See also *Mothew* (n 2) 18 (Millett LJ); *Bray v Ford* [1896] AC 44 (HL) 51 (Lord Herschell). There is a debate, beyond the scope of this chapter, about the extent to which the profit principle stands separately to the conflict principle. See, eg, *Chan v Zacharia* (1984) 154 CLR 178 (HCA) 198 (Deane J); *Warman International Ltd v Dwyer* [1995] HCA 18, (1995) 182 CLR 544, 557–58 (Mason CJ, Brennan, Deane, Dawson and Gaudron JJ); M Conaglen, *Fiduciary Loyalty: Protecting the Due Performance of Non-fiduciary Duties* (Oxford, Hart Publishing, 2010) 114–20; R Nolan, '*Regal (Hastings) Ltd v Gulliver (1942)*' in C Mitchell and P Mitchell (eds), *Landmark Cases in Equity* (Oxford, Hart Publishing, 2012) 519–27.

[119] *Re Ebbett* (n 76).

[120] *Fomsgard v Fomsgard* (n 67).

the fiduciary power also ultimately consented to its exercise.[121] The strongest model for the permission seeking fiduciary is, rather, the judicial advice category. But even here, as is discussed below, there is arguably a conceptual and practical obstacle as the fiduciary will be required fully to inform the court as to the state of affairs. As emphasised in the parallel trustee category, a trustee must 'ensure full disclosure of all relevant matters'[122] and an obligation of the fullest of disclosure would similarly bind the fiduciary in approaching the court.

Conaglen considers the case of fiduciaries who have made an unauthorised profit in good faith and in the best interests of their principals. He argues that a court *could* find jurisdiction to make orders authorising the profit, at least in relation to the profit to which the principal may have consented.[123] He points to United Kingdom's Civil Procedure Rules, Part 6, and the protections of Practice Direction 64A which conceive of a claim by a trustee asking the court to approve without a hearing a transaction affected by conflicts of interests or duties[124] and requiring inter alia that the advice of a lawyer of 10 years standing also be provided to the court.[125] Similarly, the claim form must be accompanied by a witness statement identifying those affected by the remedy sought and giving information about any consultations of those affected.[126] Thus, on this model, a court is said to be apprised of relevant information and interests in ruling ex ante on a breach of fiduciary duty.

However, as shown by fiduciary relationships arising de novo, fiduciary relationships are potentially more complex and varied than trust relationships. The scope of the fiduciary relationship, and thus the conflict or potential conflict, is very particular. As stated by Black J in *Barescape* (speaking of fiduciary disclosure and the consent of the principal), the task of 'explanation inherent in a request to be excused from a fiduciary requirement is an onerous and exacting one'.[127] The fiduciary who is unable to meet the requirements of equitable consent in obtaining the consent of the principal should arguably also be unable to secure the assistance of the court. Whatever malaise affects the giving of disclosure to the principal, such that disclosure and consent cannot be obtained, that malaise must equally impact disclosure

[121] *Drexel* (n 3) 34 (representative beneficiaries were parties). '[T]he proposals finally settled upon by the trustees … which no one sought to oppose' (ibid 36), '[t]he scheme proposed has been considered by counsel and solicitors especially appointed to consider the various categories of members and their conflicting interests' (ibid 42) (Lindsay J); *Re Ebbett* (n 76) [19]: '[t]he daughters have now notified me that they have no objection to what is proposed and I make the orders sought' (Perry J); *Fomsgard v Fomsgard* (n 67) 213 (Hodges J): 'I am fortified in this opinion by the fact that all the beneficiaries are agreed that this course is desirable.'

[122] *Joy Cottee* (n 25) [42] (Hallen J).

[123] Conaglen (n 17) 569 (speaking of existence of court's jurisdiction). Ultimately, Conaglen concludes that a court should *not* relax the fiduciary's strict obligation to account, principally since to do so would undermine the 'deterrence that the account of profits represents for fiduciaries' (ibid 577).

[124] CPR Part 64, PD 64A, r 1A.1.

[125] PD 64A, r 1A.3(b). Similar in form and function presumably to counsel's opinion in a judicial advice application under s 63 of the Trustee Act 1925 (NSW).

[126] PD 64A, r 1A.3(a).

[127] *Barescape* (n 6) [154] (Black J), citing Barrett J in *Re McGrath & Anor (in their capacity as liquidators of HIH Insurance Ltd)* [2010] NSWSC 404.

to the court. The court would surely not permit itself to circumvent the rights of the principal. Even taking account of the possibility that a court-appointed contradictor or interlocutor might speak for unrepresented interests, including potentially an absent principal(s), and the court's wide powers under the Uniform Civil Procedure Rules 2005 (NSW), reg 6.24 (court may join party if joinder proper or necessary), there may well be circumstances where such measures will be insufficient as 'the fiduciary … may be unable to discharge adequately the one obligation without conflicting with the requirement for observance of the other obligation'.[128] The nature of the conflict or potential conflict(s) may mean that these procedures merely replicate at the level of court authority the problems of disclosure and consent by the principal.[129]

The point has already been made that the source of equity's regulation of trusts is equity's commission to ensure the administration of trusts and estates.[130] Arguably, however, in the broader fiduciary context, a fiduciary invoking a parallel procedure of seeking advice and thereby gaining the protection of that procedure raises the difficulty that the court may, as a primary matter, be determining rights. Judicial advice in its nature has some *impact* on beneficiaries' rights. As explained by Perram J in *Hodges v Waters (No 7)*:[131]

> s 63 … is not the giving of an advisory opinion … [It] operates not in a vacuum but directly to curtail actual rights, namely, the rights of the beneficiaries to sue the trustee for breach of trust if the advice is followed. There is nothing therefore hypothetical or moot about judicial advice under section 63.

Assuming a fiduciary relationship exists, the effect of advice would similarly be to 'curtail' the right of the principal to sue the fiduciary for breach of duty. However, at least in the case of a fiduciary relationship de novo, which perhaps counterintuitively, may be on the application of the *fiduciary* to obtain orders declaring the *existence* of the fiduciary relationship prior to obtaining advice, the effect of the orders will also be to transform the underlying rights of the parties. However, this objection should not be overstated: a court may similarly be asked to confirm the existence of a trust and in the same proceeding to give advice to the putative trustee.[132]

There may be an additional qualitative difference between an express trust and a fiduciary relationship as would justify differential treatment, which is that trusteeship is conceived in equity as an office. This office endures notwithstanding that the occupant of that office changes from time to time. Indeed, the court has the power to appoint a trustee if the settlor has omitted to do so or if those identified are dead

[128] *Breen* (n 2) 135 (Gummow J) (footnote omitted). See also *CBA* (n 2) 392 (the Court).

[129] See, eg, *Kelly v Willmott Forests Ltd (in liq)* [2012] FCA 1446; (2012) 300 ALR 675 [63]–[64], [308]–[309] (Murphy J).

[130] See also Conaglen (n 17) 566.

[131] in *Hodges v Waters (No 7)* (n 31) [48].

[132] eg, *Re Scott (decd)* [1948] SASR 193 (SC) in which a putative trustee of a charitable trust under a bequest applied to the court under the Administration and Probate Act 1919 (SA) s 69 for advice and direction. As only the trustee (the General Assembly of the Presbyterian Church of South Australia) could apply for guidance in this way, it was necessary as a prior question to determine the existence of a valid trust.

or refuse to act.[133] A court does not similarly appoint or replace a fiduciary. The business of constituting, monitoring, and overseeing the office of trustee is in the hands of parties other than the holder of the office. The same cannot be said for the fiduciary relationship which is structurally unsupervised apart from the rights of the principal. Further, an express trustee has various positive obligations. For example, in *Byrnes v Kendle* it was stated that 'where the trust estate includes land, it is the duty of the trustee to render the land productive by leasing it, and this is so even if the trust instrument does not expressly so provide'.[134] The trustee's obligations therefore go beyond the fiduciary obligation of loyalty. Consistently with these positive obligations, equity provides a mechanism to facilitate trustee action. When conflicted opportunities arise, a fiduciary may by contrast discharge fiduciary obligations by avoiding being placed in the situation of serious possibility of conflict.[135] Therefore, despite the attractiveness of the model of a trustee who comes before the court seeking guidance, this is not a suitable model for the fiduciary.

This conclusion is also supported by reference to the normative foundations of express trusts and fiduciary obligations. Whilst recognition of both fiduciary relationships and express trusts may rest on equity's respect for the autonomy of the settlor or principal, express trusts also serve other interests. For example, the special regime applicable to charitable trusts might be seen as evidence that particular societal ends are valued.[136] In addition, the proprietary quality of trusts inevitably distinguishes the normative and policy ends achieved by the trust device.[137]

It is not the purpose of this discussion to document the evolution and history of the express trust. The trust as an institution has metamorphosed over time[138] and trusts now include the modern 'trading trust' which, as D'Angelo explains, is 'not a term of art but … describes an express trust in which the trustee is given the power to carry on business, either generally or of a particular type, with some or all of the trust assets at its disposal'.[139] Underlying the evolution of the trust is equity's commitment to the settlor's autonomy, described by Gardner as 'rooted in

[133] *Raftland Pty Ltd v Commissioner of Taxation* [2006] FCA 109; (2006) 227 ALR 598 [66] (Kiefel J): 'It is a clearly established principle of equity that it will not allow a trust to fail for want of a trustee … In accordance with that principle the Court will appoint a trustee where there is none.' See also Trustee Act 1925 (NSW), s 6.

[134] *Byrnes v Kendle* [2011] HCA 26; (2011) 243 CLR 253, [67] (Gummow and Hayne JJ) (footnote omitted).

[135] Other obligations may be placed on the fiduciary (or trustee), for example an obligation of care and skill, which may thereby be breached. However, the point is to realise that any such obligation does not arise in virtue of the fiduciary character of the relationship. See *Permanent Building Society (in liq) v Wheeler* (1994) 11 WAR 187 (SC) 237, 239 (Ipp J); *Mothew* (n 2) 16–17 (Millett LJ).

[136] See, generally, relief of poverty, advancement of education, advancement of religion and other purposes beneficial to the community not falling under the preceding heads, referred to in *Special Commissioners of Income Tax v Pemsel* [1891] AC 531 (HL) 581 (Lord Macnaghten).

[137] Eg, the proprietary effect of trusts raises the risk that property will be held in perpetuity, thus inherently posing other policy imperatives such as the need to ensure that at some point the property vests absolutely.

[138] See, eg, PJ Millett, 'Equity's Place in the Law of Commerce' (1998) 114 *LQR* 214, 216 pointing to the rise of the professional trustee.

[139] N D'Angelo, *Commercial Trusts* (Chatswood, LexisNexis Butterworths, 2014) 76.

liberalism, especially the liberal vision of the institution of property'.[140] Supporting this commitment, argues Gardner, are the following four (non-exhaustive) policies: paternalistic considerations, such that equity takes steps to ensure that a settlor is not acting against her own interests in making a trust of her property;[141] communitarian considerations, pursuant to which it is thought that 'well-being is better promoted if the potential role, interests and responsibilities of communities are made part of the reckoning';[142] utilitarian considerations which are said to involve a basis calculus of whether or not 'a trust does more good than harm';[143] and, finally, whether there are any 'rights' considerations.[144] For example, whether upholding the trust would infringe the rights of one of the beneficiaries or another party. This is an extremely brief description of Gardner's thesis, and it must also be acknowledged that on his account, differing considerations support a facilitative account of trust law to varying extents.[145] Thus, for example, balanced with the desire of the settlor to keep the property in trust is the countervailing policy consideration to ensure that ultimately, wealth is distributed and held in absolute ownership, thus being under the absolute use and control of the vested beneficiary.

However, the point of relevance is that the trust as an institution is underpinned by various policies. The trust is the particular 'package' available in equity which contains the unique ability to separate ownership, benefit and control of property. Trusts carry with them the whole panoply of pre-determined rights, duties and remedies. Allowing a (non-trustee) fiduciary to invoke one of the aspects of trusteeship, the albeit limited ability to approach the court and seek permission for future action, without subjecting that fiduciary to the balance of the trust package requires justification.

That various '[p]olicies shaping the express trust concept'[146] also sets this category apart from fiduciary relationships which, it may be argued, equity more closely aligns with the principal's autonomy. The theoretical justification for fiduciary duties is a field of intense discussion and debate.[147] Irrespective of why we think

[140] S Gardner, *An Introduction to the Law of Trusts* 3rd edn (Oxford, Clarendon Press, 2010) 31.

[141] ibid 32–34.

[142] ibid 34.

[143] ibid 38.

[144] ibid 48–53.

[145] ibid 32.

[146] ibid 28.

[147] See, generally, J Edelman, 'When Do Fiduciary Duties Arise?' (2010) 126 *LQR* 302; J Edelman, 'The Role of Status in the Law of Obligations Common Callings, Implied Terms, and Lessons for Fiduciary Duties' in Gold and Miller (eds), *Philosophical Foundations of Fiduciary Law* (n 1); J Edelman, 'The Importance of the Fiduciary Undertaking' (2013) 7 *Journal of Equity* 128; P Finn, 'The Fiduciary Principle' in TG Youdan (ed), *Equity, Fiduciaries and Trusts* (Toronto, Carswell, 1989); P Finn, 'Fiduciary Reflections' (2014) 88 *Australian Law Journal* 127; J Getzler, 'Rumford Market and the Genesis of Fiduciary Obligations' in A Burrows and Lord Rodger of Earlsferry (eds), *Mapping the Law: Essays in Memory of Peter Birks* (Oxford, Oxford University Press, 2006); J Getzler, '"As If" Accountability and the Counterfactual Trust' (2011) 91 *BUL Rev* 973; J Getzler, 'Ascribing and Limiting Fiduciary Obligations: Understanding the Operation of Consent' in Gold and Miller (eds), *Philosophical Foundations of Fiduciary Law* (n 1); M Harding, 'Trust and Fiduciary Law' (2013) 33 *OJLS* 81; P Miller, 'Justifying Fiduciary Duties' (2012) 58 *McGill LJ* 969; P Miller, 'The Fiduciary Relationship' in Gold and Miller (eds), *Philosophical Foundations of Fiduciary Law* (n 1); L Smith 'The Motive, Not the Deed' in

fiduciary duties arise, we may observe that 'in every fiduciary relationship, the fiduciary acquires control over a part (or in some cases, all) of another person's autonomy'.[148] Within the scope of the fiduciary relationship, the fiduciary holds relevant powers and discretions. Accounts of fiduciary duties which rely on the fiduciary's control of part of the principal's autonomy[149] link equity's imposition of an obligation of loyalty to the need to control the decision-making power held for on or behalf of the other person.[150] Consistently with this position, we may argue that it is only, or at least primarily, via the informed consent of the principal that fiduciary obligations may be relaxed.[151] Similarly, in an account of fiduciary obligations which emphasises the representative power of the fiduciary, the fiduciary derives her authority from the legal personality of the principal.[152] We may argue, therefore, that it is the principal who must authorise derogations from fiduciary duty, not the court.

Even an account of fiduciary obligations which argues that these obligations arise 'when they are expressed or implied into voluntary relationships'[153] since, in common with any other consensual duty, they are 'expressed or implied into voluntary undertakings'[154] of the fiduciary, part of what is thereby incorporated into the relationship includes the power of the principal to consent or release the fiduciary from breach. Whether or not the fiduciary obligation thereby undertaken is more or less onerous,[155] the observation remains that on this model the primacy of the principal's consent to derogations of duty is similarly preserved. Arguably, therefore, consistently with equity's normative commitment to the principal, a court should be reluctant to make orders which circumvent the principal as being primarily competent to authorise prior to breach a breach of fiduciary duty.

In those cases involving the protective jurisdiction of the court, it might be argued that principal's autonomy is already vulnerable or impaired.[156] Alternatively, framing such cases in terms of Miller's fiduciary power analysis, in being subject to the court of protection, a court has already determined that the protected person has limited capacity and thus arguably has limited authority with which to vest

J Getzler (ed), *Rationalising Property, Equity and Trusts: Essays in Honour of Edward Burn* (London, LexisNexis, 2003); L Smith, 'Deterrence, Prophylaxis and Punishment in Fiduciary Obligation' (2013) 7 *Journal of Equity* 87; Smith (n 1).

[148] Smith (n 1) 614.

[149] eg, ibid 614.

[150] ibid 615.

[151] Smith contemplates (ibid 625 fn 70) the fully informed consent of beneficiaries in excluding the no-conflict rules, these rules he argues themselves exist to support and protect the requirement of loyalty. On Smith's model the no-profit rule has a distinct justification, which is that the rule extrapolates the requirement of fiduciary loyalty. Thus, the no profit rule is a means of primary attribution pursuant to which benefits obtained within the scope of the fiduciary relationship are allocated to the principal.

[152] Miller, 'The Fiduciary Relationship' (n 147) 70–74 who emphasises the fiduciary's discretionary power over the practical interests of the principal.

[153] Edelman, 'When Do Fiduciary Duties Arise?' (n 147) 316.

[154] ibid 316. See also Edelman, 'The Role of Status in the Law of Obligations Common Callings, Implied Terms, and Lessons for Fiduciary Duties' (n 147) or Edelman, 'The Importance of the Fiduciary Undertaking' (n 147).

[155] See Getzler, 'Ascribing and Limiting Fiduciary Obligations' (n 147).

[156] See, eg, *AEW v BW* [2016] NSWSC 905, [57] (Lindsay J).

the fiduciary. Therefore, in these exceptional cases, it is not surprising that it is the court and not the principal who is empowered to grant prior authority to the fiduciary to enter conflicted transactions. Moreover, when exercising this protective power, amongst other matters, the court gives consideration 'to what the particular person incapable of self-management would be likely to do (acting with wisdom and prudence) if he or she possessed the capacity to act'.[157] To a very limited extent, the court is thus standing proxy for the principal in making decisions, including consenting to any fiduciary breach.[158]

In practical terms, the consequence of this position is that the cases from equity's protective jurisdiction are exceptional, and should not be considered the general template for future development of the law.[159] In the general case, orders sanctioning breach *ex parte* should not be available. Thus, the hypothetical example in which the fiduciary wishes to pursue a commercial opportunity, for the benefit of principal, in which the fiduciary will also make an as yet undisclosed and unconsented to profit, must go unexploited.[160] The practical difficulty presented by the fact that the principal has gone bushwalking in the remote Kimberley, and is thus unable to be contacted, cannot be overcome by the fiduciary disclosing relevant information to the court and seeking the court's permission to pursue the transaction in lieu of obtaining the principal's consent.

Unless akin to some adversarial proceeding with all necessary parties before the court, which would include the principal, it is respectfully submitted that equity has no general warrant to authorise fiduciary malefaction prior to breach. Further, even in this case, to the extent that orders are based on consent or fiduciary admissions of consent to breach, it would as a normative matter be difficult to distinguish between actual fiduciary consent and judicial action.[161]

V. CONCLUSION

There are limits on the ability of a court exercising equitable jurisdiction to authorise transactions which would otherwise be in breach of fiduciary duty. The analysis

[157] *C v W (No 2)* (n 102) [7] (Lindsay J).

[158] Note, however, that the court is not simply substituting what it perceives to be the subjective judgment of the claimant. Not only is the decision bounded by 'best interests', but it is to be made according to some conception of conscience since it is what a person acting with 'wisdom and prudence' who was 'right minded and honourable' would do. *C v W (No 2)* (n 102) [5] and [7] (Lindsay J).

[159] Another example is *Downie v Langham* [2017] NSWSC 113, [8], [12] (White J) in which the court confirmed that an attorney (agent) acting under an enduring power of attorney previously given by a (now) incapable person stands in a fiduciary relationship with the principal, and that the court has an inherent jurisdiction analogous to relief available to a trustee, to excuse breaches of duty, if the fiduciary has acted honestly and reasonably and ought fairly to be excused. However, note that in this instance, the agency in question 'needs to accommodate the protective jurisdiction': *Smith v Smith* [2017] NSWSC 408, [19] (Lindsay J).

[160] Any argument that the transaction is in the best interests of F is irrelevant. An obligation to act in the principal's best interests is not a fiduciary obligation such that even if this could be demonstrated to the court, it is not the obligation with which we are here concerned.

[161] Recall that the beneficiaries in *Drexel* (n 3), *Re Ebbett* (n 76) and *Fomsgard v Fomsgard* (n 67) all consented to what would otherwise have been a breach of fiduciary duty.

presented here suggests that despite some parallels between express trustees and fiduciaries, a court should only exceptionally circumvent the paradigm which protects the role of the principal's consent. Unlike an express trustee who has limited capacity to obtain court authorisation prior to action, the (non trustee) fiduciary must seek the fully informed consent of the principal. The exceptional circumstances in which a court may give a fiduciary the necessary prior permission include cases within equity's protective jurisdiction.

7

Exemption Clauses in Trusts

PHILIP SALES

I. INTRODUCTION

As explained in the Law Commission report, *Trustee Exemption Clauses*:[1]

> 2.1 A trustee exemption clause is a clause in a trust instrument which purports to exclude or restrict the trustee's liability for failure to carry out properly the duties imposed upon it by the trust instrument or by law.
>
> 2.2 In addition to clauses that seek simply to exclude or restrict liability for breach of trust, there are various other types of clause which purport to secure exemption from liability. These consist of clauses which limit the scope of the trustees' duties ('duty modification clauses'), clauses which extend the trustee's powers ('extended powers clauses') and clauses which entitle the trustee to indemnity from the trust fund ('indemnity clauses').

These techniques of exemption are similar to those which are typical in a contractual context.[2]

An issue which arises in the context of exemption clauses in trusts is, how close are the parallels between trusts and contract? As with contract, trusts depend on the voluntary assumption of obligations by trustees. On one view, this feature of trusts can be relied on in order to emphasise the similarities between trust and contract and the scope for a common approach.[3] For instance, an objective approach to the interpretation of a trust instrument is justified because trustees, in particular, need to know where they stand so far as their obligations are concerned; and it can also be said that beneficiaries should have fair notice of their rights under the instrument as well. Further, English law endorses a strong form of freedom of disposition for property owners, similar to freedom of contract, so there are arguments that the trust settlor should have maximum freedom of choice as to what obligations to impose when conveying their property to a trustee.

On the other hand, are there public policy reasons to restrict the power of a settlor to introduce limits set out in the terms of the trust in relation to the extent of liability of a trustee? Perhaps that might be thought overly paternalistic. Or is the concept

[1] Law Commission, *Trustee Exemption Clauses* Report (Law Com No 301, 2006), paras 2.1–2.2.

[2] B Coote, *Exception Clauses* (London, Sweet & Maxwell, 1964).

[3] See J Edelman, 'When Do Fiduciary Duties Arise?' (2010) 126 *LQR* 302; *F&C Alternative Investments (Holdings) Ltd v Barthelemy* [2012] Ch 613; [2011] EWHC 1731 (Ch), [222]–[225]. See also P Miller and A Gold (eds), *Contract, Status, and Fiduciary Law* (Oxford, OUP, 2017).

of repugnancy between trust terms capable of fulfilling a policing role in relation to exemption clauses and, if so, does it provide a sufficient and satisfactory control on the operation of such clauses?

At a very specific doctrinal level, consideration of the law in relation to trustee exemption clauses is illustrative of deeper themes in trust law. Operation of trusts in commercial contexts and an emphasis upon voluntary assumption of obligations by fiduciaries and trustees has tended to draw trusts law along the spectrum from status to contract, with trustees' duties identified through an increased emphasis on interpretation of the trust terms rather than by relying on a standard menu of obligations imposed by law. At the same time, contract law has arguably been moving further along the same spectrum, emphasising more forcefully the centrality of interpretation as the key concept in working out the obligations of contracting parties.[4] Is trusts law now set to follow down the same path? Are there brakes which can or ought to be applied in this process?

In the historic development of the law of trusts, the courts have sought to articulate legal standards to strike a balance, pithily expressed by Lord Hardwicke in *Charitable Corporation v Sutton*[5] thus: '... two mischiefs are to be avoided: first, not to make it unsafe or too perilous for honest men to accept offices of trust, by making them liable to losses in the execution of them; and secondly, to prevent the frauds of dishonest men in such employments.' This statement indicates a resolution of the tension between these objectives in the law itself, based upon a standard of honesty. But should there be scope for the settlor to fashion his own resolution of this tension, moulded to the particular context in which he seeks to act?

Actual application in legal proceedings of an honesty standard may not strike the balance in the way that the settlor wishes to achieve, because a potential trustee will be aware that it may be possible to fashion a *claim* of dishonesty from suggestive circumstantial materials sufficient to get a case on its feet, imposing considerable burdens on the trustee to meet it in legal proceedings, even if the trustee's defence that he acted honestly is ultimately found to be made out. The possibility of being vulnerable to future claims of dishonesty may deter the settlor's preferred trustee from agreeing to act, and that may itself lead to the settlor not being able to act and dispose of his property in the way he would wish.

Suppose a settlor, Albert, who wishes to create a trust of property in favour of beneficiaries drawn from his fractious and argumentative relatives, who are known to be willing to litigate at the drop of a hat. Albert has a longstanding friend, Bernard, in whom he has complete trust, and Albert strongly wishes Bernard to act as trustee—in fact, Albert trusts no-one else so much and thinks that no-one else will do. Bernard is willing to act as trustee, but only if given the protection of the most complete exemption from personal liability, including in relation to claims in fraud or based on dishonesty which might be brought against him by one or more of the beneficiaries. Should Albert be able to, or allowed to, fashion exemption clauses of

[4] C Mitchell, 'Obligations in Commercial Contracts: A Matter of Law or Interpretation?' (2012) 65 *Current Legal Problems* 455.

[5] *Charitable Corporation v Sutton* (1742) 9 Mod 349, 356; 88 ER 500, 504. See also Joshua Getzler, ch 10 in this volume.

such ambit and effectiveness as would persuade Bernard to act? It is not obviously irrational for Albert to want to do so, taking the risk with his eyes open that he might have misjudged his friend, but feeling confident that he has not and that proceeding in this way will afford the best opportunity for him, all things considered, to achieve what he wishes to achieve. On the other hand, of course, if it later emerges that Albert's trust was misplaced and Bernard does do something dishonest, then it can be inferred that Albert would not have wished that this should happen.

So in one sense, one can pose the key question as being whether it should be open to a settlor, if he does it clearly enough, to create a bright-line rule in advance, to protect the trustee from personal liability, which is capable of withstanding the pressures that it might come under when the future turns out differently from what the settlor hoped and expected. The brightness of the line may be important to securing values in terms of settlor autonomy which would be jeopardised if its application is diluted; but dilution of application may be important to securing values in terms of settlor and beneficiary protection which are only fully in focus at the time when a judge has to decide whether to apply and abide by the stated rule, or to disapply it.

Against this background, this chapter addresses three questions:

(1) Are there limits in law to the extent to which an exemption clause may protect or relieve a trustee from liability?
(2) What intersection is there between legislative control of contract exemption clauses and trust exemption clauses?
(3) How should exemption clauses in trust instruments be interpreted?

At the outset I should apologise for the number of question marks I have deployed in this chapter. They are indicative of the way in which, in writing it, I have felt myself pulled in different directions on the first issue, which is the most fundamental. The tugs in each direction are partly the result of a tension between conventional doctrine in the older cases, reflecting older ways of thinking about trusts law, and a more modern, contract-like interpretive approach; and partly due to a tension between different underlying values of the kind I have described above. From the perspective of a judge, ultimately one's hope would be to have some of these points argued out in court by first-rate counsel on both sides, to try to come to the best view overall.

II. LIMITS IN LAW

Trustee exemption clauses are not directly subject to tests of validity and enforceability by reference to supervening legal rules in legislation requiring that they be reasonable. This is in contrast to the legal regimes which control the enforceability of exemption clauses in contract, albeit there is a degree of intersection of trusts law with these regimes: see section III. The Law Commission initially proposed legislative reform in relation to trustee exemption clauses in its consultation paper, but changed its mind in its final report: *Trustee Exemption Clauses*.[6] Therefore, control of their effect is a function of general common law and equitable rules.

[6] Law Commission (n 1).

Are there elements inherent in the very concept of trusteeship which limit the scope for lawful application of a trustee exemption clause? Or is it always possible to achieve full exemption from personal liability, for example by exempting from liability for breach of duty as a trustee and/or, where that is not possible, by re-defining the obligations of a putative or *quondam* trustee so that he is no longer regarded as a trustee at the relevant point in time when he acts?

In an effort to achieve the latter effect, a settlor might include in the trust instrument a clause which says that 'if eventuality *x* occurs, the trustee will no longer be subject to duties as such'. *Citibank NA v MBIA Assurance SA*[7] can be explained as an illustration of this type of case. Citibank was trustee for the holders of debt notes issued in respect of Eurotunnel. There were different classes of note-holder, with the senior lenders having the benefit of a guarantee from MBIA. To protect MBIA's position, under the elaborate trust and loan instruments it had powers to give Citibank binding instructions as to how to exercise most of its powers and discretions as trustee, and where instructions were given the trust deed stated that Citibank 'need not have regard to the interests of the noteholders'. Likewise, MBIA owed no obligation to the noteholders when issuing instructions, and for good measure the trust deed included a wide exemption clause for Citibank in respect of its actions in compliance with MBIA's instructions. The Court of Appeal held that these provisions were effective to insulate Citibank from being liable as a trustee when it acted on MBIA's instructions.

In relation to exemption from liability as distinct from re-definition of duty, Millett LJ's judgment in *Armitage v Nurse*[8] remains the primary reference point for judicial discussion of trustee exemption clauses for the purposes of English law. Millett LJ held that English law would invalidate a trustee exemption clause which purports to exempt the trustee from liability for fraud (in the strict, dishonest sense) or dishonesty, but does not invalidate an exemption clause which exempts a trustee from liability for wider forms of equitable 'fraud' (ie not involving dishonesty) or for negligence or gross negligence.

In *Citibank v MBIA Assurance*, the Court of Appeal applied the framework set out by Millett LJ in *Armitage v Nurse*. His judgment was also cited with approval by the majority in the Privy Council in *Spread Trustee Company Ltd v Hutcheson*, which held that in so far as the law of Guernsey mirrored that of England, liability for gross negligence could be excluded by an appropriately drafted clause.[9] The Law Commission report states that, despite a question mark regarding Millett LJ's interpretation of Scottish authority, his statement is taken to be authoritative.[10]

In *Armitage v Nurse*, Millett LJ addressed a submission that invalidity of exemption clauses, to the extent it applies, arises either by reason of repugnancy of the exemption provision to the trusts in the context of which it appears or because

[7] *Citibank NA v MBIA Assurance SA* [2007] EWCA Civ 11; [2007] 1 All ER (Comm) 475.

[8] *Armitage v Nurse* [1997] EWCA Civ 1279; [1998] Ch 241.

[9] *Spread Trustee Company Ltd v Hutcheson* [2011] UKPC 13; [2012] 2 AC 194 [38], [46]–[57] (Lord Clarke), [106] (Lord Mance), [114] (Sir Robin Auld).

[10] Law Commission (n 1), paras 2.8–2.16.

such clauses are contrary to public policy.[11] Although he did not definitively reject the public policy reason generally,[12] the thrust of his reasoning to explain why invalidity arises in relation to exemption from liability for dishonesty but not in relation to exemption in respect of gross negligence is based on repugnancy, as follows:

> [T]here is an irreducible core of obligations owed by the trustees to the beneficiaries and enforceable by them which is fundamental to the concept of a trust. If the beneficiaries have no rights enforceable against the trustees there are no trusts. But I do not accept the further submission that these core obligations include the duties of skill and care, prudence and diligence. The duty of the trustees to perform the trusts honestly and in good faith for the benefit of the beneficiaries is the minimum necessary to give substance to the trusts, but in my opinion it is sufficient. … a trustee who relied on the presence of a trustee exemption clause to justify what he proposed to do would thereby lose its protection: he would be acting recklessly in the proper sense of the term.[13]

He also observed that if an exemption clause in respect of liability for gross negligence were to be treated as invalid, that should be a matter for legislation by Parliament rather than for the courts.[14] This appears implicitly to recognise that Parliament is the proper judge of public policy on an issue of this kind.

Millett LJ's judgment, including the statement quoted above, was subject to serious question in the minority judgments of Baroness Hale and Lord Kerr in *Spread Trustee Company v Hutcheson*, as being too narrow in saying that English law will only treat an exemption clause as invalid in so far as it purports to exclude liability for dishonesty or acting in bad faith, and not extending this principle to invalidate clauses which purport to exclude liability for gross negligence as well.[15] Indeed, there was a majority view on the judicial committee that Millett LJ had misinterpreted the leading Scottish authorities,[16] by suggesting that they turned on the construction of the specific exemption clauses at issue in them, whereas in fact they reflected a rule of public policy in Scottish law to the effect that neither liability for dishonesty nor liability for gross negligence (*culpa lata*) could be excluded.[17]

However, Millett LJ's statement can be questioned from a number of different directions as well.

First, trusts law is usually taken to be governed by a dominant principle of full autonomy on the part of the settlor—a sort of 'freedom of trust' to match 'freedom of contract'. From this angle, instead of being too generous to trustees, is Millett LJ's statement perhaps not generous enough? In fact, is it really right to look at this as

[11] *Armitage* (n 8) 251G.

[12] He simply said, 'The submission that it is contrary to public policy to exclude the liability of a trustee for gross negligence is not supported by any English or Scottish authority': ibid 254E–F.

[13] ibid 253–54.

[14] ibid 256B–D.

[15] *Spread Trustee* (n 9) [130]–[137] (Baroness Hale), [141]–[180] (Lord Kerr).

[16] *Seton v Dawson* (1841) 4 D 310; *Knox v Mackinnon* (1888) 13 App Cas 753; *Rae v Meek* (1889) 14 App Cas 558; *Carruthers v Carruthers* [1896] AC 659; *Wyman v Paterson* [1900] AC 27; and *Clarke v Clarke's Trustees* 1925 SC 693.

[17] *Spread Trustee* (n 9) [38] (Lord Clarke), with whom Sir Robin Auld agreed: [133], [137] (Baroness Hale), [169]–[174] (Lord Kerr); *cf* [108] (Lord Mance, '… I think it improbable that they would be read as involving or giving rise to an absolutely inflexible rule, effectively one of public policy, precluding any trustee from exempting him, her or itself from liability for gross negligence …').

though it is the trustee exempting *himself* from liability?[18] Should it not rather be looked at from the perspective of what the settlor specifies as defining the extent of the obligations and the ambit of liability of the trustee, in order to induce the trustee to take on that role?

There is ambiguity in the authorities, including Millett LJ's judgment in *Armitage v Nurse*, and in commentaries as to whether the principle according to which an exemption clause may be treated as invalid is based on public policy or on the concept of repugnancy. As Baroness Hale in *Spread Trustee Company v Hutcheson* summarised the position which applied in England prior to *Armitage v Nurse*, '… there was a body of opinion which considered that the law was not clear, that it might well be as the House of Lords had held it to be in the Scottish cases, and that the exclusion of liability for gross negligence "was void as being repugnant to the nature of a trust or contrary to public policy" …'.[19]

The ambiguity matters, because the extent of the principle of invalidity must depend upon the basis for it. As mentioned above, in Millett LJ's formulation the principle appears to be based on a view that an exemption clause which excludes liability for dishonesty is repugnant to the key obligations in the trust. But then, is the principle of invalidity on the basis of repugnancy a rule of law or really a rule of interpretation? If a rule of interpretation, presumably it can be overcome by sufficiently clear drafting. If, however, it is a rule of law, what is its basis? Also, as discussed below, there may be different forms of repugnancy, with different consequences.

We seem to be living through a period of increased value given to freedom of contract, evident across a range of cases.[20] For example, in *Peekay Intermark Ltd v Australia and New Zealand Banking Group Ltd*,[21] a leading authority on contractual estoppel, Moore-Bick LJ says this:

> There is no reason in principle why parties to a contract should not agree that a certain state of affairs should form the basis of the transaction, whether it be the case or not. For example, it may be desirable to settle a disagreement as to an existing state of affairs in order to establish a clear basis for the contract itself and its subsequent performance. Where parties express an agreement of that kind in a contractual document neither can subsequently deny the existence of the facts and matters upon which they have agreed, at least as far as concerns those aspects of their relationship to which the agreement was directed. The contract itself gave rise to an estoppel: see *Colchester Borough Council v Smith* [1991] Ch 448, affirmed on appeal [1992] Ch 421.

[18] As Lord Mance frames the issue in *Spread Trustee* (n 9) [108].

[19] *Armitage* (n 8) [137], citing Law Commission, *Trustee Exemption Clauses* Consultation Paper (Law Com No 171) para 2.22, referring to A Kenny, 'Living up to Expectations' (1996) 146 *New Law Journal* 348, 349; P Matthews, 'The Efficacy of Trustee Exemption Clauses in English Law' (1989) *Conv* 42; H Hanbury and J Martin, *Hanbury and Martin, Modern Equity* 14th edn (London, Sweet & Maxwell, 1993) 473–74; DJ Hayton, *Underhill and Hayton: Law Relating to Trusts and Trustees* 14th edn (London, Butterworths, 1987) 792.

[20] See *Arnold v Britton* [2015] UKSC 36; [2015] AC 1619 (construction); *Cavendish Square Holdings BV v El Makdessi* [2015] UKSC 67; [2015] 3 WLR 1373 (penalty clauses); *Marks & Spencer plc v BNP Paribas Securities Services Trust Co (Jersey) Ltd* [2015] UKSC 72; [2016] AC 742 (implied terms).

[21] *Peekay Intermark Ltd v Australia and New Zealand Banking Group Ltd* [2006] EWCA Civ 386; [2006] 2 Lloyd's Rep 511 [56].

In contract law, Catherine Mitchell argues that there has been a shift away from controls via rules of law to interpretation, with such (presumably, in theory, weaker) controls that this might offer.[22] Is trusts law ripe to follow suit? Should it?

Mitchell points out that '[t]he interpretative turn ... may be a response to the criticism that the dogma and doctrine of contract law is too rigid and unresponsive to serve commercial interests'.[23] By contrast, she suggests that on an alternative view, 'contract law cannot be concerned solely with interpreting commercial contract behavior, but directing and guiding it according to [a] moral framework ... On this basis, the point of conceptualizing fundamental breach[24] as a rule of *law* is that this expresses something about contract law's underlying values: that a promise to render performance could not be emptied of all content and the obligation rendered largely illusory through the formal operation of contract terms'.[25] On this side of the debate she goes on:

> ... a commercial contract law that perceives its primary task as one of interpretation arguably reduces its capacity to be a repository of independent and substantive normative principles concerning the importance of making and performing agreements, and its capacity to develop standards according to which commercial contractors should conduct their dealings. To be clear, this is not to say what these normative principles or external standards are, but only to say that, insofar as we believe such principles to exist and to matter, we can better manifest our commitment to them, and our pursuit of them, through rule-formulation rather than the technique of interpretation.[26]

Although the principle of settlor autonomy in disposing of property and in establishing trusts is an important one, the argument for moral guidance through legal rules rather than through techniques of interpretation can be said to be stronger in the area of the law of trusts and fiduciaries than in contract law. In relation to trustees and fiduciaries it is the power to take decisions which affect the rights and property interests of beneficiaries, who are vulnerable *cestuis que trust*, which generates an especially strong impetus for the law to provide protection. The law here is strongly informed by moral considerations and values, and this may afford some basis for resisting in trust law the interpretive turn observable in contract law.

The control of contractual exemption clauses which was attempted via the doctrine of fundamental breach, taken as a rule of law, was decisively rejected in *Photo Production Ltd v Securicor Ltd*,[27] in favour of control based on presumptions as to interpretation.[28] A contractual exemption clause can be drafted to exclude liability arising from a deliberate act or omission,[29] but it seems that on public policy grounds the law does not permit a contracting party to exclude liability for his own

[22] Mitchell (n 4).

[23] This is to emphasise the importance of freedom of contract as a value: ibid 477, 485.

[24] See text to nn 28–30.

[25] Mitchell (n 4) 479.

[26] ibid 480.

[27] *Photo Production Ltd v Securicor Ltd* [1980] AC 827.

[28] See Sir Kim Lewison, *The Interpretation of Contracts* 6th edn (London, Sweet and Maxwell, 2015) para 12-11.

[29] H Beale et al, *Chitty on Contracts* 32nd edn, Vol I (London, Sweet and Maxwell, 2015), para 15-019.

fraud in inducing the making of the contract.[30] However, it is arguable that a clause, if drafted sufficiently clearly, could exempt a principal from liability in respect of the fraud of his agent.[31] It is also debatable whether the relevant rule of public policy would extend not just to fraudulent misrepresentations in making the contract, but also to fraud of the party or of his agent in carrying it out. This would be the closest analogy with an exemption clause in relation to what a trustee does, and it may be that here the position is governed by construction of the contract rather than a rule of public policy. On the other hand, inconsistency with the main purpose of the contract will lead to an exemption clause being given a narrow construction consistent with that purpose.[32] Is there justification for a different approach to exemption clauses in trust instruments?

Can inconsistency between a contractual exemption clause and the object of the contract in which it is contained go so far as to justify a court in giving no effective meaning at all to the exemption clause, as something which the parties could not realistically be taken to have intended to include in their contract, on an objective approach to construction? This would be a very strong conclusion to draw, but is conceptually possible. In *Watling v Lewis*,[33] for example, the contract included a covenant by the defendants to indemnify the claimant from certain claims, but 'not so as to create any personal liability on [the defendants] or either of them'. The exempting proviso was treated as deleted, on the grounds of repugnancy with the main term.

However, the test of repugnancy in contract is a strict one, and the principle operates within very narrow limits. In *Forbes v Git*[34] the Privy Council said,

> If in a deed the earlier clause is followed by a later clause which destroys altogether the obligation created by the earlier clause, the later clause is to be rejected as repugnant and the earlier clause prevails. ... But if the later clause does not destroy but only qualifies the earlier, then the two are to be read together and effect is to be given to the intention of the parties as disclosed by the deed as a whole.

In accordance with conventional canons of interpretation, the court is to strive to give effect to provisions in a contract if it possibly can.[35] Probably under modern approaches to interpretation, if there is genuine repugnancy the court would not apply a strict rule of precedence according to where a clause appears in the contract, but would look to the substance of the provisions which most clearly represent the true intention of the parties, which generally will be the provisions setting out the primary obligations rather than an exemption clause.[36]

[30] *HIH Casualty and General Insurance Ltd v Chase Manhattan Bank* [2003] UKHL 6; [2003] 2 Lloyd's Rep 61, as an aspect of the old maxim that 'fraud unravels all': [15]–[16] (Lord Bingham), [76] (Lord Hoffmann), [122] (Lord Scott). See also Lewison (n 28) para 12.13.

[31] *HIH Casualty and General Insurance* (n 30) [15]–[16] (Lord Bingham), [76]–[82] (Lord Hoffmann), [96]–[98] (Lord Hobhouse), [121]–[127] (Lord Scott).

[32] *Chitty on Contracts* (n 29) para 15-010. See also *HIH Casualty and General Insurance* (n 30).

[33] *Watling v Lewis* [1911] 1 Ch 414.

[34] *Forbes v Git* [1922] 1 AC 256 (PC) 259.

[35] See G Dworkin, *Odger's Construction of Deeds and Statutes* 5th edn (London, Sweet and Maxwell, 1967) 71–73.

[36] In fact, in the construction of legal instruments the principle that one adopts an interpretation *ut res magis valeat quam pereat* (ie to uphold the substance of what is intended to be achieved by the instrument) is a very old one.

To approach interpretation of contracts in this way allows scope for inconsistency between the primary terms and exemption clauses to be addressed by rules operating at different levels of intensity and with different effects. Where the inconsistency meets the strict standard of full repugnancy, the repugnant exemption clause will be treated as being of no effect. There will be practical deletion of the repugnant clause. But at a level below that, the exemption clause will be subject to a strict construction to minimise the internal tension within the contract, with any ambiguity being resolved against the party seeking to rely on it. The approach of favouring form over substance does not end with the conclusion that there is no repugnancy, but informs the interpretation of the exemption clause which purports to take 'with one hand what had been given with the other'.[37] I consider the operation of this approach to interpretation in section IV.

Returning to the concept of repugnancy in a trust instrument, it is questionable whether the principle stated in *Armitage v Nurse* can be justified on the basis of the same strict approach to repugnancy as applies in the law of contract. Or, if the relevant principle is to be justified by reference to that approach, it is questionable whether Millett LJ was right in stating its effect, which ought then properly to be limited to the very extreme sort of case where interpretation leads to practical deletion of a clause on grounds of pure repugnancy with the terms of the trust. The difficulty here is that provisions conferring powers and duties on trustees have functions other than simply to create liability on the part of the trustees. They have other effects as well, for example in relation to governing the ability of the trustees to hold and convey trust property, to give good receipts for money received, and so on. It may well be possible to say that these powers and duties continue to have practical effect, in particular in relation to the impacts of a trustee's acts upon non-beneficiary third parties who have no notice of any breach of trust, while at the same time giving an exemption clause effect in accordance with its terms to relieve a trustee of personal liability if he acts inconsistently with the terms of those powers and duties.

In the example of Albert and Bernard, if in breach of the trust terms Bernard transfers trust property to a third party who has notice of the breach, the beneficiaries would be able to sue the third party to recover that property even though (if the exemption clause is effective) they cannot sue Bernard to establish his personal liability for breach of trust, even if he has been dishonest. Also, if Bernard still has trust property in his hands, the beneficiaries can join together to compel him to transfer it to them under the principle in *Saunders v Vautier*.[38] So the primary terms of the trust and the exemption clause can both be given meaning and effect, without being treated as repugnant according to the strict contractual standard. Moreover, it could be said that the primary terms will still have real practical effect, by telling Bernard how he is expected to behave and hence, if he is honest, guiding his actions as Albert desired.

Since there seems to be this problem with a strict contractual repugnancy model, can it be said that in trusts law a wider concept of repugnancy applies? There are

[37] *Bank of Credit and Commerce International SA v Ali* [2001] UKHL 8; [2002] 1 AC 251 [66] (Lord Hoffmann).

[38] *Saunders v Vautier* (1841) Cr & Ph 240; 41 ER 482; 4 Beav 115; 49 ER 282.

two difficulties with going down this route. The concept of repugnancy as used in relation to contracts is usually taken to be a feature of a general approach to interpretation of legal instruments, be they contracts, deeds or something else, so it is not clear why trusts should be regarded as falling into a separate category. Also, since value should be given to the principle of settlor autonomy, one needs an explanation why the emphasis on party autonomy in contract should not carry across into the realm of trusts.

It may be that, as touched on above, the trusts context is one in which the fiduciary relationship to some degree resists the influence of the contract analogy and that the moral content of that relationship justifies a more substantive, action-guiding constraint imposed as a rule of law rather than merely a rule of interpretation. The concept of repugnancy which is being invoked seems more to be repugnancy to the core moral values which the law takes to be inherent in the trust relationship, rather than repugnancy in the strict and more limited sense of logical inconsistency between terms in a legal instrument. If this is the line to be taken, then it can be argued that the approach of Millett LJ, drawing the line of the mandatory rule of law according to a standard of honesty, has the merit of reflecting a very old tradition in equity, exemplified by the statement of Lord Hardwicke in *Charitable Corporation v Sutton*, quoted above.[39] However, if repugnancy in the area of trusts is to be thought of in this way, as a constraint operating as a rule of law, the distinction between repugnancy and public policy as a justification for overriding settlor autonomy breaks down. In effect, one is then working with a principle of public policy. But then the question arises whether there is a sufficient public policy justification to override settlor autonomy. Also, since at this point one is not using a principle based on logical deduction from what has been said in the document (ie the strict model of repugnancy, which reflects settlor autonomy), other factors may become relevant to defining the applicable public policy, and hence the rule to be applied, more precisely. For example, it may become relevant to ask whether the particular nature of the trustee (paid professional versus unpaid lay-person) should have any effect as to the existence or application of the relevant rule of law.

A second line of questioning opens up here. If the principle in *Armitage v Nurse* represents a rule of law rather than an approach to interpretation, then perhaps s 61 of the Trustee Act 1925 should be taken to inform the relevant public policy standard. Section 61 re-enacts protection set out in s 3 of the Judicial Trustees Act 1896, conferring a power on the court to relieve a trustee from personal liability for any breach of trust where he has acted 'honestly and reasonably' and 'ought fairly to be excused'. It is Parliament's statement of a general rule governing exemption of trustees from liability. But Millett LJ's formula appears to allow wider scope for exempting trustees from liability via a suitably drafted clause. Also, since Parliament has legislated for a general rule of law governing the issue and displacing settlor autonomy, it might be questioned whether there is justification for the courts to find *another* general rule of law based on their own conception of public policy to do the same thing. The interaction of statute and the common law (and equity) is a large

[39] *Sutton* (n 5) 504.

topic in its own right.[40] However, there is undoubtedly scope in other areas of the law for public policy rules operated by the courts to be informed by statutory provisions operating in the same field. Millett LJ himself recognised the potential significance of Parliament's views and the priority to be given to them in respect of public policy in relation to trustee exemption clauses.[41] In opposition to the arguments arising from the importance of settlor autonomy, this line of reasoning could perhaps be taken to support the doubts of Baroness Hale and Lord Kerr in *Spread Trustee v Hutcheson* regarding the narrowness of the principle stated by Millett LJ, referred to above. On the other hand, para 7 of Sched 1 to the Trustee Act 2000, which provides for a settlor to have the ability to exclude the general implied duty of care of a trustee, might be taken to support the importance, in public policy terms, of promoting settlor autonomy.

Third, James Penner points out that there is an important distinction between relief of a trustee from personal *liability* for breach and the legal substance of a trust, comprising the duties which constitute it. As he says, '[t]he simple reason is that legal duties have more functions than serving as grounds for claims for breach of them'.[42] He pursues that line of thought to criticise Millett LJ's statement in *Armitage v Nurse* for focusing on limits given by the trustee's personal liability, rather than on his 'essential duties', which Penner identifies as (1) the duty to keep the trust property separate from his own and to keep the trust accounts, and (2) to comply with the trust terms, if any.[43] According to him, 'the claim is that so long as those with claims against the trust are truly able to falsify the trust account, the personal liability of the trustee is not essential to give substance to the trusts' and 'on the basis that we look to the "minimum" necessary to give substance to the trust, there need be no personal liability upon the trustee *at all*'.[44] But this still seems to contemplate that a clearly drafted exemption clause could not exempt a trustee from certain forms of liability, for example to restore an item of trust property if it is traced by a beneficiary into his hands.[45] Yet, in some contexts, there may be a reasonable commercial purpose in trying to do even that, to rule out the bringing of claims against a trustee desired by the settlor but who is unwilling to serve unless protected against the possibility of claims being brought against him, such as claims for dishonest misappropriation. As discussed in the Albert and Bernard example above, the proposed trustee may be unwilling to take on the role if that might involve him having to take on the burden of defending litigation in relation to claims which it might be

[40] See P Atiyah, 'Common Law and Statute Law' (1985) 48 *MLR* 1; J Beatson, 'Has the Common Law a Future?' (1997) *CLJ* 291; J Beatson, 'The Role of Statute in the Development of Common Law Doctrine' (2001) 117 *LQR* 247; A Burrows, 'The Relationship Between Common Law and Statute in the Law of Obligations' (2012) 128 *LQR* 232.

[41] *Armitage* (n 8) 256B–D. See also *Spread Trustee* (n 9) [105] (Lord Mance), making the similar though converse point that it would be surprising if the common law disallowed exempting provisions that were permitted under s 30 of the Trustee Act 1925.

[42] J Penner, 'Exemptions' in P Birks and A Pretto (eds), *Breach of Trust* (Oxford, Hart Publishing, 2002) 250.

[43] ibid 252.

[44] ibid 253.

[45] ibid 260.

thought *ex ante* to be unlikely to be made out, because the settlor believes the trustee to be especially trustworthy.

Another dimension to be taken into account is the very wide range of circumstances in which a trust relationship arises, from professional trustees offering to take on trust obligations on their own standard terms to unpaid lay-people who take on the role of trustee essentially as a favour to others or for the public benefit (for example, for charities). At the latter end of the spectrum the trustee may be almost more akin to a consumer than a service-provider in control of the relationship. The trustee may feel a moral obligation to take on the role while also being personally ill-equipped to understand or negotiate over the terms of a trust deed which are simply presented to him as a *fait accompli*. Does this affect the applicable legal limits within which valid exemption clauses can be drafted, or is it only relevant to interpretation, perhaps by extension of the *contra proferentem* approach to construction? See further section IV below.

III. INTERSECTION WITH LEGISLATIVE CONTROL OF CONTRACTUAL EXEMPTION CLAUSES

Trustee exemption clauses are not directly subject to tests of validity and enforceability by reference to supervening legal rules requiring that they be reasonable. This is in contrast to the legislative regime which controls the enforceability of exemption clauses in contract under the Consumer Rights Act 2015, in so far as they interfere with the rights of consumers, and under the Unfair Contract Terms Act 1977, which applies also to contracts where a party deals on the other's written standard terms of business.[46] However, a trust instrument may be put forward by a professional trustee as part of a contractual package to sell their services, for example for forms of investment products which may be offered to consumers or to other businesses upon standard terms, in which case there appears to be a congruence between the trust terms and the contract terms. The contract is that a trust will be formed on the stated terms, which may include exemption clauses in the trust deed.

There seems to be no reason why the trust terms and the contract terms should be treated as disaggregated in this sort of arrangement. Accordingly, it seems that the legislative controls of contract exemption clauses may apply to govern the trust exemption clauses.[47]

IV. INTERPRETATION

The courts have moved towards a general unified approach to interpretation of legal instruments of all kinds, but with considerable sensitivity to context: see for example

[46] *Chitty on Contracts* (n 29) ch 15.

[47] There may also be other protections for consumers in these sorts of cases, arising under the Financial Services and Markets Act 2000 pursuant to the protection of consumers objective in that Act or under pensions legislation.

Trump International Golf Club Scotland Ltd v Scottish Ministers.[48] Given the caveat to allow for sensitivity to context, there is no reason to apply different general rules of interpretation to exemption clauses in trusts.

Of course, in construing an exemption clause in a trust, one needs to have regard to the general background of trusts law. This provides part of the relevant context for its interpretation. Thus references to mere 'fraud' may be taken to be only to the constructive equitable form of 'fraud' rather than actual fraud in the sense of full deceit: see *Armitage v Nurse*[49] and *Barnsley v Noble*.[50]

The factual matrix will also be relevant, as it is for contracts. As stated above, there is good reason to approach interpretation of trusts in an objective way as is done with contracts. Thus the identity of the trustee and the circumstances in which they assume that role may be significant. For example, in *Barnsley v Noble* one reason for construing an exemption clause widely so as to exclude all forms of trustee liability to pay compensation in the absence of dishonesty was that it was not plausible to suppose that the testator in relation to will trusts undertaken by his executors, including his widow and brother as well as professional trustees, 'would have wanted his widow and his brother to be at risk of personal liability to pay compensation in circumstances where they would naturally feel a personal bond and moral obligation to take on the potentially onerous task of being an executor of his will and had acted honestly' in performing their duties.[51]

Moreover, in some trustee cases where the trustee is not a paid professional appointed on the basis of their own standard terms, two different forms of the *contra proferentem* rule may be in tension, namely that which operates to resolve ambiguities against the person who prepared the document, on the one hand, and that which operates to limit the effect of an exemption clause, on the other.[52] It is not altogether clear which should prevail, and that may itself depend on an examination of overall fairness assessed in light of the factual matrix.

No doubt, on usual principles, the courts will be particularly astute to lean against any interpretation of an exemption clause which appeared to relieve a trustee from liability for dishonesty (compare the judgment of Millett LJ in *Armitage v Nurse*) or from the core incidents of the trust relationship (compare Penner's position). This follows from the usual objective interpretive approach to identify what a reasonable person in the position of the parties to the trust arrangement would understand was intended to be agreed by them. Interpretation giving especially strong weight to these factors is appropriate because of the stringency of the ordinary legal rules regarding imposition of liability on trustees in these sorts of cases, which in turn

[48] *Trump International Golf Club Scotland Ltd v Scottish Ministers* [2015] UKSC 74; [2016] 1 WLR 85 [33]–[34] (Lord Hodge JSC): the case concerned the interpretation of conditions attached to a grant of planning permission, but general principles of construction were stated. See also *Evangelou v McNicol* [2016] EWCA Civ 817 [18]–[24] (Beatson LJ), in relation to interpretation of the rules of an unincorporated association.

[49] *Armitage* (n 8) 250.

[50] *Barnsley v Noble* [2016] EWCA Civ 799.

[51] ibid [30] (Sales LJ).

[52] *Nobahar-Cookson v The Hut Group Ltd* [2016] EWCA Civ 128 [12]–[20] (Briggs LJ); *Chitty on Contracts* (n 29) para 15-012; E Peel, 'Contra Proferentem Revisited' (2017) 133 *LQR* 6.

reflects the moral values which the courts regard as informing the trust institution, by reason of the vulnerability of beneficiaries, where their property or interests are exposed to the discretion and decisions of a trustee. Similarly, the courts will be slow to find that a trustee has had his trust duties removed and transformed into simple contractual duties owed to a stranger to the trust.[53]

In *Photo Production Ltd v Securicor Transport Ltd*, Lord Diplock set out the interpretive approach to be adopted where a contractual exemption clause is in issue:

> ... it is, in my view, wrong to place a strained construction upon words in an exclusion clause which are clear and fairly susceptible of one meaning only *even after due allowance has been made for the presumption in favour of the implied primary and secondary obligations*.[54]

In the trusts context, the presumption in favour of the primary and secondary obligations is stronger still, for the reasons given above. There is clear scope for the courts to inject a considerable degree of moral value or 'substantive normativity,' to use Catherine Mitchell's language,[55] in structuring the trust relationship through an interpretive approach. This in turn suggests that it might be possible to accommodate the practical essence of the approaches of both Millett LJ and Penner at the level of interpretive principle, rather than trying to account for one or both of them as a rule of law. It may be that trust law is capable of having its own *Photo Production v Securicor* moment; but if it does, it seems desirable to give underlined emphasis in the trusts context to the passage in italics quoted above from the speech of Lord Diplock.

Perhaps the most promising way forward to accommodate the competing interests in this context is through an interpretive approach of this kind. It would give real substantive content to the usual expectation that the trust relationship carries with it an especially strong emphasis on honesty and good faith, while at the same time allowing a settlor who makes it crystal clear that he wishes for reasons of his own to depart from that usual expectation to do so. The strong moral dimension of the trust relationship and respect for settlor autonomy could be practically reconciled in this way.

It would also mean that the approach to interpretation of provisions in trust instruments is assimilated to the approach to interpretation of contracts and also statutes. In the modern interpretation of statutes, legal doctrine provides for a reconciliation of democratic principle (Parliament's right to choose what law to enact[56]) and rule of

[53] *Citibank* (n 7) [82] (Arden LJ), noted A Trukhtanov, 'The Irreducible Core of Trust Obligations' (2007) 123 *LQR* 342.

[54] *Securicor* (n 27) 851 (emphasis added). See also *HIH Casualty and General Insurance* (n 31).

[55] Mitchell (n 4) 479. See also JW Carter and W Courtney, 'Unexpressed Intention and Contract Construction' (2017) 37 *OJLS* 326 on the interaction of rules of law in contract and contractual interpretation. As they say at 328, the use of rules of law presumptively to resolve certain issues of unexpressed intention in the construction of contracts 'can be rationalised on the general basis that entry into a contract is an express commitment to the institution, and therefore an agreement for such issues to be resolved by applying the law of contract ... that is what each party has led the other reasonably to believe by entering into the contract'.

[56] The functional equivalent on this analogy with settlor autonomy.

law and human rights values[57] through the operation of strong presumptions in the interpretation of statutory provisions.[58] As I have written elsewhere:

> Statutes are legal instructions transmitted into an existing, highly developed framework of legal values and expectations. The existing law, modes of reasoning and established localised value systems provide the interpretive context in which a statute is read.[59]

Much the same can be said of an instrument which sets out the terms of a trust.

[57] The functional equivalent of background moral values.

[58] See *R v Secretary of State for the Home Department, ex p Simms* [2000] 2 AC 115, 131–32 (Lord Hoffmann); P Sales, 'Modern Statutory Interpretation' (2017) 38 *Statute Law Review* 125.

[59] Sales (n 58) 128. Also, for discussion of a similar model in the law of contract, see Carter and Courtney (n 55).

8

Professional Advice

MICHAEL ASHDOWN

I. INTRODUCTION

ALTHOUGH THE LEADING trusts and equity texts each set out a wide range of defences available to trustees alleged to have committed a breach of trust, no chapter headed 'professional advice' will be found in any of them.[1] Yet from the modern practitioner's perspective, this is now one of the most important defences, and certainly one of the most frequently deployed. In its simplest form, it entails a trustee saying 'I can't possibly have committed a breach of trust: I just did what my professional adviser told me to'. In the context of the modern trust 'industry', where the trustees of occupational pension schemes, charities and substantial private trusts are typically the recipients of extensive advice on all manner of relevant matters,[2] are often professionals themselves,[3] and in many cases would not dare to take any significant decision except on the footing of having first taken and considered relevant professional advice, this is a potent answer to allegations of trustee wrongdoing. But as a feature of English equity it is the most recent of innovations, dating only to the reworking of the so-called 'rule in *Re Hastings-Bass*' by the Court of Appeal in 2011,[4] and the confirmation of Lloyd LJ's important judgment by Lord Walker in the Supreme Court in 2013.[5] The subject matter of this chapter is not, therefore, one in which it falls to the author to pick apart a tangled body of case law. The challenge is rather the converse: to try to understand and explain, with very little assistance from the decided cases, the choices which have been and will continue to be made as to how this defence will function, and whom it will protect.

[1] See, eg, Lynton Tucker, Nicholas Le Poidevin and James Brightwell, *Lewin on Trusts* 19th edn (London, Sweet & Maxwell, 2015) ch 39; David Hayton, Paul Matthews and Charles Mitchell, *Underhill and Hayton: Law Relating to Trusts and Trustees* 19th edn (London, LexisNexis, 2016) ch 23; John McGhee (ed), *Snell's Equity* 33rd edn (London, Sweet & Maxwell, 2016) ch 30.

[2] Eg, legal, investment, governance, actuarial, commercial and property matters.

[3] Though not invariably: most occupational pension schemes must have at least one third of their trustees (or, if a corporate trustee, one third of the directors) chosen by the members and pensioners, pursuant to the Pensions Act 2004 (UK), ss 241–43.

[4] *Pitt v Holt* [2011] EWCA Civ 197; [2012] Ch 132.

[5] *Pitt v Holt* [2013] UKSC 26; [2013] 2 AC 108.

II. THE DEFENCE IN *PITT v HOLT*

'*Re Hastings-Bass*' claims are now governed by the decision of the Supreme Court in *Pitt v Holt*.[6] Giving the only judgment, Lord Walker took care to distinguish clearly between two categories of trustees' wrongdoing. The first comprises trustees acting outside of or in excess of their authority, who are strictly liable for their actions. This most obviously includes the trustee who purports to exercise a power of appointment in favour of a person who is not within the class of permitted objects. It would also include an exercise in breach of some other rule of law, such as (formerly, at least) the rule against perpetuities.[7] The second comprises trustees acting within the scope of their authority, but in a manner which amounts to a breach of trust. The paradigmatic example of the second category is the trustee who exercises a power properly conferred upon the trustee but on the basis of 'inadequate deliberation'—that is, failing to take account of relevant considerations, or taking account of irrelevant considerations—but this category is, in fact, wide enough to encompass any breach of trust which is not within the first type, as long as it is 'sufficiently serious as to amount to a breach of fiduciary duty'.[8]

A beneficiary bringing a claim in respect of inadequate deliberation[9] which has caused a monetary loss to the trust fund might seek to make the trustees liable to pay money into the trust by way of reconstitution of the position it would otherwise have been in, on the well-established principles of trust accounting.[10] More commonly, the beneficiary would ask the court to set aside the exercise of power, on the footing that the trustees' inadequate deliberation amounts to a breach of trust and renders the exercise voidable. The decision to set aside a voidable decision is a matter of discretion for the court, but one to be exercised in accordance with established principle, such as where the claimant is guilty of laches, or third-party rights have intervened.[11] This is usually the preferred course for claimants, because setting aside the trustees' decision can often make any monetary loss disappear. This is most apparent where the trustees have failed to give proper consideration to the tax consequences of their decision, and have thereby incurred a tax liability they might

[6] ibid.

[7] As in *Re Hastings-Bass* [1975] Ch 25 (CA) itself. See *Pitt v Holt* (UKSC) (n 5) [13]–[15].

[8] *Pitt v Holt* (UKSC) (n 5) [73].

[9] In the past *Re Hastings-Bass* claims were usually brought by trustees seeking to set aside their own decisions, often with the concurrence of their beneficiaries. But Lord Walker made clear in *Pitt v Holt* (UKSC) (n 5) [69] that 'in general it would be inappropriate for trustees to take the initiative in commencing proceedings of this nature'. In future, it will be for beneficiaries to decide whether to protect their own interests by bringing such proceedings.

[10] See *AIB Group (UK) plc v Mark Redler & Co Solicitors* [2014] UKSC 58; [2015] AC 1503 [51]–[56]; *Ultraframe (UK) Ltd v Fielding* [2005] EWHC 1638 (Ch); [2007] WTLR 835 [1513]. See also Robert Walker, 'Some Trust Principles in the Pensions Context' in AJ Oakley (ed), *Trends in Contemporary Trust Law* (Oxford, Clarendon Press, 1996) 125; Robert Chambers, 'Liability' in Peter Birks and Arianna Pretto (eds), *Breach of Trust* (Oxford, Hart Publishing, 2002) 16–17; Charles Mitchell and Stephen Watterson, 'Remedies for Knowing Receipt' in Charles Mitchell (ed), *Constructive and Resulting Trusts* (Oxford, Hart Publishing, 2010) 123–25; *Lewin on Trusts* (n 1) paras 39-002–39-010.

[11] *Pitt v Holt* (UKSC) (n 5) [93]. See also: *Abacus Trust Co (Isle of Man) Ltd v Barr* [2003] EWHC 114 (Ch); [2003] Ch 409 [30]–[33]; Dominic O'Sullivan, Steven Elliott and Rafal Zakrzewki, *The Law of Rescission* 2nd edn (Oxford, Oxford University Press, 2014) pts V and VI.

otherwise have avoided. For example, under the Inheritance Tax Act 1984 (UK), when a chargeable transfer is set aside, liability to inheritance tax is recalculated as if the transfer had been void *ab initio*, and overpaid tax is repaid.[12]

Before *Pitt v Holt*, trustees often admitted that they were guilty of inadequate deliberation, sometimes in concert with beneficiaries, in order to procure the court to declare their decision to be void.[13] But this is now a risky course to take, since it necessarily entails admitting a breach of trust, with no guarantee that the court will set aside the decision taken: it might be upheld on the basis of one of the usual equitable bars,[14] or even on policy grounds. In *Pitt v Holt* Lord Walker expressly envisaged that:[15]

> [i]n some cases of artificial tax avoidance the court might think it right to refuse relief, either on the ground that such claimants, acting on supposedly expert advice, must be taken to have accepted the risk that the scheme would prove ineffective, or on the ground that discretionary relief should be refused on grounds of public policy.

A trustee whose questionable decision was motivated by tax planning considerations might well take pause to consider whether she could be sure of the court being willing to undo what had been done. If it did not, the trustee would likely be left bearing the loss to the trust fund.[16]

Trustees in the post-*Pitt v Holt* world are consequently much more likely to seek to defend themselves from any inadequate deliberation claim, and benefit from a stout defence fashioned by the Supreme Court for precisely this purpose. Lord Walker held that:[17]

> Trustees may be liable, even if they have obtained apparently competent professional advice, if they act outside the scope of their powers (excessive execution), or contrary to the general law ... That can be seen as a form of strict liability in that it is imposed regardless of personal fault. Trustees may also be in breach of duty in failing to give proper consideration to the exercise of their discretionary powers, and a failure to take professional advice may amount to, or contribute to, a flawed decision-making process. *But it would be contrary to principle and authority to impose a form of strict liability on Trustees who conscientiously*

[12] Inheritance Tax Act 1984 (UK), s 150. There is no equivalent express provision in relation to income tax or capital gains tax, although in the Court of Appeal in *Pitt v Holt* HMRC was prepared to proceed on the basis (without making any concession) that the position was the same in relation to those taxes: *Pitt v Holt* (CA) (n 4) [91].

[13] See *Futter v Futter* [2010] EWHC 449 (Ch); [2010] STC 982 [2]; *Pitt v Holt* (CA) (n 4) [130]; *Pitt v Holt* (UKSC) (n 5) [69]. See also *Green v Cobham* [2002] STC 820 (Ch D) 822; *Abacus Trust Co (Isle of Man) Ltd v NSPCC* [2001] STC 1344 (Ch D)[1]; *Abacus Trust Co (Isle of Man) Ltd v Barr* (n 11) [1], [2], [12]; *Sieff v Fox* [2005] EWHC 1312 (Ch); [2005] 1 WLR 3811 [1], [2], [28].

[14] See text to n 11.

[15] *Pitt v Holt* (UKSC) (n 5) [135].

[16] Subject to the defences ordinarily available in respect of any breach of trust, including the acquiescence or consent of the beneficiaries, and any exoneration clause in the trust instrument. However, a trustee guilty of inadequate deliberation would be unlikely to obtain relief under the Trustee Act 1925 (UK), s 61, on the footing that she 'acted honestly and reasonably, and ought fairly to be excused', because the individual fault inherent in a finding of 'inadequate deliberation' would usually be inconsistent with finding that the trustee acted 'reasonably'. See Michael Ashdown, *Trustee Decision Making: The Rule in Re Hastings-Bass* (Oxford, Oxford University Press, 2015) paras 5.36–5.40.

[17] *Pitt v Holt* (UKSC) (n 5) [80] (emphasis added).

> *obtain and follow, in making a decision which is within the scope of their powers, apparently competent professional advice which turns out to be wrong.*

The defence is comprised of four elements: that trustees (i) obtained 'professional advice'; (ii) did so 'conscientiously'; (iii) followed the advice received; and (iv) the advice was 'apparently competent'. None of these is entirely straightforward, and each will in future involve the courts in making choices about the scope and operation of the defence. But in order to understand and evaluate the choices that are to be made here, it is important to appreciate the principled basis for the existence of the defence. This is derived from Lord Walker's (and, in the Court of Appeal, Lloyd LJ's) approach to the operation of the *Re Hastings-Bass* principle. The law as it developed prior to *Pitt v Holt* was exemplified by the judgment of Lloyd LJ[18] in *Sieff v Fox*,[19] which treated the principle as founded primarily on whether the effect of the trustees' exercise of discretionary power was different to what they expected it to be, and 'whether, if they had not misunderstood the effect that their actual exercise of the discretionary power would have, they would have acted differently'.[20] Lloyd LJ expressly doubted that 'the application of the doctrine should be regarded as depending on a breach of duty, and whether its consequences should be aligned with those of a breach of trust'.[21] In contrast, in *Pitt v Holt* Lord Walker preferred the approach of Lightman J in *Abacus Trust Co (Isle of Man) Ltd v Barr*[22] and held that:[23]

> Breach of duty is essential (in the full sense of that word) because it is only a breach of duty on the part of the trustees that entitles the court to intervene ... It is not enough to show that the trustees' deliberations have fallen short of the highest possible standards, or that the court would, on a surrender of discretion by the trustees, have acted in a different way. Apart from exceptional circumstances (such as an impasse reached by honest and reasonable trustees) only breach of fiduciary duty justifies judicial intervention.

In other words, a successful inadequate deliberation claim will necessarily involve the court criticising the conduct of one or more trustees, whose failure must have gone beyond merely 'fall[ing] short of the highest standards of mature deliberation and judgment'.[24] That there can be no 'inadequate deliberation' without blameworthy conduct by a trustee is emphasised by Lord Walker's acceptance[25] that trustees who act in accordance with 'skilled professional advice' would commit a breach of trust only where they act 'outside the scope of their powers ... or contrary to the general law'.[26] On this analysis, breach of trust and reliance on professional advice

[18] This was the last case heard by Lloyd J (as he then was) as a Judge of the Chancery Division of the High Court, and he was elevated to the Court of Appeal prior to giving judgment.

[19] *Sieff v Fox* (n 13).

[20] ibid [77].

[21] ibid [80]. Lightman J's contrary view in *Abacus Trust Co (Isle of Man) Ltd v Barr* (n 11) was cited before Lloyd LJ and considered at [68]–[72].

[22] *Abacus Trust Co (Isle of Man) Ltd v Barr* (n 11).

[23] *Pitt v Holt* (UKSC) (n 5) [73].

[24] ibid [68].

[25] ibid [78]–[80].

[26] ibid [80].

are really just opposite sides of the same coin: an 'inadequate deliberation' claim will only succeed where the claimant can show that the trustee ought to have acted differently in the circumstances; trustees cannot fairly be criticised for not acting differently if they acted in accordance with apparently competent professional advice.[27] Whether the advice was right or wrong, the trustee who followed it in good faith could not reasonably have been expected to do anything else. No personal culpability means no breach of duty, and so no *Re Hastings-Bass* liability. This principle is the foundation of Lord Walker's re-analysis of the *Re Hastings-Bass* rule, and the justification for his expression of the professional advice defence[28] and it will determine its limits and contours as the detailed operation of the defence falls to be worked out in future cases.

III. WHAT IS PROFESSIONAL ADVICE?

The first element of the defence might be thought to be straightforward, in practice at least, if not in precise definition. Trustees may require advice on all sorts of matters which are beyond their own expertise. Legal and financial advice may be much the most common, but trustees may properly take advice on any matter which arises in the performance of their functions.[29] A precise definition of who counts as a 'professional' for these purposes may be open to argument in future cases, but the problem is essentially a practical one—and the court has in fact troubled itself relatively little with the analogous question of identifying an 'expert' for the purposes of opinion evidence given pursuant to CPR r 35.[30]

However, a more significant difficulty arises from the compendious nature of the term 'professional advice', which in practice encompasses a number of quite distinct types of advice. In the course of argument in *British Airways plc v Airways Pension Scheme Trustee Ltd*,[31] an exchange between leading counsel and Morgan J brought out a possible three-fold distinction as to the type of advice a trustee might take in relation to a matter subsequently alleged to be the subject of

[27] The 'defence' of professional advice therefore appears to operate by negating a constituent element of the 'inadequate deliberation' cause of action against a trustee, rather than as a free-standing defence. Whether it follows that the burden of proof in an 'inadequate deliberation' claim should not be upon the defendant trustee to establish reliance on professional advice, but rather upon the claimant to establish its absence, does not appear to have been considered in the case law or literature.

[28] Ie the final sentence of *Pitt v Holt* (UKSC) (n 5) [80].

[29] The cost of such advice is an expense properly chargeable to the trust fund: Trustee Act 2000 (UK), s 31. See also Trustee Act 2000 (UK), s 11; *Lewin on Trusts* (n 1) ch 21, especially para 21-033.

[30] See Civil Evidence Act 1972 (UK), s 3; Hodge M Malek and others (eds), *Phipson on Evidence* 18th edn (London, Sweet & Maxwell, 2013) para 33-24; Adrian Zuckerman, *Zuckerman on Civil Procedure: Principles of Practice* 3rd edn (London, Sweet & Maxwell, 2013) paras 21.13–21.14; Tristram Hodgkinson and Mark James, *Expert Evidence: Law and Practice* 4th edn (London, Sweet & Maxwell, 2014) paras 1-027–1-1028.

[31] *British Airways plc v Airways Pension Scheme Trustee Ltd* [2017] EWHC 1191 (Ch). Morgan J gave British Airways permission to appeal on 25 May 2017, and the appeal is due to be heard from 1 May 2018.

inadequate deliberation.[32] Type 1[33] is advice as to the identity of the relevant considerations. This would include advising the trustees to take a particular matter into account, and also advising them to exclude some matter as irrelevant. Type 2 is advice as to the content of a particular consideration. Type 3 is advice as to how the trustees should weigh the competing considerations when making a decision. For example, if the trustees were proposing to exercise a power of appointment, they might be advised that they must take account of the inheritance tax consequences of the exercise (type-1 advice), what the inheritance tax consequences would be (type-2 advice) and that they should (or should not) prioritise the other benefits of the exercise over the inheritance tax liability to be incurred (type-3 advice).

Type-2 advice is the most straightforward, and is the sort of advice that the *Re Hastings-Bass* cases are primarily concerned with. Most commonly, the problem is an assessment of likely tax liability which transpires to be incorrect.[34] The Supreme Court's decision in *Pitt v Holt* is the clearest authority that trustees who take and act on such advice do not commit a breach of trust.[35] A slightly more complex case is possible if the trustees do not receive the advice they should. For example, consider a situation where trustees say to their advisers 'we propose to exercise this power, advise us on the tax consequences' and the advice given is that 'there will be no adverse inheritance tax consequences'—but the advisers have omitted to consider the possibility of adverse capital gains tax consequences. In this case a beneficiary seeking to set aside the trustees' decision might argue that the capital gains tax consequences of the exercise of the power were undoubtedly a relevant consideration, and one in relation to which the trustees did not receive 'professional advice' and therefore could not rely on the professional advice defence. But that would be to take a very narrow view of the Supreme Court's approach in *Pitt v Holt*. It would be tantamount to requiring trustees not only to take appropriate professional advice[36] but also to make sure that their professional advisers fully address everything required to give that advice. Since the point of using professional advisers is usually that the relevant field is inaccessible to lay people without the benefit of the adviser's expertise, this is simply unrealistic. To criticise trustees for failing to appreciate that their professional advisers have gone wrong would certainly be to require the 'highest possible standards' of decision-making, contrary to Lord Walker's analysis.[37]

[32] Morgan J ultimately concluded (ibid [635]) that the trustees did in fact have regard to all relevant and no irrelevant considerations, and therefore (at [632]) that he did not have to decide whether 'any flaw in their approach should be excused on the ground that they were relying on professional advice'. The interesting questions which arose in the course of argument as to the scope of the professional advice defence were consequently not addressed in the judgment of the Court.

[33] The nomenclature as 'type 1', 'type 2' and 'type 3' is the author's, adopted for the purpose of exposition only.

[34] Eg *Burrell v Burrell* [2005] EWHC 245 (Ch); [2005] STC 569 [5], [8]–[12]; *Sieff v Fox* (n 13) [16]–[26].

[35] *Pitt v Holt* (UKSC) (n 5) [47]–[48], [54], [95]–[98].

[36] English trust law encourages trustees to make full use of professional advisers. Such advice assists them to make better decisions, and so benefits both trustees and beneficiaries: S Gardner, *An Introduction to the Law of Trusts* 3rd edn (Oxford, Clarendon Press, 2011) 193. See also Ashdown (n 16) paras 8.07–8.08.

[37] See text to n 23 and following.

The better view, consistent with the requirement of individual trustee fault for a finding of inadequate deliberation, is that it is for a professional adviser to ascertain precisely what is required in order to give the advice requested. The adviser is bound by the terms of his or her instructions—and the trustees will therefore not be protected if they do not instruct their advisers in terms sufficiently wide to encompass the advice required—but the trustees are entitled to assume that the advice given in response to those instructions is accurate and complete, save to the extent that the advice given is not 'apparently competent'.[38]

The more difficult question is whether type-1 advice affords a defence to trustees who act upon it. The starting point must be that nothing in Lord Walker's statement of the defence in *Pitt v Holt*[39] appears to rule out such a defence; there is no obvious reason why legal advice as to what is or is not a relevant consideration cannot be conscientiously obtained and followed by lay trustees like any other advice. However, in the course of argument in *British Airways plc v Airways Pension Scheme Trustee Ltd*[40] it was suggested that type-1 advice might be different. Type 1 advice is necessarily legal advice, since whether a factual consideration is one which the trustees must or must not consider is a question of law—it is a question of applying the *Re Hastings-Bass* rule in accordance with *Pitt v Holt*.[41] It was consequently suggested that to allow trustees to defend their decisions on this basis would be to oust in part the jurisdiction of the court to supervise trustees and their decision-making. On this view, a question of law must always be for the court's ultimate determination. To allow type-1 advice to afford a defence would be to allow trustees not only to take valid decisions on the basis of a wrong understanding of some relevant consideration (as where the type-2 advice they receive proves to be wrong) but to approach the decision-making process itself in the wrong way. There is some tentative support for this approach in *Top Brands Ltd v Sharma*,[42] one of the very few *Re Hastings-Bass* cases to have been decided since *Pitt v Holt*. The Court in that case had to consider reliance on professional advice in the context of a liquidator alleged to have acted in breach of duty. HHJ Barker QC held that 'a liquidator will not have taken proper advice where the instructions to the adviser were flawed (partial or incorrect) by reason of a failure on the part of the liquidator to identify relevant considerations'[43] and so appeared to rule out the possibility that the defence might itself be based on (wrong) advice as to what the relevant considerations were.

However, despite the superficial appeal of the proposed distinction, it is not well founded, and the better view is that trustees should be afforded the same defence by their reliance on type-1 advice as for type-2 advice. That type-1 advice is invariably

[38] See text to n 70 and following.

[39] See text to n 17.

[40] *British Airways plc v Airways Pension Scheme Trustee Ltd* (n 31). This point is not addressed in Morgan J's judgment, for the reasons explained at n 32.

[41] Albeit that in fact working out whether a consideration is one which the trustees must or must not take account of is not at all straightforward, the law still being very unclear as to the test for identifying relevant and irrelevant considerations. See *Pitt v Holt* (CA) (n 4) [118]; *Pitt v Holt* (UKSC) (n 5) [65], [66], [70]; Ashdown (n 16) paras 5.03–5.10.

[42] *Top Brands Ltd v Sharma* [2014] EWHC 2753 (Ch); [2015] 2 All ER 581.

[43] ibid [33].

legal is no basis for a meaningful distinction: the type-2 advice most commonly seen in the reported cases is (wrong) legal advice as to the tax consequences of a transaction.[44] The court is fully able to determine the true legal position whilst acknowledging that the trustees acted properly in the circumstances in which they found themselves by following the advice they received, and so committed no breach of trust. Furthermore, there is no real ouster of the court's jurisdiction in affording a defence based on type-1 advice. That trustees have acted on such advice would not preclude the court from refusing to give its blessing to a proposed decision,[45] or even to grant an injunction preventing the trustees from acting in the manner proposed.[46] In an appropriate case the court might even think it appropriate to exercise its inherent jurisdiction to remove trustees.[47] The *Pitt v Holt* reformulation of the *Re Hastings-Bass* rule is not about the court's ability to supervise trustees, which remains unaffected, but concerns the fault-based liability of trustees for their own past conduct. Indeed, the argument that the court's intervention in *Re Hastings-Bass* cases was merely an aspect of the supervisory jurisdiction over trusts, and was not dependent on establishing trustee fault, was pressed on the Supreme Court but ultimately rejected.[48]

As a matter of authority, HHJ Barker QC's statement in *Top Brands* is far from definitive on this point. The judge refers to the adviser's instructions being 'flawed (partial or incorrect) by reason of a failure on the part of the liquidator to identify relevant considerations'. This could be read as simply making the obvious point in relation to type-2 advice: that trustees are not protected where their advisers do not advise because the trustees have not asked. A trustee who appreciates an inheritance tax risk arising out of a proposed decision, but does not note the possibility of capital gains tax arising from the same, does not have a defence if inheritance tax advice only is requested and received. In HHJ Barker QC's language, the instructions are '*flawed*' as they did not identify capital gains tax. That is an entirely different situation from the same trustee asking her lawyer whether both inheritance tax and capital gains tax should be considered, and being told to consider inheritance tax but to ignore capital gains tax as irrelevant. However, if HHJ Barker QC were understood to be saying that a trustee's failure to appreciate relevant considerations would put the trustee beyond saving by reliance on professional advice, then this would effectively be to impose strict liability on the trustee for her default. But such an approach would be inconsistent with Lord Walker's reformulation of the *Re Hastings-Bass* rule in *Pitt v Holt*, which depends for its principled foundation on distinguishing trustees' decisions which are outside their powers from 'inadequate deliberation' *intra vires*.[49] If a trustee were strictly liable for failing to appreciate the existence of

[44] See text to n 34.

[45] Pursuant to the *Public Trustee v Cooper* [2001] WTLR 901 (Ch D) jurisdiction. See *Lewin on Trusts* (n 1) para 27–069ff.

[46] See *Lewin on Trusts* (n 1) paras 38-010–38-015.

[47] *Re Harrison's Settlement Trusts* [1965] 1 WLR 1492 (Ch D) 1497. See *Lewin on Trusts* (n 1) paras 13-062–13-073.

[48] *Pitt v Holt* (UKSC) (n 5) [71]–[76]. See also R Wilson, 'Trustee Mistakes Post-Futter and Pitt' (2013) 19 *Trusts & Trustees* 975, 979.

[49] *Pitt v Holt* (UKSC) (n 5) [60], [78]–[80].

a relevant consideration and consequently for failing to take account of its content, then the trustee would be treated as if within Lord Walker's first category of 'excessive execution'[50] or *ultra vires*, where fault is irrelevant, despite Lord Walker treating 'inadequate deliberation' as being in the second category of *intra vires* breach of trust,[51] and a failure to take a relevant matter into account as the paradigm of such 'inadequate deliberation.'[52]

This is really just another way of putting Lord Walker's central proposition in *Pitt v Holt*: that trustees only commit a breach of trust by 'inadequate deliberation' where they are individually at fault. The equivalent treatment of type 1 and type-2 advice cases must follow from this touchstone. The question to be asked in any case of alleged 'inadequate deliberation' is: what could the trustees reasonably have been expected to do in the circumstances in which they found themselves? Approached in this way, the question in a type-1 advice case is: what should the court expect trustees to do when advised by their apparently competent lawyers that a particular matter must be taken into account, or must be excluded? To pose the question in this form is to answer it: it would be absurd to treat lay trustees as being at fault for not knowing the law better than their professional legal advisers. Lay trustees should follow the advice they receive, unless there is good and apparent reason to doubt it. It is hard to see how it would ever be consistent with Lord Walker's approach, or indeed would promote good quality decision-making by trustees, for trustees to be expected to do the opposite of what their advisers recommend.[53]

Type-3 advice is advice as to the weighing of competing considerations. It is the advice given by lawyers especially when, having given full advice on what the relevant considerations are and their content, they are asked by their bemused trustee clients 'but what should we actually do?' To the client this seems a wholly reasonable question: they have asked for professional advice as to how they should exercise of a power of appointment, but what they have received in reply is a lengthy list of matters, some of which may be quite complex, together with the firm injunction to weigh the matters in their own minds before reaching a decision. But this form of advice, as unhelpful as the trustees may consider it to be, reflects the long-standing policy of the law, most pithily expressed by Robert Walker J (as then was) in *Scott v National Trust*: that it is 'for advisers to advise and for trustees to decide: trustees may not (except in so far as they are authorised to do so) delegate the exercise of their discretions, even to experts'.[54] Once the trustees have been properly advised as to the scope of their powers, what the relevant considerations are and their content, and what they must exclude as irrelevant, the process of weighing and reaching conclusions is for the trustees alone.

What then of trustees who do persuade their adviser to express a view on the outcome of the decision-making process? It appears very unlikely that such advice

[50] ibid [60].
[51] See text to n 8.
[52] See *Pitt v Holt* (UKSC) (n 5) [70] (Lord Walker) approving *Pitt v Holt* (CA) (n 4) [127] (Lloyd LJ).
[53] See text to n 71 and following.
[54] *Scott v National Trust for Places of Historic Interest or Natural Beauty* [1998] 2 All ER 705 (Ch D) 717.

would be treated as affording a defence to the trustees, despite the wide wording used by Lord Walker in describing the defence, which does not explicitly rule it out. To do so would be to cut across a core principle of the law of trusts: that the court will not interfere in trustees' discretionary decisions, as long as they are *intra vires*, taken in good faith and for proper purposes, and (at least since the rule in *Re Hastings-Bass* came into being) not in breach of duty. The decision of the House of Lords to this effect in *Gisborne v Gisborne*[55] has never been seriously called into question.[56] In other words, *Pitt v Holt* does not establish a new defence in relation to type-3 advice because no defence is needed: the process of balancing relevant considerations and reaching a conclusion is simply not open to challenge as 'inadequate deliberation'. When Lord Walker said that trustees 'who conscientiously obtain and follow … apparently competent professional advice'[57] do not commit a breach of duty, it is not likely that he meant implicitly to undermine the *Gisborne* doctrine. Rather, this statement should be understood as applying to those matters in relation to which the trustees must inform themselves in order to be in a position to make a proper decision—that is, what the relevant considerations are, and their content. It need not (and ought not) apply to the judgement the trustees exercise and the choices they make in the light of that information. Indeed, the court, if confronted with an attempted defence based on type-3 advice, might well see a risk in accepting such a submission: to give special protection to trustees who weighed competing considerations as their professional advisers directed would not merely allow trustees to abdicate responsibility for their own ultimate decision, but could open the door to trustees in future being criticised for reaching a different conclusion than that recommended by their advisers. That would wholly subvert the *Gisborne* doctrine, and, contrary to Robert Walker J's dictum in *Scott v National Trust*, would put advisers in ultimate charge of the exercise of powers conferred upon trustees. This does not, however, mean that it would be inappropriate for a professional adviser to give such type-3 advice, as long as the limits of reliance upon it are made clear to the trustees. In some cases it may also be incumbent upon the adviser to make clear that certain matters are of special importance. An obvious example would be very seriously adverse tax consequences, which must be brought home to the trustees. Another would be the obligation of the trustees of an occupational pension scheme to ensure the security of members' and pensioners' accrued rights to future benefits. But in each case it remains for the trustees to take the final decision.

Finally, there may be situations in which it is not clear whether what is said by an adviser is professional advice at all, of any of the types set out above. A practical example is the lawyer who somewhat hedges her bets on the trustees' proposed decision by saying that what the trustees intend to do would be 'very difficult', but does

[55] *Gisborne v Gisborne* (1877) 2 App Cas 300 (HL).

[56] See *Re Beloved Wilkes's Charity* (1851) 3 Mac & G 440; 42 ER 330; *Tabor v Brooks* (1878) 10 Ch D 273 (Ch D); *Tempest v Lord Camoys* (1882) 21 Ch D 571 (CA) 578; *Board of Management for Dundee General Hospital v Bell's Trustees* 1952 SC (HL) 78; *Re Allen-Meyrick's Will Trusts* [1966] 1 WLR 499 (Ch D) 503; *Re Londonderry's Settlement* [1965] Ch 918 (CA) 936; *Sieff v Fox* (n 13) [37]. See also *Pitt v Holt* (CA) (n 4) [110]–[113]; Maurice Cullity, 'Judicial Control of Trustees' Discretions' (1975) 25 *University of Toronto Law Journal* 99; Ashdown (n 16) paras 3.31–3.38.

[57] *Pitt v Holt* (UKSC) (n 5) [80].

not rule it out. In argument in *British Airways plc v Airways Pension Scheme Trustee Ltd*,[58] Morgan J tended to the view that such 'advice' would usually be an expression of mere personal opinion, and would not qualify as 'professional advice' for the purposes of the *Pitt v Holt* defence. This may just amount to saying that type-3 advice is not really advice at all, or at least that there is little to distinguish type-3 advice from statements which are not professional advice, on the assumption that advice that a proposed course of action would be 'very difficult' is really advice that the trustees *could* properly do what they propose, but the adviser would not herself reach the same conclusion.[59] But there is a risk that this analysis can easily be taken too far, so as to rule out from the professional advice defence much advice given informally or in compressed form. The proper starting point is that the advice must be properly construed and understood before it is written off as mere personal opinion. A professional adviser who says that a proposed action is 'very difficult' may simply mean that she would prefer some other course, based on a different weighing of competing considerations. But such an adviser might also be using words such as 'very difficult' as a shorthand for something else. For example, the trustees may have been advised that if they exercise a power to exclude a particular beneficiary from benefit under the trust, there will be a tax advantage. They ask their solicitor for advice, and are told 'you have the power to exclude this beneficiary, but it would be very difficult …' The solicitor may be giving this advice because she has carefully considered the beneficiary's position, and has concluded that if the beneficiary were to respond to the exclusion by bringing a claim against the trustees, there would be a 40 per cent chance of success. She might also be aware that this beneficiary is notoriously litigious, and inclined to be difficult during the litigation process. She might therefore conclude that the trustees, if they were to exercise the power, would likely be faced with a claim, and would have good—but not certain—prospects of successfully defending it. These are of course all matters upon which a solicitor could (and should) give professional legal advice. The character of that advice is plainly not changed by the solicitor summing these matters up by saying that it would be 'very difficult' for the trustees to exclude the beneficiary, such that this fairly ordinary legal advice should be treated as no advice at all.

IV. WAS THE ADVICE CONSCIENTIOUSLY OBTAINED?

The second element of the defence is that trustees must 'conscientiously obtain'[60] the professional advice they seek to rely upon. This followed from Lloyd LJ's statement in the Court of Appeal that trustees could rely upon professional advice by way of defence 'unless the process of taking and acting on the advice is itself open to challenge in some way'.[61] Lord Walker also quoted[62] from the judgment of Lightman J

[58] *British Airways plc v Airways Pension Scheme Trustee Ltd* (n 31).
[59] This point is not addressed in Morgan J's judgment, for the reasons explained at n 32.
[60] *Pitt v Holt* (UKSC) (n 5) [80].
[61] *Pitt v Holt* (CA) (n 4) [124].
[62] *Pitt v Holt* (UKSC) (n 5) [40].

in *Abacus Trust Co (Isle of Man) v Barr*, which afforded a defence to a trustee who 'identified the relevant considerations and used all proper care and diligence in obtaining the relevant information and advice relating to those considerations'.[63] To the extent that a failure to obtain professional advice 'conscientiously' is reflected in a failure to give adequate instructions, then trustees may find themselves outside the scope of the defence altogether, where in consequence of their error they have not obtained 'professional advice' in relation to the relevant consideration in issue. More difficult (though in practice likely to be much less common) is the situation where the process of obtaining professional advice is itself tainted by wrongdoing. This was British Airways' pleaded case in *British Airways plc v Airways Pension Scheme Trustee Ltd*.[64] British Airways alleged, and the defendant trustees of the Airways Pension Scheme denied, that the trustees had pressed their professional actuarial adviser to adapt and modify his advice over the course of several years, in order to obtain the advice they wished to receive. Although the trustees prevailed over British Airways at trial,[65] this serves as an example of the kind of real scenario in which the second element of the defence may prove to be crucial.

The principled basis for the requirement to 'conscientiously obtain' advice is clear from the foundations of the defence already discussed. The professional advice defence operates by negating individual fault on the part of a trustee. But where the trustee is acting improperly in seeking the advice in the first place, the trustee remains at fault, and that fault is not negated by the advice. Most obviously, the defence presupposes that the trustee obtains advice in order to inform her decision: it is obtaining and considering the advice which prevents the trustee's deliberation from being inadequate. But where the advice is obtained for some other purpose than genuinely to inform her decision, the trustee is outside the scope of the defence. This will necessarily be the case where advice is not obtained in good faith, or is obtained for an improper or foreign purpose, as where the purpose of obtaining the advice is not to guide the trustees prospectively, but merely to provide justification for a course already set.[66] It remains an open question whether mere carelessness in the process of obtaining advice should preclude reliance on the professional advice defence. In practice, this may resolve into the issue explained above as to the instructions given: if the carelessness results in inadequate instructions, then the advice may simply be insufficient to protect the trustees, irrespective of how obtained; if the instructions given are satisfactory despite the trustees' carelessness, then there is no obvious reason of policy or principle why the trustees, having acted on that advice, should not be entitled to rely upon it, just as a more diligent trustee who had obtained identical advice would be entitled to.

[63] *Abacus Trust Co (Isle of Man) Ltd v Barr* (n 11) [23]. See also *Top Brands Ltd v Sharma* (n 42) [33].

[64] *British Airways plc v Airways Pension Scheme Trustee Ltd* (n 31).

[65] The Court did not ultimately have to decide whether, if British Airways' allegations were proved, the trustees would be deprived of the professional advice defence: see n 32.

[66] *cf* Millett LJ in *Armitage v Nurse* [1998] Ch 241 (CA) 254, holding that 'a trustee who relied on the presence of a trustee exemption clause to justify what he proposed to do would thereby lose its protection'.

V. DID THE TRUSTEES FOLLOW THE ADVICE?

Whether trustees have in fact followed the professional advice they obtained is primarily a question of fact, to be answered by reference to the advice given, and any evidence of the steps the trustees took in reliance upon it. It will typically entail showing that the trustees took account of the advice in considering how to exercise their power, irrespective of what they ultimately decided.

The position may be more factually complex where advice is given on several topics, and the court must isolate the advice which is in fact relied upon in relation to a particular exercise of power or discretion. Similarly, in some cases the advice itself may be ambiguous. For example, an experienced private client solicitor might give her trustee clients tax advice, but warn that, although she is sure that her advice is correct, the trustees should nevertheless seek confirmation from specialist tax counsel before acting upon it. If the trustees are content to rely upon their solicitor's advice and decline to expend further trust funds on counsel's advice, have they 'followed' their solicitor's advice? Plainly, they have not followed it to the letter. On the other hand, there is nothing intrinsically dubious about the advice they have obtained, nor any defect in the process of obtaining it. It may be that more authoritative advice is obtainable, but it would be wrong to restrict the operation of the defence only to trustees who have taken the best possible advice.[67] The starting point must be to characterise the advice given by the solicitor: was the solicitor giving professional tax advice, but suggesting a second opinion from tax counsel to confirm; or was she effectively saying that she could not say what the tax consequences would be, and that tax counsel should therefore be consulted to obtain that advice? If the former, then the professional advice has essentially been followed. Lord Walker was quite explicit about not requiring perfection of trustees.[68] If the latter, the trustees have not in fact received professional advice on the tax position upon which they could rely. As with the question of ambiguous advice discussed above,[69] the answer will generally become clear once the advice given is precisely understood.

The court's degree of tolerance for the imperfect following of advice is really a question of policy. Plainly the court must keep the defence tied to its principled basis by restricting it to trustees whose reliance on professional advice negates individual fault. Trustees who do not diligently follow the advice received may be seen as sufficiently at fault to justify treating them as guilty of inadequate deliberation. But an overly strict approach would be likely to exclude from the defence those trustees who have followed the essentials of the advice obtained, and where a more rigorously compliant approach to the advice by the trustees would have made no difference to the outcome of their decision. What is required here is a pragmatic approach, operated case by case, and focused on whether the trustees' conduct is open to proper criticism for the approach they took to the advice they received.

[67] See text to n 71 and following.
[68] *Pitt v Holt* (UKSC) (n 5) [68].
[69] See text to n 67.

VI. WAS THE ADVICE APPARENTLY COMPETENT?

The final element of the defence is that the advice given was 'apparently competent'.[70] In other words, trustees will only be entitled to the professional advice defence where it was reasonable for them to obtain and act upon the advice they now rely upon. What is reasonable in the circumstances will always be fact sensitive, but the starting point must be that lay trustees will not be at fault if they assume that their professional advisers know much more about their own field of expertise than they do: there is no obligation on trustees to, for example, second-guess the legal expertise of their lawyers. It is perfectly reasonable for lay trustees to rely on legal advice which would appear wrong, even obviously wrong, to other lawyers and to the court. As in relation to all other elements of the professional advice defence, the touchstone is the individual fault of the trustee: is she properly open to criticism for acting as she did, in the circumstances in which she found herself?[71] Such a trustee will be free of individual fault where she acts on advice she reasonably believes to be satisfactory—which typically will entail no more than that the advice comes from a reputable source and that the trustee has no reason to believe that it is not satisfactory. The requirement that the advice be 'apparently competent' consequently serves to rule out of the scope of the defence, first, the trustee who knowingly acts on advice she does not believe to be satisfactory and, second, the trustee who does not act reasonably to obtain advice appropriate to the circumstances.

As to the first of these, a trustee who knows or believes the advice she has been given to be wrong will plainly not be free of fault in acting upon it. To afford a defence to such a trustee would be inconsistent with Lightman J's requirement that the trustee has 'used all proper care and diligence in obtaining the relevant information and advice'[72] and with the very purpose of the *Pitt v Holt* formulation of the *Re Hastings-Bass* rule, which at its heart is about ensuring that (within reason) trustees take properly informed decisions: a trustee who chose to act on advice known to be wrong or inadequate would be guilty of deliberately 'inadequate deliberation'. What of the trustee who professes not to have realised that the advice obtained was hopelessly wrong? There must logically come a point at which a reasonable lay trustee would see that the advice given was so obviously wrong-headed or insufficient that she would not seek to rely upon it. In other words, the advice is not 'apparently competent' because it no longer maintains even a veneer of competence. In practice this is most likely not where the advice reaches a wrong conclusion based on mistakes in relation to the specialist knowledge or analysis of the adviser (which could be expected to be outside the understanding of the trustee), but rather where the advice overlooks a key issue or proceeds on a mistaken factual premise. But the court must be careful not to allow, without more, the inference that because it considers the advice given to have been seriously wrong, the trustee ought to have appreciated this. The risk is particularly high in relation to legal advice, where it may

[70] *Pitt v Holt* (UKSC) (n 5) [80].
[71] See text to n 24 and following.
[72] *Abacus Trust Co (Isle of Man) Ltd v Barr* (n 11) [23].

seem absolutely plain to the court and to all the lawyers involved that the advice was wrong. But reliance on wrong advice is the very reason for the existence of the defence: it will only need to be relied upon where 'apparently competent professional advice ... turns out to be wrong'.[73] The court must instead put itself in the shoes of a reasonable lay trustee and ask: what else should the trustee have done?

As to the second, it is important, if the defence is to remain practically useful, that the court not be too exacting as to the advice a trustee should obtain. After all, it is almost invariably open to the trustees to get 'better' advice, whether from other solicitors, from junior or leading counsel, or by way of application to the court for blessing.[74] The question must be whether the trustee acted reasonably in obtaining and relying upon the advice she did in fact obtain, not whether some other advice might also have been sought. This is a question the court has had to grapple with already in relation to its jurisdiction under s 61 of the Trustee Act 1925 (UK) when considering whether to excuse from liability trustees who have 'acted honestly and reasonably, and ought fairly to be excused'. Where a trustee claims to have acted 'reasonably' on the basis that she followed professional—usually legal—advice, the court has maintained the view that it does not follow automatically that the trustee will be excused,[75] whilst in fact usually granting relief.[76] In *Re Allsop*, Sir Herbert Cozens-Hardy MR considered whether a trustee who had neglected to take legal advice had acted reasonably, and held that a trustee who paid money to someone not entitled to it[77]

> cannot be considered to have acted reasonably if he has neglected to obtain skilled advice. In considering what is reasonable, regard must be had to the estate of which he is trustee. In a large estate it may be only reasonable that he should consult counsel of the first rank or apply by originating summons for the direction of the Court, whereas it would not be reasonable to insist upon all this where the estate is small.

Just as in *Pitt v Holt* Lord Walker made clear that it does not suffice for a claim of 'inadequate deliberation' that the trustees 'fall short of the highest standards',[78] the Court of Appeal has emphasised that in s 61 relief cases 'the requisite standard is that of reasonableness not of perfection'.[79] Reasonableness in the context of obtaining 'apparently competent' advice means the kind of proportionality envisaged by the Master of the Rolls in *Re Allsop*, allowing a wide margin of discretion for trustees acting in good faith. In other words, trustees should only be treated as having obtained advice of a kind or from a source which is not 'apparently competent' where both (i) the court considers that more authoritative advice ought to have been

[73] *Pitt v Holt* (UKSC) (n 5) [80].

[74] See text to n 67.

[75] In *Marsden v Regan* [1954] 1 WLR 423 (CA) 434–35, Sir Raymond Evershed MR held that: 'The mere fact that you take a solicitor's advice, natural and prudent though such a course be, will not automatically result in relief being given.'

[76] See *Perrins v Bellamy* [1899] 1 Ch 797 (CA); *Marsden v Regan* (n 75).

[77] *Re Allsop* [1914] 1 Ch 1 (CA) 13.

[78] *Pitt v Holt* (UKSC) (n 5) [68].

[79] *Nationwide Building Society v Davisons Solicitors* [2012] EWCA Civ 1626; [2013] PNLR 12 (Sir Andrew Morritt C) [48]. See also *Santander UK v RA Legal Solicitors* [2014] EWCA Civ 183; [2014] PNLR 20 [21].

obtained and (ii) no reasonable trustee would have thought it appropriate to rely on the advice that was in fact obtained. Any more exacting standard would generate much advisory work for senior practitioners at the chancery bar, but at the cost of the wasteful employment of trust funds in obtaining such advice. It is also important to note that often trustees will rely on their advisers to tell them what further advice is required. Even in a complex case, it is likely to be reasonable for trustees to rely on their usual solicitor's advice that they do not need to obtain the opinion of specialist counsel: whether or not their solicitor is in fact competent to advise on the underlying issue, the trustees are entitled to believe that their solicitor is better placed than them to ascertain whether further legal advice is required.

The position of a trustee who is herself an expert is more difficult. Erroneous legal advice may be 'apparently competent' from the perspective of a lay trustee, but the court is likely to take a less sympathetic view of a solicitor trustee who would have been well placed to appreciate the defects in the advice. In general, a trustee acting in the course of a business or profession will be assumed to have the 'special knowledge or experience that it is reasonable to expect of a person acting in the course of that kind of business or profession'[80] and will be held to the standards of that business or profession. Plainly, there is in each case a question of fact as to the extent to which the particular professional could be expected to have appreciated that the advice was not competent: a family law solicitor acting as trustee might not be open to criticism for failing to appreciate the defects in complex advice on a commercial property transaction, where the law is wrongly stated or the analysis is faulty. But if the advice is illogical in its own terms, or makes errors in handling basic legal concepts, then it might be thought that any competent solicitor should appreciate the flaws. The professional trustee is likely to find herself in much the same position as an allegedly negligent solicitor who relies by way of defence on the advice of counsel: whilst the solicitor 'does not abdicate his professional responsibility' and must 'apply his mind to the advice received', nevertheless 'the more specialist the nature of the advice, the more reasonable is it likely to be for a solicitor to accept it and act on it'.[81]

Finally, what of the professional whose own firm gives the erroneous advice now relied upon? That was the situation in *Futter v Futter* where a partner in a firm of London solicitors, Mr Cutbill, was appointed as trustee, and incorrect tax advice was subsequently given by his firm.[82] Lord Walker did not, however, consider this a bar to Mr Cutbill being treated as having relied on the advice given by his firm and so not having committed a breach of trust in omitting to appreciate the true capital gains tax consequences of the trustees' decisions. In particular, Lord Walker preferred not to distinguish the position of Mr Cutbill and his lay co-trustee, and noted that 'most if not all of the technical tax advice given by his firm came not from

[80] Trustee Act 2000 (UK), s 1. See also *Bartlett v Barclays Bank Trust Co Ltd (No 2)* [1980] Ch 515 (CA) 534.

[81] *Ridehalgh v Horsefield* [1994] Ch 205 (CA) 237. See also *Locke v Camberwell Health Authority* [2002] Lloyd's Rep PN 23 (CA) 29; John L Powell and Roger Stewart (eds), *Jackson & Powell on Professional Liability* 8th edn (London, Sweet & Maxwell, 2017) para 11-120.

[82] *Pitt v Holt* (UKSC) (n 5) [47] and [86].

Mr Cutbill but from the assistant solicitor who was working with him'.[83] Consequently Mr Cutbill was not 'personally in breach of fiduciary duty'.[84] Although intuitively this seems to be a rather indulgent approach to take to solicitors who have given incorrect advice,[85] it follows logically from Lord Walker's starting point for 'inadequate deliberation' of requiring a finding of individual fault by a trustee. Whether Mr Cutbill had committed a breach of trust depended upon his personal conduct as trustee, not upon the actions of others in his firm. Whether he, as a solicitor himself, was entitled to rely upon his firm's advice should depend upon the principles set out above.[86] Had he himself been instrumental in giving that advice, then of course he could not rely upon it—just as any solicitor trustee could not herself rely by way of defence upon advice she had given to her fellow trustees.

VII. A WIDER DEFENCE?

In the coming years, the court will have to work out how to operate in practice the law on 'inadequate deliberation' claims set out by Lord Walker in *Pitt v Holt*. Filling in the details of the defence of reliance on professional advice will undoubtedly be an important part of this process and, perhaps, in practical terms, the most important. But other questions are also likely to be asked about the defence. Most fundamentally, it is not at all obvious that the defence should be limited to 'inadequate deliberation' claims. A trustee accused of committing a fraud on a power by exercising it for an improper purpose might well point to legal advice endorsing both her decisions and her reasons. The principled basis of the fraud on a power doctrine is far from clear, and Lord Walker acknowledged in *Pitt v Holt* that it 'may need a separate pigeon-hole somewhere between the categories of excessive execution and inadequate deliberation'.[87] Since reliance on professional advice is a defence only to the second of these, it is likely to be the resolution of such questions about the very nature of the fraud on a power doctrine, as to whether it is a form of *ultra vires*, or is concerned with trustees acting in a breach of duty,[88] which will determine the application of the defence. A related problem will arise from the difficulty of distinguishing inadequate deliberation and fraud on a power claims: an allegation that the trustees were motivated in the exercise of a power by an improper purpose might equally be pleaded as the improper taking into account of an irrelevant consideration. A similar problem will arise where the trustees' decision is alleged to be void as

[83] ibid [96].

[84] ibid.

[85] Though in *Futter v Futter* the result was far from indulgent: Mr Cutbill had not sought to rely on the professional advice defence, but rather had joined his co-trustee in seeking to rely upon their own 'inadequate deliberation' as a reason to set aside their exercise of a power of enlargement.

[86] Though Lord Walker did not expressly consider whether Mr Cutbill ought to have realised that his firm's advice was wrong.

[87] *Pitt v Holt* (UKSC) (n 5) [62].

[88] See Ashdown (n 16) ch 9.

being irrational or perverse.[89] Whilst most obviously seen as a matter of *vires*—the conferral of power on a trustee does not entitle the trustee to use that power irrationally or perversely—it might equally be said that it is not irrational for a lay trustee to follow apparently competent professional advice. If the test were wholly objective, then it would create the situation where a trustee acting on merely incorrect professional advice may have a good defence, whereas a trustee acting on outrageously wrong advice may be treated as having acted *ultra vires*, even if there were no difference in the culpability of the trustee in each case. This would be difficult to fit with Lord Walker's concern to require individual fault in cases of trustee decision making gone awry.

[89] In the context of pension trusts, this is a well-established basis for challenging the decisions of the pension trustees: *Harris v Lord Shuttleworth* [1994] ICR 991 (CA) 999; *Edge v Pensions Ombudsman* [1998] Ch 512 (Ch D) 534; *Re Merchant Navy Ratings Pension Fund* [2015] EWHC 448 (Ch); [2015] Pens LR 239 [20]; *Underhill and Hayton* (n 1) para 57.12. It is likely, though less well established, that the same doctrine applies to private trusts: Richard Nolan, 'Controlling Fiduciary Power' (2009) 68 *CLJ* 293; Geraint Thomas, *Thomas on Powers* 2nd edn (Oxford, Oxford University Press, 2012) para 10.184.

9

Want of Causation as a Defence to Liability for Misapplication of Trust Assets

PG TURNER*

I. INTRODUCTION

A NEW DEFENCE to equitable liability has recently been added to the inventory of equitable defences recognised in English and Australian law—though not, to date, in other common law jurisdictions. Among equitable defences generally, this new defence takes an unusual form. It says nothing of misconduct or impropriety by the claimant. It relates not to the demerits of the defendant's conduct, nor the passing of time. Unusually, for a defence, it concerns causation. The new doctrine is this: where a trust suffers direct loss by reason of trustees' misapplication of trust moneys, the trustees' liability therefor may be reduced—even to nil—by showing that the loss would have been suffered even had the moneys been properly applied. So far as the defaulting trustees show the loss would have been suffered but for the trustees' breach, monetary relief will be denied. Want of causation by the trustees' breach of the proved loss discharges the trustees *pro tanto* of legal responsibility for the proved loss.

Like many judicial innovations when first made, this addition to English and Australian law is prickly with questions. One is, 'Can this innovation properly be called a "defence"?' In some circumstances, it cannot. A beneficiary may seek a common accounting—that is, an accounting of all trust property received and applied by the trustee—as a means of recovery for a particular misapplication of trust moneys. Want of causation can negate the trustees' liability regarding one or more items of account, but not their liability as accounting parties for the trust assets. In other circumstances, want of causation can properly be called a defence. The onus of proving want of causation lies on the defaulting trustees. Defaulting trustees who put want of causation in issue do not merely put the claimant to proof of any fact, including that the claimant suffered personal loss or proof that the trust estate suffered a loss

* University Lecturer, Faculty of Law, University of Cambridge; Fellow of St Catharine's College, Cambridge. This paper was initially prepared while the author was a Dyason Visiting Fellow of the University of Melbourne. The author records his gratitude to that University.

that would not have occurred but for the trustees' misapplication of trust moneys.[1] Want of causation is put in issue by defaulting trustees to answer a claim that they are liable to repay the misapplied sum. The answer may even defeat a claim entirely, as where a beneficiary only claims relief from the loss directly suffered by a trust on such a transaction—rather than for a full audit. Want of causation is properly called a defence where it operates as such.

Other questions about character emerge, especially: 'Is it correct to speak of this as a defence to claims of "equitable compensation" for "loss"?'[2] The correctness of those forms of speech opens important substantive enquiries, such as whether assertions of power to grant equitable compensation ever involve 'second-guessing' the law of torts.[3] The courts speak daily of compensation as monetary relief awarded, under common law rules, to repair losses that claimants prove they have suffered personally. Trusts, however, are governed primarily by principles of equity; they are legal relations rather than legal persons with the capacity to sue and to be sued;[4] and proof of personal loss is not required of a claimant who sues for a breach of trust. Yet courts speak of compensating[5] for the loss[6] to the trust estate[7] or trust fund[8]—absent proof of loss by any individual beneficiary or object of the trust[9]—via equitable doctrine. But whether it is correct to speak of want of causation as a defence to claims of equitable compensation for loss cannot be directly answered here. Unless the correctness of the usage is provisionally assumed, the meaning of that usage cannot be discerned. And without discerning those meanings, the establishment of the defence of want of causation cannot be charted.

The boldness of suggesting that a defence of want of causation has been established must be acknowledged. No English or Australian case appears explicitly to have ruled, or even explicitly said, that such a defence now exists.[10] The little commentary that addresses the matter denies that the defence exists.[11] Without directly addressing

[1] See text following n 152.

[2] See J Edelman, 'An English Misturning with Equitable Compensation' in S Degeling and J Varuhas (eds), *Equitable Compensation and Disgorgement of Profits* (Oxford, Hart Publishing, 2017) 94.

[3] P Birks, 'Equity in the Modern Law: An Exercise in Taxonomy' (1996) 26 *University of Western Australia Law Review* 1, 49–52.

[4] See *ACES Sogutlu Holdings Pty Ltd (in liq) v Commonwealth Bank of Australia* [2014] NSWCA 402; (2014) 89 NSWLR 209 [15]–[20]; *Agricultural Land Management Ltd v Jackson (No 2)* [2014] WASC 102; (2014) 48 WAR 1 [302].

[5] *Youyang Pty Ltd v Minter Ellison Morris Fletcher* [2003] HCA 15; (2003) 212 CLR 484 [35], [40], [50]; *AIB Group (UK) plc v Mark Redler & Co Solicitors* [2014] UKSC 58; [2015] AC 1503 (*passim*).

[6] *Youyang* (n 5) [34], [35], [45], [46], [50], [51], [63]; *AIB Group* (n 5) (*passim*).

[7] *Target Holdings Ltd v Redferns* [1996] AC 421, 434; *Youyang* (n 5) [38]; *AIB Group* (n 5) [23], [65], [98], [141].

[8] *Target* (n 7) 431, 433; *AIB Group* (n 5) [106], [132], [137].

[9] For references to personal loss, see section VI.A and JD Heydon, MJ Leeming and PG Turner, *Meagher, Gummow and Lehane's Equity: Doctrines and Remedies* 5th edn (Sydney, LexisNexis Butterworths, 2015) [23-360].

[10] See Edelman (n 2) 93; *cf*, P Davies, 'Compensatory Remedies for Breach of Trust' (2016) 2 *Canadian Journal of Comparative and Contemporary Law* 65, 103. In *Barnett v Creggy* [2016] EWCA Civ 1004; [2017] 2 WLR 1054 [45] Sales LJ said a claim for misapplication of trust moneys 'is a claim which is restitutionary in nature (in the sense of being designed to restore the trust fund), albeit capable of being defeated if the defendant trustee can show that no loss was caused'.

[11] M Conaglen, 'Equitable Compensation for Breach of Trust: Off *Target*' (2016) 40 *Melbourne University Law Review* 125; Edelman (n 2). Regarding breaches of fiduciary duty as distinct from breach

its existence, the greater amount of commentary in effect denies it: either by taking Australian law to remain unaltered by the addition of such a defence,[12] or by reading the chief English decisions as changing the law more radically than by merely establishing a new equitable defence,[13] or both.[14] Thus, some observers see the English (but not the Australian) law of trustees' liability for misapplying trust assets as so confused that, evidently, no doctrine can be discerned in it, let alone a new defence.[15] Some advance further, suggesting that the chief English decisions (but not the Australian) reduce that liability to a liability to pay damages in a sum equal to the loss suffered individually by beneficiaries,[16] and deny beneficiaries' ability to keep trustees to their duty through curial accounting.[17] A defence of want of causation has been accepted in Hong Kong, but the Court of Final Appeal has not had to decide its incidents.[18] Bold as this suggestion may be, it merits an audience. Changes of law can occur without their character being at first perceived—as, it is respectfully suggested, has occurred here. Upon analysis, the authorities allow the conclusion that a defence of want of causation has been founded in English and Australian law. Since 'the doctrine of precedent, or as it is sometimes known stare decisis, is fundamental'[19] in common law systems, the English and Australian authorities in fact compel the conclusion that an equitable defence of want of causation has been founded in those jurisdictions.

It is desirable to proceed stepwise, the first step being to establish whether there has been a change in the law at all. The analysis will concentrate on the decisions of ultimate appellate courts because '[d]ecisions on points of law by more senior courts have to be accepted by more junior courts':[20] those decisions, rather than more junior courts' understandings thereof, are the law. At that level, English and Australian law currently diverge sufficiently from the law of other common law

of express trust, a defence of want of causation has been favoured by C Mitchell, 'Equitable Compensation for Breach of Fiduciary Duty' (2013) 66 *Current Legal Problems* 307, 338. See also *Libertarian Investments Ltd v Hall* (2013) 16 HKCFAR 681 [93].

[12] See Davies (n 10) 82–83, 100; J Penner, 'Distinguishing Fiduciary, Trust and Accounting Relationships' (2014) 8 *Journal of Equity* 202, 226.

[13] A Shaw-Mellor, 'Equitable Compensation for Breach of Trust: Still Missing the Target?' [2015] *Journal of Business Law* 165, 172; S Worthington, 'Four Questions on Fiduciaries' (2016) 2 *Canadian Journal of Comparative and Contemporary Law* 723, 757–64.

[14] NA Tiverios and C McKay, 'Orthodoxy Lost: The (Ir)relevance of Causation in Quantifying Breach of Trust Claims' (2016) 90 *Australian Law Journal* 233 (*passim*).

[15] Lord Millett, 'The Common Lawyer and the Equity Practitioner', *The UK Supreme Court Yearbook Legal Year 2014–2015*, 193, 199, 204; Mitchell (n 11) 323–326; Shaw-Mellor (n 13) 169, 172.

[16] Birks (n 3) 47; A Burrows, 'Limitations on Compensation' in A Burrows and E Peel (eds), *Commercial Remedies* (Oxford, OUP, 2003) 46–47; Conaglen (n 11) 158; Davies (n 10) 71, 78; Edelman (n 2) 103; W Gummow, 'Three Cases of Misapplication of a Solicitor's Trust Account' (2015) 41 *Aust Bar Rev* 5, 10–11; L Ho, 'Causation in the Restoration of a Misapplied Trust Fund: Fundamental Norm or Red Herring?' in S Degeling and JNE Varuhas (eds), *Equitable Compensation and Disgorgement of Profits* (Oxford, Hart Publishing, 2017) 170–71; Tiverios and McKay (n 14) 239; D Wright, 'Another Wrong Step: Equitable Compensation Following a Breach of Trust' (2015) 21 *Trusts & Trustees* 825, 838; M Yip, 'The Commercial Context in Trust Law' [2016] *Conv* 347, 363–64. See also *KBL Investments Ltd v KBL Courtenay Ltd* [2016] NZCA 227 [71].

[17] See n 197.

[18] *Libertarian Investments* (n 11) [93].

[19] *Willers v Joyce (No 2)* [2016] UKSC 44; [2016] 3 WLR 534 [4].

[20] *Willers* (n 19) [4].

jurisdictions that this enquiry into the establishment of this novel equitable defence requires the law of other common law jurisdictions to be placed to one side.[21] But as the English and Australian decisions are likely to have some persuasive value in other common law jurisdictions outside the United States, the chapter is written with the lawyer of the common law Commonwealth in mind.

II. A LEGAL INNOVATION

In order to appreciate that want of causation has become a defence to liability for breach of trust arising from the misapplication of trust money, it must be seen that English law and Australian law have changed as a result of deliberate judicial decision.[22] The character of the alteration—be it the establishment of a novel defence or otherwise—will be considered later because it is irrelevant to the first point to be considered: the doubt that 'traditional' doctrines of trustees' liability for breach of trust have been altered in England and Australia, either because (a) the courts when deciding the leading cases failed to apply 'traditional' doctrines[23] or (b) they could have reached the same decisions by applying 'traditional' doctrines, although they in fact did not.[24] These reasons for doubting that English and Australian law have changed are reasons concerning the authority of judicial decisions. They require that the leading decisions have no authority beyond their own facts or that they contain only *obiter dicta* on point. The reasons presumably do not require the leading cases to be read as decisions *per incuriam*, for the *per incuriam* doctrine only applies in the appellate court that decided the impugned decision: a decision *per incuriam* can in effect change the law because more junior courts may not decline to apply it,[25] whereas the point to be considered is that the law is, relevantly, unchanged because the leading decisions lack the authority of law.

If the law is unchanged, it must stand as it stood before the earliest of the three decisions of ultimate appellate courts to be considered in this chapter—*Target Holdings Ltd v Redferns*[26]—was decided in 1995. How did the relevant law stand at the beginning of that year? What features of the law, as decided in *Target* and

[21] In Canada, see DWM Waters, MR Gillen and LD Smith, *Waters' Law of Trusts in Canada* 4th edn (Toronto, Carswell, 2012) 1279–90. In Hong Kong, see *Libertarian Investments* (n 11); *cf* L Ma, *Equity and Trusts in Hong Kong* 2nd edn (Hong Kong, LexisNexis 2009) [26-33]–[26-36]. In India, see Trusts Act 1882, s 23; SK Aiyar, SK Sarvaria and S Gupta, *Commentary on the Indian Trusts Act* 7th edn (New Delhi, Universal Law Publishing, 2012) 288, 290. In New Zealand, see AS Butler (eds), *Equity and Trusts in New Zealand* 2nd edn (Wellington, Thomson Reuters, 2009) [8.3.2], [10.3.1](1), (8), [10.3.3], [10.3.5], [32.4.1], [32.5], [39.10.1]–[39.10.2]. In Singapore, see *Maryani Sadeli v Arjun Permanand Samtani* [2014] SGCA 55; [2015] SLR 96 [9]–[11]. In the United States, see AW Scott, WF Fratcher and ML Ascher, *Scott and Ascher on Trusts* 5th edn (Frederick MD, Aspen, 2007) ch 24, § 24.9.1.

[22] For sources in England, see n 16. For sources in Australia, see n 73.

[23] C Mitchell, 'Stewardship of Property and Liability to Account' [2014] *Conv* 215, 225–226.

[24] See *Agricultural Land Management* (n 4) [358]; Tiverios and McKay (n 14) 247–48; Ho (n 16) 169–74; Mitchell (n 23) 225–26. See also n 16.

[25] *Baker v R* [1975] AC 774, 788; *Miliangos v George Frank (Textiles) Ltd* [1976] AC 443, 479; *R (RJM) v Work and Pensions Secretary* [2008] UKHL 63, [2009] 1 AC 311 [65].

[26] *Target* (n 7).

since, indicate that English law as of 1 January 1995, and the corresponding law of Australia, have changed?

A. At the Outset of 1995

Owing to the way in which the subject has recently been discussed among scholars and taught in some universities, it has become common to introduce the topic of trustees' liability for misapplying trust assets through the remedy of accounting. The application of this remedy to defaulting trustees experienced long 'inattention'[27] in the period before 1995. However, principles can be traced back some centuries in printed reports.

i. Account: Trustees

How did the accounting remedy lie as against express trustees on 1 January 1995? The curial taking of trust accounts was done in order to ascertain whether trustees had kept to their duty, and was done by verifying whether an account drawn up by trustees to record their receipts, disbursements and allowances was a true account.[28] Accounts of administration were taken pursuant to orders made where the 'overall administration of a business enterprise or fund or other property [was] to be established or accounted for'.[29] Accounts of the administration of trusts could be taken in two ways. The 'usual order'[30] was for accounts in common form: an accounting of all sums received and disbursed. Beneficiaries were, it is said, entitled to the usual order 'as of right'.[31] An unusual form of order was for an accounting grounded on wilful default. Trustees shown to have committed an instance of wilful default[32] could then be ordered to account for all sums received and disbursed *and* all sums that ought to have been received had the trustees had acted as carefully and diligently as their obligations required.

Accounting relief differed according to whether the trustees' account was open or settled. An outline of the difference will suffice here.[33] Where the account was open—that is, still operating—the trustees' accounts were received as evidence of the true account, rather than an unquestionable record. Trustees swore an affidavit in answer to or defence of claimants' bills of account. The affidavit usually had

[27] Conaglen (n 11) 127, 129. An early proselytisation of the hitherto unattended learning may be found in R Ham, 'Trustees' Liability' (1995) 9 *Trust Law International* 21.

[28] A Pulling, *The Law and Usage of Mercantile Accounts* (London, Butterworths, 1850) 161–62; Conaglen (n 11) 128–45.

[29] *Glazier Holdings Pty Ltd v Australian Men's Health Pty Ltd [No 2]* [2001] NSWSC 6 [36].

[30] *Dowse v Gorton* [1891] AC 190, 202.

[31] *Libertarian Investments* (n 11) [167].

[32] The beneficiary was required to establish one or more instances of 'wilful default'. Wilful default demanded some voluntary action in breach of trust, not conscious wrongdoing: *AIB* (n 5) [54]; *Bartlett v Barclays Bank Trust Co Ltd (No 2)* [1980] Ch 515, 546.

[33] See *Pit v Cholmondeley* (1754) 2 Ves Sen 566; 28 ER 360; IP Cory, *A Practical Treatise on Accounts* 2nd edn (London, Pickering, 1839) ch 7.

four schedules. One asserted what the trustees were expected to receive. A second asserted what the trustees actually received. A third showed how the assets received were applied. A fourth listed all the papers, accounts, books, vouchers and letters relating to the matters in question.[34] Trustees were 'charged' with the items they did or ought to have received, and with any sums they took as allowances without being entitled to. Trustees were 'discharged' or 'exonerated' of items for which they were not responsible. Although the trustees' account was important, the active verbs indicate that the court drew up the true account: the court 'charged' or 'discharged'; the court 'allowed' or 'disallowed' items for which the trustees provided evidence. Except where fraud was practised on a court, therefore, a court-drawn account would contain no unverified discharges or charges. Settled accounts were different. The items of a settled account were presumed to be true; they could only be varied if a party gained leave to falsify and surcharge,[35] in which case unauthorised charges against the trust could be struck out and charges against trustees could be added. This affected the burden of proof[36] and was confined to particular items of account.[37] Recently, writers have widened the terms 'falsify' and 'surcharge' to apply generally—that is, not only in relation to settled accounts—thus following AJ Oakley[38] and DJ Hayton.[39]

ii. Account: Misapplied Trust Moneys

How did all this bear on misapplications of trust moneys as of 1 January 1995? In an open account, once trustees were found to have received moneys on trust they were charged with them. For disbursing them, the trustees remained charged with the disbursed sum unless they showed a ground of discharge.[40] In a settled account that charged *the trust* with an improper disbursement (for example, one made without power or in improper or imprudent exercise of a power[41]), that account entry could be falsified or struck out. In either case the objective was restitution at current values when restitution was made: beyond finding that the trustees disposed of a trust asset in breach of trust, no enquiry occurred into loss or the causation of loss. This was quite different to charging trustees for failing, through want of care on applicable equitable[42] or statutory[43] standards, to procure the title or custody of an asset they ought to have got in.[44] In the latter case, loss and causation were enquired into.

[34] Cory (n 33) 261–64. See also Practice Direction 40A under the Civil Procedure Rules 1998, paras 2 and 3.1.

[35] See also *Brownell v Brownell* (1786) 2 Bro CC 262; 29 ER 35.

[36] *Pit* (n 33) 565–66; 360–61.

[37] *Gething v Keighley* (1878) 9 Ch D 547.

[38] AJ Oakley, *Parker and Mellows: the Modern Law of Trusts* 7th edn (London, Sweet & Maxwell, 1998) 680–85.

[39] DJ Hayton, *Hayton and Marshall: Commentary and Cases on the Law of Trusts and Equitable Remedies* 11th edn (London, Sweet & Maxwell, 2001) [10-04]–[10-09]; *Underhill and Hayton: Law of Trusts and Trustees* 16th edn (London, Sweet & Maxwell, 2003) ch 20.

[40] See text following n 144.

[41] See Conaglen (n 11) 141–42, discussing *Re Salmon* (1889) 42 Ch D 351.

[42] *Re Speight* (1883) 22 Ch D 727, 739–40; *Learoyd v Whiteley* (1887) 12 App Cas 727, 733.

[43] Trustee Act 2000 (Eng), ss 1–2, Sch 1.

[44] *M'Donnell v White* (1865) 11 HLC 570, 581–84; 11 ER 1454, 1459–60; *Speight v Gaunt* (1883) 9 App Cas 1, 13–14. See also Conaglen (n 11) 142–43.

Before 1995, a change of practice occurred, the history of which is still unclear.[45] Relief by a general accounting diminished in use. A quicker, cheaper and more efficient procedure was adopted. Beneficiaries began to sue for particular breaches of trust, and to obtain relief for those without a full accounting, on the common or the wilful default footing. 'Equitable compensation' has, particularly since *Target Holdings*, become a favoured term to denote the equitable relief obtained by that shortened procedure. It is, Lord Reed JSC has said, the more 'direct' remedy although it is quantified as if the lengthier procedure were engaged.[46]

Each ground on which trustees were discharged of their accounting liabilities for misapplying trust moneys was a defence in the sense explained earlier.[47] As will be seen, those grounds are critical to a doctrinal statement of the change wrought in England by *Target* in 1995 and furthered in *AIB (UK) plc v Mark Redler & Co Solicitors*[48] in 2014, and in Australia by *Youyang Pty Ltd v Minter Ellison Morris Fletcher*[49] in 2003. What features of those decisions show that English law and Australian law must have changed?

B. Change

In both English cases solicitor-trustees owed obligations to hold a client's money pending the completion of conveyances by grants of security over land.

In *Target*,[50] the House of Lords denied summary judgment to a lender (Target Holdings Ltd) for whom the lender's solicitors (Redferns) undertook to hold loan moneys on trust until the solicitors received properly executed charges over land. The charges were intended to secure the repayment of the loan. The House of Lords held that the solicitors had committed a breach of trust by advancing the loan moneys to the borrower before the solicitors received the required charge instruments. Rather than enter summary judgment for the lender-beneficiary in the amount of the wrongly disbursed sum—£1,490,000—the House of Lords restored the primary judge's order giving the trustees leave to defend, allowing the case to proceed to trial.[51] Before *Target*, when monetary relief was ordered as restoration of a trust estate following the misapplication of trust assets, the sum of monetary relief was found by valuing the misapplied assets as at the date of restoration.[52] For the first time in an ultimate appellate court,[53] the House of Lords held in *Target* that events

[45] Conaglen (n 11) 21–24; Edelman (n 2) 91–92; Heydon, Leeming and Turner (n 9) [23-030].

[46] *AIB* (n 5) [90]–[91], [99]–[100], [106], [108], [134].

[47] See text following n 2.

[48] *AIB* (n 5).

[49] *Youyang* (n 5).

[50] *Target* (n 7).

[51] In a related proceeding before Sir Richard Scott V-C in 1998, the claim for breach of trust did not figure: *Target Holdings Ltd v Redferns* (1998) 95(41) LSG 45.

[52] *Re Massingberd's Settlement* (1890) 59 LJ Ch 107 (aff'd (1890) 63 LT 297); *Re Dawson (dec'd)* [1966] 2 NSWR 211, 217. Interest, dividends and the like might be included in the relief.

[53] Dicta to this effect were uttered in *Canson Enterprises Ltd v Boughton & Co* [1991] 3 SCR 534. See L Smith, 'The Measurement of Compensation Claims against Trustees and Fiduciaries' in E Bant and M Harding (eds), *Exploring Private Law* (Cambridge, CUP, 2010) ch 16.

between breach and judgment went to the *value* of the assets misapplied but also, separately, to the *extent* of the trustees' responsibility for misapplied trust moneys.

By emphasising that Lord Browne-Wilkinson's reasoning was untrue to prior authority and suggesting that *Target* could have been decided on orthodox equitable grounds, observers have doubted the authority of *Target* and the persuasiveness of its reasoning.[54] Objections to its authority cannot stand. The doctrine of precedent recognises the authority of a decision even where the court's reasons for the decision are mistaken[55] or the decision might have been reached on other grounds.[56] While doubts over the persuasiveness of Lord Browne-Wilkinson's reasoning will be pertinent in jurisdictions yet to consider the legal change made in *Target*, such doubts do not permit the decision to be ignored in English law. Even at the level of the House of Lords or, now, the UK Supreme Court, the doubts over *Target* do not allow it to be argued that *Target* was decided *per incuriam*. Decisions are not *per incuriam* merely because counsel could have made an argument better or more fully.[57] Indeed, the summary of argument in the authorised report shows *Target* was not decided *per incuriam*.[58] In particular, the beneficiary's counsel invoked doctrines of trustees' accountability, correctly saying that '[t]he primary rule in equity [had been] that the trustee must preserve and protect the trust property'[59] such that defaulting trustees must 'account and restore the trust property which has been paid away in breach of trust'.[60] The authority of *Target* cannot be ignored simply because *Target* diverges from the previous law.

The result and the reasoning in *Target* are beyond the reach of the pre-1995 doctrines of trustees' accountability, as applied to the facts assumed on the application summarily to dismiss the plaintiff's case.[61] It was orthodox that trustees who misapply or misappropriate trust property immediately become liable to restore the trust property: trustees who do so are discharged of further liability.[62] In *Target*, the misapplied trust moneys were not restored to the trust; nor was an equivalent sum of money restored to the trust (or paid to the lender-beneficiary). The proposition established by earlier authorities did not directly apply. Further facts which, if assumed or found, could have grounded an orthodox decision were not assumed or found.[63] No facts were assumed or found so as to show that the solicitor-agents had informed their principal that they had breached their authority in advancing the moneys and

[54] Conaglen (n 11) 152–54, 157; Davies (n 10) 80; Ho (n 16) 174 ('arguably' explicable 'on traditional grounds'); P Millett, 'Equity's Place in the Law of Commerce' (1998) 114 *LQR* 214, 227; *cf Target*: P Millett, 'Equity—the Road Ahead' (1995) 9 *Trust Law International* 35, 37); Tiverios and McKay (n 14) 244.

[55] *Miliangos* (n 25), 465, 473, 496, 503; *R v Knuller (Publishing, Printing and Promotions) Ltd* [1973] AC 435, 455; AL Goodhart, 'Determining the *Ratio Decidendi* of a Case' in *Essays in Jurisprudence and the Common Law* (Cambridge, CUP, 1931) 3–4.

[56] *Miliangos* (n 25) 465, 473, 496, 503.

[57] *Morelle v Wakeling* [1955] 2 QB 379, 406. See also *Nguyen v Nguyen* (1990) 169 CLR 245, 269 (Dawson, Toohey and McHugh JJ).

[58] *Miliangos* (n 25) 477–78.

[59] *Target* (n 7) 427B.

[60] ibid 425G, 426A–B.

[61] *cf* n 54; Davies (n 10) 71.

[62] See text to nn 40–44, n 82.

[63] See P Watts, 'Agents' Disbursal of Funds in Breach of Instructions' [2016] *Lloyd's Maritime and Commercial Law Quarterly* 118, 119–21.

getting in the charges, nor that the principal subsequently ratified such unauthorised action.[64] Nor were facts assumed or found so as to show that the trustee-agents' authority to get in the charges continued following the breach of authority.[65] Again, facts supporting defences of waiver or laches were not assumed or found.[66] In any of those situations, the acquisition of the charges must have been entered into the accounts, barring the lender-beneficiary from later denying the solicitor-trustees' authority to release the trust funds.[67] The effect would be to deny Redferns' recovery of the entire misapplied sum. However, as such facts were not assumed or found—and as the trustees' leave to defend was restored because causal enquiries were held relevant to the extent of the trustees' liability—the result and reasoning of *Target* were inexplicable in the terms of English law as of 1 January 1995.

The novelty of the reasoning and decision in *Target* was recognised in *AIB*. Responding to an argument that *Target* was like pre-1995 authorities in which misapplied trust assets were restored or unauthorised assets were adopted by trust beneficiaries,[68] Lord Toulson JSC said indignantly: '[t]here is something wrong with a state of law which makes it necessary to create fairy tales'.[69] Actual restoration of the misapplied moneys, and actual adoption of charges obtained otherwise than as directed, was one thing—and was permitted in law at 1 January 1995. Deemed restoration or adoption was quite another thing—and beyond the law as of that date.

AIB is the second leading case to have made clear that English doctrines of trustees' accountability as they stood before 1995 have been altered. Discussion of precisely what *AIB* decides may be deferred until later: the immediate point is that *AIB* affirms that trustees' accountability was changed by *Target*. On partly similar facts to those of *Target*, defaulting trustees effectively invited the Supreme Court to overrule the House of Lords' 1995 decision. A lender (AIB) advanced money in a refinancing transaction to its solicitors to hold on trust pending the receipt of a registered instrument of first charge over land. The solicitors breached the trust by releasing the lent moneys without obtaining the first charge: they paid a sum to the prior lender purportedly to satisfy the borrowers' indebtedness and later paid the balance of the lent sum to the borrowers. As the sum paid to the prior lender did not satisfy the borrowers' indebtedness, the prior lender refused to release its first charge over the relevant land. That the solicitors had breached the trust and that the breach related to all the moneys they had advanced (£3.3m) was not in issue.[70] However, the Supreme Court held that the claimant lender was not entitled to recover that sum. The lender's recovery was confined to the difference between the sum realised by its enforcement of its second charge (£1.2m) and the sum it would have recovered

[64] ibid 119–21.

[65] ibid 121; *cf* Millett (1998) (n 54) 227; M Conaglen, 'Explaining *Target Holdings v Redferns*' (2010) 4 *Journal of Equity* 288; Conaglen (n 11) 153.

[66] *cf* J Edelman, 'Money Awards of the Cost of Performance' (2010) 4 *Journal of Equity* 122, 128–30.

[67] Conaglen (n 65) 290; Conaglen (n 11) 153.

[68] *AIB* (n 5) [69]; Millett (1998) (n 54) 227.

[69] *AIB* (n 5) [69]. Other passages expressed in terms that no change of the law occurred in *Target* must be read as stressing the continuity of the law rather than as denying the change made in *Target*.

[70] ibid [16], [140].

under a first charge (£273,777.42). The Court held this to follow from *Target*, which it declined to overrule. Since the Supreme Court saw causal enquiries into loss and the affirming of *Target* as essential to its decision in *AIB*, the *ratio* or *rationes decidendi* of *AIB*—whatever it or they be—affirms that the doctrines of trustees' accountability have changed in England since 1 January 1995.

A corresponding change of Australian law occurred by the decision in *Youyang*.[71] That was another case in which solicitor-trustees held moneys on trust which they were to release only in exchange for security: this time, personal security in the form of a bearer deposit certificate.[72] The solicitor-trustees released the money without having obtained the required certificate. The High Court of Australia held the trustees liable to make good the misapplied sum and interest thereon from breach until judgment. Looking at the Court's order alone, *Youyang* might seem to reaffirm Australia's counterparts of the English doctrines of trustees' accountability as of 1 January 1995. Some lawyers have thought so. With respect, however, it is *nihil ad rem* that the orders in *Youyang* could have been made without changing the law.[73] It is *ad rem* when discerning the *rationes decidendi* of decisions given without reasons[74] and decisions turning on but one legal proposition.[75] However, *Youyang* turned on several legal propositions for which reasons were given in one judgment. Ordinarily, the *ratio* of such a case is identified by examining the order of the court, the material facts *and* the court's reasons for determining the issues that arose from those facts by making the particular order.[76] The reasons for judgment are not ignored, and it would be curious to do so.[77] As will be further explained, the conclusion is inevitable that the High Court in *Youyang* altered the Australian equivalents of England's doctrines of trustees' accountability as those were on 1 January 1995.[78]

The doctrine of precedent allows, and indeed requires, acceptance that the doctrines of trustees' accountability as those existed before 1995 have been altered in England and Australia.

III. ENTER CAUSATION

The nature of that change is seen by noticing the developments that produced it. Causal enquiries entered judicial analysis of breach of trust and its remedies in two relevant stages.

[71] *Youyang* (n 5).

[72] ibid [7].

[73] *Deakin v Webb* (1904) 1 CLR 585, 604–05; *cf Agricultural Land Management* (n 4) [358]–[359]; Conaglen (n 11) 158–63; Tiverios and McKay (n 14) 247–48.

[74] R Cross and JW Harris, *Precedent in English Law* 4th edn (Oxford, Clarendon Press, 1991) 47–48; *R (Kadhim) v Brent London Borough Council Housing Benefit Review Board* [2001] QB 955 [17].

[75] E Wambaugh, *The Study of Cases* 2nd edn (Boston, Little, Brown & Co, 1894), §12; Cross and Harris (n 74) 52–57. Wambaugh's position on cases in which two or more grounds of decision are given (§§ 25–26) has been mistaken by writers: see GW Paton and G Sawer, '*Ratio Decidendi* and *Obiter Dictum*' (1947) 63 *LQR* 461, 475; Cross and Harris (n 74) 54.

[76] *Kadhim* (n 74) [16]–[17], endorsing Cross and Harris (n 74) 72. See also Cross and Harris (n 74), 69; Wambaugh (n 75) § 14.

[77] *cf* Conaglen (n 11) 158–63.

[78] Text between nn 114 and 124.

A. 'Damage'

The first stage is conveniently explained by analogy with the common law distinction between damage and quantification of loss. Suppose a proceeding before 1995 in which accounting relief had been sought against trustees who misapplied trust moneys. No causal enquiry would have been made to determine whether an equitable equivalent of 'damage' occurred. The trustees might have admitted a disbursement of the trust moneys but claimed a discharge. Or they might have admitted receipt of moneys to hold on trust, but failed to explain the fate of the missing moneys. In neither case would the court's decision—that the trustees were chargeable with the missing moneys—have depended on causal enquiries. Equitable 'damage' would have been found without determining, for example, whether the moneys were lost 'by reason of' the trustees' breach. When courts before 1995 said that trust assets were lost by reason of trustees' defaults, they merely told what had happened. They did not use causal language to test whether equitable 'damage' occurred.

The judicial analysis changed upon the adoption of *obiter dicta* uttered by Street J in *Re Dawson (dec'd)*.[79] The trustee in that case improperly paid out trust moneys, being New Zealand pounds. Between breach and litigation, the Australian pound fell against the New Zealand pound. The trustee argued that his liability was fixed as at breach, while the beneficiaries asserted that the trustee's liability continued until judgment. The account being open, this was a case for (a) charging the trustee with the disbursed sum, (b) finding no ground of discharge and (c) ordering him to pay the amount in the local currency required to restore the misapplied foreign currency.[80] The result was the same as if a curial accounting had been done: the trustee was ordered to pay the equivalent in Australian pounds of the sum of misapplied New Zealand pounds, assessed at judgment. However, the plaintiff beneficiaries sued directly for relief of a particular breach of trust rather than a curial accounting.[81]

With reason Street J thus expressed himself without the language of accounting. But in doing so, he took a step taken in no previous English or Australian decision. After considering four cases[82] in which accounting parties in equity were denied a discharge after misapplying assets for which they were accountable, he said:

> The principles embodied in this approach do not appear to involve any inquiry as to whether the loss was caused by or flowed from the breach. Rather the inquiry in each instance would appear to be whether the loss would have happened if there had been no breach.[83]

To borrow common law terms again, rather than being concerned with quantification of loss this enquiry went to whether equitable 'damage' was sustained.[84]

[79] *Dawson* (n 52).
[80] See text to nn 34–37. The rule that English courts may not enter judgment in a foreign currency was abandoned in *Miliangos* (n 25) 463, 467, 497, 500, 501.
[81] See text to nn 45–46.
[82] *Dawson* (n 52) 214–16, citing *Caffrey v Darby* (1801) 6 Ves Jun 488; 31 ER 1159; *Clough v Bond* (1838) 3 My & Cr 490; 40 ER 1016; *Fyler v Fyler* (1841) 3 Beav 550; 49 ER 216; *Salway v Salway* (1831) 2 Russ & My 215; 39 ER 376.
[83] See *Caffrey* (n 82) 494, 1162; *Fyler* (n 82) 567, 223.
[84] Mitchell (n 11) 323, 325–26.

The critical point is that whether such equitable 'damage' occurred was to be determined by a causal enquiry. The novelty of this idea is obscured by grouping[85] *Re Dawson* together with pre-1995 cases. The legal analysis in *Re Dawson* is singular. It stands apart from known prior English and Australian decisions.

B. Quantum

The second development by which causal enquiries gained a relevant role was by the adoption of a simple 'but for' test to quantify equitable relief for loss. The *dicta* in *Re Dawson* did not require this. To say that the misapplied New Zealand currency in *Re Dawson* would not have been lost but for the trustee's breach is true. But according to the *dicta* in *Re Dawson*, the monetary relief payable by the trustee was not the difference between the actual position of the beneficiaries—or the trust estate—and the position that would have been, but for the breach of trust. The relief was quantified simply by valuing the misapplied asset (New Zealand pounds) in the currency in which judgment was given (Australian pounds) at judgment. Nevertheless, in *Target* counsel for the solicitor-trustees (Mr Sumption QC) submitted that on the dicta in *Re Dawson* and *Nocton v Lord Ashburton*:[86]

> the least that the plaintiff must show is that he has suffered a loss which he would have avoided but for the breach of trust. What is meant by the dicta is that once the plaintiff has established this much, the trustee is not entitled to resist liability on the ground that the misapplication will have caused no loss if it had not been for some unforeseeable intervening factor. The 'but for' test of causation, which is not normally good enough at common law, may suffice in equity …[87]

Except that the House of Lords in *Target* decided that the claimant need not prove personal loss,[88] their Lordships adopted this depiction. Speaking for the House, Lord Browne-Wilkinson employed a 'but for' causal enquiry to quantify the trustees' responsibility for their misapplication of trust moneys.[89] He derived this enquiry from *Re Dawson*.[90] *Re Dawson* has since been viewed as authority that causal enquiries determine whether a breach of trust—or a breach of either a fiduciary duty or an equitable obligation of confidence—has caused equity's equivalent of 'damage'[91] and that equitable monetary relief for loss thereby suffered is properly quantified by a test of 'but for' causation unlimited by common law notions of foreseeability and remoteness of loss, or intervening cause.[92]

All this is so. Yet the role today of causation in English and Australian law when relieving misapplications of trust moneys is not equal to the sum of the two

[85] ibid 323.
[86] *Nocton v Lord Ashburton* [1914] AC 932.
[87] *Target* (n 7) 424.
[88] See n 129.
[89] *Target* (n 7) 431G, 434E–F, 435B–C, 436C, 438B, 441A.
[90] ibid 434E.
[91] *Youyang* (n 5) [35], [69].
[92] For critical discussion of this view, see *Agricultural Land Management* (n 4) [344]–[348].

developments described above. Further analysis is needed, particularly to show that the recent use of causal enquiries into an equitable equivalent of 'damage' has not reduced actions for breach of trust to a kind of action on the case, and that 'but for' causation forms part of a defence of trustees rather than an element of a claimant's case.

C. Significance of Developments

Before considering those matters, however, a point made at the start of this section ought to be emphasised: causal enquiries have been assigned a place in judicial analysis of breach of trust and its remedies by the ultimate appellate courts of both England and Australia.

Given that *Target*, *Youyang* and *AIB* were not sued out through the remedy of account, it is unsurprising that the judges—like Street J before them—found it unnecessary to speak in the terms of that remedy. Each English decision preferred an enquiry into an equitable equivalent of 'damage'. Just as a claim to compensation at common law requires the damage to have been caused by the relevant breach, Lord Browne-Wilkinson said in *Target*, so must a claim to equitable compensation show that the defaulting trustees' 'wrongful conduct' in misapplying trust moneys 'cause[d] the damage complained of'.[93] He expressly distinguished that question of 'damage' from quantification.[94] Lord Browne-Wilkinson's distinction was noticed and affirmed by Lord Toulson JSC in *AIB*.[95] In *AIB*, Lord Reed JSC spoke without using the word 'damage' to explain the need for a causal enquiry prior to quantification. But he said a causal enquiry prior to quantification was necessary: at that prior stage, 'foreseeability of loss is generally irrelevant, but the loss must be caused by the breach of trust, in the sense that it must flow directly from it'.[96] As will be seen, *AIB* also affirms that the distinct 'but for' causal enquiry applies when enquiring into the distinct matter of quantum.[97]

Since observers have thought causal enquiries remain foreign to Australian law,[98] it may be especially emphasised that the High Court of Australia has assigned a role to causal enquiries in analysis of breach of trust and its remedies as a matter of strict decision. That occurred in *Youyang*,[99] the facts of which were outlined above.[100] In accounting terms, *Youyang* was a case for (a) charging the trustee with the moneys and (b) disallowing any asserted discharge therefor. Counsel for the beneficiary submitted, faithfully to pre-*Target* accounting doctrine:

> The obligation of a trustee in breach of trust by wrongfully paying away trust assets is to restore to the trust fund that which has been lost to it. Courts of equity ordered the

[93] *Target* (n 7) 432E.
[94] ibid 432E–F.
[95] *AIB* (n 5) [26], [63].
[96] ibid [135].
[97] ibid [31], [34], [63], [64] (Lord Toulson JSC), [116] (Lord Reed JSC).
[98] Conaglen (n 11) 158–63; Davies (n 10) 82–83; Tiverios and McKay (n 14) 247–48; Watts (n 63) 133; Penner (n 12) 225–26.
[99] *Youyang* (n 5).
[100] See text following n 71.

> defaulting trustee to restore the fund.[101] They also awarded a common account which required the defaulting trustee to be called upon to account for any deficiency in the trust fund. It involved an account of the funds actually received and what had become of them.[102] The obligation arising on breach of trust continues until restoration[103] and the amount that a defaulting trustee is bound to pay to restore the fund is an equitable debt. The relief requires the defaulting trustee to restore the trust fund or to place it monetarily in the same position as if there had been actual restoration.[104]

Counsel for the beneficiary thus eschewed causal enquiry in quantification.[105] His statement that, '[i]f there was a breach of trust, the trustee must place the trust fund in the same position as if no breach was committed',[106] properly told what had happened. It was not meant or used to quantify loss.

The High Court could have preserved the accounting doctrines traditionally applied against trustees, free of causal enquiries, by adopting the quoted submissions and ordering the trustee-solicitors to restore the $500,000 which had been lost. However, a strong bench consisting of Gleeson CJ, McHugh, Gummow, Kirby and Hayne JJ eschewed discussion of accounting relief and favoured causal enquiries. Addressing the beneficiary's claim, they said 'there is no equitable by-pass to causation'. The favoured test, that the 'loss' be caused 'by' the breach of trust, was easily satisfied: such loss happened when the trust moneys were misapplied. Echoing *Re Dawson*, they denied that the relevant breaches and loss only occurred later than the wrongful disbursements, viz 'when [the plaintiff] Youyang's investment … was lost'.[107] The Court held:

> The trust moneys were lost when paid out in breach of trust. That is the injuria with which equity is concerned, not the failure of the investment transaction. By analogy with common law terms, the damage was then suffered;[108] subsequent events went to quantification.[109]

The court's pursuit of causal enquiries did not end there, as Edelman J has noted.[110] In meticulous reasoning over 20 paragraphs,[111] the Court considered and rejected the trustees' specific submission that 'events subsequent to the completion date … show[] that Youyang seeks to render [them] accountable for a loss which is attributable to other circumstances'[112] and held that 'there was an evidentiary burden on the [solicitor-trustees], not discharged, to show that the plaintiff [beneficiary] would

[101] *Nocton v Lord Ashburton* (n 86) 952, 958.

[102] *Partington v Reynolds* (1858) 4 Drew 253, 255–56; 62 ER 98, 99.

[103] *Bartlett* (n 32) 543.

[104] *Youyang* (n 5) 486–87; *cf Agricultural Land Management* (n 4) [358]; Tiverios and McKay (n 14) 247–48, suggesting restoration via account was not sought.

[105] 'Common law principles governing causation and remoteness of damage do not apply': *Youyang* (n 5) 488.

[106] ibid 488.

[107] ibid [34].

[108] *cf Crofter Hand Woven Harris Tweed Co v Veitch* [1942] AC 435, 442; *Marks v GIO Australia Holdings Ltd* (1998) 196 CLR 494 [93].

[109] *Youyang* (n 5) [69].

[110] See *Agricultural Land Management* (n 4) [343]–[348], [355], [357].

[111] *cf* Tiverios and McKay (n 14) 245.

[112] *Youyang* (n 5) [51].

have proceeded if it had known of the absence of the bearer certificate'.[113] At that stage, the court evidently conducted a 'but for' causal enquiry.[114]

Does this matter? Sir Arthur Goodhart[115] was accredited[116] with the opinion that the *ratio decidendi* of a case is the principle derived from a court's decision on the basis of those facts treated as material by the court, and that only scant regard is due to 'the way in which the case was argued and pleaded, the process of reasoning adopted by the judge and the relation of the case to other decisions'.[117] On that view, the causal reasoning of Gleeson CJ, McHugh, Gummow, Kirby and Hayne JJ could form no part of the *ratio decidendi* of *Youyang* unless the orders made could not have been made without that reasoning.[118] However, the High Court's reasoning cannot be ignored. First, where a court treats certain facts as material to its determination of issues, the rules of law it sets forth and applies to those facts must be *rationes* or part of the *ratio* of the case.[119] Notwithstanding that point, secondly, 'any attempt to ascertain the *ratio decidendi* without paying due regard to the facts treated as material by the judge [or the court] is completely unrealistic'.[120] The High Court in *Youyang* enunciated rules of law posing two distinct causal enquiries. Over 12 paragraphs, the Court enquired into whether the trustees' breach caused an equitable equivalent of 'damage',[121] and over 20 paragraphs it enquired into whether the loss thereby suffered would have been suffered 'but for' the trustees' breach.[122] It would be unrealistic to deem the facts in those paragraphs immaterial to the determination of the case. Thirdly, since the *per incuriam* principle does not apply—for the reasons already given[123]—and since the Court explicitly adopted the submission that causation was relevant to quantum over argument to the contrary, *Youyang* must be understood to have altered Australia's counterparts of the trust accounting doctrines as they stood in England on 1 January 1995.[124]

'*Communis error facit ius*', it might be said. A New South Welsh *dictum* of 1966 has led causal enquiries to become part of the English and Australia law of trustees' accountability for misapplied moneys, rather surprisingly. Error or no, however, the law has changed. The further analysis of that change that was postponed above can now be resumed.

[113] Gummow (n 16) 11; *Youyang* (n 5) [60].
[114] See also *Youyang* (n 5) [46]–[48].
[115] Goodhart (n 55) ch 1.
[116] JL Montrose, 'The *Ostime* Case' [1960] *British Tax Review* 184, 188–89; Cross and Harris (n 74) 67–86.
[117] Cross and Harris (n 74) 67; Goodhart (n 55) 4–10.
[118] Conaglen (n 11) 158–63.
[119] Cross and Harris (n 74) 67–68. See also *Kadhim* (n 74) [16]–[17]; Wambaugh (n 75) § 14. As to the likelihood of a case having a single *ratio*, see J Stone, 'The *Ratio* of the *Ratio Decidendi*' (1959) 22 *MLR* 597, 603–15.
[120] Cross and Harris (n 74) 67.
[121] For the legal rule, see *Youyang* (n 5) [43]–[44]. For the factual analysis, see [19]–[26], [32], [34]–[35], [43].
[122] For the legal rule, see ibid [50]. For the factual analysis, see [51], [70].
[123] See text to n 57.
[124] *cf* Edelman (n 2) 108–09; *Agricultural Land Management* (n 4) [354], [358](i) where the court concluded that *Youyang* does not decide the point. See also J Ward, 'Equitable Compensation—An Overview', in S Degeling and JNE Varuhas (eds), *Equitable Compensation and Disgorgement of Profit* (Oxford, Hart Publishing, 2017) 79.

IV. A MERE ACTION FOR DAMAGES

The commonest interpretation of the English cases, *Target* and *AIB*, is that trustees' liability for misappropriating or misapplying trust assets has been reduced to a liability to pay damages for beneficiaries' individual loss. Observers offer this interpretation with regret.[125] Such a reduction of trustees' liability would, it is said, empower trustees to behave as Holmesian 'bad men',[126] free to choose between performing the trust or instead paying damages for not doing so.[127] A legal and practical weakening of trust relationships is predicted.[128] Australian law has avoided such criticisms—curiously, since similar causal enquiries have been adopted by legal innovation there and in England.

Worrying as those eventualities would be, they are unlikely. The causal enquiry, 'Has the equitable equivalent of "damage" been suffered as a direct result of the trustees' misapplication of trust moneys?' and the more 'traditional' enquiry, 'Have the trustees a discharge for their disbursement of the trust moneys (outside of power) for which they are accountable?' differ in language and form, but apply identically in practice. Thus, in *Target* Lord Browne-Wilkinson held that 'there is an accrued cause of action as soon as [a breach of trust] is committed',[129] the defaulting trustees immediately being liable to restore the misapplied moneys. Similarly, the High Court of Australia in *Youyang* held that 'the injuria with which equity is concerned' is that the trust moneys were paid out in breach of trust, not the consequential failure of a transaction for which the money was used.[130] That is why the trustees owed an immediate obligation to *restore* the misapplied moneys, just as trustees who—in terms of accounting relief—have no discharge for their misapplication of trust moneys must restore the wrongly disbursed amount. The same points were decided in *AIB*.[131] It makes no difference whether this causal enquiry is expressed to demand that the misapplied moneys were lost 'by reason of'[132] the breach (as the High Court put it in *Youyang*) or that the loss of the moneys 'flow[ed] directly from'[133] their misapplication (as Lord Reed JSC put it in *AIB*). On both formulae, the equitable equivalent of 'damage' is found by determining that trust moneys which ought to be in the trust estate are not there.[134]

Under the next heading, it will be shown that a separate causal enquiry turning on 'but for' causation can apply by way of defence where a claimant has satisfied a court

[125] Davies (n 10) 71, 78; Tiverios and McKay (n 14) 239. See also n 16; *Bronson v Hewitt* 2013 BCCA 367 [80]–[82].

[126] OW Holmes, 'The Path of the Law' (1897) 10 *Harvard Law Review* 457, 462.

[127] Davies (n 10) 68–78; Ho (n 16) 168; Millett (1998) (n 54). See also DJ Hayton, 'The Development of Equity and the "Good Person" Philosophy in Common Law Systems' [2012] *Conv* 263, 267.

[128] For a clear statement, see Conaglen (n 11) 161–62.

[129] *Target* (n 7) 437.

[130] *Youyang* (n 5) [69].

[131] *AIB* (n 5) [29]–[32], [65], [67], [71], [90], [94], [99]–[100], [105]–[108], [114]–[116], [134], [135], [162]–[171].

[132] *Youyang* (n 5) [43]–[44], quoting *Webb v Stenton* (1883) 11 QBD 518, 530; see also [32], [43], [50], [69].

[133] *AIB* (n 5) [135].

[134] Davies (n 10) 88–89.

of such 'damage'. The enquiry asks, 'Would the "loss" proved by the beneficiaries have been suffered *but for* the trustees' default?" That does yield results different from enquiring, as was done before 1995 in England, 'Have the trustees a ground of discharge for their misapplication of the trust moneys?' But the nature of this second causal enquiry is immediately notable. It is notable because it is distinct from the causal enquiry above; it puts a burden of proof on defaulting trustees, not on claimants, and in its current form it shows no real prospect of weakening trustees' obligations.

The scope of the defence will be further discussed below. Regarding the reduction of trustees' liability to a mere liability in damages:

(a) since (subject to defences) trustees' liability for misapplying trust moneys is substantively the same whether expressed in the terms of accounting or the causal enquiries set out two paragraphs above, and
(b) since a claimant's action for an accounting is not in substance a claim for damages, then
(c) it is unclear how the same claim can in substance be a mere claim for damages simply because it complains of the loss of trust moneys as a result of a causal enquiry.[135]

The doctrine that no action on the case lies for breach of trust remains the elemental doctrine it has been for above three centuries.[136]

V. A NEW DEFENCE

The *rationes decidendi* of cases make legal doctrine, whether or not the *rationes* are expressed as such in the reasoning of courts. This fact of legal authority in common law systems is apposite in the present discussion. It is true that English and Australian law have never required claimants to establish causation of loss by a 'but for' test in order to sue defaulting trustees for their misapplication of trust moneys: within the accounting remedy, a claimant must show that the moneys were disbursed by the trustees who were accountable for them, and outside the accounting remedy, the claimant must show that the moneys the loss of which the claimant complains were lost by reason of, or as the direct result of, the trustees' default. But the fact that none of *Target*, *Youyang* and *AIB* directly says that a want of 'but for' causation now exists as a defence[137] does not indicate that the defence does not exist.

Reason suggests the opposite. Since trustees who misapply trust moneys become immediately liable to restore those assets or their equivalent in money to the trust

[135] *cf* Tiverios and McKay (n 14) 240–41. See also *Target* (n 7) 434 ('Courts of Equity did not award damages but, acting in personam, ordered the defaulting trustee to restore the trust estate'), *cf* 439.

[136] *Turner v Sterling* (1671) Freem KB 15, 16; 89 ER 13, 14; *Holland v Holland* (1869) LR 4 Ch App 449, 458, 459. On the preceding period, see NG Jones, 'Uses, Trusts and a Path to Privity' [1997] *CLJ* 175, 192–98; M Macnair, 'Common Law and Statutory Imitations of Equitable Relief under the Later Stuarts' in C Brooks and M Lobban (eds), *Communities and Courts in Britain 1150–1910* (London, 1997) 125–27.

[137] Edelman (n 2) 93.

(as *Target*, *Youyang* and *AIB*[138] each reaffirm as a matter of decision) and since the quantum of loss for which the trustees are found responsible may be reduced if that initial sum is shown to include loss[139] that would have been suffered even had the trustees not misapplied the trust assets (as each of *Target*, *Youyang* and *AIB* also holds a matter of strict decision[140]), the causal enquiry into what loss would have been suffered but for the trustees' breach must be an enquiry in the trustees' defence. Proof of that fact falls outside the facts the claimant must prove in order to succeed. Where *the claimants prove* loss suffered by reason of, or directly as the result of, the trustees' misapplication of trust moneys, and *the defaulting trustees prove* that some or all of that loss initially *proved by the claimants* would have been suffered even had the trustees not committed that breach of trust, the new defence of want of causation in principle applies.

The newness of this defence is significant. However, the defence joins a detail of existing defences rather than stand without company in an open field. Presumptions and shifting onuses are often employed by the law of fiduciaries and of express trustees.[141] In the remedy of account in England as of 1 January 1995, presumptions and shifting onuses were always employed in taking open accounts. Trustees who disbursed trust moneys were also required to show why they should be discharged for doing so. The 'great difference' in settled accounts, said Lord Hardwicke LC, is that 'the *onus probandi* is always on the party having that liberty; for the court takes it as a stated account, and establishes it' subject to the party with leave proving an omission or a wrong charge.[142] In taking open accounts, the liability of trustees as one species of fiduciary was 'strict'.[143]

Grounds of discharge or defence, in the sense given earlier, are central where trustees wish to answer or escape such liability in account.[144] Apart from general equitable and statutory defences, trustees could defend themselves by obtaining a discharge on various grounds:

(a) necessity, as where the trustees placed title or custody of trust assets in another (for example, an agent) for good reason and where the asset was stolen from the trustees or an agent without fault on the trustees' part;[145]
(b) that the missing asset had been transferred to another in proper execution of some dispositive or administrative power;[146]

138 *Target* (n 7) 434, 437; *Youyang* (n 5) [35]; *AIB* (n 5) [53], [90].
139 On the meaning of 'loss', see section VI.A. See also Smith (n 53) 369–73.
140 *Target* (n 7) 437; *Youyang* (n 5) [35], [50]–[70]; *AIB* (n 5) [107]–[108], [134]–[135] (also at [72]–[74] (Lord Toulson JSC)).
141 P Finn, 'Fiduciary Law and the Modern Commercial World' in E McKendrick (ed), *Commercial Aspects of Trusts and Fiduciary Obligations* (Oxford, OUP, 1992) 40. As to presumptions in this area, see J Glister, 'Breach of Trust and Conversion in a Falling Market' [2014] *Lloyd's Maritime and Commercial Law Quarterly* 511, 529–534; Heydon, Leeming and Turner (n 9) [23-260]–[23-325].
142 *Pit* (n 33) 565–66; 360; see also text to nn 35–37.
143 Davies (n 10) 69; Ham (n 27) 21.
144 Other matters might bar such a liability from arising at all. On these, and on general defences not specific to accounts, see Cory (n 33) 249–59.
145 *Jones v Lewis* (1751) 2 Ves Sen 240, 241; 28 ER 155, 155; Cory (n 33) 277.
146 Cory (n 34) 263–64; *Re Windsor Steam Coal Co (1901) Pty Ltd* [1919] 1 Ch 151, 166.

(c) the prior restoration of the asset to the trust;[147]
(d) account stated, by which the parties' agreement on a particular account would thereafter bar them from challenging the items included in the account.[148]

Want of causation is a further defence to add to this list. It differs from the other defences. In particular, though 'necessity' presented the question of whether the loss of an asset occurred by reason of the trustees' fault, necessity went exclusively to liability or, by analogy with the common law term, 'damage'. The new defence of want of causation goes primarily to quantum, though it may reduce the trustees' responsibility to nil.[149] It resembles the defence of want of causation in cases where by wilful default the trustees failed to get in assets or, say, collect in a debt for which they were accountable as trustees.[150]

When and how will this new defence apply?

VI. APPLICATION OF THE NEW DEFENCE

Should a day come when the defence of want of causation is wholly settled, it is certain to differ in some particular from the best view available today. Current uncertainties will be resolved in ways not yet apparent. Will the defence apply only to breaches of 'commercial' trusts? Will it be limited to misapplications of trust moneys or will it extend to specie? Will it be impossible to 'falsify' unauthorised disbursements?

However, one uncertainty stands out. It presents as a discrete, perhaps difficult, technical matter but goes to what the most controversial of the cases under discussion, *AIB*, decides. The point arises as follows. Where the causal enquiry, 'Was this loss of trust moneys suffered by reason of the trustees' misapplication of those moneys?' or the causal enquiry, 'Was this loss of trust moneys suffered directly as a result of the trustees' misapplication of those moneys?' is posed, the loss whose causation is in question is straightforwardly shown: it consists of the absence of the trust moneys from the trust estate. Reason does not require that 'loss' have the same meaning where defaulting trustees argue, in their defence, a want of causation of loss. In principle and practice it ought to, it is suggested, and does in both English and Australian law. But reaching this conclusion for England entails the conclusion that the *ratio* of *AIB* must be found in the reasoning of Lord Reed JSC, not in the ostensibly 'leading'[151] judgment of Lord Toulson JSC, who delivered the other reasoned speech in the case.

[147] *Bacon v Clark* (1837) 3 My & Cr 294, 301; 40 ER 938, 941; *Re Massingberd's Settlement* (1890) 63 LT 296, 299. This would be accompanied, in appropriate cases, with a surcharge for any interest and dividends and the like received by the trustees in between breach and restoration: Conaglen (n 11) 130, 141–42.

[148] *Siqueira v Noronha* [1934] AC 332, 337–38; Cory (n 33) 250–51.

[149] An unlikely circumstance: see text to nn 191–92.

[150] *Re Brogden* (1888) 38 Ch D 546, 567–68, 572–73; Davies (n 10) 102–03.

[151] So called by S Atkins, *Equity and Trusts* 2nd edn (Abingdon, Routledge, 2016) 430.

A. But for What Losses?

The problem of what losses are relevant to the want of causation defence may be exposed by identifying the differences of reasoning between the two reasoned judgments in *AIB*. As the provisional attempt below shows, much is common to the reasoning of Lord Toulson JSC and of Lord Reed JSC. But the later steps of their reasoning reveal different conceptions of loss operating under the defence:

> Where express trustees are liable for a breach of trust by the misapplication of trust moneys, the trustees may immediately be ordered to relieve that breach by restoring the misapplied sum to the trust fund[152]—or, should the trust no longer subsist, then paying that sum directly to the person who was in equity entitled, as at the time of the breach, to those moneys as the beneficiary of the trust[153]—and remain so liable unless and until the breach of trust is satisfied.[154]
>
> However, because the sum required to satisfy the breach must be quantified at judgment with 'the full benefit of hindsight',[155] the quantum of relief that the trustees will be liable to pay will be reduced:
>
> (a) (Lord Toulson JSC): to a sum equal to the loss *the beneficiary would not have suffered* but for the breach of trust,[156] as found by deciding what course of conduct the trustees would have followed as to the proper application of the trust moneys while complying with its equitable, contractual and tortious obligations;[157] or
>
> (b) (Lord Reed JSC): to a sum equal to the loss *to the trust estate*,[158] as found by identifying the difference in value of (i) any unauthorised investment the trustees acquired with the misapplied trust moneys, provided that the beneficiaries 'accepted' the unauthorised investment as a trust asset, and (ii) any asset the trustees owed a duty to obtain for the trust.[159]

For reasons already given, the reduction-of-quantum element of each *ratio* operates by way of defence.

But consider the losses on which defaulting trustees may rely in their defence, according to each judge. Lord Toulson JSC thought that, *unlike the claimant's claim*, the defence of want of causation turns on (a) financial loss (b) suffered by the lender-beneficiary as such.[160] Except that the causal enquiry into this loss was made by way of defence—in reduction of a prima facie liability to relieve the breaches of trust by restoring the sums of misapplied trust moneys—the enquiry was the same as that

[152] *AIB* (n 5) [29]–[32], [65], [67], [71], [90], [94], [99]–[100], [105]–[108], [114]–[116], [134], [135], [162]–[171].

[153] ibid [31]–[32], [63]–[66], [106], [108], [134].

[154] ibid [33], [36], [63], [135].

[155] ibid [36], [63], [135].

[156] ibid [64], [66]–[67], [70]–[71], [73].

[157] ibid [58], [73].

[158] ibid [115]–[116], [141].

[159] ibid [141].

[160] For a view that 'equitable compensation' by definition relates to such loss, see Millett (n 15) 201.

made by a claimant who seeks damages for breach of contract.[161] In contrast, Lord Reed JSC thought that, *like the claimant's claim*, the defence of want of causation turns on (a) loss of assets (b) from a trust estate. The concepts of loss that each judge thought pertinent to the defence are essentially opposites. The concepts contradict one another.

Which—if either—forms part of the *ratio* of the case? It is submitted that the *ratio* must lie in the reasons for judgment of Lord Reed JSC.

Lord Reed JSC had the support of the greater number of judges. Each reasoned judgment had its author's support plus the support of Lord Neuberger PSC, Lade Hale DPSC and Lord Wilson JSC, who expressed agreement in both judgments without elaboration. The judgment of Lord Toulson JSC gained the support only of those four: Lord Reed JSC thought his own reasons 'substantially the same'[162] as those of Lord Toulson JSC—which is true so far as the *rationes* of their respective judgments are the same, and only so far—but did not indicate that he agreed in the reasons of Lord Toulson JSC. That he impliedly agreed is unlikely, as his views on the kinds of loss arising on the want of causation defence contradict the views of Lord Toulson JSC. In contrast, the judgment of Lord Reed JSC gained the support of all five judges—the fifth being Lord Toulson JSC. Admittedly, Lord Toulson JSC made no emphatic display of agreement when he said his own reasoning 'accords with' the reasoning and general conclusions of Lord Reed JSC. But Lord Toulson JSC immediately showed the reality of his agreement with Lord Reed JSC's reasoning by summarising and adopting key points of the latter's reasoning and then concluding that, '[o]n the facts of the present case', the result was the same as the result reached on his own analysis.[163] It is sufficiently clear, then, that Lord Toulson JSC indicated formal agreement with the reasoning of Lord Reed JSC, thus giving Lord Reed JSC the support of all five judges. In an appellate court, judge A's expressed agreement in the reasons for judgment of judge B is effective for the purpose of identifying the decision of the case even if that agreement introduces contradiction into judge A's reasoning.[164]

The judgment of Lord Reed JSC would contain the *ratio* of the case even if his reasons and those of Lord Toulson JSC each had the support of only four members of the court. For, although Lord Reed JSC said he reasoned on 'a somewhat broader basis' than did Lord Toulson JSC,[165] the grounds of the judgment of Lord Toulson JSC are much the broader in a critical sense. In *Gold v Essex County Council*,[166] Lord Greene MR made an observation seemingly applicable also to the Supreme Court:[167]

> In a case where two members of the court base their judgments, the one on a narrow ground confined to the necessities of the decision and the other on wide propositions which go far

[161] *AIB* (n 5) [71]–[74].
[162] ibid [78].
[163] ibid [76].
[164] Wambaugh (n 75) § 14; Cross and Harris (n 74) 59–63.
[165] *AIB* (n 5) [78].
[166] *Gold v Essex County Council* [1942] 1 KB 293.
[167] Cross and Harris (n 74) 90, while noting the impossibility of saying that this approach will 'always be followed in like situations'.

> beyond those necessities, and the third member of the court expresses his concurrence in the reasoning of both, I think it right to treat the narrow ground as the real ratio decidendi.[168]

It is strictly accurate, with respect, to record that the reasoning of Lord Toulson JSC went on a ground 'far beyond [the] necessities of the decision' in *AIB* in abandoning prior understanding of the concept of 'loss' in connection with the misapplication of trust moneys.[169]

That his Lordship abandoned that prior understanding is clear. First, his Lordship thought the defence of want of causation is directed to abstract financial loss.[170] However, in protecting financial interests by remedying breaches of trust, English law has, it seems, only ever been concerned with financial interests in the property that is and ought to be held on trust. At the opening of 1995—or, indeed, the opening of 2014, during which the UK Supreme Court decided *AIB*—trustees' misapplications of trust assets were remedied by ordering the restoration of the particular assets or, where that could not be done, monetary relief to the value of the misapplied assets (plus incidental relief).[171] Similarly, in wilful default cases—where the claim was that the trust estate ought to be of greater value—trustees' liability focused exclusively on assets: a charge for wilful default was in the value of *the asset* the trustees would have acquired or got in for the trust, had they acted with the required care.[172] The concentration on assets, in awarding relief, reflected trustees' obligations in carrying out the trust. This whole system of trust practice and doctrine turns on assets and financial interests therein, and knows nothing of financial interests abstracted from trust assets such as Lord Toulson JSC had in mind.

Secondly, the concentration on loss suffered by the lender-beneficiary as such likewise departs from prior understanding. It removes attention from the trust estate (an abstract quasi-entity) and places it on persons (the beneficiary). The concern ceases to be whether a quasi-person (the trust estate) holds the assets it ought to hold (and if it does not, owing to some breach, how the deficiency is to be repaired) and becomes whether a real legal person (a beneficiary) is financially any worse off as a result of the breach of trust. Thus, when he considered the pre-1995 and pre-2014 orthodoxy that a breach of trust founds 'an equitable debt, or liability in the nature of a debt',[173] Lord Toulson JSC said:

> It is one thing to speak of an 'equitable debt or liability in the nature of a debt' in a case where a breach of trust has caused a loss; it is another thing for equity to impose or recognise an equitable debt in circumstances where the financial position of the beneficiaries, actual or potential, would have been the same if the trustee had properly performed its duties.[174]

[168] *Gold* (n 166) 298.
[169] Worthington (n 13) 761–62.
[170] *AIB* (n 5) [64], [66]–[67], [70]–[71], [73].
[171] S Elliott and J Edelman, '*Target Holdings* Considered in Australia' (2003) 119 *LQR* 545, 548; Conaglen (n 11) 130, 141–42.
[172] *Re Stevens* [1898] 1 Ch 162, 171; *National Trustees Executors and Agency Co of Australasia Ltd v Dwyer* (1940) 63 CLR 1, 14.
[173] *Ex p Adamson, Re Collie* (1878) 8 Ch D 807, 819 (James and Baggallay LJJ).
[174] *AIB* (n 5) [61].

This view of financial position excluded reference to the position that ruled in all prior cases, namely the position of the trust estate as regards the assets it comprises and ought to comprise.

That the wide propositions underpinning these departures from prior understanding went far beyond the necessities of *AIB* is clear when the reasoning of Lord Toulson JSC is contrasted with that of Lord Reed JSC. Lord Reed JSC concurred in the order to dismiss the appeal on markedly narrower grounds. In his reasoning, Lord Reed JSC concentrated on loss 'to the trust estate'.[175] He indicated that relief by 'equitable compensation' differs only in procedural form from relief by way of an accounting.[176] Hence financial loss suffered by a beneficiary is not in point where equitable compensation is sought for the misapplication of trust moneys: the concern is with the misapplied trust moneys.

The relative width and narrowness of the grounds on which Lord Toulson JSC and Lord Reed JSC respectively decided the case can be seen from the way in which they each analysed the facts. Each accepted that the asset the solicitor-trustees ought to have got in was a first charge (which would have realised £1.2m) and that the asset they had got in was a 'hopelessly inadequa[te]'[177] second charge (which realised £867,697). However, the solicitor-trustees' prima facie liability to pay the sum misapplied (£3.3m) was reduced by putting causation in issue. By way of defence, the question for Lord Toulson JSC was: 'But for the breaches of trust, how much (if any) up to the amount of £3.3m would the lender-beneficiary have suffered as personal loss?' This permitted enquiries into what course of conduct the defaulting trustees might have followed, while keeping to their various duties: enquiries that could not arise had his Lordship concentrated alone on what assets the trust comprised and ought to comprise. For Lord Reed JSC the trustees' defence posed the narrower question: 'But for the breaches of trust, how much (if any) up to the amount of £3.3m would the trust estate have held as an authorised trust asset, whether as money or specie?' The ultimate value of the first charge (£1.2m) less the ultimate value of the second charge (£867,697) left a difference of £273,777.42. That was, Lord Reed JSC held, the compensable loss to the trust estate 'as a result' of the breaches of trust.[178] It was immaterial to enquire what *other acts* the trustee might have done but for the breach or what someone not privy to the trust would have done.[179] On this last point the *ratio* of *AIB* may indeed be narrower than the *ratio* of *Youyang*, where enquiries into such other acts were made at length.[180]

The judgment of Lord Reed JSC shows that abandonment of established trust practice and doctrine, with their focus on the completeness of trust estates, was unnecessary. If the reasoning of Lord Reed JSC did not command the agreement of all five members of the Supreme Court—which, it is submitted, it did—the

[175] ibid [106], [132], [137], [141].
[176] ibid [90]–[91], [99]–[100], [106], [108], [134].
[177] ibid [140].
[178] ibid [141]: as the trust was no longer on foot and £273,777.42 (plus interest) had already been paid, the appeal was dismissed.
[179] See also *Youyang* (n 5) [63]; Gummow (n 16) 5.
[180] *Youyang* (n 5) [50]–[70].

relative narrowness of the grounds of the judgment of Lord Reed JSC indicate that the *ratio decidendi* of the case is to be found therein, not in the judgment of Lord Toulson JSC.

B. Commercial vs Traditional Trusts

Uncertainty continues over whether the legal developments discussed in this chapter apply only to so-called commercial trusts, not so-called traditional trusts. The uncertainty was at its greatest immediately after *Target*,[181] where Lord Browne-Wilkinson first divined the distinction and a consequential distinction between 'basic' rules of trust law and those that presumably are 'advanced'. Only the basic rules applied to commercial trusts; traditional trusts attracted basic and advanced rules.[182] Thus, Lord Browne-Wilkinson held, the lender-beneficiary in *Target* had no entitlement to the restoration of the misapplied sum to the trust estate. He implied that a beneficiary of a traditional trust would have had such an entitlement. Apart from the uncertainty left as to what is a 'commercial' trust, *Target* left uncertainty by describing as 'basic' the 'rule' denying the lender-beneficiary an entitlement to restoration of the full misapplied sum of trust moneys to the trust estate. The adjective 'basic' was a misnomer. The 'basic rule' was complex. It depended on several features of the case, and perhaps several rules.

Such uncertainties are reduced by *AIB*, though not eliminated. Lord Reed JSC denied 'a categorical distinction between trusts in commercial and non-commercial relationships, or … that there are trusts to which the fundamental principles of equity do not apply'.[183] The application of Wambaugh's famous test[184] for distinguishing *ratio* from *obiter dictum* shows that this doctrine is *ratio* in the judgment of Lord Reed JSC—and part of the *ratio* of the case. Reversing Lord Reed JSC's denial to become an assertion, Wambaugh would ask: 'if the court had conceived this new proposition to be good, and had it in mind, [could] the decision … have been the same'?[185] Had Lord Reed JSC meant that a categorical distinction exists between commercial and traditional trusts, he would have held that the fundamental principles of equity did not apply to the trust in *AIB*. He held that those fundamental principles in fact applied.[186]

Lord Toulson JSC likewise denied that Lord Browne-Wilkinson intended a dispositive distinction between commercial and traditional trusts. He said 'commercial' facts can simply inform 'whether there has been a loss applying a "but for" test'.[187]

[181] Conaglen (n 11) 27; Mitchell (n 11) 323–24.
[182] *Target* (n 7) 435.
[183] *AIB* (n 5) [102].
[184] Wambaugh (n 75) § 11. See also Cross and Harris (n 74) 52–57.
[185] Wambaugh (n 75) § 11.
[186] *AIB* (n 5) [70], [102], [136]; *cf* J Penner, 'Falsifying the Trust Account and Compensatory Equitable Compensation' in S Degeling and J Varuhas (eds), *Equitable Compensation and Disgorgement of Profits* (Oxford, Hart Publishing, 2017) 150.
[187] *AIB* (n 5) [70] (italics added); see also [102], [106], [108] (Lord Reed).

In point of authority, that is strictly irrelevant: the *ratio* of *AIB* is to be found in the judgment of Lord Reed JSC. However, it is worthwhile to note without elaboration that while 'commercial' facts can undoubtedly inform causal enquiries, his Lordship's use of such facts in that way involved a non sequitur.[188]

C. Money and Specie

The experiment with a distinction between commercial and traditional trusts suggests some other criterion may be found to constrain the defence of want of causation. Commerce concerns money. Might the defence only apply where the misapplied trust property is money?[189] The courts in *Target*, *Youyang* and *AIB* all spoke generally of misapplications of 'trust property' or 'trust assets'. Yet all three cases concerned trust moneys alone. The *ratio decidendi* of a case rests on the facts material to the determination of the issues presented by a case; a fact can be material even though the court did not indicate as much.[190] It is conceivable that the monetary character of the trust property in these cases was material even though it was not said to be so. The defence of want of causation might prove to be limited in principle to misapplications of trust moneys.

Several matters suggest that the defence is specially suited to misapplications of money but not specie. At base, trustees who assert that trust specie would have been lost even had the trustees not misapplied it must assert that they would have had (equitable) power to deal with the specie in the supposed situation. The defence will necessarily fail if the trustees cannot show they would have had that power.[191] Supposing they would have had that power, the self-interestedness of an allegation that, but for the trustees' breach, the specie would have been lost without the trustees' fault makes the allegation implausible. A trier of fact might ask with incredulity: 'How can the misapplied specie now exist given that, on the trustees' account, it would have been destroyed without blame had the trustee committed no breach?' Further, 'if a trustee makes an unauthorised disbursement of trust funds'—or, surely, any misapplication of trust property—'it is no defence to a claim by a beneficiary for the trustee to say that if he had not misapplied the funds they would have been stolen by a stranger'.[192] Though the reasoning in *Target*, *Youyang* and *AIB* displays no plain sign that the defence might be limited to misapplications of money, these matters suggest the cogency of such a constraint.

188 Edelman (n 2) 98; Davies (n 10) 77.

189 For another perspective, see Edelman (n 2) 103–07.

190 Goodhart (n 55) 10ff.

191 See *Various Claimants v Giambrone and Law (a firm)* [2017] EWCA Civ 1193 [62] (money).

192 *AIB* (n 5) [58] (Lord Toulson JSC), relying on *Magnus v Queensland National Bank* (1888) 37 Ch D 466, 472. This doctrine is good English law, even assuming that the speech of Lord Toulson JSC does not contain the *ratio* of *AIB*. See also *Youyang* (n 5) at [63]; Heydon, Leeming and Turner (n 9) [23-425]–[23-430].

D. The Remedy of the Account

The establishment a want of causation defence in doctrine has effects on the remedy of account, as has been seen. The breadth of these effects is uncertain. All else aside, it is unknown whether the defence will come to apply to misapplications of assets by accounting parties other than express trustees, especially receivers, company directors, executors and agents.[193] Some courts have declined to apply the reasoning in *Target* where relief was sought from company directors' misappropriations of company property,[194] but the question is not settled.

Fortunately, other alleged uncertainties over the effects of the new defence on the remedy of account can immediately be dispelled. First, the possibility[195] that greater relief for a given breach of trust could be recovered through a judicial accounting than by a direct claim to recover equitable compensation has been eliminated. Trustees' liability for the one misapplication of trust property is no different according to the procedure by which relief of that breach of trust is sought.[196] Secondly, without doubt it remains possible to falsify unauthorised disbursements when those show in settled accounts, and in an open account to charge trustees with the assets for which they are responsible—as well as to find that defaulting trustees have no discharge from that obligation.[197] Establishing a want of 'but for' causation between breach and 'loss' is inapt to destroy either accounting procedure: the defence only limits the quantum of relief. That the procedures and principles of trust accounting continue is apparent, in particular, from the judgment of Lord Reed JSC in *AIB*: where the trust no longer subsists and the procedures of curial accounting are not engaged, his Lordship said, 'equitable compensation' can instead be paid in a 'measure ... the same as would be payable on an accounting'.[198]

E. Authority on Own Facts

The possibility of concluding that the want of causation defence is not law does not exist, and *Target*, *Youyang* and *AIB* decide too many general legal propositions to have no authority beyond their own facts. But a final point of current uncertainty should be recorded: namely, a doubt as to how often facts like those litigated in *Target*, *Youyang* and *AIB* will lead to limited relief like that granted in *Target* and *AIB*—but not *Youyang*.

[193] *O'Halloran v RT Thomas & Family Pty Ltd* (1998) 45 NSWLR 262, 278; *Bairstow v Queens Moat Houses plc* [2001] EWCA Civ 712; [2001] 2 BCLC 531 [53]–[54]. See also *Re Loquitur Ltd* [2003] EWHC 999 (Ch); [2003] 2 BCLC 442 [135]–[137]; *Revenue and Customs Commissioners v Holland* [2010] UKSC 51; [2010] 1 WLR 2793 [44], [49], [56], [124], [142].

[194] See Mitchell (n 23) 227–28; Heydon, Leeming and Turner (n 9) [23-250]–[23-255].

[195] See Burrows (n 16) 46–47.

[196] *AIB* (n 5) [90]–[91], [99]–[100], [106], [108], [134].

[197] *cf* Burrows (n 16) 47; Edelman (n 2) 103; Penner (n 186) 143, 144, 151.

[198] *AIB* (n 5) [91].

In view of the points for which *Target* and *AIB* stand as authority, it is ironic that the decisions on the facts in those two cases will easily be distinguishable. Indeed, they may be distinguishable in every similar case.[199] In such cases, the lender who advances money to solicitor-trustees does not thereby make a gift: the advance is to be held on trust until an instrument of conveyance is received. Should the money not be applied as the lender's directions (or the trust terms) require, the trustees—especially solicitor-trustees—must return the money to the lender-beneficiary. This was provided for by the applicable terms in *AIB*, which said: '[i]f completion is delayed, you [the solicitor-trustees] must return [the advanced sum] to us [the mortgage lender] when and how we tell you'.[200] Should completion not occur at all, it must have been so obvious as to go without saying[201] that the solicitor-trustees owe at least the same obligation to return the moneys. There must have been an implied term to that effect in *AIB*—and in *Target*.[202]

For the purpose of applying or distinguishing *Target* and *AIB* on these grounds, it does not matter whether the obligation to return the trust money is analysed as a trust obligation, a contractual promise or a debt. The material point is the result. For, in considering whether the defence of want of causation applies either as conceived by Lord Reed JSC—'But for the breaches of trust, what if any part of the misapplied £3.3m would the trust estate have held in an authorised form as money or specie?'—or as conceived by Lord Toulson JSC—'But for the breaches of trust, how much (if any) up to the amount of £3.3m would the lender-beneficiary have suffered as personal loss?'[203]—this obligation to refund must have altered the result of *AIB*. Had the solicitor-trustees not breached their obligations, what they would (lawfully) have done is return the borrowed sum—unreduced—to the lender-beneficiary.

The outcomes on the facts in *Target* and *AIB*—where such critical facts were, evidently, not the subject of submissions—may never be replicated for it is difficult to imagine that the trustees could owe no obligation to return the money (or otherwise apply it as the beneficiary directs) should the transaction not complete as the parties intend. This conclusion is not weakened by the curious view of 'completion' advanced by Lord Toulson JSC which, as one part of a minority concurring judgment,[204] can be ignored here.[205]

VII. CONCLUSION

In a development of equitable doctrines not yet considered by the ultimate appellate courts of most common law jurisdictions, a new defence has been established in

[199] See *Various Claimants v Giambrone and Law* (n 191) [61]–[63].
[200] ibid [4].
[201] *Marks and Spencer plc v BNP Paribas Securities Services Trust Co (Jersey) Ltd* [2015] UKSC 72; [2016] AC 742 [16]–[21], [23].
[202] Davies (n 10) 77; Edelman (n 2) 96, 98.
[203] See text to nn 156–59.
[204] *AIB* (n 5) [74].
[205] Davies (n 10) 74–75.

English and Australian equity by the ultimate appellate courts of those jurisdictions. Want of causation of loss is a defence that delimits the personal liability of trustees. It allows them to argue that, of the loss shown to have been suffered by reason of (or directly as the result of) the trustees' misapplication of trust moneys, the trustees' responsibility is confined to that part of the loss (if any) that would not have been suffered but for the trustees' default.

This defence has not been named as such in the leading decisions.[206] However, it is the necessary consequence of the authoritative decision of the following points as a matter of the doctrine of precedent. Before 1995 in England and before 2003 in Australia, causal enquiries were neither permitted nor required when ascertaining trustees' liability for misapplying trust property. Today, as before 1995 in England and 2003 in Australia, the remedy of account allows trustees to be charged with trust moneys and held immediately liable—without causal enquiry—to restore all of those moneys where they disburse them in circumstances giving no ground for a discharge. Claims outside the doctrines and procedures of account require the claimant to show that the loss of the misapplied moneys occurred by reason of, or as the direct result of, the trustees' misapplication of the trust moneys: such enquiries recognise an equitable equivalent of the common law concept of 'damage', but apply exactly as the enquiry whether trustees have a discharge for their disbursement of trust moneys (outside of power) applies.

Trustees who are found prima facie liable to restore the misapplied trust moneys may defend the claim by means of a distinct causal enquiry. If some only of the loss suffered by the misapplication of the trust moneys would not have been suffered but for the trustees' default, the trustees' prima facie liability will be reduced to that amount. Between the law of England and the law of Australia in point, the main difference is the scope of the 'but for' causal enquiry. The enquiry in England, under the *ratio* of *AIB* as found in the judgment of Lord Reed JSC, is into the difference in value of (i) any unauthorised investment acquired by the trustees with the misapplied trust moneys, provided that was later 'accepted' by the beneficiaries as a trust asset, and (ii) any asset the trustees owed a duty to obtain for the trust. That is, the enquiry is exclusively into what assets are and ought to be held, and their value. In Australia, however, the enquiry evidently permits and perhaps requires a wider enquiry into what conduct the trustees and others would have pursued but for the trustees' default.[207]

There is a fair likelihood that intermediate and ultimate appellate courts in England and Australia will have occasion to study the grounds on which, it is suggested, this defence of want of causation has been established. The creation of that new defence in both jurisdictions in turn suggests that the appellate courts of other Commonwealth common law jurisdictions in which English and Australian decisions are persuasive will, in time, also have cause to consider this new equitable defence.

[206] See n 10.
[207] *Youyang* (n 5) [51]ff.

10

Laying the Axe to the Root of the Tree? Shielding a Co-trustee from Liability

JOSHUA GETZLER*

He searched, beginning with the oldest and ending with the youngest; and the goblet turned up in Benjamin's bag. ... Joseph said to them, "What is this deed that you have done?" ... Judah replied, "What can we say to my lord? How can we plead, how can we prove our innocence? God has uncovered the crime of your servants. Here we are, then, slaves of my lord, the rest of us as much as he in whose possession the goblet was found."

Genesis 44:12,15,16 (New JPS Translation)

The ... objection was ... on this general point of breaches of trust and gross neglects of the several directors ... that some acts are joint, others separate, and each is answerable only for his own particular acts and neglects ... If this be so, it is *laying the axe to the root of the tree* ... But it is not so; for where there are many trustees, and some are guilty of one breach and some of others, or where there is a gross negligence, and the loss is so complicated as it cannot be apportioned, I think they are all jointly liable.

Charitable Corporation v Sutton (1742) 9 Mod 349, 356; 88 ER 500, 504 per Lord Hardwicke C (emphasis added)

I. THE PROBLEM OF CO-TRUSTEE LIABILITY

AS THE AUTHOR of Genesis and Lord Hardwicke each suggest in the quotations above, the instinct to hold group members liable for the breach of any one member goes very deep in moral and legal tradition. The mechanism is clear enough: the entire membership of a group falls liable for failing to constrain each and every member from doing the wrong thing. For hundreds of years the courts in England have held that co-trustees are jointly and severally liable for breaches of trust along these lines; but we must be careful to specify what 'joint and several' can mean here, for equity shades the meaning of this concept differently to law. The act constituting a breach of trust might be joint or shared such that all the trustees are seen to commit the wrongful act together as a finding of fact. Alternatively there might be parallel coordinate breaches, where the wrongful act of the one

* I thank Paul Davies and Aleksi Ollikainen for thoughtful comments on drafts of this chapter, and James Goudkamp, Charles Mitchell and Mark Leeming for discussion of key points. They do not share in any remaining defaults or errors.

trustee brings a concomitant breach of trust by the others for failing to monitor and restrain, with that latter style of wrongdoing registering as a separate legal claim. By holding that one trustee can commit a separate breach of trust by failing to forestall a breach by a co-trustee, the separate and various breaches of the multiple trustees can be accumulated and liability shared between the trustees, even where they do not act jointly. But these two cases—a single breach jointly done on the one hand, distinct breaches accumulated and shared on the other—do not sum to a system of vicarious liability whereby the breach of one actor is ascribed to another. Co-trustees are not agents the one for the other, nor do they as a group personally represent the beneficiaries; co-liabilities are not generated by attribution.

The distinction of co-trustees' joint and several liabilities from the mutual liabilities of partners or agents or directors can blur in practice. The ambiguity emerges most clearly when we examine claims that an 'innocent' co-trustee should not be made liable where an 'active' trustee has received and controlled assets and then loses or degrades those assets through an individual breach of trust. In many such cases the courts have visited primary liability on the active trustee only, and denied the active trustee any claim for contribution from the other co-trustees. The claim of the innocent trustee to avoid liability either directly or through contribution might here be characterised as a *defence*, that is, an independent reason adduced by the defendant when answering a completed claim that explains why a liability that would otherwise exist is undone or mitigated. But such an argument might also take effect as a *denial*, that is, an answer that the essential ingredients of liability are lacking, in that the claimant has failed to make out a case for some active participation on breach or else failure to monitor when such protective behaviour could have been expected. Perhaps we have here a third category, neither denial nor defence exactly, but rather a *dilution* of liability, a claim that *ex post* breach the errant trustee cannot share any (prima facie joint) liability with the innocent trustees via solidary liability afforced by the normal processes of contribution and apportionment because the latter parties are not sufficiently at fault. The dilution model is supported by the phenomenon that co-trustee liability in English law today has been folded into a general legislative duty of care subject to the apportionment rules for multiple tortfeasors. Where distribution of liabilities between wrongdoers is predicated on varying levels of misfeasance and the court splits the burden of liability based on some arithmetic appraisal of fault, the classical distinction between defence or denial may break down; neither category exactly fits, or else a dilution claim inhabits both the defence and denial categories simultaneously. So dilution can be framed as a particular kind of defence against double recovery: 'you may have a claim, but you can't claim against me because you've already claimed against another trustee (who may not have even a contribution claim against me)'. Or else dilution may take shape as a denial, along the lines that 'you have failed to supply an essential ingredient of the claim you are making, namely the identity of the proper wrongdoer; you have instead selected a person who was not culpable'.[1]

[1] I am grateful to Aleksi Ollikainen for discussion of the distinctions in this passage. Similar classificatory problems evoked here are found in other areas of the law, see eg A Dyson, J Goudkamp and F Wilmot-Smith, 'Central Issues in the Law of Tort Defences' in Dyson, Goudkamp and Wilmot-Smith (eds), *Defences in Tort* (Oxford, Hart Publishing, 2014) 3–24.

This is hardly simple law. To ease our way into the tangle of historical rules, it may be expedient to begin with the parallel problem of knowing assistance and shared breach of trust by parties who may not each originally be co-trustees, starting with a recent and controversial case of the highest English court.

II. PARTICIPATORY LIABILITY IN THE SHADOW OF CO-TRUSTEESHIP

In *Central Bank of Nigeria v Williams*[2] a sharply divided Supreme Court held that a party participating in a breach of trust through knowing receipt or dishonest assistance could successfully claim that liability was time-barred by operation of the Limitation Act 1980. Section 21(1)(a) of the Act exempted from limitation a claim by 'a beneficiary under a trust' where there was a 'fraud or fraudulent breach of trust to which the trustee was a party or privy'. To put the rule in positive terms, in such a case an action could be brought by the beneficiary at any distance of time, and limitation could be no defence. But this exception to limitation, it was argued by the majority, did not apply to a stranger participating in a breach of trust: first, because there was no 'true trust' existing prior to breach, but instead a personal accounting relationship that came into existence post breach, as a remedy or liability reacting to the breach;[3] and, secondly and cumulatively, because a participant liability based on breach of trust could sufficiently exist without the head trustee engaging in 'fraudulent breach of trust', as where a crooked solicitor leads an innocent trustee to misallocate trust assets; in such a case the assistant might be fraudulent but not the primary actor. On the majority's reading a *shared* fraud in making the breach was a prerequisite for exclusion of the limitation rules. One strand of the reasoning was that Parliament could not have intended the incidence of limitation for stranger participants in a breach of trust to depend on the mind-state of the trustee; ergo participant liability was not covered by the statutory exception. In the end that exception only applied to primary *and* fraudulent breaches of the so-called 'true trusts'.

Reacting perhaps to the minority judges' sharp criticism of this reading of the statute, Lord Sumption JSC in the majority offered this explanation or justification for his narrow interpretation of the statutory exception:

> These words are there to relieve trustees who acted in good faith, including the honest co-trustees of a dishonest trustee. They would be unnecessary if the provision applied to actions against strangers to the trust, because any fraudulent breach of trust must necessarily be one to which the trustee is a party or privy. The inclusion of the phrase makes sense only on the footing that the section applies to actions against trustees and that it was intended to limit the circumstances in which it applied to them.[4]

This passage is worth highlighting. Lord Sumption here acknowledges the orthodox juridical position whereby an innocent trustee would presumptively be liable in full for a dishonest co-trustee's breach on the basis of some version of joint and

[2] *Central Bank of Nigeria v Williams* [2014] UKSC 10; [2014] AC 1189.

[3] ibid 1197, 1200, 1206–08 (Lord Sumption). On this reasoning the trustee *de son tort*—that is, the trustee who assumes trust duties by intermeddling in trust affairs—does manage a 'true trust' since the law erects the duties of trust management *ex ante* any breach.

[4] ibid 1209.

several liability. The statutory exception was necessary to ensure that the innocent co-trustee's joint liability for a co-trustee's fraudulent breach could still be shielded by limitation. The fraud of the breaching co-trustee might otherwise colour the legal characterisation of the 'innocent' co-trustees as somehow sharing in the fraud of the other members of the trustee group, and so denying them the benefit of limitation protection. Why this denial of protection would have been a bad thing was not explained. Is it so very innocent for one co-trustee to tolerate, ignore or fail to see the breaches of another trustee when both are subject to a joint liability to execute the trust? It is surely significant that courts have in the past denied that the statutory discretion to excuse a trustee for 'honestly and reasonably' breaching a trust duty[5] can have any application to failures of co-trustees to monitor, even inadvertently;[6] and going beyond that it has recently been held by the Court of Appeal held that any breach of a negligence duty applied to a trustee cannot be classified as 'honest and reasonable' under the exculpatory statutory provision.[7]

Lord Neuberger PSC gave the other majority speech in *Williams*. Agreeing in the main with Lord Sumption's analysis, Lord Neuberger elaborated on the principles governing a co-trustee's negligence liability as a further reason to insist that fraudulent breach *by the trustee being sued* should be a necessary condition to suspend the normal limitation rule:

> [T]he context of [the limitation] section suggests that a claim against an innocently negligent co-trustee or professional adviser of the fraudulent trustee is not "an action ... in respect of ... fraud or fraudulent breach of trust". Rather it should be characterised as an action "in respect of [their] negligence". In the case of a co-trustee, this is borne out by what is stated in article 96.1 of *Underhill & Hayton's The Law of Trusts and Trustees*, 18th ed (2010), namely that a trustee "is not vicariously answerable for the ... defaults of his co-trustee, but only for his *own* acts or defaults".[8]

This reasoning, which was central to Lord Neuberger's interpretation of the meaning of the statutory exception on which the case turned, raises some fresh puzzles. What could the concept of the 'innocently negligent co-trustee' possibly mean? The judge may have wished simply to contrast a fraudulent or advertently dishonest breach from a non-fraudulent breach, attaching different limitation results to the two categories; but such use of 'innocent' to qualify or explicate 'negligence' would risk redundancy or even incoherence. It is basic that a negligent person cannot sustain an active mind-state purposing to breach the relevant duty of care; in that sense all negligence is inevitably 'innocent' in the sense of 'not dishonest'.[9] But perhaps we can put this puzzling language to one side (along with indiscriminate

[5] Trustee Act 1925, s 61; and see text accompanying nn 27–30.

[6] *Re Turner* [1897] 1 Ch 536, 541–42 (Byrne J).

[7] *Santander UK v RA Legal Solicitors* [2014] EWCA Civ 183; [2014] PNLR 420 [31]–[32] (Briggs LJ).

[8] *Williams* (n 2) 1221–22.

[9] Lord Clarke SCJ picks up on Lord Neuberger's odd contrast of 'innocently (as opposed to fraudulently) negligent co-trustees' (at 1244) but finds reasons to differ from the majority on alternative grounds of a likely legislative intent to treat at least a dishonest assistant in the same way as fraudulent trustee for the purposes of limitation. Negligence as a mind-state is distinguished from intentionality including deceit and recklessness in P Cane, '*Mens Rea* in Tort Law' (2000) 20 *OJLS* 533.

hybridisations of 'knowing assistance',[10] 'knowing receipt',[11] 'dishonest receipt'[12] and 'dishonest assistance')[13] as symptoms of judges writing under pressure rather than consciously developing new jurisprudence.[14] It may be more fruitful to focus on Lord Neuberger's (largely) correct statement in *Williams* of the basic principle that 'a trustee "is not vicariously answerable for the ... defaults of his co-trustee, but only for his own acts or defaults"'.

III. VICARIOUS v SHARED (SOLIDARY) LIABILITY

Some courts have specified co-trustee liabilities in terms similar to partners or joint tortfeasors engaged in common enterprise, for example Katz J in a recent New Zealand case:

> Trustees' liability is joint and several. As a result, where there are two or more trustees, a creditor can choose to pursue any one of them. ... If that trustee is found liable, he or she may then seek a contribution (or in some limited cases, an indemnity) from his or her co-trustee(s).[15]

But this may over-simplify. Co-trustees differ from partners in that they do not by virtue of the trusteeship bestow any kind of mandate on each other to bind each other personally in contract or in agency. Nor can a trustee vicariously be liable for persons who effect breaches of duty sounding in tort unless the trustee is also employing or controlling such a person (whether a co-trustee or not) as a delegate or agent in running the trust business[16] (though statutory indemnities and exemption clauses commonly exist to shield an employing trustee from full vicarious liability for delegates or principal-agent liability, such as section 23 of the Trustee Act 2000, restating earlier legislative rules). But it is also an oversimplification to speak simply of a co-trustee being liable 'only for his own acts or defaults'; and the reason for this is clear. Co-trustees generally do not act on their own in the eyes of the law but rather as a solidary group. Co-trustees are subject to a bespoke form of solidary liability born of their joint tenancy of the trust assets and their joint and collective wielding of trust powers as a unanimous collective.[17] The coordinate joint liabilities of co-trustees may resemble in operation those of partners or directors or other co-agents, but these liabilities do not find their source in shared contractual or tortious duties. They arise from shared titular trustee powers with concomitant shared duties to account, and this can mean that the breaches of any one co-trustee are

[10] *Williams* (n 2) 1202, 1209–10, 1215, 1228, 1241, 1243.
[11] ibid 1196, 1202, 1203, 1207, 1208, etc.
[12] ibid 1215.
[13] ibid 1215, 1242.
[14] See J Lee, 'Constructing and Limiting Liability in Equity' (2015) 131 *LQR* 39; PS Davies, 'Limitation in Equity' [2014] *Lloyd's Maritime and Commercial Law Quarterly* 313.
[15] *Selkirk v McIntyre* [2013] NZHC 575 [16].
[16] *Mendes v Guedalla* (1862) 2 J & H 259; 70 ER 1054 (KB).
[17] See *Luke v South Kensington Hotel Company* (1879) 11 Ch D 121; *Wilson v Moore* (1834) 1 My & K 126, 142–43; 39 ER 629, 635 (Leach MR) ('All parties to a breach of trust are equally liable'); *Taylor v Tabrum* (1833) 6 Sim 281, 282; 58 ER 599.

attributed to all co-trustees as joint actors; a fraudulent breach by one trustee which harms assets held jointly by the co-trustee collective is automatically each and every other trustee's 'own act or default' and each is severally liable for the joint action.[18] That is why it is incorrect to describe joint co-trustee liabilities arising from wrongful exercise of powers as vicarious liabilities.

The shared powers model may not even require shared title to assets. There can be trust-like duties without present assets as where there are charges for future property[19] or duties to wield powers so as to constitute a trust.[20] Multiple holders of a power of attorney are another analogue where no joint assets are held. Moreover, trusts jurisprudence makes no distinction between the joint tenancy of trusts and equitable powers when it comes to the *jus accrescendi* (that is, vesting of relevant assets or powers by survivorship).[21] All of this might suggest that a stranger participant, by joining with a trustee to effect a breach of the trust, also becomes by this act of intermeddling a solidary holder of the trust powers him or herself (if not a joint tenant in possession) and thus should be seen as akin to a primary trustee, a kind of 'trust power holder *de son tort*', if that parallel species of liability can be adapted and bent into service.[22] Such a conception of participant liability can help explain why courts continue to deploy gain-stripping, tracing and following remedies against stranger participants despite the personal origin or basis of their liability.[23]

[18] *Fletcher v Green (No 1)* (1864) 33 Beav 426, 429–30; 55 ER 433, 434 (Romilly MR).

[19] See J Getzler, 'Assignment of Future Property and Preferences' in J Glister and P Ridge (eds), *Fault Lines in Equity* (Oxford, Hart Publishing, 2012) 73–105.

[20] The unexecuted estate is just one possible example of a duty to constitute a fiduciary fund where the duty itself has fiduciary qualities: see *Commissioner of Stamp Duties v Livingston* [1965] AC 694, 707–14 (PC); (1960) 107 CLR 411 (HCA) 437–44 per Fullagar J, 448–54 per Kitto J.

[21] Trustee Act 1893, s 22(1): 'Where a power or trust is given to or vested in two or more trustees jointly, then, unless the contrary is expressed in the instrument, if any, creating the power or trust, the same may be exercised or performed by the survivor or survivors of them for the time being.'

[22] An assumption of fiduciary power by an intermeddling solicitor is in effect what North J found in *Mara v Browne* [1895] 2 Ch 69; he expressly eschewed the label 'constructive trustee' to describe the liability, preferring to speak of the intermeddler being a kind of 'partner' of the primary trustee in operating the trust (at 94). His decision was reversed by the Court of Appeal on the point that in the circumstances of the case assumption of trusteeship would have been *ultra vires qua* solicitor-agent ([1896] 1 Ch 199); but this was couched as an evidential finding rather than a rule of law. See discussion of these principles in *Dubai Aluminium Company Ltd v Salaam* [2002] UKHL 48; [2003] 2 AC 366 [131]–[141], where Lord Millett prefers to describe this as the liability of the intermeddler as a '*de facto* trust'; a similar analysis is offered in *Novoship (UK) Ltd v Mikhaylyuk* [2014] EWCA Civ 908; [2015] QB 499 [73]–[84].

[23] *Novoship* (n 22); *Grimaldi v Chameleon Mining NL (No 2)* (2012) 200 FCR 296 (FCA); C Mitchell and S Watterson, 'Remedies for Knowing Receipt' in C Mitchell (ed), *Constructive and Resulting Trusts* (Oxford, Hart Publishing, 2010) 115–58; PS Davies, *Accessory Liability* (Oxford, Hart Publishing, 2015) 264–69; PS Davies, 'Gain-based Remedies for Dishonest Assistance' (2015) 131 *LQR* 173; J Dietrich and P Ridge, *Accessory Liability in Private Law* (Cambridge, CUP, 2016) 288–303; P Ridge, 'Participatory Liability and the Hallmarks of an "Australian" Equity' in T Bonyhady (ed), *Finn's Law: An Australian Justice* (Annandale, Federation Press, 2016) 68–91. The case of *FHR European Ventures LLP & Ors v Cedar Capital Partners LLC* [2014] UKSC 45; [2015] 1 AC 250 (UKSC) may be distinguished as an instance of proprietary gain-stripping being imposed on a fiduciary office assumed *ex ante* the relevant breach; the decision further that 'true trust' attributes may be attached to non-custodial fiduciary positions. The language of 'true trust' may ultimately be misleading as there is no analytical reason to distinguish the custodial fiduciary and the holder of fiduciary power; this is to oppose the analysis offered in S Worthington, 'Exposing Third-Party Liability in Equity: Lessons from the Limitation Rules' in PS Davies and JE Penner (eds), *Equity, Trusts and Commerce* (Oxford, Hart Publishing, 2017) 331–59. It is more difficult to fit into a fiduciary model of constructive trusteeship the Australian rule allowing

IV. NATURE AND FUNCTIONS OF CO-TRUSTEE LIABILITY

The ruminations on 'innocent' co-trustees in the *Williams* decision provide a good prompt to revisit the nature and functions of co-trustee liability. This has always been a topic of great practical importance, since the vast majority of express trusts have involved multiple rather than single trustees. The great advantage of multiple trusteeship is the creation of a group functioning as a *universitatis*, a stable 'social integrate' with functional perpetual succession through the accretion of membership over time. Indeed, plural trusts served across the eighteenth and nineteenth centuries as corporation substitutes, and they increasingly provide this function today in an era of post-modern corporate capitalism.[24] Within co-trusteeships an active trustee or minority group of trustees will often take the lead in managing the trust, but if the assets are lost then passive trustees with the means to pay are often called to account. Thus having a group of conjoined trustees insures or guarantees the due performance of the trust by providing sureties, as well as adding managerial skill and reputational capital to the enterprise.[25] Courts of equity developed fine-grained principles distinguishing and balancing between the liabilities of active and passive co-trustees, but this body of law has not been raised in appellate courts nor thoroughly reviewed by jurists for some time; and this lacuna is itself of interest.[26] Perhaps co-trustee liability has diminished in importance because of legislative protection of trustees purporting

account remedies to be applied against a thief. See further J Tarrant, 'Property Rights to Stolen Money' (2005) 32 *University of Western Australia Law Review* 234; J Tarrant 'Theft Principle in Private Law' (2006) 80(8) *Australian Law Journal* 531; SB Thomas, 'Thieves as Trustees: The Enduring Legacy of Black v S Freedman & Co Ltd' (2009) 3 *Journal of Equity* 1; J Tarrant 'Thieves as Trustees: In Defence of the Theft Principle' (2009) 3 *Journal of Equity* 170; R Chambers 'Trust and Theft' in E Bant and M Harding (eds), *Exploring Private Law* (Cambridge, CUP, 2010) 223–46.

24 The literatures on this topic are vast. For some overview see J Getzler, 'Frederic William Maitland—Trust and Corporation' (2016) 35 *University of Queensland Law Journal* 171; J Getzler, 'Plural Ownership, Funds, and the Aggregation of Wills' (2009) 10 *Theoretical Inquiries in Law* 241; LE Ribstein, *The Rise of the Uncorporation* (Oxford, OUP, 2009); RH Sitkoff, 'Trust as "Uncorporation": A Research Agenda' [2005] *University of Illinois Law Review* 31. The interaction of trust-derived fiduciary duties and directors' duties remains a live issue in the interpretation of statutory corporate controls: see *Australian Securities and Investments Commission v Cassimatis (No 8)* [2016] FCA 1023 [416]–[428] (Edelman J).

25 C Stebbings, *The Private Trustee in Victorian England* (Cambridge, CUP, 2001) 98–103, 120–27.

26 The classic study is now nearly a century old: GG Bogert, 'The Liability of an Inactive Co-trustee' (1921) 34 *Harvard Law Review* 483. This invaluable article is encyclopaedic but mashes together the law of many jurisdictions and time periods into one timeless whole. American jurists studying this area were particularly interested in hybridisation of trust and corporate forms during the Gilded Age and New Deal eras: see Note, 'The Effect of Default by a Joint Trustee' (1923) 23 *Columbia Law Review* 670; Note, 'Trusts—Responsibility of Inactive Co-Trustees in New York' (1928) 37 *Yale Law Journal* 535; American Law Institute, *Restatement of the Law of Trusts* (St Paul, American Law Institute Publishers, 1935) Ch 7 'The Administration of the Trust', I, 399–807; GW Lutes, 'Does a Corporation Acting as a Trustee Hold in Joint Tenancy with its Co-trustee?' (1934) 1 *University of Chicago Law Review* 629; 'W.L.F.', 'Right of Contribution among Co-Trustees' (1936) 22 *Virginia Law Review* 804; GG Bogert, *Handbook of the Law of Trusts and Trustees* (St Paul, West Publishing Co, 1921) 476–95; AW Scott, *The Law of Trusts* (Cambridge, Massachusetts, Harvard University Press, 1940) §224, II, 1184–91. For the Anglo–Commonwealth law, the most detailed coverage is found in DJ Hayton, P Matthews and C Mitchell (eds), *Underhill and Hayton's Law Relating to Trusts and Trustees* 19th edn (London, LexisNexis, 2016) §97.1–§97.30, 1257–69. See also G Williams, *Joint Obligations: A Treatise on Joint and Joint and Several Liability in Contract, Quasi-Contract and Trusts in England, Ireland and the Common-Law Dominions* (London, Butterworths, 1949) §80–§96, 159–76.

to cut away the great bulk of joint liabilities,[27] or newer legislation subjecting the old and strict solidary duties to a generalised duty of care that can readily be reduced by exemption clauses.[28] It may also be that many conflicts involving co-trustees are resolved in the shadow of a statutory power whereby trustees may seek relief from the consequences of a breach, at the discretion of the court, if they 'acted honestly and reasonably, and ought fairly' to be excused,[29] though older cases suggested that the discretion should not be exercised in favour of a co-trustee who takes insufficient steps to monitor the active trustee's conduct.[30] Most co-trusteeship battles today find their way to court in the guise of internecine contribution actions where the essential first step of joint liability is likely conceded. But we do not need a bevy of recent litigation to see that the regime of liabilities and defences relevant to co-trustees has much to teach us about the basics of the trust institution.

V. THE EVOLUTION OF DOCTRINE: MONITORING AND RECEIPT

The courts early identified a deep dilemma in setting standards of co-trustee liability: on the one hand, joint and several liability arises from the basic duty of all trustees to act unanimously and with full monitoring and control of each other's conduct, so that each stands as surety for the right conduct of the others; on the other hand, it seems harsh to hold co-trustees to account where only one trustee has received and controlled assets and the co-trustees could do little in practice to curb defalcation or other breach of trust. This dilemma reproduced a deeper tension in trust law: there was an obvious demand for high standards of stewardship and accountability in managerial relationships, but there was also a countervailing policy not to attach too great an individual liability to trustees, maybe volunteers, who had done their best. This policy tension crops up over and again in the doctrinal statements of the courts regulating the area of co-trusteeship. Co-trustees must perforce monitor the conduct of an active trustee who controls assets on their behalf, and must not allow a dishonest or incompetent co-trustee effective disposition of assets; but they may plead innocence if assets are received without their knowledge or in circumstances where it was not unreasonable to leave the assets in the control of some other co-trustee.

For an authoritative restatement of the principles of co-trustee liability we can turn to the leading text *Underhill and Hayton*, an earlier version of which was relied upon by Lord Neuberger in the *Williams* passage excerpted earlier. The revision of that cited passage, taken here from the nineteenth edition of 2016, appears as follows:

> Trustees are liable only for their own breaches of duty, and they are not vicariously liable for breaches of trust committed by their co-trustees. However, it often happens that the beneficiaries suffer the same 'damage' as a result of various breaches of trust committed

[27] Trustee Act 1925, s 30, adapting Trustee Act 1859, s 31 and Trustee Act 1893, s 24 (repealed by Trustee Act 2000), discussed further below.

[28] Trustee Act 2000, s 1 and Sch 1(7), text to n 135ff discussed below, text to nn 140–45.

[29] Trustee Act 1925, s 61.

[30] *Re Turner* (n 6) 541–42 (Byrne J).

> by several trustees, either because the trustees have collectively done an act which entails a breach of duty by each trustee, or because one 'active trustee' has committed a breach of trust while another 'passive trustee' has committed a distinct breach of duty, eg by standing by with knowledge that the other is committing a breach of duty, or by failing to take steps to obtain redress after becoming aware that a breach has been committed. In the event that several trustees are liable for the same damage, their liability is joint and several, with the result that the whole amount of the damage can be recovered from any or all of them.[31]

The learned authors go on to note that where one co-trustee bears more than his or her fair share of the payment burden under a joint and several liability, then he or she may seek contribution from other co-trustees with coordinate liability, unless a particular co-trustee has had that liability relieved under the statutory discretion to protect a trustee who has 'has acted honestly and reasonably, and ought fairly to be excused'. The whole passage with its language of 'damage' done by 'several' trustees is quite far from older conceptions of collective accounting responsibilities. Let us see next how these classical principles worked.

***

Townley v Sherborne,[32] a Chancery case of 1633, is commonly taken to be the font of principle in this area. A trust of the rents and profits of land was made for an infant Challoner, with some four co-trustees including Townley and Foster appointed to collect the monies and administer the trust. Foster received individually approximately £1700 (equivalent to £4m in today's labour earning terms, or £11m in income value—a vast sum) without accounting for the receipt in the trust accounts. The beneficiary's executor sued Townley as co-trustee to restore the fund to the value of the missing receipts. The Lord Keeper Coventry (counted a mediocre judge by Bulstrode), 'upon mature deliberation' decided the case 'to be of great importance' and so afforced his court with a panel of five common law judges to help him. He next

> appointed presidents to be looked over, as well in this, as in other Courts, if any could be found touching the point in question; whereupon several presidents were produced before

[31] *Underhill and Hayton* (n 26) §97.2, 1258. For other concise treatments in the standard works see also B McFarlane and C Mitchell, *Hayton and Mitchell's Commentary and Cases on the Law of Trusts and Equitable Remedies* 14th edn (London, Sweet & Maxwell, 2015) §9–002, 337–38; L Tucker, N Le Poidevin and J Brightwell, *Lewin on Trusts* 19th edn (London, Sweet & Maxwell, 2015) ch 29, 39; J McGhee, *Snell's Equity* 33rd edn (London, Sweet & Maxwell, 2015) [30–001]–[30–009], [30–045]–[30–048]. The American Law Institute's first *Restatement of the Law of Trusts* (n 26) §224, I, 637–639 offers a notably elegant formulation of 'Liability for Breach of Trust of Co-Trustee' that tracks English law:

> (1) A trustee is not liable to the beneficiary for breach of trust committed by a co-trustee.
> (2) A trustee is liable to the beneficiary, if he
> (a) participates in a breach of trust committed by his co-trustee; or
> (b) improperly delegates the administration of the trust to his co-trustee; or
> (c) approves or acquiesces in or conceals a breach of trust committed by his co-trustee; or
> (d) by his failure to exercise reasonable care in the administration of the trust has enabled his co-trustee to commit a breach of trust; or
> (e) neglects to take proper steps to compel his co-trustee to redress a breach of trust.

[32] *Townley v Sherborne* (1633) Bridgman 35; 123 ER 1181 (Lord Coventry LK).

> them, some in this Court, and some in the Court of Wards, where parties trusted were chargeable onely according to their several and respective receits, and not one to answer for the other; but no president on the contrary was produced to them.[33]

Coventry LK elaborated the doctrine in these words:

> [T]hat where lands or leases were conveyed to two or more upon trust, and one of them receives all or the most part of the profits, and after dyeth or decayeth in his estate, his co-trustees shall not be charged, or be compelled in this Court, to answer for the receits of him so dying or decayed, unless some purchase, fraud or evil dealing appear to have been in them to prejudice their trust; for they being by law joyntenants or tenants in common, every one by law may receive either all or as much of the profits as he can come by.[34]

The court commended the widespread practice of heads of family vesting land on trust with a group of friends charged to collect income for the support of children, to gather legacies and to protect the family patrimony from debtors. In order to encourage such service the trusted friends should not presumptively be made accountable for each other's receipts:

> [I]f such of these friends, who carry themselves without fraud, should be chargeable out of their own estates for the faults and deficiencies of their co-trustees, who were not nominated by them, few men would undertake any such trust.[35]

But here the Lord Keeper may have relied upon a distinct line of authority holding executors who stood in the shoes of testators and were armed with wide individual powers to gather in estates and assign away bequests and legacies.

> And if two executors be, and one of them waste all, or any part of the estate, the devastavit shall by law charge him onely, and not his co-executor: and in that case, equitas sequitur legem [equity follows the law], there having been many presidents resolved in this Court, that one executor shall not answer nor be charged for the act or default of his companion.[36]

Devastavit was an ancient action for waste of an estate in the hands of an individual executor, that began in the ecclesiastical courts of probate, fell to be regulated via Magna Carta as a feudal accounting action in the common law courts, and then washed onto the shores of the Chancery Court due to its superior multipartite accounting procedure. Justice Nye Perram of the Federal Court of Australia in a recent study observed that

> *devastavit* is a manifestation of at least four or five sets of principles: a tort rule—possibly trespass, possibly trespass on the case; a principle relating to the enforcement of judgments; a corollary of a bailment possibly arising from the executor's custody of the estate (at least in respect of personalty); an aspect of an administration action; and, the remedy of the taking of accounts on a wilful default basis.[37]

[33] ibid Bridgman 37; ER 1182–83. The Trumpian spelling is authentically seventeenth century.
[34] ibid Bridgman 37; ER 1183.
[35] ibid.
[36] ibid.
[37] N Perram, 'The Origins and Present Operation of the Action in Devastavit' [2012] *Federal Judicial Scholarship* 23.

The law here struck a balance whereby executors (including joint executors) were armed with extensive sole powers of disposal in order to make for effective execution of deceased estates, allied to a penetrating action *in personam* to compensate for any losses caused to the estate or the beneficiaries by misfeasance in the exercise of those powers. It may have been a category error for Coventry LK in *Townley v Sherborne* to search the 'presidents' of every likely court including the courts of probate for basic principles of co-trusteeship, when *devastavit* had a peculiar origin and purpose in the field of control of executors. But Lord Coventry pushed the analogy hard:

> And it is no breach of trust, to permit one of the trustees to receive all or the most part of the profits, it falling out many times that some of the trustees live far from the lands, and are put in trust out of other respects then to be troubled with the receit [sic] of the profits.[38]

Another hypothetical given was wrongful assignment of trust assets. Where one co-trustee without authority assigned away the trust estate to an assignee who subsequently lost the assets and became insolvent, then the assigning co-trustee would be liable personally to restore the trust assets,[39] but not so any of the other co-trustees unless they themselves had received any proceeds arising from the assignment. Individual liability thus seemed to be based on one of two aspects: (1) exercising authority over the trust by way of assignment or (2) by receipt, with the two often coinciding. But the passive trustee who neither assigned nor received seemed to be insulated from liability, subject to one important exception:

> [I]f upon the proofs or circumstances the Court be satisfied, that there be dolus malus, or any evil practice, fraud or ill intent in him that permitted his companion to receive the whole profits, he may be charged though he received nothing.[40]

Some judges went further and fastened on formal joint receipt as a sufficient base for joint liability, even if one trustee in reality took in the assets. In 1684 Guilford LK stated: 'Each trustee shall be charged for no more than he actually received; but where they join in receipts, there they shall be all charged'.[41]

The problem of relating liability to level of receipt was discussed again in 1705 by Cowper LK in *Fellows v Mitchell and Owen*,[42] where two co-trustees joined in accepting a sale of a mortgage security. After the sale each received half of the £2000 proceeds with the consent of the *cestui* who was present at the sale; one trustee then declared bankruptcy and his moiety was lost. The *cestui* sued the solvent trustee on the basis of his joining in the sale transaction. The court held the trustee's liability to that portion of the proceeds he had actually received, following *Townley*. The court noted that not all the authorities accepted the principle that receipt should set a cap

[38] *Townley* (n 32) Bridgman 37–38; ER 1183.

[39] A later case suggested that the assignor would also have to restore missing profits: *Vandebende v Levingston* (1674) 3 Swan 625; 36 ER 999: 'To charge the assignee of a trustee who comes in by breach of trust alone, or to charge both assignor and assignee with the profits respectively received, is error; for both ought to be liable to the *cestuique trust*, and the assignor must answer the whole if the assignee be a beggar.'

[40] ibid Swan 38; ER 1183.

[41] *Spalding v Shalmer & St Amond* (1684) 1 Vern 301, 303; 23 ER 483, 483–84.

[42] *Fellows v Mitchell and Owen* (1705) 1 P Wms 81; 24 ER 302.

on liability, but nonetheless upheld the defence in this case, partly on a *volenti* basis as the *cestui* had himself split the receipt between the two co-trustees, and partly because '[i]t seems to be *substantial* injustice, to decree a man to answer for money which he did not receive, at the same time that the charge upon him by his joining in the receipts, is but *notional*'.[43] It might be different if the differing levels of receipt simply reflected poor control and understanding by the co-trustees, in which case he might be attached on the basis of a presumption that he had indeed received the whole:

> It may be reasonable, where upon the proof it cannot be distinguished, how much was received by the one trustee, and how much by the other, to charge each with the whole. For in such case the trustees are to blame for not keeping distinct accounts. It is like one throwing corn or money into another's heap, where there is no reason that he who made this difficulty should have the whole: on the contrary, because it cannot be distinguished, he shall have no part [that is, each shall be responsible for the whole].[44]

The notion of blameworthiness in accounting could be used to reshape and intensify co-trustee liability, with courts holding that a simple failure to monitor the conduct of active co-trustees was itself a type of default that could expose the passive co-trustee to liability. So much emerges from the famous case of *Charitable Corporation v Sutton*,[45] which is often counted as the foundation of the law of director's duties, decided in 1742 by Lord Hardwicke C. The Charitable Corporation was a very large fund set up by the Crown using money appropriations from consolidated revenue, whose purpose was to extend loans to tradesmen secured by collateral of chattels to be stored in a warehouse. The fund was 'charitable' in that it was not operated to turn a profit but rather to support middling folk during a severe trade downturn, serving as a form of outdoor relief as well as supplying purchasing power in a depressed economy. The collateral being chattels deposited in the warehouse may not have been intended fully to secure the loans but rather served to reduce the moral hazard of debtor default. There was a large governing committee of some 50 trustees or directors, who did very little and certainly failed to monitor the conduct of some five active trustees and their agents who had bilked the fund with fraudulent loans, often without collateral, given to fictitious borrowers. Through such collusive devices the enormous fund was almost entirely depleted. There was good suspicion that the less involved committee men had turned a blind eye or even in some cases actively connived in those frauds. The defence was raised that only where active fraud was proved in each individual trustee's case could there be an attribution of liability for the misconduct of the five directing trustees. Lord Hardwicke's sharp and detailed response to this argument was recorded in the Modern report:

> The … objection was, that the nature of this case is such as it is impossible for the Court to decree for the plaintiffs on this general point of breaches of trust and gross neglects of the

[43] ibid P Wms 82–83; ER 302. To like effect, *Churchill v Lady Hobson* (1713) 1 P Wms 241, 243; 24 ER 370, 371; *Murrell v Cox and Pitt* (1706) 2 Vern 570; 23 ER 971.

[44] *Churchill* (n 43) P Wms 82–83; ER 302.

[45] *Charitable Corporation v Sutton* (1742) 9 Mod 349; 88 ER 500; 2 Atk 400; 26 ER 642 (Lord Hardwicke).

several directors, for that some acts are joint, others separate, and each is answerable only for his own particular acts and neglects; and from thence there is a general inference, that this case is so complicated, and of such a nature, as is out of the jurisdiction of any Court of Equity. If this be so, it is laying the axe to the root of the tree, and I have been stating all this to no purpose. But it is not so; for where there are many trustees, and some are guilty of one breach and some of others, or where there is a gross negligence, and the loss is so complicated as it cannot be apportioned, I think they are all jointly liable. And I will never establish this, that breaches of trust, or any matters of fraud, are above the reach or out of the jurisdiction of this Court. The King's Courts are to redress every wrong and protect every innocent person; and if the laws do not extend to do this, new and more ample ones will be provided, for two mischiefs are to be avoided: first, not to make it unsafe or too perilous for honest men to accept offices of trust, by making them liable to losses in the execution of them; and secondly, to prevent the frauds of dishonest men in such employments. Therefore at present, as far as I can be certain, I will determine that the conspiracy called "The Partnership of Five, Four, and Three," are answerable in the first degree; but as to the others, I shall not now determine how far they are answerable, but at most it will be only in the second degree: and this method I took in a similar case that was before me the twenty-eighth of May 1739, The Lead Company v. Hall, their treasurer. Their bill was for a satisfaction in respect of frauds committed by Hall, and connived at, or assented to, or acted under by the directors; and I held Hall to be first liable, and if he proved deficient, then the directors. So here I am of opinion, that if it appears any others of the directors, committee-men, or assistants, are liable, it will be only in the second degree, and upon the deficiency of the partnership.[46]

Here a principle of joint and several liability was established, but governed by a rule of recovery akin to the contemporaneous jingle rule in partnership debt whereby recovery would be exhausted against inside partnership funds before resorting to the outside personal estates of the partners.[47]

The more succinct Atkyns report of *Sutton*[48] states the relevant principles as follows. First, passivity by a non-paid trustee might turn out to be a *per se* breach of co-trustees' duties:

Next as to *mal-feasance* and *non-feasance*. To instance in non-attendance; if some persons are guilty of gross non-attendance, and leave the management intirely to others, they may be guilty by this means of the breaches of trust that are committed by others. By accepting of a trust of this sort, a person is obliged to execute it with fidelity and reasonable diligence; and it is no excuse to say that they had no benefit from it, but that it was merely *honorary*; and therefore they are within the case of common trustees. *Vide Coggs* v. *Bernard*, 1 *Salk*. 26.[49]

These comments are cryptic, but seem to indicate that where active participation by co-trustees might be expected due to the nature of the trust enterprise, then

[46] ibid Mod 356; ER 504; *cf* (1742) 2 Atk 400, 406; 26 ER 642, 645.

[47] The jingle rule is described and explained in J Getzler and M Macnair, 'The Firm as an Entity before the Companies Acts' in P Brand, K Costello and WN Osborough (eds), *Adventures in the Law: Proceedings of the 16th British Legal History Conference, Dublin* (Dublin, Four Courts Press, 2005) 267–88. See also H Hansmann, R Kraakman and R Squire, 'Law and the Rise of the Firm' (2006) 119 *Harvard Law Review* 1335.

[48] *Charitable Corporation v Sutton* (1742) 2 Atk 400; 26 ER 642.

[49] ibid Atk 405–06; ER 644–45.

failure to so participate is a presumptive breach opening the door to full solidary liability. Concomitantly a bare trust with static assets might not place much demand on the passive co-trustee as 'common trustees' (in Lord Hardwicke's phrase). The reference to *Coggs v Bernard*[50] is significant, for there Lord Holt CJ introduced the Roman concepts of *culpa levis* and *culpa lata*, with differential measures of duty *in abstracto et concreto* to structure the duties of paid and unpaid bailees. In *Sutton* we seem to have a standard of *culpa lata*, gross negligence, but *in concreto*, that is, driven by the expectations due from the specific persons charged with the direction of that particular enterprise. *Culpa lata in concreto* will be a more demanding standard here than in a non-professional or non-commercial context. In other words breach by a paid professional manager or director could be presumed from the simple fact of non-activity:

> But if, upon inquiry before the Master, there should appear to be a supine negligence in all of them, by which a gross complicated loss happens, I will never determine that they are not all guilty.[51]

Lord Hardwicke cited in support a 1733 judgment of Jeckyll MR, which had stated:

> The forbearance of the trustees in not doing what it was their office to have done, shall in no sort prejudice the *cestuy que trusts*, since at that rate it would be in the power of trustees, either by doing, or delaying to do, their duty, to affect the right of others; which can never be maintained.[52]

To sum up, the *Sutton* doctrine is based on wrongdoing by co-trustees in failing to monitor the conduct of active trustees who are left to carry on with misfeasances that a minimal care by colleagues might have stopped. But could joint and several liability be raised in the absence of such neglect? In *Leigh v Barry*[53] in 1747 Lord Hardwicke C revisited the issue and found two alternative paths to liability. The first was individual receipt itself. This rule applied even if the co-trustees did not use an indemnity to negative their individual liability: '*they shall not be liable for the acts of one another*, yet this court will not make them liable for more than each has received'.[54] Lord Hardwicke was at pains to make clear that liabilities were capped by levels of actual not notional individual receipt; formal collective receipt where all trustees signed to acknowledge the entrance of an asset into the accounts did not create collective liabilities where one trustee actually took and controlled the asset:

> The court has even gone further; for where they all join in a receipt for money, it will make that trustee liable only who received it, for they are all obliged to join in the receipt; otherwise as to the executors, for there is no necessity for their joining, but may act severally if they think fit.[55]

[50] *Coggs v Barnard* (1703) 2 Ld Raym 909; 92 ER 107, discussed in the trusts context by J Getzler, 'Duty of Care' in P Birks and A Pretto (eds), *Breach of Trust* (Oxford, Hart Publishing, 2002) 41–74.
[51] *Sutton* (n 48) Atk 406; ER 645.
[52] *Lechmere v Carlisle* (1733) 3 P Wms 211, 215; 24 ER 1033, 1035.
[53] *Leigh v Barry* (1747) 3 Atk 583; 26 ER 1136.
[54] ibid Atk 584; ER 1337 (emphasis in original).
[55] ibid.

In other words co-trustees by this rule enjoyed the same protection as executors, and the court ignored the formal requirement of unanimous co-trustee assents to receipt and disbursement in order to reach that position. The other path to liability identified by Lord Hardwicke was contractual, or at least based on assumption of responsibility: 'if the trustees will bind themselves to be liable for the acts of each other, the court will not relieve them',[56] modelling such full joint and several liability on the analogy of co-sureties of a debt. Such an assumed liability did not depend on the level of receipt of each individual trustee: one could be liable for property received and then lost by another.[57] That left open the question as to which words or conduct of trustees amounted to such an assumption of joint and several liability; covenant was clearly sufficient; but what of an informal agreement or a common understanding? In the present case the co-trustees, who were also creditors seeking liquidation of the fund assets, had made a covenant guaranteeing payment in the trust, so in the result each co-trustee was found to have a full joint and several liability. It may be that *Leigh* can be reconciled with the reasoning in *Sutton* not only in its result, but also in its reasoning, in that the co-trustees or directors in *Sutton* had also signed on to accept full joint and several liability when they took offices in the Charitable Corporation. But that leaves in place the question why Lord Hardwicke emphasised negligence in *Sutton* as the reason for extending liability to every member of the co-trustee group, rather than basing liability on consent or receipt. Analysis of judicial reasons is impeded by the cryptic nature of surviving reports of Lord Hardwicke's opinions; further research into manuscripts (including his judicial notebooks) may cast a brighter light.

In *Ex parte Belchier*[58] Lord Hardwicke C further explained the interaction between joint receipt by co-trustees or executors and undertakings of joint liability. In that case the defendant had taken assignment of her son's estate as trustee in insolvency, and had entrusted a large consignment of tobacco to a broker for sale by auction, who then absconded with the proceeds. The defendant trustee's conduct in delegating to an agent was found to be reasonable and indeed necessary by the

[56] ibid.

[57] It is tolerably clear that liabilities spoken of here are external, between co-trustees and *cestui*, and not agreements establishing or varying contribution between co-trustees; the interaction of contribution with contract were yet to be explored prior to the decision of Eyre LCB in *Dering v Earl of Winchelsea* (1787) 1 Cox CC 318, 321; 29 ER 1184, 1185 (Exch of Pleas), 'find[ing] that contribution is bottomed and fixed on general principles of justice, and does not spring from contract; though contract may qualify it'. Doctrinal history of this point is explored in *Zurich Insurance plc UK Branch v International Energy Group Ltd* [2015] UKSC 33; [2016] AC 509; *Lavin v Toppi* (2015) 254 CLR 459 (HCA); *Friend v Booker* (2009) 239 CLR 129 (HCA); *Burke v LFOT Pty Ltd* (2002) 209 CLR 282 (HCA); *Caledonia North Sea Ltd v British Telecommunications plc* [2002] UKHL 4; [2002] Lloyds Rep IR 261; *BP Petroleum Development Ltd v Esso Petroleum Co Ltd* 1987 SLT 345 (HL(Sc)); *Albion Insurance Co Ltd v Government Insurance Office* (NSW) (1969) 121 CLR 342 (HCA). See also C Mitchell, *The Law of Contribution and Reimbursement* (Oxford, OUP, 2003) §8.23, 164–65; D Heydon, MJ Leeming and PG Turner, *Meagher Gummow and Lehane's Equity: Doctrines and Remedies* 5th edn (Sydney, LexisNexis, 2015) 395–416.

[58] *Ex parte Belchier; In the Matter of Parsons, Bankrupt* (1754) Amb 218; 27 ER 144.

trading norms around her, and hence she was not chargeable on the trust account to restore the assets.

> If [the assignee] is chargeable in this case, no man in his senses would act as assignee under commissions of bankrupt. This Court has laid down a rule with regard to the transactions of assignees, and more so of trustees, so as not to strike a terror into mankind acting for the benefit of others, and not for their own.
>
> Courts of law, and equity too, are more strict as to executors and administrators; but where trustees act by other hands, either from necessity, or conformable to the common usage of mankind, they are not answerable for losses.[59]

Lord Hardwicke used the same measure of necessity to justify a trustee delegating receipt or conversion of assets to a delegate or co-trustee, and also explained why executors were treated differently:

> There are two sorts of necessities: 1st, Legal necessity. 2d, Moral necessity.
>
> As to 1st, A distinction prevails where two executors join in giving a discharge for money, and one of them only receives it, they are both answerable for it, because there is no necessity for both to join in the discharge, the receipt of either being sufficient; but if trustees join in giving a discharge, and one only receives, the other is not answerable, because his joining in the discharge was necessary.[60]

Thus the co-executor by joining in a receipt that was not legally required, and without himself taking possession or control, was in effect guaranteeing due accounting by the other executor. The decision was soon cited as a leading authority, and was used a century later by Jessel MR and Lord Blackburn in constructing a new negligence standard for trustees and moving the law away from stricter account measures for stewardship of assets.[61]

The *Belchier* necessity principle with its harsh rule for executors came to be affirmed many times in the Court of Chancery, and was also applied to any co-trustee who accepted a supererogatory responsibility for the actions of the trustee group. So in *Westley v Clarke* in 1759 Lord Northington LK held:

> it is a general rule in this court, that if executors join in a receipt, they make themselves all liable *in solido*, because it is an unnecessary act, as each executor has an absolute power over the personal assets and rights of the testator. And that the contrary rule holds with respect to trustees; that they are not answerable for joint receipts each *in solido*, but only in proportion to what they actually receive.
>
> But though there are distinctions in the books concerning the acts of trustees and those of executors, according to the cases cited for that purpose, yet those distinctions seem not to be taken with precision, sufficient to establish a general rule; for a joint receipt will charge trustees *in solido* each, if there is no other proof of the receipt of the money.[62]

[59] ibid Amb 219; ER 145.
[60] ibid.
[61] *Re Speight; Speight* v *Gaunt* (1883) 22 Ch D 727; (1883) 9 App Cas 1 (HL), analysed in Getzler, 'Duty of Care' (n 50).
[62] *Westley v Clarke* (1759) 1 Eden 357, 360; 28 ER 723, 724.

This implied that co-trustees would presumptively be liable for each other's acts regarding trust assets unless they could establish absence of receipt. Lord Thurlow C doubted this blurring of the line between executors and trustees in a case of 1786, and restated the principle as follows:

> where one executor takes the money but of his own authority, his companion shall not be charged; but if he puts the money into the hands of his companion, he shews he had it in his power to secure it; and that his companion, for some reason, was permitted to obtain the possession of the money.[63]

This principle was used numerous times to make an executor jointly and severally liable for the receipts of another co-executor if the former executor joined in the receipt without taking control, as in effect the non-controlling executor was volunteering his or her own power of receipt to another. The judges sometimes expressed discomfort at the strictness of this rule, especially when contrasted with the lenience showed to non-testamentary co-trustees who had not directly involved themselves in the management of the trust assets.[64] But the strict approach won out; in the 1805 decision of *Brice v Stokes* Lord Eldon C restated the rule in still stronger terms that put the onus of proving non-receipt on a co-trustee if the co-trustee was to avoid liability, reverting to Lord Northington LK's speculation expressed earlier in *Westley v Clarke*:

> At Law, where trustees join in a receipt, *prima facie* all are to be considered as having received the money. But it is competent to a trustee, and, if he means to exonerate himself from that inference, it is necessary for him, to shew, that the money, acknowledged to have been received by all, was in fact received by one; and the other joined only for conformity. In the case of executors it has been said, and well said, to be otherwise. An executor, as it is not necessary for him to join, interfering in the transaction unnecessarily, the inference is just the other way; he is to be considered as assuming a power over the fund; and therefore answerable for the application; as far as it is connected with the particular transaction, in which he joins.[65]

In *Lord Shipbrook v Lord Hinchinbrook* (also decided in that year of 1805)[66] Lord Eldon C extended the principle and held that even where a co-executor had been shown to be the sole recipient of funds, without any sign of receipt by the other executors, then an *ex post* liability could arise by failure to monitor the active holder of the fund. In that case it might have been expected after a time that the funds would be sent to the due beneficiary, but the active executor seemed unwilling

[63] *Sadler v Hobbs* (1786) 2 Bro CC 114, 116; 29 ER 66, 67.

[64] See *Scurfield v Howes* (1790) 3 Brown CC 90; 29 ER 425 (Arden MR); *Hovey v Blakeman* (1799) 4 Ves Jun 596; 31 ER 306 (Arden MR); *Chambers v Minchin* (1802) 7 Ves Jun 186 198–99; 32 ER 76, 80–81 (Lord Eldon). A laxer approach to 'necessary' deposit is shown in the earlier case of *Attorney-General v Randell* (1734) 21 Vin Abr 354 pl 9 (Lord Macclesfield), where money was deposited with one co-trustee for four years and then lost; the co-trustees were excused on the analogy of an unforeseen failure by a banker. In the later case of *Re Gasquoine* [1894] 1 Ch 470 (CA), an executor allowing sole receipt to a co-executor was not held liable for loss, as that manner of several control was in the normal course of business.

[65] *Brice v Stokes* (1805) 11 Ves Jun 319, 324–25; 32 ER 1111, 1113; followed in *Langford v Gascoyne* (1805) 11 Ves Jun 333; 32 ER 1116.

[66] *Lord Shipbrook v Lord Hinchinbrook* (1805) 11 Ves Jun 252; 32 ER 1085.

or unable to do so; the legatees then sued the other executor for payment. The co-executor's neglect of the duty to ensure due execution over a period of time attracted full solidary liability such that the non-recipient was required to pay over the requisite equitable debt. The principle was applied still more firmly to normal co-trustees who were supposed to act unanimously to protect trust assets; in a 1790 case where a co-trustee lost trust money by lending it to a friend without security, Lord Thurlow C stated that 'if a trustee will suffer a co-trustee to detain a sum of money belonging to the trust estate, they are both liable'.[67] The doctrine was later extended back into executorships by Langdale MR in 1838, holding that a co-executor who was assured by the *cestui* that he would not be assuming any duty or responsibility by taking the trust office and did not take receipt of any assets was nonetheless accountable if he knew or ought to have known of mismanagement or breach of trust by the other trustee:

> It is important that it should be well understood that no one can safely act in that manner, and that the law will not permit a party to neglect the duty which, by proving the will, he has undertaken. ... he became liable for the performance of the trusts, and for any consequences arising from a breach of them.[68]

***

An important extension of the solidary liability principle evoked by Lord Eldon was made by Sir William Grant MR in the insolvency case of *Lingard v Bromley* (1812).[69] The case involved a sale of a property by co-trustees being assignees under a commission of bankruptcy, charged with maximising the value of the bankrupt's estate for the benefit of creditors. Lingard, one of the trustees, took an active role in the business of liquidation, and Bromley, another trustee, passively accepted the other's decisions concerning the estate. A secured creditor proposed the sale of a property in the estate, but on Lingard's prompting the trustees declined to accept the sale and refused conveyance, arguing that they did not necessarily accept the validity of the security claim nor the verity of the instructions issued by those creditors. When the first sale, that would have raised £3400, was thus refused, the creditors won an order enforcing a resale, which only raised £2820. The creditors then successfully sued Lingard for the deficiency of £580, which with added interest and costs rose to the sum of nearly £1140, caused by the denial of the earlier sale under what was now proved to be an authoritative commission. Lingard as trustee paid up in full; he now prayed a Bill in Chancery for 'Account and Contribution', that is, a suit to recover an equal share of the account by contribution from his co-trustee Bromley. Bromley's defence was that Lingard

> acted principally in the Bankruptcy; the Defendants relying on his Representations and Advice; and concurring only in Form; and Evidence was produced of the Plaintiff's

[67] *Keble v Thompson* (1790) 3 Bro CC 112; 29 ER 112.

[68] *Booth v Booth* (1838) 1 Beav 125, 129; 48 ER 886, 888 (Langdale MR). See also *Styles v Guy* (1849) 1 Mac & G 422; 41 ER 1328 (Lord Cottenham); *Underwood v Stevens* (1816) 1 Mer 712; 35 ER 833.

[69] *Lingard v Bromley* (1812) 1 Ves & Beam 114; 35 ER 45.

> Declarations, that he would take the Management of the Law Business upon himself; and, on one of the Defendants observing, that they wished to have nothing to do with Law, that he would bear them harmless, &c.[70]

The report lays out the arguments of two formidable counsel, with Romilly arguing for contribution from Bromley to Lingard and Leach arguing in defence that there was no initial solidary liability for Bromley and hence no possibility of contribution:

> Sir *Samuel Romilly* ... for the Plaintiff. This Court is in the Habit of decreeing Contribution and Average between Persons, one of whom has paid the Debt of all; and that Principle applies here; no one of these Persons having a greater Interest than another. The modern Cases on this Head are but few: the Principle being universally admitted; but it was formerly much acted upon. ... The Effect of refusing Contribution, leaving one Party, who had paid the whole, without Remedy, would be the greatest Injustice. Though the Plaintiff took the active Part, they all signed the Petitions.
>
> Mr. *Leach* ... for the Defendants. The Proposition, that Contribution and Average constitute a common Head of Equity, where the Demand arises out of Contract, cannot be disputed: but its Application is denied, where a Party is charged with respect to a Tort.
>
> Sir Samuel Romilly, in Reply. If this Case is to be determined upon the Distinction between Tort and Contract, the Consequences will be most prejudicial. In Equity there is no such Distinction: Torts being only known at Law. Suppose a Breach of Trust, committed by one Trustee, selling out Stock, receiving the Amount, and persuading his Co-trustee to join him. In Justice the one receiving ought to pay: but the Decree is against both; and according to this Doctrine, if Payment were enforced against him, who received nothing, there could be no Contribution. If one Trustee by acting and giving Advice to another loses his Right to Contribution, the Effect would be a Premium to Trustees to be idle; as the most active would incur the Responsibility.[71]

Leach here argued that a breach of trust sounds as a primary equitable wrong, to be assimilated to tort and therefore not subject to contribution as the rules then stood. Romilly's rebuttal of the defence holds that it is incoherent to label every breach of a duty, including a breach of the positive managerial duties of trusteeship, as a 'wrong' and then apply the apparatus of common-law tort to that breach; better to acknowledge that co-trustees shared an identical primary equitable duty including a shared duty to give an account and make good in the event of any default however it had come to pass. Sir William Grant MR agreed with Romilly, holding as follows.

> The first Defence made in this Case seems to me to be quite untenable. Where entire Damages are recovered against several Defendants guilty of a Tort, a Court of Justice will not interfere to enforce Contribution among the Wrong-doers: but here is nothing but the Non-performance of a civil obligation. The Lord Chancellor held, in the first Place, that the Assignees were bound to convey; and secondly, that, a Loss being occasioned by their not having conveyed, they were bound to make good that Loss, with the Costs, arising by their Refusal. The Liability therefore is not at all ex Delicto; unless every Refusal to comply with a legal Obligation makes a Party guilty of a Delictum. As to the second Defence, there are, no Doubt, many Cases, in which Persons may be all liable, severally as well as

[70] ibid Ves & Beam 115; ER 45.
[71] ibid Ves & Beam 115–16; ER 45.

jointly, to indemnify a third Party; and yet ought not in Equity to bear the Burthen equally among themselves. But what are the Circumstances of Distinction between these Persons? It is not alledged, that the Plaintiff derived any exclusive Benefit from the Acts, in which he concurred with the Defendants. Their Refusal produced Loss to others; but no Advantage either to him or them. The Defence is of a Kind, which a Court of Justice is very unwilling to listen to: that, having undertaken a Trust, they abdicated all Judgment of their own in the Performance of it; and did whatever the Plaintiff desired: "without examining" (as they say in so many Words) "into the Matter, or Ground, of the Proceeding." Nothing could be more mischievous than to hold, that Trustees may thus act; and avoid Responsibility by throwing the Burthen upon the Person, in whom they have reposed this blind Confidence. The Case is not, that they abstain merely from interfering; but they enter upon the Trust; make themselves Parties to every Proceeding; give the Sanction of their Names to each Transaction; and now say, they are to be considered as total Strangers; and all, that has been done, is to be taken as the Act only of their Co-trustee. If this will do to protect them from Contribution, why would it not be sufficient to throw back the Burthen upon the Plaintiff, if the Defendants had been the Persons called upon to pay in the first Instance? It was at first a voluntary Act in them to take the Judgment of the Plaintiff, as a Guide for theirs. There is nothing to shew, that he fraudulently professed that to be his Judgment, which really was not such. … I see nothing sufficient to exempt [the co-trustees] from the Liability to answer for Acts, in which they joined; and to enable them to throw the whole Responsibility for those Acts upon the Plaintiff. He is therefore entitled to the Contribution he prays, with the Costs of the Suit.[72]

Grant MR sets out two conjoined principles: that the duty of trustees is a primary duty of performance that the Court of Chancery will positively enforce, not a secondary duty to correct damage caused by wrongdoing where each trustee is treated severally without sharing of liability or contribution; and that this primary duty requires all trustees to take cognisance of the needs of the trust management and to exercise their own judgments in parallel with the more active trustees, not hiding behind the decision of an active trustee. In other words, every co-trustee must proffer an engaged performance born of the basic duty of account for their shared office, and failure by one is translated into a failure by all that opens the door to contribution and equal bearing of liability.

The strict accounting requirement that each co-trustee should ensure personal knowledge of the state of the assets was soon after restated by Lord Eldon C in the 1818 case of *Walker v Symonds*.[73] Together with *Lingard* this case establishes the classical solidary liability of co-trustees, and is worth investigating closely as a result. The facts as recited in the Bill and Answer were lengthy and tangled, but in essence involved two passive trustees inexperienced in business allowing an active trustee to take funds drawn from a large testamentary estate and invest these in his own business rather than in gilts and land securities as was the regular and proper practice. To leave the assets in one trustee's unsafe hands for many years in this way was a clear breach of trust; and the incidence of solidary liability could not be lessened by the negotiation of a release of the two trustees from their duties by a deed executed with the *cestui que trust* when she reached her majority. This agreement was set

[72] ibid Ves & Beam 116–18; ER 45–46.
[73] *Walker v Symonds* (1818) 3 Swan 1; 36 ER 751.

aside as the trustees could not inform the *cestui* of the state of the trust management and the location of the assets, and thus had not won her informed consent. Had the deed been valid, then the *cestui* could not have sued for the loss of her share of the estate, and might have been liable for contribution if her assent had engineered loss to other innocent *cestuis*.[74] The two passive trustees were therefore charged with restoring the fund when the active trustee lost the assets in a business failure. Lord Eldon acknowledged that a *cestui* could overtly or even by acquiescence waive or excuse a breach of trust or release trustees from their duty, but only with the fullest information. Analysis of the requisite level of trustee duty and ensuing liability was complicated by the fact that different types of trustees had distinct several powers. Trustees in bankruptcy were always to act collectively; but trustee-executors could conceivably have a normal authority to act singly in handling the trust assets. However in neither category did the law excuse co-trustees from the duty to monitor each other's conduct and sustain full awareness of the state of the trust: 'it would be impossible to maintain this proposition, that, because trustees are not aware that they have committed a breach of trust, they are not responsible'.[75] It was particularly egregious for the passive trustees to claim that they 'had a co-trustee who had been guilty of a shameful violation of his duty', but had failed to discover this and exert themselves to put right the breach until it was too late.[76] This restated principles that Lord Eldon had developed earlier to control the managing committees of large joint stock partnerships, where it was an 'Abuse of Trust ... that Persons will not according to their Duty attend to the Interest of the Concern'.[77] Lord Eldon in *Walker v Symonds* set the duty to monitor co-trusteeship very high:

> This is a case of great importance to trustees in general, and illustrates the necessity of attending to every word in transactions of this nature. It is one of the cases which convince me at a mature period of my judicial life, that it is impossible [for trustees] to comprehend such questions without minute examination of every fact, and reference to all the documents.[78]

***

The principles set out by Lord Eldon were ratified many times in later case law.[79] But not all judges accepted the strictness of the Eldonian rule. In the 1835 case of

[74] Lord Eldon's exclusion of the release as lacking informed consent reversed the finding of the trial judge Sir Thomas Plumer MR. Counsel for the plaintiff indeed put the breach of trust almost entirely in terms of failure by the trustees to locate the assets and inability explain to the *cestui* the state of the trust: ibid Swan 58; ER 772.

[75] ibid Swan 69; ER 776.

[76] ibid Swan 70–71; ER 776.

[77] *Carlen v Drury* (1812) 1 Ves & Beam 154, 158; 35 ER 61, 62. The duty of trustee managers of a company to avoid tortious harm to outsiders was also conceived early as a kind of breach of trust bring liability via the person of the corporate servants and their employers the trustees so as to attach to beneficial assets: see *'The Mersey Docks and Harbour Board' Trustees v Gibbs* (1866) 11 HLC 686; 11 ER 1500 (HL).

[78] ibid HLC 74; ER 777.

[79] *Re Pauling's Settlement Trusts (No 1)* [1962] 1 WLR 86 (Ch D); *McEvoy v Belfast Banking Co Ltd* [1935] AC 24 (HL); *London General Omnibus Co Ltd v Holloway* [1912] 2 KB 72 (CA); *Fletcher v Collis* [1905] 2 Ch 24 (CA); *Chillingworth v Chambers* [1896] 1 Ch 685 (CA); *Re Brogden*

Tarleton v Hornby in the Exchequer of Pleas[80] the beneficiary interest was harmed not by a transactional delay of the co-trustees causing the value of assets to decay, but rather the reverse—a too-hasty sale by trustees who had failed to seek a high enough price. The beneficiary was a debtor whose estate was placed under administration for bankruptcy. The debtor resented the grant of a commission of bankruptcy over his estate, and sought to undermine the commission by claiming that sales of his assets had been collusive and at undervalue—a mischief often brought before the courts of equity. One particular trustee was sued on the basis of joint and several liability for the shortfall. Scarlett LCB (soon to become Lord Abinger) suggested that no single trustee in bankruptcy could be sued unless all were joined, this because the taking of an account against joint trustees in bankruptcy must intrinsically be a collective act:

> The principle is no doubt just, that mere wrong doers, who have no other connexion with each other than the common injury they do, may be brought to account for their transactions either singly or altogether. It is a familiar principle of law that an action of trespass may be brought either against all the joint trespassers or against each of them singly; it is equally true that at law the joint trespassers cannot sue inter se for contribution. The question is whether these principles apply to the present case and bring it within the rule that where trustees are guilty of a breach of trust they may be sued either jointly or separately, which is the case of Walker v. Symonds (3 Swanst. 75). That case, however, appears to me inapplicable. This bill calls the defendants to account as assignees, and nothing can be done completely in the suit till they do account. It would be unjust to say that one of these persons—who, it is to be recollected, are made trustees by act of Parliament—that one only shall be called upon to give that account, which possibly the other only could justly give. The other might be the very person who could best inform the Master or the other parties upon the subject. This is not like an account required of one specific sum; on the contrary, the assignees are called upon to give an account of joint transactions. If we were to take it pro confesso that the whole of the debts were paid, and that a certain sum remained in their hands, which was misapplied by them, then the case of Walker v. Symonds might require application. In the present case, however, we have not arrived at that stage of the proceedings, but only at the account. Then the question is whether an uncertificated bankrupt, who has not superseded his commission, but has resisted it, shall be allowed to call his assignees to an account of their proceedings under the bankruptcy; and that has been already decided [against the bankrupt].[81]

(1888) LR 38 Ch D 546 (CA); *Re Flower and Metropolitan Board of Works* (1884) 27 Ch D 592; *Farrant v Blanchford* (1863) 1 De GJ & S 107; 46 ER 42; *Mendes v Guedalla* (n 16); *Bright v Legerton* (1861) 2 De GF & J 606; 45 ER 755; *Thompson v Finch* (1856) 22 Beav 316; 52 ER 1130; 8 De GM & G 560; 44 ER 506 (CA) (discussed below); *Raby v Ridehalgh* (1855) 7 De GM & G 104; 44 ER 41 (QB); *Burrows v Walls* (1855) 5 De GM & G 233; 43 ER 859; *Macleod v Annesley* (1853) 16 Beav 600; 51 ER 912; *Ex parte James James and James Cushion* (1853) 3 De GM & G 493; 43 ER 193; *Thornber v Sheard* (1850) 12 Beav 589; 50 ER 1186; *Knight v Marjoribanks* (1848) 11 Beav 322; 50 ER 841; *Ex Parte Eyre* (1843) 1 Ph 227; 41 ER 618; *Clough v Dixon* (1841) 10 Sim 564; 59 ER 734; *Lowry v Fulton* (1839) 9 Sim 104; 59 ER 298; *Munch v Cockerell* (1836) 8 Sim 219; 59 ER 88; *Wilson* (n 17) 142–43; *Twyford v Trail* (1834) 7 Sim 92; 58 ER 771; *Stiles v Guy* (1832) 4 Y & C Ex 571; 160 ER 1137; *Hanbury v Kirkland* (1829) 3 Sim 265; 57 ER 998.

[80] *Tarleton v Hornby* (1836) 1 Y & C Ex 333; 160 ER 135.
[81] ibid Y & C Ex 336–37; ER 137.

The requirement of complete joinder arose in the bankruptcy context to prevent a singling out of one commissioned trustee for a wrongful sale; the same joinder rule was then applied to executors,[82] company directors[83] and charitable trustees.[84] But this rule might be seen purely as adjectival law; once joinder had occurred, so permitting a collective accounting, then the facts establishing joint-several liability might be established so that any single trustee within the defaulting group could be attached, with sharing out of the burden of liability being left *ex post* to the contribution rules.

Sir John Romilly MR restated the Eldonian solidary liability principle in strong terms in the 1855 case of *Trutch v Lamprell*.[85] The court found the defendant trustee liable for putting the proceeds of an authorised sale of trust property into the hands of a co-trustee, who promised to pay the money to the beneficiary once the beneficiary's liabilities had been offset. The beneficiary contested these liabilities but the co-trustee nonetheless retained the money by way of set-off without seeking a judgment. The defendant trustee was held to be fully accountable for the sum retained; the court rejected the defence that the defendant had only been involved with the sale passively, for the sake of conformity, and had no part in the contest between the beneficiary and co-trustee in receipt of the assets. Romilly MR stated:

> This is one of those painful cases which, unfortunately, this Court has constantly to deal with, where trustees, innocent of any desire to benefit themselves, have failed to perform their duties, and the Court is compelled to make them responsible. It is constantly argued by counsel, but the conclusion is as constantly rejected by the Court, that a person who acts is not an active trustee, and is not liable, because he has only acted for conformity's sake. It is a contradiction in terms to say that a trustee who acts is not an active trustee; by taking upon himself the office of trustee, and acting, he becomes, in that transaction at least, an active trustee, and is bound properly to perform all the duties appertaining to his office.[86]

Romilly MR and the Court of Appeal again endorsed solidary principles in the authoritative 1856 case of *Thompson v Finch*.[87] Finch stood as co-trustee of a widow's estate together with Hayward, a well-regarded solicitor. On Hayward's advice and with the consent of the *cestui* the two co-trustees authorised the conversion of government stock held on trust into funds for mortgage investment; those sums were collected by Hayward alone and paid on loan to a favoured client of his without taking good mortgage security. A decade passed without Finch (or the *cestui*) raising any questions about the performance of the trust investments, and ultimately the funds were lost. Romilly MR held Finch jointly and severally liable for the whole

[82] *Wilson* (n 17) 142–43 (Leach MR).

[83] See *Seddon v Connell* (1840) 10 Simons 58; 59 ER 534, where joinder was said to be necessary for breach of trust by company directors, but not where the breach was concurrently a tortious fraud.

[84] See *Attorney-General v Daugars* (1864) 33 Beav 621, 624; 55 ER 509–11, where charitable trustees wrongfully applied trust funds to the costs of defending themselves against a suit for breach of duty involving the same trust; those still living were held to be jointly and severally liable, but the court would only attach those joined and appearing in the suit, and left the other co-trustees to be pursued for contribution.

[85] *Trutch v Lamprell* (1855) 20 Beav 116; 52 ER 546.

[86] ibid Beav 118; ER 547.

[87] *Thompson v Finch* (1856) 22 Beav 316; 52 ER 1130; 8 De GM & G 560; 44 ER 506 (CA).

loss, Hayward having been bankrupted. First, Finch had authorised Hayward to take the converted funds, and the rule 'that a trustee would be liable for his own receipts only, do[es] not apply to a case where a trustee assists or enables another trustee to receive the money'.[88] And, second, Finch had failed to check over a ten-year period if proper real security had been acquired for trust investments, but had accepted without inquiry his co-trustee's undertakings. The consent and quiescence of the *cestui* could not serve as a bar in this case. The correct approach was

> that if a *cestui que trust*, being *sui juris*, having a knowledge of the breach of trust by a trustee, assents to it, or takes no steps to obtain redress for a long lapse of time, he cannot afterwards complain of the breach of trust sanctioned by him, and of which for a great length of time he had not thought fit to complain. But here the case made is not one of notice to the Plaintiff of a breach of trust, but of its performance … it is not the business of a *cestui que trust* to inform a trustee of his duty. It was his duty, without any request, to see that the money had been laid out on proper and sufficient security.[89]

The *cestui* with no ready access to the accounts could not have imposed upon her a duty to monitor the trustees and keep them to their duty; and failure to detect the incorrect investments could not be taken as a ratification in these circumstances.[90]

Knight Bruce LJ in the Court of Appeal affirmed. Finch's ready belief in Hayward's honest execution of the investments could not morally be condemned; but such complete reliance was nonetheless a ceding of Finch's trustee role to his co-trustee:

> [U]nfortunately it was Mr. Finch's duty to ascertain whether the facts were as he may be taken to have understood them to be. In truth the facts were not so. There was no mortgage at all, or no proper mortgage, and if there had been a mortgage proper in any sense (which there was not) it was an improper proceeding, because it was not in the names of the two trustees.[91]

The appeal judges confirmed that Hayward was discharged of trust liability as a bankrupt, leaving Finch to bear the full liability—and then called for Hayward to be struck off the rolls for his abuse of his position as solicitor in the running of the trust.

By the time of the Judicature Acts 1873–75 the proactive duties of co-trustees to monitor closely each other's conduct had been well established as a core element of due administration. In the 1878 case of *Lewis v Nobbs*[92] the defendant, a friend of a deceased testator, was appointed co-trustee of assets from the deceased estate alongside a solicitor who appeared to be honest and competent. This was a post-execution arrangement so the trustees were no longer serving as executors. They were authorised to invest beyond safe local government stock, and they bought Russian railway bonds, each taking half of the bond instruments into possession. These bearer bonds were disposable by the individual controlling the paper, and the solicitor disposed of the bond and absconded, so that half the value of the investment was lost outright. The defendant trustee also made a loan to the son of a *cestui que trust* at her request,

88 ibid Beav 323; ER 1132.
89 ibid Beav 323–25; ER 1132–33.
90 On ratification of breach in relation to investment, see *Re Salmon* (1889) 42 Ch D 351 (CA).
91 *Thompson v Finch* (n 87) De GM & G 564; ER 509.
92 *Lewis v Nobbs* (1878) 8 Ch D 591.

taking a simple promissory note or personal security only; that money also was lost. Hall VC found the defendant liable for both losses. Although the Russian investment was authorised as a general category of investment, it was wrong to arm a single trustee with sole power to dispose, without dual control:

> [T]he Defendant ... did not discharge his duty in allowing his co-trustee to retain possession of one half of the bonds, and the course pursued enabled the co-trustee to improperly deal with them. The duty of the trustees was to make an investment in the names of both, so that the bonds should not be transferable without the action of both, or, as the bonds were transferable by delivery, care should have been taken that there could not be any improper disposition of them.[93]

And likewise the trustee was imprudent to have relied solely on the personal credit of the borrower from the family, nor should he have allowed himself to have been influenced by the request of the *cestui* to make the loan to her son, and so he had to replenish those lost funds as well. Hall VC made clear that the defendant had committed no fraud and had done no subjective wrongdoing in relying on others to perform their duty. In order to emphasise the honesty of the ill-fated trustee, Hall VC criticised the plaintiff for making personal imputations against the trustee and applied the sanction of refusing a costs order. In effect Hall VC thereby made the co-trustee jointly and severally liable for the conduct of the co-trustee on a demanding objective standard. The duty of the co-trustee was apparently to mistrust the other co-trustees, put in all reasonable controls that might have curbed any tendency to defalcation, and pay restitution on a but-for causal basis if a defalcation occurred in the absence of control. If this was not vicarious liability in name it was coming very close in effect.

VI. CONTRIBUTION RULES AND CO-TRUSTEE LIABILITIES

After the Judicature Act reforms the solidary liabilities of co-trustees tended to be explored largely via claims for contribution. The first notable case after the Act was *Asshurst v Mason* in 1875.[94] A director of a company who had been allocated unpaid shares wanted to resign his directorship and return the shares, thus to eliminate any future liability. The board led by Asshurst as chairman resolved that the company manager should take those shares to his name on trust for the company, not appreciating that this transaction was *ultra vires*. Asshurst and the board then asked Mason, another director and board member, to take joint title to the shares as co-trustee as this was a more secure practice. Fearing liability Mason objected; 'but upon the express arrangement that his co-directors should hold him harmless against all consequences—"see him through it"—he agreed';[95] the company then entered him on the register as joint owner of the shares on trust. The company became insolvent and Asshurst, prompted by the receiver, sought full payment from Mason

[93] ibid 594–95.
[94] *Asshurst v Mason* (1875) LR 20 Eq 225 (VC).
[95] ibid 226.

of the value of the unpaid shares as the owner, the manager and co-trustee lacked all means to pay. Mason brought suit for contribution from the other members of the board as *cestuis* of a trust who owed him an indemnity for liabilities incurred in his capacity as trustee, and alternatively because of the board's informal guarantee and indemnity. Bacon VC ordered full contribution from all board members, on an equity that was not fully explained. He first 'referred to the legendary case of a suit by a highwayman against his comrade of the road for a partnership account of his share of the plunder' as a kind of *reductio ad absurdum*;[96] but went on to hold that the *ultra vires* nature of the share transaction in this case did not eliminate the board members' equitable duty to contribute when the illegal common project failed and resulted in loss. The assurances offered to and reliance invited from Mason established liability: 'they who have procured his name to be used, who have adopted his name to carry into effect their design, must reasonably contribute to the loss, since loss has happened. That rests upon universal principles'.[97] It was clear that the base of liability was neither contractual indemnity nor co-trusteeship by the board members; nor was it stated that the board members became *cestuis* in lieu of the company;[98] nor could this be an estoppel as the claim was raised as a sword rather than a shield. Perhaps the best interpretation was that the board members had made themselves partners of the co-trustees, making for a participatory liability in the absence of breach. So far as co-trusteeship principles apply, the case signifies an expectation by the courts that a co-trustee who enters into office explicitly refusing solidary liability will nonetheless owe such liability as intrinsic to the office.

Policy reasons to support an onerous and non-avoidable co-trustee duty, and also detailed principles of contribution, were articulated in *Bahin v Hughes* in 1886.[99] In that case one of two trustees of a family trust took the lead in reinvesting funds from low yield municipal bonds into higher yield mortgages. The active trustee, relying on poor advice and without a proper understanding of her trust powers, made an *ultra vires* investment in a mortgage of a leasehold at undervalue and the money was lost. The other trustee had passively stood by during the reinvestment process, but had later written protesting the investment and demanding dual control of future decisions. On being joined in the suit for restitution of the fund the passive trustee claimed in defence that he had not been responsible for the poor investment, and in the alternative that if joint liability did apply then the active trustee should indemnify him, that is, he was exempted from the usual equitable duty of equal contribution as the co-trustees were not *in pari delicto*. Both defences failed, and full solidary liability with full equal contribution was ordered. Cotton LJ held it was a negligent breach of trust for the one passive trustee to let the fund into the control

[96] ibid 232. In a note on this point the reporter added: 'The case referred to is that of John Everet v. Joseph Williams, about 1725: see Pothier on Obligations, vol. ii. p. 3; Lindley on Partnership, p. 188. It appears that the Plaintiff, or a highwayman of that name, was hanged at Tyburn, February 1729–30; the Defendant at Maidstone 1735; and the solicitor was convicted of robbery 1735, but reprieved and only transported.' This was contribution with a vengeance.

[97] *Asshurst* (n 94) 233–34.

[98] As interpreted by Swinfen Eady J in *Jackson v Dickinson* [1903] 1 Ch 947 (Ch D).

[99] *Bahin v Hughes* (1886) 31 Ch D 390.

of another inexperienced and ill-advised co-trustee who misapplied the fund, and hence both were responsible for the ensuing breach of trust. Moreover 'it would be laying down a wrong rule to hold that where one trustee acts honestly, though erroneously, the other trustee is to be held entitled to indemnity who by doing nothing neglects his duty more than the acting trustee'.[100] Bowen LJ raised a doubt as to whether the post-dated protest of the passive trustee might amount to a *locus poenitentiae*, whereby the active trustee was put on notice that she should either withdraw the poor investment or indemnify her co-trustee; but he did not press his doubts in a formal dissent.[101] Fry LJ vehemently rejected Bowen LJ's supposition that the co-trustees were not *in pari delicto*, and delivered an analysis of co-trustee contribution that was taken by later courts to be definitive:

> [T]he Courts ought to be very jealous of raising any such implied liability as is insisted on, because if such existed it would act as an opiate upon the consciences of the trustees; so that instead of the cestui que trust having the benefit of several acting trustees, each trustee would be looking to the other or others for a right of indemnity, and so neglect the performance of his duties. Such a doctrine would be against the policy of the Court in relation to trusts.[102]

In the instant case, the active trustee caused loss 'through simple ignorance and want of knowledge', but at the same time the passive trustee could have averted the loss had he used ordinary diligence.[103]

The principle established in *Bahin* was that unequal culpability between co-trustees would only seldom displace the principle of equal contribution by the erection of an indemnity to protect the less culpable co-trustee. Cotton LJ set out some exceptions as follows:

> [T]here are very few cases in which one trustee, who has been guilty with a co-trustee of breach of trust and held answerable, has successfully sought indemnity as against his co-trustee … Of course, where one trustee has got the money into his hands, and made use of it, he will be liable to his co-trustee to give him an indemnity. … Now I think it wrong to lay down any limitation of the circumstances under which one trustee would be held liable to the other for indemnity, both having been held liable to the cestui que trust; but, so far as cases have gone at present, relief has only been granted against a trustee who has himself got the benefit of the breach of trust, or between whom and his co-trustees there has existed a relation, which will justify the Court in treating him as solely liable for the breach of trust.[104]

The most prominent relationship erecting an indemnity was the case of the solicitor-trustee who instigated a breach of trust. In such cases co-trustees who reasonably relied on the solicitor, whilst liable to the *cestuis*, were presumptively not bound to share equally in the loss with the solicitor for the solicitor's errors of

[100] ibid 396.
[101] ibid 397.
[102] ibid 398.
[103] ibid 398; principle affirmed in *Robinson v Harkin* [1896] 2 Ch 415; *Bacon v Camphausen* (1888) 58 TLR 851.
[104] *Bahin* (n 99) 395–96.

judgment as they had a good claim to rely on the solicitor's professional judgment.[105] However the presumption that the solicitor-co-trustee could not require contribution was displaced where it was shown that the other co-trustees were active participants in the breach and had not simply entrusted decision-making to the expert solicitor. This made it possible for the solicitor to seek contribution from active but not passive trustees.[106]

The important case of *Re Brogden* in 1888[107] put the solidary duty of co-trustees still higher. The court refused indemnity against contribution even where a trustee had actively tried to protect the trust interests against the wishes of his co-trustees. In that case three co-trustees had a responsibility to bring in assets from a family iron firm into the trust fund and raise monies from those assets to pay out legacies. A five-year period was allowed under the testamentary trust before the trustees would have to effect final execution. After the five years had passed the two family members of the trustee group were loath to extract the funds from the firm which was then facing trading difficulties. The third trustee, Budgett, pressed for liquidation and payment over so as to complete execution of the trust, but backed off to avoid a quarrel over the likely disintegration of the family firm. The firm soon went into administration leaving no surplus for distribution; the *cestui que trust* then claimed funds equivalent to the unpaid legacy from the three co-trustees. The two family members of the trust acknowledged their liability, but Budgett claimed indemnity on the basis that he had honestly tried to execute the trust but had been defeated by the lack of will or obstruction of the other two co-trustees. North J in Chancery, and then a strong Court of Appeal, expressing some reluctance, found Budgett equally liable as trustee. Despite the pressures of the family situation and the opposition of his co-trustees, he ought to have pressed for full and prompt execution at the time when the trust was due for completion, bringing legal action to force payments of all legacies. He had failed to act reasonably by backing off until the business had been run down and it was too late to realise the trust assets. According to Lopes LJ: 'No consideration of delicacy, and no regard for the feelings of relatives or friends, will exonerate him'.[108]

Extending the principle established in *Re Brogden,* it has been stated that a co-trustee has both the power and the duty to sue co-trustees in order to prevent or remedy a breach of trust, and may do this in his or her personal capacity without joining the *cestuis* to the action; that is, the co-trustees can sue each other in their own right to ensure the primary performance of the trust, for example by seeking a *quia timet* injunction to safeguard assets, to force specific performance of the

[105] ibid citing as *locus classicus Lockhart v Reilly* (1856) 25 LJ 697; (1857) 1 De GG & J 464; 44 ER 803. This indemnity rule was upheld in a series of cases suggesting an endemic problem of abuse by solicitor-trustees: see *Re Bell's Indenture* [1980] 1 WLR 1217 (Ch D); *Re Munton* [1927] 1 Ch 262 (CA); *Re Linsley* [1904] 2 Ch 785 (Ch D); *Jackson v Dickinson* (n 98); *Head v Gould* [1898] 2 Ch 250 (Ch D); *Re Turner* (n 6); *Chillingworth v Chambers* (n 79); *Blyth v Fladgate* [1891] 1 Ch 337 (Ch D); *Re Partington* (1888) 57 LTR 654 (Ch D); *Price v Price* (1880) 1 TLR 626 (Ch D).

[106] *Head* (n 105) 265 (Kekewich J).

[107] *Brogden* (n 79).

[108] ibid 574–75.

trust, and in an extreme case to displace or replace errant co-trustees.[109] A colonial New South Wales case stated interestingly that breach of trust by active co-trustees is 'duplex'—simultaneously a breach of duty owed to *cestuis*, and a breach of duties owed to the other co-trustees who have a 'negative' interest in due performance due to their own exposure to solidary liability upon breach.[110] The co-trustee's action to enforce the trust *inter se* must be distinguished from a suit for equal contribution for the consequences of breach.[111] The analysis differs where it is a *cestui* rather than a co-trustee who insists that the trust duties not be rigorously enforced. In such a case of a *cestui* assenting to breach, a full defence by way of indemnity would be afforded to the co-trustees.[112] In a further variation, the courts have on occasion had to deal with a *cestui* who was also a co-trustee being liable for breach of trust causing loss to the beneficial estate (including loss to the *cestui*'s own assets). The relevant rule, harking back to *dicta* of Lord Eldon in *Walker v Symonds*, was that the *cestui*-trustee had his or her beneficial interest impounded by the court and charged with the losses to the trust fund; in addition the *cestui*-trustee was barred from seeking contribution from co-trustees up to the value of loss suffered by the *cestui* in that capacity. By so partially barring contribution, a *cestui*-trustee had to give the entire value of his or her trust share over to the innocent *cestuis*, and then pay *pro rata* for any further losses to the trust estate, without sharing in that restitution.[113] A parallel rule held that where a trustee received a personal benefit from a breach of trust, the defaulting trustee had first to contribute the amount of the personal benefit received before equal accounting would be ordered; but such partial indemnity could only protect the other trustees if they had not actively participated in the breach.[114] No contribution could be claimed by a fraudulent trustee where an element of the wrongdoing included fraudulent misrepresentations or fraudulent misconduct towards the co-trustees who themselves did not actively share in the breach of trust.[115] It has

[109] *Re Forest of Dean Coal Mining Co* (1878) 10 Ch D 450; *Young v Murphy* [1996] 1 VR 279; *Nicholson Street Pty Ltd v Letten and Lane* [2016] VSCA 157.

[110] *Wentworth v Tompson* (1859) 2 Legge (NSW) 1238, 1241 (Stephen CJ).

[111] *Fletcher v Green (No 2)* (1864) 33 Beav 513; 55 ER 467.

[112] This refers to consent *ex ante*, which binds the beneficiary with regard to each co-trustee. It appears that a *release* or *compromise* of liability *ex post* given by a beneficiary to a co-trustee does not necessarily embrace all co-trustees, depending on their individual position and merits: *Blackwood v Borrowes* (1843) 4 Dr & War 441, 475 (Lord St Leonards); *Thompson v Australian Capital Television Pty Ltd* (1996) 186 CLR 574 (HCA) n 128 (Gummow J).

[113] *Booth* (n 68) 888 (Langdale MR); *Birks v Mickelthwait* (1864) 3 Beav 40; 55 ER 426; *Re Rhodesia Goldfields Ltd* [1910] 1 Ch 239; *Re Towndrow* [1911] 1 Ch 662; *Chillingworth v Chambers* (n 79) 707 (Kay LJ); *Selangor United Rubber Estates v Cradock (No 4)* [1969] 1 WLR 1773 (Ch D); *Goodwin v Duggan* (1996) 41 NSWLR 158 (Handley and Beazley JJA). Where cestuis are not only co-trustees but partners with mutual agency powers, full joint and several liability is rigorously enforced: *Gillespie and Paterson v City of Glasgow Bank and Liquidators* (1879) 4 App Cas 632 (HL).

[114] See *Powlet v Herbert* (1791) 1 Ves 297; 30 ER 352; *Greenwood v Wakeford* (1839) 1 Beav 576, 578; 48 ER 1064, 1065 (Langdale MR); *May v Selby* (1842) 1 Y & C CC 235; 62 ER 869; *Baynard v Woolley* (1855) 20 Beav 583; 52 ER 792; *Butler v Butler* (1877) 5 Ch D 554; *Wynne v Tempest* [1897] 1 Ch 110, 113 (Chitty J); *Re Smith* [1896] 1 Ch 71 (Ch D); *Goodwin* (n 113).

[115] *Belemore v Watson* (1885) 1 TLR 241. In *Burke v LFOT Pty Ltd* (2002) 209 CLR 282 (HCA) at [17] and [143], it is stated that a contribution claim between co-trustees requires that the parties to be *in pari delicto*, and additionally is disbarred by any fraud on the part of the claimant; this risks some imprecision as it is clear enough that a co-trustees with differential levels of fault may still claim contribution from each other.

been stated more recently in the Commonwealth that co-trustees who participate in a common fraud are likewise disbarred from seeking contribution.[116] These rules preventing contribution claims by persons tainted by fraud have been overtaken in England since 1978 by legislation bestowing a power of 'just and equitable' apportionment on the court with no presumptive bar against a wrongdoer;[117] the details of this apportionment regime, and also statutory apportionment regimes applying to the primary co-trustee liabilities in other jurisdictions,[118] need not concern us here.

***

The last great case in the development of co-trustee liability was *Head v Gould*, decided in 1898.[119] In that case two trustees, each solicitors, held funds and properties on trusts to support a widow for life, with powers to appoint to the three children, and, in default of appointment, to hold for the three children in equal shares. Some but not all of the trust properties were covered by additional powers of advancement. The widow, acting in concert with her daughter, one of the beneficiaries or objects under the trusts, wrote repeatedly to the trustees requesting appointment or advancement of the properties to the mother and to the two adult children to support them in expensive lifestyles commensurate with their social class. The assets were rapidly spent, up to the third share of the properties that were to be preserved in default of appointment for the infant. When the trustees proved unwilling to appoint that last portion of capital into the control of the widow and daughter as well, they were asked to resign from their trust offices and make way for new trustees, being the daughter herself and a compliant junior solicitor. The old trustees acceded to this change, and finding some sale proceeds of trust assets left in their hands, transferred these to the widow as a final appointment as they stepped down from office. Once the new trustees had taken title and control, the last parts of the capital were soon transferred into the widow's control and spent.

The infant son, for whom none of the trust wealth survived, then sued the old trustees for breach of trust or participation in breach, seeking restitution of his third share of the fund. He also sued his sister as new trustee for acting under the control of their mother in order to commit the breach of trust. The daughter claimed she had no real control as trustee and was completely passive and unaware of what her co-trustee had done, shielding behind his status as a solicitor and professional adviser. She with her mother also claimed that the trust wealth had correctly been applied for the advancement of the *cestuis*, including the infant; this claim was rejected on the evidence. Kekewich J further found that the daughter was an untrustworthy witness, was largely under her mother's sway, and had actively worked to extract the trust

[116] See also *Selkirk* (n 15); *Goodwin* (n 113); *Belan v Casey* [2003] NSWSC 159; *McNally v Harris* [2008] NSWSC 659; JD Heydon and MJ Leeming, *Jacob's Law of Trusts in Australia* 8th edn (Sydney, LexisNexis, 2016) [21–17]–[21–25], [22–09]; A Gurr, 'Accessory Liability and Contribution, Release and Apportionment' (2010) 34 *Melbourne University Law Review* 481.

[117] Civil Liability (Contribution) Act 1978, ss 1(10), 2(1).

[118] See Wrongs Act 1968 (Vic), Parts IV and IVA (as amended in 2003).

[119] *Head v Gould* (n 105). Interestingly the Trustee Act 1893, s 11, granting a presumptive power for a co-trustee to be retired from a trust office and discharged from liability, was not discussed in this case.

assets for her own and her mother's unauthorised use. He held that her active role in drawing off her brother's trust share meant she had no automatic indemnity against the solicitor co-trustee's claim for contribution. Kekewich J next found that the old trustees were fully aware that the daughter was under the sway of her mother and that both had a relationship of influence over the new solicitor-trustee. He further found that the old trustees had acceded to the change of trusteeship out of exasperation, exhaustion and reluctance to continue in an anxious and thankless role, but they were not cognisant that a breach of trust of the sort that happened must follow as a consequence of their resignation from office, and were at no times dishonest. The great question of the case is whether they could be held accountable for the predictable misconduct of the trustees who succeeded them. Kekewich J framed the problem as follows:

> [T]he alleged liability of the former trustees is of vast importance, affecting, as it does, not only the two large classes to one or both of which most men belong, trustees and cestuis que trust, but also all members of the legal profession to which the position and duties of trustees are a source of constant anxiety.[120]

Kekewich J found judicial utterances suggesting that where old trustees knew or contemplated that new trustees appointed to replace them would breach the trust, then that knowledge constituted an ostensible or constructive agency so that the wrongful acts of the new trustees were ascribed as actions of the old trustees themselves; in other words, a vicarious liability continued after the changeover binding the old trustees to accept liability for the acts of the new. But the learned judge preferred to cast the liability not in agency terms but as a part of the primary accounting duties of the old trustees, which duties were breached at the moment they parted with the property with knowledge that this would lead to abuse:

> It is the duty of trustees to protect the funds intrusted to their care, and to distribute those funds themselves or hand them over to their successors intact, that is, properly invested and without diminution, according to the terms of the mandate contained in the instrument of trust. This duty is imposed on them as long as they remain trustees and must be their guide in every act done by them as trustees. On retiring from the trust and passing on the trust estate to their successors—and this whether they appoint those successors or merely assign the property to the nominees of those who have the power of appointment—they are acting as trustees, and it is equally incumbent on them in this ultimate act of office to fulfil the duty imposed on them as at any other time. If therefore they neglect that duty and part with the property without due regard to it, they remain liable and will be held by the Court responsible for the consequences properly traceable to that neglect.[121]

To find negligence, however, the old trustees' act of resignation had to amount to a participation in the ensuing breaches that would be the foreseeable consequence of that resignation. He put the standard thus:

> [I]in order to make a retiring trustee liable for a breach of trust committed by his successor you must shew, and shew clearly, that the very breach of trust which was in fact committed

[120] *Head* (n 105) 267.

[121] ibid 268–69, building on *Webster v Le Hunt* (1860) 8 WR 534; (1861) 9 WR 918 (Ch); *Palairet v Carew* (1863) 32 Beav 564; 55 ER 222; *Clark v Hoskins* (1867) 36 LJ 689; (1868) 37 LJ Ch 561.

> was not merely the outcome of the retirement and new appointment, but was contemplated by the former trustee when such retirement and appointment took place. ... It will not suffice to prove that the former trustees rendered easy or even intended, a breach of trust, if it was not in fact committed. They must be proved to have been guilty as accessories before the fact of the impropriety actually perpetrated.[122]

In this case the old trustees, despite their reservations about the daughter, had no reason to believe that the new trustees would breach the trust as they did, and hence were not accountable. They were however accountable for the smaller sum of sale proceeds they had handed over to the widow at the end of their trusteeship; and they could not be excused by the court under statutory discretion as it was not reasonable to entrust any trust assets to the rapacious widow. To show his disapproval of the behaviour of the widow and daughter he refused any cost order against the old trustees.

Head v Gould is almost the last major judicial authority adding to the jurisprudence of co-trusteeship in English jurisprudence. Kekewich J was himself puzzled over the lack of recent litigation or judicial exploration of the problem, offering these ruminations:

> It is strange that so little authority should be forthcoming on a point of such importance, and especially as no one presumes to cast a doubt on the doctrine, which may be regarded as an integral part of accepted legal lore. In former days, when students learned law and practice not only by reading books and attending lectures (means, of course, which cannot be safely neglected), but at least equally as much from the precept and example of a master and animated discussion in the pupil room, doctrines such as this not calling for frequent practical application were passed from one generation to another, and became engrained in the minds of practitioners without being formulated in reported cases unless a precise question was raised between litigants in a concrete form. This possibly explains why, for a doctrine in substance undisputed, there is so little authority to be found. ... the few cases cited ... are admitted to be all that can be discovered in the books.[123]

One possible answer to the puzzle of missing co-trusteeship was the rise of trustee corporations providing professional fiduciary services governing private and commercial trusts, a process of displacement beginning in the later nineteenth century[124] and accelerating in the past few generations.[125] Another was that privately negotiated indemnity clauses, and then legislative protections modelled on such instruments, had gradually choked off paths to co-trustee liability. We will conclude by examining this aspect.

[122] *Head* (n 105) 273–74. See also YL Tan, 'Must Retiring Trustees be Replaced? (1989) 9 *Legal Studies* 323. Unanimous beneficiaries can also force an inadequate trustee or co-trustee to retire via a court order, subject to discharge of extant liabilities: *Miller v Cameron* (1936) 54 CLR 572 (HCA).

[123] *Head* (n 105) 269.

[124] See *Perpetual Executors and Trustees Association of Australia, Limited v Swan* [1898] AC 763 (PC). I am grateful to Mark Leeming for this point.

[125] A recent example of a corporation offering investment trust services and then seeking to use corporate form to limit the directors' liability is afforded in *Australian Securities* (n 24) (Edelman J).

VII. THE RISE OF INDEMNITY CLAUSES

It is a commonplace of positive economic analysis that parties will bargain around the extant legal rules to reach a new equilibrium of rights and duties better reflecting their respective interests or power; or else promote optimal shifts in the rules by repeated litigation or lobbying for legislation. This model is complicated in the arena of trusts law as settlors, trustees and beneficiaries are not necessarily or normally in direct contractual privity. Nonetheless, constant negotiation and re-negotiation of liability levels aiming to vary the general law can be seen across the history of trust institutions,[126] including co-trusteeship.

The law reports reveal very early use of indemnity clauses to attempt to shield co-trustees from solidary liability or indeed any liability for less than fraudulent misappropriations. In *Brice v Stokes*, an 1805 case already met in relation to presumptions of liability for joint receipt, we find that a wide indemnity clause was incorporated by a testator into his testamentary trust around 1783, the relevant clause stating that

> his said trustees and executors should not be answerable or accountable for any loss, which might happen, of all or any part of his real and personal estate, so as such loss be not through their wilful neglect or default; and that one of them should not be answerable for the others or other of them, or for the acts, receipts, payments, or defaults of the other or others of them, but each of them for himself and for his own acts, receipts, and defaults, only.[127]

Lord Eldon C managed to read this clause *contra proferentem*, holding that it did not apply where one trustee left monies in the hands of another trustee without monitoring to ensure due accounting and security. The question for the court was 'not, whether the receipt of the money was right, but, whether the use of it, subsequent to that receipt, was right, after the knowledge of the trustee, that it had got into a course of abuse'. He concluded: 'as soon as a trustee is fixed with knowledge, that his co-trustee is misapplying the money, a duty is imposed upon him to bring it back into the joint custody of those, who ought to take better care of it'.[128] In other words the defendant by failing to control the other trustee had committed an 'act' of breach and a 'wilful default' of trust himself, and the indemnity could not save him.

Chantal Stebbings in her history of nineteenth-century private trusteeship[129] has shown how the newly intensified co-trustee obligations evoked in the time of Lord Eldon C and Sir William Grant MR led to still wider indemnity clauses being

[126] See R Sitkoff, 'The Economic Structure of Fiduciary Law' (2011) 91 *Boston University Law Review* 1039; J Getzler, 'Legislative incursions into modern trusts doctrine in England: The Trustee Act 2000 and the Contracts (Rights of Third Parties) Act 1999' (2002) 2(1) *Global Jurist Topics* §2; J Getzler, 'Ascribing and Limiting Fiduciary Obligations: Understanding the Operation of Consent' in A Gold and P Miller (eds), Philosophical Foundations of Fiduciary Law (Oxford, OUP, 2014) 39–62; JH Langbein, 'The Contractarian Basis of the Law of Trusts' (1995) 105 *Yale Law Journal* 625; *cf* L Smith, 'Contract, Consent, and Fiduciary Relationships' in P Miller and A Gold (eds), *Contract, Status, and Fiduciary Law* (Oxford, OUP, 2016).

[127] *Brice v Stokes* (n 65) 117–38. Ves Jun 320; ER 1111.

[128] ibid Ves Jun 327; ER 1114.

[129] Stebbings (n 25).

incorporated into trust settlements as a common practice. She adduces a typical clause of 1807 from a trust deed, worth reproducing in full:

> [Trustees] shall be chargeable … only for such monies as they shall respectively actually receive by virtue of the Trusts hereby in them reposed notwithstanding his or their signing or giving any Receipt or Receipts for the sake of Conformity and any one or more of them shall not be answerable or accountable for the others or other of them but each and every of them only for his own Acts Receipts Neglects or Defaults respectively. And that they or any of them shall not be answerable or accountable for any Banker Broker or other person with whom or in whose Hands or Custody any part of the said Trust monies and premises shall or may be deposited for safe custody nor for the insufficiency or deficiency of any Security or Securities Stocks or Funds in or upon which the said Trust Monies and premises … shall be placed out or invested or for any Misfortune or Loss which may happen in the execution of the … trusts … except the same shall happen by or through their or his own wilful Misconduct Neglect or Default respectively.[130]

Despite the sweeping language of such clauses, it seems that all they really achieved was to reverse the burden of proof by requiring beneficiaries to evidence wilful default or direct actions in breach of trust, rather than simply demand a strict account of assets and leave it to the trustee to assert a defence.[131] In courts of equity using bill and answer procedure even this probative effect could be slight. On occasions the judge did not even bother to read around the indemnity clause but simply ignored its existence.[132] In 1854 Sir John Romilly MR stated bluntly: 'The ordinary trustee indemnity clause affords no security to a trustee who neglects to take the steps necessary to secure the fund'.[133] Four years later he repeated the message more urgently when striking down yet another typical indemnity clause defence:

> I am of opinion that this clause does not exonerate a trustee from the consequences of any acts by which the money has been misapplied.
>
> This clause is constantly brought forward to sanction the misapplication of trust moneys; but until it is provided, by the instrument creating the trust, that the trustee shall be liable for no breach of trust, provided he does not obtain a personal advantage, I shall not consider the clause as giving a trustee the right or liberty of conniving at a breach of trust.
>
> Even if an instrument containing such an inconsistent clause were brought before me, I express no opinion on the result; but until it is, I cannot allow a trustee to say that it is not his business to act properly in the performance of his duty as trustee. The Defendant is liable, because, by signing the receipt, he has enabled his co-trustee to obtain and misapply the trust money.[134]

The Master of Rolls was in effect identifying an irreducible core of co-trusteeship that no indemnity clause could shave away—the requirement to execute a trust without wilful default or knowing or reckless indifference.

[130] ibid 123.
[131] See *Re Brier* (1881) 26 Ch D 238, 243–44 (Lord Selborne).
[132] See *Pride v Fooks* (1840) 2 Beav 430; 48 ER 1248 (Langdale MR).
[133] *Dix v Burford* (1854) 19 Beav 409, 413; 52 ER 408, 410. See also *Styles* (n 68) (Lord Cottenham).
[134] *Brumridge v Brumridge* (1858) 27 Beav 5, 7; 54 ER 2, 3.

The common clauses may have had little impact in mitigating liability, yet trustees would refuse to serve without them, and by the mid-nineteenth-century such clauses had become a ubiquitous element of trust settlements, serving perhaps as a kind of legal placebo. Finally, Lord St Leonards promoted legislation in 1859 reading an indemnity clause in common form into every trust instrument as a matter of course.[135] Such default clauses added to the complexity of trust interpretation, supervision and litigation but achieved little else. On occasion, a non-standard indemnity might shield from liability, as in the 1861 case of *Wilkins v Hogg* where a clause of a will trust stated 'that any trustee who should pay to his co-trustee, or enable him to receive monies, for the general purposes of the will, should not be obliged to see to the due application thereof, or be responsible by express or implied notice of the misapplication'.[136] Two co-trustees allowed a payment to a third who immediately misappropriated it. Sir John Stuart VC found no carelessness or wilful default in so trusting a co-trustee with an instant receipt, and further held that the testatrix had specifically authorised and consented to such a vesting. So the indemnity clause was effective. But such enforcement of very wide exemption clauses was exceptional and against the greater tradition of equity jurisprudence, and Stuart VC's decision was quarantined and not followed. It is a shame that this case, lying outside the greater tradition, was revived by Lord Millett in *Armitage v Nurse* in 1997 in order to justify wide trustee exemption clauses excusing normal negligence in English law;[137] and used again to even wider effect by the Privy Council in *Spread Trustee Co Ltd v Hutcheson* in 2011 to permit indemnity against gross negligence in a Guernsey trust.[138] On one reading the effect of these modern decisions has been to cut down the irreducible core so as to excuse any conduct falling short of fraud, in the sense of conscious awareness of wrongdoing going beyond what older lawyers described as 'wilful default', or conscious action that breaches duty. This is to fly against the long tradition of control of trusteeship where the judges have been concerned precisely to ensure that co-trustees are required diligently to monitor each other as a central protection of the beneficiaries' rights. It may match a deeper hostility to joint and several liability that is gathering force in the common law world, whereby solidary duties are fragmented into individualised liabilities and apportionment displaces contribution.[139] But these themes take us outside the bounds of this study into a much wider debate about the aims of private law.

[135] Trustee Act 1859, s 31, adopted in similar terms by the Trustee Act 1893, s 24 and the Trustee Act 1925, s 30(1), which latter clause reads: 'A trustee shall be chargeable only for money and securities actually received by him notwithstanding his signing any receipt for the sake of conformity, and shall be answerable and accountable only for his own acts, receipts, neglects, or defaults, and not for those of any other trustee, nor for any banker, broker, or other person with whom any trust money or securities may be deposited, nor for the insufficiency or deficiency of any securities, nor for any other loss, unless the same happens through his own wilful default.'

[136] *Wilkins v Hogg* (1861) 3 Giff 116; 66 ER 346 (VC).

[137] *Armitage v Nurse* [1998] Ch 241, 253–54.

[138] *Spread Trustee Co Ltd v Hutcheson* [2011] UKPC 13; [2012] 2 AC 194.

[139] See also T Weir, 'All or Nothing?' (2003) 78 *Tulane Law Review* 511; AS Burrows, 'Should One Reform Joint and Several Liability' in N Mullany and A Linden (eds), *Torts Tomorrow: A Tribute to John Fleming* (Sydney, Law Book Company, 1998) 102–18.

VIII. CODA

This story of doctrinal metamorphosis reaches its terminus with the elimination of the common form statutory indemnity and abandonment of the juristic language of wilful default and solidary liability by the Trustee Act 2000. The Act replaces the juxtaposition of relatively strict primary accounting duties with statutory indemnities by erecting in their place a general duty of care applying to trustees in the exercise of all powers and discretions. The duties of the trustee, including the special duties of co-trustees to monitor and control each other, now fall to be measured by a general duty to 'exercise such care and skill as is reasonable in the circumstances',[140] subject to any party-designed clauses exempting such general duty, exemptions that now take their validity from legislative fiat.[141] Free delegation of trust functions now allows co-trustees acting collectively to vest their powers in a sub-set of active trustees, provided this delegation or concentration of powers passes the generic 'reasonableness' test.[142] The move to such a generalised test was adumbrated in *Re Lucking's Will Trusts* in 1967, where Cross J asked simply if it was unreasonable or negligent[143] for a passive co-trustee to delegate most trust functions to an active trustee and then fail to monitor; the judgment gave no attention to the detailed nineteenth-century rulings cited by counsel, and accorded the co-trustee partial relief from liability based on a metric of fault based on the conventions of the relevant market relationships.[144]

With the embrace of the negligence standard (and putting to one side the remaining operation of contribution rules), the intricate historical law of co-trusteeship in England in a sense came to an end. We no longer ascribe liability to a co-trustee based on a prima facie requirement of due administration of receipts or a duty to monitor, subject to pleas showing some excuse for not so administering or monitoring. It is all about duty of care now, driven forward by the comparative measurement of fault, but also limited by the pervasive contracting out from initial liability. Whether the removal of traditional equitable controls on groups of trustees charged with the stewardship of vast wealth on behalf of banks, mutual funds and pension funds has led to improved performance and discipline after 1967—or 2007—is a question that remains to be answered.[145]

Did we lay an axe to the root of the tree?

[140] Trustee Act 2000, s 1.
[141] ibid, Sched 1(7).
[142] ibid, s 11.
[143] Following the rule in *Speight v Gaunt* (n 61).
[144] *Re Lucking's Will Trusts* [1968] 1 WLR 866 (Ch D) 874–78 per Cross J.
[145] See further J Getzler, 'Financial Crisis and the Decline of Fiduciary Law' in C Morris and D Vines (eds), *Capital Failure: Rebuilding Trust in Financial Services* (Oxford, OUP, 2014) 193–208, and other essays in that volume; J Armour et al, *Principles of Financial Regulation* (Oxford, OUP, 2016).

11

Marshalling Marshalling

CHRISTOPHER HARE

MARSHALLING SEEKS TO achieve an equitable result between creditors secured over the same collateral. The doctrine has defied judicial categorisation and there has been long-running judicial and academic disagreement as to how exactly that doctrine works. Rather than contending for the adoption of either the coercion or post-realisation models of marshalling, this chapter argues in favour of a 'hybrid' model that views marshalling as a defence operating against either the senior secured creditor or the debtor depending upon the circumstances. Such an approach is consistent with both the origins of marshalling and the modern desire to retain as much flexibility in that doctrine as possible.

I. INTRODUCTION

Despite its clear insolvency and enforcement advantages, a secured creditor still runs not-inconsiderable risks, whether statutory invalidation,[1] subordination to subsequent lenders[2] or loss in the collateral's value.[3] The position of a creditor holding a second- or third-ranking security over an asset is even more precarious, however, since the value of its junior security-interest can be prejudiced by the senior-ranking creditor's commercial decision to make further advances or enforce its security.

[1] Insolvency Act 1986, ss 238–39, 245.

[2] For example, a prior equitable interest can lose priority to a subsequently created legal interest provided the latter's holder does not have notice (see L Gullifer and J Payne, *Corporate Finance Law: Principles and Policies* 2nd edn (Oxford, Hart Publishing, 2015) [7.4.4]); a creditor with security over accounts receivable may lose priority to a subsequent secured lender who gives notice first (see *Dearle v Hall* (1828) Russ 1; 38 ER 475); a creditor with a subsequent purchase-money security interest by way of title retention (rather than charge) will take priority over the holder of a prior global security (see *Abbey National Building Society v Cann* [1991] 1 AC 56); and a subsequent fixed chargeholder without notice will take priority over an earlier floating charge (see *Re Ind Coope & Co Ltd* [1911] 2 Ch 223; *Re Rayford Homes Ltd* [2011] BCC 715 [97]), as will a subsequent floating charge over a smaller class of assets (*Re Automatic Bottle Makers Ltd* [1926] Ch 412, 420, 423, 427). It might be possible to prevent such a loss of priority by means of an appropriately drafted negative pledge clause, which now constitutes a registrable particular under the Companies Act 2006, s 859D(2)(c): see *English and Scottish Mercantile Investment Co Ltd v Brunton* [1892] 2 QB 700.

[3] Such a loss in value may be attributable to the initial valuation being negligent or to a subsequent drop in the value of the particular asset or asset prices more generally: see *South Australia Asset Management Corporation v York Montague Ltd* [1997] AC 191; *AIB Group (UK) plc v Mark Redler & Co* [2014] UKSC 58, [2015] AC 1503.

Whilst a junior secured creditor's position has to a degree been ameliorated in the first scenario by the common law rule against 'tacking'[4] and its statutory replacements,[5] the courts have been understandably reluctant to trench upon the senior creditor's right of enforcement.[6] Indeed, given that the commercial calculation undertaken by the junior security-holder when lending must include the risk that the senior creditor might enforce its prior interest over the asset, and thereby leave insufficient equity for the junior creditor, any other stance would be unjustifiably paternalistic. By way of exception to this traditional common law reluctance,[7] however, the courts of Equity considered that a junior secured creditor should not be 'squeezed out' of its collateral solely as a result of another creditor (with a prior-ranking security over the asset in question) electing to enforce its claims against that 'common asset' rather than employing the alternative enforcement options at its disposal (such as security over other collateral). Indeed, the unconscionability[8] in such a scenario derives from the fact that if the senior secured creditor had acted differently, the junior secured creditor would have recovered all, or at least more, of the sums due to it. To counter such unfairness, the courts extended the doctrine of marshalling, which had already been developed in other specific contexts,[9] to the context of competing security interests in general.[10] In essence, the marshalling of securities is '... a principle for doing equity between two or more creditors, each of whom are owed debts by the same debtor, but one of whom can enforce its claim against more than one security

[4] *Hopkinson v Rolt* (1861) 11 HL Cases (Clark's) 514, 533–35, 538–39; 11 ER 829, 837–40; *Deeley v Lloyds Bank Ltd* [1912] AC 756, 769–74, 780–85; *cf* Law of Property Act 1925, s 94(3)–(4); *McCarthy & Stone Ltd v Julian S Hodge & Co Ltd* [1971] 1 WLR 1547, 1556–57; *Macmillan Inc v Bishopsgate Investment Trust plc* [1995] 1 WLR 978, 1002–05; *Re Rayford* (n 2) [31].

[5] Law of Property Act 1925, s 94(1)–(2); Land Registration Act 2002, s 49(1)–(2).

[6] *China and South Sea Bank Ltd v Tan Soon Gin* [1990] 1 AC 536, 545; *Cheah Theam Swee v Equiticorp Finance Group Ltd* [1992] AC 472, 476.

[7] *Wallis v Woodyear* (1855) 2 Jur NS 179, 180; *Manks v Whiteley* [1911] 2 Ch 448, 466.

[8] *Earl of Oxford's Case* (1615) 1 Ch Rep 1; 21 ER 485. See also FW Maitland, *Equity* 2nd edn (Cambridge, CUP, 1936) 18–19.

[9] *Burgh v Francis* (1673) Rep temp Finch 29; 23 ER 16; *Anonymous* (1679) 2 Ch Cas 5; 22 ER 819. See also *Clifton v Burt* (1720) 1 PW 678; 24 ER 566. Whilst this chapter focuses upon marshalling as it applies to competing security interests, the doctrine has had a broader application, such as determining the respective claims of specific and residuary legatees following the discharge of a mortgage in the context of the administration of estates (see *Re Roberts* [1902] 2 Ch 834; *Re Fry* [1912] 2 Ch 86; *Re Ross* [2013] EWHC 2724 (Ch) [86]–[87]) and dealing with the competition between master's wages and bottomry bonds in the early admiralty jurisdiction (see *The Edward Oliver* (1865–1866) LR 1 A&E 379; *The Eugenie* (1872–1875) LR 4 A&E 123). Whilst these other applications of the marshalling doctrine can sometimes provide useful analogies, they have largely developed as distinct and separate jurisdictions (see *Re Townley* [1922] 1 Ch 154) and their significance has diminished since the passing of the Administration of Estates Act 1925: see J Ross Martyn and N Caddick, *Williams, Mortimer and Sunnucks, Executors, Administrators and Probate* 20th edn (London, Sweet & Maxwell, 2012) [75-18]; J Ross Martyn et al (eds) *Theobald on Wills* 18th edn (London, Sweet & Maxwell, 2016) [32-034]; *cf* J McGhee, *Snell's Equity* 33rd edn (London, Sweet & Maxwell, 2015) [32-046].

[10] *Aldrich v Cooper* (1803) 8 Ves 382, 389; 32 ER 402, 405; *Dolphin v Aylward* (1869–1870) LR 4 HL 486, 505; *The Eugenie* (n 9); *Duncan, Fox & Co v The North and South Wales Bank* (1880) 6 App Cas 1, 12–13; *Wegg-Prosser v Wegg-Prosser* [1895] 2 Ch 449, 451. See also *Tegel Foods Ltd v Coastal Cuisine NZ Ltd* [2013] NZHC 899 [21]; *Highbury Pension Fund Management Co v Zirfin Investments Ltd* [2014] Ch 349 [1], [18].

or fund and the other can resort to only one'[11] by regulating the manner in which the creditors can access the value in the common asset(s) subject to both the senior and junior creditor's security interest. In this regard, it has been suggested that the marshalling of securities is effectively an application of the equitable maxim that 'equity is equality'[12] as between the debtor's secured creditors (although due care must always be taken with such tropes) and 'a principle of maximum distribution' as between the debtor's secured and unsecured creditors.[13]

Whilst an accretion of case law over time, including a recent decision of the UK Supreme Court,[14] has helped to crystallise and clarify marshalling's doctrinal elements and commercial rationale, the doctrine has long defied juridical classification.[15] That issue will be the focus of this chapter. By way of background, however, this chapter starts by mapping the historical origins and traditional justifications for the marshalling of securities,[16] before outlining the scope of the marshalling doctrine, the requirements for its operation and its limits.[17] Thereafter, two key controversies will be tackled: the marshalling doctrine's theoretical underpinnings and consequently its nature, legal classification and practical operation. This chapter will argue that the theoretical approach to the marshalling of securities (at least as traditionally conceived) indicates that the doctrine operated as an equitable defence that a junior creditor could raise directly against a senior creditor in order to restrict the latter's enforcement options against assets that the former viewed as collateral;[18] and that, even if one accepts the alternative theoretical basis for marshalling advocated in more recent times, marshalling should still be viewed as a defence, albeit one raised against the debtor (and, in an insolvency context, the debtor's unsecured creditors and liquidator).[19] The conclusion will suggest that the traditional and modern conceptions of marshalling as a defence are not necessarily mutually inconsistent and that the courts may wish to adopt (if they have not already) a 'hybrid' approach to marshalling that retains the doctrine's traditional flexibility.[20] Indeed, that flexibility, which has been a key source of confusion in the past, may ultimately prove to be marshalling's greatest advantage.

[11] *Re Bank of Credit and Commerce International SA (No 8)* [1998] AC 214, 230–31.

[12] *Khan v Khan*, unreported, Privy Council Appeal No 116 of 1936, 7 April 1938, 8, applying *Deering v Earl of Winchelsea* (1787) 2 Bos & P 270; 126 ER 1276; *International Energy Group Ltd v Zurich Insurance plc* [2015] UKSC 33; [2016] AC 509 [61]. See also D Heydon, M Leeming and PG Turner, *Meagher, Gummow and Lehane's Equity: Doctrines and Remedies* 5th edn (Sydney, LexisNexis, 2015) [3-135].

[13] *National Crime Agency (formerly Serious Organised Crime Agency) v Szepietowski* [2011] EWCA Civ 856; [2011] Lloyd's Rep FC 537 [2].

[14] *National Crime Agency (formerly Serious Organised Crime Agency) v Szepietowski* [2013] UKSC 65; [2014] 1 AC 338. See further W Gummow, 'Marshalling and Protected Assets: *Miles v The Official Receiver*' (1965) 5 *Sydney Law Review* 120.

[15] *Across Australia Finance Pty Ltd v Kalls* [2008] NSWSC 783 [10], [22].

[16] See section II below.

[17] See section III below.

[18] See section IV below.

[19] See section V below.

[20] See section VI below.

II. ORIGINS AND JUSTIFICATIONS FOR THE MARSHALLING OF SECURITIES

Even in the context of competing security interests, the doctrine of marshalling has a long pedigree stretching back to the late seventeenth century, although it has been argued that it may even be a Roman Law derivative.[21] Although the earliest suggested[22] application of the marshalling doctrine to security interests is *Bovey v Skipwith*,[23] it is submitted that that case is more concerned with the consolidation of mortgages, than a nascent doctrine permitting the marshalling of securities.[24] Accordingly, that doctrine's origins arguably lie in *Povye's Case*,[25] the significance of which has to date been under-appreciated.[26] That case involved a debtor with total liabilities of £1,500 (one debt of £500 being secured by a mortgage over land and the remaining debt being secured by a bond) who transferred leasehold interests worth £1,200 to trustees for the purpose of repaying his debts. Following the debtor's death, the debtor's heir and the trustees used the leasehold land to repay the mortgagee (despite the fact that this creditor could have recovered the debt pursuant to the terms of the mortgage) and consequently left one of the other creditors unpaid. Upon that creditor's bill, Lord Finch LC (later the Earl of Nottingham) held that 'the trust lands should be applied in the first place for the other debts, because the mortgagee could be at no damage, being secured by his mortgage; but on the contrary, if the mortgage should be first satisfied, the other creditors might lose their debts'. In reaching this conclusion, his Lordship justified the emergent doctrine by stating that '[a] creditor who has a double fund to resort to, will not be allowed, *by his option* to disappoint another who has only one'.[27] In this way, marshalling avoids the value of the junior security-holder's interest over the common asset (and consequently the extent of any recoveries) depending upon the enforcement whims or caprices of the senior security-holder,[28] especially when the debtor is insolvent and *both* secured creditors would otherwise have recovered in full from the debtor's

21 M Bigelow, *Story's Commentaries on Equity Jurisprudence* 13th edn (London, Little, Brown & Co, 1886) [635]–[636]; *cf* P Ali, *Marshalling of Securities: Equity and the Priority-Ranking of Secured Credit* (Oxford, OUP, 1999) [2.10]–[2.13].

22 Ali (n 21) [2.02].

23 *Bovey v Skipwith* (1671) 1 Ch Cas 201; 22 ER 762. For further confusion between marshalling and the consolidation of mortgages, see *Titley v Davies* (1743) 2 Y&C Ch Cas 399; 63 ER 177.

24 In essence, *Bovey* involved a situation where A had security over *x* and *y* and B had security over *y* alone, but then B purchased C's senior-ranking security over both *x* and *y*. In these circumstances, Sir Orlando Bridgeman held that B could 'hold against' A both *x* and *y* until the former had been paid everything due in respect of both his securities; *cf Szepietowski* (SC) (n 14) [28]. For other examples of confusion between the doctrines of marshalling and consolidation, see *Heyman v Dubois* (1871) LR 13 Eq 158; *Re Stratton, ex p Salting* (1884) LR 25 Ch D 148; *New Zealand Loan and Mercantile Agency Company Ltd v Loach* (1912) 31 NZLR 292. See also Heydon, Leeming and Turner (n 12) [11-145]–[11-155].

25 *Povye's Case* (1680) 2 Free 51; 22 ER 1052. Although the slightly later decision in *Culpepper v Aston* (1682) 2 Ch Cas 115; 22 ER 873 has sometimes been identified as the origin of the marshalling doctrine (see J Nehf, 'Marshaling Assets', in J McDonnell (ed), *Secured Transactions under the Uniform Commercial Code* (Matthew Bender, 2009) Ch 7G), that case concerned the marshalling of legacies rather than securities.

26 There have been references to, and brief discussions of, *Povye's Case* both academically (Ali (n 21) [2.02]) and judicially (*Szepietowski* (SC) (n 14) [28]), but the analysis has to date been rather cursory.

27 *Povye's Case* (n 25) Free 52; ER 1053 (emphasis added).

28 *New Zealand Loan and Mercantile Agency* (n 24); *Khan* (n 12) 8.

encumbered assets if the senior security-holder had refrained from using the 'common asset' as its first port-of-call.[29] To a large extent, this remains the classical justification for the marshalling of securities even today. As Lewison LJ put the point in *Highbury Pension Fund Management Co v Zirfin Investments Ltd*:[30]

> ... the way in which the original principle in its classic form is framed fastens on the conduct and conscience of the doubly secured creditor. It is the fact that he has the choice which fund to resort to and the power at law to disappoint the singly secured creditor which brings the equity into play.

Indeed, such protection from the impact of the senior creditor's election has two further advantageous consequences. First, the marshalling of securities avoids (or at least minimises) any unfair prejudice to, or discrimination against, those junior security-holders with insufficient resources to help themselves[31] by first redeeming the higher-ranking security (thereby promoting their own second-ranking security to a first-ranking security over the common asset) and then enforcing the redeemed security against the other (non-common) assets available for that purpose.[32] Second, marshalling securities will also minimise the extent to which an unscrupulous senior security-holder can derive an unwarranted and uncovenanted-for benefit (flowing from its freedom to choose between different enforcement options) by 'auctioning' that election between the junior security-holder and the debtor's general unsecured creditors (or liquidator), both of whom might make the commercial decision that it is better to pay some further sum to avoid being prejudiced by the senior security-holder's enforcement action.[33]

As well as seeking to protect a junior security-holder from the actual or potentially unconscionable conduct of the senior security-holder, Lord Finch's speech in *Povye's Case* also appears to contain an alternative, broader view of the marshalling of securities that is based upon perceived unconscionability on the debtor's part (whether directly or through its representatives)—'as the trust lands were not sufficient to satisfy the whole debt, the heir and the trustees and the mortgagee should not juggle together to cheat other creditors, by paying the mortgage first off'.[34] This statement is particularly important for this chapter since it views the marshalling doctrine, at its very origins, as operating to regulate not only the relations between the junior and senior creditors over the common asset, but also the relations between the junior creditor and the debtor (or his representatives). Indeed, it is argued below that this view of marshalling should be given something of a renaissance,[35] since the junior creditor-debtor aspect of the doctrine became somewhat obscured during the course of the eighteenth century, largely as a result of conflating the doctrine of marshalling

[29] *Szepietowski* (SC) (n 14) [1]–[2], [32].
[30] *Highbury Pension Fund* (n 10) [18]. See also *McLean v Berry* [2016] EWHC 2650 (Ch); [2017] Ch 422 [17], [25].
[31] *Szepietowski* (SC) (n 14) [36].
[32] *Downsview Nominees Ltd v First City Corporation Ltd* [1993] AC 295, 315; *Silven Properties Ltd v Royal Bank of Scotland plc* [2003] EWCA Civ 1409; [2004] 1 WLR 997 [18].
[33] *Szepietowski* (SC) (n 14) [36].
[34] *Povye's Case* (n 25) Free 51; ER 1052.
[35] See section V below.

of *securities* with the glut of cases dealing with the marshalling of *legacies* in the wills context.[36] In fact, a number of cases from that period that have been used as authority for the marshalling of securities either have little to do with the competing claims of secured creditors,[37] have involved situations in which the doctrine could have no application[38] or have subsequently been treated as incorrectly decided.[39] Indeed, even the supposed leading case from the eighteenth century—*Lanoy v Duchess of Athol*[40]—did not involve the marshalling of securities *stricto sensu*. Nevertheless, in one of the key passages from *Lanoy* concerning the marshalling of securities, Lord Hardwicke constrained the doctrine to performing an essentially inter-creditor role, ignoring the fact that marshalling might also operate between the junior creditor and debtor: 'Is it not then the constant equity of this court that if a creditor has two funds, he shall take his satisfaction out of that fund upon which another creditor has no lien'.[41] It was this view of marshalling that the Chancery courts adopted at the beginning of the nineteenth century, in cases such as *Aldrich v Cooper*,[42] where Lord Eldon stated that 'it is the ordinary case to say a person having two funds shall not by his election disappoint the party having only one fund; and equity, to satisfy both, will throw him, who has two funds on that, which can be affected by him only'. By force of repetition,[43] this inter-creditor view of marshalling ultimately crystallised in the House of Lords' decision in *Dolphin v Aylward*,[44] and has since cast a long shadow over the doctrine for the best part of a century.[45] The consequences of suppressing the junior creditor-debtor function of marshalling will be developed through this chapter.

III. SCOPE AND LIMITS OF THE MODERN MARSHALLING OF SECURITIES DOCTRINE

Before considering the more theoretical issues, it is possible to clear some ground by referring to the doctrinal requirements and limitations of the marshalling of securities doctrine. These were comprehensively formulated by the House of Lords in the aforementioned decision in *Dolphin v Aylward*[46] and have not produced significant controversy in the interim. That said, those early developments must now be considered in light of the United Kingdom Supreme Court's decision in

36 For a comprehensive case list in this regard, see Ali (n 21) [2.05].

37 See, for example, *Carter v Barnadiston* (1718) 1 P Wms 506; 24 ER 492; *Clifton* (n 9); *Galton v Hancock* (1743) 2 Atk 427; 26 ER 658; *A-G v Tyndall* (1764) Amb 614; 27 ER 399.

38 *Finch v Winchelsea* (1715) 1 P Wms 277; 24 ER 387.

39 *Robinson v Tonge* (1735) 3 P Wms 398; 24 ER 1117.

40 *Lanoy v Duchess of Athol* (1742) 2 Atk 444; 26 ER 668.

41 ibid Atk 446; ER 669.

42 *Aldrich* (n 10) Ves 395; ER 407. See also *Trimmer v Bayne* (1803) 9 Ves Jun 209, 211; 32 ER 582, 583: '[A] person having resort to two funds shall not by his choice disappoint another, having one only.'

43 *Ex p Kendall* (1811) 17 Ves 514, 527; 34 ER 199, 204; *Webb v Smith* (1885) 30 Ch D 192, 199–200; *Flint v Howard* [1893] 2 Ch 54, 72. The development of the marshalling doctrine would have been assisted during this period by the passage of the Common Law Procedure Act 1854, 17 & 18 Vict c 125, ss 83–86.

44 *Dolphin* (n 10) 505.

45 *Highbury Pension Fund* (n 10) [18].

46 *Dolphin* (n 10).

National Crime Agency (formerly Serious Organised Crime Agency) v Szepietowski,[47] which has authoritatively re-stated the elements of the marshalling doctrine. *Szepietowski* arose out of the National Crime Agency ('NCA') obtaining an interim receiving order over a number of properties registered in the name of the first defendant, and subsequently bringing a civil recovery claim in respect of those properties under the Proceeds of Crime Act 2002 ('PCA 2002'). These proceedings were compromised in full and final settlement of the NCA's claims and the terms of that agreement were set out in a consent order stipulating that the defendant's properties listed in the schedule would be vested in the Trustee for Civil Recovery and that the other properties (including the defendant's family home) would be released from the receiving order and returned to the first defendant. Two of the properties listed in the consent order's schedule ('the transfer properties') were already subject to a first mortgage in favour of the second defendant, the Royal Bank of Scotland ('RBS'), which also had mortgages over several of the investment properties that had been released by the NCA back to the first defendant ('the Claygate properties'), as well as the first defendant's family home. As the two charged transfer properties were sold first and the proceeds used to reduce the RBS mortgages, the NCA automatically obtained (pursuant to the terms of the consent order) a second-ranking charge over the Claygate properties. When the Claygate properties were eventually sold for a much lower price than anticipated, the proceeds of those sales were only just sufficient to discharge the remaining indebtedness to RBS. Accordingly, the NCA sought a declaration that it should be entitled to marshal the charge held by RBS over the family home with NCA's second charge over the Claygate properties, so that it could look to the former to satisfy its claim under the PCA 2002.

For differing reasons,[48] the Supreme Court unanimously rejected the NCA's marshalling attempt, although there was broad consensus regarding the six pre-conditions identified by Lord Neuberger as triggering the court's equitable jurisdiction to

[47] *Szepietowski* (SC) (n 14).

[48] ibid. A majority of the Supreme Court (Lords Neuberger, Sumption and Reed) denied the availability of marshalling *inter alia* on the basis that, whilst the National Crime Agency ('NCA') could recover certain properties to the extent that they represented the proceeds of crime, once the properties in question had been sold there was no underlying debt that the NCA could enforce against the debtor. Nor did the settlement deed between the parties in that case create or acknowledge any debt. According to Lord Neuberger (at [46], [49], [53]–[54]), the justification for insisting that there be an underlying indebtedness between the junior creditor and the person against whose property the security could be enforced was that otherwise the doctrine of marshalling would operate to the latter's detriment. Consider, in this regard, *Brigham v Chambers* (1880) OB&F 66, 69. Dissenting on the issue, Lord Carnwath (at [99]–[104]) did not consider that the absence of any underlying indebtedness to the NCA precluded marshalling, although his Lordship did doubt the significance of the division in the Supreme Court's reasoning outside the immediate context of cases like *Szepietowski* given that 'the concept of a charge without an underlying personal debt seems sufficiently unusual' to apply widely. Lord Hughes (at [107]–[108]) agreed. Lord Carnwath justified (at [103]) the irrelevance of an underlying debt by looking at matters from the chargor's perspective and enquiring 'whether [marshalling] is within the scope of the risk which the chargor has undertaken at the time the charges were granted'. A slightly differently constituted majority (Lords Neuberger, Sumption, Reed and Hughes) also rejected the availability of marshalling on the basis that the consent order and surrounding documentation, when properly construed, excluded that possibility. Although Lord Carnwath agreed with this conclusion, his judgment placed more emphasis on the statutory context in which the consent order was made.

marshal securities.[49] First, the claimant[50] must have a second-ranking security over the debtor's property in respect of an underlying debt[51] and, second, the defendant[52] must be a creditor of the same debtor[53] with a first-ranking security over the same property as the claimant.[54] As well as making clear that an unsecured creditor is unable to marshal another creditor's securities,[55] these first two requirements give rise to a further subsidiary question concerning the nature of the creditors' interests in the 'common asset' for the doctrine to be triggered. Marshalling would certainly be available when the junior and senior security-holders have interests by way of mortgage or charge,[56] but it is less clear whether that doctrine would also encompass the case where one of those creditors has a possessory security (whether a pledge or lien)[57] or some other form of proprietary interest performing a security function (such as a retention of title clause[58] or a *Quistclose* trust[59]). How expansive the English courts are likely to be in this last regard will largely depend upon the extent to which they are prepared to recharacterise quasi-security as a true security interest for these purposes[60] and/or upon whether English law ever finally adopts a comprehensive UCC-style personal property securities regime. To avoid like cases being treated radically differently, however, the courts should be encouraged to adopt a functional approach to the notion of security for marshalling purposes.

Third, in relation to its debt, the defendant must also have another form of security to which the claimant cannot have recourse. This particular condition in turn

[49] ibid [31]. See also *Highbury Pension Fund* (n 10) [1].

[50] The term 'claimant' is used here in a neutral manner to refer to the junior security-holder who has invoked the court's jurisdiction to marshal securities, whilst the term 'defendant' is similarly neutrally employed to indicate the person against whom the jurisdiction has been invoked. The use of those terms should not be taken as in any way prejudging the later discussion (in sections IV and V) concerning the nature of marshalling, since this chapter's contention is that marshalling is frequently used in a defensive manner in practice.

[51] *Re BCCI (No 8)* (n 11) 230–31; *Szepietowski* (SC) (n 14) [40]–[56], [65], [79], [85]–[86]. Although the requirement of an underlying debt was the issue upon which the majority and minority differed in *Szepietowski*, Lord Neuberger was not prepared (at [58]–[59]) to foreclose entirely an 'exceptional case' where marshalling might be available without any such underlying indebtedness to the claimant. That said, his Lordship (at [58]) found it hard to conceive of what such 'an exceptional case' might be 'absent express words which permit or envisage marshalling'.

[52] See n 50 above.

[53] *Ex p Kendall* (n 43).

[54] When there is no 'common asset' against which the two creditors have claims, there is no scope for marshalling: see *Tegel Foods* (n 10). The same may be true in circumstances where the senior-security holder has access to two different forms of collateral, but only in respect of different debts or liabilities: see *Finance Corporation of Australia Ltd v Bentley* (1991) 5 BPR 11,833.

[55] *Re Professional Life Assurance Company* (1866–67) LR 3 Eq 668, 679–81; *Re International Life Assurance Society* (1876) 2 Ch D 476, 482–83.

[56] *Re Mower's Trusts* (1869) LR 8 Eq 110; *Webb v Smith* (n 43). It does not matter whether the charge is consensual or statutory in nature: see *McLean* (n 30) [24]–[25] (charge created pursuant to the terms of the Agricultural Credits Act 1928). The fact that marshalling applies to charges means that the doctrine cannot be a form of mortgage consolidation: see Ali (n 21) [5.02], [5.22]–[5.27].

[57] *Re Stratton* (n 24), 152–53. In support of the view that marshalling should extend to possessory security, see Ali (n 21) [9.12]–[9.24].

[58] *Re Stratton* (n 24) 152–53; *Re Burge, Woodall & Co, ex p Skyrme* [1912] 1 KB 393. Consider *Esanda Finance Corporation Ltd v Plessnig* (1989) 63 AJLR 238, 246; *Associated Alloys Pty Ltd v Metropolitan Engineering and Fabrications Pty Ltd* (2000) 171 ALR 568.

[59] *Barclays Bank Ltd v Quistclose Investments Ltd* [1970] AC 567.

[60] Gullifer and Payne (n 2) [7.2.2]–[7.2.5].

gives rise to two sub-issues. The first sub-issue is similar to the one just considered above, namely the form that the senior security-holder's alternative means of recourse must take in order to justify marshalling. The most obvious situation covered by the doctrine is when the senior security-holder has recourse to other assets by way of mortgage or charge, but (as with the first and second requirements), it is unclear whether the possibility of alternative recourse to possessory security or security-like devices would count. The functional approach advocated above should be equally applicable to this issue. Beyond these situations, however, it is clear that the possibility of the senior security-holder relying upon the enforcement of the debtor's underlying personal obligation by way of fallback position will not (and should not) suffice for these purposes; any other conclusion would mean that the marshalling doctrine would be too readily available to junior security-holders, since any creditor would be able to avail himself of this alternative route.[61] Nor does the doctrine apply when the senior security-holder has an alternative *personal* claim that performs a security function,[62] such as the ability on the part of a banker to combine accounts or (if different) exercise a right of set-off.[63] By way of exception to this position, however, the courts have consciously extended the doctrine of marshalling to include the situation where the senior security-holder also has an alternative claim against a third party under a personal guarantee.[64] The second sub-issue concerns whether, in circumstances where the senior security-holder's alternative means of recourse takes the form of a charge or mortgage, the assets in question must also belong to the debtor. Whilst this has certainly been the traditional understanding of marshalling,[65] there are indications that the courts have tried to avoid applying this requirement too slavishly. For example, in *McLean v Berry*,[66] Norris J applied the marshalling doctrine to the situation where the 'common asset' over which both creditors had security was property belonging personally to the partner of a firm, but the senior security-holder also had security over property that constituted partnership assets. Similarly, where the debtor disposes of the relevant asset that is subject to the senior security-holder's interest alone, then the junior security-holder's ability to marshal ought not to be defeated if the transferee has notice of the junior security-holder's interest[67] or the transfer is expressly made subject to the senior or junior creditor's rights.[68]

[61] *The Arab* (1859) 5 Jur (NS) 417. See also *Re International Life Assurance Society* (n 55) 482–483.

[62] *Webb v Smith* (n 43) 198–203.

[63] *cf Smit Tak International Zeesleepen Bergingsbedrijf BV v Selco Salvage Ltd* [1988] 2 Lloyd's Rep 398, 406, where Warner J considered that the doctrine of marshalling could apply to an equitable set-off, although the court's powers in that regard were limited to funds that had been paid into court and over which it exercised control, so that the court would not order particular funds owned by a third party to be paid into court in order to assist with the marshalling process. As *Smit Tak* has been roundly and convincingly criticised, it has not been followed in the text: see R Derham, 'Set-off Against an Assignee: The Relevance of Marshalling, Contribution and Subrogation' (1991) 107 *Law Quarterly Review* 126. See also *On Faith Woollen Weaving Factory v Star Industrial Corporation* [1968] HKDC 8.

[64] *Ex p Kendall* (n 43) Ves 527; ER 204; *Re Stratton* (n 24) 152–53; *Highbury Pension Fund* (n 10) [2]–[4], [15]–[17].

[65] *The Chioggia* [1898] P 1, 5–6. See also Heydon, Leeming and Turner (n 12) [11-050].

[66] *McLean* (n 30) [3], [15]–[28].

[67] *Dolphin* (n 10); *cf Cheesebrough v Millard* (1815) 1 Johns Chan 408; *Gwynne v Edwards* (1825) 2 Russ 289n. See also Ali (n 21) [11.51].

[68] Ali (n 21) [8.01], [11.50]–[11.51].

Fourth, the defendant must have been repaid from the sale of the 'common property' over which the claimant also has security, and, fifth, the claimant's debt must remain unpaid. Whilst the fourth requirement might be seen as being rather uncontroversial, it should be noted that it is closely associated with the particular theoretical approach to marshalling advocated by Lord Neuberger in *Szepietowski*,[69] namely the post-realisation theory, which is considered further below. Accordingly, it follows that, if one were to adopt an alternative theoretical explanation of marshalling, then the requirement that the senior security-holder have been repaid might no longer be a prerequisite to marshal securities. Sixth, the other property subject to the defendant's security must not be required at all (or must only be required in part) to satisfy the debtor's liability to the first-ranking secured creditor. The precise ambit of these various requirements, however, awaits significant judicial analysis *post-Szepietowski*.[70]

Even when the above conditions have been satisfied, however, there is no guarantee that marshalling will be available, since there are a number of established circumstances in which the junior security-holder's ability to marshal the senior creditor's securities may be limited or excluded entirely. As the equitable doctrine protects the junior creditor from the senior creditor's caprices,[71] it should have no role when the senior creditor has limited its options by contractually obliging itself to look to its other security first[72] or to enforce first against the assets over which the junior creditor also has security.[73] Similarly, the doctrine has no application when the terms of the second-ranking charge itself,[74] or some collateral arrangement[75] to which the junior secured creditor is a party (when properly construed against all the admissible background circumstances),[76] either expressly or impliedly excludes the ability to marshal securities.[77] In *Szepietowski*, Lord Neuberger refused, however, to

[69] *Szepietowski* (SC) (n 14).

[70] See *McLean* (n 30).

[71] *Aldrich* (n 10) Ves 389, 395; ER 405, 407–08; *Trimmer* (n 42) Ves Jun 211; ER 583; *Highbury Pension Fund* (n 10) [18].

[72] *Szepietowski* (SC) (n 14) [38], applying *Re Holland* (1928) 28 SR (NSW) 369; *Miles v Official Receiver in Bankruptcy* (1963) 109 CLR 501.

[73] *Szepietowski* (SC) (n 14) [75]. Lord Neuberger appeared to accept the possibility that estoppel principles might operate to negate the ability to marshal securities.

[74] ibid [61]–[63], [68]–[72]. Lord Neuberger held that, in determining whether it is equitable or not to marshal securities in a particular case, the starting point must be the terms of the second-ranking security at the time of its creation, although a court can also have regard to 'what passed between the parties prior to its execution' and 'relevant subsequent developments'. See also *Official Assignee v Kirk* [2006] NZHC 1359 [14].

[75] In *Highbury Pension Fund* (n 10) [18], [20]–[21], Lewison LJ considered that the ability to marshal could be excluded by a contract between the senior and junior creditors, but not between the senior creditor and a guarantor of the debtor's liabilities.

[76] See generally *Investors Compensation Scheme Ltd v West Bromwich Building Society* [1998] 1 WLR 896; *Chartbrook Ltd v Persimmon Homes Ltd* [2009] UKHL 38; [2009] 1 AC 1101; *Re Sigma Finance Corporation* [2009] UKSC 2; [2010] 1 All ER 571; *Rainy Sky SA v Kookmin Bank* [2011] UKSC 50; [2011] 1 WLR 2900; *Belmont Park Investments Pty Ltd v BNY Corporate Trustee Services Ltd* [2011] UKSC 38; [2012] 1 AC 383; *Arnold v Britton* [2015] UKSC 36; [2015] AC 1619; *Wood v Capita Insurance Services Ltd* [2017] UKSC 24; [2017] 2 WLR 1095.

[77] *Szepietowski* (SC) (n 14) [61]–[62], [88]–[92], [107].

introduce a further limitation[78] to a junior creditor's ability to marshal based upon the fact that the charged properties included the debtor's family home.[79] The existence of other encumbrances over the assets to which the junior creditor initially has no claim may also limit (although not necessarily exclude entirely) the availability of marshalling, since the doctrine will only apply to the extent that third-party encumbrancers are not prejudiced.[80] In *Flint v Howard*,[81] Kay LJ articulated the difficulty faced by the courts in such cases, and its solution, in characteristically lucid terms:

> ... if a person having two estates mortgaged both to A and then one only to B, who had not notice of A's mortgage, B might, as against the mortgagor, compel the payment of the first mortgage out of the estate on which he had no charge, according to the ordinary doctrine of marshalling. ... But if there was a second mortgage of one estate to B, and also subsequently a second mortgage of the other estate to C, the matter is more complicated. C, although he had no notice of the prior mortgage on both properties to A, would not then be able to throw it on the property mortgaged to B, but the equity between B and C would be to apportion the first mortgage between the two properties according to their respective values.

This power of rateable apportionment (or 'marshalling by apportionment'[82]) does not appear to depend upon whether one or other of the junior creditors had notice of the senior creditor's security,[83] although, if the instrument creating the first junior creditor's security contains a negative pledge clause, then the existence of a subsequent junior security over different assets should not affect the marshalling ability of the junior secured creditor that comes first in time.[84]

IV. COERCION IN THE MARSHALLING OF SECURITIES

Having set out the relatively uncontroversial requirements for, and limitations upon, the marshalling of securities in light of *Szepietowski*,[85] this chapter's focus shifts to the far more uncertain question of that equitable jurisdiction's theoretical

[78] The argument that there should be some 'home exception' to the marshalling doctrine was based upon a combination of the Administration of Justice Act 1970, s 36 and the Human Rights Act 1998, Sch 1, Art 8: see *Szepietowski* (SC) (n 14) [75].

[79] *Szepietowski* (SC) (n 14) [73]–[77].

[80] *Dolphin* (n 10) 501–03.

[81] *Flint v Howard* (n 43) 72. See also *Lanoy* (n 40) Atk 446; ER 669; *Barnes v Racster* (1842) 1 Y&C Ch 401, 409–10; 62 ER 944, 947–48; *Bugden v Bignold* (1843) 2 Y&C Ch 377, 398; 63 ER 167, 176. In *Gibson v Seagrim* (1855) 20 Beav 614, 619; 52 ER 741, 743, Lord Romilly stated: '... if two estates are mortgaged to A, and one is afterwards mortgaged to B and the remaining estate is afterwards mortgaged to C, B has no equity to throw the whole of A's mortgage on C's estate, and so destroy C's security. As between B and C, A is bound to satisfy himself the principal, interest and costs due to him out of the two estates rateably, according to the respective values of such two estates, and thus to leave the surplus proceeds of each estate to be applied in payment of the respective incumbrances thereon'. See also *Smyth v Toms* [1918] 1 IR 338.

[82] Heydon, Leeming and Turner (n 12) [11-110], although the authors express the view that such apportionment has more to do with notions of contribution than marshalling *stricto sensu*.

[83] *Gibson* (n 81) Beav 619; ER 743; *Flint* (n 43) 72–73; *Smyth* (n 81) 346–47.

[84] *Flint* (n 43) 73.

[85] *Szepietowski* (SC) (n 14).

underpinnings. One's theoretical preferences in this regard will in turn guide one's determination of marshalling's nature, legal classification and practical operation (in the sense of what a court is actually being asked/is entitled to do when it deploys its marshalling jurisdiction).[86] As indicated above,[87] courts in the eighteenth and nineteenth centuries viewed the marshalling of securities as involving an inter-creditor equity, which traditionally resulted in the courts (albeit that there was some limited dissent on this point)[88] feeling justified in compelling or ordering the senior security-holder to have recourse first to the other assets over which it alone had security, rather than to the 'common asset' over which the junior creditor also had security,[89] thereby leaving the 'common asset' for the satisfaction of the junior security-holder's claims. That the marshalling of securities operated by compulsion of the senior security-holder had been made explicit by the mid-eighteenth century in *Lanoy v Duke and Duchess of Athol*,[90] in which Lord Hardwicke stated that 'the court in order to relieve the second mortgagee, have *directed* the first to take his satisfaction out of that estate only which is not in mortgage to the second mortgagee, if that is sufficient to satisfy the first mortgage, in order to make room for the second mortgagee'.[91] As this approach to marshalling focuses on regulating *ex ante* the manner in which the senior security-holder could enforce its security, it has subsequently been termed the 'coercion theory'.[92] This theory was embraced wholeheartedly during the course of the nineteenth century with Lord Eldon, in *Aldrich v Cooper*,[93] indicating that a junior secured creditor has 'a right in equity to *compel* the [senior secured creditor] to resort to [its alternative collateral], if that is necessary for the satisfaction of both' and, in *Ex p Kendall*,[94] stating that '[t]he equity is clear upon the authorities, that … the [senior secured creditor] shall be *thrown upon* that fund, to which the other cannot resort'. In fact, the judicial language hardened somewhat in the latter half of the nineteenth century, with the references to the senior creditor being 'required' to act in a particular way increasingly replaced by the language of him being 'compelled' to do so.[95] Indeed, as well as representing

[86] This statement assumes that the availability of marshalling is conditional upon the exercise of an equitable judicial discretion, rather than involving the enforcement of any particular right that is the correlative of a duty owed by the senior secured-creditor (as in the case of a claim based upon a breach of fiduciary duty) or involving the exercise of some self-help remedy (as in the case of rescission).

[87] See section I above.

[88] *Re Mower's* (n 56). See also *Wallis* (n 7) 180.

[89] *Aldrich* (n 10) Ves 388, 391, 395; ER 405–07; *Ex p Kendall* (n 43) Ves 527; ER 204; *Webb* (n 43) 199–200; *Flint* (n 43) 72; *Mallott v Wilson* [1903] 2 Ch 494, 505; *Public Trustee v Allder* [1922] 1 Ch 154, 159–60.

[90] *Lanoy* (n 40). See also *A-G v Tyndall* (n 37) Amb 615–16; ER 399, per Lord Henley: '[W]here a person had a double fund to resort to, and another person had a demand upon one of those funds, *the Court has turned the person having the double security upon that fund,* which was not liable to the other person's demand, in order to leave open the fund which was' (emphasis added). See further *Trimmer* (n 42); *Lord Rancliffe v Lady Parkyns* (1818) 6 Dow 149; 3 ER 1428; *Tidd v Lister* (1853) 3 De GM & G 857; 43 ER 336; *Gibson* (n 81); *Re Loder's Trusts* (1886) 56 LJ Ch 230.

[91] *Lanoy* (n 40) Atk 446; ER 669 (emphasis added).

[92] Ali (n 21) ch 3.

[93] *Aldrich* (n 10) Ves 388–89; ER 405 (emphasis added), applied in *Duncan* (n 10) 12.

[94] *Ex p Kendall* (n 43) Ves 527; ER 204 (emphasis added).

[95] *Lawrance v Galsworthy* (1857) 3 Jur (NS) 1049, 1050; *The Arab* (n 61); *Webb* (n 43) 198; *Flint* (n 43) 72.

the generally preferred approach in the United States[96] and (to a lesser extent) Scotland[97] and Ireland,[98] the coercion theory has persisted in England,[99] despite the advent of an alternative theoretical conceptualisation, as considered in the following section.[100] Indeed, in *Bank of Credit and Commerce International SA (No 8)*,[101] Lord Hoffmann made (albeit *obiter*) what subsequently became the authoritative restatement regarding the modern process of marshalling in this jurisdiction:

> … a principle for doing equity between two or more creditors, each of whom are owed debts by the same debtor, but one of whom can enforce his claim against more than one security or fund and the other can resort to only one. It gives the latter *an equity to require the first creditor to satisfy himself (or be treated as having satisfied himself) so far as possible out of the security or fund to which the latter has no claim.*

Even the most recent English decisions concerning the marshalling of securities may be interpreted as lending some support to the continued validity of the coercion theory, albeit that such support is admittedly more tentative than has been the case in the past. Certainly, in *Highbury Pension Fund Management Co v Zirfin Investments Ltd*,[102] Lewison LJ's statement that marshalling 'gives the second creditor a right in equity to *require* that the first creditor satisfy himself or be treated as having satisfied himself so far as possible out of the security or fund to which the latter has no claim'[103] is certainly consistent with the coercion theory of marshalling (albeit that, as considered further below,[104] other statements in *Highbury* tend to support the alternative theoretical approach). Similarly, while a bare majority in *Szepietowski* adopted the other theory considered further below,[105] Lord Carnwarth considered that the majority were looking at the issue 'from the wrong end' by focusing on 'the position after the common property has been sold by the first chargee'[106] and (applying the dictum of Lord Hoffmann in *BCCI (No 8)*, set out above) explained the doctrine in the more traditional terms of 'an equity to *require* that the first creditor satisfy himself … out of the security or fund to which the latter has no claim'.[107] Moreover, support for Lord Carnwath's view of marshalling can be garnered from Lord Reed, who indicated that the Scottish doctrine of 'catholic securities' would

[96] Ali (n 21) [3.35]–[3.37]. See also *Union Bank of Georgetown v Laird*, 15 US 147, 148–49 (1817); *Sowell v Federal Reserve Bank*, 268 US 449, 456–57 (1925); *Meyer v United States*, 375 US 233, 236 (1963); *Shedoudy v Beverly Surgical Supply Co*, 161 Cal Rptr 164 (1980). Although there is no specific provision dealing with marshalling in the Uniform Commercial Code (UCC), Art 9, the equitable doctrine survives by virtue of UCC, s 1-103: see UCC, s 9-610, Comment 5. See also *Re Computer Room Inc*, 24 BR 732 (ND Ala, 1982).

[97] *Littlejohn v Black* (1855) 18 D 207, 212; *Nicol's Trustees v Hill* (1889) 16 R 416, 421, considered in *Szepietowski* (SC) (n 14) [81]–[86].

[98] *Averall v Wade* (1835) L&G temp Sugd 252, 253; *Re Lawder's Estate* (1861) 11 Ir Ch R 346; *cf Re Fox* (1856) 5 Ir Ch R 541.

[99] *Smit Tak* (n 63) 407–08.

[100] See section V below.

[101] *Re BCCI (No 8)* (n 11) 230–31 (emphasis added). See also *Szepietowski* (SC) (n 14) [1]–[2].

[102] *Highbury Pension Fund* (n 10).

[103] ibid [1], [18] (emphasis added).

[104] See section V below.

[105] See section V below.

[106] *Szepietowski* (SC) (n 14) [103].

[107] ibid [101].

sometimes operate in just such a coercive manner.[108] Accordingly, whilst support for the coercion theory is undoubtedly diminished nowadays, when compared to earlier centuries, it is arguably premature to dismiss this theory as a 'historical curiosity'[109] at least in England (albeit that this comment may be more accurate in respect of other jurisdictions[110]).

The significance of this continued acceptance of the coercion theory is that it supports a particular view of how marshalling operates in practice and consequently the juridical nature of that doctrine. In essence, the coercion theory provides a junior creditor with the means to stop the senior creditor from continuing with the enforcement of its claims against the 'common asset' once such steps have been initiated.[111] As some prior enforcement step by the senior secured creditor accordingly appears to be a pre-requisite of the doctrine's operation,[112] albeit that enforcement must not have been completed,[113] the coercion theory of marshalling effectively operates in a defensive manner *vis-à-vis* the senior secured creditor.[114] Whilst the doctrine may not operate in the same way as a traditional defence by negating or reducing liability that exists between the junior creditor (as claimant) and the senior creditor (as defendant),[115] marshalling in its coercive form nevertheless operates to negate or reduce the effectiveness of the senior creditor's proprietary rights by trenching upon its usual enforcement mechanisms and thereby protecting the junior creditor from the usual legal consequences of senior creditor enforcement. On this basis, it is not unduly stretching the term to classify (coercive) marshalling as a defence exigeable against the senior creditor.[116]

Such a classification does, however, give rise to two subsidiary issues. The first sub-issue is whether the coercion theory would enable a junior creditor to marshal in an offensive manner, *before* the senior creditor has taken enforcement steps against the 'common asset' and *in anticipation* of such action; and, if so, whether this undermines the suggested legal classification as an equitable defence. Whilst courts should generally be slow to order interlocutory or final injunctive relief that would interfere with the senior creditor's enforcement of its security,[117] a court would certainly be justified in granting a *quia timet* injunction when the senior creditor's threatened conduct will deprive the junior creditor of an established ability to marshal.[118]

[108] ibid [81]–[86].

[109] Ali (n 21) [3.02].

[110] Heydon, Leeming and Turner (n 12) [11-015].

[111] *Aldrich* (n 10) Ves 395; ER 407.

[112] Heydon, Leeming and Turner (n 12) [11-160]–[11-170], citing *Bondi Securities Pty Ltd v AGC (Advances) Ltd*, unreported, 31 August 1990, NSWSC, Windeyer M. See also Ali (n 21) [2.17] n 35.

[113] *Smit Tak* (n 63) 407.

[114] For the defensive qualities of marshalling, see *Jacomb v Wikeley* [2013] NZHC 707 [67]–[70], in which Kós J allowed the doctrine of marshalling to be successfully raised by a guarantor as a defence to the enforcement of the guarantee. See further n 212 below.

[115] Marshalling operates to maintain the *status quo ante*, rather than extinguishing or reducing an established liability.

[116] Classifying coercive marshalling as a defence would not pose any difficulty in terms of its survival under the judicature system: see Judicature Act 1873, s 24(2)–(3).

[117] *Tan Soon Gin* (n 6) 545.

[118] Ali (n 21) [2.27]; Heydon, Leeming and Turner (n 12) [11-045], citing *Deta Nominees Pty Ltd v Viscount Plastic Products Pty Ltd* [1979] VR 167, 192; *Chase Corporation (Australia) Pty Ltd v North*

The possibility of such protective steps being taken should not, however, refute the earlier classification as an equitable defence.[119] Recognising injunctions in support of marshalling does, however, risk opening the door more generally to junior creditors pre-emptively seeking such interlocutory or permanent relief against senior secured creditors on wider and wider bases, including on the mere ground that the senior creditor's enforcement might cause detriment to the junior security-holder or deny them some other tangible benefit. Any such broader development should be strongly resisted[120] as being inconsistent with the approach adopted in *China and South Sea Bank Ltd v Tan Soon Gin*[121] that a secured creditor has a fundamental freedom of choice in enforcement matters and, in *Downsview Nominees Ltd v First City Corporation Ltd*, that 'powers conferred on a [senior creditor] may be exercised although the consequences may be disadvantageous to the [junior creditor]'.[122]

The second sub-issue concerns whether the coercion theory (by engendering expectations that senior creditors should act in a particular manner towards junior encumbrancers) might result in the imposition of enforceable duties upon senior secured creditors, which, if breached causing loss to the junior secured creditor, might sound in damages or alternatively result in some form of gain-based award, such as an account of profits[123] or the imposition of a trust over the enforcement proceeds from the 'common asset'.[124] Such losses could result, for example, from the manner in which the senior security-holder enforces its claims, the surrender of part of its security interest to the borrower[125] or the failure to take some enforcement step that might have resulted in more significant recoveries. Although there was previously some (limited) English[126] and (more extensive) Australian[127] support for the enforcement of the equity between senior and junior encumbrancers through compensatory or restitutionary awards against the senior security-holder, Dowsett J (in a strong *obiter* comment in the Australian Federal Court of Appeal) has recently rejected this possibility in *Naxatu Pty Ltd v Perpetual Trustee Company Ltd*.[128] The English and New Zealand courts have effectively adopted a similar stance by making clear that a senior security-holder's duties to a subsequent encumbrancer (and accordingly its potential liability to pay damages) are limited to '[exercising] his powers in good faith and for the purpose of obtaining repayment of the debt owing

Sydney Brick and Tile Co Ltd (1994) 35 NSWLR 1, 24; *cf Naxatu Pty Ltd v Perpetual Trustee Company Ltd* [2012] FCAFC 163 [83]–[84].

[119] *Lanoy* (n 40).

[120] *Naxatu* (n 118) [83]–[84].

[121] *Tan Soon Gin* (n 6) 545. See also *Cheah Theam Swee* (n 6) 476; *Highbury Pension Fund* (n 10) [22]–[23]. See also *Union Bank of Georgetown* (n 96).

[122] *Downsview Nominees* (n 32) 312.

[123] *Sarge Pty Ltd v Cazihaven Homes Pty Ltd* (1994) 34 NSWLR 658, 655.

[124] *South v Bloxam* (1865) 2 H&M 457; 71 ER 541; *cf Commonwealth Trading Bank v Colonial Mutual Life Assurance Society Ltd* [1970] Tas SR 120, 131–32.

[125] *Chase Corporation* (118) 21.

[126] *Bloxam* (n 124).

[127] *Sarge* (n 123) 655; *Chase Corporation* (n 118) 20–21; *Oamington Pty Ltd v Commissioner of Land Tax* (1997) 98 ATC 5051, 5051.

[128] *Naxatu* (n 118) [83]–[84].

to his mortgagee'[129] and, more particularly, 'if the mortgagee decides to sell, [taking] reasonable care to obtain a proper price'.[130] More generally, a senior secured creditor's deliberately harmful conduct may result in the imposition of liability for one or more of the 'economic torts'.[131] Beyond these more egregious forms of senior security-holder opportunism, however, Lord Templeman, in *Downsview Nominees Ltd v First City Corporation Ltd*,[132] expressly refused to impose any wider duties or forms of liability upon senior to junior encumbrancers even in relation to the former's negligent conduct. On the basis of the current authorities, therefore, it would be surprising if the senior secured-creditor were liable to compensate a junior secured creditor, or account for any gains, on the basis that its actions had frustrated the latter's ability to marshal the securities; some more serious form of conduct on the senior creditor's part would be required to trigger a compensatory or restitutionary award as a legal consequence. This reluctance is entirely consistent with the coercion theory, which is unconcerned with adjusting *ex post facto* the position between the creditors once the senior creditor has enforced its security.[133]

V. THE POST-REALISATION MARSHALLING OF SECURITIES

Set against the traditional coercive approach considered in the previous section, there is a more modern, competing theory that the marshalling of securities does not operate *ex ante*, by compelling the senior security-holder to adopt one particular course or another, but rather only operates *ex post*, once the senior creditor has completed enforcement. According to this approach, if the senior creditor decides to realise its

[129] *Downsview Nominees* (n 32) 311–12, 316, 317. Such a duty might be breached if the senior secured creditor has refused to assign its security interest to the junior creditor for some personal reason that is collateral to the recovery of the debt (as in *Downsview* itself), has deliberately misled the junior creditor about its enforcement steps (see *Tomlin v Luce* (1889) 43 Ch D 191) or has deliberately failed to take the necessary steps to preserve the value of the charged assets (see *McHugh v Union Bank of Canada* [1913] AC 299, 312).

[130] *McHugh* (n 129) 315. See also *Cuckmere Brick Co Ltd v Mutual Finance Ltd* [1971] Ch 949, 966; *Yorkshire Bank plc v Hall* [1999] 1 WLR 1713, 1728; *Silven Properties* (n 32) [27]; *Anton Durbeck GmbH v Den Norske Bank ASA* [2005] EWHC 2497; [2006] 1 Lloyd's Rep 93 [61]; *Alpstream AG v PK Airfinance Sarl* [2013] EWHC 2370 (Comm); [2014] 1 All ER (Comm) 441 [8]. There appears to be some uncertainty as to whether the duty in *Cuckmere Brick* is equitable in nature (see *Parker-Tweedale v Dunbar Bank plc (No 1)* [1991] Ch 12) or based upon common law principles (see *Medforth v Blake* [2000] Ch 86, 102). For the rejection of this duty, see *Citicorp Australia Ltd v McLoughney* (1984) 35 SASR 375, 381; *Westpac Banking Corporation Ltd v Kingsland* (1991) 26 NSWLR 700, 707–09.

[131] For example, if the senior security-holder were to act in concert with the debtor or unsecured creditors in order to deprive the junior creditor of some of the value of its security, it might be possible to rely upon the tort of lawful means conspiracy (see *Lonrho v Fayed* [1992] 1 AC 448) or, if the senior security-holder induced the junior creditor by deliberate misstatements to desist from acting in a particular manner, the tort of deceit might be available (see *Smith New Court Securities Ltd v Scrimgeour Vickers (Asset Management) Ltd* [1997] AC 254). There may also be liability on the part of the senior security-holder where it uses unlawful means to interfere with the enforcement of the junior creditor's security (see *OBG Ltd v Allan* [2007] UKHL 21; [2008] 1 AC 1) or conspires with others to do so (see *Total Network SL v HMRC* [2008] UKHL 19; [2008] AC 1174).

[132] *Downsview Nominees* (n 32) 315, applying *Murphy v Brentwood District Council* [1991] 1 AC 398.

[133] Ali (n 21) [3.16]–[3.17].

security over the 'common asset', thereby prejudicing the junior creditor's position, the latter should be entitled to enforce its security against the other collateral to which the senior creditor might otherwise have had recourse and to which the junior creditor did not previously have recourse. This now represents the preferred approach to marshalling in New Zealand,[134] Australia[135] and Canada.[136] In England, the position remains judicially (but not academically[137]) unsettled. Whilst support for this 'post-realisation theory' of marshalling can be found in some of the early English jurisprudence—for example, in *Re Mower's Trusts*,[138] Lord Romilly MR allowed a marshalling creditor to enforce his mortgage against a fund that was previously only subject to the senior creditor's security interest—it is only relatively recently that this theory has gained traction. Certainly, in *Highbury Pension Fund Management Co v Zirfin Investments Ltd*,[139] Lewison LJ formulated the marshalling doctrine in terms consistent with the post-realisation theory when he stated that 'if the first mortgagee with more than one security satisfies his debt out of the property over which the second mortgagee has his only security, the second mortgagee is entitled to stand *pro tanto* in the place of the first mortgagee in relation to the property over which the second mortgagee has no legal security'[140] and that 'if the doubly secured creditor resorts to the fund over which both creditors have security, then the singly secured creditor is entitled to stand in the place of the doubly secured creditor as regards the remaining securities'.[141] Indeed, in *McLean v Berry*,[142] Norris J recently interpreted *Highbury* as supporting the post-realisation theory. That said, it is not clear that *Highbury* can be taken as finally determining the correct theoretical

[134] *Re Tremain* [1934] NZLR 369; *Bissett v Australia and New Zealand Banking Corporation* [1961] NZLR 687; *National Bank of New Zealand Ltd v Caldesia Promotions Ltd and Jenkins Roberts & Associates Ltd* [1996] 3 NZLR 467; *New Zealand Associated Refrigerated Food Distributors Ltd v Simpson* [2008] NZHC 951 [28]–[30]; *MFT Properties Ltd v Country Club Apartments Ltd* [2012] NZHC 1116 [12]–[17]; *Jacomb* (n 114) [67]–[70]; *Tegel Foods* (n 10) [21]–[41]; *Adams v Sun* [2014] NZHC 912, [80]; *Napier v Waimana Investments Ltd* [2017] NZHC 265 [27].

[135] See, eg, *Jenkins v Brahe & Gair* (1902) 27 VLR 643, 648; *Miles* (n 72) 510–11; *Bank of New South Wales v City Mutual Life Assurance Society Ltd* [1969] VR 556, 557; *Commonwealth Trading Bank* (n 124) 130; *Mir Projects Pty Ltd v Lyons* [1977] 2 NSWLR 192, 196; *Chase Corporation* (n 118); *Takemura v National Australia Bank Ltd* [2003] NSWSC 339 [37]–[41]; *Elnic Holdings Pty Ltd v New Wave Development (NSW) Pty Ltd* [2005] NSWSC 1226 [15]–[24]; *Across Australia Finance* (n 15) [30]; *Naxatu* (n 118) [62]–[70], [73]–[84]. See also *Friend v Brooker* [2009] HCA 21; (2009) 239 CLR 129 [38]. The marshalling doctrine is not impacted by the statutory personal property securities regime in Australia: see Personal Property Securities Act 2009 (Cth), s 254(1)(c).

[136] *Ernst Bros Co v Canadian Permanent Mortgage Corporation* (1920) 57 DLR 500, 505; *Seel Investments Ltd v Greater Canadian Securities Corporation Ltd* (1967) 65 DLR (2d) 45; *Williamson v Loonstra* (1973) 34 DLR (3d) 275; *First Investors Corporation Ltd v Veeradon Developments Ltd* (1988) 47 DLR (4th) 446; *Farm Credit Corporation v Nelson* (1993) 102 DLR (4th) 743.

[137] Ali (n 21) [3.18]–[3.27]; Ross Martyn and Caddick (n 9) [75-18]; L Gullifer, *Goode on Legal Problems of Credit and Security* 5th edn (London, Sweet & Maxwell, 2013) [5-34]; A Guest, *Guest on the Law of Assignment* 2nd edn (London, Sweet & Maxwell, 2015) [6-80]; Heydon, Leeming and Turner (n 12) [11-020]; McGhee, (n 9) [39-085].

[138] *Re Mower's* (n 56). See also *Wallis* (n 7) 180; *Manks* (n 7) 466; *Re Broadwood* [1911] 1 Ch 277.

[139] *Highbury Pension Fund* (n 10).

[140] ibid [15].

[141] ibid [18].

[142] *McLean* (n 30) [17], [25]–[26].

approach to marshalling in England, since, as considered already above,[143] there are also aspects of Lewison LJ's judgment that can only be interpreted as lending support to the coercion theory.[144]

The theoretical uncertainty in *Highbury* has now been compounded by the Supreme Court decision in *Szepietowski*.[145] In considering how marshalling should operate, Lord Neuberger doubted whether a court was ever entitled to interfere with the senior security-holder's freedom to realise its securities 'in such manner and order as he thinks fit'.[146] Accordingly, his Lordship viewed marshalling as operating, not by restricting the senior security-holder's enforcement options, but rather by making the other assets subject to the senior creditor's security available *pro tanto* to satisfy the junior secured creditor's claim by a process akin to subrogation.[147] Lord Hughes appeared to explain the operation of marshalling in similar terms to Lord Neuberger,[148] as did Lord Sumption,[149] who viewed marshalling as giving the junior security-holder the ability to 'proceed in addition against a different asset which was never charged to him'. As considered already above,[150] however, the approach suggested by Lords Carnwath and Reed appears more consistent with an essentially coercive notion of marshalling. Accordingly, whilst there seems to be a bare majority in *Szepietowski* supporting the post-realisation, rather than the coercion, model of marshalling, it is not clear how much weight can be given to their Lordships' views or the differences between them. In terms of Lords Sumption, Hughes and Reed, their judgments dealt only very briefly or peripherally with the issue of how the marshalling process actually operates, so there is a risk of reading too much one way or the other into their throwaway phrases. Although Lords Neuberger and Carnworth dealt with the issue more fully, *Szepietowski* was not a case where the practical outcome was in any way affected by the particular theoretical view adopted, since marshalling was not available on the particular facts (due to the absence of an underlying personal obligation owed to the NCA), and, even if that doctrine had applied, there was little scope for the application of any coercive measures in *Szepietowski* given that the senior security-holder had already enforced against the 'common asset' and had had its claim satisfied in its entirety. In effect, post-realisation-style marshalling was the only approach realistically available on the facts of *Szepietowski* and, therefore, it is unclear how far one can take Lord Neuberger's views as representing a decisive shift towards the post-realisation theory more generally.

This is an unsatisfactory state of affairs, since the determination of marshalling's theoretical underpinnings is not merely of academic interest, but, as considered

[143] See section IV above.

[144] *Highbury Pension Fund* (n 10) [1], [18].

[145] *Szepietowski* (SC) (n 14).

[146] ibid [34]. See also *Wallis* (n 7) 180; *Manks* (n 7) 466.

[147] *Szepietowski* (SC) (n 14) [32]. A similar theoretical approach was adopted by Rose LJ in *Re BCCI (No 8)* [1996] Ch 245, 271. See also *Petterson v Ross* [2013] EWHC 2724 (Ch), [86].

[148] *Szepietowski* (SC) (n 14) [107].

[149] ibid [79].

[150] See section IV above.

above,[151] can have significant practical consequences for the parties, including whether injunctive relief against the senior security-holder might in principle be available (the availability of such relief being more consistent with the *ex ante* nature of the coercion theory) or whether some form of monetary award might be available where the junior creditor's ability to marshal has been prejudiced (although, as discussed above,[152] a compensatory or restitutionary award against the senior creditor is unlikely to be generally available in England or other jurisdictions,[153] the post-realisation model may well justify a monetary award as part of 'an accounting exercise' carried out by the court[154] when the assets to which the junior creditor might have had access through the marshalling doctrine no longer exist[155]). Additionally, one's choice of model may have an impact on the amount that the junior security-holder ultimately recovers by marshalling the securities, and consequently the assets available for distribution to the debtor's general unsecured creditors. This is particularly the case when the debt due to the junior security-holder is greater than the amount owing to the senior security-holder: the post-realisation model views marshalling as only conferring a *pro tanto* protection upon the junior security-holder, since the junior security-holder is only entitled to resort to the other (non-common) assets to the extent that they secured the senior creditor's claim, with the result that the junior creditor's recovery through marshalling is limited to the amount due to the senior creditor;[156] whereas the only potential limit upon the junior security-holder's recovery under the coercion model would be the value of the 'common asset' at the time of enforcement.[157] Accordingly, whilst the coercion theory can produce a more

[151] See section IV above.

[152] See section IV above.

[153] *Naxatu* (n 118) [83]–[84]. An award of damages might be available in England when the senior creditor has acted in bad faith: see *Downsview Nominees* (n 32) 311–12, 316, 317 (as considered in n 129 above).

[154] *McLean* (n 30) [27]. See also *Naxatu* (n 118) [62]. See further Heydon, Leeming and Turner (n 12) [11-020]: 'On the taking of accounts between mortgagor and first and second mortgagee, since equity regards as done that which ought to be done, the accounts will be taken on the footing that the first mortgagee has marshalled the securities as equity requires'.

[155] Essentially, the post-realisation model of marshalling seeks to protect the junior secured creditor by providing them with access to the assets that the senior creditor could have used, but did not. Where the other assets are simply insufficient in value to cover the amount owed to the junior creditor, there will be no scope for further relief as this would be prejudicial to the debtor (see *Ex p Kendall* (n 43) Ves 527; ER 204; *Szepietowski* (SC) (n 14) [107]) and be tantamount to conferring a greater *total* priority on secured creditors over the debtor's unsecured creditors than was originally affected by the debtor. A monetary award as a result of an accounting exercise may, however, be appropriate in circumstances where the asset to which the junior creditor would have had access is no longer owned by the debtor so that the junior creditor's 'marshalling equity' is transferred to the equivalent of that assets' proceeds by a process similar to overreaching: see Heydon, Leeming and Turner (n 12) [11-020].

[156] *Re Broadwood* (n 138) 281–82 (marshalling of deceased's estate); *Miles* (n 72) 510–11 (marshalling of securities); *New Zealand Associated Refrigerated Food Distributors* (n 134) [28]–[30] (marshalling of securities); *Naxatu* (n 118) [62]–[63]; *cf Szepietowski* (SC) (n 14) [107], where Lord Hughes appears to suggest that the junior security-holder may potentially recover more than the senior security-holder could have done.

[157] An instructive worked example is where the senior creditor's claim for £5,000 is secured over asset 'A' worth £13,000, as well as being secured over asset 'B', which is worth £7,000 and is in turn subject to a second-ranking security in respect of £8,000 advanced by the junior creditor. If the senior security-holder were to enforce against asset 'B', the junior security-holder would only receive £2,000 from its security interest and accordingly might consider marshalling. According to the post-realisation model, the

attractive result for the junior security-holder, the post-realisation model arguably achieves a more subtle balancing of the respective interests of the junior-security holder and the debtor's unsecured creditors.

Assuming for present purposes, however, that the post-realisation model of marshalling applies, it is necessary to determine (in the same manner as was done for the coercion theory above[158]) what the practical operation of the doctrine indicates about its juridical nature. Unfortunately, a frequent academic response to this kind of conundrum has been to fall back onto labeling marshalling as *sui generis*.[159] Whilst there may well be some truth in this description of marshalling, it is hardly likely to promote clarity, predictability or understanding. Before examining possible conceptualisations, however, it is probably worth clearing the ground of two early misconceptions/misdescriptions of marshalling. The first such misconception was to use the term marshalling as a synonym for 'priority', such as when the court is asked to rank two or more claims against a fund remaining in the hands of an insolvent agent,[160] since marshalling in fact only arises as an issue once the priority of any competing claimants has been determined. Accordingly, the determination of a particular claim's priority is logically prior to the issue of whether marshalling is available in the first place. The second misconception was to use the term marshalling as referring to a rule for the appropriation of payments in a mixed fund,[161] but once again this should be rejected as a misnomer, since (like priority) appropriation involves a logically prior question to that of marshalling. Putting these two wrong-turns aside, the possible theoretical explanations for post-realisation marshalling that will be canvassed below are,[162] first, whether it should be viewed as involving a cause of action or claim designed to vindicate some underlying right of the junior creditor and/or enforce some pre-existing duty of the senior creditor; second,

junior security-holder would only be able to enforce its claim to asset 'A' to the extent of £5,000 (being the value of the senior security-holder's interest in that asset), whereas the coercion model, by compelling the senior creditor to enforce against asset 'A', would enable the junior security-holder to realise the full amount of £7,000 from asset 'B'.

158 See section IV above.

159 Ali (n 21) [11.13].

160 *Re State Fire Insurance Co* (1863) Hem & M 457; 71 ER 200; *Re Professional Life Assurance Company* (n 55) 679–81; *Re Holland, ex p Alston* (1868–69) LR 4 Ch App 168.

161 *Re Barned's Banking Company* (1867) LR 4 Eq 458.

162 There have been suggestions in other jurisdictions that marshalling is 'a process, not an entitlement' (see *Bentley* (n 54), 11,841; *Adams* (n 134) [75]), so that the doctrine should be considered as part of procedural law (in much that same way as tracing is part of evidential law). Whilst marshalling does indeed resemble a form of interpleader procedure (without the requirement that there must be a 'stakeholder' without any interest in the property in dispute: see Civil Procedure Rules r 86.2(4)(a)), the suggestion that that doctrine is merely an aspect of *English* procedure suffers from two principal weaknesses: first, on this assumption, it would be difficult to explain how marshalling survived the Judicature Act 1873, ss 24–25; and, second, it would be difficult to justify its total absence from the CPR given their extensive coverage (although these rules are not necessarily intended to be comprehensive and some common law procedural rules continue to operate outside the CPR regime: consider, eg, *Norwich Pharmacal Co v Customs & Excise Commissioners* [1974] AC 133, 175–76, 182, 188, 190, 199). That said, such a characterisation has the merit of going some way towards explaining why there has been such uncertainty in the past about both the theoretical underpinnings and juridical nature of marshalling and why the trend in the most recent jurisprudence seems to be towards a more flexible and less dogmatic version of that doctrine (see further section VI below).

whether marshalling might be characterised as a remedy responding to some pre-existing cause of action or claim; and, finally, whether marshalling might best be treated as a species of equitable defence.[163]

As regards the question of whether the post-realisation model of marshalling might be characterised as a cause of action or claim designed to vindicate some underlying right of the junior security-holder or enforce a correlative duty of the senior security-holder, it is clear that, in *Szepietowski*, Lord Neuberger at several points referred to the 'right to marshal'[164] (language similarly employed by Lords Sumption[165] and Carnwath[166]) and classified marshalling as an 'equitable right'[167] that could be invoked by the junior security-holder as a claimant upon satisfying certain precisely formulated conditions.[168] On this view, marshalling is effectively used in an offensive manner. Such a characterisation, however, gives rise in turn to a question concerning the precise nature of the right (and/or duty) that justifies invoking the marshalling doctrine. Consistently with the post-realisation theory, there are a number of possible 'rights' and/or 'duties' that have been rejected over the years by the courts as potential explanations for marshalling. One such possibility rejected by the Australian courts is that marshalling operates to enforce an immediate equitable proprietary right or interest that the junior security-holder automatically and immediately obtains (even before the matter has been determined judicially) in the other assets subject to the senior creditor's security interest.[169] A similar view is evident in England, since the House of Lords in *Dolphin v Aylward*[170] rejected a junior creditor's attempt to marshal securities when this would have operated to the detriment of a third-party volunteer without notice.[171] Whilst a junior creditor will certainly acquire a proprietary interest in new collateral by virtue of the court's order, at its strongest, a junior creditor's 'right' in this regard before such judicial intervention[172] has been described (rather cryptically) as 'an 'inchoate equity' (which, whilst falling short of an equitable interest or estate, is superior to a 'mere equity')'.[173] Equally untenable has been the argument that the senior security-holder could be treated as holding the assets subject to its security on trust for the junior security-holder and

[163] It should be noted, however, that Lord Neuberger in *Menelaou v Bank of Cyprus UK Ltd* [2015] UKSC 66; [2016] AC 176 [96] has warned against trying to draw too-clear a dividing line between these different categories.

[164] *Szepietowski* (SC) (n 14) [38], [54], [56], [57], [62]–[63], [75]–[76].

[165] ibid [79]. Lord Carnwath (at [94]–[95]) referred to there being a 'marshalling claim'.

[166] ibid [79], where Lord Carnwath referred to marshalling as involving a 'claim'. See also *CAN 077 991 890 Pty Ltd v National Australia Bank Ltd* [2007] NSWSC 358 [8].

[167] *Szepietowski* (SC) (n 14) [55], [61]. See also *Miles* (n 72) 510–11 referring to a 'right in equity'.

[168] ibid [31], [55].

[169] *Commonwealth Trading Bank* (n 124) 128–30; *Naxatu* (n 118) [84]. Consider *Highbury Pension Fund* (n 10) [62].

[170] *Dolphin* (n 10).

[171] This conclusion cannot be explained on the basis of the usual bona fide purchaser defence that defeats equitable proprietary interests, as the third party in *Dolphin* was a mere volunteer.

[172] *Sarge* (n 123) 664–65.

[173] Ali (n 21) [11.13]. See also M Waters, E Ovey and M Fell, *Retail Mortgages: Law, Regulation and Procedure* (London, Sweet & Maxwell, 2013) [5-02]. See also *National Provincial Bank Ltd v Ainsworth* [1965] AC 1175, criticised by K Gray, 'Property in Thin Air' [1991] *CLJ* 252, 292–93.

accordingly be liable to account for the manner in which it realises its security.[174] Treating the senior creditor as a trustee, who owes fiduciary duties to the junior creditor when realising its security, would seriously compromise the former's freedom to enforce its security as he sees fit and would contradict a number of judicial decisions to the contrary.[175] Accordingly, it is hardly surprising that in *Commonwealth Trading Bank v Colonial Mutual Life Assurance Society Ltd*,[176] Neasey J stated:

> … counsel were unable out of the very many cases on marshalling to be found in the books to cite one case in which a prior encumbrancer was held liable to a subsequent encumbrancer for damages for breach of trust where the subsequent encumbrancer had not sought the court's intervention before the reconveyance of the security upon which he relied for marshalling.

Indeed, as discussed above in the context of the coercion theory,[177] the courts have generally been hostile to the imposition of any general equitable[178] or common law[179] duty on the senior security-holder towards junior encumbrancers. Although, as similarly discussed above, there remains the possibility in England of the junior security-holder bringing a claim against the senior creditor for breach of its duty of good faith[180] or on the basis of the economic torts, such forms of liability cannot easily provide a juridical explanation for marshalling: neither bad faith nor fault more generally have been viewed as pre-requisites to marshalling[181] with the consequence that that doctrine potentially operates in a much broader range of situations than are presently covered by either the duty of good faith or the economic torts. Moving beyond wrong-based claims,[182] it is also not compelling to see marshalling as a species of unjust enrichment claim (given that it will be difficult either to envisage the senior creditor's enforcement of its security as being 'unjust' when this is precisely the security for which the junior creditor bargained or to treat the senior creditor as having been 'enriched at the expense of' the junior creditor)[183] or as a form of contractual claim (given that there will usually be no privity between the two creditors).[184]

[174] *Commonwealth Trading Bank* (n 124) 121–22.

[175] *Kennedy v De Trafford* [1897] AC 180, 185; *Tan Soon Gin* (n 6) 545. See also *Nash v Eads* (1880) 25 Sol Jo 95; *Farrar v Farrars Ltd* (1888) 40 Ch D 395, 410–11; *Saltri III Ltd v MD Mezzanine SA SICAR* [2012] EWHC 3025 (Comm) [123(g)–(h)], [124], [127(b)–(c)].

[176] *Commonwealth Trading Bank* (n 124) 121–22.

[177] See section IV above.

[178] *Naxatu* (n 118) [73], in which Dowsett J indicated that 'the doctrine of marshalling imposes no duty upon the first mortgagee' and (at [84]) that 'it is simply too late to create a fiduciary relationship between first and second mortgagees in respect of properties over which the second mortgagee has no security interest'.

[179] *Downsview Nominees* (n 32) 315.

[180] ibid 311–12, 316–17.

[181] *Szepietowski* (CA) (n 13) [52]. See also *Across Australia Finance* (n 15).

[182] Academically, the view that marshalling might be a species of contribution has also been rejected, as the former does not involve co-debtors or any notion of equal or proportionate burden-sharing: see Ali (n 21) [5.28], [5.37]–[5.48].

[183] Ali (n 21) [4.39]–[4.54]; McGhee (n 9) [39-091].

[184] Although there is no requirement that creditors of the same debtor have a contractual relationship, it is possible for there to be a subordination agreement, deed of priority or inter-creditor agreement between secured creditors regulating the manner of enforcement of their security, but such arrangements are likely to exclude the marshalling doctrine in any event: see *Szepietowski* (SC) (n 14) [61]–[62], [88]–[92], [107]. That said, as considered further below, there is some recent judicial support for the

Indeed, as the post-realisation model operates on the assumption that the senior creditor has 'left the scene' so to speak, it is difficult to envisage how exactly marshalling might constitute a claim for the enforcement of any type of right against the senior creditor, even though the weight of authority views marshalling as an *inter-creditor* equity.[185] Accordingly, it is submitted that a different juridical explanation is required.

Given the difficulty in characterising the post-realisation model of marshalling as a claim to enforce an underlying right/duty between the secured creditors, an alternative suggestion might be to treat marshalling as an equitable 'remedy', which is a view that does appear to garner more judicial support. In *Commonwealth Trading Bank v Colonial Mutual Life Assurance Society Ltd*,[186] Neasey J certainly referred to marshalling as being 'remedial' and as involving an 'equitable remedy'. Such a classification similarly appears to have been the preferred view of Lord Carnwath in *Szepietowski*,[187] and Lord Neuberger on several occasions used the language of remedialism when describing marshalling.[188] In determining the nature of marshalling as a remedy, the courts have tended to reason by analogy with other forms of remedy (although one should keep in mind Lord Carnwath's warning in *Menelaou v Bank of Cyprus UK Ltd*[189] against distorting concepts by becoming overly fixated on analogies with cognate areas). With that cautionary note in mind, there are two particular suggestions evident in the case law.[190] First, given that, as mentioned above, the junior creditor only obtains an equitable proprietary interest (under the post-realisation theory) from the moment that the court makes an order for marshalling, the Australian courts have suggested that marshalling should be viewed as a discretionary proprietary *remedy* that arises for the first time upon a judicial declaration to that effect.[191] On this approach, however, the marshalling doctrine starts to resemble the remedial constructive trust, although there is the difference that the junior security-holder has pre-existing proprietary rights, whereas the remedial constructive trust is often invoked to turn obligation into property. Despite this difference, the general aversion of the English courts to the discretionary adjustment of property rights (as evidenced by the reluctance to admit the remedial constructive trust[192]) may well make it difficult for English law to follow Australia down this particular path.[193] Second, given that the post-realisation theory of marshalling entitles the junior security-holder

view that marshalling is based upon the enforcement of an implied term in the contractual relationship between the junior secured creditor and the debtor: see *Szepietowski* (SC) (n 14) [54], [63]. Acceptance of this suggestion would require a change in thinking (advocated in this chapter) away from treating marshalling as a purely inter-creditor equity.

[185] *Re BCCI (No 8)* (n 11) 230–31; *Highbury Pension Fund* (n 10) [18]; *Szepietowski* (SC) (n 14) [101], [107].

[186] *Commonwealth Trading Bank* (n 124) 126–28, approved in *Naxatu* (n 118) [64]–[67].

[187] *Szepietowski* (SC) (n 14) [101], [104].

[188] ibid [55], [58], [61].

[189] *Menelaou* (n 163) [117].

[190] Marshalling should not be considered a form of specific performance, since there is often no contractual relationship between the junior and senior security-holders: see Ali (n 21) [5.49]–[5.53].

[191] *Commonwealth Trading Bank* (n 124) 128; *Sarge* (n 123) 644–55.

[192] See, eg, *Bailey v Angove's Pty Ltd* [2016] UKSC 47; [2016] 1 WLR 3179 [18]–[32].

[193] The fact that the Australian courts have embraced the notion of the remedial constructive trust (see *Muschinski v Dodds* (1985) 160 CLR 583, 614) may explain why they have been so willing to treat marshalling as a discretionary proprietary remedy.

'to stand *pro tanto* in the place of the [senior security-holder]' in relation to the (non-common) asset,[194] there have been suggestions in the United Kingdom,[195] New Zealand[196] and Australia[197] that marshalling is a species of subrogation (which was itself characterised as a form of equitable remedy in *Menelaou v Bank of Cyprus UK Ltd*).[198] Despite this weight of authority, it is interesting that more recent courts have been at pains to avoid losing marshalling altogether within the nebula of subrogation and have stressed that, whilst the two doctrines may bear a superficial resemblance, they are not the same thing.[199] For example, in *Naxatu*, Dorsett J considered that 'the doctrine of marshalling is closely aligned to the doctrine of subrogation'[200] and 'a remedy akin to subrogation',[201] but did not go so far as to suggest it actually *was* subrogation. Similarly, in *Highbury*, Lewison LJ was only prepared to go so far as to say that 'the second mortgagee is *in effect* subrogated to the rights of the first mortgagee'.[202] Indeed, in the most recent marshalling decision of *McLean v Berry*,[203] Norris J was even more explicit in this regard:

> ... the principle of marshalling is not identical with the doctrine of subrogation. ... As Lewison LJ explained [in *Highbury*], the principle is that the second mortgagee 'is entitled to stand *pro tanto* in the place of the first mortgagee'; and '*it is in this sense* that we say that the second mortgagee is *in effect* subrogated to the rights of the first mortgagee' (emphasis added). The imagery must not distort the reality.

This is probably the correct approach since, unlike in the subrogation context, the junior creditor's funds are not being used to discharge the debtor's indebtedness to the senior creditor. Equally, it has never been a requirement of subrogation, unlike marshalling, that the creditors have a common debtor. Indeed, two consequences probably flow from these more recent judicial statements. First, if marshalling is not really a species of subrogation, then one may wonder how helpful it is to continue referring to the former doctrine as a species of 'quasi-subrogation' (to use a particularly inelegant label); it is probably now better to avoid reference to subrogation entirely in the marshalling context. Secondly, once one casts marshalling adrift from subrogation, the debate surrounding the nature of marshalling becomes that little bit more uncertain than might otherwise have been the case if marshalling could simply have been subsumed within subrogation. Accordingly, whilst the view of marshalling as an equitable remedy has probably garnered the most judicial support, considerable doubt continues to surround whether this remains the most appropriate

[194] *Highbury Pension Fund* (n 10) [15].

[195] *Re Mower's* (n 56) 114; *Nuclear Cameron (PX) Ltd v AMF International Ltd* [1982] 16 NIJB (14 August 1980).

[196] *New Zealand Loan and Mercantile Agency* (n 24); *Caldesia Promotions* (n 134) 474; *New Zealand Associated Refrigerated Food Distributors* (n 134) [28]–[30].

[197] *City Mutual Life Assurance Society* (n 135) 557; *Miles* (n 72) 512; *Naxatu* (n 118) [83].

[198] *Menelaou* (n 163). See further *Banque Finance de la Cité SA v Parc (Battersea) Ltd* [1999] 1 AC 221; *cf Bofinger v Kingsway Group Ltd* [2009] HCA 44; (2009) 239 CLR 269.

[199] *Szepietowski* (CA) (n 13) [2].

[200] *Naxatu* (n 118) [74].

[201] ibid [68].

[202] *Highbury Pension Fund* (n 10) [15].

[203] *McLean* (n 30) [26].

classification, especially in light of the difficulty in identifying the underlying right that such a remedy is intended to vindicate.

As it appears unsatisfactory to characterise the post-realisation model of marshalling as either a claim or remedy, an alternative might be to classify the doctrine as an equitable defence. Certainly, from a historical perspective, marshalling was used in other contexts as a defence against the enforcement of bottomry bonds in the admiralty jurisdiction[204] and against the claims of residuary legatees in the context of the administration of estates.[205] Unlike the suggestion made above[206] in the context of the coercion theory (to the effect that marshalling provides the junior creditor with an equitable defence against the *senior creditor*), the present argument is that post-realisation model also operates as a defence (existing in tandem with the coercion approach as a part of 'hybrid model' of marshalling),[207] albeit that this form of marshalling operates against the *debtor* and those claiming through the debtor.[208] At the outset it must be admitted that the latter suggestion is problematic in light of the modern leading cases, such as *BCCI, Naxatu*, *Highbury* and *Szepietowski*, since not only was marshalling generally used in an offensive manner by the junior secured creditor in those cases, but those courts also stressed that marshalling was an inter-creditor equity, rather than one arising between the junior creditor and the debtor.[209] It is submitted, however, that modern courts have lost sight of the fact that in its origins marshalling was a doctrine that operated as against *both* the senior secured creditor and the debtor. As explained in detail above,[210] this is precisely what Lord Finch envisaged in *Povye's Case*.[211] Indeed, there are clearly circumstances where marshalling in its post-realisation form might be employed defensively by the junior creditor against the debtor or (more likely) its representatives. The most obvious such situation is when a liquidator or administrator seeks directions from the court as to how to distribute the surplus from the sale of an asset by the senior security-holder, as occurred recently in *McLean v Berry*.[212]

Indeed, a novel conceptualisation of marshalling suggested by Lord Neuberger in *Szepietowski* may provide fertile ground for the suggestion that the post-realisation model of marshalling effectively involves a species of defence against debtor action.[213]

204 *The Edward Oliver* (n 9); *The Eugenie* (n 9).
205 *Re Roberts* (n 9); *Re Fry* (n 9); *Re Ross* (n 9) [86]–[87].
206 See section IV above.
207 See section VI below.
208 McGhee (n 9) [39-086].
209 *Re BCCI (No 8)* (n 11) 230–31; *Highbury Pension Fund* (n 10) [18]; *Szepietowski* (SC) (n 14) [101], [107].
210 See section II above.
211 *Povye's Case* (n 25) Free 51; ER 1052.
212 *McLean* (n 30) [14]. See also *Jacomb* (n 114) [67]–[70] (in which Kós J allowed the doctrine of marshalling to be raised successfully by a guarantor as a defence to the enforcement of the guarantee); *Adams* (n 134) [75]–[94] (in which Heath J allowed several junior secured creditors to employ the marshalling doctrine to resist a liquidator's claim to surplus proceeds from the sale of mortgaged property). See also *HSBC Bank (China) Ltd v Yip Kim Po* [2008] 5 HKC 224 [8].
213 Whilst there is nothing in the judgments of Lords Sumption, Reed and Hughes that overtly endorses this conceptualisation of marshalling, Lord Carnwath does reference a somewhat watered-down version of this contractual right approach when he suggests that marshalling might be influenced by 'the scope of the risk which [the debtor] has voluntarily accepted': see *Szepietowski* (SC) (n 14) [103].

After approving the post-realisation theory, his Lordship suggested that the ability to marshal arises 'as an incident of the second mortgage when it is granted', since '[i]t is normally easy to imply a common intention on the part of the parties to the second mortgage ... that there should be a right to marshal'.[214] Accordingly, by virtue of an implied term in the junior creditor-debtor arrangements,[215] the junior secured creditor has the ability to resist the debtor's (or its liquidator's or unsecured creditors') claim to any additional collateral not required by the senior creditor and to utilise those assets to satisfy its own claim first. As the scope of such an implied term would be conditioned by the requirement of 'necessity',[216] it would not arise in every case involving multiple secured creditors, but only in those circumstances identified above in *Szepietowski*.[217] As the debtor's interest in the asset (which was originally subject to the senior creditor's security interest alone) would be subject to a 'flaw' in favour of the junior creditor (in a similar way to express flawed-asset arrangements that have been recognised by the courts),[218] it would be effective as against the debtor's liquidator and unsecured creditors, but not necessarily subsequent third-party acquirers of the collateral.[219] Conceptualising marshalling in this manner would not fall afoul of fundamental insolvency concerns, such as the *pari passu* principle[220] or the anti-deprivation principle,[221] nor would it unduly impact upon the statutory priority afforded to preferential unsecured creditors[222] or the liquidator's expenses,[223] as long as marshalling is not used as a guise for unduly promoting floating chargeholders ahead of such statutorily preferred claims. Indeed, courts are likely to be alert to such risks.[224]

That said, there are potentially three difficulties with Lord Neuberger's novel approach. First, by grounding the doctrine of marshalling in an implied contractual limitation upon the debtor's proprietary rights, his Lordship has potentially opened the door to the possibility that the junior security-holder might be able to have recourse to the senior creditor's other assets without the need for any prior

[214] *Szepietowski* (SC) (n 14) [54], [63]. See also *City Mutual Life Assurance Society* (n 135) 557, applying *Flint v Howard* (n 43) 73; *cf Duncan* (n 10) 12.

[215] Although the better view would be that the term is one implied by law, Lord Neuberger's language in *Szepietowski* (at [54]) is more consistent with the suggestion that the term is actually implied in fact.

[216] This remains the case whether the term is viewed as one implied by law (see *Liverpool City Council v Irwin* [1977] AC 239, 254, 258, 262, 266) or in fact (see *Marks and Spencer plc v BNP Paribas Securities Services Trust Co (Jersey) Ltd* [2015] UKSC 72; [2016] AC 742 [17]–[23]).

[217] See section III above.

[218] *Re BCCI (No 8)* (n 11) 225, 227; *Money Markets International Stockbrokers Ltd v London Stock Exchange Ltd* [2002] 1 WLR 1150 [91]; *Fraser v Oystertec plc* [2004] EWHC 1582 (Ch) [12]; *Belmont Park* (n 76) [89]; *Re Lehman Brothers International (Europe)* [2012] EWHC 2997 (Ch); [2014] 2 BCLC 295 [47].

[219] *Dolphin* (n 10).

[220] Given that a creditor invoking marshalling will have some form of security from the outset, there is no problem in terms of *pari passu* distribution as this is usually limited to the context of unsecured creditors.

[221] *Belmont Park* (n 76).

[222] Insolvency Act 1986, s 386(1), Sch 6.

[223] ibid, s 176ZA.

[224] For a similar issue in the context of deeds of priority, consider *Re Portbase Clothing Ltd* [1993] Ch 388, 399–401, 407; *cf Re Woodroffes (Musical Instruments) Ltd* [1986] 1 Ch 366, 373.

court order—as a form of extra-judicial self-help[225]—and that, when there is an application to the court, marshalling would be automatically available if the criteria above were satisfied, rather than its availability being dependent upon an exercise of a broad judicial discretion.[226] This would certainly improve predictability in this area, but would represent an approach to marshalling that has little prior judicial support.[227] Second, it is unclear how much weight one can afford to Lord Neuberger's suggestions in *Szepietowski* that marshalling operates between the junior secured creditor and the debtor, given that this would represent a significant break with the dominant judicial review of marshalling[228] and yet no explicit recognition of that fact is contained in his Lordship's judgment. Indeed, there are references by the other Supreme Court Justices in *Szepietowski* itself (albeit the dissenting minority) that are inconsistent with Lord Neuberger's novel approach—for example, Lord Carnwath viewed marshalling as 'a remedy which operates primarily between security holders, not between them and the common debtor or chargor'[229] and Lord Hughes stated 'that it is of the essence of marshalling that it is neutral so far as the chargor/debtor is concerned'.[230] More worryingly, Lord Neuberger is himself unclear in *Szepietowski* as to how marshalling should be characterised, frequently referring to the doctrine interchangeably as being a 'right' or 'remedy'[231] (as discussed above) and similarly endorsing the idea of debtor neutrality.[232] Thirdly, in a similar manner to other attempts to explain marshalling, Lord Neuberger's novel approach is unable to explain some of the continuing procedural oddities of the doctrine,[233] such as the fact that marshalling is only available 'if the funds are in Court and when the Court can exercise a jurisdiction over them'[234] and the fact that (at least in Australia) courts have been prepared to marshal securities *sua sponte*, without any specific request from the parties.[235] It may be that these features of the doctrine will

[225] *Szepietowski* (SC) (n 14) [33].

[226] ibid [55]–[58], [61].

[227] *Adams* (n 134) [78]: '... the adjustment of priorities may only be effected through a court order ...'; *cf Westpac Banking Corporation v Daydream Island Pty Ltd* [1985] 2 Qd 330, 332. For academic support for the approach in *Daydream Island*, see Ali (n 21) [7.04].

[228] Having overlooked *Povye's Case* (n 25), marshalling has generally been viewed as an equity arising only between the secured creditors themselves (see *Re BCCI (No 8)* (n 11) 230–31; *Highbury Pension Fund* (n 10) [18]) and effectively neutral as regards the debtor (see Ali (n 21) [4.48], adopted in *Szepietowski* (SC) (n 14) [32]). Certainly marshalling should not operate to prejudice the debtor's overall liability position: see *Ex p Kendall* (n 43) Ves 527; ER 204.

[229] *Szepietowski* (SC) (n 14) [101].

[230] ibid [107].

[231] ibid [55], [58], [61].

[232] ibid [32].

[233] These 'oddities', however, might arguably be consistent with the alternative procedure-based explanation of marshalling canvassed in n 162 above.

[234] *Naxatu* (n 118) [71]–[72], applying *Lawrance v Galsworthy* (n 95) and *Webb v Smith* (n 43). See also *Smit Tak* (n 63) 406; *Adams* (n 134) [75].

[235] *Gibbs v Ougier* (1806) 12 Ves Jr 413, 416–17; 33 ER 156, 157. See also *Daydream Island* (n 227) 332; *Oamington* (n 127); *Naxatu* (n 118) [61]. The fact that a court is prepared to raise marshalling of its own motion is not necessarily inconsistent with the characterisation of that doctrine as an equitable defence, since an English court is required to ensure that, as far as reasonably practicable, all issues (including potential claims and defences) between the parties are resolved irrespective of the state of the pleadings: consider Senior Courts Act 1981, s 49; CPR rr 1.1, 1.4.

ultimately be abandoned or limited to particular jurisdictions, but, until then, they may weaken the explicatory force of Lord Neuberger's approach.

VI. CONCLUSION

This chapter has sought to highlight the confusion in thinking surrounding the theory and practice of marshalling, to demonstrate why characterising marshalling as a claim or a remedy is problematic and to argue that a better approach might be to view that doctrine as a species of defence. It has also been argued that the operation of that defence differs according to the model of marshalling that one adopts: the coercion model provides the junior secured creditor with a defence exigeable against the senior secured creditor, whilst the post-realisation model confers a defence against the debtor. Whichever model is followed though, marshalling remains an essentially defensive tool. It has not been an aim of this chapter, however, to argue that one model of marshalling is superior to the other, but rather to suggest, on the basis of *Povye's Case*,[236] that both models should have a continuing role to play and should operate side-by-side as part of a 'hybrid model' of marshalling. In that regard, the attempt has been made to show that there is both continuing modern judicial support for the coercion model[237] and (as yet) a lack of overwhelming judicial acceptance of the post-realisation model.[238] On this basis, the courts should resist the temptation to be too dogmatic or prescriptive about how marshalling should operate, since the post-realisation model is the only approach that can cope with the situation where the senior creditor has already enforced its security and there may well be situations where it remains entirely appropriate to compel some form of action on the part of the senior security-holder.[239]

Indeed, it is possible to find some positive support for a more flexible or 'hybrid' model of marshalling pursuant to which the court is free to pick and choose the most appropriate way of protecting the junior security-holder without necessarily being constrained by either the coercion or post-realisation approaches.[240] As well as some support in New Zealand[241] and Canada,[242] the Scottish doctrine of 'catholic securities' appears to operate on the basis of the court having a choice between either compelling the senior security-holder to act in a particular manner or allowing the junior security-holder to step into the senior creditor's shoes. For example,

236 *Povye's Case* (n 25).

237 See section IV above.

238 See section V above.

239 Whilst a court applying the coercion model of marshalling must be careful not to infringe too much upon the senior creditor's freedom of action (see section IV above), compulsion may be appropriate in the (admittedly limited) circumstances where there is no legal, economic or commercial advantage to the senior creditor enforcing against one asset or another and yet enforcement against the 'common asset' would cause significant detriment to the junior creditor. Indeed, in the United States, the coercive form of marshalling is only available when the senior secured creditor would not be prejudiced by its operation: see *Lieberman Music Co v Hagan*, 394 NW 2d 837 (Minn Ct App, 1986).

240 For an academic rejection of the 'hybrid' model of marshalling, see Ali (n 21) [3.35]–[3.39].

241 *Gillespie v Cameron* (1996) 7 TCLR 376.

242 *Butler Engineering Ltd v First Investors Corporation* [1986] 1 WWR 469 [17].

in *Littlejohn v Black*,[243] Lord President McNeill indicated that 'the primary creditor will be compelled either to take his payment in the first instance out of that one of the subjects in which no other creditor holds a special interest, or to assign his right to the second creditor, from whom he has wrested the only subject of his security' and, in *Nicol's Trustees v Hill*,[244] Lord Adam indicated that 'the prior creditor is bound either to adopt that course [that is less injurious to the junior creditor], or by assignation to put the postponed creditor into his right'.[245] Similarly, it may be that a better explanation of the theoretical confusion in the current English jurisprudence (as considered above)[246] is that the English courts are already operating a 'hybrid' approach to marshalling, rather than committing unequivocally to one or other of the classic theories. Support for such an approach is explicit in *Smit Tak International Zeesleepen Bergingsbedrijf BV v Selco Salvage Ltd*,[247] in which Warner J stated:

> [The authorities] show ... beyond doubt that, where the relevant funds are wholly under the control of the Court, the Court will give effect to the doctrine of marshalling in a way that will bind [the senior secured creditor]. They show also, at the other extreme, that where the [senior creditor] has satisfied himself before proceedings are brought, the Court will confine itself to giving effect to the equities as between the subsequent claimants.

Such flexibility of approach may be precisely what Lewison LJ had in mind in *Highbury* when he indicated that marshalling 'gives the second creditor a right in equity to *require* that the first creditor satisfy himself or *be treated as having satisfied himself* so far as possible out of the security or fund to which the latter has no claim'.[248] This similarly finds echoes in *McLean v Berry*,[249] in which Norris J indicated that the marshalling of securities may often boil down to little more than 'an accounting exercise' carried out by the court.[250] If a 'hybrid' version of marshalling is indeed what the English courts are already employing, then this should be encouraged.

[243] *Littlejohn v Black* (n 97) 212.
[244] *Nicol's Trustees* (n 97) 421.
[245] For the possibility of adopting a similar assignment-based approach to marshalling, see Ali (n 21) [3.28]–[3.29].
[246] See sections IV–V above.
[247] *Smit Tak* (n 63) 407.
[248] *Highbury Pension Fund* (n 10) [1], [18] (emphasis added). See also *Re BCCI (No 8)* (n 11) 230–31.
[249] *McLean* (n 30) [26]–[27].
[250] ibid [27]. See also *Re Holland* (n 160) 173; *Naxatu* (n 118) [62]. See further Ross Martyn and Caddick, *Williams, Mortimer and Sunnucks* (n 9) [75-17], referring to marshalling as a 'process of adjustment'.

12

Illegality in Equity

PAUL S DAVIES

I. INTRODUCTION

THE OPERATION OF the maxims *ex turpi causa non oritur actio* ('no action arises from a wrongful act') and *in pari delicto potior est conditio defendentis* ('where both parties are equally in the wrong the defendant is in the stronger position') have long proved to be problematic in private law. Indeed, each of the previous volumes in this series on *Defences* includes (at least) one chapter dealing with some of the difficulties involved.[1] Those essays sought to explain how the law might develop, but since they were written the significant decision of the Supreme Court in *Patel v Mirza*[2] has, for better or worse,[3] changed the legal landscape. The majority of the Supreme Court clearly thought that the approach of the House of Lords in *Tinsley v Milligan*[4] should no longer be followed, and that earlier decision has now effectively been overruled.[5] *Tinsley v Milligan* laid down a 'reliance principle', which meant that a claim would fail if claimants had to rely upon their own illegality. But *Patel v Mirza* favoured a more flexible test which involves the balancing of a range of factors. The crucial passage of Lord Toulson's leading judgment is worth setting out in full:[6]

> I would say that one cannot judge whether allowing a claim which is in some way tainted by illegality would be contrary to the public interest, because it would be harmful to the

[1] B McLachlin, 'Weaving the Law's Seamless Web: Reflections on the Illegality Defence in Tort Law' in A Dyson, J Goudkamp and F Wilmot-Smith (eds), *Defences in Tort* (Oxford, Hart Publishing, 2015); J Goudkamp and L Mayr, 'The Doctrine of Illegality and Interference with Chattels' in A Dyson, J Goudkamp and F Wilmot-Smith (eds), *Defences in Tort* (Oxford, Hart Publishing, 2015); G Virgo, 'The Defence of Illegality in Unjust Enrichment' in A Dyson, J Goudkamp and F Wilmot-Smith (eds), *Defences in Unjust Enrichment* (Oxford, Hart Publishing, 2016); R Toulson, 'Illegality: Where Are We Now?' in A Dyson, J Goudkamp and F Wilmot-Smith (eds), *Defences in Contract* (Oxford, Hart Publishing, 2017).

[2] *Patel v Mirza* [2016] UKSC 42; [2016] 3 WLR 399.

[3] This chapter does not seek to rehash the well-worn debate between the 'reliance' principle and the 'balancing of factors' approach, and proceeds on the assumption that the latter will now become commonplace following *Patel v Mirza*.

[4] *Tinsley v Milligan* [1994] 1 AC 340.

[5] *Patel* (n 2) [114]; see also [134] (Lord Kerr). Lady Hale, Lord Kerr, Lord Wilson and Lord Hodge agreed with Lord Touslon. Lord Neuberger also ultimately endorsed Lord Toulson's approach: see [174]. Lord Clarke, Lord Mance and Lord Sumption took a different view, more sympathetic to *Tinsley v Milligan*.

[6] ibid [101] (Lord Toulson).

> integrity of the legal system, without a) considering the underlying purpose of the prohibition which has been transgressed, b) considering conversely any other relevant public policies which may be rendered ineffective or less effective by denial of the claim, and c) keeping in mind the possibility of overkill unless the law is applied with a due sense of proportionality. We are, after all, in the area of public policy.

The ramifications of *Patel v Mirza* clearly need to be understood. The case concerned the recovery of money paid under an illegal contract, but its impact cannot sensibly be limited to claims brought at common law. Although *Tinsley v Milligan* concerned a trusts dispute, which was a very different context from *Patel v Mirza*, it would take a very bold judge indeed to continue to apply *Tinsley v Milligan* in the face of *Patel v Mirza*. Admittedly, it is in many respects unsatisfactory for the Supreme Court to quasi-legislate across the whole of private law, given its inability to work out the potential impact in all affected areas when deciding one particular case.[7] Moreover, it does not appear that counsel on either side actually asked the Supreme Court to adopt an approach which balanced a 'range of factors' when deciding whether to apply the illegality defence, and that this step was taken of the Court's own volition.[8] Nevertheless, it is at least understandable why the Supreme Court decided to 'venture further'[9] and deal with the law of illegality more broadly than the narrow context of restitution: the law was a mess, strongly criticised,[10] and it was unlikely that a better opportunity would soon present itself to the Supreme Court to deal with the law concerning trusts, for example.[11] Before *Patel v Mirza*, lower court judges continued to feel constrained to apply *Tinsley* in the context of trusts.[12] In order to move away from that situation, the majority justices clearly intended that their favoured approach be applied broadly.

Patel v Mirza itself concerned a claim in unjust enrichment, and seems to make it easier for a briber to recover the value of a bribe from the bribee. This could conceivably affect the equitable jurisdiction to grant relief in the context of bribery and breach of fiduciary duty. Bribery is an important area of the law;[13] in *Patel v Mirza* Lord Toulson recognised that '[b]ribes of all kinds are odious and corrupting'.[14] It will be suggested in section II that it is doubtful whether bribers really should be able to recover their bribes, and in section III it will be argued that *Patel v Mirza* should not alter the right of a beneficiary to recover the bribe under a constructive trust, or affect the beneficiary's ability to bring personal claims against the briber or bribee. Claims brought against fiduciaries more generally will then be considered in

[7] This is why Lord Goff in *Tinsley v Milligan* called for legislative intervention after a full and broad investigation by the Law Commission: *Tinsley* (n 4) 364.

[8] *Patel* (n 2) [261] (Lord Sumption); *cf* [20] (Lord Toulson).

[9] ibid [166] (Lord Neuberger).

[10] See the comments of Gloster LJ in the Court of Appeal in *Patel v Mirza* [2014] EWCA Civ 1047; [2015] Ch 271, cited by Lord Toulson in the Supreme Court at [15].

[11] See *Patel* (n 2) [133] (Lord Kerr).

[12] *Hniazdzilau v Vajgel* [2016] EWHC 15 (Ch).

[13] *FHR European Ventures LLP v Mankarious* [2014] UKSC 45; [2015] AC 250 [42] (Lord Neuberger). For general discussion, see P Davies, 'Bribery' in P Davies and J Penner (eds), *Equity, Trusts and Commerce* (Oxford, Hart Publishing, 2017).

[14] *Patel* (n 2) [118].

section IV; most claims brought by a fiduciary against a principal should continue to be barred if pursuant to an illegal transaction. Finally, in section V some comments will be made about illegality in trusts disputes.[15] It now seems very unlikely that a claim to enforce a trust will be barred on the basis of illegality, unless, perhaps, the illegality is very serious indeed.[16]

II. THE DECISION IN *PATEL v MIRZA*

Mr Mirza was a city trader. Mr Patel transferred sums totalling £620,000 to Mirza. The money was to be used for betting on the price of RBS shares. Mirza expected to obtain insider information from contacts at RBS regarding an anticipated government announcement which would affect the price of the shares. In the end, the government announcement never materialised, and the money was never used for the purpose of the intended betting. However, Mirza refused to repay the money to Patel. The claim was framed in both contract and unjust enrichment.

Mirza sought to resist Patel's claim on the basis of illegality. The agreement between the parties amounted to a conspiracy to commit an offence of insider dealing under section 52 of the Criminal Justice Act 1993. Since both parties were tainted by this illegal scheme, Mirza argued that Patel could not enforce the contract, and that the claim in unjust enrichment should also fail: *in pari delicto potior est conditio defendentis*. Nevertheless, the Supreme Court unanimously held that Mirza had to repay the money to Patel.

Lord Toulson suggested that resort to Latin maxims in this area is often unhelpful,[17] and that there are in fact two broad policy factors which underpin the illegality defence.[18] The first is that a person should not profit from his illegal conduct. The second is that the law should be 'coherent and not self-defeating'.[19] Lord Toulson was greatly influenced by the work of the Law Commission in this area,[20] and concluded that '[t]he law should strive for the most desirable policy outcome, and it may be that it is best achieved by taking into account a range of factors'.[21] His Lordship emphasised the importance of identifying both the purpose of the relevant prohibition and any other public policies that might be affected, as well as a need for proportionality.[22]

Lord Toulson clearly thought that, taking these factors into account, Patel's claim for restitution should succeed. But it is not at all clear why this result was obviously correct. The judgment does not consider the purpose underpinning the law against

[15] This issue is dealt with more fully elsewhere: P Davies, 'Ramifications of *Patel v Mirza* in the Law of Trusts' in A Bogg and S Green (eds), *Illegality after Patel v Mirza* (Oxford, Hart Publishing, forthcoming).

[16] *Patel* (n 2) [110] (Lord Toulson); *cf* [254] (Lord Sumption).

[17] ibid [95]–[96] (Lord Toulson).

[18] ibid [99].

[19] ibid. See also *Hall v Hebert* [1993] 2 SCR 159 (SCC) 165.

[20] This is unsurprising, given that Lord Toulson was the Chair of the Law Commission for part of the very long lifetime of the Commission's project.

[21] *Patel* (n 2) [91].

[22] ibid [101].

insider trading, or how other public policies might be balanced on the facts of the case. It is somewhat unsatisfactory that the Supreme Court does not illustrate how its own test should be applied to the facts of the very case before it.[23] This is perhaps exacerbated by the impression that the Supreme Court's primary concern was to reform the illegality defence throughout private law. Yet effectively quasi-legislating in a very broad manner seems to be difficult for the Supreme Court to do on the basis of a single appeal.[24] The lack of clarity surrounding how the test applies to the facts of *Patel v Mirza* might give credence to the observation of Lord Clarke that the majority of the Supreme Court has come 'close to reviving the public conscience test'.[25] That test was favoured by the Court of Appeal in *Tinsley v Milligan*,[26] but was rejected by the House of Lords for being arbitrary and unpredictable.[27] It is striking that their Lordships in *Tinsley v Milligan* thought that primary legislation would be needed for a test based upon balancing various factors to be adopted,[28] whereas the Supreme Court in *Patel v Mirza* was much more bold. Over 20 years after the decision in *Tinsley v Milligan* that provoked such a long investigation by the Law Commission,[29] the Supreme Court in *Patel v Mirza* has reversed the House of Lords and in substance favoured the approach of the Court of Appeal.

In any event, the Supreme Court supported the view that parties should generally be restored to the position they were in before there was any illegality. For example, Lord Toulson said that 'a person who satisfies the ordinary requirements of a claim in unjust enrichment will not prima facie be debarred from recovering money paid or property transferred by reason of the fact that the consideration which has failed was an unlawful consideration'.[30] Similarly, Lord Neuberger said that 'the general rule should in my view be that the claimant is entitled to the return of the money which he has paid',[31] which was consistently referred as 'the Rule'.[32] The minority judges held similar views. Lord Sumption commented that restitution 'merely recognises the ineffectiveness of the transaction and gives effect to the ordinary legal consequences of that state of affairs. The effect is to put the parties in the position in which they would have been if they had never entered into the illegal transaction, which in the eyes of the law is the position which they should always have been in'.[33] Unfortunately, the minority judges employed the language of 'rescission' to describe

[23] ibid [107], Lord Toulson stating that '[p]otentially relevant factors include the seriousness of the conduct, its centrality to the contract, whether it was intentional and whether there was marked disparity in the parties' respective culpability', but did not clearly apply these to the facts of *Patel v Mirza*.

[24] Which seems unsatisfactory: see text to n 28.

[25] *Patel* (n 2) [219].

[26] *Tinsley v Milligan* [1992] Ch 310.

[27] *Tinsley* (n 4) 363 (Lord Goff).

[28] ibid 364 (Lord Goff).

[29] See Law Commission, *Illegal Transactions* Consultation Paper (Law Com No 154, 1999); Law Commission, *The Illegality Defence in Tort* Consultation Paper (Law Com No 160, 2001); Law Commission, *The Illegality Defence: A Consultative Report* Consultation Paper (Law Com No 189, 2009); Law Commission, *The Illegality Defence* Report (Law Com No 320, 2010).

[30] *Patel* (n 2) [116].

[31] ibid [146].

[32] ibid [176].

[33] ibid [250]; see also [199] (Lord Mance), [210] (Lord Clarke).

the process of restoring the parties to their original positions.[34] This is confusing. An illegal contract is void, so there is nothing to rescind. It is suggested that the judges were simply emphasising the primacy of the restitutionary remedy in order to restore the parties to the status quo ante through achieving *restitutio in integrum*.

However, Lord Kerr appeared to adopt a slightly different approach. His Lordship was influenced by Birks' contention that to allow restitution would 'stultify' the law's refusal to enforce the contract.[35] This may be because restitution would be tantamount to enforcing the contract,[36] or because the restitutionary claim would provide a 'safety net' in the event that the contract could not be enforced due to the illegality. Relying upon such an analysis,[37] Lord Kerr thought that returning the parties to the status quo ante should not necessarily be the prima facie rule. Instead, he preferred the balancing approach set out by Lord Toulson as better-equipped to achieve principled and just results. There is much force in Lord Kerr's analysis, but his views seem more cautious as regards restitution than Lord Toulson and are somewhat isolated given the tenor of all the other judgments.

The thrust of the reasoning in *Patel v Mirza* is to encourage the award of restitution. But it is unclear on what grounds restitution is justified. It had previously been understood that a transaction could, generally, only be unwound if the contract remained wholly unperformed,[38] but the very result in *Patel v Mirza* suggests that it no longer needs to be the case that the contract is wholly executory. Lord Toulson refers to 'failure of consideration', but, perhaps tellingly, not to *total* failure of consideration.[39] Indeed, Lord Neuberger thought it was 'not necessarily the correct analysis'[40] that 'the Rule' be explained on the ground of total failure of consideration, and that in any event 'the law should not regard an inherently criminal act as effective consideration'.[41] It would appear that the emphasis placed upon restoring the parties to their original positions is so strong that even if some shares had been bought with the money advanced by Patel to Mirza, restitution would still have been ordered.[42] Since restitution might be ordered even when the illegal contract has been fully executed,[43] the better view seems to be that the illegality itself justifies the practical response of the courts to put the parties—so far as it is possible to do so—back into their original positions before the illegal transaction.

Another consequence of *Patel v Mirza* seems to be to sideline the *locus poenitentiae*, or 'time for repentance'. After all, the balancing approach necessarily takes into account whether the illegal purpose has been fulfilled.[44] Moreover, in *Patel v Mirza*

[34] ibid [197]–[198] (Lord Mance), [210] (Lord Clarke), [253] (Lord Sumption).

[35] See P Birks, 'Recovering Value Transferred Under an Illegal Contract' (2000) 1 *Theoretical Inquiries in Law* 155.

[36] *cf Boissevain v Weil* [1950] AC 327.

[37] *Patel* (n 2) [141]–[142].

[38] See N Strauss, 'Ex turpi causa oritur actio?' (2016) 132 *LQR* 236, 258–59.

[39] *Patel* (n 2) [13].

[40] ibid [170].

[41] ibid [176].

[42] ibid [169] (Lord Neuberger).

[43] ibid [253] (Lord Sumption).

[44] ibid [44], [116] (Lord Toulson); see also [169] (Lord Neuberger); *cf* [202] (Lord Mance); [247]–[253] (Lord Sumption).

itself there was no withdrawal, let alone repentance, but simply a change of circumstances which meant that the illegal purpose could no longer be performed. If a claimant does genuinely withdraw before any illegal purpose is carried out then that further strengthens his or her claim to restitution, but even without such withdrawal it now appears to be highly likely that restitution will be granted anyway.

The major limitation on the ability to obtain restitution may be where the illegality is particularly serious. Lord Toulson gave the example of participation in a drug trafficking operation,[45] but recognised that such instances are likely to be 'rare'.[46] On the other hand, Lord Sumption stated that 'I would also reject the dicta, beginning with *Tappenden v Randall* (1801) 2 B&P 467, 470 and *Kearley v Thomson* (1890) 24 QBD 742, 747, to the effect that there may be some crimes so heinous that the courts will decline to award restitution in any circumstances'.[47] His Lordship thought it impossible to distinguish between degrees of illegality, and unnecessary to do so since restitution should presumptively always be available. It is of course true that distinguishing between different types of illegal conduct will often be very difficult to do, and it is not even clear why the offence of insider dealing was not thought by Lord Toulson to be particularly serious. Nevertheless, it may well be unsatisfactory to award restitution no matter the nature of the illegality, and regardless of whether or not the illegal conduct has occurred. These issues will be analysed in the next section when considering the particular context of bribery.

III. THE IMPACT OF *PATEL v MIRZA* ON BRIBERY

Bribery poses important and difficult problems, for both the criminal law and private law. In *FHR European Ventures LLP v Mankarious* Lord Neuberger said:[48]

> As Lord Templeman said giving the decision of the Privy Council in *Attorney General for Hong Kong v Reid* [1994] 1 AC 324, 330H, 'bribery is an evil practice which threatens the foundations of any civilised society'. Secret commissions are also objectionable as they inevitably tend to undermine trust in the commercial world. That has always been true, but concern about bribery and corruption generally has never been greater than it is now: see for instance, internationally, the OECD Convention on Combating Bribery of Foreign Public Officials in International Business Transactions 1999 and the United Nations Convention against Corruption 2003, and, nationally, the Bribery Acts 2010 and 2012.

However, there is still no recognised tort of bribery.[49] As a result, many claims tend to be brought in equity. After all, the recipient of a bribe is often induced to breach an obligation of loyalty, and courts tend to be flexible when finding that there has

[45] ibid [110].
[46] ibid [116].
[47] ibid [254]; see also [176] (Lord Neuberger). This has an impact on the hitman example, see text to nn 69–70.
[48] *FHR* (n 13) [42].
[49] K Handley, 'Civil Liability for Bribery (No 2)' (2001) 117 *LQR* 536; *cf* C Mitchell, 'Civil Liability for Bribery' (2001) 117 *LQR* 207. It is sometimes said that the fraud claim for loss suffered by a bribe is *sui generis*: *Petrograde Inc v Smith* [2000] Lloyd's Rep 486, 490 (Steel J).

been a 'fiduciary relationship' which facilitates the availability of gain-based relief against a bribee. For example, in *Reading v Attorney General*,[50] an army sergeant accepted bribes to ride on lorries in full military uniform. The sergeant suspected that the lorries were used to transport drugs, and that his presence was designed to facilitate this. It was held that the sergeant acted in breach of fiduciary duty and had to account for the profits he made. In the House of Lords, Lord Porter agreed[51] with Asquith LJ's observation in the Court of Appeal[52]

> that the words 'fiduciary relationship' in this setting are used in a wide and loose sense and include, inter alia, a case where the servant gains from his employment a position of authority which enables him to obtain the sum which he receives.

The breadth of the equitable jurisdiction is able to offer strong protection to the vulnerable beneficiary whose fiduciary has acted disloyally as a result of bribery. The beneficiary may be able to sue the fiduciary either for the personal remedies of an account of profits or equitable compensation, or for a proprietary remedy on the basis that the fiduciary holds the bribe on constructive trust.[53] The beneficiary may also be able to sue the briber for dishonestly assisting a breach of trust, which could lead either to an award of compensation or an account of profits.[54] The beneficiary may even be able to combine claims against both the briber and the bribee.[55]

The remedies available to the beneficiary are discussed more fully elsewhere.[56] But whilst the beneficiary may have a claim against the briber in one direction, and the bribee in another, what about the remaining side of the triangle between the briber and bribee? It was previously thought that the briber could not recover the bribe. After all, as Lawrence Collins J noted in *Daraydan Holdings Ltd v Solland International Ltd*, bribery 'corrupts not only the recipient but the giver of the bribe'.[57] As a result, it was generally thought that both parties were equally tainted, and that the *in pari delicto* rule meant that the briber could not recover anything from the bribee. Yet if *Patel v Mirza* is understood to lay down a general desire to restore the parties to the status quo ante, then that may no longer be true. However, *Patel v Mirza* dealt with a relatively simple two-party situation; it is suggested that the same sort of reasoning should not readily be applied where the bribee is a fiduciary, since the interests of a third party, the beneficiary, should be taken into account.

Before *Patel v Mirza*, a leading decision that was taken to govern similar claims was *Parkinson v College of Ambulance Ltd*.[58] The secretary of the defendant charity, Harrison, told the claimant, Parkinson, that either he or the charity had

[50] *Reading v Attorney General* [1951] AC 507. See also *University of Nottingham v Fishel* [2000] ICR 1462.

[51] *Reading* (n 50) 517.

[52] *Reading v Attorney General* [1949] 2 KB 232, 236 (Asquith LJ).

[53] *FHR* (n 13).

[54] *Novoship (UK) Ltd v Mikhaylyuk* [2014] EWCA Civ 908; [2015] QB 499.

[55] See *Salford v Lever* [1891] 1 QB 168 (CA); *cf Mahesan S/O Thambiah Appellant v Malaysia Government Officers' Co-Operative Housing Society Ltd* [1979] AC 374 (PC).

[56] Davies (n 13).

[57] *Daraydan Holdings Ltd v Solland International Ltd* [2004] EWHC 622 (Ch); [2005] Ch 119 [1].

[58] *Parkinson v College of Ambulance Ltd* [1925] 2 KB 1.

the power to nominate people for honours, and that in return for a large donation Parkinson could expect to receive a knighthood. Parkinson did indeed make a sizeable donation, but did not receive a knighthood. He later sued both Harrison and the charity for the return of the money either on the basis of deceit, or money had and received. The contractual claim was obviously hopeless because it is unlawful to undertake that an honour will be conferred by the Sovereign in return for money or services.[59] Lush J was clear that both Parkinson and Harrison knew that the contract was illegal.[60] As a result both were *in pari delicto,* and the fact that Harrison had made fraudulent representations did not affect this conclusion. The claim in deceit therefore failed, as did the claim in unjust enrichment. Lush J held that Parkinson could not invoke the *locus poenitentiae* because he had not really resiled from the contract at all, but was instead bringing his action because he had failed to obtain the promised title.[61] Even if that were not the case, Lush J found that restitution could not be awarded simply because the contract was executory.[62]

It is suggested that the decision in *Parkinson v College of Ambulance Ltd* is both principled and appropriate. It fits better with the idea of 'stultification'[63] discussed above,[64] and also seems more likely to deter illegal activities. If Parkinson had been able to recover the money, then he may have been encouraged to try again to buy a knighthood through a different party. This does not sit entirely easily with a general principle of 'buyer beware', where the risk lies with the person paying. It would be better to deter people from paying over money in the first place. If Parkinson knew that the charity could keep the money regardless of whether or not a knighthood was bestowed upon him, then it would seem foolish for Parkinson to go ahead with the transaction anyway: there would be little incentive for the charity to try to obtain a knighthood for Parkinson. Parkinson should be deterred from entering into a very bad, and illegal, deal. If determining whether it would be better to deter a party from paying money over, or from asking for money, it is surely better to deter the actual payment—at least where neither party is vulnerable to the other.[65] Furthermore, if the money is not returned then it remains amenable to confiscation under the Proceeds of Crime Act 2002.[66]

However, *Parkinson v College of Ambulance* now seems to be wrongly decided. In *Patel v Mirza* Lord Toulson said '[i]f today it transpired that a bribe had been paid to a political party, a charity or a holder of public office, it might be regarded it [*sic*] as more repugnant to the public interest that the recipient should keep it than that it should be returned'.[67] His Lordship thought that the Supreme Court was 'not directly concerned with such a case' but the emphasis placed on restitution

[59] ibid 13.
[60] ibid 15.
[61] ibid 16.
[62] ibid.
[63] See text to n 35.
[64] Although, arguably, arguments that seek to avoid stultification may be better accommodated through confiscation of illegal gains: see below.
[65] *cf Kiriri Cotton Co Ltd v Dewani* [1960] AC 192 (PC).
[66] See text to nn 72–77.
[67] *Patel* (n 2) [118].

makes it difficult to see how the judgment of Lush J in *Parkinson* can be consistent with the decision in *Patel v Mirza*. Lord Neuberger was clear that *Parkinson v College of Ambulance* was 'wrongly decided'.[68] Indeed, Lord Neuberger[69] and Lord Sumption[70] even thought that a person who hires a hitman to commit murder would be able to recover the money paid to the hitman (regardless of whether the murder actually takes place!), which seems a much stronger case than *Parkinson v College of Ambulance*. It is difficult to accept that this result is satisfactory, or sits easily with a general principle of 'buyer beware'.

Virgo has argued that deterrence is an unsatisfactory basis to deny restitution.[71] This is for three principal reasons, although in the context of bribery none is ultimately compelling. First, a claimant may not know that the transaction is illegal; this is unlikely to apply to instances of bribery. Secondly, the defendant may be encouraged to participate in the transaction if restitution is denied. Although it is true that the defendant would be deterred by granting restitution, it has been suggested above that prevention is better than cure and the law should primarily seek to deter parties from paying over bribes. Thirdly, Virgo argues that if the illegal conduct also constitutes a crime, then if the parties have not been deterred by the criminal law, then the private law is unlikely to be an effective deterrent. This is not clear. It may be that the parties take the view that the criminal sanctions would not have as severe consequences as a civil claim, and that the chances of a criminal prosecution being brought are slim—perhaps because of a lack of resources. It is very difficult to detect certain types of illegal behaviour, such that the parties themselves may be the most likely candidates to disclose the illegality. This is a bit odd, but obviously does happen. In both *Parkinson v College of Ambulance* and *Patel v Mirza*, for example, it is striking that these claims were brought despite revealing the illegal conduct and potentially exposing the claimants (and defendants) to criminal charges.

All this suggests that it is not as clear as the Supreme Court appeared to think that a person should make restitution of money received under an illegal transaction. This may be especially significant where the recipient of a bribe is a fiduciary. It is suggested that it would be unsatisfactory for the approach of *Patel v Mirza* to mean that a fiduciary should have to make restitution to the briber, to the detriment of the beneficiary. After all, it is already difficult enough for beneficiaries to discover fraud or instances of bribery; if beneficiaries do manage to establish an available claim, it is to be hoped that a meaningful remedy will be available. But a fiduciary should not be mulcted twice over; if the fiduciary has already restored the briber to the position he or she was in prior to the illegal transaction, then the fiduciary may be able to argue that he or she is unable also to satisfy the beneficiary's claim (beyond, perhaps, compensation for losses shown to have been caused by the breach of fiduciary duty). However, that result would be unfortunate, and a number of responses to *Patel v Mirza* might be made in order to avoid that outcome.

[68] ibid [170].
[69] ibid [176].
[70] ibid [254].
[71] Virgo, 'The Defence of Illegality in Unjust Enrichment' (n 1) 174.

First, and least likely, *Parkinson v College of Ambulance* could be maintained in instances of bribery. Lord Toulson did say that the Supreme Court in *Patel v Mirza* was not 'directly concerned' with such a case, and perhaps this could be exploited to restore a rule that fiduciaries who accept bribes do not have to make restitution. In such a scenario, beneficiaries' claims would be able to proceed as they always have done. However, as suggested above, it is difficult to see how such a stark rule would be consistent with the general tenor of the judgment in *Patel v Mirza*.

Secondly, bribery might be thought to raise particular concerns because the bribe itself could be confiscated as the proceeds of crime.[72] Giving and receiving a bribe is a criminal offence,[73] as is continuing to have possession of a bribe which is criminal property.[74] Where a criminal offence has been established, then it is possible for the State to bring a claim to confiscate the bribe.[75] The general rule is that '[i]f ... the court is satisfied that any property is recoverable, the court must make a recovery order'.[76] This is mandatory: it follows that a confiscation order must be made when the fiduciary has committed the criminal offence of bribery under section 2 of the Bribery Act 2010. This should therefore take priority over both the claims of the principal and the briber.[77] The coherent operation of the Proceeds of Crime Act 2002 should not be disturbed by the approach to the illegality defence advanced in *Patel v Mirza*.[78] However, the National Crime Agency lacks the resources to seek confiscation of all proceeds of crime, and civil courts are unlikely to change their approach just because confiscation proceedings *might* be brought in the future. Indeed, it would appear that the money paid over in *Patel v Mirza* itself was amenable to confiscation, yet restitution was nevertheless ordered. Bribery was not viewed by Lord Toulson as especially serious, and certainly not in the same bracket as drug trafficking such that restitution should not be awarded.

The next three possibilities are perhaps more promising. Thirdly, it might be argued that fiduciaries are in a special position because of the obligation of loyalty owed to a third party, the beneficiary. This may be one of the factors that the court should consider. Lord Toulson was careful 'not [to] attempt to lay down a prescriptive or definitive list'[79] of the factors to be taken into account, and as a result the position of the recipient of the bribe could well remain relevant. This would also help to protect the beneficiary's position.

A fourth possibility might be to conclude that the fiduciary is not enriched if the fiduciary holds the bribe for the benefit of the principal. Indeed, one reason for the decision in *FHR* that a fiduciary holds a bribe on constructive trust for his or her

[72] Admittedly, where there has been an illegal transaction then there may often be gains which could be confiscated.

[73] Bribery Act 2010, s 2.

[74] Proceeds of Crime Act 2002, s 329(1)(c).

[75] ibid Part 5.

[76] ibid s 266(1).

[77] For further discussion of the relationship between confiscation and other private law claims, see Davies (n 13) 229–232.

[78] *Patel* (n 2) [108] (Lord Toulson), [185] (Lord Neuberger), [254] (Lord Sumption). Lord Mance was more circumspect: [198].

[79] ibid [107].

principal was the need to combat bribery effectively.[80] Since the beneficial interest in the bribe resides in the principal from the moment of receipt, it is arguable that the fiduciary is not enriched such that no claim in unjust enrichment should lie.[81] Moreover, a claim brought by the briber against the beneficiary in unjust enrichment should fail since there is a good basis for the beneficiary's enrichment provided by the nature of the fiduciary relationship.

A further, fifth option may be to look at the three-party situation differently. Although the Supreme Court in *Patel v Mirza* rejected the notion that the court had a free-standing jurisdiction to punish the parties to an illegal transaction by requiring disgorgement to a third party,[82] this principle would not be infringed simply by recognising the beneficiary's equitable proprietary rights. In order to favour the beneficiary's claim the court would not have to disgorge the recipient's profits in favour of a third party extraneous to the dispute. Rather, the court could give effect to the proprietary rights acquired by the beneficiary on the point of receipt,[83] and find that such rights outweigh the interest in restoring two parties—who are both tainted by illegality—to their respective original positions. Given the wide range of considerations that might be relevant to the balancing approach when deciding whether the illegality defence applies, it is suggested that this is a likely outcome. There is no need to deter the beneficiary, who has done nothing wrong, but every reason to seek to deter the conduct of both the briber and bribee. It would be unfortunate if a desire to unwind a transaction were to prejudice an innocent beneficiary to the advantage of a party tainted by illegality.

It is, however, possible to envisage situations where the fiduciary makes restitution to the briber before the beneficiary becomes aware of the bribe. Given the decision in *Patel v Mirza*, a fiduciary might genuinely think that restitution would be necessary. But it is suggested that this should not be encouraged or condoned. Since a constructive trust in favour of the beneficiary arises at the moment the fiduciary receives the bribe, paying back the bribe can be viewed as a breach of trust. It is suggested that the fiduciary should remain liable to account to the beneficiary, and that the beneficiary may be able to trace his or her equitable interest into the hands of the briber to whom restitution has been made.

IV. BREACH OF FIDUCIARY DUTY: BEYOND BRIBERY

The illegality defence does not play a prominent role in claims for breach of fiduciary duty beyond the context of bribes and secret commissions. It has been said that

[80] *FHR* (n 13) [42].

[81] See *Challinor v Bellis* [2015] EWCA Civ 59 [113] (Briggs LJ). This has been criticised as 'confusing the factual and legal interpretations of enrichment': G Virgo, *The Principles of the Law of Restitution* 3rd edn (Oxford, OUP, 2016) 73. But it is suggested that there is no confusion, and indeed a similar approach has been maintained in cases concerning freezing orders: see *Federal Bank of the Middle East Ltd v Hadkinson* [2000] 1 WLR 1695; *Lakatamia Shipping Co Ltd v Su* [2014] EWCA Civ 636; [2014] C P Rep 37.

[82] *cf Nelson v Nelson* [1995] HCA 25; (1995) 184 CLR 538.

[83] *FHR* (n 13) [36]–[47]. See also P Millett, 'Bribes and Secret Commissions Again' [2012] *CLJ* 583.

even where a fiduciary pleads illegality to try to defeat a claim brought by his or her principal for breach of duty, the illegality should not, generally, bar the claim since it would be unconscionable for the fiduciary to be better off as a result of the breach of duty.[84] This is sensible. It is, however, less clear whether, as a result of *Patel v Mirza*, a fiduciary may now be able to bring a claim in unjust enrichment against his or her principal, even though the parties both participated in an illegal scheme.

In *Re Thomas*,[85] a principal handed over money to his solicitor to be used for conducting certain litigation. The principal later sought to obtain an account from the solicitor and a taxation of his bill of costs. The solicitor sought to resist the claim on the basis that the money had come from illegal agreements. That defence failed. The Court of Appeal was adamant that an officer of the court could not rely on such illegality to protect himself. Lindley LJ pointedly asked:

> Is every rascally solicitor to invoke his own rascality as a ground of immunity from the jurisdiction of the Court? Or is the Court to listen to a solicitor who, after acting for and advising his client and taking his money, is mean enough to denounce him and set up the illegality of the client's conduct as a reason why the Court should not call its own officer to account?[86]

Clearly not. A court could not allow a fiduciary to act in such a reprehensible manner.

In *Harse v Pearl Life Assurance*[87] a claimant paid insurance premiums under a policy that was assumed to be illegal. The defendant insurer had made innocent misrepresentations to induce the claimant to take out the policy, but the court nonetheless held that the claimant could not recover the value of the premiums since the parties were *in pari delicto*. The outcome of the case may now be different following *Patel v Mirza*. However, Collins MR was clear that if the claimant had been able to establish a 'difference in the position of the parties which created a fiduciary relationship to the [claimant] so as to make it inequitable for the defendants to insist on the bargain that they had made with the [claimant]',[88] then the claimant would have been able to obtain restitution. Where the defendant abuses a fiduciary relationship with the principal then he or she should not be able to invoke the illegality defence to resist a restitutionary claim.[89]

But what if it is the fiduciary who seeks restitution? The answer to this question is not clear. In *Wild v Simpson*[90] a solicitor entered into an illegal agreement with a client. The client promised to pay to the solicitor a percentage of certain sums he recovered. The client successfully recovered various monies, and the solicitor brought a claim for his costs. The claim failed: the agreement between the parties was illegal, and the solicitor could not bring a claim against the client. The outcome

[84] J Heydon, M Leeming, P Turner, *Meagher, Gummow & Lehane's Equity: Doctrines & Remedies* 5th edn (Sydney, LexisNexis, 2014) [5-305].

[85] *Re Thomas* [1894] 1 QB 747.

[86] ibid 749.

[87] *Harse v Pearl Life Assurance* [1904] 1 KB 558.

[88] ibid 563.

[89] Unless, perhaps, the illegality is very serious indeed: see text to nn 45–47.

[90] *Wild v Simpson* [1919] 2 KB 544 (CA).

has been criticised as unfair,[91] since the solicitor was not seeking to enforce the illegal contract and recover a percentage of the client's money, but only to recover the value of the work the solicitor provided in a restitutionary claim. Such criticisms perhaps chime well with the emphasis placed upon the availability of restitution by the Supreme Court in *Patel v Mirza*, and it may be that *Wild v Simpson* could now be decided differently. However, it is suggested that since the enrichment of the defendant consisted of services rendered, rather than money received (as in *Patel v Mirza*), it is harder to achieve *restitutio in integrum*. Moreover, there are good reasons why a fiduciary (the stronger party) should not be able to bring a claim against his or her principal (the vulnerable party) once the parties have entered into an illegal arrangement. After all, the principal should be able to place trust and confidence in the fiduciary, and in order to hold fiduciaries up to higher standards the courts may well continue to be reluctant to allow fiduciaries even a restitutionary remedy in circumstances such as those in *Wild v Simpson*.

V. ILLEGALITY AND TRUSTS[92]

Patel v Mirza purports to set down an approach to illegality throughout the private law. As a result, even in the context of trusts disputes it is to be expected that courts will balance various factors when deciding whether the illegality defence should apply. This is a very different approach from that favoured in *Tinsley v Milligan*, but will often lead to the same results.[93] Moreover, it is possible to exaggerate the importance of the illegality defence in the context of trusts: in its 'Impact Assessment for Reforming the Law of Illegality in Trusts' in 2010, the Law Commission was only able to identify 19 reported cases in the previous 9 years.[94]

It is important to remember that *Patel v Mirza* was not a trusts case, and that Lord Sumption's warning that the majority's approach could lead to 'unforeseen and undesirable collateral consequences'[95] might be particularly prescient where third-party rights are involved. The emphasis placed upon restitution throughout *Patel v Mirza* does not fit very well with many trusts cases. For example, in *Tinsley v Milligan* itself Miss Milligan's ability to enforce a beneficial share in the property did not reverse any illegality.[96] Instead, the decision of the House of Lords gave effect to the illegal scheme: Miss Milligan was able to hide her beneficial interest so that she could fraudulently claim benefits from the Department of Social Security. It was impossible to restore Miss Milligan and Miss Tinsley to any status quo ante, since the property in question could not be returned to the original vendors.

91 Virgo, 'The Defence of Illegality in Unjust Enrichment' (n 1) 172.

92 This section draws upon a more extensive analysis of these issues in Davies (n 15).

93 In *Patel v Mirza*, the only trusts case which the Supreme Court identified that should now be decided differently is *Collier v Collier* [2002] EWCA Civ 1095; [2002] BPIR 1057, discussed at text to n 101.

94 Law Commission, *The Illegality Defence* Report (n 29) 80.

95 *Patel* (n 2) [226]; see also [165] (Lord Neuberger).

96 Compare [201] (Lord Mance); for criticism see [135]–[136] (Lord Kerr). For further discussion of this case, see Nicholas McBride, ch 13 in this volume.

Nevertheless, the outcome in *Tinsley v Milligan* would be the same after *Patel v Mirza*; the Supreme Court Justices were clear that any other result would be 'disproportionate'.[97] Similarly, unwinding the transaction in *Tribe v Tribe*,[98] where a father transferred shares to his son to conceal them from his creditors, would still occur following *Patel v Mirza*, even if some of the illegal purpose had in fact been performed.[99] It is interesting to note that these cases of intentional fraud do not seem to be treated as involving illegal conduct of a particularly serious nature,[100] even though conspiracy to defraud may be punished with a custodial sentence of up to 10 years.

One case that would be decided differently after *Patel v Mirza* is *Collier v Collier*.[101] The Law Commission observed that '[t]he facts of the case were complex and hard to discern, the judge concluding that both parties had lied to the court'.[102] Essentially, a father, who owned the freehold to two properties, gave his daughter a lease over both premises, together with an option to purchase the freehold at a later date. The purpose of this transaction was to deceive the father's creditors and the Inland Revenue; the father intended to continue to control both properties. Aldous and Chadwick LJJ held that the grant of the leases had not been by way of gift, because of the requirement that the daughter pay rent and a sum of money to exercise the option, so the presumption of advancement did not apply. Mance LJ, on the other hand, thought that the leases were shams and the presumption of advancement did apply. All three judges agreed that, if the presumption of advancement did apply, then it could not be rebutted by the father because of *Tinsley v Milligan*. That reasoning would no longer be followed, and it seems likely that if the transfer had been gratuitous then the father would now be able to establish a beneficial interest under a resulting trust.

The father also argued that there was an express trust in his favour. Chadwick LJ rejected this claim due to a lack of evidence; Aldous LJ held that any agreement included illegal terms and so could not be relied upon; Mance LJ thought that the father would have to rely on the proof of the purpose of their agreement, which was not allowed. Yet had the father been able to produce a simple document recording the express trust, then this would have been sufficient to establish a trust without leading any evidence of illegality. It is clearly unsatisfactory for the outcome of cases to depend upon whether an 'untainted' document can be produced as an 'objective fact', and the distinction drawn between relying upon an agreement and relying upon a neutral fact seems to be very fine indeed. The outcome of the case is, *prima facie*, that the daughter is rewarded for her duplicitous behaviour.[103] As the Law

[97] *Patel* (n 2) [112] (Lord Toulson), [181] (Lord Neuberger).
[98] *Tribe v Tribe* [1996] Ch 107.
[99] *Patel* (n 2) [171].
[100] See also *Silverwood v Silverwood* (1997) 74 P & CR 453.
[101] *Collier* (n 93).
[102] Law Commission, *The Illegality Defence: A Consultative Report* Consultation Paper (n 29) para 6.41.
[103] Lord Mance called the decision 'unsatisfying', having been reluctant to reach that result in *Collier v Collier* itself: *Patel* (n 2) [105]–[106], [187].

Commission noted, 'it seems nonsensical that the courts might decide the outcome of the case by looking at selective pieces of the relevant evidence'.[104] Happily, *Patel v Mirza* suggests a different outcome would now be reached.[105] The court would take into account the purpose of the prohibition and a sense of proportionality, such that the father would now be able to claim an interest under a trust.

Patel v Mirza will also affect the law concerning constructive trusts, or at least common intention constructive trusts. In *Tinsley v Milligan*, Lord Browne-Wilkinson thought that the same result should be reached regardless of whether the claim is brought for a beneficial interest under a resulting trust or under a common intention constructive trust.[106] This view received some support from the Court of Appeal[107] prior to *Patel v Mirza*, but in some situations it would have been difficult to establish any agreement sufficient for a 'common intention' without leading evidence of illegality.[108] Following *Patel v Mirza*, such a formalistic approach is not required: courts can look at all the evidence and decide whether a party should be prevented from enforcing a beneficial interest due to the illegality.[109] It is now even less likely that a party will be unable to claim a beneficial interest under a common intention constructive trust because of an illegal transaction.

It is suggested that, after *Patel v Mirza*, participation in an illegal transaction will prevent a claimant from enforcing a beneficial interest under a trust only in very unusual and rare circumstances. It is likely that the illegality will have to be particularly serious (such as terrorism offences).[110] Yet it is difficult to state definitively what outcomes will be reached, since an approach involving the balancing of various relevant factors is inherently somewhat uncertain.

Lord Toulson was highly influenced by the work of the Law Commission on illegality, but it should be remembered that the law of trusts was the one area where the Law Commission recommended statutory reform.[111] Admittedly, this was largely because the Commission did not think it likely that *Tinsley v Milligan* would be departed from judicially, but the Commission was perhaps also influenced by many responses to its consultations which emphasised the need for certainty in the context of property rights.[112] Lord Toulson thought that 'people contemplating unlawful activity' do not perhaps 'deserve' that the law be entirely certain.[113] But where the claim in a trust dispute concerns third parties, such reasoning is obviously weakened.

[104] Law Commission, *The Illegality Defence: A Consultative Report* Consultation Paper (n 29) para 6.51.

[105] 'It is I think now accepted on all sides that, if *Collier v Collier* [2002] BPIR 1057 came before the courts today it would be decided differently': *Patel* (n 2) [221] (Lord Clarke).

[106] *Tinsley* (n 4) 376.

[107] *O'Kelly v Davies* [2014] EWCA Civ 1606; [2015] 1 WLR 2725.

[108] *Barrett v Barrett* [2008] EWHC 1061 (Ch); [2008] BPIR 817.

[109] And this may include considerations of remoteness: *Q v Q* [2008] EWHC 1874 (Fam); [2009] 1 FLR 935 [137] (Black J).

[110] *cf Tinsley* (n 4) 362 (Lord Goff).

[111] See the Draft Trusts (Concealment of Interests) Bill attached to Law Commission, *The Illegality Defence* Report (n 29).

[112] See Law Commission, *The Illegality Defence: A Consultative Report* Consultation Paper (n 29) paras 6.87–6.88; Law Commission, *The Illegality Defence* Report (n 29) para 3.46.

[113] *Patel* (n 2) [113]; see also [137] (Lord Kerr).

As Lord Neuberger rightly observed, innocent third parties are entitled to expect the law to be clear, and 'there is a general public interest in certainty and clarity in all areas of law'.[114]

It remains unclear what the effect of illegality should be upon third parties to the trust.[115] For example, the claimant may not be a tainted beneficiary, but instead the beneficiary's creditor[116] or executor.[117] The more flexible approach adopted by the Supreme Court in *Patel v Mirza*, and the desire to reach more transparently just outcomes, might suggest that the claims of an innocent creditor or executor should trump the claims of a defendant tainted by illegality.[118] Indeed, given the support extended to Lord Browne-Wilkinson's view in *Tinsley v Milligan* that the effect of illegality is procedural rather than substantive,[119] it seems possible for a court to say that whilst a beneficiary cannot personally enforce his or her rights due to the illegality defence, creditors or executors suing through the beneficiary may be able to.

It is also to be hoped that one factor to be taken account should be that the intended 'victim' of the concealment may have an interest in the value of the assets of the beneficiary.[120] The Law Commission gave the example of a husband who may transfer property to his mistress in order to hide it from his wife. If a dispute were to arise between the husband and mistress over the ownership of the property, the court should be able to take into account the possibility that the wife might in the future bring a claim against her husband under the Matrimonial Causes Act 1973, and that the value of the wife's possible claim could be reduced if the court were to decide that the husband did not in fact have an interest under a trust in the property transferred to the mistress because of the illegality defence.

One issue that remains unclear is what consequences should follow if a trust is unenforceable as a result of illegality. The Law Commission's Draft Bill thought that there were four options regarding who should be entitled to the equitable interest: (i) the beneficiary;[121] (ii) the trustee;[122] (iii) the settlor;[123] and (iv) another beneficiary under the same trust.[124] The Law Commission concluded that these options were mutually exclusive, and that the illegality defence should operate in an all-or-nothing manner.[125] This is consistent with a traditional approach to the doctrine, but it is interesting to speculate whether the more flexible approach favoured in *Patel v Mirza* might have an impact upon the remedies awarded as well. It may be that an

[114] ibid [158]; see also [263] (Lord Sumption).

[115] The Law Commission accepted that 'the position is simply not clear': Law Commission, *The Illegality Defence: A Consultative Report* Consultation Paper (n 29) para 6.65.

[116] See the discussion of Mance LJ in *Collier* (n 93).

[117] See *Silverwood* (n 100).

[118] *cf Stone & Rolls Ltd v Moore Stephens* [2009] UKHL 39; [2009] 3 WLR 455; criticised in *Bilta (UK) Ltd v Nazir* [2015] UKSC 23; [2016] AC 1.

[119] *Tinsley* (n 4) 374, cited in *Patel* (n 2) [20] (Lord Toulson), [193] (Lord Mance).

[120] Draft Trusts (Concealment of Interests) Bill, Clause 5(1)(f).

[121] The default position: see ibid Clause 3(1).

[122] ibid Clause 4(4)(a).

[123] ibid Clause 4(4)(b).

[124] ibid Clause 4(4)(c).

[125] ibid Clause 4(3)(a), although if a particular class contains more than one party, then the interest can be split between those parties: ibid Clause 4(3)(b).

all-or-nothing approach is too inflexible, just as the reliance principle in *Tinsley* has been recognised as too inflexible, and that in some instances the court might have a discretion to split property between the settlor and beneficiary, for example.[126]

VI. CONCLUSION

Patel v Mirza is a significant decision that is bound to have an impact upon the operation of the illegality defence in every area of private law. It is to be hoped that an approach which requires a range of factors to be balanced will lead to more transparent reasoning. But it is difficult to predict how the court's discretion will be exercised.[127] Of course, under *Tinsley v Milligan* the 'reliance principle' had proved to be sufficiently malleable to undermine commercial certainty as well, but the prospect of successfully appealing against the decision of a trial judge now appears to be very remote indeed. Unless a judge has taken into account irrelevant factors, or failed to take into account clearly relevant factors, then it should be very difficult to appeal on the basis that the judge weighed those factors incorrectly. A trial judge who has heard all the evidence is in the best position to exercise a discretion in this area.

In any event, *Patel v Mirza* suggests that, as a general rule, it is only in instances of serious illegality that a claim seeking to restore the parties to the status quo ante will be barred. Yet this will not inevitably lead to satisfactory results. In particular, where a fiduciary has been bribed to act disloyally towards his or her principal, the parties should not simply be restored to their status quo ante, and the position of the principal should be protected. Indeed, courts should be wary about awarding restitution to a briber in all circumstances. It is clear that the task of the courts in applying the illegality defence in equity remains far from easy.

[126] *cf Taylor v Bhail* [1996] CLC 377, CA, 383 (Millett LJ).

[127] Lord Neuberger thought that the majority's approach 'is not akin in practice to a discretion', but in substance it is suggested that judges do have a wide discretion regarding the effect of illegality: *Patel* (n 2) [175].

13

The Future of Clean Hands

NICHOLAS J McBRIDE

DOES THE EQUITABLE defence of clean hands[1] have a future? Some might think not, arguing that it should be swallowed up by the defence of illegality. In this chapter, I argue that this would be a mistake: the defence of clean hands can be seen as having a distinctive role to play in future in determining whether there are grounds for withholding from the claimant what I will call a *supererogatory remedy*.

I. CURRENT SCOPE

Let's begin by sketching out the current scope of the defence of clean hands. The defence is, in theory, available whenever a claimant (C) seeks an equitable remedy against a defendant (D) but C's past behaviour is such that it would be inequitable to grant him that remedy. In order for this to be made out it has to be shown that C's behaviour was both (i) improper, and (ii) bears 'an immediate and necessary relation to the equity sued for'.[2]

Zechariah Chafee identified 16 cases where the maxim 'he who comes to equity must do so with clean hands'[3] might be relevant;[4] but we can confine ourselves to four:

(1) Cases where C seeks to prevent D from violating a *legal* right of C's. Examples would be where C seeks an injunction against D's committing a private

[1] Some might prefer '*un*clean hands' but 'clean hands' is less of a mouthful.

[2] *Dering v Earl of Winchelsea* (1787) 1 Cox 318, 319; 29 ER 1184 (Eyre LCB).

[3] A maxim which R Francis, *Maxims of Equity* (London, 1727) is generally credited with coining.

[4] Z Chafee, 'Coming Into Equity With Clean Hands' (1949) 47 *Michigan Law Review* 877 and 1065. Chafee actually identified 18 cases, but I disregard his eighth case ('Miscellaneous tort suits by person charged with crime') as clean hands are *not* relevant in that kind of case, and his eighteenth case ('Miscellaneous proceedings in equity'), which Chafee himself does not discuss. All of Chafee's other 16 cases can be sorted into the four different categories identified in the text, as follows (with Chafee's numbering shown in bold): **1** (suits to enforce illegal or immoral trusts) fall into categories (2) or (3), depending on the facts of the case; **2** (suits to undo deeds for fraud or mistake), **4** (suits to undo an executory transaction arising out of wrongful conduct) and **5** (suits to remove cloud on title) fall into category (4); **3** (suits to undo completed transactions in fraud of creditors) and **15** (matrimonial litigation) fall into categories (3) or (4) depending on the facts of the case; **6** (suits for specific performance of contract), **9** (suits to protect copyright), **10** (patent suits), **11** (suits to protect trade marks), **12** (labour litigation) and **13** (suits

nuisance, or where C seeks an order of specific performance, compelling D to perform a contract that he has with C.

(2) Cases where C seeks to prevent D from violating an *equitable* right of C's.

(3) Cases where C seeks to be granted some kind of equitable right against D. An example would be where C seeks to establish that she has an equitable charge over, or trust interest in, D's property.

(4) Cases where C seeks the assistance of equity to divest D of some right that D would otherwise normally have. Examples would be where C seeks to rescind (in equity) a contract that she has with D, thereby depriving D of the legal right to enforce that contract, or where C asks a court to award her a freezing order over a bank account of D's, thereby depriving D of the legal right to draw on that bank account.

The fact that C has acted unlawfully—which, for the purposes of this chapter, I will identify with breaching some kind of legal or equitable duty (whether or not that breach also amounts to a crime)—will, of course, potentially bring C within the reach of the clean hands maxim. But it is not necessary for C to have acted unlawfully for the courts to conclude that C's hands are too dirty for her to be granted some kind of equitable remedy. For example, in *Falcke v Gray*,[5] specific performance of a contract to sell two Chinese vases was denied on the basis that the price the claimant had agreed to pay for the vases (£40) was far below their real value (£200) and the claimant had known that when he struck the deal to purchase them. While 'clean hands' was never mentioned in the case, Kindersley V-C as much as admitted that was the basis of the denial of the claimant's claim for specific performance when he observed that 'this Court is not a court of honour, but it appears to me that, although Mr Falcke had done nothing he was legally bound not to do, yet, consistently with the authorities and the justice of the case, I must refuse specific performance'.[6]

'Clean hands' *was* mentioned in *Quadrant Visual Communications Ltd v Hutchison Telephone (UK)*,[7] where the claimants sought an order of specific performance of a contract that they had entered into with the defendants to sell their telephone company to the defendants. The price payable under the contract was dependent on the number of subscribers that the telephone company had; the more subscribers, the greater the price. Without telling the defendants they were doing so, the claimants launched a marketing campaign to increase the number

to enjoy torts of various kinds) fall into category (1); **14** (suits to enforce building restrictions and other equitable servitudes) falls into category (2); **16** (suits concerning corporate and stock transactions) falls into categories (2) or (3), depending on the facts of the case; and **17** (suits for contribution or subrogation) falls into category (3).

[5] *Falcke v Gray* (1859) 4 Drew 651; 62 ER 250. I am grateful to Mindy Chen-Wishart for drawing this case to my attention.

[6] ibid 665 (Drew); 255 (ER). See also *Young v Clerk* (1720) Prec Ch 538; 24 ER 241 (specific performance of contract to renew lease to claimant at rent that was far less than the rents the claimant was earning from sub-letting the land to various tenants refused on basis that while 'there was no direct fraud proved ... it appeared ... to be an unreasonable and shameful contract'). My thanks to Julius Grower for bringing this case to my attention.

[7] *Quadrant Visual Communications Ltd v Hutchison Telephone (UK)* [1993] BCLC 442 (CA).

of their subscribers. The Court of Appeal refused to specifically enforce the contract on the ground that the claimants' 'trickery', which 'exposed the defendants to the risk of very serious losses without giving them any proper opportunity to consider ... whether or not they wanted to complete',[8] meant that they were not coming to equity with clean hands.

The courts have also in the past refused equitable relief on the basis of the applicant's 'iniquity'.[9] In *Glyn v Weston Feature Film Company*,[10] where the claimant—the author of a novel, *Three Weeks*, about a sexual relationship between a young Englishman and a queen travelling incognito—sought to sue the defendant film-makers for breach of copyright, claiming that they had filmed a spoof version of her novel. Her claim for an injunction preventing distribution of the film, and delivery up of all copies of the film, was denied by Younger J on the basis that *Three Weeks* amounted to a 'glittering record of adulterous sensuality masquerading as superior virtue' and that 'to a book of such cruelly destructive tendency no protection will be extended by a Court of Equity'.[11] More recently, in *Pitt v Holt*,[12] the UKSC indicated that the equitable jurisdiction to rescind a mistaken disposition of trust assets would not extend to 'some cases of artificial tax avoidance [where] the court might think it right to refuse relief ... on grounds of public policy [because] artificial tax avoidance is a social evil which puts an unfair burden on the shoulders of those who do not adopt such measures'.[13] However, as the dispositions in *Pitt v Holt* were not 'at the extreme of artificiality ... it [was] unnecessary to consider ... further on these appeals'[14] this particular limit on the equitable jurisdiction.

II. THE CASE FOR ABOLITION

The case for abolishing the defence of clean hands can be quickly stated, before being elaborated. The case rests on two propositions.

(*A*) In a case where C is seeking some kind of equitable remedy against D, and C's hands are said to be unclean because C has acted unlawfully in the past, the defence of

[8] ibid 451 (Stocker LJ).

[9] *cf Stephens v Averay* [1988] 1 Ch 449 (Ch D) 453 (Browne-Wilkinson V-C): 'I entirely accept the principle ... that a court of equity will not enforce ... a duty of confidence relating to matters which have a grossly immoral tendency'—though he did not think that the existence of a lesbian relationship between the claimant (who was seeking to enforce a duty of confidence in relation to that relationship) and a murder victim counted as 'grossly immoral' and Eady J took the view in *Mosley v News Group Newspapers Ltd* [2008] EWHC 1777 (QB) 106, that while '"there is no confidence in iniquity" ... it is highly questionable whether in modern society that is a concept that can be applied to sexual activity, fetishist or otherwise, conducted between consenting adults in private'. It is noticeable that while in *Gartside v Outran* (1857) 36 LJ Ch 113, 114 Wood V-C said that 'there is no confidence as to the disclosure of iniquity', all his examples of 'iniquity' involved unlawful conduct: 'You cannot make me the confidant of a crime or fraud, and be entitled to close up my lips upon any secret which you have the audacity to disclose to me relating to any fraudulent intention on your part'.

[10] *Glyn v Weston Feature Film Company* [1915] 1 Ch 261 (Ch).

[11] ibid 270.

[12] *Pitt v Holt* [2013] UKSC 26, [2013] 2 AC 108.

[13] ibid [135] (Lord Walker).

[14] ibid.

illegality should exclusively determine whether or not C should be denied the remedy she seeks because of her past unlawful conduct.

(*B*) Where C has *not* acted unlawfully, the law would be left in an unsatisfactory state were C to be denied an equitable remedy against D simply because C had in the past engaged in conduct that is regarded as 'tricky' or 'iniquitous' or 'unconscionable' or whichever disapproving adjective one prefers.

If both (*A*) and (*B*) are correct, there is no room for the defence of clean hands to operate to determine whether C should be denied the remedy that she seeks against D. The only basis on which her past conduct could be relevant to the question of whether she should be awarded the remedy sought is if she acted unlawfully, and in such a case, it should be up to the law on illegality—not the law on clean hands—to determine whether or not C should be denied the remedy she seeks. Let us now expand on each of these propositions.

A. Where C has Acted Unlawfully

The case for thinking that (*A*) must be true may be illustrated by discussing *Tinsley v Milligan*. In that case, Tinsley and Milligan both contributed to the purchase of a house. The house was put into Tinsley's name, so that Milligan could, in making claims for benefits from the Department of Social Security (DSS), represent that she was poorer than she was. When Tinsley and Milligan fell out, Milligan claimed that the house was held by Tinsley on trust for Tinsley and Milligan in equal shares. Tinsley argued that Milligan's claim was barred because of her involvement in the scheme to defraud the DSS by misrepresenting the state of her interest in Tinsley's house. Both the Court of Appeal[15] and the House of Lords[16] held that the defence of illegality did not prevent Milligan claiming a half interest in Tinsley's house—in the Court of Appeal, because Milligan's claim did not 'affront the public conscience';[17] in the House of Lords, because Milligan could assert that she had an interest in Tinsley's house without relying on the illegal scheme that she entered into with Tinsley.[18] The UK Supreme Court (UKSC)'s recent decision in *Patel v Mirza* seems to make it clear that the UKSC would come to the same conclusion, though through different reasoning.[19]

Even if the law on illegality did *not* bar Milligan for claiming that Tinsley held the house on trust in equal shares for Tinsley and Milligan, could Milligan *still* have been barred from making such a claim on the basis that her illegal scheme with Tinsley meant that her hands were 'unclean'? It would seem strange if she could be.

[15] *Tinsley v Milligan* [1992] Ch 310 (CA).

[16] *Tinsley v Milligan* [1994] 1 AC 340 (HL).

[17] *Tinsley v Milligan* (CA) (n 15) 321 (Nicholls LJ), 339 (Lloyd LJ).

[18] *Tinsley v Milligan* (HL) (n 16) 367 (Lord Jauncey), 368 (Lord Lowry), 376 (Lord Browne-Wilkinson).

[19] *Patel v Mirza* [2016] UKSC 42; [2016] 3 WLR 399 [112] (Lord Toulson), [164] and [181] (Lord Neuberger) (in both cases, relying on the 'disproportionate' impact on Milligan that denying her claim against Tinsley would have on her).

How can two areas of law—the law on illegality and the law on clean hands—reach different conclusions as to whether Milligan's crimes should prevent her from being able to make a claim against Tinsley? Consistency would seem to demand that if the law on illegality sees no problem with Milligan being able to make a claim against Tinsley, then neither should the law on clean hands.

As it happens, of the nine judges who ended up considering *Tinsley v Milligan*, only Lord Goff (and, by extension, Lord Keith of Kinkel, who agreed with Lord Goff) was willing to dismiss Milligan's claim against Tinsley on the basis that her hands were 'unclean'.[20] However, even Lord Goff did not see any distinction between the way the law on the defence of illegality operated and the way the defence of clean hands operated. Rather, Lord Goff thought that in the case where 'A puts property in the name of B intending to conceal his (A's) interest in the property for a fraudulent or illegal purpose' with the result that 'equity will not assist [A] in asserting an equitable interest in [the property]',[21] the reason why B would be able to raise a defence of illegality to A's claim was that A 'has not come to equity with clean hands'.[22] So, for Lord Goff, the defence of clean hands *underpinned* the law on illegality, and did not operate independently of it.

The relationship between the maxims '*ex turpi causa non oritur actio*' and 'He who comes to equity must come with clean hands' was most fully considered by the Court of Appeal in *Tinsley v Milligan*, as one of the grounds of Milligan's appeal to that court was that the first instance judge had 'wrongly equated the equitable doctrine of "clean hands" with the common law doctrine *ex turpi causa non oritur actio*'.[23] While the Court of Appeal judges considered how those maxims separately applied to Milligan's case, they did not seem to see any potential for the two maxims to get out of lock-step with each other. Having concluded that Tinsley could not raise a defence of illegality to Milligan's claim against her, Nicholls LJ held that the defence of clean hands did not apply in Milligan's case either: 'The equitable maxim "he who comes to equity must come with clean hands" is to be applied no less flexibly than its common law counterparts.'[24] Lloyd LJ agreed, observing that 'the two maxims are closely related' and that 'I see no reason why the court should not, in the exercise of its equitable jurisdiction, follow and adopt the more flexible attitude shown by the common law'[25] in cases involving illegality.

So all of the judges in *Tinsley v Milligan* seem to have agreed that (*A*) is correct. If, in a case where D is arguing that C should be barred from obtaining some equitable remedy, R, on the basis that C committed some illegal act in the past, the law would become incoherent and unprincipled if C were *not* barred from obtaining R on the basis that *ex turpi causa non oritur actio* but *were* barred on the basis that 'he who comes to equity must do so with clean hands'. The law must speak with one voice

[20] *Tinsley v Milligan* (HL) (n 16) 357–58, 362.
[21] ibid 356.
[22] ibid 357.
[23] *Tinsley v Milligan* (CA) (n 15) 313.
[24] ibid 324.
[25] ibid 341.

on the issue of whether P's illegality prevents her from obtaining R, and that voice is provided by the law on illegality.[26] The law on clean hands must go along with whatever its slightly older sibling[27] has to say on that issue.[28] And that is what (*A*) says.

B. Where C has Not Acted Unlawfully

It might be thought that the defence of clean hands would come into its own where it is argued that C should be barred from seeking an equitable remedy against D because her past behaviour—while *not* unlawful—means her hands are unclean. In such a case, the defence of illegality has nothing to say on whether C should be refused the remedy she seeks—for example, it is quite clear from the UKSC's decision in *Patel v Mirza* that the defence of illegality can only be raised against a C who has actually acted unlawfully[29]—and so there is room in this sort of case for the defence of clean hands to climb out of the shadow of the defence of illegality and take an independent stand on whether C's past misconduct should count against her obtaining the remedy she seeks. However, if we return to our fourfold classification of the kinds of cases where a defence of clean hands might be raised, we can set out a strong case for thinking that the law would be left in an unsatisfactory state if a

[26] *cf* D Dobbs, *Law of Remedies* 2nd edn (St Paul, MN, West Publishing Co, 1993) 152 para 2.6(1): 'When the unclean hands defence is equivalent to some legal defense like fraud or illegality, it adds nothing except confusion'. See also, to the same effect, *Nelson v Nelson* (1995) 184 CLR 538 (HCA) 551 (Deane and Gummow JJ).

[27] The maxim *ex turpi causa non oritur actio* was first authoritatively recognised by Lord Mansfield in *Holman v Johnson* (1775) 1 Cowp 341, 343; 98 ER 1120, 1121. It was 12 years later, in *Dering* (n 2) 319 (Eyre LCB) that the maxim that 'a man must come into a Court of Equity with clean hands' first appeared in the law reports.

[28] Which is not to say that the law on illegality has nothing to learn from the law on clean hands. Contrast the aggressive way in which the clean hands defence is used to deny equitable relief to people who have told lies in order to advance their case (*Armstrong v Sheppard & Short Ltd* [1959] QB 384 (CA) 397; *J Willis & Son v Willis*, unreported, 17 October 1985; *Gonthier v Orange Contract Scaffolding Ltd* [2003] EWCA Civ 873) with the courts' pusillanimous attitude (criticised in A Zuckerman, *Zuckerman on Civil Procedure: Principles of Practice* 3rd edn (Sweet & Maxwell, 2013) paras 11.269–11.275) towards striking out deceitfully inflated claims for damages made by the admitted victims of a tort: *Summers v Fairclough Homes Ltd* [2012] UKSC 26; [2012] 1 WLR 2004. The stricter attitude in equity towards lying to advance one's case *is* mirrored by the courts' treatment of deceitfully inflated claims under an insurance policy, where even the valid part of the claim will be struck out on the basis that '[t]he fraudulent insured must not be allowed to think: if the fraud is successful, then I will gain; if it is unsuccessful, I will lose nothing', *Manifest Shipping Co Ltd v Uni-Polaris Insurance Co Ltd* [2001] UKHL 1; [2003] 1 AC 469 (HL) [62] (Lord Hobhouse).

[29] The two key paragraphs in Lord Toulson's majority judgment in *Patel* (n 19) are [99] and [101]. Paragraph [99] identifies when a claimant *might* be denied a remedy on the ground of illegality: (i) when allowing a remedy would allow the claimant to profit from their own wrongdoing, and (ii) when allowing a remedy would render the law '[in]coherent and … self-defeating, condoning illegality by giving with the left hand what it takes with the right hand'. Paragraph [101] identifies the considerations the courts should take into account in deciding whether to deny a claimant a remedy because either (i) or (ii) applies: (a) whether denying a remedy would undermine the 'underlying purpose of the prohibition which has been transgressed', (b) whether denying a remedy would render 'any other relevant public policies … ineffective or less effective', and (c) whether denying a remedy would amount to 'overkill'. These two paragraphs make it tolerably clear that Lord Toulson did not envisage any role for the defence of illegality outside a case where a claimant has 'transgressed' a 'prohibition'—that is, acted unlawfully.

shady C—a claimant who has engaged in improper, but lawful, behaviour in the past—were to be denied an equitable remedy because of her shady nature.

Let's begin with category (1), where a shady C seeks an equitable remedy to protect her *legal* rights from being violated by D. Where D is guilty of an *ongoing* violation of C's legal rights (say, for example, that D is running an operation on his premises that amounts to a private nuisance in relation to C's land), it is clear that D will *not* be able to rely on a defence of clean hands to defeat C's claim for an injunction against D where C has done nothing unlawful but may have engaged in some 'improper' behaviour that has an 'immediate and necessary relation' to C's claim against D (say, for example, the reason why D is creating a private nuisance in relation to C's land is that C slept with D's wife). This is because C will have a good claim at law for damages against D for violating her legal rights—the fact that C has done nothing unlawful will mean that D cannot raise a defence of illegality to defeat C's claim for damages, and it is not possible to rely on a defence of clean hands to defeat a claim for damages in law.[30] So, if an injunction is not granted against D to bring his wrongdoing to an end, C will be able repeatedly to sue D for damages every time D's ongoing wrongdoing causes her harm. In order to avoid this 'multiplicity of actions', the courts will grant C an injunction against D's wrongdoing, no matter how stained her hands might be in the eyes of the courts.[31] So long as C has not actually done anything unlawful that might disqualify her from suing D for damages at law, she will be able to get an injunction to bring D's persistent wrongdoing to an end.

But if a shady C *can* get an injunction against D to protect her from D's *continuously* violating her legal rights, then it would seem to follow—for the sake of consistency—that C should *also* be able to obtain an injunction against D in a category (2) type case where D is guilty of continuously violating some equitable right of C's. And if an injunction may be granted to a shady C where D is continuously violating her rights—whether legal or equitable—then consistency would also seem to demand that a shady C should *also* be able to obtain equitable relief in a category (1) or category (2) case where C is seeking to prevent D committing a *one-off* violation of C's rights. That the law should apply the same rule to threatened one-off violations of C's rights as it does to continuous violations of C's rights seems particularly obvious in cases (such as intellectual property cases or cases where D is in possession of C's property) where it can be difficult to tell whether what we are dealing with is a one-off violation of C's legal rights, or an ongoing violation of those rights.

30 *Hurley v Mustoe (No 2)* [1983] ICR 422 (EAT) 426 (Browne-Wilkinson J): 'the introduction of the equitable doctrine of "clean hands" into the assessment of common law damages is, so far as we are aware, a novelty. The equitable doctrine of coming to equity with clean hands is dealing with the exercise by a court of equity of its powers to grant an equitable remedy; it does not apply to claims for damages at common law.' TL Anenson, 'Treating Equity Like Law: A Post-Merger Justification of Unclean Hands' (2008) 45 *American Business Law Journal* 455 valiantly tries to argue for the existence of a clean hands defence in the common law, but in vain. See also TL Anenson, 'Beyond Chafee: A Process-Based Theory of Unclean Hands' (2010) 47 *American Business Law Journal* 509 and TL Anenson, 'Limiting Legal Remedies: An Analysis of Unclean Hands' (2010–11) 99 *Kentucky Law Journal* 63.

31 *Angelides v James Stedman Hendersons Sweets Ltd* (1927) 40 CLR 43 (HCA) 63 (Isaacs ACJ).

So, the argument goes, in a category (1) or category (2) case where a shady C seeks equitable relief to protect her rights from being violated by D, C's shady nature should *never* be taken into account in determining whether C should be allowed some form of equitable relief against D. That leaves category (3) and category (4) cases where a shady C seeks the assistance of equity either to vest her with some right against D, or to divest D of some right that he would otherwise enjoy. The case for thinking that a shady C should *never* be denied the equitable relief she seeks in a category (3) or category (4) case rests squarely on rule-of-law considerations. To deprive a shady C of remedies she would otherwise have enjoyed based on an evaluation of her behaviour as 'iniquitous', 'tricky', 'extreme' or 'unconscionable', would seem to fall foul of the ideal, memorably articulated by Peter Birks,[32] that 'A judge must be able to say: "It is not me who does this to you, but the law. Look I will show you."' 'It is the judgment that does the showing', Birks contended, 'and the judgment must be rational, intelligible, and consistent with others.' Given this, Birks argued, there can be no room for 'the gut reaction' or 'intuitive decision-making' that the law seems to fall into when it says that a shady C can be deprived of a remedy in a category (3) or category (4) type cases (or, indeed, category (1) or (2) type cases) because actions of hers that were not actually unlawful have nonetheless made her hands 'unclean'.

III. THREE TYPES OF REMEDIES

This ends the case for abolishing clean hands as an equitable defence. If the defence were to be abolished, it seems unlikely that many would lament its passing.[33] Certainly, the practical effect of abolishing the defence would be very small.[34] However, in the rest of this chapter I would like to make the case for retaining the defence, at least in certain cases where C seeks to obtain an equitable remedy against D.

[32] P Birks, 'Equity, Conscience, and Unjust Enrichment' (1999) 23 *Melbourne University Law Review* 1, 21.

[33] O Herstein, 'A Normative Theory of the Clean Hands Defence' (2011) 17 *Legal Theory* 171 advances a couple of arguments in favour of the clean hands defence, but his case for the defence is weakened by his assumption that C will be guilty of some 'wrongdoing' in any case where P's hands will be held to be unclean. If this were true, then the defence of clean hands could be subsumed within a general defence of illegality without losing anything. Similarly, §63 of the *Restatement 3d Restitution and Unjust Enrichment* (American Law Institute, 2011) acknowledges that there is a defence of clean hands to claims in restitution when it provides that '[r]ecovery in restitution to which an innocent claimant would be entitled may be limited or denied because of the claimant's inequitable conduct in the transaction that is the source of the asserted liability'. But all of the examples provided of this rule at work are cases where the claimant has been guilty of some illegal behaviour—so, again, any defence of clean hands to claims in restitution could be subsumed within a general defence of illegality without losing anything.

[34] *cf Moody v Cox* [1917] 2 Ch 71 (CA) 87 (Scrutton LJ): 'I think the expression "clean hands" is used more often in the text-books than it is in the judgments, though it is occasionally used in the judgments'. Nothing has changed: a Westlaw UK search of recent cases where 'clean hands' has been invoked as a defence reveals that it is invoked almost as a matter of routine whenever a claimant seeks some form of equitable remedy, but the courts almost never allow the cleanliness or otherwise of the claimant's hands to affect their decision as to whether or not to find in favour of the claimant.

In this section I want to distinguish between three different kinds of remedy: (1) a remedy that C has a *right to*; (2) a remedy that it is *necessary* to award C in order to preserve the law's legitimacy; (3) a remedy that is *supererogatory*—that is, a remedy that C has no right to, and which it is not necessary to award to C. My argument will be that the clean hands defence can be justifiably retained in cases where the remedy that C is seeking against D is supererogatory. We will get a better sense of what kinds of remedies are supererogatory by first of all discussing what remedies a given C can claim to have a right to; which discussion will also lead into a discussion of what remedies are necessary in order to preserve the law's legitimacy.

A. Discretion and Rights

In discussing when C can say that she has a right to a particular remedy R, we must first brush aside a misconception. The misconception is that: (i) C *will* have a right to R if the courts have no (or very little) discretion as to whether or not to award R to C under the rules governing the award of R; whereas (ii) C will *not* have a right to R if the rules governing the award of R *underdetermine* the circumstances in which R will be awarded[35] with the result that the courts enjoy a strong discretion as to whether or not to award R to C.[36]

Peter Birks assumed that (i) and (ii) were correct when he said:

> If the court regards its order [that C should be granted R] as strongly discretionary, its content cannot reflect an [a]nterior right. The discretion which is interposed between the claimant and the order shows that he has no right to that which he wants ordered. The word 'strongly' needs to be added. Many judicial orders are weakly discretionary. Orders for specific performance and injunctions and all others rooted in the Court of Chancery are weakly discretionary. The discretion has been settled over the centuries. To speak of a right to specific performance or an injunction is not nonsense. We know on what facts a person is entitled to such orders.[37]

Dan Dobbs made the same assumption when he observed of equitable remedies, which are often said to be discretionary in nature: 'The chancellor's discretion to deny relief is a peculiar tradition to encounter in a democratic society where citizens possess rights under the law, not merely the hope of indulgence'[38] and 'why is it that one has no right to equitable relief? The answer is that one has no right to equitable relief because equity has discretion to deny it.'[39]

[35] The rules governing the award of R will underdetermine the circumstances in which R will be awarded either because those rules do not fully specify the facts that a judge is supposed to take into account in deciding whether or not to award R, or because those rules do specify what facts the judge is supposed to take into account but do not specify what weight the judge is to give those facts in reaching his or her conclusion as to whether or not to award R.

[36] For this sense in which a remedy can be said to be discretionary, see M Harding, 'Equity and the Rule of Law' (2016) 132 *LQR* 278, 289–90, building on HLA Hart, 'Discretion' (2013) 127 *Harvard Law Review* 652, especially 658–61.

[37] P Birks, 'Rights, Wrongs, and Remedies' (2000) 20 *OJLS* 1, 16.

[38] Dobbs (n 26) 115.

[39] ibid 119.

Despite this distinguished support for (i) and (ii), I don't think either (i) or (ii) is correct. As we are interested in knowing when C *has* a right to a particular remedy R, let's focus on (i). Contrary to what (i) claims, I don't think it follows that because the courts enjoy no (or very little) discretion over whether to award R to C, that C has a *right* to R.[40] This point is easily demonstrated. My close friends know that if they ask me to buy something for them or their children, I will buy it for them. So if a close friend X asks me to buy her daughter a hair dryer for Christmas, I will not regard myself as having any kind of choice over whether or not to buy the hair dryer: I *must* buy it. But neither X nor her daughter could sensibly say that they have a *right* that I buy them a hair dryer. Closer to home, there is no right of appeal to the UK Supreme Court.[41] When the Divisional Court delivered its ruling in *R (on the application of Miller) v Secretary of State for Exiting the European Union*[42]—that the UK government could not invoke the procedure for leaving the European Union under Article 50 of the Lisbon Treaty without prior Parliamentary approval—there was no prospect at all that the UK Supreme Court would *not* hear the government's appeal against the Divisional Court's ruling. But that does not mean that the UK government had a *right* to have its appeal against the Divisional Court's ruling heard by the UK Supreme Court.

B. Determining Whether There is a Right to a Remedy

If the non-discretionary nature of a remedy R tells us nothing about whether a particular C has a *right* to R, what *does* tell us whether C has a right to R? We can begin by saying that if you have a right (whether moral or legal), that right will be based on: (i) who you are (both in terms of what interests you have, and in terms of what your status is); (ii) what you have done; or (iii) what has been done to you. This taxonomy of the sources of rights seems to be exhaustive in that it is difficult to think of an example where someone could plausibly claim to have a right (whether moral or legal) that is not based on one of (i), (ii) or (iii). If this is correct, then we can see whether, and if so when, C can claim that she has a right to R, based on any of (i), (ii) or (iii).

i. Who You Are

Can C ever claim that he has a right to R based on who she is? Many people think that C can. They think that C will be able to argue: 'I am someone who is endowed

[40] For the reverse point—that just because someone has a right in relation to the award of a remedy that does not necessarily mean that the award of that remedy will be non-discretionary—see S Evans, 'Defending Discretionary Remedialism' (2001) 23 *Sydney Law Review* 463, 470, criticising Birks for overlooking 'those remedies … where it can be said that the claimant had an anterior right to *a* remedy but where the court has a discretion … as to the *form* of the remedy' (emphasis in original).

[41] There used to be a right to appeal to the House of Lords, but that was abolished by the Administration of Justice (Appeals) Act 1934 (UK).

[42] *R (on the application of Miller) v Secretary of State for Exiting the European Union* [2016] EWHC 2768 (Admin).

with various (primary) legal rights, and because I am endowed with those rights, I have a right to certain remedies when any of these primary rights are violated.'

So William Blackstone argued that 'it is a settled and invariable principle in the laws of England, that every right when withheld must have a remedy, and every injury its proper redress'.[43] In *Marbury v Madison*,[44] Marshall CJ quoted Blackstone's words with approval, and added some of his own to the same effect: 'The very essence of civil liberty certainly consists in the right of every individual to claim the protection of the laws, whenever he receives an injury. One of the first duties of government is to afford that protection'[45] and 'where a specific duty is assigned by law, and individual rights depend upon the performance of that duty, it seems equally clear that the individual who considers himself injured has a right to resort to the laws of his country for a remedy'.[46]

These claims do not support the view that if a primary legal right of C's has been violated, then C has a right to a remedy for the violation of that right. It may be true—as many legal academics have recently argued[47]—that it is inherent in the nature of having a legal right against someone else that you will also have access to a remedy in the event of that right being violated: a remedy that will undo the violation or provide you with a 'second best' version of what you should have had in the first place. Let's call this the *Rights-Based View of Remedies*.[48] However, the *Rights-Based View of Remedies* does not establish that you have a *right* to a remedy when your rights have been violated. In order to make out that you have a *right* to such a remedy, you would have to establish that you have a *right to the legal right* that is the foundation of the remedy. If you do not have such a right, then the law does nothing wrong *to you* in withholding the remedy that you would have expected to come with the right that the law has said that you have. On the *Rights-Based View of Remedies*, the corollary of *ubi ius, ibi remedium* is 'No remedy, no right'.[49] By withholding a remedy from you, the law has gainsaid its earlier assertion that you had a legal right, and if you had no right to that right you cannot complain that the law has done anything wrong *to you* by going back on its earlier statement.

Can such a right—a right to a legal right—be based on who you are? Again, some people might think that this is not a problem. They might argue that given the interests we have, and the dignity we possess as human beings, the government is duty-bound to recognise us as having certain legal rights. As Arthur Ripstein argues,

43 W Blackstone, *Commentaries on the Laws of England* (Oxford, Clarendon Press, 1769) Book III, 109.

44 *Marbury v Madison*, 5 US 137 (1803).

45 ibid 163.

46 ibid 166.

47 See, eg, A Ripstein, *Private Wrongs* (Cambridge, MA, Harvard University Press, 2015) ch 8, and references contained therein.

48 As will be clear in at the start of the next section, I don't accept the *Rights-Based View of Remedies*: the fact that a legal right of C's has been violated does not necessarily mean that C will or should be granted a remedy in respect of that violation.

49 *cf* DH Zeigler, 'Rights Require Remedies: A New Approach to the Enforcement of Rights in the Federal Courts' (1987) 38 *Hastings Law Journal* 665, 678: 'a right without a remedy is not a legal right; it is merely a hope or a wish'.

'[t]he state only has standing to do anything if it is doing so on behalf of all citizens' and acting 'on behalf of all citizens' requires that the state create and sustain 'a social world in which no person is in charge of another'—a world in which every citizen 'has the ability to make what they will of their own lives' and is able 'to each enjoy their private rights in a way that is consistent with the ability of others to do the same'.[50] But this all supposes that there *exists* a state that can do all these things. It seems doubtful that C, by virtue of who she is, has a *right* to live under a government that can endow C with the kind of legal rights against other people that will allow C to make what she will of her own life—and if C does not have such a right, then she has no right to be endowed with such legal rights or the remedies that (on the *Rights-Based View of Remedies*) come as part and parcel of those rights.

A much simpler explanation of Blackstone's 'settled and invariable principle in the laws of England' is available to us, which does not claim that C invariably[51] has a right to a remedy when her legal rights have been violated. It has already been hinted at: the law *looks bad* if it takes back with one hand what it appeared to give with the other. It seems (and, indeed, is) hypocritical of the law to say to C that she has a right that D not walk on C's land, and then give C no effective remedy when D does precisely that. No one has a right that the law not make itself look bad, but it is not a good idea either for the law to bring itself into disrepute—the effects of its doing so are wide ranging, unpredictable and never good. It is a concern for the law's legitimacy, and not its rightfulness, that accounts for the law's giving C a remedy against the trespassing D, and in most other cases where someone violates C's rights.

ii. What You have Done

But this is to anticipate. It may be that in a case where the law grants C a remedy R, C can argue that she had a right to R based on something C did. The most obvious example of this is where C has *relied* in some way on the expectation of obtaining R. In this way a necessary remedy—a remedy that is customarily granted to someone whose rights have been violated in order to ensure that the law's legitimacy is not brought into question—can turn into a remedy that you have a right to, because the customary award of that remedy has created an expectation that it will be awarded to you, and you have relied on that expectation. A victim of a breach of contract might be able to use this kind of argument to establish that she has a right to be paid

[50] Ripstein (n 47) 290. *cf* Blackstone (n 43) Book I, 124: '[T]he principal aim of society is to protect individuals in the enjoyment of those absolute rights, which were vested in them by the immutable laws of nature, but which could not be preserved in peace without that mutual assistance and intercourse which is gained by the institution of friendly and social communities. Hence it follows, that the first and primary end of human laws is to maintain and regulate these absolute rights of individuals.'

[51] Of course, it might be that the constitution of the state or country in which C lives requires that C not be denied a remedy when he is the victim of a legal wrong. For a very good discussion of the case law interpreting provisions in US state constitutions guaranteeing people a remedy for injuries done to them in their 'goods, land or person' or for injuries done to their 'person, property or reputation', see TR Phillips, 'The Constitutional Right to a Remedy' (2003) 78 *New York University Law Review* 1309.

compensatory damages as she will probably have relied on the practice of awarding such damages in deciding to enter into the contract that was breached rather than some other arrangement to assure herself she would get whatever it was that she was contracting for. Outside this kind of case, it is hard to see a *reliance-based* argument getting off the ground to establish that a particular C has a right to a particular remedy R. Not many people are aware *ex ante* of what the law promises to do for them, and of those who are, not many are in a position to structure their affairs around those promises. So it is doubtful that there will be many cases where you can say you have a right to a remedy based on what you have done.

iii. What has Been Done to You

This third basis might provide a more promising ground for finding that you have a right to a remedy. This thought has been pursued by John Goldberg and Benjamin Zipursky. Their theory of tort law[52] takes as its starting point the observation that in civilised societies, the state claims a monopoly over the ability to use violence.[53] By claiming this monopoly, the state has deprived us of the abilities we would otherwise enjoy to protect ourselves from those who would do us serious wrong, and to seek recourse from those who have done us such serious wrong.[54] Having deprived us of those abilities, we have a right against the state that it provide us with alternative forms of recourse against those who would or have wronged us.[55]

One problem with what we can call the '*G/Z Argument*' has been pointed out by Arthur Ripstein: 'Fairness requires those who prohibit others from doing something to provide a substitute *only* if those others were *entitled* to do the

[52] For an overview of Goldberg and Zipursky's theory of tort law, see their 'Torts as Wrongs' (2010) 88 *Texas Law Review* 917.

[53] *cf* B Zipursky, 'Rights, Wrongs, and Recourse in the Law of Torts' (1998) 51 *Vanderbilt Law Review* 1, 84: 'It is essential to our ordered society and our legal system that we do not permit private retribution for the violation of … rights. Having been wronged is neither an excuse nor a justification for violence against or taking from another, except in rare cases. The law prohibits and criminalizes violence as a reaction to … wrongs.'

[54] *cf* J Goldberg, 'The Constitutional Status of Tort Law' (2005) 115 *Yale Law Journal* 524, 606: 'Government, by taking on the task of maintaining civil society, obtains from individuals a variety of powers that they would otherwise be entitled to exercise. Thus, apart from special cases as self-defense, the victim of a wrong is by law disabled from responding to the wrong on his own, or with the aid of his friends or kin. If he attacks or seizes another or expropriates her goods in an effort to obtain satisfaction for the wrong done to him, he will be subject to liability … as well as criminal punishment.'

[55] *cf* J Goldberg and B Zipursky, 'Rights and Responsibility in the Law of Torts' in D Nolan and A Robertson (eds), *Rights and Private Law* (Oxford, Hart Publishing, 2011) 268–69: 'Government … is obligated to provide a body of law that defines wrongs and empowers victims of wrongs to respond to those who have wronged them. This is obviously a right to redress in a very different sense than the Hohfeldian power conferred on tort victims to obtain remedies from wrongdoers. To invoke the language of an old US Supreme Court opinion, it is a "right to *a law* for the redress of wrongs"—ie an affirmative right to be provided with a means of responding, through the legal system, to certain kinds of mistreatment at the hands of others' (quoting *Missouri Pacific Railway Co v Humes*, 115 US 512 (1885) (Field J, emphasis added by Goldberg and Zipursky)). See also Goldberg (n 54) 606: 'With resort to self-help blocked by the law, government is obligated, at least to some degree, to provide an alternative path for the attainment of satisfaction. Granting the victim a right to redress is an obvious way for government to fulfill that duty'.

prohibited thing.'[56] So under the *G/Z Argument*, you can *only* say that you have a right to a remedy R against me if the state prevents you from taking steps that you would otherwise be *entitled* to take to extract from me whatever R would give you. If (a) I or my property poses an unjust threat to you or your property, then you could plausibly argue that you have a 'natural right' to take steps to protect yourself from that threat by acting against me or your property, with the result that if the state forbids you from taking such steps, it comes under an obligation to provide you with a remedy that is effective to protect you or your property. Similarly, if (b) I am in possession of your property, then you could plausibly argue that you have a 'natural right' to take steps to retrieve your property from my possession, with the result that if the state prevents you from taking such steps, it comes under an obligation to provide you with a remedy that will give you what you would get if you were allowed to retrieve your property back from me. However, in a situation where neither (a) nor (b) are true, it is hard to see how you could argue that you have a 'natural right' to act against me or my property to extract some advantage for yourself—and that is so whatever I might have done to you (or failed to do for you) in the past or whatever might have happened between us in the past. And even where (a) is true, the *G/Z Argument* does *not* work to establish that you have a right to a remedy against me because the state does not actually forbid you from taking steps to protect yourself or your property against the unjust threat that I or my property represent. It is only in case (b)—where the state *does* place severe limits on your ability to recover your property from my possession[57]—that you can plausibly claim that you have a right to a remedy against me.

So the *G/Z Argument* does not go very far to establish that we have a right to certain remedies that we currently enjoy under the law. A different argument, which also purports to find a right to a remedy that is rooted in what has been done to you, can be made. The argument goes like this: If a *public body* (PB) has treated you in a way that means it is morally required to undo what it did to you (or make up for what it failed to do for you), then you could claim that the state has a moral duty to provide you with a remedy that will have the effect of undoing what PB did to you (or making up for what PB failed to do for you). This is because PB is an organ of the state, and so PB's moral duty is also the state's moral duty. Transplanting this argument into the legal realm, we can say that if a public body has violated a legal right of yours, you will have a moral right to a remedy to repair the violation of that legal right provided that the public body in question is morally required to

[56] Ripstein (n 47) 268 (emphases added).

[57] What powers people enjoyed under the common law to use force against others (*R v Milton* (1827) 1 M & M 107; 173 ER 1097; *Devoe v Long* [1951] 1 DLR 203) or to enter onto other people's land (*Patrick v Colerick* (1838) 3 M & W 483; 150 ER 1235; *Anthony v Haney* (1832) 8 Bing 186, 192; 131 ER 372, 374) to recover their property were abolished in England and Wales by the Tribunals, Courts and Enforcement Act 2007 (UK), which (by virtue of a combination of s 65 and Sch 12) abolishes any self-help remedy involving taking goods which are in another's possession unless one is doing so in order to pay off a debt.

repair that violation.[58] So in the case where a public body has violated a legal right of yours, it might be possible to make a plausible case for saying that you have a right to a remedy requiring the public body to repair the violation. This might, in turn, provide some basis for the view that 'the historic function of the common law judiciary' has been 'to preserve and provide legal remedies for violation of rights by the government'[59]—for it is where *the government* has violated your legal rights that you have, if the arguments made in this section are correct, the most plausible case for arguing that you have a right to a remedy for what has been done to you.

C. Necessary and Supererogatory Remedies

The number of remedies that we can plausibly say that we have a *right* to turns out to be very small. *At best*, such remedies fall into three classes: (1) remedies requiring a contract breaker to pay compensatory damages to the victim of his breach of contract; (2) remedies requiring someone in possession of C's property to return the property, or its value, to C; (3) remedies requiring a public body that has violated C's legal rights to repair that violation.

These remedies are dwarfed in significance by the number of remedies that are *necessary*, in the sense that their award is necessary to preserve the legitimacy of the law. We have already noted that an award of compensatory damages that is made against a tortfeasor can be explained as necessary in this sense. For the law to acknowledge that D has violated C's rights but not to require D to make up for that violation calls, at the very least, for some explanation. In some cases an explanation can be given. For example, where D's rights-violation has caused C no relevant harm, the presumption should be in favour of letting things be and not awarding C any kind of remedy against D—though the presumption can, of course, be displaced if C can provide us with a good reason why D *should* be held liable for his harmless wronging. But in cases where D's violating C's rights has caused C to suffer relevant harm, *not* to award C some kind of remedy against D—not necessarily full compensation, but at least fair compensation[60]—would seem to bring into question the law's integrity: to recognise that C had a right that D should not act as he did but then not award C fair compensation for the relevant harm that she has suffered

[58] It has been argued that so long as the legal right that the public body (PB) violated is morally justified, you will always have a moral right that the PB repair its violation of your right under something called the 'continuity thesis' where the reasons that justify the existence of the legal right that PB violated also require PB to repair the violation of that right: see J Gardner, 'What is Tort Law For? Part 1. The Place of Corrective Justice' (2011) 30 *Journal of Law and Philosophy* 1. I am skeptical as to whether the 'continuity thesis' is defensible given the vast disparity that is normally involved between observing a legal right, and repairing the violation of that same right: see NJ McBride and R Bagshaw, *Tort Law* 5th edn (Harlow, Pearson Education, 2015) 802–03.

[59] DE Edlin, 'A Constitutional Right to Judicial Review: Access to Courts and Ouster Clauses in England and the United States' (2009) 57 *American Journal of Comparative Law* 67, 92.

[60] For the distinction, see J Goldberg, 'Two Conceptions of Tort Damages: Fair v Full Compensation' (2006) 55 *DePaul Law Review* 435.

at D's hands, seems hypocritical.[61] The same explanation can be provided of compensatory awards against other kinds of private wrongdoers, such as contract breakers, and defaulting trustees and other fiduciaries.

However, not all remedies are necessary in the sense that their award is necessary to preserve the legitimacy of the law. An obvious example is an order for specific performance of a contract. Given the substantial costs involved in making such an order against D for C's benefit—the need to supervise D to see whether he complies with the order, the risk that if D breaches the order the courts will have to send him to prison for contempt, and the opportunities that the existence of the order creates for C to abuse the power it gives her over D to extort money from D—no one could seriously think that avoiding these costs by abolishing the power to make orders for specific performance against contract breakers would bring the law's legitimacy into question.[62] The fact that orders of specific performance are only supposed to be made where damages would be an inadequate remedy might prompt the thought that abolishing the power to make such orders would create an unacceptable hole in the law's armoury of remedies against a contract breaker. However, this is untrue: there is no case where specific performance is currently made available as a remedy against a contract breaker D where a substantial award of damages could not be made[63] against D in lieu of specific performance.[64] The same is true of most

[61] It is not necessarily the case that the compensation has to come from D. So in a jurisdiction—such as New Zealand—where C is able to claim from a government body compensation for the harm she has suffered as a result of D's wrong, then it is *not* necessary for the law to give C a right to sue D for fair compensation in order to preserve its own legitimacy.

[62] In discussion, Robert Chambers advanced the view that nowadays people might be able to argue that they have a *right* to specific performance of contracts that are specifically enforceable, based on the fact that the specifically enforceable nature of a contract gives rise to equitable interests in the subject matter of the contract under *Walsh v Lonsdale* (1882) 21 Ch D 9 (CA) and people may have relied on the expectation that they have such equitable interests in arranging their affairs. In support of this argument, he pointed to the disruption that was caused by the Supreme Court of Canada's suggestion in *Semelhago v Paramadevan* [1996] 2 SCR 415 that contracts for the acquisition of an interest in land might not be routinely specifically enforceable. Against this, it could be argued (and has been by Magda Raczynska, in as yet unpublished work on the foundations of equitable security) that it is possible to break the link between a contract being specifically enforceable and a party to that contract having an equitable interest in the subject matter of that contract. The need to break this link is made more pressing by the powerful criticisms of *Walsh v Lonsdale* that have been advanced by W Swadling, 'The Vendor-Purchaser Constructive Trust' in S Degeling and J Edelman (eds), *Equity in Commercial Law* (Sydney, Law Book Company, 2005).

[63] Of course, in a jurisdiction where fair compensation (whatever its source) could not be awarded to the victim of a wrong, then it would become much more necessary for specific performance to be awarded against a contract breaker whose contract could still be performed. However, we do not live in such a jurisdiction today and given the considerations advanced in the previous paragraph, we are not ever likely to live in such a jurisdiction. I am grateful to Lusina Ho for pressing me on this point.

[64] *Beswick v Beswick* [1968] AC 58 (HL) (breach of a promise to pay allowance to promisee's widow after the promisee's death, in return for the promisee's coal business) provided the most formidable counter-example to the position taken in the text until the Contracts (Rights of Third Parties) Act 1999 (UK) allowed third-party beneficiaries of a contractual promise to sue for breach of that promise. Even before the 1999 Act, a creative judge could have solved the problem posed by *Beswick v Beswick*—how to stop the promisor getting something for nothing—without resorting (as the House of Lords did in the case) to an order of specific performance. The courts could have prevented the promisor being unjustly enriched not by requiring the promisor to return the value of coal business to the promisee's estate but by paying the promisee's widow a sum of money equal to the present value of all the future payments that it was anticipated that he would make to the widow when the coal business was transferred to him.

injunctions. However, some injunctions *must* be awarded to prevent the law's legitimacy bring brought into question. Examples are: (1) an injunction that is awarded to prevent C being forced to bring multiple claims for damages against D, a persistent wrongdoer;[65] and (2) an injunction that is awarded to prevent D violating C's rights in a way that would also amount to a crime. Not to award an injunction in (1) would make the law seem uncaring and, in (2), the law would appear unwilling to do as much as any police officer would be expected to do, which is to prevent crime. Other injunctions (such as injunctions against a private nuisance, or against an invasion of privacy) are supererogatory in nature—their award does (one hopes) more good than harm, but denying them would not violate anyone's rights to a remedy nor bring the law's legitimacy into question.[66]

Other remedies are on the necessary/supererogatory borderline. 'Cost of cure' damages for breach of contract are orders for specific performance tricked out in money form—they effectively force a contract breaker to sub-contract performance to someone else and cover the cost of doing so. If (contrary to the arguments tentatively advanced in part (ii) of the previous section) the victim of a breach of contract is not entitled to such damages as a matter of right, are such damages necessary or supererogatory? Given the analogy between such damages and specific performance, one might think that they are supererogatory in the same way that specific performance is. However, cost of cure damages are much cheaper to award than specific performance, and a failure to award cost of cure damages in a case where D has breached a contract with C might lead C to believe the law was not being entirely sincere when it said that C had a right that D perform his contract.[67] Given this, awards of such damages should probably be regarded as necessary to preserve the legitimacy of the law, just like other awards of compensatory damages (or equitable compensation) against a wrongdoer.

Punitive (or exemplary) damages are awarded against a tortfeasor (D), who has cynically violated C's rights, where (i) D's conduct would not otherwise receive an adequate sanction and (ii) (in England and Wales) where D either works for the state or was motivated by the prospect of making a gain for himself in

[65] See text at n 31.

[66] As is demonstrated by the UK Supreme Court's decision in *Lawrence v Fen Tigers Ltd* [2014] UKSC 13; [2014] AC 822. That decision, which recalibrated the law on what factors should be taken into account in deciding whether to award an injunction against a private nuisance with the result that such injunctions might be awarded less often in future, might be criticised as *unwise*, but not as *improper* or *damaging*. See, eg, the discussion of *Lawrence* in P Davies, 'Injunctions in Tort and Contract' in G Virgo and S Worthington (eds), *Commercial Remedies: Resolving Controversies* (Cambridge, CUP, 2017) section II.

[67] I remember attending a conference in All Souls that was organised by Peter Birks, and which happened to coincide with the release of the House of Lords' decision in *Ruxley Electronics & Construction Ltd v Forsyth* [1996] AC 344 (HL). As I recall, the more senior academics at the conference were very satisfied with the decision to deny cost of cure damages in *Ruxley* on the ground that their award would be wasteful. The more junior academics were more doubtful, wondering whether the decision in *Ruxley* meant that a client would not actually have a right that a contractor ensure that his work fulfilled certain specifications if curing the contractor's failure to do this would inevitably be wasteful. On reflection, the senior academics were correct: denying cost of cure damages in *Ruxley* brought the law into *less* disrepute than would have been the case had cost of cure damages been awarded.

violating C's rights. If the power to award such damages were abolished tomorrow,[68] would the legitimacy of the law be brought into question? One argument that is commonly made in favour of awards of punitive damages is that such awards help to vindicate the rule of law.[69] Abolishing the ability of the courts to make such awards might be seen to make the law imbalanced. For example, *Rich* would be left free to ride roughshod over *Poor*'s rights, safe in the knowledge he would have enough money to compensate *Poor* for any harm suffered by *Poor* as a result of his conduct; while *Poor*'s lack of means would deter him from doing the same to *Rich*. Similarly, a public body might be emboldened by the abolition of awards of punitive damages to disregard *Subject*'s rights, knowing that any criminal response its wrongdoing might be muted by the police's reluctance to bring other organs of the state to account for what they have done, while the police would feel no such reluctance in bringing the full force of the law to bear on *Subject* were *Subject* to commit a criminal offence by violating someone else's rights. It is therefore clear that abolishing the ability of the courts to award punitive damages would bring the legitimacy of the law into question, and that such awards are necessary and not supererogatory. By contrast, awards of aggravated damages—which are designed to assuage C's feelings of anger at the contemptuous way in which she has been treated by a tortfeasor, D—seem to be supererogatory, rather than necessary. Were such awards to be abolished tomorrow with the result that C was forced to live with her feelings of anger towards D, it is hard to see how the legitimacy of the law would be brought into question.

Ben McFarlane has interestingly argued that remedies for unjust enrichment—at least in the context of C's paying money to D—are necessary to preserve the legitimacy of the rules on the transfer of title to money: were such remedies not available then those rules would come to be seen as unfairly prejudicial to people who, for example, have transferred money to someone else by mistake.[70] Stephen A Smith has advanced a similar view.[71] I have argued—drawing on a little noted remark of Lord Kames'[72]—that such remedies are supererogatory.[73] They are a useful way

[68] Something which has been made impossible by Parliament's enthusiastic embrace of such awards in the Crime and Courts Act 2013 (UK), ss 34–35.

[69] *Rookes v Barnard* [1964] AC 1129 (HL) 1226 (Lord Devlin); *Kuddus v Chief Constable of Leicestershire* [2001] UKHL 29; [2002] 2 AC 122 (HL) [63] (Lord Nicholls).

[70] B McFarlane, 'Unjust Enrichment, Rights, and Value' in Nolan and Robertson (n 55).

[71] S Smith, 'The Restatement of Liabilities in Restitution' in C Mitchell and W Swadling (eds), *The Restatement Third: Restitution and Unjust Enrichment—Critical and Comparative Essays* (Oxford, Hart Publishing, 2013); S Smith, 'A Duty to Make Restitution' (2013) 26 *Canadian Journal of Law and Jurisprudence* 157. See also R Zimmermann, *The Law of Obligations: Roman Foundations of the Civilian Tradition* (Oxford, OUP, 1996), 867: '[I]n the words of the great pandectist Heinrich Dernburg, it is by means of an enrichment action that the law attempts to heal the wounds that it itself inflicts (by virtue of the abstract transfer of ownership).'

[72] Lord Kames, *Principles of Equity* 3rd edn, first published 1778 (Indianapolis, Liberty Fund, 2014) 300: '[I]f a debtor were not secure by voluntary payment, no man would venture to pay a shilling by any authority less than that of the sovereign court; and how ruinous to credit this would prove, must be obvious without taking a moment for reflection.'

[73] NJ McBride, 'Restitution and Unjust Enrichment: The Coming Counter-Revolution' (Obligations VIII conference, Cambridge, July 2016).

of giving people the confidence they need to engage in valuable transactions (such as paying debts, or making gifts). But they are no more than that—they are certainly not remedies that people are entitled to as of right, and were they not to exist, the law's legitimacy would not (in my view) come into question. McFarlane is on stronger ground, I think, in arguing that remedies that are awarded under the law on proprietary estoppel are necessary to preserve the legitimacy of the law.[74] McFarlane argues that such remedies help to mitigate the 'harshness ... of the classic rules of contract formation' that might otherwise cause people to question the justice of those rules.[75] McFarlane offers a similar explanation of the rules allowing a party to a contract to rescind that contract[76]—though, again, it could be argued that the remedy of rescission is supererogatory: a remedy that seeks to increase the good that the law does by empowering us to enter into certain transactions (such as making a contract or making a gift) by allowing particular instances of those transactions to be unwound when it is clear that the goods that would normally be realised by engaging in those transactions are absent.[77]

D. Summary

This section of this chapter has drawn a distinction between three kinds of remedies: (1) remedies that someone is entitled to; (2) remedies that are necessary to preserve the legitimacy of the law; and (3) remedies that are supererogatory because they do not fall into class (1) or (2). As can be seen from the table below (which does not, of course, cover all the remedies available in a private law action), this classification cuts across the traditional divide between legal and equitable remedies, though remedies that are traditionally classified as equitable in nature tend (but only tend) to fall into class (3), while remedies that are traditionally classified as legal in nature tend to fall into class (2).

Entitled	Necessary	Supererogatory
Remedies for recovery of property or its value	Compensatory damages for common law wrong	Specific performance
Remedies requiring public body to repair violation of right	Equitable compensation	Most injunctions
		Aggravated damages

(continued)

[74] B McFarlane and P Sales, 'Promises, Detriment, and Liability: Lessons from Proprietary Estoppel' (2015) 131 *LQR* 610, 632–33.
[75] ibid. See also B McFarlane, 'Equitable Estoppel as a Cause of Action: Neither One Thing Nor One Other' in S Degeling, J Edelman and J Goudkamp (eds), *Contract in Commercial Law* (Sidney, Thomson Reuters, 2016) para IV; and Harding (n 36) 298–99.
[76] McFarlane (n 70) 604.
[77] See NJ McBride, 'Rescission' in Virgo and Worthington (n 66).

(Continued)

Entitled	Necessary	Supererogatory
Compensatory damages for breach of contract (?)	Injunctions against persistent or criminal wrongdoers	Rescission?
	Punitive damages	Remedies for unjust enrichment (in case of money payments)?
	Remedies arising under proprietary estoppel	
	Rescission?	
	Remedies for unjust enrichment (in case of money payments)?	

IV. THE PLACE OF CLEAN HANDS

In *Tinsley v Milligan*, Lloyd LJ, having observed that it had been argued by counsel for Tinsley 'that equitable remedies are more fragile than remedies at common law', asked '[b]ut why should this be so?'[78] There is, of course, no reason why an equitable remedy should be more fragile than any other kind of remedy. But what I want to suggest in this section is that *supererogatory* remedies should be more fragile than other remedies precisely because they are supererogatory and it is therefore open to the courts to take a greater range of considerations into account in determining whether or not to make such a remedy available, and those considerations may legitimately include the cleanliness of the hands of the person who is seeking to be awarded that remedy.

A. The Fragility of Remedies

Remedies that a given C is entitled to should not be fragile at all: there are no grounds that would justify denying that remedy to C.[79]

A remedy (R) that would normally be awarded to C on the ground that doing so is necessary in order to preserve the legitimacy of the law should be denied if it is actually the case that awarding R to C would bring the law into more disrepute than would be the case were R *not* awarded to C.[80] The defence of illegality identifies one

[78] *Tinsley v Milligan* (CA) (n 15).

[79] It is no accident, then, that the courts are hostile to the defence of illegality being raised to deny a C a remedy for the recovery of property that was formerly in C's possession or its value (*Costello v Chief Constable of Derbyshire Police* [2001] 1 WLR 1437 (CA)), as we have identified that remedy as being one which C can plausibly claim to be entitled to.

[80] See the explanation of the House of Lords' decision in *Ruxley* (n 67).

such situation—a situation where awarding a remedy to a C who has been involved in serious criminal misconduct would make the law look like it was encouraging or endorsing C's behaviour.

When it comes to a supererogatory remedy (SR), the factors that are taken into account in deciding whether or not to award such a remedy are much wider. As the remedy is not one which a C can claim to be entitled to, and is not one which it would normally be necessary to award C in order to preserve the legitimacy of the law, the remedy—where it is awarded—is simply awarded on the basis that doing so would do more good than harm. So a SR should be denied where its award would do more harm than good. And in determining whether awarding a SR would do more harm than good, it would seem irrational not to have regard to the question of whether awarding C a SR would encourage people to engage in undesirable forms of behaviour. Where (i) C has behaved in an undesirable way and (ii) C's behaviour has 'an immediate and necessary relation to the [remedy] sued for',[81] a good case can be made for saying that awarding C a SR would encourage the kind of undesirable behaviour that C has behaved in. So where (i) and (ii) are true, there should be a presumption against awarding C an SR unless further facts show that denying C that SR would actually do more harm than good. Should that be the case, C should be awarded the SR despite having unclean hands.[82]

B. The Future of Clean Hands: Where C has Acted Unlawfully

If the argument made in the previous paragraphs is correct, we can immediately see a problem with proposition (*A*), above, that:

> (*A*) In a case where C is seeking some kind of equitable remedy against D, and C's hands are said to be unclean because C has acted unlawfully in the past, the defence of *illegality* should exclusively determine whether or not C should be denied the remedy she seeks because of her past unlawful conduct.

The argument that was made above, in favour of thinking that (A) is true, assumed that the law on illegality and the law on clean hands are basically concerned with the *same* issue: whether C's past unlawful behaviour should count against C being awarded the remedy that she seeks. The previous paragraphs show that that assumption is not necessarily correct: the law on illegality and the law on clean hands

[81] *Dering* (n 2) 319 (Eyre LCB).

[82] It should be noted that if (as was argued above, text at n 69) it is the case that aggravated damages are an SR, then in principle it should be possible to raise a defence of clean hands against a claim for aggravated damages. Such might be the case where D, a landlord, deliberately made it impossible for C to continue living in premises let to C by D in revenge for C's having an affair with D's wife. While claims for aggravated damages have been made in the past against landlords who have cynically forced out tenants from their premises (see, eg, *McMillan v Singh* (1984) 17 HLR 120 (CA)), it is not clear how the courts would currently handle such a claim in our hypothetical. Perhaps the courts would dismiss the claim on the basis that C's feelings of anger at the way he has been treated by D are unreasonable, given C's past behaviour.

should be seen as being concerned with fundamentally different issues.[83] The law on illegality should be seen as being concerned with whether awarding a remedy that would normally be awarded in order to preserve the legitimacy of the law will in fact do more harm than good *to the law's legitimacy*. By contrast, the law on clean hands should be seen as being concerned with whether awarding a supererogatory remedy will do more than harm than good *in general*, given the way that the person seeking that remedy has behaved in the past.

It follows that if the remedy R that C is seeking is a necessary one—one that would normally be awarded on the ground that it is necessary to do so in order to preserve the law's legitimacy—then the law of illegality should be the *only* area of law we look to, in order to see whether C's past misconduct should count against her being awarded R. But if the remedy R that C is seeking is supererogatory in nature, then the fact that awarding R to C would not bring the law into disrepute does not necessarily mean that C should be awarded R.[84] If it can be established that awarding R to C would do more harm than good *overall*—because awarding R to C would have a tendency to encourage people like C to engage in the kind of undesirable behaviour that C has been guilty of in the past—then R should still be denied to C on the basis of C's having unclean hands.

As we saw, the judges who decided *Tinsley v Milligan* simply assumed that the law on illegality and clean hands operated in lock-step together, at least in cases where the person seeking an equitable remedy had been guilty of some past unlawful conduct. How would *Tinsley v Milligan* be resolved if the understanding of the (non-) relationship between illegality and clean hands set out in the previous paragraph were accepted by the courts? The UKSC has made it clear that the defence of illegality would *not* apply to defeat the claim for a trust interest in Tinsley's house, even after the UKSC's decision in *Patel v Mirza*.[85] But could Milligan's claim to such an interest have been defeated on the basis that Milligan's hands were unclean? The answer is 'maybe' if (i) Milligan was seeking a remedy in *Tinsley v Milligan*, and (ii) that remedy was supererogatory in nature.

It is not at all clear that (i) is true, because it is not clear that Milligan, by seeking a *declaration* that she had a trust interest in Tinsley's house, was seeking to be awarded a remedy. A declaration does not seem to remedy anything, but rather state the existing position. However, what is the position if we say that (i) is true, because Milligan was seeking *both* a declaration of her rights over Tinsley's house and follow-up remedies to protect those rights? Because those follow-up remedies were designed

[83] *Contra* A Burrows, 'Remedial Coherence and Punitive Damages in Equity' in Degeling and Edelman (n 62) 386: 'I make no apology for reiterating that, in my opinion, there are common law counterparts to the famous equitable defences. The defence of illegality equates to the clean hands principle'; S Smith, 'Form and Substance in Equitable Remedies' in A Robertson and M Tilbury (eds), *Divergences in Private Law* (Oxford, Hart Publishing, 2016) 335: 'The clean hands doctrine is closely related to the general defence of illegality'.

[84] Of course, if the law on illegality indicates that awarding R to C *would* bring the law into disrepute, then R should be denied C, as awarding R to C will do more harm than good overall. So the law on illegality should be our first port of all in determining whether a supererogatory remedy should *not* be awarded to C; but it should not be our last.

[85] *Patel* (n 19).

to help Milligan recover her property or its value, it is arguable that Milligan had a right to those remedies.[86] If this is true, then denying Milligan those follow-up remedies on the basis that her hands were unclean would have been *wrong*—a violation of Milligan's rights—and, in fact, it would have been equally wrong to deny Milligan those remedies on the basis of illegality.[87]

What is the position if we say that (i) is true, on the basis that Milligan was seeking to be *granted* a trust interest in Tinsley's house as a remedy to prevent Tinsley's being unjustly enriched at Milligan's expense?[88] If we follow McFarlane,[89] and regard remedies for unjust enrichment as necessary to preserve the legitimacy of the law, then it would have been *inappropriate* to deny Milligan's claim to a trust interest over Tinsley's house simply on the basis of unclean hands. It is only if one views remedies for unjust enrichment as supererogatory[90] that it *might have* been appropriate to deny Milligan's claim on the basis of unclean hands. But even then, one would have to ask whether denying Milligan's claim would do more good than harm overall; in other words, whether discouraging people like Milligan from engaging in social security fraud is better than allowing people like Tinsley to get something for nothing from people like Milligan. It is doubtful whether this is the case and, therefore, doubtful whether there was ever any basis on which Milligan's claim could have been denied because of her unclean hands.

C. The Future of Clean Hands: Where C has Acted Lawfully

Let's now look at proposition (*B*), above, which—together with proposition (*A*)—formed the basis of the case for abolishing the defence of clean hands:

> (*B*) Where C has *not* acted unlawfully, the law would be left in an unsatisfactory state were C to be denied an equitable remedy against D simply because C had in the past engaged in conduct that is regarded as 'tricky' or 'iniquitious' or 'unconscionable' or whichever disapproving adjective one prefers.

The argument for thinking that (*B*) was correct began with category (1) type cases where a *shady* C is seeking equitable relief against D's continuously violating C's legal rights, and concluded that if the cleanliness of C's hands could not be taken into account in that kind of case then it should not be taken into account in any other kind of category (1) type case, and by extension should not be taken into account in a category (2) type case where a shady C is seeking equitable relief against her equitable rights being violated. Moving on to category (3) and category (4) type cases, it was observed that rule of law concerns militate against denying a shady C a remedy on the basis of unclean hands in those cases (and, indeed, in type (1) and (2) cases),

[86] See n 57.
[87] See n 79.
[88] *Contra* the analysis adopted by the House of Lords in *Foskett v McKeown* [2001] 1 AC 102 (HL) 109 (Lord Browne-Wilkinson).
[89] McFarlane (n 70).
[90] See n 72.

as the law could not claim to be operating in a certain, predictable and intelligible manner if it allowed its operation to turn on judgments about whether a particular C's behaviour violated some extra-legal standard of proper behaviour.

However, the distinction drawn in this chapter between necessary and supererogatory remedies undermines the starting point of this argument in favour of (*B*). An injunction that is awarded to a shady C1, whose common law rights are being persistently violated, is a necessary remedy[91] and therefore one that should not be denied on the basis of C1's hands being unclean. But it isn't necessary to award an injunction to a shady C2, whose rights are threatened with a one-off violation, where that violation does not amount to a crime. In such a case, an injunction is a supererogatory remedy and there is no inconsistency in refusing to award an injunction to a shady C2 on the grounds of C2's hands being unclean when an injunction *is* awarded to a shady C1 regardless of how dirty C1's hands are. Once we accept that a shady C may be denied an injunction against a common law wrong on the basis of unclean hands then there seems nothing inconsistent in *also* refusing an injunction to a shady C whose equitable rights are being violated on the basis of unclean hands. The distinction that the law should really be making, if it is to be consistent, is between cases where a shady C is the victim of persistent wrongdoing—where an injunction is necessary and cannot be denied on the basis of unclean hands—and cases where a shady C is the potential victim of a one-off wrong—where an injunction is supererogatory and can therefore be denied on the basis of unclean hands.

If this is right then the *only* argument that can be made in favour of (*B*) is the 'rule of law' argument that we made in favour of not allowing a defence of clean hands to be raised against a shady C who is seeking equitable relief in a category (3) or (4) type case. Such an argument could also work in favour of not allowing a clean hands defence to be raised against a shady C who is seeking equitable relief in a category (1) or (2) type case. So if this rule of law argument goes through, then it provides enough of a foundation to prop (*B*) up. But does it? In a case where C's past behaviour was not unlawful but was sufficiently undesirable that a court declined to grant C a supererogatory remedy that C was seeking, Peter Birks insisted that a judge must be able to say to C: 'It is not me who does this to you, but the law. Look I will show you.'[92] Can a judge do this? I think a judge can. This is what the judge can say:

> You are asking to be given something to which you have no positive right, and which no one could criticise the law for not granting you. In these circumstances, the law tells me that I can help you out, but only if doing so will do more good than harm. In judging whether or not granting you this remedy will do more good than harm, the law also tells me to have regard to your past behaviour and how desirable it was; and if it was clearly undesirable, to think about whether awarding you this remedy will encourage such undesirable behaviour in future. If it will, then even then that is not the end of your case. The law tells me to look at all the circumstances, and if there is some good that would be done by awarding you this remedy that outweighs the harm that this would do in terms of encouraging people to do as you have done, then the law tells me that I should still award you the remedy you seek.

[91] See n 65.

[92] See n 32 and associated text.

> I have done what the law told me to do, and I have concluded I should *not* award you this remedy. Your past behaviour was clearly undesirable. Awarding you this remedy would encourage others to follow your example. And I can find no sufficient good that would be done by awarding you this remedy that would outweigh the harm that would be done by granting you this remedy.

It is hard to see how C could complain when told this, or think that justice *according to the law* has not been done in her case.

So none of the arguments that were made in favour of (*B*) really work. In the case where C seeks a supererogatory remedy from the courts, there should still be room for the courts to deny C that remedy on the basis that C's hands are unclean, even though C's behaviour was not unlawful.

V. CONCLUSION

I hope I have managed to make the case for thinking that there is still a place for a defence of clean hands in the law. The rush to decry and destroy any differences between legal and equitable remedies must not result in the defence of clean hands being subsumed within the defence of illegality. While it would clearly be senseless to argue that the difference between legal and equitable remedies always reflect a distinction of substance rather than form, it would be equally senseless to argue that all remedies are fundamentally the same. There are a few remedies that we have a right to obtain from the courts. Many more remedies are awarded to us because otherwise the law would be brought into disrepute. And some remedies are awarded to us because some measure of good is done through their award. The defence of clean hands still has a role to play in determining when this last class of remedies will and should be awarded.

14

'Not Slavishly Nor Always'—Equity and Limitation Statutes

MARK LEEMING*

I. INTRODUCTION

IN JUDGMENTS DELIVERED at the beginning and the end of some three decades as a member of the United States Supreme Court, Scalia J observed that 'courts of equity can no more disregard statutory and constitutional requirements and provisions than can courts of law'.[1] That passage confirms that the way in which equity is understood and analysed in the United States is of continuing interest,[2] as well as introducing the theme of this chapter, which is equity's relationship with limitation statutes. That relationship is complex and subtle. Its nuances are more accurately captured by the familiar statement in Cardozo CJ's dissent in the New York Court of Appeals in *Graf v Hope Building Corpn* from which this chapter's title derives. Unlike the majority, the Chief Judge would have issued relief against the lender's opportunistic foreclosure following the borrower's trivial mistake and delay. In support of the availability of equitable relief, Cardozo CJ said, using characteristically[3] evocative language: '[E]quity follows the law, but not slavishly nor always'.[4] Cardozo CJ was referring to common law, and, obviously enough,

* I acknowledge the assistance of Ms Elizabeth Daley and Ms Lindi Todd, and the helpful comments of conference participants. All errors are mine.

[1] *Immigration and Naturalization Service v Pangilinan* 486 US 875, 883 (1988) and *Armstrong v Exceptional Child Centre* 135 S Ct 1378, 1385 (2015), both citing *Hedges v Dixon County* 150 US 182, 192 (1893).

[2] Scalia J's reasons were both directed to innovative equitable remedies created by the Ninth Circuit, reasoning which reads a little strangely to Anglo-Australian eyes. However, that is not to deny the ongoing interest and importance in the United States of what has been called 'the New Equity': S Bray, 'The Supreme Court and the New Equity' (2015) 68 *Vanderbilt Law Review* 997. See, also, many of the chapters in P Turner (ed), *Fusion and Fission* (Cambridge, Cambridge University Press, forthcoming).

[3] In B Cardozo, 'Law and Literature' (1925) 14 *Yale Review* 699, Cardozo had endorsed '[t]he mnemonic power of alliteration and antithesis' and '[t]he terseness and tang of the proverb and the maxim'. See M Hall (ed), *Selected Writings of Benjamin Nathan Cardozo* (New York, Matthew Bender, 1975) 338, 342.

[4] *Graf v Hope Building Corpn* 254 NY 1, 9; 171 NE 884, 887 (1930). The merits of the dissent were recognised even at the time: see A Bergman, 'Equitable Relief from the Effect of an Acceleration Clause in a Mortgage' (1930) 5 *St John's Law Review* 55. The division anticipates that more recently seen in *Cukurova Finance Ltd v Alfa Telecom Ltd (No 4)* [2013] UKPC 20; [2016] AC 923.

if equity had invariably followed the common law, there would never have been a distinctive equitable jurisprudence. However, the Chief Judge's aphorism may also be read as applying to statute. Understood in that way, there is no inconsistency with Scalia J's observation, for to follow is certainly not to disregard. Naturally, a court adjudicating an equitable claim will and must apply a statute which applies in terms. But equity goes further, and sometimes 'follows' limitation statutes even when they do not directly apply. The result is significant: equitable relief which would otherwise be available is denied by reason of a statute which does not in terms apply to a claimant's claim. How that occurs is a matter of no little complexity and subtlety. It is easier to point out, as Cardozo CJ did, what equity is *not* doing than to explain the processes at work in such cases.

As this chapter will explain, two quite distinct processes are in play. The first is statutory construction—and statutory construction which presents difficult and interesting issues relating to the interplay between equity and statute. The second, which only operates where the statute (as construed) does not apply, is the equitable doctrine of applying the statute by analogy. This doctrine also gives rise to difficult and interesting questions, but of a different nature. This chapter will consider how the requisite 'analogy' is identified, and how any such analogical application operates, something which has been closely considered by appellate courts in New South Wales.

This chapter adopts the following structure. First, it mentions, but only so as to put to one side, some superficial complexities in this area. It then outlines the historical background, in order to expose how the sources of doctrinal obscurity have arisen. The main portions of the chapter focus upon the processes of statutory construction and application by analogy mentioned above. It will be seen that each process involves the relationship between equity and statute, in ways which are more nuanced than may at first be appreciated.

A. Some Superficial Complexity

Ashburner's overview discloses a straightforward account of the relationship between equity and limitation statutes:[5]

> Lapse of time operates in itself as a defence … under one or other of the following circumstances. (a) A statute of limitation may apply in terms to equitable rights. (b) It may apply to legal rights, and courts of equity in aiding legal rights act in obedience to the statute. (c) It may apply to legal rights to which equitable rights correspond, and courts of equity in dealing with these equitable rights act by analogy to the Statute.

It is easy to see why the situation is more complex—indeed, *much* more complex—than stated by Ashburner. It is convenient at the outset to sketch some of the sources of complexity. I do so not with a view of providing a full analysis, but, instead, so as to be able to put them to one side, in order to focus without peripheral distraction on the relationship between equity and limitation statutes.

[5] D Browne, *Ashburner's Principles of Equity* 2nd edn (London, Butterworth & Co, 1933) 501–02.

i. Complexity from Overlapping Equitable Doctrines

Limitation statutes typically state in terms that they do not affect 'the rules of equity concerning the refusal of relief on the ground of laches acquiescence or otherwise'.[6] Even so, there remains a large question as to whether and if so how, in cases where a limitation statute applies directly or by analogy, other delay-based equitable defences might apply.[7] Consistently with two other aspects in this chapter, it is submitted that there is no simple answer applicable to all statutes of limitation, but that the analysis is essentially the same irrespective of whether the statute applies directly or by analogy. The analysis will turn on the particular statute and the particular equitable defence on which reliance is placed. The issue is whether the statute precludes reliance on the equitable defence, which is to say, that the statute is the exhaustive of the circumstances when relief is not available. That will depend upon the construction of the Act as a whole, in which task provisions which are expressly directed to the relationship between statute and equitable defences are apt to be highly influential (although falling short of being conclusive).[8] In the common case where a defendant points not merely to delay but to delay coupled with prejudice, it would seem unlikely that the statute (whether applying directly or by analogy) would exclude the equitable defence.[9]

Although this chapter is directed to the interaction between statute and equitable defences where both may be available, it passes over the question of the relationship between equitable defences such as laches, waiver and release as between themselves and their relationship with doctrines such as estoppel by acquiescence.[10] There are competing views as to the extent to which those overlapping defences are, or else should be, rationalised. One approach is to remove that which adds nothing save confusion. For example, 'acquiescence' is an imprecise term which on one view adds nothing to what is more precisely connoted by laches (understood as delay coupled with prejudice) and waiver, release and estoppel by acquiescence.[11] A more elaborate approach is to seek to rationalise those doctrines so that they cease to overlap.[12]

[6] See, eg, Limitation Act 1980 (UK), s 36(2); Limitation Act 1969 (NSW), s 9; see also Limitation of Actions Act 1936 (SA), s 26; Limitation of Actions Act 1974 (Qld), s 43; Limitation Act 1974 (Tas), s 36; Limitation Act 1958 (Vic), s 31; Limitation Act 2005 (WA), s 80. There are minor differences in the wording of these provisions, which most probably are immaterial: see *Re Loftus (decd)* [2006] EWCA Civ 1124; [2007] 1 WLR 591 [33] ff.

[7] See the 11 Australian, Canadian and English cases collected in G Dal Pont, *Law of Limitation* (Sydney, LexisNexis, 2016) [3.31]–[3.32].

[8] See (albeit in a different context) *John Holland Pty Ltd v Victorian Workcover Authority* [2009] HCA 45; 239 CLR 518 [20] 'such a statement is only a statement of intention which informs the construction of the Act as a whole. It must be an intention which the substantive provisions of the Act are capable of supporting.'

[9] See *Lallemand and Stevenson v Brown and Swan* [2014] ACTSC 235; 9 ACTLR 313 [140]–[155].

[10] See Lusina Ho, ch 15 in this volume.

[11] See J Edelman, 'Money Awards for the Cost of Performance' (2010) 4 *Journal of Equity* 122, 129.

[12] See Lusina Ho, ch 15 in this volume; *cf Fistar v Riverwood Legion and Community Club Ltd* [2016] NSWCA 81; 91 NSWLR 732 [49]–[51] and *Perera v Genworth Financial Mortgage Insurance Pty Ltd* [2017] NSWCA 19; 94 NSWLR 83 [44].

ii. Complexity from Historical Legislative Haphazardness

Another aspect of complexity derives from the fact that statutes of limitation have evolved haphazardly. The Law Commission has said that 'The current law on limitations has developed in an *ad hoc* way over a period of several centuries. Little thought has been given to the overall coherence of limitations law.'[13]

The problem is more acute in Australia, where there are significantly different approaches in different jurisdictions. One leading Australian commentator, referring to this historical dimension, has observed that the 'Australian States and Territories are at very different stages of development'.[14] In very general terms, the South Australian law reflects nineteenth-century English statutes. The Victorian, Tasmanian and Queensland laws reflect the English reforms of the late 1930s. New South Wales and the Northern Territory have statutes based on a 1967 New South Wales Law Reform Commission report,[15] while the laws of Western Australia and the Australian Capital Territory are modern and distinctive (for example, they apply directly to all equitable claims).

iii. Complexity from Australian Federal Considerations

A third aspect of complexity is peculiarly Australian. It derives from the absence of a general federal statute of limitations,[16] the substantial divergence between the Australian States and Territories, and the nature of the Australian federation.

There is no general federal limitation law, so that, ordinarily, Australian courts (state and federal) will be directed to state limitation statutes, which are far from uniform. Uniform legislation enacted in the 1990s had provided that for choice-of-law purposes limitation laws were regarded as substantive,[17] a result which was shortly thereafter confirmed (realigning the general law to the result achieved by statute)[18] by the High Court.[19] There are further complexities in the exercise of federal jurisdiction, which turn on the operation of sections 79 and 80 of the Judiciary Act 1903 (Cth), which has very recently been reinterpreted by the High Court and the operation

[13] Law Commission, *Limitation of Actions* (Law Com CP No 151, 1998) [11.2].

[14] P Handford, *Limitation of Actions* 3rd edn (Sydney, Thomson Reuters, 2011) vi; see, further, Dal Pont (n 7) [1.10]–[1.13], summarising the legislative history in each Australian jurisdiction.

[15] Australian Law Reform Commission, *First Report on the Limitation of Actions* (No 3, 1967).

[16] The specific limitations under federal legislation such as the Corporations Act 2001 (Cth) and intellectual property legislation falls far short of providing for a limitation period in all matters in federal jurisdiction.

[17] Choice of Law (Limitation Periods) Act 1993 (NSW); Choice of Law (Limitation Periods) Act 1993 (Vic); Limitation of Actions Act 1936 (SA), ss 38, 38A; Limitation of Actions Act 1974 (Qld), s 43A; Choice of Law (Limitation Periods) Act 1994 (WA); Limitation Act 1974 (Tas), ss 32A–32D; Choice of Law (Limitation Periods) Act 1994 (NT); Limitation Act 1985 (ACT), Pt 4, Div 4.4.

[18] This is perhaps an example of common law following statute: see M Leeming, 'Theories and Principles Underlying the Development of the Common Law: The Statutory Elephant in the Room' (2013) 36 *University of New South Wales Law Journal* 1002, 1021–26.

[19] *John Pfeiffer Pty Ltd v Rogerson* [2000] HCA 36; 203 CLR 503 [100].

of which in relation to choice of law rules may fairly be regarded as unsettled.[20] And the choice-of-law rules governing trusts are not straightforward, particularly in relation to trusts created by operation of law to which one aspect of this paper is directed.[21] But enough is enough. For the balance of this chapter, I shall put to one side Australian federal complexities.

B. Historical Overview

This chapter considers two deeper aspects of complexity in the relationship between equity and limitation statutes: the way in which statute has addressed equitable principle in terms, giving rise to complex questions of construction, and the nature of the equitable doctrine of itself. Neither aspect may be considered without regard to the historical development of this area of the law. This section provides a brief (and somewhat simplified) summary.

For present purposes, the starting point is the statute of 21 Jac 1 c 16 enacted in 1623,[22] which is the source of the rule that most claims in tort and contract have a six-year limitation period.[23] The actions specified in s 3 'shall be commenced and sued within … six years next after the cause of such Accions or Suit, and not after' in most cases. There were exceptions for accounts between merchants, and the statute did not apply to speciality debts. It was not until another two centuries had passed that the Civil Procedure Act 1833[24] provided that speciality debts be barred after 20 years.

A series of eighteenth-century cases made it clear that courts of equity would apply the statute, but fell short of clearly explaining how that would occur. Two decisions of Lord Redesdale at the beginning of the nineteenth century have proven to be influential. His Lordship reached the following conclusion in *Hovenden v Annesley*:[25]

> I think it is a mistake in point of language to say that Courts of Equity act merely by analogy to the statutes; they act in obedience to them. … I think therefore that Courts of Equity are bound to yield obedience to the Statute of Limitations upon all legal titles and legal demands and cannot act contrary to the spirit of its provisions. I think the statute must be taken virtually to include Courts of Equity; for when the legislature by statute limited

[20] See *Rizeq v Western Australia* [2017] HCA 23; 91 ALJR 707.

[21] See JD Heydon and M Leeming, *Jacobs' Law of Trusts in Australia* 8th edn (Sydney, LexisNexis, 2016) 626.

[22] For earlier statutes, including the Statutes of Fines and Non-Claim and the statute of 32 Hen 8 c 2, see J Brunyate, *Limitations of Actions in Equity* (London, Stevens and Sons, 1932) 2–4.

[23] Section 3 was directed to 'all Accions or Trespass, Quare clausum fregit, all Accions of Trespas, Detinue, Accion sur Trover and Replevyn for taking away of Goods and cattell, all Accions of Accompt and upon the Case, all Accions of Debt grounded upon any lending or contract without specialitie, all Accions of Debt for Arrerages of Rent, and all Accions of Assault Menace Battery Wounding and Imprisonment'.

[24] Civil Procedure Act 1833, 3 & 4 Will 4 c 42.

[25] *Hovenden v Lord Annesley* [1806] 2 Sch & Lef 607, 630.

> the proceedings at law in certain cases and provided no express limitation for proceedings in equity, it must be taken to have contemplated that equity followed the law, and therefore it must be taken to have virtually enacted in the same cases a limitation for Courts of Equity also.

In *Cholmondeley v Clinton*, Lord Redesdale dealt with a claim in equity's exclusive jurisdiction, saying that 'I conceive therefore that the very words of the Statute of James 1, if it is a statute which has any application to a Court of Equity, apply to such a case as this'.[26] His Lordship said that Parliament was to be taken to know that 'all large estates and every considerable property was constantly turned into an equitable property' and explained what he had said in *Hovenden v Annesley* as follows:[27]

> I take it, therefore, to be a positive law which ought to bind all Courts and for that reason I have taken the liberty in another place to say that I considered it not simply a rule adopted by Courts of Equity by analogy to what had been done in Courts of Law under the statute but that it was a proceeding in obedience to the statute and that the framers of that statute must have meant that Courts of Equity should adopt that rule of proceeding.

The equitable doctrine thereafter became settled, notably by *Knox v Gye*,[28] and as will be seen in the next section of this chapter, statute itself came to recognise the existence of a doctrine of application by analogy when there was a gap in the statute.

Precisely how the doctrine operated remained debatable. John Brunyate, who later revised Maitland's lectures in Equity,[29] won the Yorke Prize in 1929 for his influential essay, later published, on how limitation statutes applied in equity.[30] He said there were two views:[31]

> The first, Lord Redesdale's opinion, that in cases in which equity was accustomed to follow the law the statutes were adopted by virtue of this custom, and that in other cases they were adopted by analogy as part of the law of laches; the second, the later opinion, that in deciding questions that might have arisen at law, being questions within their auxiliary and perhaps also their concurrent jurisdiction, the Courts of Equity were as much bound by the statutes as were the Courts of Law, and that in other cases they adopted the statutes by analogy.

The difference in approach turns in part on a question of statutory construction—whether the statute spoke directly to courts of equity. The difference had practical consequences, because equity would only follow the law when it was not inequitable to do so. Hence, to the extent that equity's approach turned on equity following the law, there would *in all such cases* be a residual discretion to disapply the statute. On the other hand, if the statute were regarded as applying directly to a suit, then there would be no such discretion.

[26] *Cholmondeley v Clinton* (1821) 4 Bli 1; 4 ER 721.
[27] ibid Bli 119–20; ER 736.
[28] *Knox v Gye* (1872) LR 5 HL 656.
[29] *Equity—A Course of Lectures* rev edn (Cambridge, Cambridge University Press, 1936).
[30] Brunyate (n 22).
[31] *Cholmondeley* (n 26).

C. Construing Statutes Which Draw upon Equitable Doctrine

The intertwined history of equitable doctrine and statutes means that the question of construction can be especially complex. Although this is 'merely' a question of statutory construction, the following examples illustrate some recurring themes.

i. First Example: Statutory Recognition of Equitable Principle

A ready example of the interrelationship may be found in s 36 of the Limitation Act 1980 (UK) and s 23 of the Limitation Act 1969 (NSW). Each section provides that the statutory time limits for many common law actions: '[do] not apply to any claim for specific performance of a contract or for an injunction or for other equitable relief, except in so far as any such time limit may be applied by the court by analogy …'. Conversely, section 27 of the Limitation Act 2005 (WA) imposes a six-year limitation period for actions 'in which the relief is sought in equity and for which … the limitation period would not be determined in equity by analogy to the limitation period for any other cause of action'.

The former example is best seen as recognising longstanding equitable principle, rather than being the source of or authority for applying statutes by analogy.[32] It is an example of statute responding to and preserving an equitable doctrine which itself depended upon the *absence* of statute applying to a particular class of case. It may be said to be a case of statute following equity (resembling the exceptions now found for resulting and constructive trusts in the modern equivalents of the Statute of Frauds),[33] reflecting the result reached by equity prior to those exceptions being enacted. The Western Australian legislation is, of course, unintelligible without recourse to the equitable principle displaced by it. Both examples reflect an aspect of the important point once made by Gleeson CJ: 'Legislation and the common law are not separate and independent sources of law; the one the concern of parliaments, and the other the concern of courts. They exist in a symbiotic relationship.'[34]

ii. Second Example: The Meaning of Constructive Trustee

The decision of the United Kingdom Supreme Court in *Williams v Central Bank of Nigeria* confirmed that even though the statute applied in terms to a claim against a 'trustee', and even though 'trust' and 'trustee' were expressly defined to include a constructive trust, the statute did not apply to a knowing recipient of trust funds who was accountable as a constructive trustee.[35] Lord Sumption JSC referred with

[32] A point made in *Alec Finlayson Pty Ltd v Royal Freemason Benevolent Institution of New South Wales Nominees Ltd* [2013] NSWSC 1168 [41].

[33] Law of Property Act 1925 (UK), s 53; Conveyancing Act 1919 (NSW), s 23C(2). See A Burrows, 'The relationship between common law and statute in the law of obligations' (2012) 128 *LQR* 232, 248–51.

[34] *Brodie v Singleton Shire Council* [2001] HCA 29; 206 CLR 512 [31]; *Commonwealth Bank of Australia v Barker* [2014] HCA 32; 253 CLR 169 [17].

[35] *Williams v Central Bank of Nigeria* [2014] UKSC 10; [2014] AC 1189.

a measure of understatement to the 'rather complicated interaction between the successive statutes of limitation and the equitable rules regarding the limitation of actions against trustees'.[36] The legislative history pointed squarely in support of the conclusion reached, which was that a person said to be accountable as a constructive trustee could not plead the statute of limitations applicable to trustees. The legislative history is essentially as follows.

First, the Judicature Act 1873 confirmed the traditional position that express trusts were not within the Statute of Limitations.[37] However, the Trustee Act 1888 reversed the position and extended the benefit of the statute of limitations to trustees in special cases.[38] Section 8(1) applied:

> In any action or other proceeding against a trustee or any person claiming through him, except where the claim is founded upon any fraud or fraudulent breach of trust to which the trustee was party or privy, or is to recover trust property, or the proceeds thereof still retained by the trustee, or previously received by the trustee and converted to his use …

If the section applied, the trustee was entitled to the same period of limitation as would have applied if he or she were not a trustee. 'Trustee' was defined to include an executor or administrator 'and a trustee whose trust arises by construction or implication of law as well as an express trustee'.[39] In *Taylor v Davies*,[40] a Canadian appeal based on a cognate statute, where a person in knowing receipt of trust assets sought to invoke the statute, the Privy Council held that the statute did not apply 'to a case where a person having taken possession of property on his own behalf, is liable to be declared a trustee by the Court'. Despite the consideration of a Law Revision Committee chaired by Lord Wright in 1939,[41] the Limitation Act 1939 repealed the Trustee Act 1888 and re-enacted s 8 of that Act by s 19, in substantially similar terms to s 21 of the current Act. According to Lord Sumption, the result was to confirm that the legislation did not deal with constructive trusts, but rather (as had been held in *Taylor v Davies*) to persons who, at the time of misapplication of trust assets, had assumed the responsibilities of a trustee, whether expressly or de facto.[42] Although that aspect of the reasoning has been criticised, its force is that the Wright Committee made no mention of *Taylor v Davies* nor did it recommend the abolition of a distinction for this purpose between constructive trusts and express trusts. Modern English cases have so held,[43] and they were confirmed in *Williams v Bank of Nigeria.*

[36] ibid [6].
[37] Judicature Act 1873, s 25(2).
[38] Trustee Act 1888, 51 & 52 Vict c 59.
[39] ibid s 1(3).
[40] *Taylor v Davies* [1920] AC 636 (PC (Can)).
[41] See P Mitchell, *A History of Tort Law 1900–1950* (Cambridge, Cambridge University Press, 2015) 243 ff for the creation and operation of this committee.
[42] *Williams v Bank of Nigeria* (n 35) [24]–[27].
[43] See *Paragon Finance plc v DB Thakerar & Co (a firm)* [1999] 1 All ER 400 (CA); *JJ Harrison (Properties) Ltd v Harrison* [2001] EWCA Civ 1467; [2002] 1 BCLC 162; *Dubai Aluminium Co Ltd v Salaam* [2002] UKHL 48; [2003] 2 AC 366, [139]–[143]; *Gwembe Valley Development Co Ltd v Koshy (No 3)* [2003] EWCA Civ 1048; [2004] 1 BCLC 131; *Halton International (Holdings) Inc Sarl v Guernroy Ltd* [2006] EWCA Civ 801; [2006] WTLR 1241; *Cattley v Pollard* [2006] EWHC 3130 (Ch); [2007] Ch 353; and *Peconic Industrial Development Ltd v Lau Kwok Fai* [2009] 5 HKC 135.

The position in Australia is different, and for two quite different reasons. For one thing, Australian State legislatures have made different choices. The Victorian decisions, which closely follow the 1888 legislation, have preserved the result that constructive trusts are outside the statute.[44] However, in its First Report on the Limitation of Actions,[45] the New South Wales Law Reform Commission addressed the point directly, referring squarely to *Taylor v Davies* and altering the statutory language.[46] The position was thoroughly examined by the New South Wales Court of Appeal in *Sze Tu v Lowe*, where it was concluded:[47]

> By contrast, when one looks at the definitions of 'trust' and 'trustee' in s 11(1) of the Limitation Act, the reference to 'and whether or not the trust arises only by reason of the transaction impeached', makes clear that it was intended that 'constructive trustee' or 'trustee' was to have a wider meaning than that which they had been given by the Courts of Equity previously, such as in *Taylor v Davies*.

There is another, and more subtle, distinction between the United Kingdom and Australian positions. Not only is there a different legislative history, but there is now a different formulation of equitable principle. Take the case of a person accountable as a constructive trustee for knowing assistance. Lord Sumption observed:[48]

> it is now clear that knowing assisters are liable on account of their own dishonesty, irrespective of the dishonesty of the trustees: *Royal Brunei Airlines Sdn Bhd v Tan* [1995] 2 AC 378. There is no rational reason why the draftsman of section 21(1)(a) should have intended that the availability of limitation to a non-trustee should depend on a consideration which had no bearing on his liability, namely the honesty or dishonesty of the trustee.

In Australia, Lord Browne-Wilkinson's reformulation basis of liability is inconsistent with what was held by the High Court in *Consul Development Pty Ltd v DPC Estates Pty Ltd*, and is not good law in Australia until and unless the High Court so determines.[49] In Australia, such a person cannot be liable under this limb of

[44] *Paragon* (n 43) and *Nolan v Nolan* [2004] VSCA 109.

[45] New South Wales Law Reform Commission, *First Report on the Limitation of Actions* (Law Com 3, 1967).

[46] The Limitation Act 1969 (NSW) as initially enacted had a sidenote which included 'cf *Taylor v Davies* [1920] AC 636 at 653', and 'trusts' was defined to include 'express implied and constructive trusts.' The Commission wrote at 103:

> The reference to a trust arising only by reason of a transaction impeached and the marginal reference to *Taylor v Davies* ([1920] AC 636) are made so as expressly to comprehend what might appear to many minds to be a typical constructive trust, namely, the case of a man in a fiduciary position acquiring, in breach of his duty, property in relation to which he is a fiduciary. In *Taylor v Davies* (above) however, Viscount Cave, giving the reasons of the Privy Council, said that such a man was not a trustee within a definition similar to that in the Trustee Act and was thus not disentitled to plead a statute of limitations. ... We think that a fiduciary who becomes a constructive trustee by taking property in breach of his duty should not be in a better position in relation to the limitation of actions than other trustees and the references inserted in the definition of 'trust' will ensure that he is not.

[47] *Sze Tu v Lowe* [2014] NSWCA 462; (2014) 89 NSWLR 317 [338].

[48] *Williams* (n 35) [35].

[49] *Farah Constructions Pty Ltd v Say-Dee Pty Ltd* [2007] HCA 22; 230 CLR 89 [163].

Barnes v Addy unless the breach of duty by the fiduciary amounts to a fraudulent and dishonest design.[50]

My point is not merely to identify small textual and doctrinal differences between the United Kingdom and Australia. It is to observe that, underneath those superficial differences, a broader identicality of reasoning may be seen. In all cases, the tangled legislative history of statutes of limitation, which engage directly with equitable doctrine, requires a close analysis, and one which is sensitive to fine distinctions.

iii. Third Example: Concealed Fraud

Similar themes may be seen in relation to the doctrine of concealed fraud. Eighteenth-century cases in equity upheld claims made after the six-year period where there was fraud.[51] In 1806, in *Hovenden v Lord Annesley*,[52] Lord Redesdale held that in cases of fraud, the period of limitation would not run in equity until the fraud was discovered.[53] That judicial development was reflected in the Real Property Limitation Act 1833,[54] which repealed the 1623 Act insofar as it applied to land and replaced it with a fuller body of rules, including s 26 which applied in terms to 'every case of a concealed fraud'.

Once again, the law here was, at least until recently, quite confused. Sheridan put the position vividly:[55]

> If any branch of the law can be described as a muddle, the doctrine of concealed fraud has no rival for that epithet; presenting, as it does, an impression of multitudes of decisions confusing to such a degree that it seems incredible that the judges are speaking of the same doctrine.

A series of decisions confined the availability of the doctrine to equitable claims.[56] However, a subtler analysis was given by *Metacel Pty Ltd v Ralph Symonds Ltd*,[57] holding that either the doctrine was a 'peculiar doctrine of equity' limited to claims in equity's exclusive jurisdiction, or else, to the extent that it applied to claims in the concurrent jurisdiction, courts either regarded themselves as bound by the limitation statute or acted by analogy to it. Six members of the High Court of Australia said, in *Commonwealth v Cornwell*:[58]

> First, in cases of 'concealed fraud' courts of equity refused to apply by analogy statutes of limitation which operated upon actions at law. Secondly, this doctrine of 'concealed fraud' did not furnish an answer on equitable grounds to a plea in a common law court of the

[50] A result which does not prevent other forms of ancillary liability: see *Hasler v Singtel Optus Pty Ltd* [2014] NSWCA 266; 87 NSWLR 609 [68]–[82].

[51] For example, *Booth v Lord Warrington* (1714) 4 Bro PC 163 and *South Sea Co v Wymondsell* (1732) 3 P Wms 143.

[52] *Hovenden v Lord Annesley* (n 25).

[53] Concealed fraud is considered in the following section of this chapter.

[54] Real Property Limitation Act 1833, 3 & 4 Will 4 c 27.

[55] L Sheridan, *Fraud in Equity* (London, Sir Isaac Pitman & Sons Ltd, 1956) 159.

[56] Including *Bulli Coal Mining Co v Osborne* [1899] AC 351 (PC (Aust)) and *John v Dodwell & Co Ltd* [1918] AC 563 (PC (Ceylon)), cited with approval in *R v McNeil* (1922) 31 CLR 76, 99–100.

[57] *Metacel Pty Ltd v Ralph Symonds Ltd* (1969) 90 WN (Pt 1) (NSW) 449.

[58] *Commonwealth v Cornwell* [2007] HCA 16; 229 CLR 519 [9] (citations omitted).

1623 Act or other limitation statute to, for example, an action in tort; it was not possible to plead by way of replication on equitable grounds that the existence of the plaintiff's cause of action had been fraudulently concealed from the plaintiff by the defendant. Accordingly, in *Metacel Pty Ltd v Ralph Symonds Ltd*, Sugerman JA said:

> 'Concealed fraud remains a special doctrine of courts of equity applicable where relief is sought in those courts and is not applicable in bar of the Statute of Limitations in a pure common law action.'

That narrow but principled approach nevertheless provided scope for claimants to avoid defeat by the statute, because Exchequer decisions had established the rule made it clear that the fraudulent concealment by the defendant *itself* gave rise to a cause of action. Thus in *Imperial Gas Company v London Gas Company* the claim for conversion was barred, notwithstanding the defendant's interference with the claimant's pipes, but a separate action in trespass in concealing the wrongful acts was allowed.[59] Martin B observed during argument that '[i]t constantly happens that the owner of a coal mine takes coal from an adjoining mine, and by fraud prevents its being found out for more than six years, yet that is no answer to the Statute of Limitations'.[60] *Hunter v Gibbons* was another such case: the equitable replication of concealed fraud in answer to the statute which was pleaded in defence to an action for trespass for taking underground coal was not allowed, but the court said that the claimant could sue in a court of equity making fraud the gist of the action.[61]

Finally, the equitable doctrine of concealed fraud was then extended, by statute, to legal claims. The joint judgment in *Cornwell* explains the process whereby the equitable doctrine was enacted, with modifications, in s 26(b) of the Limitation Act 1939 (UK) and then s 32 of the Limitation Act 1980 (UK).[62] This is an instance of limitation statutes not only recognising equitable doctrine in terms, but expanding the scope of its area of operation.

D. Conclusions

It would be idle to multiply examples.[63] The richness of the analysis tends to confirm the hypothesis that the interaction between statute and equity is rich and distinctive. That is a consequence of a lengthy history, where equity has responded to perceived gaps in the statutory scheme, *and* where statute has responded—in a variety of ways—to equitable principle. It is an example of what I have elsewhere referred as the temporal dimension to the interaction between legislative and judicial changes in the law, a phenomenon which recurs throughout the law.[64]

[59] *Imperial Gas Light Company v London Gas Light Company* (1854) 10 Exch 39; 156 ER 346.
[60] ibid Exch 42–3; ER 348.
[61] *Hunter v Gibbons* (1856) 26 LJ Ex 1; 156 ER 1281.
[62] *Commonwealth v Cornwell* (n 58) [40]–[44].
[63] eg, in *Creggy v Barnett* [2016] EWCA Civ 1004; [2017] PNLR 4, the Court of Appeal divided on whether a claim against a trustee for the recovery of trust money which was wrongly paid away or for compensation in respect of other trust assets wrongly misapplied was a 'liquidated pecuniary claim' in s 29(5)(a) of the Limitation Act 1980 (UK).
[64] Leeming (n 18) 1002, 1021–6.

II. THE NATURE OF THE ANALOGICAL REASONING

Let it be assumed that the question of construction has been resolved, and that a limitation statute does *not* apply directly to an equitable claim. A quite different process then takes place. It is necessary to consider whether the statute is to be applied by analogy, and, if so, how that is to occur, bearing in mind that equity has its own doctrines directed to delay. These issues are interesting, and have given rise to confusion. Indeed, it has been said that 'The reason why a statutory limitation period is applied to a circumstance which was not recognised in the terms of the statute has never been clearly explained'.[65] That is unfortunate, particularly from the perspective of the claimant whose claim is denied only because of a statute which does *not* apply in terms. There is thus good reason to attempt to unpack the considerations which apply.

The starting point must be to compare the legal right which is barred by the direct operation of the statute with the equitable claim at hand. For example, in *Cohen v Cohen*,[66] Dixon J upheld a wife's claim that her estranged husband was required to account specifically for the proceeds of sale of her furniture as not being barred by the statute by analogy, but came to the opposite conclusion regarding her claim to be repaid the proceeds of converting a sum of German marks into pounds, because he was found not to be required to hold the amount specifically for her. Dixon J observed (by reference to authority) that 'courts of equity have refused to see any analogy when a person, intending to act in a capacity which is fiduciary, has received, as and for the beneficial property of another, something which he is to hold, apply or account for specifically for his benefit'.[67]

How does this process of analogical comparison operate? One looks at the elements of the legal and equitable rights, and in particular to whether the claimant's entitlement to a common law or equitable remedy is derived from the same conduct. Thus, for example, it has been said that 'one could scarcely imagine a more correspondent set of remedies as damages for fraudulent breach of contract and equitable compensation for breach of fiduciary duty in relation to the same factual situation, namely, the deliberate withholding of money due by a manager to his artist'.[68] However, *Cohen v Cohen* shows that quite fine distinctions may be drawn.[69] By way of further examples, *Harris v Harris*[70] and *Re Robinson; McLaren v Public Trustee*[71] were cases where a trustee had mistakenly paid the wrong beneficiary and, many years later, the underpaid beneficiary had sued and was met by a limitation defence. The different outcomes reflected the facts that Mr Harris, 12 years later, sought and

[65] *Agricultural Land Management Ltd v Jackson (No 2)* [2014] WASC 102; 42 WAR 1 [207].

[66] *Cohen v Cohen* (1929) 42 CLR 91.

[67] This was the critical distinction applied in *Re Robinson; McLaren v Public Trustee* [1911] 1 Ch 502 (Ch D).

[68] *Coulthard v Disco Mix Club Ltd* [2000] 1 WLR 707 (Ch D) 730.

[69] So, too, does *P & O Nedlloyd BV v Arab Metals Co* [2006] EWCA Civ 1717; [2007] 1 WLR 2288 [34]–[53].

[70] *Harris v Harris* (1861) 29 Beav 107; 54 ER 567.

[71] *Re Robinson; McLaren v Public Trustee* (n 67).

obtained orders for the specific property he should have received (5,000*l* Consols, rather than 5,000*l* sterling), while Mrs McLaren sought merely an order for the payment of money. She failed, on the basis that 'although, owing to the fact that the claimant is not the person who paid the money, the action is one which could not have been maintained at common law, it is in substance a mere money demand to which a Court of Equity, acting by analogy to the statute, would apply the same period of limitations'.[72]

What justifies those distinctions? They are an instance of the important general phenomenon in legal analysis of ascribing the right level of abstraction or particularity. This may also be seen in the identification of the 'risk of harm' and the kind of harm which must be reasonably foreseeable for the purposes of the law of negligence,[73] and the identification of the 'purpose' of a statute or a contract;[74] there are many other examples. Professors Twining and Miers have said that '[t]here are no categorical rules to direct judges about the selection of appropriate levels of generality'.[75] That is one reason, not without force, in favour of limitation legislation which speaks directly to equitable claims.[76]

It seems to me that it is also necessary to look to the limitation statute itself, to consider whether it is consistent with its application by analogy to the equitable claim.[77] For the statute may be aligned with, or quite foreign to, the values vindicated by equity. Take for example the relatively short limitation periods which tend to apply to applications for judicial review. A claimant who seeks injunctive relief preventing reliance on an administrative decision which has been made through misuse of the claimant's confidential information may have a strong case for contending that the limitation period should have no application by analogy. Conversely, a short limitation period aimed at protecting government revenue may not be applicable either in terms or by way of analogy to an equitable claim for pecuniary relief.

Considerations of that nature suggest that the process may resemble that adopted in Australia where statutory illegality is relied on in answer to an equitable claim. In Australia, where a contract or trust is 'not directly contrary to the provisions of the statute by reason of any express or implied prohibition in the statute' but which is 'associated with or in furtherance of illegal purposes', then 'the courts act not in response to a direct legislative prohibition but, as it is said, from 'the policy of

[72] ibid 513.

[73] See *Uniting Church in Australia Property Trust (NSW) v Miller* [2015] NSWCA 320; 91 NSWLR 752 [110]–[122] and the authorities there considered.

[74] See *Perpetual Custodians Ltd as custodian for Tamoran Pty Ltd as trustee for Michael Crivelli v IOOF Investment Management Ltd* [2013] NSWCA 231; 304 ALR 436 [90]–[102] and the authorities there considered.

[75] W Twining and D Miers, *How To Do Things With Rules* 5th edn (Cambridge, Cambridge University Press, 2010) 150.

[76] See, eg, the observation by the Western Australian Law Reform Commission: 'The doctrine of analogy, already reduced to a shadow of its former self by the fact that most equitable claims are now directly the subject of Limitation Act provisions, will disappear. The Commission sees this as a wholly desirable development': Law Reform Commission of Western Australia, *Limitation and Notice of Actions* (Project 36II, 1997) [13.76].

[77] See *Johns v Johns* [2004] NZCA 42; [2004] 3 NZLR 202 [78]–[80].

the law'.[78] That bears some resemblance to the analysis where it is said that a limitation statute applies by analogy.

Finally, a threshold question, which can be overlooked, is the nature of the limitation statute itself. That is not merely because regard must be had to the text and purpose of the particular limitation statute. It is also because limitation statutes themselves come in a wide variety of types. As Windeyer J said:[79]

> Statutory provisions imposing time limits on actions take various forms and have different purposes. Some are for preventing stale claims, some for establishing possessory titles, some for the protection of public authorities, some in aid of executors and administrators. Some are incidents of rights created by statutes. Some prevent actions being brought after, some before, a lapse of time.

For example, if the statute is merely an incident of the statutory right, then it will be inapplicable directly, and unlikely to be applicable by analogy.[80]

III. THE WAY IN WHICH EQUITY APPLIES A LIMITATION STATUTE BY ANALOGY?

Next, let it be assumed that a limitation statute is considered to apply by analogy to an equitable claim. A key idea is that if equity applies a limitation statute by analogy, it means just that. There is no *analogical* application of the statute if it is merely a contributing consideration to a more general exercise of discretion. Most limitation statutes provide bright line and necessarily arbitrary resolutions to questions of delay. If the statute applies by analogy to an equitable claim, then there will be no scope for a further, residual discretion, although that is not to deny that separate equitable defences such as acquiescence or estoppel may also be available in a particular case.

There was a measure of authority for the limitation statute to apply *as part of* the law of laches, thereby retaining a 'residual discretion', reflecting the position favoured by Brunyate. Typical was the statement in a South Australian case that 'before applying the statutory time limit by analogy, I must be satisfied that in all the circumstances it is just to do so'.[81] For the most part, the position was stated without analysis, and may not even have been argued. *Gerace v Auzhair Supplies*[82] reviewed the position from first principle.

[78] *Nelson v Nelson* (1995) 184 CLR 538, 552; *Miller v Miller* [2011] HCA 9; 242 CLR 446 [26]. Contrast the position in the decisions that culminated in *Patel v Mirza* [2016] UKSC 42; [2017] AC 417.

[79] *Australian Iron & Steel Ltd v Hoogland* (1962) 108 CLR 471, 488.

[80] See, eg, the analysis in *Airey v Airey* [1958] 2 QB 300 (CA).

[81] *The Duke Group Ltd (in liq) v Alamain Investments Ltd* [2003] SASC 415 (appeal dismissed *Barker v Duke Group Ltd (in liq)* [2005] SASC 81; 91 SASR 167). See also *Hewitt v Henderson* [2006] WASCA 233 [25]; *KM v HM* (1993) 96 DLR (4th) 289, 333; and *Williams v Minister, Aboriginal Land Rights Act 1983* (1994) 35 NSWLR 497 (CA) 509–10.

[82] *Gerace v Auzhair Supplies* [2014] NSWCA 181; 87 NSWLR 435, noted (2014) 88 *Australian Law Journal* 621. For criticisms, see *Issa v Issa* [2015] NSWSC 112 [41]–[81] and A O'Dea and P O'Dea, 'The Application of Statutory Time Limitation Provisions by Analogy to Claims in Equity's Exclusive Jurisdiction' (2015) 4 *Journal of Civil Litigation and Practice* 56.

The appellants were three brothers who were the sole directors and shareholders of Auzhair Supplies. In 2002 and 2003, two lenders advanced funds to Auzhair, and received interest payments over the next six years. However, in 2005, the appellants and the lenders agreed to transfer the company's assets to a different company, Auzhair 1 Pty Ltd, a company in which the lenders as well as the brothers were shareholders. The first company was then deregistered following a declaration that it had no liabilities. The declaration was incorrect, for it still owed its lenders, but it was not alleged that anyone had acted dishonestly (it seems that all parties assumed that the assignment was effective to assign the company's liability as well as its assets). It was accepted that in transferring the company's assets to Auzhair 1 Pty Ltd for little or no consideration, the appellants had acted in breach of fiduciary duty.

Auzhair was reinstated in 2010 on its lenders' application and sued Auzhair 1 Pty Ltd and the three brothers. By then, more than six years had elapsed. The Corporations Act 2001 (Cth) provides for a six-year limitation period for claims for compensation for breaches of directors' statutory duties.[83] Auzhair had, of course, only sued in equity, but the directors sought to apply the statute by way of analogy to the equitable claims made against them. In opposition to this, it was pointed out that for most of that six-year period, Auzhair had ceased to exist.

At first instance, it was held that the claim for breach of fiduciary duty in equity was 'as close as possible' to a claim for breach of statutory duties to act in good faith in the best interests of the corporation and for a proper purpose, and not to gain an advantage for themselves or to cause detriment to the corporation.[84] No challenge was made to that assessment on appeal. However, the primary judge took the view that there was a residual discretion to be exercised, and held that it would be inequitable to apply the limitation period, in light of the fact that the company and its liquidator could not exercise their rights against the former directors after it had been deregistered and until such time as it had been reinstated, and in light of the absence of any evidence of prejudice.[85] The brothers' appeal was allowed.

Meagher JA, with whom Beazley P and Emmett JA agreed, reviewed the authorities extensively and concluded:[86]

> None of the authorities to which reference has been made so far suggest, as Brunyate does, that where there is a limitation statute and closely analogous remedy at law, equity applies the statute as part of the law of laches and allows, as exceptions to the application of the statute, 'any exceptions that are allowed in the law of laches'. Brunyate's analysis fixes upon Lord Redesdale's distinction between equity acting in obedience to the statute and it acting by analogy. This analysis suggests that when equity was acting in obedience to the statute, its application of the bar was 'peremptory'. In such a case only fraudulent concealment would suspend the statute from operating. Whereas, when equity was acting by analogy it applied the statute as part of the law of laches so that the running of time would be suspended by the plaintiff's ignorance of his rights, and without the need to establish fraudulent concealment or some other equitable ground.

83 Corporations Act 2001 (Cth), s 1317K.
84 ibid ss 181–82.
85 *Re Auzhair Suplies Pty Ltd (in liq)* [2013] NSWSC 1; 272 FLR 304 [90].
86 *Gerace* (n 82) [51].

Meagher JA observed that Lord Redesdale's distinction had neither been generally nor consistently adopted, and did not accord with Isaac J's statement in *R v McNeil* that equity applied the statute unless a greater equity operated to prevent a defendant from relying on it.[87] There was a clear rejection of the proposition that equity retains a general residual discretion to decline to apply the statute.[88]

An application for special leave to appeal was dismissed,[89] and the result was confirmed by the subsequent decision of the Court of Appeal in *Sze Tu v Lowe*,[90] from which decision an application for special leave to appeal was also dismissed.[91]

Even so, the position established by those decisions has, so far, proven to be a little controversial.[92] Although the point is a narrow one, it goes to something which is fundamental to the relationship between equity and statute. Subject to two matters, once equity has determined that the statute applies by analogy, then that is how a defence of delay is applied, and *in the manner specified by the statute*, rather than as some ingredient in a broader discretion. That accords with orthodox notions of legislative supremacy, especially where the legislature has itself endorsed the existence of the equitable doctrine. The two qualifications are (a) the statute itself might confer a discretion, and (b) there seems to me to be no reason why familiar doctrines concerning unconscientious reliance on a statute need not apply.

Thus, in Australia, if a limitation statute does not apply directly to an equitable claim, one asks whether the equitable claim 'corresponds' to a legal claim to which it does apply. If not, then no application by analogy is possible and the only question is whether some other equitable defence is available. If there is a corresponding legal claim to which the statute applies, then the statute is to be applied by analogy in its terms, subject to any discretions it may contain, and subject to other doctrines precluding a party from relying on a statute, but not subject to some further 'residual' discretion which lacks foundation in the statute. If that were not so, then to use Meagher JA's language, equity 'would not truly be acting by analogy and following the law'.[93]

IV. CONCLUSION

Lord Sumption once wrote that: 'issues of limitation are bedevilled by an unarticulated tendency to treat it as an unmeritorious procedural technicality. Limitation in English law is generally procedural. But it is not a technicality, nor is it necessarily unmeritorious'.[94] I respectfully agree. The topic is interesting and complex, in part because much of the legislation (particularly the older legislation)

[87] *R v McNeil* (n 56) 100.
[88] *Gerace* (n 82) [74].
[89] [2014] HCASL 231.
[90] *Sze Tu v Lowe* (n 47) [365].
[91] *Lowe v Sze Tu* [2015] HCA Trans 179.
[92] *Issa* (n 82) [41]–[81], O'Dea and O'Dea (n 82) and Dal Pont (n 7) [13.40]–[13.41].
[93] *Gerace* (n 82) [74].
[94] *Abdulla v Birmingham City Council* [2012] UKSC 47; [2012] ICR 1419 [41].

is directed to the vast majority of litigation: actions at common law in tort and contract, as opposed to suits in equity. Further the legislation tends to involve a direct legislative engagement with legal taxonomy, which is apt to give rise to dispute in cases where the categories are evolving.[95] One result has been the creation of equitable doctrine responding to a perceived gap in the statute, consistently with equity's traditional role of supplementing the law. That in turn has given rise to a rich interaction between equitable principle and statute. In *Gerace*, federal legislation had in substance incorporated directors' obligations in equity as a new statutory obligation, such that the analogy between the statutory and equitable claims and remedies was 'as close an analogy as one can conceive'.[96] But it will not always be thus, leading to a contestable question of judgment, based upon the nature and purpose of the statute in question, as well as the similarity or otherwise of the equitable claim to the legal claim which engages the statute. These questions of statutory construction and the process of determining whether a statute applies by way of analogy are different facets of what the High Court of Australia has described as: 'the constitutional relationship between the arms of government with respect to the making, interpretation and application of laws'.[97]

Two final observations may be made. The first is that the relationship is more nuanced than is commonly considered. The second is that this is another instance where equity has interacted and continues to interact with statute differently from other areas of the law.[98]

[95] eg, the leading provision in the Limitation Act 1969 (NSW), imposing a six-year limitation period on actions founded on contract and tort extends contract to 'including quasi contract': s 14(1)(a).

[96] *In the Matter of Auzhair Supplies Pty Ltd (in liq)* [2013] NSWSC 1 [79].

[97] *Zheng v Cai* [2009] HCA 52; 239 CLR 446 [28].

[98] See M Leeming, 'Equity: Ageless in the "Age of Statutes"' (2015) 9 *Journal of Equity* 108.

15

The Importance of Being Earnest: The Doctrines of Laches and Acquiescence

LUSINA HO*

I. INTRODUCTION

A CLAIMANT WHO fails to exercise his right may be barred from relief by laches or acquiescence, but he may also be caught by the enveloping folds of other doctrines such as concurrence, release or estoppel. The contents of these overlapping defences and their relationship with each other are far from clear. Historically, the Court of Chancery would dismiss a bill pleaded after a long lapse of time by inferring an abandonment of the right,[1] or by refusing relief as a matter of discretion after balancing the personal equities of the parties. In exercising such discretion, the Court referred to the broad maxim that 'Equity aids the vigilant, not those who slumber on their rights', which partakes of another equitable maxim, 'He who seeks equity must do equity'.[2]

Yet there has been little analysis as to the precise moral or legal premise behind these abstract exhortations and balancing exercises. After all, having a right does not mean that one must exercise it. Even though the law can stipulate a conditional duty to act with reasonable diligence that arises only if the right-holder chooses to exercise his right, there still remains the question why he is less deserving than someone who commits a civil wrong and infringes his right? At what point would the merits tilt in favour of the party acting in violation of his right? Furthermore, on closer examination laches and acquiescence overlap between themselves and with concurrence, release and estoppel. It is time that these confusing labels were clarified and their respective boundaries rationalised.

* Lusina Ho, Faculty of Law, The University of Hong Kong. The author thanks Nicholas McBride for the title of the chapter, Rebecca Lee, participants of the Symposium on Defences in Equity held in January 2017 and, in particular, Simon Douglas for comments and Yulin Cheng for research assistance.

[1] *Clarke v Hart* (1858) 6 HL Cas 633, 655; 10 ER 1443, 1452 (Lord Chelmsford). Where inaction did not provide sufficient evidence of abandonment on the facts, it might still be used to strengthen a presumption in favour of abandonment drawn from other circumstances of the case: *Blake v Gale* (1886) 32 Ch D 571, 579.

[2] See J McGhee (ed), *Snell's Equity* 33rd edn (London, Sweet and Maxwell, 2016) ch 5.

The present chapter has three goals. First, it argues that laches is best understood as giving effect to the duties to honour one's promise and not to cause irreversible prejudice by one's own inaction. A claimant's inaction may affect his claim in at least four ways:

(1) it may be evidence from which a *promise* not to exercise his right is inferred; such a promise may establish the defence of concurrence, release,[3] acquiescence and the first strand of laches;[4] if detrimental reliance on this promise is also established, relief may be denied on the additional ground of estoppel;
(2) it may be evidence from which a *representation* that he has no rights is inferred; if the defendant has detrimentally relied on the representation, estoppel will apply;
(3) it may, in the absence of any inferred promise or representation, encourage the defendant's *mistaken belief* that he has rights; if he has detrimentally relied on such a belief, estoppel will apply;
(4) it may, in the absence of any conduct of the parties (including detrimental reliance on the part of the defendant), cause *irreversible prejudice* to the defendant, in which case the second strand of laches may apply.[5]

Section II of this chapter will examine how the duty to honour one's promise and the duty not to cause irreversible prejudice by one's own inaction run through and justify time-related defences in these four situations. In particular, the duty not to cause irreversible prejudice is constant, but the concrete actions required by it varies depending on factors such as the nature of the right, the nature of the remedy sought, the nature of the subject matter, the conduct of the parties, and the effect of their conduct on each other, to name but a few. This section will also show that even though the duty mandates positive action, such as to act promptly to bring a claim or to speak up to disabuse the other party of his mistaken belief, it does not conflict with the time-honoured principle against the imposition of legal responsibilities for omissions.

Second, it argues that the defence of acquiescence, if it has existed as an independent defence at all, is otiose and should be reclassified under other defences. In so far as acquiescence refers to inaction (with or without delay) from which consent to a continuing violation can be inferred, it should be incorporated within the doctrine of concurrence. In so far as it refers to inaction from which consent to a past breach can be inferred, it overlaps with the doctrines of release and the first strand of laches, and should also be incorporated within the doctrine of release. Finally, if it simply

[3] Legal terms such as 'affirmation', 'confirmation', 'acquiescence', 'abandonment', 'waiver' or 'accord and satisfaction' have been used interchangeably with 'release' of a breach that has been committed. Despite minor differences between these labels, this chapter will use 'release' in lieu of the other terms in order to avoid unnecessary confusion. Where the claimant accepts a continuing breach, the term 'concurrence' will be used.

[4] There are two strands of laches, the first of which involves inaction that amounted to 'waiver': *Lindsay Petroleum v Hurd* (1874) LR 5 PC 221, 239–40 (Lord Selbourne).

[5] The second strand refers to situations where the delay causes such prejudice that it would not be just and equitable to grant relief: ibid 239–40.

encourages the defendant's mistaken belief that he has rights, and further his detrimental reliance upon such a belief, it is a subset of estoppel and can be subsumed under estoppel. Re-classifying acquiescence will significantly avoid the injustice arising from the mysterious and convoluted scaffolding of time-related defences.

Third, the present chapter notes that release, laches and acquiescence overlap to a large extent with the doctrine of estoppel, and in particular promised-based and acquiescence-based estoppel.[6] The common thread between these time-related defences and estoppel is that the claimant's inaction is material not in itself as a bar to relief but as evidence from which acts giving rise to the defendant's detrimental reliance or prejudicial change of circumstance can be established. Notwithstanding, this does not call for the drastic step of unifying laches, release and concurrence under the doctrine of estoppel. There remain significant differences that justify keeping them distinct from estoppel. For example, while estoppel can be pleaded as a cause of action, these defences only impose a disability to bring an action. Besides, reliance is necessary for establishing estoppel but not laches.[7] Similarly, release is enforceable on contractual grounds,[8] whether because there is a formal release by deed, the release is supported by valuable consideration (ie accord and satisfaction), or because the release is treated as binding in the eyes of equity. Detrimental reliance is not necessary.

II. RELEASE, LACHES AND THEIR UNDERLYING DUTIES

Although a party who has a valid claim never owes a duty to bring the claim, if he delays doing so his delay may bar his relief. The delay may affect his entitlement to relief in four ways: it may allow the inference of an implied promise not to exercise his rights in the *future*; it may allow an implied representation of an *existing* fact that the claimant has no right to be inferred; it may provide encouragement of such a mistaken belief and detrimental reliance upon it; or it may simply subject the defendant to an irreversible prejudice without any of these accompaniments. This section argues that the availability of defences in these situations is best explained by the well-recognised duty to honour one's promise and by recognising the right-holder's duty to not subject the defendant to irreversible prejudice by his own inaction. It will examine how these duties shape the defences of release, laches and estoppel, and argue that they are consonant with existing principles in the law of obligations.

[6] See B McFarlane, *The Law of Proprietary Estoppel* (Oxford, Oxford University Press, 2014) ch 2. The author uses the label of 'acquiescence-based estoppel' to refer to the traditionally labelled category of 'estoppel by standing by', and 'promise-based estoppel' to refer to 'estoppel by encouragement'. See also B McFarlane and P Sales, 'Promises, Detriment, and Liability: Lessons from Proprietary Estoppel' (2015) 131 *LQR* 610.

[7] *Thorner v Major* [2009] UKHL 18; [2009] 1 WLR 776 [29] (Lord Walker).

[8] H Beale (ed), *Chitty on Contracts* 32nd edn (London, Sweet and Maxwell, 2015) paras 22-003, 22-012; J Heydon, M Leeming and P Turner, *Meagher, Gummow and Lehane's Equity: Doctrine & Remedies* 5th edn (Sydney, LexisNexis Butterworths, 2015) 1079 [37.005].

A. Release

The doctrine of release of a *past* breach involves a promise not to exercise rights, and is a corollary to the doctrine of concurrence to a *continuing* breach.[9] It is no surprise, therefore, that a single rule applies to both doctrines, which are based on consent.[10] Their justifications depend on the context in which the promise is made, which can be organised into three situations.

First, it is incontrovertible that if the release is made by a formal deed of release, or an agreement supported by valuable consideration (ie accord and satisfaction), the defence is justified on contractual grounds at common law.[11]

Second, in the absence of an enforceable contract, the release may be upheld in equity on the basis of the test laid down by Wilberforce J in *Re Pauling's Settlement Trusts*, namely whether having considered all circumstances, it would be unfair and inequitable for a claimant who has made the promise to turn round to sue the defendant.[12] There is very little elaboration of what unfairness and inequity require. At first glance, this test appears to be based on estoppel or laches rather than consent. On closer examination, however, the court's enquiries in *Re Pauling's Settlement Trusts* and subsequent cases focused on whether the promise was made with full information and knowledge, and free from misrepresentation, undue influence and terror.[13] Very little attention is paid to establishing detrimental reliance as in estoppel or irreversible prejudice as in laches, thus showing that the doctrine of release is based on consent rather than estoppel or laches. For example, the main contention settled in *Re Pauling's Settlement Trusts* is that the claimant must know the facts giving rise to his rights and understand what he is doing,[14] but he does not need to know that the wrongful act amounted to an infringement of his right.[15]

[9] Except that concurrence to a future or continuing breach can also be justified on the basis of *volenti non fit injuria* as the claimant brought upon the loss complained of: *Fyler v Fyler* (1841) 3 Beav 550, 559–60 (Lord Langdale). By contrast, release of a breach which has already taken place cannot be so justified, as the claimant in no way brought about the loss or consented to the risk of the loss.

[10] See the earlier cases of *Trafford v Boehm* (1746) 3 Atk 440; 26 ER 1054 and *Brice v Stokes* (1805) 11 Ves Jr 319; 32 ER 1111 on inducement and approbation, followed by *Walker v Symonds* (1818) 3 Swans 1; 36 ER 751 on release. See also L Tucker, N Le Poidevin and J Brightwell, *Lewin on Trusts* 19th edn (London, Sweet and Maxwell, 2015) 1907 [39.123].

[11] *De Bussche v Alt* (1878) 8 Ch D 286; Beale (n 8) paras 22-003, 22-012. For examples of formal release, see *Wilkinson v Parry* (1826) 4 Russ 272; 38 ER 808; *Cresswell v Dewell* (1863) 4 Giff 460; 66 ER 787; *French v Hobson* (1803) 9 Ves Jr 103; 32 ER 540; Heydon, Leeming, and Turner (n 8) 1079 [37.005].

[12] *Re Pauling's Settlement Trusts* [1962] 1 WLR 86, 108, affirmed [1964] Ch 303. It was applied in *Holder v Holder* [1968] Ch 353; *Re Freeston's Charity* [1978] 1 WLR 741; *Spellson v George* (1992) 26 NSWLR 666. More recently, see *Pullan v Wilson* [2014] EWHC 126 (Ch); [2014] WTLR 669. See also the earlier case of *Walker* (n 10).

[13] Tucker, Le Poidevin and Brightwell (n 10) 1907 [39.122]–[39.123]; *Leonard v Leonard* 2 Ball & B 171; *Jarvis v Duke* (1681) 1 Vern 19; *Wedderburn v Wedderburn* (1836) 2 Keen 722 (imperfect information will be regarded as concealment of fact).

[14] *Re Pauling's Settlement Trusts* [1962] (n 12) 107.

[15] ibid, citing *Walker* (n 10); *Evans v Benyon* (1887) 37 Ch D 329, and distinguishing *Re Garnett* (1885) 31 Ch D 1; *Re Somerset* [1894] 1 Ch 231; *Chillingworth v Chambers* [1896] 1 Ch 685. This dictum in *Re Pauling's Settlement Trusts* (n 12) was endorsed in *Holder* (n 12) 394 (Harman LJ); *Goldsworthy v Brickell* [1987] Ch 378, 411; *Brundell-Bruce v Moore* [2014] EWHC 3679 (Ch); [2015] WTLR 373 [195]–[197]. *Holder* (n 12) was endorsed in *Re Freeston's Charity* (n 12) 754–55.

Thus, Wilberforce J considered that when a well-educated and highly intelligent beneficiary who had come of age understood that he was handing over money advanced to him in a trust in favour of his parents' joint banking account, he had sufficient knowledge, even if he did not know the legal nature of a settlement and an advancement.[16] Significantly, these factors of full information and lack of undue influence closely approximate those that determine whether a principal consents to or authorises an act of the fiduciary that would otherwise be a breach of fiduciary duty. As equity does not treat a seal as having binding effect, it determines whether a promise not to sue or consent to release a breach should be binding by examining such factors as full disclosure of information and lack of undue influence. In the eyes of equity, these substantive criteria are more relevant than the formality of the seal; they are also long established before the common law doctrine of consideration. Once the criteria are established, the court has no hesitation in inferring consent, but significantly in doing so it does not look into whether the principal has suffered detrimental reliance or irreversible prejudice, let alone whether the common law doctrine of consideration is satisfied. As such, the underlying basis of equitable release is the duty to honour one's promise. Such a promise does not need to meet the common law requirement of consideration, and hence is not contractual in the strict sense of the word, but it must have satisfied the legal scrutiny for it to have binding effect in equity.

Third, on some occasions the court did refer to the detrimental reliance of the defendant on the release as rendering it unfair and inequitable for the claimant to sue. These instances of release may be accommodated under estoppel.[17] *Aveline v Melhuish* provides a neat illustration. In this case, a beneficiary signed a release of a wrongful distribution of trust assets to her father, and on his death his estate was distributed to her together with other children. The trustee would have set the wrongfully distributed amount aside from the father's estate had she not released the breach, but was precluded from doing as a result of relying on the release. The Court held that the release had 'materially altered the position of the trustee', such that she could not maintain the claim against him.[18] Nonetheless, in assessing whether it is unfair and inequitable to allow a claimant who has released a breach to sue the defendant, detrimental reliance is relevant but not necessary. As such, the underlying basis of release remains that of contract or the duty to honour one's promise, and not estoppel. It is also worth noting that even though it is possible for release to be inferred from inaction,[19] such instances are likely to require exceptional facts. They also overlap with the strands of laches and acquiescence that are based on consent and should be classified as part of the doctrine of release.

[16] *Re Pauling's Settlement Trusts* [1962] (n 12) 107, 109.

[17] J Payne, 'Consent' in P Birks and A Pretto (eds), *Breach of Trust* (Oxford, Hart Publishing, 2002) 300, fn 14.

[18] *Aveline v Melhuish* (1864) 2 De G J & S 288, 293; 46 ER 386, 388.

[19] *Wright v Vanderplank* (1856) 8 De G M & G 133, 146–47; 44 ER 340, 345 (Turner LJ): 'I am not of opinion that a positive act is necessary to render the transaction unimpeachable.' See also *Walker* (n 10).

B. Laches

i. Delay Allowing an Inference of Release and Delay Causing Prejudice

Laches bars relief if there is delay in prosecuting a claim. Yet it is practically settled that mere delay, no matter how long, does not amount to laches. Derived from old French, laches means 'slackness or negligence, or not doing',[20] which imports a focus on the claimant's conduct or neglect rather than mere effluxion of time. This reinforces the thesis of the present chapter that laches *in its strict sense* is based on the duty to not subject the defendant to irreversible prejudice by one's own inaction.

Two strands of laches can be identified from Lord Selbourne's oft-cited passage in *Lindsay Petroleum Co v Hurd* below:[21]

> Now the doctrine of laches in Courts of Equity is not an arbitrary or a technical doctrine. Where it would be practically unjust to give a remedy, either because the party has, by his conduct, done that which might fairly be regarded as equivalent to a waiver of it, or where by his conduct and neglect he has, though perhaps not waiving that remedy, yet put the other party in a situation in which it would not be reasonable to place him if the remedy were afterwards to be asserted, in either of these cases, lapse of time and delay are most material.

The first strand involves inaction that permits an inference of waiver,[22] and is hence consent-based, and grounded on the duty to honour one's promise.[23] Such instances are likely to be exceptional, such as when the claimant ought to speak up, so that his inactivity is no longer ambiguous but gives rise to an inference that he has released the defendant from the breach. Nonetheless, even though they are uncommon and the release is inferred from inaction rather than positively established, it should still be treated as based on consent; as shown in Lord Selbourne's statement, this strand of laches can be established without the finding of any prejudice on the part of the defendant or a third party. To avoid confusion, it is better to treat this strand as belonging to the doctrine of release and use the label of laches only for the second

[20] *Partridge v Partridge* [1894] 1 Ch 351, 360 (North J), quoting from *Coke Upon Littleton*, Co Litt 380b.

[21] *Lindsay Petroleum* (n 4) 239–40. See also *Streeter v Western Areas Exploration Pty Ltd (No 2)* [2011] WASCA 17; (2011) 278 ALR 291 [635] (Murphy JA), suggesting that laches encompasses two themes: 'One is delay implying not just quiescence, but rather acquiescence and assent, and the other is delay involving prejudicial change of circumstances'.

[22] *Lindsay Petroleum* (n 4) 239–40. An example of such waiver can be found in *Allcard v Skinner* (1887) 36 Ch D 145, where the young nun had consulted a solicitor after she left the nunnery and made a conscious decision not to bring an action, but changed her mind and did so after six years had elapsed. While Lindley and Bowen LJJ held that laches was made out, the former accepted that there was conduct beyond mere delay that amounted to confirmation of her gift: ibid 186.

[23] Earlier authorities typically treated inaction as evidence that the claimant had promised not to exercise his rights: *Stiles v Cowper* (1748) 3 Atk 692; 26 ER 1198; *Aston v Aston* (1750) 1 Ves Sen 396; 27 ER 1103; *Jackson v Cator* (1800) 5 Ves Jr 688; 31 ER 806. The court may also infer an abandonment of the rights: *Clarke* (n 1) (Lord Chelmsford). Where inaction did not provide sufficient evidence of abandonment on the facts, it might be used to strengthen a presumption in favour of abandonment drawn from other circumstances of the case: *Blake* (n 1). These cases may now be dealt with under limitation statutes.

strand, the strict sense of laches.[24] This strand involves substantial delay coupled with prejudice to others that renders it practically unjust (or inequitable[25]) to grant the remedy. The essential ingredients for proving this strand support the contention that it is based on the duty not to prejudice others due to one's own inaction.

First, even though earlier authorities might have treated lapse of time as a bar in its own right,[26] by the end of the nineteenth century, and certainly in *Lindsay Petroleum Co v Hurd*, there was strong judicial support that lapse of time was but evidence rendering it unjust to grant the remedy.[27] This view has received extensive support in authorities[28] and academic commentary,[29] albeit the debate remains unsettled. The New Zealand Supreme Court refrained from ruling out that mere delay could be a bar on its own right.[30] The English commercial court has recently denied an anti-suit injunction on the ground of lack of promptness alone, albeit prejudice could also be found on the facts.[31] While the United Kingdom Supreme Court also declined to resolve the debate in a decision that involved drawing an analogy to laches rather than applying it, it went on to say that laches 'generally requires (a) knowledge of the facts, and (b) acquiescence, or (c) detriment or prejudice'.[32] It is fair to say that the trend of authorities favours treating mere delay, no matter how long, as evidence to establish laches, but not laches itself. Such a trend supports the proposal in this chapter to rationalise laches on the basis of duties governing the private relationship of the parties, and not merely as a rule mandating the expiry period of a right based on public policy.[33]

[24] This was strongly advocated by Heydon, Leeming and Turner (n 8) 1087 [38.020]; citing J Edelman, 'Money Awards of the Cost of Performance' (2010) 4 *Journal of Equity* 122, 129, referencing D O'Sullivan, S Elliott and R Zakrzewski, *The Law of Rescission* 2nd edn (Oxford, Oxford University Press, 2014) 484 [24.17].

[25] *Frawley v Neill* [1999] EWCA Civ 875; [2000] CP Rep 20.

[26] *Smith v Clay* (1767) 3 Bro CC 646; 29 ER 743, 744 (Lord Camden LC): 'A court of equity … has always refused its aid to stale demands, where the party has slept upon his right and acquiesced for a great length of time. Nothing can call forth this court into activity, but conscience, good faith, and reasonable diligence; where these are wanting, the Court is passive, and does nothing'; *Milward v Earl Thanet* (1801) 5 Ves 720n; 31 ER 824, stating that relief would be refused to a claimant who was not 'ready, desirous, prompt, and eager'.

[27] *Lindsay Petroleum* (n 4) 239–40; *De Bussche* (n 11) 314; *Pickering v Lord Stamford* (1795) 2 Ves Jr 581; 30 ER 787; and *Life Association of Scotland v Siddal* (1861) 3 De G F & J 58; 45 ER 800.

[28] *Burroughes v Abbott* [1922] 1 Ch 86; *Weld v Petre* [1929] 1 Ch 33; *Nelson v Rye* [1996] 1 WLR 1378, 1392; *Jones v Stones* [1999] 1 WLR 1739; *Fisher v Brooker* [2009] UKHL 41; [2009] 1 WLR 1764 [64]; *Brudenell-Bruce, Earl of Cardigan v Moore* [2012] EWHC 1024 (Ch); [2012] WTLR 931; *Pullan v Wilson* (n 12) [29]; *Salt v Stratstone Specialist Ltd (t/a Stratstone Cadillac Newcastle)* [2015] EWCA Civ 745 (England); [2015] All ER (D) 195; *Savage v Lunn* [1988] NSWCA 203; *Crawley v Short* [2009] NSWCA 410; (2009) 262 ALR 654 [163]–[164] (New South Wales Court of Appeal, Australia).

[29] McGhee (n 2) 114 [5.016]; Tucker, Le Poidevin and Brightwell (n 10) 1904 [39.113]; Heydon, Leeming and Turner (n 8) 1093 [38.065]; D Hayton, P Matthews and C Mitchell, *Underhill and Hayton: Law of Trusts and Trustees* 19th edn (London, LexisNexis, 2016) 1250 [95.10].

[30] *Eastern Services Ltd v No 68 Ltd* [2006] NZSC 42; [2006] 3 NZLR 335 [29]–[39].

[31] *Essar Shipping Ltd v Bank of China* [2015] EWHC 3266 (Comm) (two months' delay in bringing the anti-suit injunction to challenge the Chinese court's jurisdiction and a further seven months' delay after expiry of the deadline for bringing arbitration proceedings in London).

[32] *Adamson v Paddico (267) Ltd* [2014] UKSC 7; [2014] AC 1072 [31], [34].

[33] For a contrary view, see G Watt, 'Laches, Estoppel and Election' in Birks and Pretto (n 17) ch 12.

Second, time only begins to run when the claimant acquires knowledge of the facts constituting the title to relief (but not necessarily the legal entitlement itself).[34] It is not sufficient knowledge that a claimant who has made reasonable enquiries would have become aware of the breach.[35] Interestingly, the test of knowledge is formulated not in terms of the claimant's cognition alone but the requisite knowledge that compels him to take action. As Lord Blackburn put it, it must be 'such notice or knowledge as to make it inequitable to lie by'.[36] His Lordship explained that after acquiring such knowledge, 'a Court of Equity requires that those who come to it to ask its active interposition to give them relief, should use due diligence'.[37] In saying that the requisite knowledge is one that makes it unjust to stand by, the court accepts that the claimant owes a duty to speak up if he wishes to exercise his right, and the failure to discharge this duty will lead to loss of the remedy. The need for the duty to speak is *a fortiori* where a promise to release a past breach is inferred from inaction. As inactivity itself is equivocal, to infer a promise from silence is an exceptional matter that should happen only if there is a duty to speak in the circumstances.[38]

At this point, it is tempting to conclude from Lord Blackburn's reference to 'due diligence' that the duty is one to exercise reasonable diligence. The same language is also used in *Barclay v Messenger* when the Court denied specific performance to a purchaser who failed to perform its side of the bargain knowing that it would render the vendor in breach of its agreement with a third party.[39] Sir George Jessell MR explained that the plaintiffs had 'not used that diligence which was incumbent upon them to use to obtain the aid of the court'.[40] This would have been an adequate formulation of the duty if the claimant's procrastination were, as is typically in the second strand of laches, due to neglect alone. However, some procrastination may be out of a calculated, opportunistic decision to stand by in order to reap the benefit of the other party's efforts, or a change of mind after making a conscious decision not to prosecute the claim. The nun in *Allcard v Skinner*[41] and Sir Elton John in *Elton John v James*[42] are well known examples of the latter situation, albeit they are better

[34] *Lindsay Petroleum* (n 4); *Stafford v Stafford* (1857) 1 De G & J 193, 202; 44 ER 697, 701 (knowledge of facts gives rise to presumption of knowledge of the rights arising from them); *Hourigan v Trustees Executors and Agency Co Ltd* (1934) 51 CLR 619, 651; *Holder* (n 12) 394; *Savage v Lunn (No 2)* [1998] NSWCA 204; *Crawley v Short* (n 28) [163]–[164]. It has been suggested by Heydon, Leeming and Turner (n 8) 1094 [38.070] that where laches consists of release, knowledge of the entitlements is necessary whereas if laches consists of detriment and prejudice, knowing of the facts is enough: *Nowell v Palmer* (1993) 32 NSWLR 574 (Mahoney JA), see also DL Mahoney, 'Delay ... A Judge's Perspective' (1983) 57 *Australian Law Journal* 30.

[35] *Betjemann v Betjemann* [1895] 2 Ch 474.

[36] *Erlanger v New Sombrero Phosphate Co* (1878) 3 App Cas 1218, 1279 (Lord Blackburn).

[37] ibid.

[38] See discussion in the context of offer and acceptance in E Peel, *Treitel on the Law of Contract* 14th edn (London, Sweet & Maxwell, 2015) 35–40. Furthermore, it has been said in the context of a breach of trust that the trustee ought to observe the trust, and cannot be exonerated from a breach by '[throwing] upon the *cestui que trust* the obligation of ... cautioning him to observe it': *Life Association of Scotland* (n 27) De G F & J 73; ER 806.

[39] *Barclay v Messenger* (1874) 30 LT 351, citing *Eads v Williams* (1854) 4 De G M & G 674; 43 ER 671 and *Milward v Earl of Thanet* (n 26).

[40] ibid 355.

[41] *Allcard* (n 22).

[42] *Elton John v James* [1991] FSR 397.

explained on the basis of release, estoppel and acquiescence. Formulating the duty narrowly as the duty to exercise reasonable diligence would necessitate a separate duty to deal with deliberate delay or change of mind, and unduly complicate the picture.

Third, Lord Selbourne in *Lindsay Petroleum* has made it clear that laches requires not just delay but prejudice on the part of the defendant.[43] Lord Neuberger recently emphasised in *Fisher v Brooker*, a case of the second strand, that prejudice or detrimental reliance was usually necessary.[44] Some English authorities go further. In *Frawley v Neill*, Ardous LJ considered it unnecessary to fit the circumstances 'within the confines of a preconceived formula derived from earlier cases'.[45] Instead, there should be a 'broad approach' asking 'whether it would in all the circumstances be unconscionable for a party to be permitted to assert his beneficial right'.[46] Even though the broad approach shifts the emphasis to the overall assessment of unconscionability, it is not intended to remove the requirement of detriment or prejudice.

In the context of the second strand of laches, such detriment can be established when the defendant alters his position in reliance upon an implied representation or encouragement that can be inferred from the delay.[47] For example, he may have expended money or given up opportunities.[48] He may also have incurred liabilities that he cannot now recoup, such as in purchasing a farm from a trust that he believed he was at liberty to acquire.[49] Where the detriment arises from relying on the claimant's representation or encouragement, such instances of laches overlap with estoppel. However, the detriment can also arise where there is a continuing dispute between the parties as to their legal rights (and hence there is neither implied representation nor mistaken belief about the parties' rights), and where the detriment or prejudice is suffered by a third party. In these instances, estoppel cannot apply. An independent defence of laches is still needed.

Apart from causing detrimental reliance, lapse of time may cause prejudice due to a change of objective circumstance. Evidence may have been lost through no fault of any party,[50] witnesses might have passed away,[51] the property may have deteriorated

[43] *Lindsay Petroleum* (n 4) 239, endorsed by the House of Lords in *Erlanger* (n 36) 1279 as the most 'distinct and definite' statement of the doctrine of laches.

[44] *Fisher* (n 28) [64], [79].

[45] *Frawley* (n 25).

[46] *Frawley* (n 25), endorsed in *Patel v Shah* [2005] EWCA Civ 157, [2005] WTLR 359 [32]–[33] (Mummery LJ); *Re Loftus* [2006] EWCA Civ 1124; [2007] 1 WLR 591 [42] (Chadwick LJ); *P&O Nedlloyd BV v Arab Metals Co* [2006] EWCA Civ 1717; [2007] 1 WLR 2288 [61]; *Sheffield v Sheffield* [2013] EWHC 3927 (Ch); [2014] WTLR 1039 [100], [106], [109].

[47] If the inaction gives rise to an implied promise, his detrimental reliance will be relevant to the doctrine of release.

[48] *Turner v Collins* (1871) LR 7 Ch App 329; *Shaw v Applegate* [1977] 1 WLR 970; *Fysh v Page* (1956) 96 CLR 233, [1956] ALR 474.

[49] *Holder* (n 12).

[50] *Watt v Assets Co Ltd* [1905] AC 317; *Hourigan* (n 34) 629, 651; *Hughes v Schofield* [1975] 1 NSWLR 8, approved in *Orr v Ford* [1989] HCA 4 [16]; (1989) 167 CLR 316, 344; 84 ALR 146, 163 (Deane J).

[51] *Fernandes v Fernandes* [2015] EWHC 814 (Ch) [67], provided the value of the witness' evidence is not purely speculative.

or its condition may have changed,[52] and third-party rights may have intervened.[53] For example, in *Baburin v Baburin (No 2)*, a mother's plea to set aside a transfer of shares to her son made 19 years ago on the ground of unconscionability was barred by laches because one of the witnesses had died, documents had been lost or destroyed and some of the shares had been transferred to third parties.[54] In *Orr v Ford*, when the beneficiary of a constructive trust claimed his share 20 years after the legal owner asserted that he was the sole owner, the majority of the High Court held that there was no laches. The Court was divided on the application to the facts but the judges were agreed that whether the evidence was lost and whether third parties have suffered prejudice were relevant factors.[55] In these cases, the irreversible prejudice arose from the change of circumstances that occurred during the period of delay. It was not necessary that the defendant had detrimentally relied on the inaction, and the case for maintaining a separate defence of laches independent from estoppel is even more compelling.

The requirement of detriment or irreversible prejudice over and above unreasonable delay shows that the underlying purpose of laches is to protect the defendant or third parties from irreversible prejudice[56] arising from the claimant's knowing inaction. Such a purpose can be achieved by imposing on a claimant who wishes to exercise his rights a duty not to subject others to irreversible prejudice by his own inaction. One might doubt the existence of such a duty on the ground that its breach does not lead to any obligation to make amends, but just the loss of an advantage. However, the loss of the right to sue is itself a substantial loss. Furthermore, in other legal contexts, the failure to discharge this duty does lead to legal liability. For example, under proprietary estoppel, breach of this duty can give rise to the legal liability to compensate loss or provide other remedies. Accordingly, the postulation of this duty provides a uniform underlying explanation of the legal doctrines in both situations.

ii. Content of the Duty Not to Cause Irreversible Prejudice

Just like the doctrine of laches, the underlying duty not to subject others to irreversible prejudice is simple and constant, but the concrete action required by it varies from situation to situation. This is because the prejudices suffered by the defendant and third parties arise from an infinite variety of circumstances that defy any hard and fast rule. Courts increasingly favour adopting the broad discretionary test of unconscionability to accommodate the need for flexibility.[57]

[52] *Lindsay Petroleum* (n 4) 239; *Erlanger* (n 36) 1231, 1247.

[53] *Hourigan* (n 34) 649–51; *Bonney v Ridgard* (1784) 1 Cox Eq Cas 145; 29 ER 1101; *Lamshed v Lamshed* (1963) 109 CLR 440; [1964] ALR 321.

[54] *Baburin v Baburin (No 2)* [1991] 2 Qd R 240.

[55] *Orr v Ford* (n 50).

[56] If a monetary award can be used so it would not be practically unjust to grant the remedy sought, the prejudice is not irreversible. See, eg, *Fitzgerald v Masters* (1956) 95 CLR 420, 433; *Fisher* (n 28); [2009] 1 WLR 1764; *Shaw* (n 48).

[57] *Frawley* (n 25), endorsed in *Patel* (n 46) [32]–[33]; *Re Loftus* (n 46) [42]. Earlier authorities simply suggested that the court would examine all acts and circumstances: *Eads* (n 39); *Lehmann v McArthur* (1868) LR 3 Ch App 496; *Barclay* (n 39); *Lamshed* (n 53).

It is submitted that some degree of certainty can be injected into this open-ended test by identifying the factors that determine when delay becomes unacceptable. These include: the nature of the right, the nature of the remedy claimed; the nature of the subject matter; the length of the delay; and the nature of the acts done in the interval which might affect either party.[58] A brief account might illustrate their relevance.

First, as to the nature of the claimant's right, it has been well established that a bare trustee cannot rely on laches to defeat an absolute beneficial owner's claim to obtain legal title.[59] Equally, lapse of time is no bar when a beneficiary seeks to recover trust property retained by the trustee, for he is simply recovering property which he owns.[60] In a similar vein, although the court does not rule out a defence of laches in a claim to enforce beneficial interest, it is 'extremely rare' to find a beneficiary of a traditional (as opposed to commercial) trust to be unconscionable in doing so.[61] The beneficiary is not expected to look after his self-interest like a contractual party; in fact, he is entitled to expect the defendant trustee to look after his interest.

Second, the remedy sought also matters. In *Fisher v Brooker*, laches was held not to apply to a copyright owner's claim for a declaration of his right, as no discretionary equitable remedy was sought in the process.[62] The court's expectation also differs across these discretionary remedies. Laches applies most strictly to a claim for interlocutory injunction, because of the traditional need for promptitude in these reliefs.[63] Equally, specific performance[64] and rescission traditionally require greater promptitude,[65] because the feasibility of these reliefs is vulnerable to change of circumstance.

Third, the subject matter of the claim is also crucial. Greater expedition is asked for if the property is of a speculative, fluctuating or wasting character, such as shares[66] or speculative mining transactions,[67] where a few months' delay will bar

[58] *Lindsay Petroleum* (n 4); *Nelson* (n 28) 1392 (Laddie J) suggesting that the factors to be taken into account are: 'the period of delay, the extent to which the defendant's position has been prejudiced by the delay and the extent to which that prejudice was caused by the actions of the plaintiff'. See also *Boyns v Lackey* (1958) 58 SR (NSW) 395 (Hardie J).

[59] *Frawley* (n 25).

[60] *Mills v Drewitt* (1855) 20 Beav 632, 638; 52 ER 748, 750; *Harcourt v White* (1860) 38 Beav 303, 308; 54 ER 382, 384; *Thomson v Eastwood* (1877) 2 App Cas 215, 236, 252; *Rochefoucauld v Boustead* [1897] 1 Ch 196, 209.

[61] *Patel* (n 46); *Zarbafi v Zarbafi* [2014] EWCA Civ 1267; [2014] 1 WLR 4122 [70]; *Fernandes v Fernandes* (n 51).

[62] *Fisher* (n 28). The declaration in effect gives the claimant rights to future shares, but he had not sought to claim his past entitlements.

[63] See, eg, *Essar Shipping* (n 31), where the court explained that delay in seeking an anti-suit injunction may increase the risk of the injunction being seen as an inappropriate interference with the foreign court's jurisdiction.

[64] *Milward* (n 26), a party seeking specific performance must be 'ready, desirous, prompt, and eager' (Lord Alvanley); *Eads* (n 39) De G M & G 691; ER 678; *The Oriental Inland Steam Co (Ltd) v Briggs* (1861) 4 De G F & J 191; (1861) 45 ER 1157.

[65] *Simner v New India Assurance Co* [1995] LRLR 240, 258–60.

[66] *Erlanger* (n 36).

[67] *Norway v Rowe* (1812) 19 Ves Jr 144; 34 ER 472; *Turner v Trelawny* (1841) 12 Sim 49; 59 ER 1049; *Clements v Hall* (1858) 2 De G & J 173; 44 ER 954; *Huxham v Llewellyn* (1873) 21 WR 570; *Glasbrook v Richardson* (1874) 23 WR 51; *Boyns* (n 58); *Wilson v Winton* [1969] Qd R 536.

specific performance, albeit these are exceptional circumstances.[68] This is to discourage opportunistic claimants who stood by to see how their bargain turns out, and use equitable relief to obtain an unfair windfall.[69] In contrast, if the right is only capable of enjoyment from time to time, length of time does not operate to the same extent. In *Hatch v Hatch*, the grantor of a gift advowson was allowed to set it aside after a lapse of 20 years, as the grantee was himself incumbent, and might not have the opportunity to exercise the right for some 30 years.[70]

Fourth, the conduct of both parties and their effect on each other also affect the court's evaluation. In *Lamshed v Lamshed*, a purchaser who delayed seeking specific performance of a contract for the sale of land for five years was barred by laches because the vendor acted in detrimental reliance and resold the land to a third party.[71] Conversely, in *Re Loftus*, which involved a spiteful family dispute, the claimants and the defendant administratrix had mutual claims against each other.[72] The claimants delayed their claim to avoid disclosing their tax evasion in the litigation process, whereas the defendant did so in the hope that the claimants would also not pursue their claim against her. The Court held that since the claimants did not encourage such a hope, and it suited the defendant not to pursue her claim, it was not unconscionable for the claimants to now assert theirs.[73]

These factors have laid down the boundaries and operation of the duty not to prejudice others. For example, beneficiaries of traditional trusts who are entitled to have the claimant-trustee look after their interests are exonerated from the duty. In contrast, the court is less forgiving to a claimant who seeks to obtain an unfair windfall through a calculated delay, or even one who simply changes his mind. Between these two extremes, the effect of delay on the practical feasibility of the remedy, on the state of belief and detrimental reliance of the defendant, and on the prejudice suffered by any third party are all important factors in the balancing exercise.

iii. Justification of the Duty

Examination of the rules of laches shows that despite its traditional association with lapse of time, laches imports a broader principle than the mere effluxion of time. It is concerned with the claimant's conduct (or rather the lack thereof) in the face of an assertion of a conflicting right. The particular conduct at issue is inaction that causes prejudice on others; hence, the duty that informs laches is the duty not to subject others to irreversible prejudice by one's own inaction.

Importantly, its nature as a negative duty cannot be avoided by recasting it as a positive duty to bring a claim, for a right-holder does not owe any duty to enforce

[68] *Wroth v Tyler* [1974] Ch 30, 53.
[69] *Clegg v Edmondson* (1857) 8 De G M & G 787, 814; 44 ER 593, 604.
[70] *Hatch v Hatch* (1804) 9 Ves Jr 292; 32 ER 615; *Wright v Vanderplank* (n 19) De G M & G 150; ER 347 (Turner LJ).
[71] *Lamshed* (n 53).
[72] *Re Loftus* (n 46).
[73] ibid [45].

his right. Nor will it help to frame it as a positive, conditional duty to bring a claim where failing to do so will likely cause prejudice, because even if the right-holder is in the position to avert such foreseeable prejudice, the law still does not impose a duty on him to bring the claim to do so. He may avert it by speaking up to disabuse the other party of his mistaken belief. This shows that ultimately, his duty is a negative one to not cause irreversible prejudice. Such a formulation best reflects the legal doctrine at hand, namely that a claim would not be allowed if doing so would cause prejudice. At first glance, this negative duty may fall foul of the imperative against imposing legal responsibilities on omissions, which is captured by the policy of 'no action, no liability'.[74] However, it is submitted that the proposed duty is different from private law duties in three important ways, and hence the imperative is not breached.

First, it is not a legal duty breach of which amounts to a legal wrong. In a typical private law duty, say, the duty of care in tort, breach of the duty entitles the victim to bring a claim to the court to seek remedies; once the claim is accepted, the wrongdoer will be subject to liabilities to comply with remedies ordered by the court.[75] However, breach of the duty not to cause prejudice only subjects the duty-bearer to a disability in exercising his right, not a liability. It does not fall foul of the policy of 'no action, no liability'. It is more analogous to the so-called duty to mitigate in contract law, breach of which is not a civil wrong. It is but a duty that justifies and explains the doctrine of laches (and also the defence of estoppel).

Second, the duty is hypothetical and not categorical, because it prescribes what a claimant ought to do only if he intends to achieve the particular purpose of exercising his rights. It does not compel him to exercise his rights. In fact, even if he intends to exercise his rights, the duty only arises after he has acquired knowledge of the relevant facts. Conversely, if he does not intend to do so, even if he has acquired the requisite knowledge, he still does not owe any duty to take action.

Third, needless to say, it is possible for the law to prescribe a categorical legal duty not to subject others to irreversible prejudice. Acquiescence-based proprietary estoppel is a good case on point. This doctrine allows an action to be brought against X a right owner who stood by in the face of Y's mistaken belief that Y had a right and hence encouraged Y's belief, such that Y detrimentally altered his position in reliance on the belief. As this strand of proprietary estoppel does involve responsibility for omission, it needs special justification.[76] The present duty is different, however. Unlike in proprietary estoppel, it is invoked only as a defence and not as a sword. In any event, it does not impose a general duty on right-owners to exercise diligence to scout around for potential infringers, as the duty arises only upon the acquisition of actual knowledge of facts constituting title to relief. Constructive knowledge based on what a reasonable person would have found out is not sufficient.[77]

[74] I Samet, 'Proprietary Estoppel and Responsibility for Omissions' (2015) 78 *MLR* 85, 91, referencing AP Simester, 'Why Omissions are Special' (1995) 1 *Legal Theory* 311; T Honoré, 'Are Omissions Less Culpable?' in *Responsibility and Fault* (Oxford, Hart Publishing, 1999) 54.

[75] S Smith, 'Duties, Liabilities, and Damages' (2012) 125 *Harvard Law Review* 1727.

[76] Samet (n 74).

[77] *Betjemann* (n 35).

III. THE RECLASSIFICATION OF ACQUIESCENCE

The doctrine of acquiescence has been heavily criticised as a term of 'a chameleon-like quality which adds little besides confusion'.[78] It overlaps with concurrence, release, laches and estoppel, and is thus best reclassified as part of these doctrines to avoid confusion.

Even in its strict sense, acquiescence overlaps with concurrence and is a subset of it. The strict sense refers to knowingly standing by during a continuing violation which makes it inequitable to bring a claim subsequently. In the words of Lord Cottenham in *Duke of Leeds v Earl of Amherst*:[79]

> If a party, having a right, stands by and sees another dealing with the property in a manner inconsistent with that right, and makes no objection while the act is *in progress*, he cannot afterwards complain. That is the proper sense of the word acquiescence.

This formulation does not mention, let alone require, any inference of assent from the inaction. It is wide enough to encompass inaction that gives rise to an inference of an implied representation, or simply inaction that encourages the defendant's mistaken belief. Nonetheless, this passage has been widely explained on the basis of assent. In *De Bussche v Alt*, Thesiger LJ remarked as follows:[80]

> If a person having a right, and seeing another person about to commit, or in the course of committing an act infringing upon that right, stands by in such a manner as really to induce the person committing the act, and who might otherwise have abstained from it, *to believe that he assents to its being committed*, he cannot afterwards be heard to complain of the act. This, as Lord Cottenham said in the case already cited, is the proper sense of the term 'acquiescence', and in that sense may be defined as quiescence under such circumstances as that assent may be inferred from it.

On this formulation, acquiescence refers to silent assent to a *contemporaneous* act, and has nothing to do with delay. This narrower formulation has been widely adopted in earlier authorities,[81] and recently in Deane J's detailed analysis of the doctrine of acquiescence in *Orr v Ford*[82] and in *Brynes v Kendle*.[83] Its proper place is within the doctrine of concurrence, as an alternative way to establishing assent from active conduct.[84] As is well established in the authorities, the conditions for establishing concurrence and acquiescence are the same,[85] just that the former typically involves positive acts of assent, whereas the latter involves implied assent inferred from silence.

[78] *Orr v Ford* (n 50) HCA 4 [10]; CLR 337; ALR 157 (Deane J).

[79] *Duke of Leeds v Earl of Amherst* (1846) 2 Ph 117, 123; (1846) 41 ER 886, 888 (emphasis supplied).

[80] *De Bussche* (n 11) 314 (emphasis supplied).

[81] *Dann v Spurrier* [1802] Eng R 233; (1802) 7 Ves Jr 231; 32 ER 94; *Archbold v Scully* (1861) (1861) 9 HLC 360, 383; (1861) 11 ER 769, 778; *Life Association of Scotland* (n 27); *Glasson v Fuller* [1922] SASR 148, 161; *Holder* (n 12) 385.

[82] *Orr* (n 50).

[83] *Brynes v Kendle* [2011] HCA 26; (2011) 243 CLR 253 (Heydon and Crennan JJ).

[84] These active conducts can involve inducement, participation or express consent: see *Re Pauling's Settlement Trusts* [1964] (n 12).

[85] Tucker, Le Poidevin and Brightwell (n 10) 1903 [39.107] citing *White v White* (1798–1804) 5 Ves Jr 554; 31 ER 735; *Brice* (n 10); *Nail v Punter* (1832) 5 Sim 555; 58 ER 447; *Griffiths v Porter* (1858)

Apart from this strict sense, Deane J in *Orr v Ford* also pointed out a loose sense of acquiescence, where the label is also used:[86]

> in a context where laches is used to indicate either mere delay or delay with knowledge, to refer to conduct by a person, with knowledge of the acts of another person, which encourages that other person reasonably to believe that his acts are accepted (if past) or not opposed (if contemporaneous).

Prima facie, this loose sense closely approximates its strict sense (of inaction permitting an inference of contemporaneous assent). They differ only in two aspects. First, the mistaken belief encouraged by inaction is not limited to assent to contemporaneous acts, but also includes release of past acts. As such, acquiescence refers to inaction that permits a reasonable inference of release of past acts. This meaning completely overlaps with release, and can be subsumed under it. Second, the loose sense refers to inaction *coupled with delay* in permitting a reasonable inference of assent to a contemporaneous act, not mere inaction as in the strict sense. But such a difference relates only to the factual context by which the assent arises, and does not reveal any conceptual difference that warrants a doctrine that is independent from concurrence.

The ensuing question is whether the two senses of acquiescence should be re-classified under release and concurrence, or whether directly under estoppel.[87] The case law is replete with judicial suggestions for subsuming acquiescence under estoppel.[88] Lord Cottenham's classic statement of the strict sense of acquiescence in *Duke of Leeds v Earl of Amherst* is stated in terms of estoppel, as his Lordship refers to a party's standing by during violations of his right, which means that 'he cannot afterwards complain'.[89] In more explicit terms, Thesiger LJ in *De Bussche v Alt* considered that acquiescence 'is no more than an instance of the law of estoppel by words or conduct'.[90] These two authorities were cited by Poole J in *Glasson v Fuller* as support for the view that acquiescence implies either an abandonment of rights or that the claimant was estopped by it, and hence the five probanda of *Willmott v Barber*[91] on estoppel by acquiescence are applicable to this defence.[92] In a similar vein, Sachs LJ in *Holder v Holder* approved the view of Halsbury's Laws of England

25 Beav 236; 53 ER 627; *Life Association of Scotland* (n 27) De G F & J 73; ER 806; *Ex p Barnewall* (1855) 6 De G M & G 801; 43 ER 1444; *Evans* (n 15), where the trustee acquired his beneficial interest after the breach; *Re Pauling's Settlement Trusts* [1962] (n 12) 106–07; [1964] (n 12) 335. See and *cf Chillingworth* (n 15) especially 697–700 (Lindley LJ); Tucker, Le Poidevin and Brightwell (n 10) 1907 [39.123]; Hayton, Matthews and Mitchell (n 29) 1246 [95.1].

[86] *Orr* (n 50) (Deane J), who also referred to other loose usages of acquiescence as an alternative to laches, estoppel and release (or abandonment).

[87] For support in academic commentaries, see T Economou, 'The Defence of Acquiescence to a Breach of Trust' (2013) *Flinders Law Journal* 115.

[88] For cases that adopt the estoppel rationale, see *Swan v Perpetual Executors and Trustees Association of Australia Ltd* (1897) 23 VLR 293, 309; *Phillipson v Gatty* (1848) 7 Hare 516, 523; 68 ER 213, 217; *Chillingworth* (n 15) 704, 708.

[89] *Duke of Leeds* (n 79) (emphasis supplied).

[90] *De Bussche* (n 11) 314.

[91] *Willmott v Barber* (1880) 15 Ch D 96.

[92] *Glasson* (n 81) 161–62.

that 'acquiescence operates by way of estoppel', and that in the case at hand, 'if the facts are sufficient to create an estoppel then a fortiori, a plea of acquiescence must succeed'.[93] Significantly, even though Sachs LJ endorsed treating acquiescence as assent, he applied the doctrine on the basis of estopping the claimant from denying an implied representation generated from his inaction. He considered that in condoning the defendant-executor's purchase of the farm from the trust estate, and urging for its speedy execution, the claimant-brother had 'expressly and impliedly represented that [the defendant] could properly do the very act to which he now objects—purchase the property'.[94] There also are numerous authorities that explain release or concurrence as forever estopping the claimant from turning around to enforce his rights.[95]

It is submitted that while the defence of acquiescence should be reclassified under release or concurrence, the latter two defences should not be subsumed under estoppel, even though a large part of them overlaps with it. As the two recognised senses of acquiescence are, upon closer analysis, a subset of release or concurrence respectively, acquiescence has no role as an independent defence. Furthermore, while consent or promise can give rise to estoppel (as in *Walton Stores (Interstate) Ltd v Maher*),[96] and many cases of release and concurrence can be subsumed under this strand of estoppel, there still are considerable cases whether the release is binding on the basis of contract or equitable considerations.[97] Moreover, the test for release and concurrence as laid down in *Re Pauling's Settlement Trusts* refers to concepts of unfairness and equity, which are broader than and not limited to detrimental reliance as required for estoppel. There is thus a need to keep release and concurrence distinct, while appreciating that it overlaps with estoppel.

This section of the chapter has argued that acquiescence is a mongrel concept that is drawn from other doctrines, but does not have a distinct breed of its own. It is relevant only in showing that the consent required for release and concurrence can be established not only by active conduct, but also by knowing inaction (ie acquiescence). Accordingly, the doctrine can be reclassified as falling within release and concurrence, which embrace both actual and implied consent. Such a step better reflects the conceptual place of acquiescence within consent-based defences. It will significantly remove the mystery shrouding equitable defences and enable justice and transparency in the law. This new set of organising principles also allows judges and litigants to better understand how the defences interact, and in doing so promotes the efficient and rational application of the law for the ends of justice.[98]

[93] *Holder* (n 12) 403.
[94] ibid 404.
[95] *Phillipson* (n 88); *Chillingworth* (n 15) 704, 708.
[96] *Walton Stores (Interstate) Ltd v Maher* [1988] HCA 7; (1988) 164 CLR 387.
[97] See *De Bussche* (n 11) (Thesiger LJ).
[98] See R Epstein, *Simple Rules for a Complex World* (Cambridge MA, Harvard University Press, 1995).

IV. A UNIFIED DOCTRINE OF ESTOPPEL?

This chapter began with four situations in which a claimant's conduct or inaction in the face of a defendant's violation causes irreversible prejudice to the latter if the claimant subsequently enforces his right: (1) he has promised not to exercise his rights;[99] (2) he has represented that he has no rights; (3) through inaction he has encouraged the claimant's mistaken belief; and in all these three situations there is detrimental reliance on the part of the defendant; and (4) in the absence of the parties' conduct but due to a change of objective circumstances during the lapse of time the defendant has suffered an irreversible prejudice.

The current law tackles these situations by an overlapping and confusing, if not mysterious, array of defences. First, a promise not to exercise rights against a continuing violation is concurrence if expressly made and acquiescence (in the strict sense) if inferred from inaction. Delay is not relevant to this. In contrast, a promise not to exercise rights against a past violation is release if made explicitly, but can be treated as release, laches in the first strand, or acquiescence in the loose sense if inferred from inaction. Delay is relevant evidence for inferring such a promise, but it is also necessary to show that the claimant knowingly stands by during the defendant's violation. Although judges often suggest that such concurrence or release estops the claimant from complaining, estoppel is but a convenient label. The court's enquiry focuses on whether the promise is valid and binding rather than whether there was detrimental reliance. Second, if a representation not to exercise rights is expressly made or implicitly inferred from conduct (including inaction), estoppel applies. Third, if by knowingly standing by during the defendant's violation the claimant encourages the defendant's mistaken belief that he has rights, an acquiescence-based estoppel can be raised but this is a separate legal doctrine from the strict or loose senses of acquiescence. Fourth, if the inaction is unaccompanied by any of the above circumstances but still causes irreversible prejudice to the defendant due to change of objective circumstances, the second strand of laches applies.

The present chapter proposes a new set of organising principles to streamline these defences. It advocates abolishing the first strand of laches and re-classifying acquiescence as part of release or concurrence, which are consent-based defences that tackle promises not to exercise rights, whether made explicitly or implicitly. Then, representation-based and acquiescence-based estoppels will be used to analyse situations where there is a representation or mere knowing inaction that encourages a mistaken belief. Finally, laches in its strict sense will focus on delay that causes prejudice. This trilogy—of consent-based defences (release and concurrence), estoppel and laches—is founded upon the simple duties to honour one's promise and to not subject others to irreversible prejudice.

Such a proposal does not take the most radical approach of subsuming acquiescence, release, concurrence and even laches under a unified doctrine of estoppel

[99] The promise may be enforceable on contractual principles or because equity is satisfied that it should be binding, in which case it is not necessary for it to have been detrimentally relied upon by the defendant.

based on unconscionability. Deane J alluded to this idea in *Orr v Ford*, albeit he did not find it necessary to decide on the issue.[100] Aldous LJ in *Frawley v Neill* also advocated for replacing the confines of the doctrines laid down in the old cases with a broad test of unconscionability,[101] which smacks of the broad-brush balancing of personal equities in the very early cases.[102]

It is submitted, however, that assimilation of these four defences under estoppel would lose sight of the unity of consent-based defences (such as release and concurrence), which encompass both contractually made and estoppel-based consents. It would also fail to respect the distinct role of laches in protecting defendants who suffer prejudice not because of their detrimental reliance but merely a change of circumstance. If release and laches were to fit into the straitjacket of estoppel, which requires detrimental reliance, the law may be tempted to stretch the meaning of detrimental reliance at the expense of coherence in the doctrine of estoppel. Finally, while estoppel is capable of creating a cause of action, the duty not to subject the defendant to irreversible prejudice is much more limited, and is not intended to transgress the important boundary of not imposing legal responsibilities by omission.

V. CONCLUSION

The interrelated defences of concurrence, release, laches and acquiescence are bedeviled by their overlapping scopes and lack of uniformity in the use of their labels. Litigants often cast their net wide by pleading more than one of them indiscriminately in a case. The present chapter has sought to examine the moral premise underlying time-related defences and argued that they are of a wider import than the mere effluxion of time. They aim at regulating the conduct of the parties, in that laches, acquiescence and estoppel are based on the duties to honour one's promise and to not subject others to irreversible prejudice due to one's own inaction.

In particular, the duty not to cause irreversible prejudice achieves multiple purposes: to give just regard to the stability of the defendant's private right; to give allowance to gratuitous trustees who responded to importunities made by family members;[103] to observe the public policy against hearing stale claims where material evidence may have been lost;[104] and, most importantly, to regulate the conduct of the parties by discouraging calculated manipulation, change of mind and tardiness of attitude that cause irreversible prejudice to others. The duty is of a hypothetical, not categorical nature, in that it arises only if the right-holder intends to enforce his

[100] *Orr v Ford* (n 50) HCA 4 [11]; CLR 338; ALR 158.

[101] *Frawley* (n 25).

[102] *Fellows v Mitchell and Owens* (1705) 1 P Wins 81; 24 ER 302; *Smith and Helen his Wife v French* (1741) 2 Atk 243; 26 ER 550.

[103] *Smith and Helen his Wife* (n 102) 551–52 (Lord Hardwicke LC), referring to 'a very strong equity for the mother' trustee, who made an unauthorised loan of the trust fund to the husband of her beneficiary daughter at the latter's request, and where the daughter had afterwards offered repeatedly to execute a release.

[104] *Bright v Legerton* (1861) 2 De G F & J 606, 617; 45 ER 755, 760 (Lord Campbell).

right. While this duty closely approximates a duty of the same content in estoppel, it does not give rise to any liability, but only imposes a disability in the exercise of the right. Thus, it does not transgress the important imperative of not imposing legal responsibilities on omission.

This chapter also suggests re-classifying acquiescence and the first strand of laches as falling within the wider defences of release and concurrence. These simple changes to the law will provide a rational set of principles for organising time-related defences based on consent, estoppel and the prevention of irreversible prejudice. The new framework allows a better appreciation of the connection and interaction amongst these defences and ultimately justice and transparency in the law. At the same time, as estoppel itself is not a uniform doctrine and the defences of laches and acquiescence overlap with but are not sub-sets of estoppel, it is premature to subsume them under a unified doctrine of estoppel.

Index

www.ingramcontent.com/pod-product-compliance
Ingram Content Group UK Ltd.
Pitfield, Milton Keynes, MK11 3LW, UK
UKHW051416150926
475561UK00005B/195

9 781509 941117